American Reform Responsa

American Reform Responsa

Collected Responsa of the
Central Conference of American Rabbis
1889-1983

Edited by Walter Jacob

Central Conference of American Rabbis
5743 New York 1983

LIBRARY OF CONGRESS CATALOGING IN PUBLICATION DATA

Central Conference of American Rabbis.
   American Reform responsa.

   Includes index.
   1. Reform Judaism—Customs and practices.
2. Responsa—1800-   . I. Jacob, Walter, 1930-
II. Title
BM197.C46   1983   296.8'346   83-7565
ISBN 0-916694-83-6 (pbk.)

This book was produced by the Committee on Responsa of the
Central Conference of American Rabbis

Solomon B. Freehof, *Honorary Chair*
Walter Jacob, *Chair*

Leonard S. Kravitz   Rav A. Soloff
Isaac Neuman   Sheldon Zimmerman
Harry A. Roth   Bernard Zlotowitz

Ex Officio: Simeon J. Maslin

Copy editing and word processing provided by: SPECIAL EDITION, P.O. Box
09553, Columbus, Ohio 43209 (614-231-4088)

To Irene
in gratitude for twenty-five good years

אין ברכה מצויה בתוך ביתו של אדם
אלא בשביל אשתו

CONTENTS

Yoreh De-a

PREFACE

This Collected Volume of Responsa contains the complete text of all responsa issued by the Central Conference of American Rabbis until 1982. We have appended the "Report of the Committee on Patrilineal Descent on the Status of Children of Mixed Marriages." This important resolution was adopted by the Central Conference of American Rabbis in March, 1983. The unique significance of this resolution and the need to have the precise text readily available, has led to its inclusion in this volume.

A few of the responsa of this volume antedate the formation of a formal Responsa Committee. The transliteration has been standardized, and only minor stylistic changes have been made, mostly in the earlier responsa.

The responsa have been organized to follow the pattern of the **Shulchan Aruch** wherever possible. In some instances responsa were placed in a different section as it seemed more logical, and therefore easier for the reader. The references at the beginning of each responsum are to the appropriate volumes of the **Yearbook** of the Central Conference of American Rabbis. However, if no reference to the **Yearbook** appears, the responsa are the work of the Responsa Committee Chairman and have not been previously published.

The texts are complete with one exception; that responsum has been abridged, as large sections were irrelevant. On some occasions additional notes have been provided. These have been discussed by the entire current committee.

This volume contains cross-references to resolutions of the Central Conference of American Rabbis, the Union of American Hebrew Congregations, and the National Federation of Temple Sisterhoods, and to the volumes of Reform Responsa written by Solomon B. Freehof in an effort to be reasonably comprehensive.

It is the current practice of the Responsa Committee to circulate important responsa for the reactions of the members of the committee after the responsum has been written by the chairman. Other responsa continue to be written by the chairman without circulation. It is the hope of the Responsa Committee that this volume will serve the Central Conference of American Rabbis and Reform Jews throughout North America.

Thanks are due to the following individuals who have helped in the process of editing this volume of responsa: Leonard Kravitz, Eugene J. Lipman, Stephen M. Passamaneck, W. Gunther Plaut, Harry A. Roth, Herman

Schaalman, Rav A. Soloff, Sheldon Zimmerman, and Bernard
Zlotowitz.   Most notes have been written by Walter
Jacob, Eugene J. Lipman, Harry A. Roth, Rav A. Soloff,
and Bernard Zlotowitz. The thanks of the committee are
also extended to my secretary, Louise Marcovsky, for her
devotion to the typescript of this volume.

Walter Jacob
Editor

Rodef Shalom
Pittsburgh, Pennsylvania
May, 1983
Iyar, 5743

INTRODUCTION

The Jewish Reform Movement began with vigorous responsa and an exchange of essays on halachic issues in Germany and in Hungary. Within a decade of the first reforms, efforts were made to establish a rabbinic foundation for the changes which had been introduced. The earliest responsa represented attempts to justify the reforms before the traditional community. The most extensive writings along these lines were produced by Aaron Chorin of Arad in Hungary. In his volume, **Kin-at Ha-emet**, he wrote extensively on ritual matters which had aroused controversy. He dealt with such issues as the **Minyan**, the text and language of prayer, the chanting of Torah and **Haftara**, instrumental music, marriage questions, synagogue architecture, etc. These responsa led to a violent reaction on the part of the Orthodox community, which published volumes of counter-responsa.

The writing of responsa was halted because of the pace of the Reform revolution. The life of our people was changing rapidly, and it became impossible to argue about each detail. When thousands were using streetcars on Shabbat, an essay justifying the practice was hardly necessary. The path then taken was akin to that of all revolutions: it began rather brusquely, pushed much aside, but always with the understanding that these areas were valuable and needed attention after the main struggle was won. That task could not be accomplished by the revolutionary generation; in such a grand effort, minute details did not have to be justified. Yet, from the outset, Halacha was important to our leaders.

Abraham Geiger included large sections on Halacha in his **Urschrift**, his **magnum opus** in which he traced the development of Judaism from the Biblical period of Hellenistic times. Both his **Urschrift** and his **Sadducaeer und Pharisaeer** deal extensively with halachic developments. In addition, Geiger wrote a lengthy and much used introduction to the language of the Mishna (**Lehrbuch zur Sprache der Mischnah**). It paralleled the efforts of the more conservative reformer Zacharias Frankel. Although Frankel walked out of the Rabbinic Conference in Frankfurt in 1845, he remained a leader of non-Orthodox Judaism; his emphasis on history, when seen a century later by Ismar Elbogen, was not too different from that of Geiger. Frankel's scholarly efforts also dealt with the Septuagint and Biblical exegesis, and were then followed by a variety of Talmudic studies, including his **Mevo Hatalmud**, a beginning of a history of the responsa, the start of a critical edition of the Talmud Yerushalmi, as well as practical works.

In all these books historical development and changes were stressed, and it is no accident that both Geiger and Frankel established non-Orthodox Jewish seminaries. In both schools traditional literature, history, Bible, and philosophy were studied. Since most of the non-Orthodox rabbis of Germany attended both schools, their ties with the halachic past were never broken. The same pattern emerged in Hungary; for example, the works of Leopold Loew clearly showed his interest in the development of the Halacha. His lengthy essays on marriage law, first published in various issues of **Ben Chananya**, dealt not only with the development of marriage Halacha, but also with the external influences on Jewish law and customs. (Those three hundred pages treated history as well as contemporary problems). In addition to such studies, Loew also wrote short essays on such subjects as **dina demalchuta dina**, proselytes, intermarriage, bare-headedness in worship, etc. His methodology was similar to that of the American scholar, Jacob Z. Lauterbach. Matters were not very different in the United states, either. Isaac Mayer Wise considered the Talmud important to Jewish life, especially when viewed historically. Although Kaufmann Kohler was a son-in-law and follower of the radical David Einhorn, the Central Conference of American Rabbis, when establishing a responsa committee, made Kohler its chairman.

Halachic considerations and ties to the rabbinic past were on the agenda of most of our formative thinkers. Such considerations faded for a generation in America, but never completely, as the work of the Responsa Committee, essays in the **CCAR Yearbook**, and numerous scholarly efforts through the decades have attested.

We have looked at Halacha in a different and, we believe, more creative way than other Jewish groups. We have not looked to the Orthodox for approval; rather, our responsa and the guides which we have written have linked the past to the present and sought to make Halacha meaningful to new generations.

When we recognize that we are children of our age and are deeply influenced by it, we do not differ from those who lived in the creative periods of the past as we seek to understand the underlying principles and develop specifics, i.e., Halacha. A century of study by Geiger, Frankel, Lauterbach, Freehof, Cohon, and Agus, to name a few, has clearly shown the enormous role which historical development and outside influence have played in every phase of Jewish law and custom.

The Responsa Committee of our Conference was established in 1906, but no responsa were printed in the **Yearbook** until 1911, and all were written in English.

The earliest chairman, Kaufmann Kohler (from 1908 until 1922), was interested primarily in the theological overtones of the questions. Thus, his discussion of Bar Mitzvah (Vol. 23, 1913) dealt with the idea of progress, the equality of men and women, and the psychology of the congregant. The discussion was carried further by David Neumark. His responsum on the blowing of the Shofar on Shabbat emphasized "the leading principles" which were embodied by Reform and progress. Bible and Talmud were cited, but rarely any later authorities.

Jacob Lauterbach, who served as chairman from 1923 till 1933, used the responsa for thorough studies of the entire rabbinic past. His responsa presented normative material as well as other avenues. His historical approach emphasized the underlying principle which could be discovered in the developing tradition. An appropriate example might be the responsum on the naming of children (Vol. 42, 1932), or worshiping with covered heads (Vol. 38, 1928), which presented material from the Bible, the Apocrypha, the Talmud and responsa, as well as modern studies.

His successor, Jacob Mann, who was chairman for a shorter time (1934 to 1939), answered briefly with a handful of citations (as, for example, on games of chance in fundraising; Vol. 46, 1936), but did not develop any lengthy discussion of either principles or historical background.

Israel Bettan (Chairman, 1940 to 1954) sought to address himself only to the question at hand and supplied virtually no references. His concern was the contemporary mood of Reform Judaism. His responsum on Masonic services at a funeral (Vol. 56, 1946) did not contain a single reference to any source; even that on euthanasia (Vol. 60, 1950) contained only one post-Talmudic citation. This approach is interesting when we remember that he wrote his doctoral dissertation on the struggle over Reform in both Orthodox and Reform Responsa literature.

Solomon B. Freehof (Chairman, 1955 to 1976) continued the pattern set by Jacob Lauterbach, but with less emphasis on detail. His responsa are often lengthy and provide ample background, but they do not become learned essays. He frequently used the questions addressed to him as an educational device. Through his citations, he opened the pages of tradition as well as the responsa literature to many colleagues. Solomon B. Freehof has, of course, written a large number of volumes on the responsa literature and specifically on Reform responsa. Many questions have been addressed to him during the last two decades. His volumes of Reform responsa, along with those on Reform Jewish practice, have served as practical guides to the American Reform Movement.

Others in our movement have also written responsa, and they reflect a mixture of these approaches. Some responsa were discussed by the Conference, but these debates rarely added substantively to the material. They reflected differing opinions about the conclusions reached.

As we look at the total responsa of the CCAR and those of Solomon B. Freehof, the following becomes clear: guidance has been sought in almost every area of life; the approach to the questions is realistic; patterns which seemed fixed by tradition have been shown to be much more flexible than ever imagined by a thorough study of their development. Permissive answers predominate, but they are often accompanied by cautionary strictures.

The current Responsa Committee (1976-), under my direction, has constituted itself as a working committee. This is part of an attempt to involve a broader group in this important area, and, thereby, to reflect a wider spectrum of opinions. The responsa are written by the chairman, and those of wider import are circulated to the committee for comment. The fact that 57 responsa (approximately one third of the total) have been written by me during the last decade demonstrates the increasing interest in Jewish law within the Reform Movement. These responsa, the recent volumes of responsa by Solomon B. Freehof, and over one hundred of my own yet unpublished responsa--all indicate vigorous halachic developments within the Reform Movement.

The roots of Reform Halacha lie partially in our nineteenth-century past, for we have been provided with firm halachic foundations through the efforts of Geiger, Frankel, Loew, and others. They are, however, more deeply rooted in the distant rabbinic past. On occasion we may be as radical as those Tana-im and Amora-im who created Rabbinic Judaism, and thereby created anew. Frequently, we will find appropriate solutions within the tradition, broadly perceived. The authority of the Central Conference of American Rabbis and its Responsa Committee lies in its ability to persuade and reach a consensus. Halachic discussions will bring us closer to consensus and agreement on basic principles. As often in the past, we will proceed inductively, and specific statements will evolve into general principles.

Walter Jacob
Chairman, Responsa Committee

1. PROPRIETY OF USING DISCARDED PRACTICES
IN REFORM SERVICES
(Vol. LXV, 1955, pp. 88-90)

QUESTION: In the area in which my Temple is located, we increase our membership by attracting men
and women from Orthodox and Conservative homes.
The new members, when principals in a wedding ceremony, will often ask that the older forms to which
they are accustomed be retained in the service.
These include the covering of the head by all participants, the reading of the traditional **Ketuba**,
and the breaking of the glass.

Similar requests come at times from the parents of a Bar Mitzvah. To please an older member
of the family, they would have the boy wear **Talit**
and skull-cap during the Bar Mitzvah ceremony.

The members of our Ritual Committee take the
stand that the rabbi of the Temple, when acting as
officiating minister, must conform to the practices
of Reform Judaism. They likewise insist that the
Bar Mitzvah ceremony as conducted in our Temple
must be viewed as a form of initiation into the
ways of Reform Judaism, and should therefore present no feature that is glaringly inconsistent with
our established practices.

What do you think of the position taken by the
Ritual Committee?

ANSWER: There is an erroneous impression abroad, which
we have done little to dispel, that while the undevising
traditionalists are ruled by a sense of loyalty to
Torah, we who have espoused the principle of Reform are
guided by such motives as personal convenience and temp-
eramental preference.

Of course, the student of our religious history
knows quite well that the forms and customs sanctified
by tradition had their origin not in a special divine
revelation but in the compelling conditions of human
living. As life changes and new situations arise, there
also springs up the need for other ways and methods by
which the high purposes of our faith may best be fulfilled.

What passes for Torah-true Judaism reflects very
often a contemptuous disregard for the needs of the
present, and not solely a tender attachment to the
teachings of the past; and what draws so often the fire
of our opponents against us, carrying the taunt that we
play fast and loose with tradition, issues just as often
from a deep conviction that the discipline of religion,

even as the spirit of religion, must be rooted in reality and not in sheer fantasy.

Reform Judaism has eliminated the **Ketuba** from the marriage ceremony for the good and sufficient reason that the changes which have taken place in Jewish life and law have divested the document of its ancient meaning and importance. Long before the rise of Reform, the judicious curtailment of the right of the husband to divorce his wife against her will nullified the practical usefulness of the **Ketuba**, making its retention in our time an empty, meaningless formality (Mielziner, **The Jewish Law of Marriage and Divorce**, pp. 88-89).

Nor is the omission of the breaking of the glass from our marriage ceremony dictated by anything other than the very doubtful nature and value of the explosive gesture. Whether the practice was originally intended to curb excessive hilarity on a joyous occasion, or to recall the destruction of the Temple at Jerusalem, or--as Lauterbach would have--to frighten away evil spirits (Freehof, **Reform Jewish Practice**, vol. 1, p. 98), it is certain that the crude dramatic performance tends to distract rather than to inspire, to mar rather than to enhance the impressiveness of the occasion.

As to the clamorous insistence that we must keep the head covered while at prayer, one need but read Lauterbach's exhaustive and illuminating study of the subject to realize the restricted and uncertain character of the custom (**CCAR Yearbook**, vol. 38, pp. 589-603). While in Babylonia Jews worshiped with heads covered, in Palestine it was the custom to worship bareheaded. In the early medieval period, the Spanish Jews followed the Babylonian practice, while the French and German Jews followed the Palestinian practice. As late as the 18th century, the Wilna Gaon, unable to find support for the custom in Jewish law, reduced the question to a mere matter of good manners. Since in our time, and in this land, it is the very best of manners to express respect by uncovering the head, we should think it an act of willful and useless self-isolation when an American Jew chooses to make of the skull-cap an important symbol of Jewish piety.

Of course, there is here, as elsewhere, the important person, the "older member of the family," whose fixed habits make him uncomfortable in the presence of change; but then, there is also the rebuke administered to Joseph by the Patriarch: "Shall I and thy mother and thy brethren come to bow down to thee?"

The firm stand taken by the Ritual Committee augurs well for the continued stability of our Reform religious practices.

Israel Bettan

2. DISCARDED PRACTICES
(1979)

QUESTION: What shall be the attitude of Reform Judaism towards practices once discarded? May they be adopted again? What is the attitude of Reform Judaism towards the change in rituals and practices generally?

ANSWER: A fundamental distinction between traditional Judaism and Reform Judaism lies in our attitude towards change. Orthodox Judaism insists that the tradition has remained constant and unchanging since its inception. Everything was revealed on Sinai or implied in that revelation (Meg. 19b); nothing may be added or removed from the law (Deut. 4:21; 13:1). Although a historic view of Judaism clearly indicated that radical changes had occurred often, Orthodox Judaism has denied them and sees such as a reinterpretation of existing traditions.

Reform Judaism has emphasized change and has reviewed Judaism through the eyes of history. The radical differences between Biblical Judaism, Hellenistic Judaism, and Rabbinic Judaism and its varieties, have been acknowledged and explained as a reaction to new environments. This view of Judaism was implied in the earliest changes made by Israel Jacobson at the outset of the 19th century. It was clearly stated in historical and theological terms by Holdheim, Geiger, Kohler, and others in Europe and America in the middle of the last century, and perhaps earliest by Joseph Dernburg in the **Wissenschaftliche Zeitschrift** vol. IV, 1839, pp. 14ff). The views of such individual thinkers formed the basis of the questions and debates at the various Reform rabbinic meetings held in the last century in Germany. They adopted no statements of principle, but passed resolutions on practical matters which implied such a view of the past. In the United States guiding principles of Reform Judaism were at first presented and accepted by the Philadelphia Conference of 1869 and the Pittsburgh Conference of 1885. Both recognized the changing nature of Judaism. This was, perhaps, most ᶜlearly stated in the opening paragraph of the Columbus Platform of 1937: "Judaism is the historical religious experience of the Jewish people. Though growing out of Jewish life, its message is universal, aiming at the union and perfection of mankind under the sovereignty of God. Reform Judaism recognizes the principle of progressive development in religion, consciously applies this principle to spiritual as well as to cultural and social life" (CCAR **Yearbook**, vol. 47, p. 97). This indicates that Reform Judaism has not remained static, but is willing to adapt itself to the needs of each generation. We do not make such changes lightly, and we root ourselves in the past. Minor adaptations may be readily made, but major changes take place only when no alternatives exist. "The Torah, both written and oral, enshrines Israel's ever-growing consciousness of God and of the moral law; it preserves the historical precedents, sanctions, and norms of Jewish life and seeks to mold it in the pattern of goodness and holiness. Being a product of historical processes, certain of its laws have lost their binding force with the passing of the conditions that called them forth, but as a repository of permanent spiritual ideals, the Torah remains the dynamic source in the life of Israel" (**ibid.**, p. 97).

Thus, we can readily accept new customs and celebrations such as Yom Ha-atsma-ut, Berit Chayim, etc., or ideas such as the complete equality of men and women, which has led to women rabbis and cantors. We willingly move also in the other direction as history and the mood of our people re-emphasize older customs as well, demonstrated by the **Gates of Mitzvah** (1979). This has always been so in traditional Judaism as well, and has led to innumerable changes in **minhagim** in our history. Even a cursory glance at the **Shulchan Aruch** and its commentaries or any of the books of **minhagim** demonstrate how much has been adopted, omitted, and sometimes readopted. This is especially true of customs and ceremonies of life-cycle events, such as Bar Mitzvahs, weddings, funerals, etc.

Nothing would, therefore, hinder us as Reform Jews from readopting customs once omitted if a new generation finds them meaningful and useful in its practice of Judaism. We have always understood that such customs, when adopted by us, do not represent a divine enactment. In other words, we are willing to change in both directions. This would apply both to private practices and to those of the synagogue. Synagogue practices should be discussed by the appropriate committee which acts in an advisory capacity to the rabbi under whose aegis changes may be made.

Walter Jacob, Chairman
Leonard S. Kravitz
Eugene Lipman
W. Gunther Plaut
Harry A. Roth
Rav A. Soloff
Bernard Zlotowitz

3. LESS THAN A MINYAN OF TEN AT SERVICES
(Vol. XLVI, 1936, p. 127)

QUESTION: A member of my congregation has suggested that we conduct services on Friday night, even if attendance--counting men and women--is less than the customary Minyan of ten. Is it permissible to conduct a regular service in a Temple with fewer than ten persons--men and women--present?

ANSWER: Whereas the general rule is to require a Minyan, there was the practice in Palestine in olden times to be satisfied with six or seven people (see Mas. Sof., 10.8). While every attempt should be made to have a full Minyan, the importance of regular services in the Temple is such as to conduct them even when there are fewer than ten people present in accordance with the above-mentioned old Palestinian custom.

Jacob Mann and Committee

4. WOMAN WEARING A TALIT
(Vol. LXXX, 1970, pp. 55-56)

QUESTION: In some of our congregations it is the custom that whoever comes up to the pulpit to participate in the service puts on a Talit. In young people's services for our high schools, boys and girls participate, and often the girl puts on the Talit at that occasion. According to Jewish law and tradition, is it proper for a girl to wear a Talit at service?

ANSWER: The commandment to wear a **Talit** with fringes
is based upon Numbers 15:37-41.   Upon the basis of this
commandment, the anonymous baraita in Menachot 43a says
that women, too, are in duty bound to wear the garment
with fringes.   However, Rabbi Simon says there that they
are free from that obligation.   He bases his opinion
upon the fact that Scripture in the passage in Numbers
uses the phrase: "Ye shall see them and remember," etc.
Since Scripture says, "Ye shall see them," that proves
that the proper time for **Talit** and **Tsitsit** is the day-
time, not the nighttime.   This conclusion puts the commandment to wear fringes into the special class of positive commandments "limited by time" (**shehazman geramo**),
and it is a general rule that women are free from the
obligation to fulfill positive commandments that are
dependent upon time.   Of course, being free from the
obligation to fulfill the commandment of fringes does
not mean that they are forbidden to wear them.   It means
only that they are not in duty bound to wear them.

When the law is discussed in the **Shulchan Aruch**,
Orach Chayim 17.2, Joseph Caro says, following Rabbi
Simon in the Talmud (quoted above), that women and
slaves are free from putting on the fringes, since it is
a commandment based upon time; but Isserles adds: "At
all events, if they wish to put on the fringed garment
and even recite the blessing over it, they are free to
do so, as is the case with all time-limited positive
commandments" (that is, they are not compelled to obey,
but they are permitted to do so if they wish).   However,
he adds, if they do put it on, it would appear to be a
show of extra pride of piety (**yohara**).   But if they are
not to put it on because it would look like a show of
extra pride of piety on their part, then it becomes
necessary to explain the fact that women observe the
commandment of the **Lulav** and recite blessings over it.
Is not the **Lulav** also a positive commandment limited by
time?   The explanation of this difference is given by
the **Magen David**: that the **Lulav** is a stricter commandment than the one concerning fringes, because if a person does not have a square garment (the fringes must be
on the corners of a four-cornered garment) he need not
put fringes on at all.   It is true that it is now our
custom always to wear a **Talit Katan** with four corners
and fringes.   Nevertheless, according to law, it is only
if a man has a four-cornered garment that he must put
fringes on.   In other words, the obligation depends on
the garment.   But with regard to the **Lulav**, a man must
get a **Lulav** and say the blessings.   In this case the
obligation is incumbent upon the man himself (**chovat
gavra**), not on whether he has the object or not; he must
get it if he lacks it.

One of the later deciders, Yechiel Epstein, in his
Aruch Hashulchan, Orach Chayim 17, says that we should
not allow women to put on the fringed **Talit**. But then
Epstein has the problem of explaining why women bless
the **Lulav** and formally eat the **Matzah** at the **Seder**,
which are positive commandments limited by time. He
explains by saying that these positive time-limited
commandments come only once a year, but the **Talit** should
be worn every day.

However, all the great (and earlier) authorities
permit it. The only question that seems to divide the
earlier authorities (none of whom doubts the right of
women to put on the **Talit**) is the question as to whether, when a woman puts on the **Talit** she may make the
regular blessing or not. There is a full discussion of
this problem in the **Tosafot** to Rosh Hashana 33a, **s.v.**
"**Ha.**" This **tosefet** is mainly the opinion of Rabbenu
Tam. The discussion is on the general principle of
whether anyone (such as women and the blind) who is free
from the obligation to fulfill "positive commandments
limited by time" should (when he fulfills such commandments voluntarily) pronounce the blessing over them or
not. The **tosefet** is based mainly on the discussion in
Bava Kama 87a, where Rabbi Joseph, who was blind, had
voluntarily fulfilled such commandments as he was not
obligated to fulfill. See, also, the **tosefet** in Eruvin
96a, **s.v.** "**Michal**," where the **tosefet** discusses the
statement in the Talmud that Michal, the daughter of
Kushi (or the daughter of King Saul) used to put on
Tefilin, and the wife of Jonah used to make the festival
pilgrimage to Jerusalem. Both of these were "positive
commandments limited by time." Rabbenu Tam holds the
opinion that women may pronounce the blessing over the
fringed **Talit**. But Maimonides, in **Yad**, Hilchot Tsitsit
III.9, says that women may put on the fringes if they
wish, yet may not say the blessing, and he adds: "So
with all the other positive commandments that women are
free from, if they wish to fulfill them without reciting
the blessings, we do not prevent them." The **Hagahot**
Maimoniyot at that passage in the **Yad** says in the name
of Rashi that he, too, was opposed to their reciting the
blessing.

So the law is clear enough: One authority believes
that a woman is actually in duty bound to wear the
fringes. All agree that she may wear them if she wishes
to, except for the limitation that it might look like
the pride of extra piety. This solitary objection can
hardly apply to the young women if we put the **Talit** upon
them. They would simply consider it part of the ceremony. Besides, in our Reform Movement, where special
emphasis is placed upon the religious equality of men
and women, there can be no real objection to young women

putting on the **Talit** when they participate in the service.

Solomon B. Freehof

5. WORSHIPING WITH COVERED HEADS
(Vol. XXXVIII, 1928, pp. 589-603)

QUESTION: Where can one find the Rabbinic law prescribing that men should cover their heads when participating in Divine worship or when entering a synagogue? If there is no law to this effect, will you please tell me where and when did the custom of covering one's head, now generally observed in Orthodox synagogues, originate among the Jews?

ANSWER: There is no law in the Bible or Talmud prescribing the covering of the head for men when entering a sanctuary, when participating in the religious service, or when performing any religious ceremony.   The saying in the Mishna (Berachot 9.5), "**Lo yakel adam et rosho keneged sha-ar hamizrach**," does not mean "one should not bare his head in sight of the Holy of Holies," as understood by some scholars (comp. K. Kohler, "The Origin and Function of Ceremonies in Judaism," in CCAR **Yearbook**, 1907, p. 7). For one must distinguish between **giluy rosh**, which means "bareheadedness" and **kalut rosh**, which means "lightheadedness." The latter is considered a sin. The former is no sin at all and no prohibition against it can be found in either Mishna or Talmud.   It is true that among the garments prescribed for the priests (Exod. 28:4 and 40) a headgear is mentioned. This headgear was to be worn by the priests only when officiating at the altar or performing any other priestly function in the sanctuary. (This may have been intended to distinguish the priests in the Temple at Jerusalem from the priests of some heathen deity, who sit on seats in their temples "and nothing upon their heads" (**Epistle of Jeremy** 31; comp. note in Charles's **The Apocrypha and Pseudepigrapha**, vol. 1, p. 604, though some heathen priests, like the Roman, were also in the habit of sacrificing with covered head.) But it cannot be justifiably concluded from this that any person performing any religious ceremony must cover his head.   The priests of old performed all their functions at the altar and in the Temple barefooted.   Yet the conclusion was never drawn from this fact that one

must be barefooted while performing any religious ceremony. And, certainly, the custom of covering one's head
when entering a synagogue has no precedent in the practice of the priests in the Temple at Jerusalem. For,
the priests were not forbidden to enter the Temple bareheaded (see Jacob Reischer in his responsa **Shevut Ya-
akov** III, no. 5; Metz, 1789, 2b). Indeed, from B. Yoma
25a, it is evident that when not performing any priestly
function, the priests in the Temple would go without
hats. I do not know on what ground I. Scheftelowitz
makes the statement that the priests, while being allowed to enter the Temple bareheaded, were not permitted
to come within four yards of the altar with uncovered
head (**Alt-Palaestinischer Bauernglaube**, Hanover, 1925,
p. 154). The midrash **Genesis R.**, XVII and **Numbers R.**,
V., to which Scheftelowitz referred, do not contain any
saying that would justify such a statement. (Comp. my
review of Scheftelowitz's work in the **Hebrew Union College Monthly**, December, 1925, pp. 15-17.)

The practice of covering the head when entering a
synagogue, and when reciting prayers or performing any
other religious ceremony, is not based upon any Talmudic
law and cannot be supported by any express statement in
the Talmud. Many express statements and implied teachings of the Talmud rather point to the contrary. This
practice is merely a custom, **minhag**, that first appeared
among the Jews in Babylon. In the course of time it
spread to other countries and gradually became a generally observed custom among Orthodox Jews. Its origin
probably goes back to a non-Jewish source. It furnishes
another instance of how sometimes the Jews in one country, subject to the influence of their environment,
would borrow a ceremony or custom from their non-Jewish
neighbors and pass it on to Jews of other countries, and
how in the course of time such a borrowed non-Jewish
custom is interpreted by Jewish teachers as having some
Jewish significance and regarded as a genuinely Jewish
custom. In the following I present a brief account of
the origin and the development of this supposedly Jewish
custom of covering the head during religious devotion or
when in a holy place.

Now, as regards its origin, no such custom can be
found in ancient Israel. The Jews in Palestine, in so
far as Biblical and Talmudic records show, would ordinarily not wear any headgear. The covering of the head
was an expression of grief or a sign of mourning, as is
evident from II Samuel 15:2. When a person was in
mourning he would cover his head (B., M.K. 15a and
24a), but not while the people came to comfort him and
recite the comforting prayers and benedictions (comp.
saying from **Evel Rabbati**, as cited by R. Nissim to Alfasi and quoted by N. Bruell in his **Jahrbuecher**, vol. 1,

p. 54). Sometimes a person would cover his head as a protection from cold or excessive heat (see Midrash **Lev. R.** XIX.4). But this was done with a shawl or some other protective covering, not by wearing a headgear in our sense of the word. The shawl occasionally used to cover one's head because of being a mourner or for the sake of protection from heat or cold, the **sudar harosh**, was not considered a regular garment or part of a man's outfit, and hence was not subject to the law of **Tsitsit** prescribed for garments only (saying from **Sifre**, cited by R. Eshtori Haparchi in his **Kaftor Vaferach**, ch. 60, ed. A.M. Luncz, Jerusalem, 1897, p. 781, though not found in our editions of the **Sifre**). This also points to the fact that Jewish men ordinarily would not wear a hat nor otherwise cover their heads. One of the innovations forced upon the Jews by Antiochus Epiphanes, to which the pious Jews objected very much, considering it against Jewish law or practice, was that the young men were made to "wear a hat" (II Macc. 4:12, according to the authorized version, though Charles has "wear the **petasus**," that is, a broad-brimmed felt hat, which, being the mark of Hermes, may have been especially objectionable). (Compare, however, A.T. Olmstead, "Wearing the Hat," in the **American Journal of Theology**, January 1920, pp. 94ff). From the saying of Rabbi Meir that every day, "when at sunrise the kings of the earth put their crowns upon their heads and bow down to the sun, God gets angry" (Berachot 7a, Avoda Zara 4b), it also appears that it was the non-Jewish custom of covering one's head when worshiping.

The mishna Nedarim 3.8 takes it for granted that men go bareheaded and only women and children cover their heads. (The remark in the Gemara, B. Nedarim 30b, "**Uketanim le-olam miglo**," cannot be harmonized with the plain meaning of the Mishna, unless it refers only to infants or reflects a different Babylonian custom.) According to a story found in Tractate Kalla, it was, therefore, considered impudence on the part of young boys to walk on the street, and especially to pass older people, without covering their heads. The conclusion drawn from this story in Kalla Rabbati II, "**Giluy harosh azut takifa hi**," is to be understood that it is marked impudence on the part of a young boy to go bareheaded, and not, as R. Isaac Aboab (**Menorat Hama-or**, ch. 337, Warsaw, 1890, p. 325) seems to have understood it, that even on the part of adults it would be impudent to walk with uncovered heads. For, according to the Mishna, it was the usual thing for grown-up men to go bareheaded.

And when Paul said: "Every man, praying or prophesying, having his head covered, dishonoreth his head.... For a man, indeed, ought not to have his head veiled forasmuch as he is the image and glory of God" (I

Corinthians XI:4-7), he merely stated the Palestinian
Jewish practice of his time and did not express any new
or non-Jewish doctrine.   It is a mistake--and one that
involves reasoning in a circle--to interpret this passage in the Epistle as aiming to sever the Christian
worshipers from the synagogue by distinguishing their
appearance of worship from that of the Jewish worshipers, and then to assume that it was Paul's insistence
upon his followers worshiping without a hat that, in
turn, caused the Jews to attach great importance to the
covering of the head during religious service (W. Rosen-
au, **Jewish Ceremonial Institutions and Customs**, Balti-
more, 1912, p. 49; also M. Gaster, as reported in the
Jewish Chronicle of London, March 17, 1893, p. 17).   In
the first place, Gaster's alleged statement that the
founder of Christianity "in one of his Epistles" said,
"My followers, pray bareheaded to distinguish yourselves
from the Jews," is without any justification.   No such
saying of Jesus is found in the New Testament or among
the Agrapha of the New Testament (comp. the **Jewish
Chronicle**, London, April 17, 1893, "Question" by "a
Subscriber" to which, as far as I could see, no answer
was given by Gaster).   And if Gaster had in mind the
saying of Paul in I Corinthians, he gave it the wrong
interpretation.   Paul could not have meant by his saying
to put himself and his followers in opposition to Jewish
custom or traditional practice, since what he recommends
actually was the Jewish practice of his day ("Against
Jonathan Alter," in his **Antwort auf das Sendschreiben
eines Afrikanischen Rabbi**, Prague, 1826, 30a,b).
    Secondly, had the later Jewish custom of covering
the head during religious worship been the result of the
Jewish reaction to the Christian practice intended as a
protest against the Pauline doctrine, it is but reasonable to expect that traces of it would be found in Palestinian Jewish sources.   For, during the Talmudic period, it was in Palestine, more than in any other country,
that the Jews came into close contact with the Christians, and there, if anywhere, surely the teachers would
have had good reason to introduce such customs as were
calculated to prevent Jews from following Christian
practice.   But, as a matter of fact, we do not find in
Palestine Jewish sources of Talmudic times the least
indication of any decree or enactment by the Rabbis
requiring the covering of the head during religious
service or while in a synagogue.   On the contrary, we
find many indications and a few express statements to
the effect that in Palestine men would usually go bareheaded and remain bareheaded even when entering the
synagogue and reading from the Torah or reciting their
prayers.   Thus, R. Joshua b. Chananiah, a younger contemporary of Paul, states that the reason why a man, as

a rule, goes bareheaded and a woman covers her head is because the woman is ashamed of her sin in having listened to the serpent (XVII.13; also **Avot deR. Natan,** Version B., pp. 148ff). The implication is that man need not be ashamed of having listened to his wife. Evidently R. Joshua b. Chananiah did not know of any custom of men covering their heads during religious service. From the Palestinian Talmud, Berachot 2.3 (4c), it appears that R. Jochanan would cover his head during the winter as a protection against the cold, but would go bareheaded during the summer. Compare the commentaries, and especially the discussion of this passage by R. Menahem de Lunsano (in the Wilna edition of the Yerushalmi, Wilna, 1922, 14a-15a).

From another story in the Palestinian Talmud (M.K. III, 82c; also **Gen. R.** 100, 7), it is also evident that in Palestine it was the usual thing to go bareheaded. For we are told that the two sons of Rabbi Yehuda Hanasi differed in their observing the mourning for their father. On the Sabbath day during the mourning period, one of them would cover his head, as on weekdays. The other, however, would not observe this custom of mourning on the Sabbath day, and hence on the Sabbath during the mourning period he would go out bareheaded. This passage in the P. Talmud has been misunderstood by I. Scheftelowitz (**op. cit., l.c.**) and by A. Marmorstein in **Ha-olam,** December 24, 1926, no. 53, pp. 1010-1011, and in **Monatschrift fuer die Geschichte und Wissenschaft des Judentums,** 1926, p. 211. They understood it to mean that even on the weekdays of the mourning period one of the sons of Rabbi would disregard the custom for mourners, and go around bareheaded. Scheftelowitz, therefore, draws the conclusion that "in some places in Palestine it was customary for **every mourner** to go bareheaded." But the two sons of Rabbi lived in the same place, and Marmorstein concludes, that "the one son of Rabbi, for reasons of his own, refused to observe the mourning rites for his father" (**Ha-olam,** l.c., p. 1011), or "that in the time of Judah ha-Nasi it was not yet the general custom for mourners to cover their heads" (**Monatschrift,** l.c.). From a correct understanding of the passage, however, neither one of these conclusions can be justified.

In **Lev. R.** 27.6 (also **Pesikta deR. K.** IX [Buber, 77a]) and **Tanchuma,** Emor 10 (Buber, 13, p. 47a), it is implied that the Jew need not trouble himself to remove his hat, if he has one on, or to stand up, if he happens to be sitting, when he is about to recite the "Shema", but may do it even while sitting and even with his head covered. From this it is evident that not only could there be no objection to reciting the "Shema" bareheaded, but that it would ordinarily be more reverential to do so (see R. Solomon Lurya in his Responsum no. 72, and comp. Gronemann in Rahmer's **Literaturblatt**, 1880, no. 42; also M. Duschak, **ibid.**, 1881, p. 36). The Targum to the Prophets, a Palestinian work in origin if not in form (comp. W. Bacher, **Jewish Encyclopedia** XII, p. 61), interpreting Judges 5:9 as speaking in praise of the scholars and teachers in Israel who in times of trouble and persecution did not cease to study the Torah, expressly says that "it is fitting that these scholars and teachers sit in the synagogues with uncovered heads, teaching the people the words of the Torah and reciting praises and prayers of thanksgiving to God" ("**Vekadu ya-ei lehon deyatevin bevatei keneshata bereish galei ume-alefin yat ama pitgamei oraita umevarechin umodin kedam Adonai**").

And in another Palestinian work, the Tractate Soferim XIV.15 (ed. Joel Mueller, Leipzig, 1878, p. XXVI), it is expressly stated that one with uncovered head may act as the reader, leading the congregation in the recital of the "Shema": "**Mi sherosho meguleh pores al Shema**" (comp. Mueller's remark on pp. 198-199 and I. Elbogen, **Der Juedische Gottesdienst**, pp. 497 and 515). It is true that the Tractate Soferim in the same passage also mentions another opinion that would not allow one who is bareheaded to utter the name of God in prayer. But, as will be shown presently, this latter opinion reflects the Babylonian custom. For, in Palestine throughout the entire Talmudic period and even later, people would not hesitate entering a synagogue, reading from the Torah, and participating in the religious service with uncovered head.

It was different in Babylon, though even in Babylonian Jewish sources of Talmudic times, one could not find any express regulation for covering the head during religious service. Nay, from the Babylonian Talmud it might even be proved that one is allowed to recite prayers with uncovered head. For, in B. Berachot 60b, the Talmud prescribes certain benedictions to be recited every morning before one covers his head (comp. also **Shulchan Aruch**, Orach Chayim 46.1, and especially R. Elijah Gaon of Wilna in his commentary **Be-urei Hagra**, to Sh. Ar., O. Ch. 8.6). But there did develop in Babylon during Talmudic times, especially among very pious people, the custom of covering the head when reciting prayers or performing any religious ceremony, as well as the practice of avoiding going bareheaded. Thus, R. Huna, the son of R. Joshua, a Babylonian Amora of the fifth generation, second half of the fourth century (not Rav Huna, the disciple of Abba Areka and his successor as the head of the academy at Sura, who died about 297 C.E., see below), prides himself on the fact that he never walks four yards with uncovered head (Shabbat

118b, also Kiddushin 31a).   This, however, could not
have been the general practice for all scholars and for
those who read the prayers, as Scheftelowitz assumes
(op. cit., l.c.).   For in that case Huna could not have
prided himself on observing this practice.   Scheftelowitz's other statement (ibid., l.c.) that from the second century on, it became the general "custom of always
keeping the head covered," is likewise without any foundation in the sources.   The covering of the head was
especially considered a sign of respect which one must
show to his elders or to scholars.   Thus we are told (B.
Kiddushin 33a) that R. Jeremiah of Difte considered it
impudent on the part of a man passing him without showing him the respect of covering his head.   It is evident
from the context there that R. Jeremiah did not mind the
man's going without a hat, for even in Babylon it was
not a generally observed custom for men to cover their
heads (see Rabbinnovicz in Rahmer's **Literaturblatt** XXII,
1893, no. 15, p. 58).   But R. Jeremiah expected the man
to show him the respect due to a scholar by not passing
him without covering his head.   Rabina, who happened to
be with R. Jeremiah, however, sought to mitigate the
man's offense by suggesting that that man might have
come from Mata Mahasya, where the people were rather on
familiar terms with the rabbis and not so punctilious in
the usual manner of showing respect to scholars.
    The covering of the head seems also to have been
considered as tending to help one acquire the fear of
God.   Thus, the mother of R. Nachman b. Isaac, whom the
astrologer had told that her son Nachman was destined to
become a thief, would never allow him to go around bareheaded, evidently fearing that such conduct on his part
might tend to hasten the evil destiny predicted for him
by the astrologers.   She would also say to her son:
"Kasei reishach, ki heichi detiho alach eimta dishmaya,"
"Cover your head so that the fear of Heaven may be upon
you" (B. Shabbat 156b).   According to J.H. Schorr
(**Hechalutz** VII, p. 34), the practice of covering the
head, and especially the idea that it is disrespectful
to go without headgear, was borrowed by the Babylonian
Jews from the Persians.   One is also justified in sur-
mising that there were some elements of primitive superstition connected with this practice (comp. Hastings,
Encyclopedia of Religion and Ethics, vol. VI, p. 539).
But be this as it may, this much is certain, that among
the Babylonian Jews already in Talmudic times the covering of the head was considered a sign of respect.   It
was observed especially in the presence of prominent
men.   It was also regarded as conducive to inculcate in
one the fear of God.   Pious people would be careful not
to walk around with uncovered head.   A prominent scholar's outfit included also a headgear (B. Kiddushin, 8a,

case of R. Kahana), though even prominent scholars would
not wear a headgear before they were married (**ibid.**,
29b, case of R. Hamnuna. According to R. Abraham ibn
Yarhi in **Hamanhig Tefila** 43, Berlin, 1855, p. 15, it
would have been regarded as presumption or haughty
pride, "**demechezei keyohara,**" on the part of an unmarried scholar to cover his head. But for the people in
general, there was no fixed rule. Some of them would
cover their heads and some would go bareheaded: "**Anashim, zimnin demichso reishehu vezimnin demiglo reishehu**" (B. Nedarim 30b). As to how they appeared in the
synagogue we have no record. Scheftelowitz's statement
that the scholars in general and those who read the
prayers would always keep their heads covered (**op. cit.**,
l.c.) has no basis in the Talmudic sources. Some pious
people, however, would, no doubt, cover their heads when
praying. For, we are told in the Talmud (B. Berachot
51a) that R. Ashi (not Asi as in the printed editions;
see Rabbinnovicz, **Dikdukei Soferim, ad loc.**) would cover
his head when reciting the benediction after the meal.
We may justly assume that he would also cover his head
when reciting other benedictions and prayers.

In the very early post-Talmudic times, however, we
find that the Babylonian Jews considered it already
forbidden to utter the name of God in prayer with uncovered head. (This is the opinion of "**yesh omerim,**" "Some
say," in Tractate Soferim, which, as already suggested
above, represent Babylonian authorities.) In the
Chilufei Minhagim (published by Joel Mueller in **Hasha-
char** VII), it is stated that one of the differences in
custom and ritual between the Palestinian and Babylonian
Jews was that among the former the priests would recite
their benedictions bareheaded, while among the latter,
the priests were not permitted to recite their benedictions with uncovered head: "**Benei Bavel oserim sheyeva-
rechu hakohanim leYisra-el verosham parua; be-Erets
Yisra-el mevarechim kohanim leYisra-el verosham parua.**"

This is the correct reading (comp. Mueller's discussion there, no. 44). This, by the way, also implies
that even in Babylon it was not absolutely forbidden to
enter the synagogue and participate in the religious
service with uncovered head. Had this been the case,
the special mention of a law prohibiting the priests
from pronouncing their blessings bareheaded would have
been gratuitous.

There was, accordingly, a difference in custom
between Palestine and Babylon regarding wearing hats.
In the former, the people would not cover their heads
while praying or when in the synagogue, and in general
would be bareheaded; in the latter, however, it was the
custom of pious people to cover their heads. This custom, however, had not been brought to Babylon from Pale-

stine by Abba Areka, as Marmorstein assumes (**Ha-olam**, 1926, p. 1010, and **Revue des Etudes Juives**, 1928, pp. 66-69). The custom could not have been imported from Palestine where it did not exist. And we have no indication in the Talmud that Abba Areka ever observed it. The Geonim do mention among the ten practices of extreme piety (**asara milei dechasiduta**) observed by Rav, the practice not to walk four yards with uncovered head (see responsa of the Geonim, **Sha-arei Teshuva**, no. 178, Leipzig, 1858, p. 18, and **Sefer Ha-ora** of Rashi, ed. Buber, Lemberg, 1905, p. 4). They also add that his disciple R. Huna followed this practice. But the Talmud reports this practice only of R. Huna, the son of R. Joshua, who lived one century after R. Huna (the disciple of Rav), and nowhere does the Talmud say that Rav himself observed this custom.

Marmorstein's arguments for his theory that the Palestinians would cover their heads and the Babylonians would go bareheaded (**ibid.**, l.c., also **Ha-olam**, 1926, no. 8, pp. 159ff) are not at all convincing. The contradiction which he finds between B., M.K. 24a and B., Berachot 60b, can be explained without recourse to his theory (comp. also A.S. Hirschberg, **Ha-olam**, November 1926, no. 47, pp. 889-890).

Like the two centers in Asia--Palestine and Babylon--the European countries in the Middle Ages (at least up to the 13th century) were also divided as regards the propriety of covering the head during prayer or not covering it. Spain followed Babylon, while France and Germany followed Palestine. The Spanish rabbinical authorities require the covering of the head during prayer and in general consider it praiseworthy to avoid going bareheaded. Thus, Maimonides declares that one should not recite his prayers with uncovered head (**Yad**, Hil. Tefila IV.5) and he also says that it is the proper thing for a scholar not to go bareheaded (**ibid.**, De-ot V.6). The **Zohar** in Va-etchanan (Lublin, 1872, p. 520) likewise says that one must cover his head ("**Uva-ei lechafaya reisheh**") when praying. R. Abraham ibn Yarhi in **Hamanhig**, Tefila, 43 (Berlin, 1855, p. 15), states that it is a custom to pray with covered head, and he recommends this custom as well as the general practice of covering the head; but he expressly characterizes them as the custom and practice of the Jews in Spain. (This plainly contradicts the statement of David ben Yehuda Chasid as quoted by A. Marmorstein in **Monatschrift fuer die Geschichte und Wissenschaft des Judentums**, 1927, p. 41). R. Jeroham b. Meshullam, in his **Toledot Adam VeChava** I, Nativ 16 (Kopys, 1808, p. 118b), requires the covering of the head when reciting benedictions. Judah Asheri, in his responsa **Zichron Yehuda**, no. 2 (Berlin, 1846, 4a) recommends the covering of the head when studying the Torah, but would not insist upon it in hot weather, when one feels uncomfortable to have his head covered. And Joseph Caro, in **Shulchan Aruch**, Orach Chayim 91.3, merely mentions that some authorities forbid the uttering of the name of God in prayer with uncovered heads, and also that some authorities would even prevent people from entering the synagogue with uncovered head, but he himself does not decide the question. He recommends, however, as a pious practice (**midat chasidut**), not to go around bareheaded (**ibid.**, 2.6, according to R. Abraham Abali Gumbiner in his commentary **Magen Avraham** to 91.3; comp. also **Tur**, O. Ch. 2 and the discussion of Isserles in **Darchei Mosheh** and especially of R. Joel Sirkes in **Bayit Chadash**, ad loc.).

In France and Germany, however--following the Palestinian custom--there was no objection to praying or reading from the Torah with uncovered head. Thus R. Isaac b. Moses (**Or Zarua**) of Vienna (1200-1270) expressly reports that it was the custom of the French rabbis to pray with uncovered heads: "**Minhag raboteinu shebeTsarefat schemevarechin berosh meguleh**" (**Or Zarua** 2.43, Zitomir, 1862, p. 20), though he does not favor it. Likewise, R. Meir of Rothenburg (1215-1293) is quoted by his disciple R. Shimshon b. Zadok in **Tashbaz** 547 (Warsaw, 1875, p. 93) as having said that it was not forbidden to go around bareheaded. He is said to have explained the conduct of R. Huna the son of R. Joshua (reported in Kiddushin 31a and Shabbat 118b) as having been an exceptional case of extreme piety which the average man need not follow. Compare also **Kol Bo**, Tefila, XI (Lemberg, 1860, 8a).

Beginning, however, with the 13th century, the Babylonian-Spanish custom began to penetrate into France and Germany. We accordingly find Ashkenazic authorities of the thirteenth century and of the following centuries favoring the Spanish custom and recommending or requiring that one should cover his head when praying or reading from the Torah (cf. R. Isaac of Vienna, in **Or Zarua**, l.c., and R. Moses Isserles in **Darchei Mosheh** to **Tur**, Orach Chayim 282.3, arguing against the French custom, and in **Shulchan Aruch**, Orach Chayim 282.3, forbidding one to read the Torah bareheaded, and many others). But even as late as the 16th century it was in German-Polish countries not generally considered as forbidden to read the Torah or to pray bareheaded. R. Solomon Lurya, one of the greatest rabbinical authorities of his time (1510-1573), in his responsum no. 72, referring to the above, expressly says: "**Ein ani yodea isur levarech belo kisui harosh**" ("I do not know of any prohibition against praying with uncovered head"). (Comp. also Joseph Solomon Delmedigo in his **Matsref Lechochma**, Odessa, 1864, p.

76.)   In the 17th century, R. David Halevi of Lemberg (1586-1667), in his commentary **Turei Zahav**, to Shulchan Aruch, Orach Chayim 8.3, advanced the argument that praying with uncovered head be forbidden on the ground that, since it is a custom generally practiced by non-Jews, it should be regarded as **Chukat Hagoy**. This argument, however, is fallacious. For, according to the definition given by R. Moses Isserles in Sh. A., Yoreh De-a 178.1 (comp. also **Tosafot** to Avoda Zara 11a, s.v. "**ve-i chuka**"), only such non-Jewish practices as are observed by the non-Jew because of some foolish superstition (**leshem shetut**) or because they express or symbolize some of his peculiar religious beliefs are to be regarded as **Chukat Hagoy**, which the Jew is forbidden to imitate.   But practices which the non-Jew observes for the sake of comfort and convenience or because they are expressions of politeness and good manners, not involving any particular doctrine, cannot be classed as **Chukat Hagoyim**, and the Jew need have no scruples in practicing them as the non-Jew does (comp. A. Chorin in **Igeret El-asaf**, Prague, 1826, pp. 23-24).   And, indeed, many great rabbinical authorities of the 17th and 18th centuries utterly disregarded this argument on the ground of the law against **Chukat Hagoy** and declared that there is no prohibition against praying with uncovered head.   Thus, R. Hezekiah Silva (1659-1698) in his commentary **Peri Chadash** to Sh. A., Orach Chayim 93.1, says: "The opinion of those who permit the utterance of the name of God in prayer with uncovered head seems to be reasonable and valid" ("**Mistabera keman dematir lehotsi azkara berosh maguleh**").

And R. Jacob Reischer (died 1733) in his responsa **Shevut Ya-akov** III, referring to the above says: "**Ve-isur giluy harosh ein lo ikar umakom barur baShas.**"   And the famous Gaon of Wilna in his commentary **Be-urei Hagra** to Sh. A., Orach Chayim 8.6, expressly says: "According to Jewish law it is permitted to enter a synagogue and to pray without covering one's head" ("**Demidina afilu lehitpalel velikanes leveit hakeneset, hakol mutar**"). And after some discussion in which he cites many proofs for his statement, he closes with the following words: "There is no prohibition whatever against praying with uncovered head, but as a matter of propriety it would seem to be good manners to cover one's head when standing in the presence of great men, and also during the religious service" ("**Kelala demilta, ein isur kelal berosh meguleh le-olam, rak lifnei hagedolim vechen be-et hatefila**").

In the 19th century, as a reaction to the first attempts of modern Reform, which suggested the removal of the hat by the worshipers in the synagogue (see **Igeret El-asaf** by A. Chorin, Prague, 1826, pp. 17-24 and

29b-31b), the strict Orthodox rabbinical authorities
became more emphatic in their insistence upon the requirement of covering the head when entering a synagogue
and when praying or performing any religious ceremony
(comp. Chayim Chizkiya Medini in his **Sede Chemed**, vol.
II, **Ma-arechet Beit Hakeneset**, Warsaw, 1896, pp. 159-
160, where most of the authorities are quoted). But
none of these authorities succeeded in proving that
there is in Jewish law or tradition an express prohibition against praying with uncovered head. (Recently it
has been argued that the custom of covering the head
during prayer is against the Halacha; see Kahan in **Revue
des Études Juives**, vol. LXXXIV, 1927, pp. 176-178.)
Neither do the reasons for the custom of covering the
head in the synagogue and the arguments for retaining
it, advanced by modern Orthodox authorities, have any
validity. Thus, to mention but a few of them: Gaster,
as reported in the **Jewish Chronicle**, referring to the
above, said that one of the reasons why the Jews covered
their heads when praying was because the Roman slaves
used to go bareheaded. The Jews did not wish to appear
as slaves, hence they covered their heads when praying.
But according to Rava (B. Shabbat 10a), it is the proper
attitude when reciting the prayers to appear like a
slave: "Ke-avda kamei mareh." An anonymous writer in
Orient-Literaturblatt VII, p. 388, arguing in favor of
retaining the custom of covering the head in the synagogue, although ordinarily it is a sign of respect to
remove the hat, gives two reasons for it. The first one
is that we need not be so formal with God as to show him
the ordinary outward signs of respect, for only man
looketh on the outward appearance, but the Lord looketh
on the heart: "Dem alten Gotte des Judentums sollen
keine Komplimente gemacht werden, er soll ueberhaupt
nicht auf aeussere Erscheinung sehen sondern in den
Herzen lesen." But according to this argument, God
would not mind if we came to him without a hat but with
a pure heart. His second reason is that the covering of
the head while in the synagogue shows that the worshipers are like one family and feel themselves at home in
the synagogue without any need of observing the social
convention of removing the hat while there. But by such
an argument one might excuse any lack of decorum in the
synagogue. Compare further G. Deutsch, **Jewish Encyclopedia** II, pp. 530ff, **s.v.** "Bareheadedness"; and "The
Covering of the Head," in **The Jewish Chronicle** of London, October 10, 1919, p. 15).
      In summing up the discussion, I would say that from
the point of view of Jewish law or ritual there can be
no objection to either covering or uncovering the head
in the synagogue, or when praying or reading the Torah.
The custom of praying bareheaded or with covered head is

not at all a question of law. It is merely a matter of social propriety and decorum. As such it cannot, and need not, be the same in all countries and certainly not remain the same for all times. For it depends on the ideas of the people as to what is the proper attire for worshipers in the temples or what is the proper thing to wear or not to wear at solemn occasions and at public worship. These ideas are, of course, in turn subject to change in different times and in different places. Hence, in countries where the covering of the head is a sign of showing respect and reverence, it certainly would be improper to appear before God in the house of prayer with uncovered head. And even in countries where it is generally regarded more respectful to remove the hat, if there be congregations who still feel like their grandfathers and consider it disrespectful to pray with uncovered heads, they are within their right if they retain the custom of their fathers. We can have no quarrel with them and should rather respect their custom. In visiting them in their synagogues or when participating in some religious service at their homes, we should do as they do. For their motive and their intentions are good, and they observe these practices out of a feeling of respect and a sense of propriety, misguided as they may appear on this point to the occidental and modern mind. On the other hand, no one should find any fault with those people who, living in countries where it is considered to be disrespectful to keep the hat on while visiting in other people's homes or in the presence of elders and superiors, deem it proper to show their respect for the synagogue by removing the hat upon entering it. These people also observe the practice with the best intentions and with a respectful spirit. They are not prompted by the desire to imitate non-Jewish practice. Their motive, rather, is to show their respect for the synagogue and to express their spirit of reverence by praying with uncovered head. And although in the last century this question of "hat on or hat off" was the subject of heated disputes between the Conservative and Liberal groups of Jewry, we should know better now and be more tolerant and more liberal towards one another. We should realize that this matter is but a detail of custom and should not cause arguments between Orthodox and Reform. It is a detail that is not worth fighting about. It should not separate Jew from Jew and

not be made the cause of breaking up Jewish groups or
dividing Jewish congregations.

Jacob Z. Lauterbach

6. PARTICIPATION OF NON-JEWS IN A JEWISH PUBLIC SERVICE
(1979)

QUESTION: To what extent may non-Jews participate
in a Jewish public service? (Committee on Education)

ANSWER: In order to answer this question properly, we
must first inquire about the status of Christians in
Jewish law.   It is clear that from the Middle Ages onward, Christians and Moslems were considered as monothe-
ists rather than pagans. The pattern for this may very
well have been set by Hiyya bar Abba, who stated that
Gentiles outside of the Land of Israel were not to be
considered idolaters, but merely as people who were
following the practices of their ancestors (Chullin
13b). Maimonides (12th century) viewed Christians and
Moslems akin to **Benei Noach**.   In that capacity, they
were assisting the preparation for the messianic era
(**Yad**, Hil. Melachim II, **Moreh Nevuchim** I.71; **Responsa**,
II, no. 448 (ed. Blau). A French contemporary of Maimonides, commenting on Talmud Bechorot 2b, expressed the
same feeling about Christians. All placed Christians in
these special categories. We should, of course, remember that good treatment and many privileges were extended to pagans in earlier times, both in Israel and in
Babylon, **mipenei darchei shalom**. We comforted their
dead, visited their sick, helped their poor, etc. (Git.
59b, 61a; **Tur**, Choshen Mishpat 266). Proper consideration was to be extended, as they were human beings despite their pagan beliefs.
The classification of Christians as **Gerei Toshav**
had theological implications and also important economic
consequences; for example, wine made by a Gentile was
permitted to be handled by Ashkenazic Jews. Although it
could not be consumed by Jews, Jews could trade in it
(**Tosafot** to San. 63b; Isserles to **Sh.A.**, Y.D. 123.1).
Sephardic Jews did not follow this practice and had no
pressing need to do so as they were not involved in
extensive wine growing and lived among Moslems whose
consumption of wine was limited (Maimonides, **Responsa**,
II, no. 448; **Tur**, Y.D. 124).

As we turn to worship, we must remember that non-Jews were welcome to pray in the ancient Temple and Solomon had already asked that their prayers be heard by God (I Kings 8:41ff). Sacrifices of pagans were acceptable in the Temple (Men. 73b) and the permanent gift of an item such as a **Menora** to a synagogue was also considered as perfectly acceptable (Arachin 6b). There was nothing improper about a non-Jew handling a Torah or reading from it; it is not subject to ritual uncleanliness (Ber. 22a; **Yad**, Hil. Sefer Torah X.8; **Sh.A.**, Y.D. 282.9). Statements about Gentiles studying Torah contradict each other; so on the one hand we have the phrase that non-Jews who studied Torah deserved death (i.e., are punishable by heaven), and on the other hand, an individual who studied in this fashion is considered equal to the High Priest (B.K. 38a). In the latter section, we hear of a Roman emperor who sent students to study Torah from the Rabbis. David Hoffman (**Melamed Leho-il**, Y.D. 77) stated that we should teach everything except specific commandments so that the Gentile not disrespect erring Jews. Despite this friendly attitude of Judaism towards Christianity, all of the traditional authorities made it quite clear that major distinctions continue to exist. Maimonides felt that many Christians were actual idolaters and, therefore, sought to restrict relationships with them (**Yad**, Hil. Akum X.2) and also prohibited Jews from dealing in any way in Christian wine (**Yad**, Hil. Ma-achalot Asurot XVII); and he and all the other medieval authorities felt that both Christianity and Islam had mixed strange concepts (**shituf**) into the absolute unity of God as expressed by Judaism (Isserles to **Shulchan Aruch**, Orach Chayim 156; Maimonides, **Pe-er Hador**, 50; etc.). In secular relationships Christians could be treated as **Benei Noach**, but in religious matters distinctions were to remain.

Now, let us deal with the specific matter of prayer recited by an idolator or a Christian. If an idolator recited a prayer, i.e., a private prayer, in the name of God, those who heard it were to respond with "Amen" (Ber. 44a; Isserles to **Sh.A.**, O.Ch. 215.2). The only references to Christians participating in Jewish public worship in Rabbinic literature which I have been able to find consisted of singers, who honored the bride and groom by singing for them on Shabbat (H. Benvenisti, **Keneset Hagedola**, quoted in Palligi, **Lev Chayim** II.9). A similar statement has already been made by Eliezer ben Joel Halevi (**Raviah**, 796). In these cases, we are dealing with instrumental music played on the Sabbath in honor of the bride and groom by non-Jews. Citations, both for and against this practice, are listed in **Sede Chemed**, Ma-arechet Chatan Vechala, no. 13.

From Babylonian times onward, public prayers for rulers of the country, parallel to those for scholars and students in the academies, were included in the liturgy and have remained there ever since. These rulers, of course, were pagans, Moslems, or Christians. We, in modern times, have gone a number of steps further than this. For example, we regularly recite the names of non-Jewish dead in the lists of deceased read before the **Kaddish.** In most cases, these are relatives of converts; although the convert is not duty-bound to mourn for his parents, he should be encouraged to do so out of respect (**Yad,** Hil. Evel 2.3; Radbaz to **Yad;** **Sh.A.,** Y.D. 374.5; and many subsequent authorities). We have, however, also added the names of notable Christians from time to time. In addition, we have participated frequently in interfaith services, which have generally been associated with national holidays or events; these have usually been non-liturgical in character, i.e., consisted of Biblical readings and various prayers without following the strict order of the service. Furthermore, we have invited non-Jews, including ministers and priests, to address our congregations during our public services. This practice has been widespread in the Reform and Conservative movements. Thus, there is no doubt that we have included priests, ministers, and non-Jewish participants in our services in a manner not known heretofore. In addition, nowadays, because of intermarriage we find the non-Jewish parent involved in a Bar/Bat Mitzvah. It would be appropriate to have that parent participate in some way in the service, but not in the same way as a Jewish parent. For example, he or she should **not** recite the traditional blessing over the Torah which includes the words "**asher bachar banu.**" It would be well if he/she recite a special blessing, perhaps akin to the words suggested by Solomon B. Freehof: "Praised be Thou, Lord our God, King of the Universe, Who has given His sacred law unto all His children that we may learn, observe, and serve Him in righteousness" (**Current Reform Responsa**, p. 91).

We have, therefore, gone much further than any generation before our time by permitting non-Jews a larger role in our public services; this is part of a more open and friendly interreligious attitude which the Reform Movement has encouraged and led. Yet, these steps have remained within definite limits. We have not included non-Jews, no matter how friendly, in the essential elements of the service.

If we follow the line of reasoning which divides between the essential service and supplemental prayers and statements, we may conclude that Christians, Moslems, and other non-Jews who fall into the category of **Benei Noach** may participate in a public service in any of the following ways: (1) through anything which does not require specific statement from them, i.e., by standing and silently witnessing whatever is taking place (e.g., as a member of a wedding party or as a pallbearer); (2) through the recitation of special prayers added to the service at non-liturgical community-wide services, commemorations, and celebrations (Thanksgiving, etc.); (3) through the recitation of prayers for special family occasions (Bar/Bat Mitzvah of children raised as Jews, at a wedding or funeral, etc.). All such prayers and statements should reflect the mood of the service and be non-Christological in nature.

> Walter Jacob, Chairman
> Leonard S. Kravitz
> Eugene Lipman
> Harry A. Roth
> Rav A. Soloff
> Bernard Zlotowitz
> W. Gunther Plaut

See also:

S.B. Freehof, "Gentile Bridesmaids," **Reform Responsa**, pp. 190ff; "Gentile Stepfather at Bar Mitzvah," **Current Reform Responsa**, pp. 91ff; "Gentile's Part in the Sabbath Service," **New Reform Responsa**, pp. 33ff; "Pre-Convert Participating in Services", **Current Reform Responsa**, p. 88ff.

7. ORDINATION OF WOMEN AS RABBIS
(Vol. XXXII, 1922, pp. 50-51)

The discussion of the responsum, "Shall Women be Ordained as Rabbis?" was led by Rabbi Jacob Z. Lauterbach.

The following participated in the discussion: Rabbis Max Heller, Levinger, Witt, Weiss, Brickner, Charles S. Levi, Rauch, Englander, Abrams, Raisin, Baron, J.G. Heller, Cohon, Frisch, and Nathan Stern; Mrs. Frisch, Miss Baron, and Mrs. Berkowitz. The discussion was closed by Rabbi Lauterbach.

It was moved and adopted that the courtesy of the floor be extended to the wives of rabbis, in order to ascertain their views on this subject.

It was moved and adopted that the President appoint a committee to formulate a statement which shall express the sentiment that the Central Conference of American Rabbis has repeatedly made pronouncements urging the fullest measures of self-expression for woman, as well as the fullest utilization of her gifts, in the service of the Most High, and that it gratefully acknowledges the enrichment and enlargement of congregational life which has resulted therefrom.

Whatever may have been the specific legal status of the Jewish woman regarding certain religious function, her general position in Jewish religious life has ever been an exalted one. She has been the priestess in the home, and our sages have always recognized her as the preserver of Israel. In view of these Jewish teachings and in keeping with the spirit of our age and the traditions of our conference, we declare that woman cannot justly be denied the privilege of ordination.

Henry Cohen and Committee

8.   ORDINATION OF WOMEN
(Vol. XXXII, 1922, pp. 156-177)

The very raising of this question is due, no doubt, to the great changes in the general position of women, brought about during the last half century or so. Women have been admitted to other professions, formerly practiced by men only, and have proven themselves successful as regards personal achievement as well as raising the standards or furthering the interests of the professions. Hence the question suggested itself, why not admit women also to the rabbinical profession?

The question resolves itself into the following two parts: first, the attitude of traditional Judaism on this point, and second, whether Reform Judaism should follow tradition in this regard. At the outset it should be stated that from the point of view of traditional Judaism there is an important distinction between the rabbinate and the other professions in regard to the admission of women. In the case of the other professions there is nothing inherent in their teachings or principles which might limit their practice to men exclusively. In the case of the rabbinate, on the other hand, there are, as will soon be shown, definite teachings and principles in traditional Judaism, of which the rabbinate in the exponent, which demand that its official representatives and functionaries be men only. To

admit women to the rabbinate is, therefore, not merely a
question of liberalism; it is contrary to the very spirit of traditional Judaism which the rabbinate seeks to
uphold and preserve.

It should be stated further, that these traditional
principles debarring women from the rabbinate were not
formulated in an illiberal spirit by the Rabbis of old
or out of a lack of appreciation of women's talents and
endowments. Indeed the Rabbis of old entertained a high
opinion of womanhood and frequently expressed their
admiration for woman's ability and appreciated her great
usefulness in religious work. Thus, e.g., they say,
"God has endowed woman with a finer appreciation and a
better understanding than man" (Nida 45b); "Sarah was
superior to Abraham in prophecy" (**Tanchuma**, Exodus,
beginning); "It was due to the pious women of that generation that the Israelites were redeemed from Egypt"
(Sota); and "The women were the first ones to receive
and accept the Torah" (**Tanchuma**, Buber, Metsora, 18, p.
27a); and "They refused to participate in the making of
the golden calf." These and many other sayings could be
cited from Rabbinic literature in praise of woman, her
equality to man and, in some respects, superiority to
him. So we may safely conclude that their excluding of
women from the rabbinate does not at all imply deprecia-
tion on their part of woman's worth.

But with all their appreciation of woman's fine
talents and noble qualities, the Rabbis of old have also
recognized that man and woman have each been assigned by
the Torah certain spheres of activity, involving special
duties. The main sphere of woman's activity and her
duties centered in the house. Since she has her own
duties to perform, and since especially in her position
as wife and mother she would often be prevented from
carrying on many of the regular activities imposed upon
man, the law frees her from many religious obligations
incumbent upon men, and especially exempts her from such
positive duties the performance of which must take place
at certain fixed times, like reciting the "Shema" or at
prescribed seasons, like Sukkot (M. Kiddushin 1.7):
"**Vechol mitsvat aseh shehazeman geramah, anashim
chayavim venashim peturut.**"

This fact, that she was exempt from certain obligations and religious duties, necessarily excluded her
from the privilege of acting as the religious leader or
representative of the congregation (**Sheliach Tsibur**).
She could not represent the congregation in the performing of certain religious functions, since, according to
the Rabbinic principle, one who is not personally obliged to perform a certain duty, cannot perform that duty
on behalf of others and certainly cannot represent the
congregation in the performance of such duties: "Kol

she-eino mechuyav badavar eino motsi et harabim yedei chovatan" (R.H. III.8; Berachot 20b).

On the same principle, she was expressly disqualified from writing Torah scrolls. Since she could not perform for the congregation the duty of reading from the Torah, the text prepared by her was also not qualified for use in connection with the performance of that duty (Gittin, 45b; Mas. Soferim 1.14). Women were also considered exempt from the obligation to study the Torah (Eruvin 27a; Kiddushin 29b-30a). Some Rabbis even went so far as to object to women studying the Torah (M. Sota III.4). This opinion, of course, did not prevail. Women were taught the Bible and given a religious education, and there were some women learned in the law even in Talmudic times. But to use the phrase of the Talmud (M.K. 18a), "Isha bei midrasha la shechicha," women were not to be found in the Beit Hamidrash, in the academies and colleges where the rabbis assembled and where the students prepared themselves to be rabbis. Evidently, the reason that they could not aspire to be rabbis, was that the law excluded them from this religious office.

This law, that women cannot be rabbis, was always taken for granted in the Talmud. It was considered to be so generally known and unanimously agreed upon that it was not even deemed necessary to make it a special subject of discussion. The very idea of a woman becoming a rabbi never even entered the mind of the Rabbis of old. It is for this reason that we find only few direct and definite statements to the effect that women cannot be rabbis. Only occasionally, when the discussion of other questions involved the mentioning of it, reference--direct or indirect--is made to the established law that women cannot act as judges or be rabbis. Thus, in a baraita (Pal. Talmud Shevu-ot 4.1, 35b, and Sanhedrin 4.10, 21c) it is stated "Harei lamedan sheha-isha einah dana," "We have learned that a woman cannot act as judge," i.e., cannot render decisions of law. The same principle is also indirectly expressed in the Mishna (comp. Nida 6.4 and Shevu-ot 4.1). In the Talmud (Gittin 5b), it is also indirectly stated that a woman cannot be a member of a Beit Din, i.e., a rabbi or judge. For there it is taken for granted that she could not be one of three who form a tribunal or Beit Din to pass upon the correctness of a bill of divorce or of any other document (see Rashi, ad loc.).

In the Midrash (Num. R. 10.5) it is also quoted as a well-known and established principle that women may not have the authority to render decisions in religious or ritual matters: "Shehanashim einam benot hora-a."

These Talmudic principles have been accepted by all medieval Jewish authorities. Maimonides (Yad, Sanhedrin II.7) declares that the members of every tribunal or

Beit Din in Israel, which means every rabbi, **dayan**, or **moreh hora-a** in Israel must possess the same qualities which characterized the men whom Moses selected to be his associates and whom he appointed judges and leaders in Israel. These qualities, Maimonides continues, are expressly stated in the Torah, as it is said: "Get you from each one of your tribes **men**, wise and understanding and full of knowledge, and I will make them heads over you" (Deut. 1:13). Maimonides here has in mind the idea, entertained by the rabbis of all generations, that the rabbis of each generation continue the activity and are the recipients of the spirit of those first religious leaders of the Jewish people. For, as is well known, Mosheh Rabbenu and the Seventy Elders who formed his Council were considered the prototypes and the models of the rabbis of all subsequent generations (comp. Mishna, R.H. II.9). Likewise, R. Aaron Halevi of Barcelona (about 1300 C.E.) in his **Sefer Hachinuch** (nos. 74, 75, 77, 79, 81, 83), Jacob Asheri in **Tur**, Choshen Mishpat VII, and Joseph Caro in **Shulchan Aruch**, Choshen Mishpat VII.3--all expressly state the principle that a woman cannot officiate as judge or rabbi. It hardly need be stated that when some of the sources use in this connection the term "Judge" (**dayan**) they, of course, mean rabbi, for which **dayan** is but another name. In rabbinic terminology the functions of a rabbi are spoken of as being "**ladin ulehorot**," to judge and decide religious and ritual questions. And even in our modern rabbinical diploma we use the formula "**Yoreh yoreh, yadin yadin**," giving the candidate whom we ordain the authority to judge and decide religious questions and to give authoritative ruling in all religious matters.

To be sure, the Rabbis do permit the women to be religious teachers, like Miriam, who, according to the Rabbis, taught the women while Moses and Aaron taught the men (**Sifrei Zuta**, quoted in **Yalkut Shim-oni**, **Behaalotecha**, 741 end), and Deborah, whom the Rabbis believed to have been merely teaching the law (**Seder Eliyahu R.** IX-X, Friedman, p. 50; compare also **Tosafot**, B.K. 15a, **s.v.** "**asher tasim**" and parallels). Some authorities would put certain restrictions upon woman even in regard to her position as teacher (see Kiddushin 82a, and Maimonides, **Yad**, Talmud Torah II.4), but in general, the opinion of the Rabbis was that women may be teachers of religion (see **Chinuch**, 152, and comp. Azulai in **Birkei Yosef** to Choshen Mishpat VII.12); and as a matter of fact, there have always been learned women in Israel. These women-scholars were respected for their learning in the same manner as learned men were respected (see **Sefer Chasidim**, 978, and comp. also **Sede Chemed** I, letter **Kaf**, no. 99), and some of these women scholars would occasionally even give lectures in rabbinics; but they have never been admitted to the rabbinate, since all the rabbinic authorities agree, at least implicitly, that women cannot hold the office of a rabbi or of a **Sheliach Tsibur** and cannot perform any of the official functions requiring the authority of a rabbi.

This is the attitude of traditional Judaism towards the question of women rabbis, a view strictly adhered to by all Jewry all over the world throughout all generations, even unto this day.

Now we come to the second part of our question; that is, shall we adhere to this tradition, or shall we separate ourselves from Catholic Israel and introduce a radical innovation which would necessarily create a distinction between the title Rabbi as held by a Reform rabbi and the title Rabbi in general? I believe that hitherto no distinction could rightly be drawn between the ordination of our modern rabbis and the ordination of all the rabbis of preceding generations. We are still carrying on the activity of the Rabbis of old who traced their authority through a chain of tradition to Moses and the Elders associated with him, even though in many points we interpret our Judaism in a manner quite different from theirs. We are justified in considering ourselves the latest link in that long chain of authoritative teachers who carry on their activity of teaching, preserving, and developing Judaism. For our time we have the same standing as they had (comp. R.H. 25a). The ordination which we give to our disciples carries with it, for our time and generation, the same authority which marked the ordination given by Judah Hanasi to Abba Areka or the ordination given by any teacher in Israel to his disciples throughout all the history of Judaism.

We should therefore not jeopardize the hitherto indisputable authoritative character of our ordination. We should not make our ordination entirely different in character from the traditional ordination, and thereby give the larger group of Jewry that follows traditional Judaism a good reason to question our authority and to doubt whether we are rabbis in the sense in which this honored title was always understood.

Nor is there, to my mind, any actual need for making such a radical departure from this established Jewish law and time-honored practice. The supposed lack of a sufficient number of rabbis will not be made up by this radical innovation. There are other and better means of meeting this emergency. This could be accomplished if our rabbis would follow the advice of the men of the Great Synagogue, to raise many disciples and thus encourage more men to enter the ministry. And the standard of the rabbinate in America, while no doubt it could be improved in many directions, is certainly not

so low as to need a new and refining influence such as
the influence brought by women to any profession they
enter. Neither could women, with all due respect to
their talents and abilities, raise the standard of the
rabbinate. Nay, all things being equal, women could not
even raise it to the high standard reached by men, in
this particular calling. If there is any calling which
requires a wholehearted devotion to the exclusion of all
other things and the determination to make it one's
whole life work, it is the rabbinate. It is not to be
considered merely as a profession by which one earns a
livelihood. Nor is it to be entered upon as a temporary
occupation. One must choose it for his life work and be
prepared to give to it all his energies and to devote to
it all the years of his life, constantly learning and
improving and thus growing in it. It has been rightly
said that the woman who enters a profession must make
her choice between following her chosen profession or
the calling of mother and home-maker. She cannot do
both well at the same time. This certainly would hold
true in the case of the rabbinical profession. The
woman who naturally and rightly looks forward to the
opportunity of meeting the right kind of man, of marrying him, and of having children and a home of her own,
cannot give to the rabbinate that wholehearted devotion
which comes from the determination to make it one's life
work. For in all likelihood she could not continue it
as a married woman. For, one holding the rabbinical
office must teach by precept and example, and must give
an example of Jewish family and home life where all the
traditional Jewish virtues are cultivated. The rabbi
can do so all the better when he is married and has a
home and a family of his own. The wife whom God has
made as helpmate to him can be, and in most cases is, of
great assistance to him in making his home a Jewish
home, a model for the congregation to follow.

In this important activity of the rabbi--exercising
a wholesome influence upon the congregation--the woman
rabbi would be deficient. The woman in the rabbinical
office could not expect the man to whom she was married
to be merely a helpmate to her, assisting her in her
rabbinical activities. And even if she could find such
a man, willing to take a subordinate position in the
family, the influence upon the families in the congregation of such an arrangement in the home and in the family life of the rabbi would not be very wholesome. (Not
to mention the fact that if she is to be a mother she
could not go on with her regular activities in the congregation.)

And there is, to my mind, no injustice done to
woman by excluding her from this office. There are many
avenues open to her if she chooses to do religious or

educational work. I can see no reason why we should
make this radical departure from traditional practice
except the specious argument that we are modern men and,
as such, we recognize the full equality of women to men,
hence we should be thoroughly consistent. But I would
not class the rabbis with those people whose main characteristic is consistency.

Jacob Z. Lauterbach

Discussion

Rabbi Levinger: I feel very strongly on this question. When we look at the various denominations in this
country who are opposed to ordaining women as ministers
we find that they are those who, like the Episcopalians
and the Catholics, look upon their ministers as priests.
To us the rabbi is merely a teacher and preacher. The
question is not whether there are a great many women who
want to become rabbis. Perhaps there are none at all.
But we are called upon to act on a matter of principle,
and if in the next thirty or forty years we produce but
one Anna Howard Shaw, we want her in the rabbinate.

Rabbi Witt: I was present at the meeting of the
Board of Governors when the matter came up, and it was
decided to refer it to the Conference. After reading
the responsa that were prepared by Rabbi Lauterbach, I
feared that there would be much opposition. I trust
that our action in this matter will be unanimous. It is
not a matter of tradition at all. I must confess I was
not in the least interested in Rabbi Lauterbach's presentation. It seemed reactionary to me. I did not feel
that it was the proper presentation of the subject.
I need not say that I honor Dr. Lauterbach for the
learning contained therein, but the point he presents is
not the point at issue. We have witnessed the revolution in the status of women. Five years ago I had to
argue in favor of women's rights when that question came
up in the Arkansas legislature, but I did not feel that
there would be need to argue that way in a liberal body
of men like this.
There is a principle involved, and I hope that the
stand we take will be one in line with all the progressive tendencies of our day; that we will have the vision
to see what is before us. From the standpoint of today,
shall we say to women that they shall not have the right
to function as we are functioning?

The question is: Have they the qualifications to function as spiritual leaders?

What does it require to be a spiritual guide? It requires a great spirit and the quality of leadership. Some women have it and some women have not. Some men have it and some men have not. If we had a great leadership we would not have the questions which were so ably presented yesterday among the practical questions of the ministry. The one thing that was stressed was that if we had devoted leaders who could inspire following, all the problems would vanish.

I believe that this body of men should do nothing that would stand in the way of any forward movement in behalf of the womanhood of America. I cannot believe that a religion that is so splendidly spiritual and forward-looking as our religion will stand in the way of such a movement. I feel that this Conference can only act in one way, and that is to fall in line with what is the destiny of the women of the future.

Rabbi Weiss: In a large measure I agree with the previous speakers. I agree with all that has been said in favor of ordaining women as rabbis. I believe I am second to none in the rabbinate in the matter of idealism. But a vast measure of compromise must enter into all situations of life. I do not believe that we can have life exactly as we would like to have it. There is a vast debt due to cold austere justice, but there are fourteen million Jews in the world, and they must be considered. In the city of New York alone there are a million and a half who look upon you with a degree of respect but who have their own mode of procedure and who would look upon any radical action on your part as a line of cleavage in the House of Israel. I merely mean that we should proceed slowly. I believe that some compromise can be effected, such as allowing women to be teachers or superintendents; but I believe that it would be unwise at the present time to have them ordained as rabbis. Let me give one concrete illustration. Suppose a woman were to sign a marriage document. To many in New York today such a ceremony would hardly be recognized as binding.

Rabbi Brickner: There is much merit in what Dr. Lauterbach has said. He has not stressed the question of opinion, but the question of practicability. Modern psychologists agree that women do not differ from men so much in intellect. In fact, experiments prove that women are the peers of most men. There are women occupying positions in modern industry in which they could not be equaled by many men. It is not a question of equality. All that Dr. Lauterbach has said has already been said against women entering other professions. The question with us is one of practicability. The tendency in modern Judaism is to conserve Jewish values. We wish to be in touch with the masses of Jewish people. When I came away from Toronto the other day I clipped from the newspaper the vote of the Methodist Church in Canada. It represents the liberal traditions in Canada. And yet it voted by a small majority against permitting women into the ministry. It is not a question of principle or equality--on that we are all agreed. It is purely a question of practicability.

Rabbi Charles S. Levi: The matter before you is not a matter of the hour, but a matter of all times. It is a matter that touches upon the acknowledged leadership of our people, and reaches the lives of uncounted thousands of our American co-religionists. We are the links in the chain of time. We are the spokesmen who give expression to the great truths which bind the past to the future, and it is for us to keep alive the chain of tradition.

Rabbi Rauch: I listened with great interest to Dr. Lauterbach's presentation and was at first inclined to agree with him, but as he proceeded it struck me that there was a great omission. He gave a fine presentation of the traditional point of view and even hinted at certain modern needs, but I regret to say that he failed to touch on what Reform Judaism has to say on the subject. And yet our whole interpretation of religious life is supposedly based on the principles of Reform Judaism. Now what has the philosophy of Reform Judaism to say in regard to woman? I know from experience because I was born in an Orthodox environment. There was a very clear line of distinction between the boy and the girl, and the education given to the boy and girl. The boy had to learn Scriptures, while the girl was not expected to learn them. Many duties were imposed upon the boy, few upon the girl. This went on for centuries. What happened when Reform came in? One by one the barriers separating the boy from the girl educationally began to be broken down. We admitted the girls into the same schools, and we tried to teach them the same things. Even in the important ceremony of Bar Mitzvah we brushed aside the traditional point of view and we said that the girl should be educated and confirmed the same as the boy. And in our congregations, which is the practical side of our religious life, we have given to women exactly the same status as to men. In my own congregation women conduct the summer services, and they conduct them just as well as--if not better than--they used to be when we got someone temporarily for the sum-

mer. In every line of endeavor in our temples we have
proceeded on the theory that woman is the equal of man.
What do they ask us to do? They want us to make it
possible for women to work along the same lines as we
men are working. We do not ask privileges for them.
Let there be the same demands, the same rigorous training, and let the congregation decide whether the woman
is doing the work well or not. I do not think that our
course will be hurt by a liberal attitude.

Rabbi Englander: Personally, I was surprised to
learn that the Board of Governors submitted this question to the Conference. I thought that after the facul-
ty--a body composed of the teachers--had taken action,
that would be sufficient guidance for action on the part
of the Board of Governors. However, I wish to touch on
one argument which has been raised to the effect that if
we admit women as rabbis we would tend to create a
schism in Israel. During all the conferences in recent
years there have been many actions that we would not
have taken had we feared this. We would not have set
ourselves on record against Zionism. Had fear been
taken into consideration, we would not have taken a
stand on many subjects. Twenty years ago, this Conference put itself on record favoring absolute religious
equality of women with men. Are we going back on our
own action? In spite of all the arguments advanced by
Dr. Lauterbach, the faculty set itself on record as
favoring the ordination of women, although it stated
that at the present time it believed it was impractical
for women to enter the rabbinate. But I do not believe
that the question of practicability is for us to decide.
The only question before us is: Shall we, in the light
of Reform Judaism, put ourselves in favor of admitting
women to the rabbinate?

A motion is made that further discussion be discontinued.

Rabbi Morgenstern: I do not care to express any
opinion upon this subject, because--you can readily
understand--inasmuch as this question has been submitted
by the College authorities to the Conference to get an
expression of opinion, I am here rather to listen than
to offer any opinion I myself may have. I realize that
the time of the Conference is very precious and that you
cannot afford to give more time than is necessary to the
discussion of this question, but I believe that the
question is of such importance that it ought to justify
the expenditure of as much time as may be necessary for
a thorough discussion of the question. Several of the
men lay emphasis upon the significance of the principle

of not breaking with Catholic Israel. We have heard the arguments, but there are several valuable thoughts which have not yet been presented. And there is one phase of the question which has not been adequately discussed. We can all accept the opinion of Dr. Lauterbach as authoritative, namely, that from the point of view of traditional Judaism the ordination of women would not be permitted. We need not discuss that. But the practical aspect of the question has not been discussed. Namely, is it expedient, and is it worthwhile?

Rabbi Abrams: It seems to me that the question resolves itself into three parts. First, what is the principle? Second, is it consistent? Third, is it practical?

As a matter of principle, women ought to be ordained, as we now recognize that they are entitled to the same privileges and rights as men. Our ancestors never asked, is it practical? They asked, is it the will of God? And thus they settled the question for themselves. But we must ask the question, is it in keeping with the tradition of the past? In the whole paper of Rabbi Lauterbach we do not find the statement that women could not be ordained as rabbis. Indirectly we inferred that they may not be ordained because we do not find any women who were ordained. At the most, sentiment was against it; but sentiment has been against women going into many of the professions even today. But that does not mean that they should not be ordained or could not be according to traditional laws.

What is our ordination today? In spite of our claim that we are the descendants of the ancient Rabbis, we must admit that the function of the modern rabbi is entirely different from the function of the Rabbi of old. In olden times, he was the judge. That was his chief function. Preaching and teaching were secondary. If we were to lay claim to be lineal descendants of the ancient teachers, we must go to the prophets of the Bible. We are the followers of the prophets more than of the Rabbis. And if we would follow the example of the women of the Bible, we would find that many women served as prophets and that during Talmudic times many of them taught. So we are not inconsistent with the past if we put ourselves on record as favoring the ordination of women.

Rabbi Joseph L. Baron: I enjoyed thoroughly the scholarly paper of my teacher on the negative view of the question, and I shall not deny that the admission of women into the rabbinate will, like any innovation, shock some people and call forth opposition and ridicule. But I wish to point out several flaws in the negative argument. Professor Lauterbach intimates that the matter has hitherto never arisen as a practical issue because it has been taken for granted that a woman cannot, in the capacity of a rabbi, carry out, or represent the people in, a function in which she is not personally obliged to participate. How, then, can we infer from this that with the full entry of woman in all the religious functions of home and synagogue, she must still be denied the privilege of ordination? We broke with tradition long ago when we granted women an equal standing with men in all our religious functions.

I disagree entirely with the remark that by taking the proposed step, we shall create a schism. The Russian Jews, to whom reference has been made, do recognize and follow women leaders, as in the radical factions. And if women are not recognized as leaders in the Orthodox synagogue, let us not forget that neither are we recognized as such. There is a distinct difference made, even in the Yiddish terminology, between a **Rav** and a **Rabbi**. Again, we broke with tradition long ago when we declared that a rabbi need not be an authority on questions of **kashrut**; and I need not mention which, from the point of view of Orthodoxy, is the greater offense.

When I received the responsum of Dr. Lauterbach a week or two ago, I inquired as to the attitude of the members of a Unitarian Church in Moline, where a woman has been officiating for about half a year, and the reply was very favorable. That minister is not falling behind her male predecessors in her zeal and ability in handling all the problems of the church. So, as to the practicality of the matter, I believe that should be left entirely with the individual congregation.

Rabbi James G. Heller: I do not believe that the Conference has the right to appeal to its duty to "Catholic Israel" in order to settle this question. In the past, many decisions have been taken which evidenced no regard for mere keeping of the peace. The one question at issue, the one question that should be discussed by this Conference, is whether in principle the admission of women into the rabbinate is desirable, and whether it is in accordance with the historic teachings of Reform Judaism. The entire content of Dr. Lauterbach's responsum can, to my mind, be summed up in that very logical inconsistency to which he refers toward the end of his paper in so laudatory a manner. He must complete the syllogism contained in his remarks. Since traditional Judaism, Orthodoxy, did not require women to perform certain duties or functions, did not permit them to share in certain duties or functions, did not permit them to share in certain religious acts, it could not allow them to become teachers of these same duties.

And, per contra, since Reform Judaism requires and asks of women the performance of every religious duty in the catalogue, it cannot deny them the right to become teachers and preachers.

Rabbi Samuel S. Cohon: I wish to call your attention to the fact that in other professions there is a great deal of prejudice against women even where they administer with considerable success. You would imagine that women would welcome the services of women physicians; but in actual practice it is stated that women are more bitterly opposed to female practitioners than are men.

In the legal profession we also know that in many instances women are debarred from practice. But I believe that many of us who realize how much our wives have helped us, how they have cooperated with us, how they have borne many of the responsibilities, also realize that they should be given the opportunity to assume this work on their own accord, if they so desire. Of course, there will be prejudice against women in the rabbinate, but if one congregation is found that will welcome a woman, the opportunity should be granted.

Rabbi Frisch: We have made greater departures from tradition in Reform Judaism than the one which is before us, so we can afford to dismiss this question without further discussion. But I regard the ordination of women as the last step in the removal of restrictions in the Jewish faith. She is fitted by temperament and by all of her qualifications to the position of teacher, and she has been granted the right to participate in all our congregational activities as the equal of man. Civilization has had cause to regret every restriction which it has placed in the way of those who wanted to be free.

I have been wondering whether we are not denying ourselves a new source of strength, a new source of inspiration, by our reluctance to admit women to the rabbinate. I recognize the handicaps, but I believe that the women who surmount the obstacles will be greater spirits than the men who are in the rabbinate today. Will it be any greater reproach for a woman to give up the ministry for the sake of maternity than it is for a man to give it up to seek a livelihood in other work? I think it will be for a nobler reason. If we get women into our midst as rabbis, I believe that we will be enjoying some of the inspiration and strength which we feel we need. So I plead that we place ourselves on record as in full sympathy with a further emancipation of women by their ordination as rabbis in Israel.

Rabbi Stern: Emotionally I am conservative and I do not like to break with the past, but I cannot agree with Rabbi Lauterbach in this instance. Is it not essential for us first to decide what is the principle? I believe the practical will take care of itself. It is very interesting to note that in the city of New York a professor in the Seminary, the rabbi of an Orthodox congregation, had a Bar Mitzvah of girls. This is very interesting and shows that the other wing of Judaism is also making progress.

A motion that the opinions of members which have been sent in should be read was introduced. The motion lost.

Rabbi Morgenstern: I think there is one possible source of information that we have not heard from and whose opinion would be very helpful to us. I mean the wives of the rabbis present. It would help us to get an expression of opinion from the women, if some of the wives would be willing to give us their ideas based on many years of experience in this work. I would ask that this opportunity be given to the ladies to express their opinions.

It was moved that the courtesy of the floor be extended to any of the ladies present who cared to take part in the discussion.

Mrs. Frisch: When I entered the hall this morning, I was opposed to the ordination of women as rabbis. I am now in favor of it. I have been much impressed with what I have heard.

The reason I was opposed to the ordination of women was what you would call the practical reason. I now feel that whatever practical reasons I may have had cannot be compared in value with the matter of principle which has been mentioned here this morning.

The practical reason that I had in mind was that I, as a wife and mother, did not understand how a woman could attend to the duties which devolve upon a rabbi and at the same time be a true home-maker. Candidly, I do not see at this moment how it can be accomplished. I cannot solve this question, but there may be some women who would prefer a life of celibacy in order to minister to a congregation.

Personally, I am selfish enough not to be willing to give up the happiness of wifehood and motherhood for this privilege, great though it may be. But I love the work of the rabbinate so much that could I have prevailed upon myself to forget the joys that come with home-making, I should have become a rabbi. I do not

believe that privilege should be denied women, and it
behooves us to go on record as being in favor of this
development.

Miss Baron: I am connected with Jewish work in New
York City and I know that since the Jewish woman has
entered this work it has intensified the value of Jewish
education. I believe that should the Jewish woman enter
the rabbinate, she will be able to intensify the religious feeling of our people.

Mrs. Berkowitz: I am more than satisfied to be the
silent member of our partnership, but I believe that it
is the function of women to give spiritual value to the
world, and especially the Jewish woman--imbued with the
Jewish spirit--will naturally bring a certain quality to
the ministry which some of our men lack. I think that
might be enlarged and strengthened, and therefore I
should like to see our women become rabbis, if they wish
to do so.

A motion that action on this resolution be postponed until next year lost.

A motion that a referendum vote of the members of
the Conference be taken lost.

A motion that this resolution be referred to the
Committee on Resolutions lost.

Rabbi Joseph Leiser: The objections of Professor
Lauterbach concerning the admission of Jewish women to
the rabbinate are inadequate. His thesis, that the
rabbinical profession is a career and involves the totality of life to the preclusion of even the function
and offices of motherhood, is not valid and is no more
applicable to the Jewish woman as rabbi than it is to
the Jewish woman as lawyer, doctor, dentist, newspaper
writer, musician, businesswoman, or teacher. In all
these trades and professions, Jewish women are actively
engaged beyond the consideration or limitations of sex,
and in spite of previous sex taboos. As a profession,
the rabbinate ought to be open to women on a parity with
that of men, provided women receive a degree for academic training carried on according to approved standards.
But my objection to the position maintained by
Professor Lauterbach rests on more fundamental conten-
tions than of sex discrimination in the rabbinate. The
Professor fails to analyze the rabbinate in the light of
its function and activity in the world today. He carries over into America, a modern America, the methodology and outlook of an Orthodox rabbi whose function is

that of a lawyer, one who renders decisions in an ecclesiastical court from codes drawn up by established standards of behavior. Orthodox Judaism rests upon laws of conformity: one discharges his duties; one learns them and fulfills them. Whereas Reform Judaism releases the individual and enables him to realize his own nature, and therefore allows him to contribute whatever there is implanted within his soul and mind in humanity.

This difference in motivation is translated to the profession of the rabbi, as it is interpreted in Reform Judaism.

The mere repudiation of the authority of the Talmud and **Shulchan Aruch** is not sufficient to constitute one as a Reform rabbi; nor does the acceptance of these make one an Orthodox rabbi. To be sure, the Orthodox rabbi is learned in the law, since the very nature and constitution of his profession require it. But the Reform rabbi is not primarily a legal expert. The modern rabbinate has become an institution, just as the synagogue has developed functions other than those pertaining to worship and the discharging of ceremonial observances. In these days it serves more than one purpose, and therefore requires more than one type of professional labor.

The variety of activities that are now released in the ordinary synagogue calls for a number of workers, all of whom must be filled with the knowledge of God. The new work recently developed in the synagogue appeals particularly to the woman, who by nature and training is singularly fitted to undertake it.

It will be said in rebuttal that while the need and ability of these modern activities within the synagogue may require the professional assistance of women, these functions do not require the training and professional equipment of a rabbi. This is a mistake. Mere inclination provides access to those qualities of emotionalism and undisciplined enthusiasm which endanger the assistance of a woman. Professional training is required for the expert in the religious institution of the synagogue. In the departments of education, as our synagogues are elaborating them, a Jewish woman is particularly well qualified, providing her training in rabbinics is grounded in a thorough knowledge of the literature.

A Jewish woman is the logical adjunct to young people's societies and organizations, and no synagogue is complete without these new features.

The social activities of a congregation are dependent on the social instincts of a woman. Her rabbinical training enables her to link up these activities with tradition and provides the background of Jewish consciousness to this work.

The pulpit, and whatever pertains to it, is--and
remains--a plane wherein man is by nature and temperament best qualified, although not exclusively so. But
woman, by reason of self-limitation, is not disqualified. Viewing the rabbi in the light of a prophet and
the man of vision, he--more than woman--responds to this
unusual endowment. Men are prone to be idealists. They
are quick to see visions. They are the dreamers. To
men is given the gift of prophecy, but not exclusively
(as the careers of Hulda and Deborah testify). Men are
called upon by God to be pathfinders, liberators, pro-
tagonists of right, brandishing the shining sword of
justice before the hosts of evil-doers. In the defense
of right, men will face the outrages of the world alone.
     On the other hand, women are conservative, and
seldom are impelled to stand forth and proclaim these
eternal convictions. They are pacifists, importunists,
moderators, trimming their sails to whatever winds blow
on the seven seas of thought. Remember that while it
was due to the merit of women that the children of Israel were redeemed from Egypt, it was only merit, not the
fierce rebellion of a Moses, saying, "Let my people go
free!" that wrought the miracle.
     Were the woman as rabbi merely confined to pulpit
discourses and the formal aspects of ceremonials, her
admission to the profession would be inept and otiose.
The synagogue, however, has enlarged its tent cords of
service. It is an institution of which the pulpit is
part, not the totality. Being only a feature of the
institutional labor, there are spheres of activity in
the synagogue that not only can be filled by woman, but
are primarily her province.

     Rabbi Neumark: I. "This fact that she was exempt
from certain obligations...she could not...represent the
congregation in the performance of such duties" (R.H.
III.8; Berachot 20b). Against this argument the following can be said:
     First, the traditional functions of the rabbi have
nothing to do with representation of the congregation in
the performance of certain religious duties from which
women are freed. There are certain categories of men,
such as are deformed and afflicted with certain bodily
defects, who could not act as readers, but could be rabbis for decisions in ritual matters and questions of
law. The same holds true of people with a "foreign
accent" in Hebrew.
     Second, women are not free from the duties of pray-
er, grace after meal, and **Kiddush,** and they can read for
others (cf. Mishna and Bab. Gemara, Berachot, 20a,b).
Thus, even in our modern conception of the function of
the rabbi, which includes reading, woman can act as

representative according to traditional law. Of course, "Tefila" here is used in its technical meaning--"Eighteen Prayers"--while Prayer in its general meaning of Divine Service had the "Shema" in its center, and woman was freed from its obligatory reading. But no Orthodox Jew ever waited with the obligatory reading of the "Shema" for the public service; it has, at least in post-Talmudic times, always been done right in the morning, privately.

Third, the practice within Reform Judaism has decided in favor of admitting women as readers of the Divine Service. And since we are interested in the traditional law on the subject only in order to take from it a clue for Reform practice, this argument would be of no consequence even if it were valid, as it is not. If a woman is to be debarred from the rabbinate in Orthodox Judaism because she cannot serve as a reader, then the only logical consequence would be that Reform Judaism, which has decided in favor of the woman reader, should disregard the Orthodox attitude, and admit women to the rabbinate.

II. The reason why a Torah Scroll written by a woman was considered unfit is not, as Dr. Lauterbach claims, because she could not be reader of the Torah, but quite a formal one: Whosoever has not the obligation of binding (Tefilin), has not the fitness of writing (a Torah Scroll) (Gittin 45b; Men. 42b). The above reason is given in Soferim I.13, but there, woman is not debarred from writing a Torah Scroll.

III. In Bavli, Mo-ed Katan 18a, it is not said that "women were not to be found in the academies and colleges where the rabbis assembled and where the students prepared themselves to be rabbis." It is only said "Isha bei midrasha la shechicha," "A woman is not often to be found in Beit Hamidrash. The academies and colleges of those days were not institutions for training rabbis, but institutions of learning, most of whose students were pursuing other vocations. A woman in those days was supposed to keep away from all public places, such as courts and the like, and even, as much as possible, from the streets: "Kol kevodah bat melech penima."

IV. As to the direct question of the legal situation, I have discussed that matter in the opinion which I have submitted to the faculty of the Hebrew Union College. I want to add the following remarks: 1. The statement of Yerushalmi Sanh. 21c and Shev. 35b, that a woman cannot serve (occasionally) as judge, is not from a baraita, as Dr. Lauterbach claims, but occurs in a discussion between two Amoraim. 2. "Lamadnu" does not mean "we have learned," but is a technical term for an inference on the virtue of an hermeneutical rule; in this case, **Gezera Shava**. 3. Nowhere in Talmudic but always by **Tanya** literature is a baraita introduced by "**tanei**," "**lamadnu**," and the like. 4. The emphasis on "men" in the quotation from Maimonides is not justified.

V. As to the practical question of the advisability to ordain women at the Hebrew Union College, I do not believe that the Orthodox will have any additional reason to object. They themselves employ women in their schools as teachers and readers, and our women rabbis will not do more than this. In fact, the entire question reduces itself to this: women are already doing most of the work that the ordained woman rabbi is expected to do, but they do it without preparation and without authority. I consider it rather a duty of the authorities to put an end to the prevailing anarchy by giving women a chance to acquire adequate education and an authoritative standing in all branches of religious work. The practical difficulties cannot be denied. But they will be worked out the same way as in other professions, especially in the teaching profession, from the kindergarten to post-graduate schools. Lydia Rabbinowitz raised a family of three children and kept up a full measure of family life while being a professor of bacteriology. The woman rabbi who will remain single will not be more, in fact less, of a problem than the bachelor rabbi. If she marries and chooses to remain a rabbi--God blesses her--she will retire for a few months and provide a substitute, just as rabbis generally do when they are sick or are involved in an automobile accident. When she comes back, she will be a better rabbi for the experience. The rabbinate may help the women, and the women rabbis may help the rabbinate. You cannot treat the Reform rabbinate from the Orthodox point of view. Orthodoxy is Orthodoxy and Reform is Reform. Our good relations with our Orthodox brethren may still be improved upon a clear and decided stand on this question. They want us either to be Reform or to return to the fold of real, genuine Orthodox Judaism whence we came.

See also:

"Resolution," **CCAR Yearbook**, vol. 3, 1893, p. 40; vol. 32, 1922, p. 51; vol. 85, 1975, p. 70.
"Resolution," **National Federation of Temple Sisterhoods**, 1961, 1963.

9. LIMITATION OF CONGREGATIONAL MEMBERSHIP
(1980)

QUESTION: May a congregation limit its membership on the basis of geographic boundaries? (Rabbi Martin S. Rozenberg, Sands Point, New York)

ANSWER: The basic matter of excluding individuals from membership in a congregation has been dealt with in a previous responsum.   That question, however, hardly dealt with limitations based on geographic consideration.   The main concern was the establishment of at least one synagogue in all sizable communities.

Although it was always possible to establish private or semi-private places of worship in a community, each community sought to establish at least one public synagogue, and the majority could force the minority to contribute to that synagogue (**Yad, Hil. Tefila, XI.1;** Jacob ben Asher, **Tur**, Orach Chayim, 1050).   In fact, small congregations could make attendance at daily services mandatory if that was necessary to insure a **Minyan** (Adret, **Responsa V**, 222; Isaac bar Sheshet, **Responsa I,** #518, 531; Finkelstein, **Jewish Self-Government in the Middle Ages,** p. 268--the **Takanot** of Candia).   Problems arose when many medieval governments limited the Jewish communities to a single synagogue.   When massive immigration occurred, as for example of Sephardic Jews into Ashkenazic lands, or vice versa, they were often not admitted to membership or only reluctantly admitted.

We may draw some parallel of limiting a congregation to a geographical area from the medieval Jewish community.   In this case, community and congregation were the same, and the community often restricted its membership by not permitting others to settle in the area.   This ban against outsiders (**Cherem Hayishuv**) was of Talmudic origin (B.B. 21b, 22a).   It was revived through a **takana** ascribed to Rabbenu Gershom, but was actually already found earlier (Moses Mintz, **Responsa,** 89; Jacob Weil in Isserlein, **Pesakim,** #126).   This right of settlement was interpreted strictly or loosely, according to contemporary needs.   For example, Rashi generally was strict and insisted that the **Cherem** was a valid Talmudic ordinance which could not be changed (Rashi to B.B. 21b).   On the other hand, his grandson, Rabbenu Tam, interpreted it loosely and stated that the Talmudic law applied only to individuals unwilling to pay local taxes (**Or Zarua I,** 115; Meir of Rothenburg, **Responsa,** #11).   These ordinances were usually taken strictly, and most authorities followed the opinion of Rabbi Meir ben Baruch (**Responsa,** #382).   This view continued to be dominant in Germany througout the Middle Ages.

We have, then, definite restrictions on communal membership within a circumscribed geographical area. Of course, these proscribed actual settlement in a certain area. This right was refused on the grounds that this might harm the economic or general status of Jews who had already settled in the area. Such considerations play no part in modern synagogue regulations. Nor should any limitation of membership to a geographic basis be construed as an indication that the area is the "province" of a particular congregation or that anyone in such an area may not join other congregations. Any Jew has the right to join any congregation he or she wishes.

It is clear, therefore, that there are some grounds for restricting membership to geographical locations, but we would hesitate to recommend this except when it will prevent conflict between two congregations seeking to establish themselves in the same area.

Walter Jacob, Chairman
Leonard S. Kravitz
W. Gunther Plaut
Harry A. Roth
Rav A. Soloff
Bernard Zlotowitz

10. SYNAGOGUE MEMBERSHIP OF A MIXED COUPLE
(Vol. XCII, 1982, pp. 215-216)

QUESTION: In these days of rising mixed marriages, should we extend Temple membership to the non-Jewish member in a mixed family? (Rabbi Prystowsky, Lafayette Hill, Pennsylvania)

ANSWER: It is clear from tradition that such marriages cannot be considered as **Kiddushin** (**Yad**, Hil. Ishut 15; **Shulchan Aruch**, Even Ha-ezer 154.23) and, of course, the CCAR has expressed its views for the Reform Movement (Resolution, **CCAR Yearbook**, vol. 83, p. 97; Responsum, **CCAR Yearbook**, vol. 90, pp. 86ff). However, we have recognized these marriages as civil marriages and are quite willing, even eager, to have the children raised as Jews. Clearly, the children of such marriages will often become Jewish, and so a major portion of the family--father or mother and children--will have a role in the religious life of the synagogue.

This need not involve full synagogue membership of the non-Jewish family partner. Most synagogues, on their application forms, require some sort of statement of identity with Judaism as the religion, and certainly such an individual could not in good conscience sign this if he/she remains a Christian. Naturally, we would expect the Jewish party to assume his/her full responsibilities for the financial maintenance of the synagogue, especially as children will be educated by the synagogue.

Full membership in the congregation would also imply the ability to become a member of the Board of Trustees and an officer of the congregation. This could very likely lead to an absurd condition in which a Jewish congregation would have a non-Jewish officer whose knowledge of the workings of the synagogue would be gained only from the practical organizational experience but without any Jewish background. Rather than risking these kinds of conditions, it would be better for the synagogue to arrange that membership be held by the Jewish partner, even in those congregations in which the membership is normally held by the entire family. This would spare the congregation and the individual embarrassment.

This has been the traditional response of Reform Judaism (Solomon B. Freehof, **Recent Reform Responsa**, pp. 63ff) and continues to be our view.

We would continue to encourage the non-Jewish partner to be buried in our cemetery, provided that there were no specific Christian ritual or no specific markings on the tombstone. Even if that individual chose not to become Jewish, he or she would certainly be welcome at all functions of the synagogue but would not qualify for membership.

Walter Jacob, Chairman
Joseph Glaser
Leonard S. Kravitz
Simeon Maslin
Isaac Neuman
W. Gunther Plaut
Harry A. Roth
Herman Schaalman
Rav A. Soloff
Sheldon Zimmerman
Bernard Zlotowitz

11. AN UNMARRIED COUPLE JOINING THE SYNAGOGUE
(Vol. XC, 1980, pp. 83-84)

QUESTION: A young couple that is living together
has applied for synagogue membership as a family.
Should they be permitted to join as a family and be
recognized as such, or should they be asked to join
as individuals? The local rabbi has recognized the
couple as married. (S.K., Trenton, New Jersey)

ANSWER: It is the task of the Responsa Committee to
provide guidance. The authority of the local rabbi, of
course, remains supreme within his community. He knows
both the Halacha and the specific circumstances which
may lead him to a decision. In this instance, the local
rabbi has decided to consider the couple as married by
stating that this was demonstrated through their public
and private conduct (**Shulchan Aruch**, Even Ha-ezer 26-
33). Although marriage through intercourse (**bi-a**) alone
was frowned upon, it has always been considered valid
bedi-avad (**Shuchan Aruch**, Even Ha-ezer 42.1). We do not
quarrel with the decision made in that specific case,
but must now turn to the general question of our reaction to such young couples.

The tenor of halachic literature from the Talmud to
the present is against casual sexual relationships and,
is opposed to individuals living together without being
married. The restrictions, which were rather puritanical in nature, actually went considerably further than
that (A.Z. 20a,b; **Lev. Rabba**, 23; **Yad**, Hil. Yom Tov,
6.21; **Shulchan Aruch**, Even Ha-ezer 21). A young man was
not to converse with women alone, should not shake hands
(**Sede Chemed**, Chatan Vechala 26a). Generally, intercourse with an unmarried girl fell under the concept of
zenut, which was prohibited. If an act of intercourse
was intended as a mode of lawful betrothal, the betrothal was indeed lawful (Mishna, Kid. 1.1). Children born
of such liaisons, conducted without contemplation of
marriage, were completely free of any blemish and there
was no question about their legitimacy (Kid. 4.1,2; Yev.
100b). Such alliances have been reported in the Talmud,
in the Golden Age of Spain, and in Renaissance Italy, as
well as during modern times. They appeared less frequently in other periods.

There is also considerable discussion in the halachic literature about those who are engaged and might
live together for some time. During a portion of the
Talmudic period, this was not considered objectionabl
in Judea (Ket. 7b), but was rejected in Galilee (Ket
12a). Finally, a stricter view prevailed, although su

relationships were fairly common (**Otzar Hage-onim**, Kiddushin 18ff, etc.), and that strict prohibition has been recorded in **Shulchan Aruch** (Even Ha-ezer, 55.1, etc.). The halachic literature does make it clear that very often little could be done about such arrangements, and no public action was taken except during the more puritanical periods (L. Epstein, **Sex Laws and Customs in Judaism**, pp. 128ff).

We now have a problem between the rather strict tradition and its ideals and modern circumstances. We must also ask about the difference between quietly condoning a certain style of life and publicly accepting it, as would be the case through congregational membership. On the other hand, we do not want to discourage young people from joining congregations. We would suggest that this couple that is living together has demonstrated their intent to give public recognition to their union and have expressed this by their desire to join a congregation. While we would continue to encourage the couple to get married and accept the full responsibility of the status whose privileges they seek, we in the meantime willingly accept both parties as single members in all respects. Those who consider them as sinners would not be justified in withholding synagogue membership from them, for sinners remain Jews with normal rights (San. 44a; **Shulchan Aruch**, Yoreh De-a 334.2, Orach Chayim 150.1, etc.). We would, therefore, recommend that this couple be admitted to membership as single individuals.

Walter Jacob, Chairman
Leonard S. Kravitz
W. Gunther Plaut
Harry A. Roth
Rav A. Soloff
Bernard Zlotowitz

See also:

S.B. Freehof, "Unmarried Couple and Temple Membership," **Reform Responsa for Our Time**, pp. 238ff.

12.   FORFEITURE OF CONGREGATIONAL MEMBERSHIP
BY INTERMARRIAGE
(Vol. XXVI, 1916, pp. 133-134)

Whether the congregational bylaw, reading that members who contract a forbidden marriage forfeit their membership and no person married to a non-Jew may be a member of the congregation, should be changed, is, in my opinion, an altogether different question (for burial of a non-Jew in a Jewish cemetery or the duty of a rabbi to officiate in a non-Jewish cemetery, see p. 25). It seems to me that the law should stand. **Forbidden marriages** have disastrous results, especially in regard to the offspring, while, on the other hand, the second sentence simply aims at **preventing mixed marriages** in the congregation, but does not imply that they entail forfeiture of membership when concluded before the affiliation to the congregation. Self-preservation dictates the retention of the bylaw.

K. Kohler and Jacob Z. Lauterbach

See also:

S.B. Freehof, "Temple Membership of Mixed Couple," **Recent Reform Responsa**, pp. 63ff; "Gentile Membership in Synagogue," **Reform Responsa for Our Time**, pp. 221ff.

13.   JUDAISM AND HOMOSEXUALITY
(Vol. LXXIII, 1973, pp. 115-119)

QUESTION: A rabbi on the West Coast, the regional director of the Union of American Hebrew Congregations, has organized a congregation of homosexuals. He has said: "These are people facing their own situation. They have become a social grouping." Is it in accordance with the spirit of Jewish tradition to encourage the establishment of a congregation of homosexuals? (Alexander M. Schindler, President-elect of the Union of American Hebrew Congregations)

ANSWER: There is no question that Scripture considers homosexuality to be a grave sin. The rabbi who organized this congregation, justifying himself, said that being Reform, we are not bound by the Halacha of the Bible. It may well be that we do not consider ourselves bound by all the ritual and ceremonial laws of Scripture, but we certainly revere the ethical attitudes and judgments of the Bible. In Scripture (Lev. 18:22), homosexuality is considered to be "an abomination." So, too, in Leviticus 20:13. If Scripture calls it an abomination, it means that it is more than violation of a mere legal enactment: it reveals a deep-rooted ethical attitude. How deep-rooted this aversion is can be seen from the fact that, although Judaism developed in the Near East, which is notorious for the prevalence of homosexuality, Jews kept away from such acts, as is seen from the Talmud (Kiddushin 82a), which states that Jews are not "under the suspicion of homosexuality." In other words, the opposition to homosexuality was more than a Biblical law; it was a deep-rooted way of life of the Jewish people, a way of life maintained in a world where homosexuality was a widespread practice. Therefore, homosexual acts cannot be brushed aside, as the rabbi in the West is reported to have done, by saying that we do not follow Biblical enactments. Homosexuality runs counter to the **sancta** of Jewish life. There is no side-stepping the fact that from the point of view of Judaism men who practice homosexuality are to be deemed sinners.

But what conclusion is to be drawn from the fact that their homosexual acts are sinful acts? Does it mean, therefore, that we should exclude them from the congregation and thus compel them to form their own religious fellowship in congregations of their own? No! The very contrary is true. It is forbidden to force them into a separate congregation. The Mishna (Megila IV.9) says that if a man in his prayer says "Let good people bless Thee, O Lord," the man who prays thus must be silenced. Bartenura, explaining why we silence the man who says "Let the **good** praise Thee," states that it is a sin to pray this way because the man implies that only righteous people shall be in the congregation. The contrary is true. He adds that the chemical **chelbena** (Galbanum) has an evil odor, yet it is included in the recipe of the sacred incense offered in the Temple in Jerusalem. Bartenura bases this idea specifically on the statement in the Talmud (Keritot 6b) in which the presence of ill-smelling **Galbanum** in the sacred incense is used as proof for the following statement: "No fast-day service is a genuine service unless sinners of Israel are included among the worshipers." That is to say, that if we were self-righteous and considered the community to be entirely composed of noble people, we would then be far too smug and self-satisfied for a truly penitential fast-day service. That is why Maharil, in the 14th century, followed the custom of saying before the "Kol Nidrei" that we must pray side by side with the sinners. This has become our Ashkenazic custom before the "Kol Nidrei" prayer and, in fact, it has become a universal Jewish custom since Joseph Caro, the Sephardi, mentioned it as a law in the Shulchan Aruch, Orach Chayim 619.1 (and compare the Ba-er Heitev to the passage). In other words, not only do we not exclude sinners, we are actually forbidden to do so; they are a necessary part of the congregation. That is the significance of the law in the Mishna that we silence the reader if he says "Let only the righteous praise Thee."

This throws light on the present situation. We do not exclude them. We are fobidden by our tradition to do so. They are excluding themselves, and it is our duty to ask: Why are they doing it? Why do they want to commit the further sin of "separating themselves from the congregation"?

Part of their wish is, of course, due to the "Gay Liberation" movement. Homosexuals, male and female, fighting the laws which they deem unjust, are conducting a strong agitation on behalf of their status, and therefore are in the mood to extract formal recognition from all possible groups. If they can get the Union of American Hebrew Congregations to acknowledge their right to form separate congregations, it will bolster their propaganda for other rights. In fact, the press recently carried a demand on the part of women homosexuals for a separate congregation of their own (I believe these were Christian women).

It seems to be also that it is not unfair to ascribe an additional motive for their desire to be grouped together, to the exclusion of others: in this way they know each other and are available to each other, just as they now group together in separate bars and saloons in the great cities. What, then, of young boys who perhaps have only a partial homosexual tendency, who will now be available to inveterate homosexuals? Are we not thereby committing the sin of "aiding and abetting sinners" (Mesayea yedei overei avera)?

To sum up: Homosexuality is deemed in Jewish tradition to be a sin--not only in law, but in Jewish life practice. Nevertheless, it would be in direct contradiction to Jewish law to keep sinners out of the congregation. To isolate them into a separate congregation and thus increase their mutual availability is certainly wrong. It is hardly worth mentioning that to officiate at a so-called "marriage" of two homosexuals and to describe their mode of life as "Kiddushin" (i.e., sacred in Judaism) is a contravention of all that is respected in Jewish life.

Solomon B. Freehof

See also:

S.B. Freehof, "Homosexuality," **Current Reform Responsa**, pp. 236ff.
"Resolution," **CCAR Yearbook**, vol. 87, 1977, pp. 50ff.
"Resolution," **National Federation of Temple Sisterhoods**, 1965.

14.   HOMOSEXUALS IN LEADERSHIP POSITIONS
(Vol. XCI, 1981, pp. 67-69)

QUESTION: Should a congregation engage a known homosexual as a religious school teacher in the high school department? What should our attitude be toward engaging a known homosexual as Executive Secretary? Both of these individuals are quite open about their homosexuality.

ANSWER: The Central Conference of American Rabbis has concerned itself with the problems of homosexuals for a number of years.   In 1977 the following resolution was adopted:

Whereas, the Central Conference of American Rabbis consistently supported civil rights and civil liberties for all people, especially for those from whom these rights and liberties have been withheld, and
Whereas, homosexuals have in our society long endured discrimination,
Be it therefore resolved, that we encourage legislation which decriminalizes homosexual acts between consenting adults, and prohibits discrimination against them as persons, and
Be it further resolved, that our Reform Jewish religious organizations undertake programs in cooperation with the total Jewish community to implement the above stand.

We will not discuss the modern Jewish attitude toward homosexuals which has been shaped by two factors: (a) the attitude of tradition towards homosexuality, and (b) our contemporary understanding of homosexuality, which understands it as an illness, as a genetically-based dysfunction, or as a sexual preference and life-style. There is disagreement whether homosexuality represents a willful act or a response to which the individual is driven.

The Biblical prohibition against homosexuality is absolutely clear, as seen in two sample verses: "Do not lie with a male as one lies with a woman; it is an abhorrence" (Leviticus 18:22); "If a man lies with a male as one lies with a woman, the two of them have done an abhorrent thing; they shall be put to death--their blood-guilt is upon them" (Leviticus 20:13). Other statements are equally clear. The Talmudic discussion of the matter makes no substantive changes and continues the prohibition. It deals with the question of minors, duress and various forms of the homosexual act (San. 53aff, Yev. 83b, Ker. 2aff, Ned. 5.1a, etc.). In the subsequent codes, the matter is briefly mentioned with the same conclusions (Yad, Hil. Isurei Bi-a 1.5, 22.2; Tur and Shulchan Aruch, Even Ha-ezer 24). There is very little material in the responsa literature which deals with homosexuality, as it does not seem to have been a major problem. The commentators to the above-mentioned section of the Shulchan Aruch felt that suspicion of homosexuality could not arise in their day, and so various preventive restrictions were superfluous. For example, Moses Rifkes (17th-century Poland) stated that this sin did not exist in his time (Be-er Hagola). Until the most recent modern period there has been no further discussion of this matter.

Let us turn to the question of the homosexual as a role model and begin by examining the status given to those in leadership positions by our tradition. Statements such as, "Whoever teaches the son of his fellow-man is seen as having begotten him" (San. 19b), or "A teacher is given priority over the natural father in matters of honor" (B.M. 2, 11), demonstrate the high regard for persons in leadership positions. The commandment "Honor your father and your mother" was applied to teachers as well as parents (Bamidbar Rabba 15.17). The medieval codes provide a long list of duties which a student must fulfill in order to honor his teacher (Yad, Hil. Talmud Torah 5.5-7; Tur and Shulchan Aruch, Yoreh De-a 242.15, 16).

The highest personal and moral qualities were associated with these leaders of the community (M. Guedemann, Geschichte des Erziehungswesens und der Kultur der abendlaendischen Juden, vol. 1, pp. 93ff,

vol. 3, pp. 31ff). When accusations of impiety or improper behavior were brought against a rabbi, he could
be removed from office if they were proven. Such problems were rarely mentioned in the responsa literature,
and the authorities urged caution and rigorous investi-
gation of the accusations and the motivation of the
accusers (Moses Sofer, **Responsa,** Choshen Mishpat 162;
Mordecai Schwadron, **Responsa II,** no. 56). There was
more discussion about cantors and improper behavior.
Their position was somewhat different as they were not
primarily teachers, but were in the position of **Sheliach
Tsibur** and, therefore, had to possess an absolutely
proper moral character (**Machzor Vitry** 233 and 271), and
among Ashkenazim they were sometimes dismissed on rumor
alone (**ibid. Isserles** to **Shulchan Aruch,** Orach Chayim
53.2). This was not to be taken lightly (Moses Sofer,
Chatam Sofer, Orach Chayim 11.205). The Sephardic community was more lax in this regard (Maimonides, **Respon-
sa--Friemann,** #18), but would also dismiss instantly if
a charge was proven (R. Hai, **Sha-arei Teshuva,** #50).
These standards referred to all kinds of overt improper
sexual behavior, as well as to other unacceptable acts.
I have found only one reference to an accusation of
homosexual practices; although this was not proven, the
cantor was dismissed as a preventative measure (Elijah
Ibn Hayim, **Responsa,** #41). The community always sought
leaders who were above reproach and continues to do so.

Overt heterosexual behavior or overt homosexual
behavior which is considered objectionable by the community disqualifies the person involved from leadership
positions in the Jewish community. We reject this type
of individual as a role model within that Jewish community. We cannot recommend such an individual as a
role model nor should he/she be placed in a position of
leadership or guidance for children of any age.

Walter Jacob, Chairman
Leonard S. Kravitz
W. Gunther Plaut
Harry A. Roth
Rav A. Soloff
Bernard Zlotowitz

15. REFUSING A JEW MEMBERSHIP
(Vol. LXIII, 1953, pp. 154-155)

QUESTION: Does the Board of a Temple have the
right to refuse to accept the application for mem-

bership in the congregation of a Jew whose character and business activities are thought to be reprehensible? Should it exercise such a right?

ANSWER: The pertinent principle that has always obtained in Judaism finds its best expression in the Talmudic dictums: "Even though sinful, one remains an Israelite" (Sanh. 44a). A Jew does not cease to be a Jew
because of any dereliction of duty. Yet the heads of
the synagogue may refuse to accept a financial contribution from a man who they know has acquired his
possessions dishonestly (B.K. 119a). Thus, while a
notoriously dishonest person may be excluded from membership in a congregation, since such membership entails
the payment of dues, he must not be denied any of the
services which the synagogue can offer.
    It is questionable, however, whether the method of
exclusion, even where legally permissible, is calculated
to achieve the end which the heads of the congregation
have in view. Much more, it would seem, could be accomplished by bringing the Jew of ill repute under the
influence of the synagogue and its teachings.

                                        Israel Bettan

16.   THE EXPULSION OF A MEMBER FROM THE CONGREGATION
            (Vol. LXXIV, 1964, pp. 104-106)

QUESTION: Is it in accordance with the spirit of
Jewish tradition for a congregation to provide in
its bylaws for the expulsion of a member? The
proposed bylaw is as follows:

Suspension and Expulsion

I.   For Financial Cause.
II. For Other Causes. The Board shall have the
authority to remove, expel, or suspend any member
in the interest of the general welfare of the congregation. Such action on the part of the Board
shall be preceded by notification by certified mail
to the party concerned at least two (2) weeks prior
to a meeting of the Board, and the party involved
may request a hearing before the Board.

ANSWER: The question which is asked is of great deli-
cacy because of the long and complex history of the
legal instruments for exclusion of a Jew from the Jewish
community.   The various instruments of exclusion, the
ban, the excommunication--well known as instruments of
discipline in the Catholic Church--were from early days
instruments of discipline in Judaism (**Nidui** and **Cherem**),
and even have a Biblical root.   When Ezra wished to
summon the entire community to a special assembly, the
proclamation was accompanied with this threat of penalty
(Ezra 10:8): "Whosoever came not within three days,
according to the counsel of the princes and the elders,
all his substance should be forfeited and himself separated from the congregation of the captivity."   In other
words, merely for absenting himself from this assembly,
the man was "separated from the congregation."

The Talmud, in Berachot 19a, mentions twenty-four
causes for which a person may be excommunicated.   These
are not enumerated in the Talmud, but all the twenty-
four are given in Maimonides' **Yad** (Hilchot Talmud Torah,
VI.14) and also in the **Shulchan Aruch**, Yoreh De-a,
334.43.   Among these causes for excommunication would be
some of the motivations akin to the suggestions for
expulsion in your proposed bylaws: For example, he who
despises the head of the congregation, or insults his
neighbor, or refuses to accept the decisions of the
congregation, or who uses the name of God in vain--in
other words, a troublemaker.

In the Middle Ages, the ban was used to enforce the
various decisions of the community.   Many of them were
financial decisions.   It is doubtful whether the isolated, struggling Jewish communities could have maintained themselves without this instrument of exclusion
to help enforce their regulations.

However, this instrument, so indispensable for
communal continuity, was used in the last centuries as
an instrument against all liberalism and modernization
of Judaism, and so was particularly disliked by liber-
als.   For the use of the ban by rabbinical authorities
against liberal tendencies, see particularly the end of
Wiesner's **Der Bann**.   We may say, in general, that the
use of the traditional (and once indispensable) instrument of exclusion should be distasteful to any modern
Reform congregation and should be sparingly used, if at
all.   The instrument of expulsion--if the congregation
feels it is necessary for self-protection--should be
hedged in with many safeguards.   Let us, therefore, go a
little more deeply into the traditional provisions with
regard to the exclusion of people from the community,
and see which might possibly be applicable or acceptable
today.

There are obvious differences between what your congregation desires to do and what was done in the past in the matter of exclusion. In one way, what you intend to do by excusing a man from membership is equivalent to what was done in some of the provisions of the traditional ban. The man could not be counted in the **Minyan** for the service and could not even participate in the joint grace after meals, etc. (Yoreh De-a 334.13).

However, there were certain important differences. First of all: what you are doing is, from one point of view, much more serious. The old excommunication presumably lasted only thirty days (Yoreh De-a 334.13), and you mean to exclude the person permanently from participating in congregational affairs. On the other hand, what you are doing is much less serious than what was done in the past. In the Middle Ages, when these laws were most frequently applied, the community was identical with the congregation. When a man was excluded, he was excluded from the entire community. Here you are excluding him only from one separate organization, and he can still join other congregations. Furthermore, the old excommunication forbade anybody, except his immediate family, from doing business with him or even from conversing with him. You are merely removing him from membership and not isolating him personally.

However, there is one element about the old laws of exclusion which is important to notice. Every ban was presumed to last for thirty days only, unless there was ground for its renewal. Furthermore, there was a method immediately provided for the lifting of the ban at any time (see Yoreh De-a 334.13). Therefore, if there would be any objection to your proposed bylaw, it would be as follows:

1. The old laws contained an earlier stage, **Nezifa**, which means "rebuke." Sometimes a man was put under "rebuke" and needed no further discipline. Your bylaws do have the statement that a man should receive two weeks' prior notification by mail, but that is hardly enough. There should be a preliminary punishment, such as suspension, which might be as effective as the old "rebuke," and may make the final expulsion unnecessary.

2. Since the Jewish law puts a time limit on the exclusion and makes provisions for reinstatement, your bylaws should do likewise and make provision for a man applying for readmittance.

In general, we would conclude as follows: Since the exclusion is only from one congregation and not from the community, you have the right to determine who shall cease to be a member. Your Membership Committee, which has the unquestioned right to determine who shall become a member in the first place, should also have the right to determine who shall cease to be a member (especially since the expulsion is only from one congregation and not from the entire community). However, since Jewish law has certain safeguards, you should surround the by-law with the two traditional safeguards mentioned: first, a preliminary suspension, and second, if the punishment of expulsion is carried out, there must be an opportunity for reinstatement.

Solomon B. Freehof

17. COLLECTING SYNAGOGUE PLEDGES THROUGH CIVIL COURTS
(Vol. LXII, 1961, pp. 127-129)

QUESTION: One of our congregations has used legal processes in collecting delinquent building pledges. Summonses have been issued to defaulting members, placing liens upon their property. Are there any precedents for this action?

ANSWER: The very fact that the question is asked reveals a feeling that it is wrong to bring Jewish religious disputes to the secular courts. Of course, it does happen in modern times that such matters have occasionally been brought to the courts in the United States, as, for example, disputes in Orthodox synagogues on the question of mixed seating, or questions of disinterment from Orthodox cemeteries. Nevertheless, whenever such lawsuits do come up, there is a general feeling in the Jewish community that the disputes should never have been brought to the courts--that to have done so was a **Chilul Hashem.**

This strong feeling against such actions is the product of a long tradition in Jewish law. The Talmud (B. Gittin 88b) denounced the resort to Gentile courts. The **Takanot** of the various medieval Jewish communities forbade Jews to resort to Gentile courts. This tradition is recorded in vigorous language in the **Shulchan Aruch**, Choshen Mishpat 26.1: "Whoever brings his case before the Gentile courts is a wicked man, whose action amounts to blasphemy and violence against the Law of Moses, our teacher."

Of course, that does not mean that Jews in the past never had recourse to the civil courts. There were circumstances when there was no other way to obtain their rights. If, for example, a debtor was influential and stubborn and refused to be sued in the Jewish courts, he could be sued in the civil courts, usually with the creditor getting express permission from the Jewish authorities (Choshen Mishpat 26.2,4, Isserles). This procedure, as a last resort, is valid because Gentile courts may (according to Jewish law) deal with matters of business debts. This limited validity is acknowledged by Jewish law because the "Children of Noah" are understood to have been commanded to maintain courts dealing with civil law, **Dinei Mamonot** (cf. B. Gittin 9a-b).

If the building pledges discussed in our question are to be considered merely as notes of debt, then, if there is no other way to collect them, it would be permissible to bring them to the civil courts for collection. But surely they are not precisely of the same nature as a business debt. They are rather what the law calls a **Shetar Matana**, a Document of Gift (Choshen Mishpat 68.1). Jewish Documents of Gift cannot legally (in the eyes of Jewish law) be dealt with by the non-Jewish courts (Choshen Mishpat 68.1).

In Jewish law itself, such pledges, certificates of gift, are valid, legal documents. If, for example, Jewish law still had the executive authority which it possessed in past centuries, these pledges could be collected by force. The building pledges are equivalent to charity gifts in general, and are deemed collectible even if the maker of the pledge changes his mind. The law is that the members of the Jewish community may compel each other to give charity--"**kofin**" (Yoreh De-a 256.5).

To give **Tsedaka** is considered an inescapable religious obligation, **Chova**, which even the poor must fulfill (Yoreh De-a 248.1). In fact, a promise made to give **Tsedaka** has the sacred status of a religious vow, **Neder** (Yoreh De-a 257.3), and, therefore, must be fulfilled without delay.

This serious concern with the legal validity of Jewish charity pledges is exclusively a matter of Jewish law. Non-Jewish law can have no relevance to it, unless we say that the pledges are also to be considered analogous to the taxes and imposts which the medieval community imposed upon its members. These, too, were collectible by compulsion. In fact, with regard to taxes and imposts, there are indications that occasionally, in some localities, the power of the civil government was called in to enforce payment. This resort to the secular arm seems to have been confined to Italy. Joseph Colon (Italy, 15th century) says (Responsa, #17) that he sees nothing wrong in asking aid from the government in collecting the taxes imposed by the Jewish community upon its members. In fact, he adds, this has been the custom of many (Italian) communities.

Yet, after all, these taxes were to be paid over to the government, and the Jewish community would be endangered if they were not forthcoming. It was understandable, then, that the Italian communities might, in desperation, call for secular aid in collecting them. But even in the case of taxes, there seems to be no evidence that the resort to government help was made by Jewish communities in other countries. Certainly this practice is not recorded in the general codes.

The taxes and imposts were by their nature secular and civil. But a gift to the community for the building of a synagogue was a religious gift which was to remain within the Jewish community. Gentile authorities could not and would not be used to enforce an intra-community religious duty. There is only one exception to this, namely, the situation mentioned in the Mishna (Gittin 9.8) in the case of a man ordered by the Jewish court to give his wife a divorce. If he refused to do so, Gentiles may be asked to compel him to obey the mandate of the Jewish court. But even in that case the divorce is not a fully valid divorce (cf. **Tur** and **Perisha**, ad loc.).

Within the Jewish community and in Jewish law, a pledge to the building of the synagogue is valid and enforceable. The same phrase used in the case of charity gifts is used for synagogue building gifts, namely: "The members of the community may compel each other," **"Kofin zeh et zeh"** (Orach Chayim 150.1). To enforce payment, the older communities used the power of excommunication (**Cherem**).

When the Russian government forbade the Jewish communities to employ the **Cherem**, the phrase "to compel" used in the **Shulchan Aruch** seemed to reveal a violation of government decree. Therefore, in the **Shulchan Aruch** printed in Wilna, at the word "compel" there is an asterisk pointing to a footnote which reads: "By means of the government." This, of course, did not mean that the Jewish communities ever called on the Russian government to enforce this religious obligation. The footnote either was added by the censor, or else was added to disarm the censor and to say that the community would not use the forbidden instrument of **Cherem**.

It is clear, then, that except for the time when Italian communities called for government aid in collecting taxes, the Jewish communities did not call upon secular courts to help them collect charitable or religious pledges. Jewish law considered that secular law could not validly deal with charitable pledges, and in general, the resort to Gentile courts was held to be a sin.

Therefore, the action of the congregation referred
to is contrary to both the letter and the spirit of
Jewish legal tradition.

Solomon B. Freehof

18. ORIENTATION OF THE SYNAGOGUE
(1979)

QUESTION: Must a synagogue face east? Should the
Ark of the Torah be in the east wall? Must the
entrance be on the eastern side of the building?
Is any other orientation of the synagogue possible?

ANSWER: We can best deal with this question by turning
to archaeology, as well as to the traditional literature. The literary source for turning eastward comes
from the Book of Daniel (6:11): "Now his windows were
open in his upper chamber towards Jerusalem and he knelt
upon his knees three times a day and prayed and gave
thanks before his God as he did afore-time." This verse
led to synagogues being oriented toward Jerusalem and to
the placement of windows or portals on the Jerusalem
side of the building (Ber. 31a, 34b). Here we have an
insistence that the site of prayer, which was interpreted to include private homes and synagogues, needed
windows. Additional emphasis on orientation of worship
is provided by the Tosefta (Meg. IV.21), which stated
that the Ark should be set in front of the people with
its back toward the Temple in Jerusalem. This statement, of course, referred to those early days when the
Ark was not yet permanently placed in the synagogue, but
was carried in and out; therefore, the congregation was
to remain within the synagogue until the Ark with the
Torah scrolls had been removed (Sota 39b). The orientation toward Jerusalem has been stressed in the Mishna
and Talmud repeatedly so that if one is riding and cannot dismount one should at least direct one's eyes or
one's heart toward Jerusalem (Mishna, Ber. IV.5; Ber.
30a; J. Ber. IV.5). The general rule is that outside of
Israel, one should turn toward Israel; in Israel toward
Jerusalem; in Jerusalem toward the Temple. Maimonides
has codified (**Yad**, Hil. Tefila XI.1; **Shulchan Aruch**,
Orach Chayim 150.5) that the Ark should be placed in the
direction of Jerusalem and opposite the entrance. This
has meant that synagogues in North Africa, Europe, and
America have usually faced east, while those of Babylon-

ia and Asia Minor have faced west. We can see this clearly in the third-century synagogue of Dura Europos on the Euphrates, which had its entrance in the east and a niche for the Ark in the western wall.

Although this orientation became dominant, we should remember that there was a period when it had not yet been fixed, so we find the Talmudic statements of Rabbis Oshaia and Ishmael, which state that there is no orientation at the time of prayer, as the Divine Spirit is everywhere (B.B. 25a). We also find various midrashim which deal with the orientation of the worshiper during prayer; for example, he might face north for wealth or south or wisdom. This would account for various synagogues in Israel being oriented differently, for that could not have been done purely on topographical grounds. These synagogues would also comply with the statement in the Tosefta: "Synagogue gates should open toward the east as did the gates of the Tent of Meeting" (Num. 2:2,3; Tos., Meg. IV.22). Following the destruction of the Temple, the Tent of Meeting may have been taken as a model for the synagogue building. Landsberger ("The Sacred Direction in Synagogue and Church," **The Synagogue**, ed. Gutmann, p. 188ff) used this explanation to interpret the wide variety of orientation of synagogues in Israel and in Jordan. In the city of Ostia in Italy, we find a synagogue, later remodeled, that originally had its entrance in the eastern wall. After the Ark was installed in the east side, according to the new style, the entrance could no longer be moved to the opposite side, and remained beside the Ark. In the case of Beit Shearim in Israel, one of the entrance doors was blocked and remodeled into an Ark, while the portals on both sides remained as entrances. In later synagogues, such awkward arrangements were avoided.

Occasional efforts were made in various sections of Europe to orient the synagogue more precisely toward Jerusalem, and therefore a number of these synagogues face south rather than eastward. This led to considerable controversy about the orientation of the synagogue, whether it should be changed and in which direction the worshipers should actually face (Judah Altman, **Mei Yehuda**, #17; Naftali Zvi Berlin, **Meshiv Davar** 1.10; **Sede Chemed**, Ma-arechet Beit Hakeneset, #42; **Ba-er Heitev** to **Shulchan Aruch**, Orach Chayim, #94). The last source cites two responsa which came to totally opposing conclusions.

After the Ark became a permanent part of the synagogue, it was placed in the eastern wall, as mentioned earlier. In most of the early synagogues of Israel, the niche in the eastern wall served as a temporary place for the Torah. It was without doors or coverings of any kind. Sometimes it was decorated with a painting of the Temple to show the intent of the orientation.

Modern synagogues have sometimes gone to great lengths in order to face eastward. For example, the B'nai Israel Synagogue in Pittsburgh (A. Sharove and H. Hornbostel, Architects, 1923-24) has its entrance in the east, which is followed by circular rising interior walkways which lead to the actual synagogue. The Ark is placed above exterior doorways within the building. The Spanish-Portuguese Synagogue on Central Park in New York built an elaborate facade on its eastern street front, but without an entrance, so that this side of the building, used for the Ark, would remain unbroken.

In most cases, an orientation toward the east or toward the southeast is possible with the entrance in the west. If that is not possible, the entrance may be on any other side. If it is absolutely impossible to build or reconstruct in this manner, then the worshiper would simply orient his heart toward Jerusalem (**Shulchan Aruch**, Orach Chayim 94.2).

We may, therefore, conclude that synagogues should be oriented east or south in accordance with tradition, whenever this is possible. This would express our spiritual unity with the Jewish people throughout history and our love for Jerusalem and Israel.

Walter Jacob, Chairman
Leonard S. Kravitz
Eugene Lipman
W. Gunther Plaut
Harry A. Roth
Rav A. Soloff
Bernard Zlotowitz

19. POSITION OF SYNAGOGUE ENTRANCE AND ARK
(Vol. XXXVII, 1927, p. 203)

There was, for instance, the question as to the orientation of the synagogue. The chairman answered briefly that it is not absolutely necessary to have the synagogue so built as to have the main entrance on the west side and the pulpit and the Ark opposite the main entrance at the eastern wall. While this has been the rule in European countries, there have also been exceptions to the rule.

Jacob Z. Lauterbach

See also:

S.B. Freehof, "Ark Not Centered," **Reform Responsa,**
pp. 65ff.

20. PLACING OF PIANO IN FRONT OF ARK
(Vol. LXV, 1955, p. 91)

QUESTION: We are making plans for a series of
concerts to be given in our Temple. Would it be
proper to place a grand piano on the pulpit, so
close to the Ark?

ANSWER: The Rabbis held that when the Ark was closed
it was as if the Torah were housed in a separate chamber
(**Tur,** Yoreh De-a 282).   This is the reason why the
preacher is permitted to face the congregation with his
back to the Torah in the Ark.
   But the Ark itself, housing the Torah, assumes a
special sanctity which ought to be respected. It might
not be amiss, therefore, to place a stage screen in
front of the Ark and thus render it inconspicuous without, at the same time, detracting from the general appearance of the pulpit.

Israel Bettan

21. NATIONAL FLAGS AT RELIGIOUS SERVICES
(Vol. LXIV, 1954, pp. 79-80)

QUESTION: In our Temple we have two flags on the
pulpit: one is the United States flag and the other
is the flag of Israel. Some members of the congregation seem much disturbed by the practice. They
feel that these flags have no place in the auditor-
ium where religious services are held and should
therefore be removed to the social hall.
   The matter has been referred to our Committee
on Religious Practice. We are anxious to avoid
unnecessary emotional conflicts among our members.
We should like to bring to them a proposal that
would rest on sound principle and could be followed
by all factions.

ANSWER: In Judaism, devotion to the welfare of the
country in which one lives has long assumed the character of a religious duty.

When, in the sixth century B.C.E., the people of
Judah had been carried into captivity by the Babylonian
conqueror, it was the prophet Jeremiah who proclaimed
God's message to the captives in the following words:
"And seek the peace of the city whither I have caused
you to be carried away captive, and pray unto the Lord
for it; for in the peace thereof shall ye have peace"
(Jer. 29:7).

Centuries later, when the Roman emperors ruled over
many kingdoms, including Palestine, it was the Rabbis
who pronounced the same religious principle. "Pray for
the welfare of the government," they said, "since but
for the fear thereof men would swallow one another
alive" (Avot 3.2).

Accordingly, a special prayer for the ruling power
soon found its way into the fixed liturgy of the synagogue (**Abudarham**, p. 47c).   On the Sabbath Day, during
the morning services, immediately after the Scriptural
lesson, the prayer for the welfare of the government is
recited in all the synagogues of the world.   In every
country the Jew thus affirms his faith from week to week
that loyalty to the institutions of the particular country of which he is a citizen is a solemn religious obligation.

The presence of the American flag in the synagogues
of the land, far from being an intrusion, may well serve
to strengthen in us the spirit of worship.   Symbolizing,
as it does, the duties we owe to our country, obedience
to its laws, and zealous support of its rights and interests, our national flag speaks to us with the voice
of religion and partakes, therefore, of the sanctity of
our religious symbols.

What the American flag is to the American Jew, the
British flag is to the British Jew; the French flag is
to the French Jew; and the Israeli flag, to the citizens
of Israel. The American flag has no proper place in the
synagogues of Israel, even as the Israeli flag is quite
out of place in an American synagogue.

The United States army regulations governing the
display of any national flag other than our own--and
these regulations have now become the standard civilian
practice as well--are quite broad and adequate.   While
frowning on the practice of habitually flying a foreign
flag alongside the American flag, these regulations
provide that (1) in the presence of a visiting dignitary
of a foreign land or (2) on some notable anniversary of
that land, its national flag may be displayed as a token
of respect.

American Jewish congregations, if they so desire, may therefore display the Israeli flag when a representative of the State of Israel is present in their midst, or when the State of Israel celebrates a special anniversary, such as the Day of Independence.

Israel Bettan

22. ISRAELI FLAG ON A SYNAGOGUE PULPIT
(1977)

QUESTION: Should an Israeli flag be displayed on the pulpit of an American Reform synagogue? In this case, an American flag is already so displayed. (Rabbi R. Goldman, Chattanooga, Tennessee)

ANSWER: The six-pointed Star of David is now commonly recognized as a symbol of Jews and Judaism throughout the world, both by ourselves and by our non-Jewish neighbors. There is no clear distinction between Jews and Judaism, between our religious and our national aspirations.

Since the Babylonian diaspora, our prayers have constantly contained petitions for the return to Zion and the re-establishment of Israel. In the traditional Shabbat morning Torah service, we find in addition a prayer (a) for the academies in Israel, Babylonia, and the Diaspora, (b) for the local congregation, and (c) for the Gentile government under which we live (**Abudarham**, 47b; **Machzor Vitry**; Rokeach). These prayers have been part of the service either since the Talmudic period or, at the latest, since the 14th century. In other words, the service has for a long time contained side-by-side prayers expressing the desire for a return to the Land of Israel, gratitude for the land in which we live, and hope for the welfare of our own communities. The flags of the United States and Israel on a pulpit might be said to symbolize the prayers which have always been said in the synagogue. For this reason, there is no religious objection to placing an American flag on the pulpit, nor to placing an Israeli flag alongside it. (Of course there are specific secular regulations about the placement of such flags which should be followed.) It might be helpful to look at the historical background, especially as there is no ancient record of a Jewish flag or symbol for the entire people of Israel.

The six-pointed star was rarely used by the early Jewish community. It is found carved on a stone in the Capernaum synagogue and also on a single tombstone in Tarentum, Italy, which dates from the third century. Later Kabbalists used it, probably borrowing it from the Templars (Ludwig Blau, "Magen David," **Jewish Encyclopedia**, vol. 8, p. 252). It is also found in some non-Kabbalistic medieval manuscripts. None of these usages, however, was widespread.

The first time a Jewish flag is mentioned was during the rule of Charles IV of Hungary, who prescribed in 1354 that the Jews of Prague use a red flag with David's and Solomon's seal. Also, in the 15th century, the Jews of that city met King Matthias with a red flag containing two golden six-pointed stars and two five-pointed stars. Aside from this, we have no record of the use of a flag by any Jewish community, and, of course, the six-pointed star now so commonly used was rarely used as a Jewish symbol before the late 18th century and early 19th century. In that period, the newly emancipated Jewish community wished to possess an easily recognizable symbol akin to that of Christianity and so adopted the six-pointed star, which was then used frequently on books, synagogues, cemeteries, tombstones, etc. The star soon became recognized as a sign of Judaism. In 1799 it was already used in anti-Semitic literature. In 1822, the Rothschilds utilized it for their coat of arms, and it was adopted by the Zionist Congress in Basel in 1897 as its symbol. Subsequently, the State of Israel has used it in its national flag, although the official symbol of Israel is the **Menora**. Naturally, all of us also remember that the Nazis used the six-pointed star on their badges which identified Jews.

If you wish detailed information about this material see M. Gruenewald, "Ein altes Symbol...," **Jahrbuch fuer juedische Literatur**, 1901, pp. 120ff; L. Blau, "Magen David," **Jewish Encyclopedia**, vol. 8, pp. 25f; and G. Scholem, "Magen David," **Encyclopedia Judaica**, vol. 11, pp. 687ff.

Various synagogues have found other solutions to the desire for honoring both the United States and Israel. Thus, some have placed both flags in the foyer of the community hall, but have no flags on their pulpits. In any case, both the loyalty of our communities to the United States and our common concern for Israel are clear with or without the placement or possession of flags.

Walter Jacob, Chairman
Stephen M. Passamaneck
W. Gunther Plaut
Harry A. Roth
Herman E. Schaalman
Bernard Zlotowitz

23. WALKING ACROSS RELIGIOUS SYMBOLS
(Vol. LXIII, 1953, pp. 153-154)

QUESTION: The entrance to the foyer of our new Temple is embellished with a mosaic outlining the seven-branched **Menora** and the Tablets of the Law. As one enters the Temple, he unavoidably walks across these two important symbols of Judaism. Is it proper to do so? To tear up the floor at this time would, of course, involve considerable expense.

ANSWER: In a religion such as Judaism, which has always stressed the disciplinary value of symbols and symbolic acts, reverence for the consecrated objects must of necessity play an important role.

Accordingly, when sacrifices prevailed as modes of worship, the Altar assumed a holy character and had to be kept from any form of profanation. Even the ashes on the Altar, partaking of the sanctity of the Altar itself, had to be removed "without the camp unto a clean place" (Lev. 6:4).

When the book displaced the Altar, and prayer and study became the delights of the worshiper, the written word, as embodied in the Bible and Prayerbook, rose to the place of the sacred and received reverential treatment. Scrolls and religious books, worn with use, were stored temporarily in special hiding places to await ultimate burial with due ceremony.

This reverence for religious objects, long fostered in the synagogue, has taken root in our Western civilization. Modern nations cherish their national emblems and treat them with a reverence bordering on religious piety. Shall we, who have come to view the Decalogue as the symbol of our faith, allow men to trample on it?

The expense involved in rectifying the error is as nothing compared with the sure impairment of the sense of reverence in a not-too-reverent generation.

Israel Bettan

See also:

S.B. Freehof, "Menorah Decoration in Floor," **Reform Responsa**, pp. 68ff.

24. DECORATIONS IN THE FLOOR OF A SYNAGOGUE
(1979)

QUESTION: May the floor of a synagogue or entrance hall be decorated with Jewish symbols or with any other kind of decoration employing the figures of people or animals?

ANSWER: The floors of the worship area of most modern synagogues remain undecorated in contrast to many ancient houses of worship, as we usually have fixed seating, and the major area of the synagogue is covered by permanent seats. The specific question of decorating the floor of a synagogue has only been rarely treated in the traditional literature. We know that many ancient synagogues had floors of inlaid mosaics which have been found in our century, like that of Beit Alfa, probably built between 517 and 525 C.E. It contained a mosaic of the **Akeda** with human figures and a Divine Hand stretching out from heaven. In addition, there were decorative symbols depicting the seasons of the year and the signs of the zodiac. We also find an ark, a candelabrum, a **shofar**, a **lulav**, incense shovels, etc. in the mosaic of the floors at Beit Alfa, Jericho, Yafia, Ashkelon, Maon, etc.

Michael Avi-Yonah ("Ancient Synagogues," **The Synagogue**, ed. J. Gutmann, pp. 108ff) stated that the early Palestinian synagogues used only abstract patterns in their mosaic floors, as Jewish and Christian leaders refused to allow anything which might have tempted the worshiper toward idolatry. From the fifth century onward, a richer Christian iconography developed, although the emperor Theodosius II specifically prohibited the use of figures in mosaic floors of churches in 427 C.E. A similar iconographic development had taken place among

Jews, but the prohibition against the use of such elements did not affect them. For this reason, many Biblical subjects, including Noah's Ark, the Sacrifice of Isaac, Daniel in the Lions' Den, etc., were used. In the middle of the sixth century, the Rabbinic attitude seemed to change. Human figures disappeared and only animals, along with various ritual objects, were used.

The only Rabbinic discussion which has dealt with this matter was related to the verse in Leviticus 26:1: "You shall not make an **even maskit** to bow down upon in your land." Rashi has interpreted this to mean any smooth stone floor, while Rambam (**Yad**, Hil. Tefila V.14; Hil. Avoda Zara VI.6,7) interpreted it as either a decorated or a paved stone akin to those used in idol worship. The Talmud has recorded (Meg. 22b) that Rav was unwilling to prostrate himself while worshiping in the synagogue in Babylon because it had a stone floor. Despite these statements, stone floors were used in synagogues throughout the Middle Ages, and the medieval commentators stated that only full prostration was prohibited upon them (Asher ben Yehiel to Meg. 22b; Isserles to **Shulchan Aruch**, Orach Chayim 131.8; Joseph Caro in **Kesef Mishneh** to **Yad**, Hil. Avoda Zara VI.6). When full prostration was necessary, then straw or carpeting was spread on the floor, as on Yom Kippur. In other words, even in the Middle Ages, a cut or decorated stone floor was acceptable. There was absolutely no thought of objecting to walking across such a floor.

It is clear, therefore, that any kind of decoration in the floor of the synagogues has long since gone beyond the ancient concern for possible idolatrous expression, and our synagogues contain representative figures, cut and decorated stone, metal, and woodwork. Such decorations must, of course, not contain the Divine Name of God. The custom of some modern synagogues of copying the mosaics of floors from ancient Jewish synagogues should be encouraged as another link to our past and to the land of Israel.

Walter Jacob, Chairman
Leonard S. Kravitz
Eugene Lipman
W. Gunther Plaut
Harry A. Roth
Rav A. Soloff

25.   CARILLON MUSIC
(Vol. LXIII, 1953, pp. 155-56)

QUESTION: I would be very grateful if you would
advise me concerning the use of carillon music in a
proposed Temple tower. Those who have it in mind
are thinking in terms of a Memorial Tower from
which would be played at festival times hymns out
of the Jewish background.

ANSWER: The carillon is but a mechanical device to
draw elaborate tones from the play on bells.   Some interesting and extensive studies have been done on the
origin and use of bells (A. Gattey, **The Bell: Its Origin, History and Uses**; G.S. Tyack, **A Book About Bells**).
     Some students of the subject are inclined to trace
the origin of the use of bells to sheer superstition.
It was thought, they hold, that the sound of bells had
the magic power to safeguard against demons and other
evil influences. They further claim that we may discern
vestiges of that superstition in the use and treatment
of bells all through the Middle Ages.
     But whatever the origin and early use of bells, it
is certain that from the sixth century to the present
day, bells have been closely associated with the Church
and its worship. Even the Protestant Reformation, which
put an end to many things it regarded as unneeded ap-
pendages to Christian worship, carefully avoided laying
hands on the popular church bells. Today the ringing of
bells is a preliminary to prayer in Protestant as in
Roman Catholic churches. In the Church of England, the
clergy is required by canon law to toll a bell before
the daily service. Bells are as indigenous to worship
in the church as the **Shofar** to the service in the synagogue.
     Richly equipped as the synagogue is with adequate
and satisfying symbols of its own, it stands to profit
little from this glaring imitation of the church.

Israel Bettan

26.   WORK ON NEW SYNAGOGUE ON SABBATH BY NON-JEWS
(Vol. XXXVII, 1927, pp. 203-206)

QUESTION: Is it permissible to let a non-Jewish
contractor, building a synagogue, work on the
building on the Sabbath?

ANSWER: The Jewish religious law forbids the Jews to do any work on the Sabbath or to have his servant or agent do it for him. The Jew is, therefore, not allowed to hire laborers to do work for him on the Sabbath. He may, however, let out work to a non-Jew and need not concern himself whether the non-Jew does it on Sabbath or not, provided that the non-Jew has the time and could do the work on weekdays. Since the Jew does not profit by the work being done on the Sabbath, he is not responsible for the non-Jew's choosing to do the work on the Sabbath. For the Jew is not commanded to try in any way to make the non-Jew observe the Jewish Sabbath. In any case, then, where the non-Jew is not a hired laborer (i.e., paid wages by the day or week or month), but receives payment for the finished job or contracts to do the whole work and receives payment for the delivered product (**bekablanut** or **bekibolet**) and not for the hours of labor put in, the Jew may let him do on the Sabbath the labor contracted for. The non-Jew in such cases--having contracted for the job and not for so many days of labor--is his own master and not the servant or agent of the Jew. He may do his work whenever he pleases, and the Jew need not concern himself whether the non-Jew observes the Sabbath or not, for it is not the duty of the Jew to make the non-Jew observe the Jewish Sabbath.

There is only one consideration that might keep the Jew from letting the non-Jew do any work for him on the Sabbath, even when the work is contracted for by **kablanut**. This is the consideration of **mipenei haro-im**, lest other Jews, seeing the non-Jew doing the Jewish work on the Sabbath, and not knowing that it was contracted for by **kablanut**, might suspect the Jew of letting his hired laborer or agent work for him on Sabbath. This might lead to a laxity in the observance of the Sabbath on the part of other Jews. To avoid suspicion (**mishum chashda**) the Jew should not let a non-Jew do work for him on Sabbath, even **bekablanut**, when conditions are such as to cause other people to think that the Jew for whom the work is done is violating the Sabbath. Accordingly, therefore, it depends on conditions. Where there is no danger that the people, seeing the work done, might think it is done by hired day-laborers and not **bekablanut**, the Jew need have no hesitation at all to let the non-Jew do the work for him. Of course, even when there is such danger, one might argue, why consider other people's unjustified suspicions? But the Rabbis did consider the effect of any action of ours upon innocent and ignorant people.

However, R. Jacob Tam (1100-1171) somehow disregarded the consideration for other people's unjustified suspicions and permitted the building of a Jewish home by a non-Jew on the Sabbath, in case the non-Jew

has a contract for the work **bekibolet** and is not a day
laborer (**Tosafot**, Avoda Zara 21b, **s.v.** "**arisa**"). But
another Tosafist, R. Isaac, probably a younger contemporary of R. Tam, decided against R. Tam. His argument
was that since it was customary in those days, when
building a house, to hire the builders and laborers by
the day, people would not know that in the specific case
the work was done by the non-Jews on contract, and would
suspect the Jew of hiring day-laborers to do work on the
Sabbath: "**Aval bevinyan bayit regilot liskor midei yom
beyom, veharo-eh eino omer kablanutei avid, ela sechirei
yom ninhu**" (**Tosafot**, Avoda Zara, **ibid.**, l.c.). This
view of R. Isaac has been accepted in the **Shulchan
Aruch**, Orach Chayim 244. It should be remembered, however, that even according to this view it is only forbidden **mipenei haro-im** or **mishum chashda**, i.e., lest the
people seeing the work done on Sabbath might suspect the
Jew of having hired day-laborers. Accordingly, in a
country where the general custom is that the work on
buildings is done by contract, **bekablanut**, and where the
people would not suspect the Jew, it would be permissible to let the non-Jewish contractor build a Jewish home
on the Sabbath. R. Ezekiel Landau, in his **Noda BiYehuda
Kemo Orach Chayim** (no. 2, Prague, 1776, p. 5a), was
inclined to favor such a permission, since, as he says,
in his time it was customary in Prague to have all work
on Jewish buildings done by contract.

I have so far discussed the law in regard to a
private building. In cases of community buildings it is
even more to be allowed, since the fear that the people,
seeing the work done on Sabbath, might suspect a violation of the Sabbath law (**chashda**) does not enter into
the question. According to Rabbinic law (cf. Talmud
Bavli, R.H. 24b, near bottom of page; also **Tur**, Yoreh
De-a 141, and **Shulchan Aruch**, Yoreh De-a 141.4 Isserles
note), a community need not fear misunderstanding or
suspicion. Since it is a community business and every
one knows the true state of affairs and is acquainted
with the prevailing conditions, no one will unduly suspect the community of doing wrong.

Rabbi Abraham Abele Gumbiner, a great Polish rabbinical authority (1635-1683), in his commentary **Magen
Avraham** to **Shulchan Aruch**, Orach Chayim 244.8, therefore, says that a community should be allowed to have a
synagogue built by non-Jews on the Sabbath, if the work
is done by contract. He adds, however, that some authorities refused to permit it on the following grounds:
Since the non-Jews do not let any person do any public
work on their Holiday or Sunday, it would be a disgrace,
a sort of **Chilul Hashem** if we would permit work on our
buildings to be done on our Sabbath: "**Ve-im ken haya
nir-eh lehatir livnot beit hakeneset beshabat bekabla-**

nut; umikol makom ra-iti shehagedolim lo ratsu lehatiro, ki bazeman hazeh ein hagoyim manichin leshum adam la-asot melechet parhesya beyom chagam, ve-im naniach anachnu la-asot, ika chilul hashem." In other words, it would be a disgrace because it would look as if we do not care for our Sabbath as much as others care for theirs. This is a rather poor argument, and Rabbi Akiva Eiger in his notes on the **Shulchan Aruch, ad loc.**, rightly remarks that he cannot see any disgrace in our not imitating other people by forcing our Sabbath upon others. He says: "**Uve-ikar hadavar nir-eh, lefi aniyut da-ati, de-ein bazeh mishum chilul hashem bema de-ein manichin hagoyim leshum adam la-asot melacha.**"

And we today who object strongly to other people's seeking to force Sunday laws upon us, certainly cannot consider it disgraceful to refrain from forcing other people to observe our Sabbath. Since the law does not forbid us to give out work to a non-Jew **bekablanut**, we need not consider that some people might think that we do not care for our Sabbath as much as others do for theirs. R. Yehuda Ashkenazi (first half of the 18th century) in his commentary **Ba-er Heitev** to **Shulchan Aruch**, Orach Chayim, **ad loc.**, declares that if there is any apprehension that by refusing to let the non-Jews work on our Sabbath the building of the synagogue might not be able to progress or be carried out, we should not insist on the work being done on weekdays only, and we should allow the non-Jewish contractor to proceed with his work on the Sabbath. The same opinion is held by Zevi Hirsch Zamosz (1740-1807) in his responsa **Tif-eret Tsevi**, quoted in **Sha-arei Teshuva, ad loc.**, though Zamosz suggests the device of a fictitious sale of the building to a non-Jew (**Shetar Mechira**), which, of course, we cannot at all consider.

Solomon Yehuda Rappaport in his responsum published in **Beit Talmud** II (Wien, 1882, pp. 354-355) also hesitates to forbid a synagogue to be built on the Sabbath by non-Jews. After a rather lengthy discussion he finally arrives at at the following decision: If there is an absolute need for the new Temple, it is to be permitted. If, however, there is no absolute need for it, i.e., if the congregation has a house of worship, but merely wants to have a better, more convenient, and more beautiful Temple, then we should first make all efforts to arrange with the contractors--even at the risk of additional expense--that they do not work on it on the Sabbath. If this cannot be done, at least let no one representing the congregation be seen there on the Sabbath supervising the work or watching the laborers.

I think that this decision of Rappaport should be followed in your case. Since it is a matter of sentiment more than of law, you should make all efforts to arrange, if possible, not to have the work done on the Sabbath, even if it should involve extra outlay on the part of the congregation. I make this decision with great hesitancy because my sentiments are against giving the permission, but I must, in truth, state that the law does not offer any serious objection to it.

Jacob Z. Lauterbach

27. BUILDING A CHAPEL ON A CEMETERY
(1979)

QUESTION: The congregation plans to build a chapel on the cemetery. Could provisions be made for an Ark and a Torah? May that chapel eventually be used for other kinds of services as well? (Rabbi Roy A. Walter, Congregation Emanu-El, Houston, Texas)

ANSWER: In order to answer this inquiry properly, we must briefly discuss the possibility of erecting a synagogue on the cemetery. No synagogues have been intentionally built on a cemetery, but occasionally graves were found after the process of building a synagogue or converting an existing building had begun, and so the matter is discussed in the literature. For example, David Oppenheimer of Prague has a responsum (published at the end of **Chavat Yair**) which dealt with the problem of bones being found in land purchased for the construction of a synagogue. Suddenly, the congregation realized that it was building above a former Gentile cemetery. He stated that if the ground was dug and it was assured that four feet under the building were free of any human bones, one would then be allowed to build a synagogue upon it. At the beginning of this century, a congregation in the English city of Hull bought a chapel and intended to convert it into a synagogue, but then discovered that hundreds of bodies were buried in crypts beneath the basement. Rabbi Israel Daiches of Leeds permitted the building to be used as a synagogue if the vaults were cemented over. There were, however, some subsequent discussions which disagreed with his decision. These discussions show that there has been great reluctance to build a synagogue anywhere where it might be in contact with graves, even of non-Jews. For that matter, the Mishna already tried to regulate the location of cemeteries, and insisted that they be at least two hundred feet from the city and so, of course, at a distance from any synagogue (B.B. II.9; **Shulchan Aruch,** Choshen Mishpat 155.23).

As far as a Torah is concerned, it is prohibited to bring a Torah into the cemetery (Ber. 18a). For that matter, an individual is not allowed to wear **Tefilin** or **Tsitsit** into the cemetery, and these stipulations are contained in the later codes **(Shulchan Aruch,** Yoreh De-a 367.2, etc.). It was considered mocking the dead to bring these sacred objects into the cemetery, as the dead could no longer benefit from them. Naturally, such prohibition would mean that no formal services would be held on the cemetery. This would, of course, not keep anyone from saying prayers in the cemetery as an individual, as has been done throughout the ages (Ta-anit 16a; **Shulchan Aruch,** Orach Chayim 579.30), or occasionally holding a special congregational memorial service in the cemetery. Yet, traditionally we have been reluctant to hold any kind of service there. The chapel at the cemetery, therefore, should be constructed without an Ark and have no provisions for the inclusion of a Torah.

Walter Jacob

See also:

S.B. Freehof, "Synagogue Near a Cemetery," **Recent Reform Responsa,** pp. 41ff.

28. SALE OF A SYNAGOGUE
(Vol. XXIX, 1919, p. 85)

QUESTION: An Orthodox congregation has a synagogue in the downtown district of the city. A considerable number of its members--representing the wealthiest element--moved from the neighborhood to a more desirable part of the town, and--finding it impossible to attend the old synagogue on account of the great distance--propose to sell it and to use the proceeds for the erection of another synagogue in their new neighborhood. The members who remained in the old neighborhood object to the sale. The attorney representing the advocates of the sale wishes to obtain information on the Jewish law in the case.

ANSWER: The constitutional law of the congregation is chiefly defined by local practice, and the legal authorities often differ on these questions.

Shulchan Aruch, the authoritative law book (Orach Chayim 153.7) says: A synagogue may be sold by the seven trustees (the usual number) of the congregation in a convention of the members, which can only mean that the latter have but a consulting vote.

All financial affairs of the congregation, such as assessment and expenditures, are arranged through a vote in which the membership, paying more than half of the taxes, decides (**Shulchan Aruch,** Choshen Mishpat 163.3).

Solomon Ibn Adret (**Responsa,** no. 1091) declares that a majority of the membership, regardless of the tax payment, is decisive.

Asher ben Jehiel (**Responsa,** no. 7.3) is for decision on the ground of tax payment.

The usual practice of the congregation is that both factors are to be taken into consideration, e.g., if a congregation has 100 members, a vote of 51 is necessary, provided these 51 pay more than 50 percent of the congregational taxes. Mendel Krochmal (**Responsa,** no. 1-2) declares that in personal questions (such as the election of a paid official), the majority of the taxpayers is always necessary, so that in a case which is submitted to him, where, of a membership of fifty, five men pay more than half of the congregational assessment, their veto cannot prevent the election of a congregational official.

Conclusion: If a majority of members, whose dues represent more than half of the income of the congregation raised by assessment, decide upon the sale of the synagogue, their action is legal. This is the rigorous view, but authors of considerable authority declare that a vote of the trustees is sufficient, as long as the membership is ratified.

G. Deutsch

NOTE:

Since every congregation has a constitution and bylaws, such should be checked before any property is sold. However, whether or not the constitution and bylaws make provision for the sale of property, it is wise to consult an attorney. Furthermore, legal counsel may be essential because many states have laws requiring the courts to approve the sale of any property owned by a religious institution.

Responsa Committee (1980)

See also:

S.B. Freehof, "Selling Synagogue to Black Muslims," **Contemporary Reform Responsa**, pp. 13ff.

29. THE HOSPITAL CHAPEL
(Vol. LXXVII, 1967, pp. 81-82)

QUESTION: Is it permitted to put a Jewish symbol such as the Ten Commandments in a hospital chapel where there already are crosses and other Christian symbols?

ANSWER: Unfortunately, Jewish legal tradition would make it seem that Christians are more liberal in this matter of material symbols than we. Christians would very likely not object to having a Jewish symbol such as the Two Tablets of stone in the same sanctuary in which the cross has been erected. That is because they believe in both New and Old Testaments. Also, according to Jewish law, Christians are "Children of Noah," and under that covenant are not forbidden to add other semi-deities to that of God (saints, etc.). It is no sin for a Christian to invoke the Trinity (this is the opinion of the French Halacha, and was adopted by the later Halacha, see Orach Chayim 156). But Jews are forbidden to add other divinities to God (**Shituf**), and therefore, in this case, it would be a sin for us to permit crosses side by side with Jewish religious symbols.

Of course, if it were a question of emergency and there were no other place to pray, a Jew has been permitted to pray in a place where there are crosses. The **Trumat Ha-Deshen** (Israel Isserlein, Responsum #6) permits a Jewish wayfarer to pray in a Christian inn even though there are crosses there; but even then, he says, it would be preferable if the man prayed by the roadside if he thought he would not be disturbed. If, of course, he cannot pray in the open without being disturbed, Israel Isserlein says: "Let him find a separate room in the inn, if possible, or a corner, and pray there." And he continues: "After all, all our prayers are recited in cities that are full of images." His statement, quoted by Isserles, is in Orach Chayim 94.9.

Therefore, if we were dealing with an **emergency** where there was no other place to pray, a Jew would be permitted to pray in the chapel, even though there are crosses there. But this is not a situation of emergency; it is a situation which we are creating, and we have some choice in the matter.

A similar question was asked by a Mr. James McGuire of the Western Pennsylvania Hospital in Pittsburgh. Following is the suggestion made to him:

> Let me suggest a possible solution. If, for example, a niche with an eternal light were put near the entrance of the chapel with some extra chairs near it, this would do for private Jewish prayer, especially if the worshiper facing the niche would be facing East.

Of course, this solution would not work if the entire chapel already faces east, i.e., if the Christian altar faces east. But if the Christian altar is not in the east, then you may call attention to our custom of praying towards the east and have such a niche built. There you could put Jewish symbols, since we could well consider it a separate enclosure (**rashut**).

Solomon B. Freehof

30. BAR MITZVAH
(Vol. XXIII, 1913, pp. 170-173)

In this connection I wish to touch upon a subject involving the very principle of Reform, being well aware of the fact that we can only discuss congregational customs as to their correctness, but not dictate Reform and Progress. We should enlighten our people, working for a gradual advancement, following **evolutionary**, not **revolutionary** methods, as we want to build up, not to destroy. We want peace and harmony while aiming at true progress. The fact is beyond dispute that the introduction of the **Union Prayer Book** meant to bring about Union and Unity in our progressive American Jewry. Now I ask: Is the calling up of the thirteen-year-old lad to become Bar Mitzvah (Son [Bearer] of Religious Duty) by reading or by listening to the reading of the Torah--which is still the practice in many Reform Congregations--in harmony with the whole spirit of our Reform service?

To be sure, it was a grand and glorious privilege of each individual member of the congregation to be called up--like the Priest, the Aaronide, and the Levite, the original teachers of the Israelitish community--to read aloud from the Book of the Law and thus be made the participant in the great heritage of the people of God. Let me say in parenthesis that the seven men called up each Sabbath to read from the Law were, in my opinion, originally none other than the seven principal men of each town, the seven **Tovei Ha-ir**, called "the seven judges" by Josephus (**Antiquities** IV,8,14,38), who, being familiar with the whole Law, and otherwise the true representatives of the community, sat on the platform of the synagogue, having at least one Aaronide and one Levite endowed with the rights of priority in their midst. As the study of the Law spread among the Jewish people and all the members of the congregation were able to read, the reading rotated, and all were in turn called up to take the place of the seven **Tovei Ha-ir**. Accordingly, it was the greatest privilege that could be bestowed upon the youth who had just attained--according to the juridical view of the time--the age of duty and responsibility, and the Bar Mitzvah, after having received his training in Scriptural reading (see article on "Bar Mitzvah" in **Jewish Encyclopedia**, and esp. Mas. Soferim XVIII.5; **Bereshit R.** LXIII.14), to be called up to the Torah like any of the learned men and thus be solemnly admitted into the membership of the congregation. And this custom prevailed even after the congregation had been so enlarged as to admit many of those unable to read aloud from the Torah, so the Reader (**Chazan** or **Sheliach Tsibur**) had to read the portion for them, while they simply recited the benediction preceding and following the Torah reading. The young Bar Mitzvah at least took special pride in being amply conversant with the law so as to be able to read his **Parasha** when called up on the Sabbath marking the entrance into his fourteenth year.

But there is a greater principle involved. When Confirmation--a rite borrowed from the Church but sanctioned even by Conservative congregations and rabbis all over Europe, notwithstanding its denunciation as **Chukat Hagoy** (a pagan rite?) by strict Orthodoxy--was introduced into the modern synagogue, the early Reform leaders had chiefly one object in view, viz., to emancipate religion from the Oriental view which regards religion in the main as the concern of man only, and not of woman, and, therefore, essentially and intently neglects the religious training of the girl (Loew, **Die Lebensalter**, pp. 218-222; Herxheimer in Geiger's **Wiss. Zeitsch. f. Jued. Theol.** I, pp. 68-96; the article "Confirmation" in **Jewish Encyclopedia**; and **The Reform Move-**

ment in Judaism by Philipson, Index, s.v. "Confirmation"). In clear and emphatic opposition to such Orientalism as still prevails wherever the Shulchan Aruch or the Talmudic code is regarded as authoritative, the religious instruction was systematically extended so as to include the girls, and after the conclusion of the course of instruction, the young woman was as solemnly initiated into the faith of the fathers at the age of maturity as the young man. As a matter of fact, the Confirmation introduced by enlightened religious educators in Germany bore originally the character of a solemn Religious School graduation rather than that of a specific religious or synagogal ceremony.

Only gradually the Confirmation was transferred to the synagogue, there to become a prominent and impressive feature of the divine service. And finally it was rendered an integral part of the Shavuot service in the Reform synagogue, expressive of the grand idea that, just as our fathers stood on that day at the foot of Mt. Sinai to receive the Law amidst the solemn vow "Na-aseh venishma"--"We shall do and shall hearken!"--so is the whole congregation, in common with its young men and women, each year reconsecrated to Israel's mission on God's Holy People and His Kingdom of Priests.

How, then, can a Bar Mitzvah ceremony, as a survival of a dead past, claim any importance beside the Confirmation? Is it not an altogether false pretense that the young man is a more important factor of religious life in the community than is the young woman? Granted for argument's sake that the individual allegiance entered into by the Bar Mitzvah is of some value and impressiveness, let us see whether these very Benei Mitzvah are kept from violating the Sabbath as soon as they enter business life. On the other hand, watch the girls after Confirmation and see how eagerly and conscientiously most of them become and remain attendants at the divine service and prove powerful influences for religion at home! Disregarding altogether the false claim of mental maturity of the thirteen-year-old boy for a true realization of life's sacred obligations, I maintain that the Bar Mitzvah rite ought not to be encouraged by any Reform rabbi, as it is a survival of Orientalism like the covering of the head during the service; whereas the Confirmation, when made, as it should, by the rabbi to be an impressive appeal to the holiest emotions of the soul and a personal vow of fealty to the ancestral faith, is a source of regeneration of Judaism each

year, the value of which none who has the spiritual
welfare of Israel at heart can afford to underrate or to
ignore.

K. Kohler

31. BAT MITZVAH
(Vol. XXIII, 1913, pp. 183-185)

The lesser part of women in religious life is not
Orientalism. As far as Israel is concerned (to say
nothing of our other Semitic peoples, such as Babylonians, Assyrians, etc.), the women maintained a leading
role in religious life as far down as the time of Jeremiah and Ezekiel. The women were considered of equal
standing not only as worshipers but also as functionaries in the religious life. It was on account of the
Istar-worship which the women in Israel, as well as
elsewhere, favored, that they were excluded from the
religious functions in post-exilic Judaism, and later,
in Talmudic times, from certain religious duties which
depend on fixed times and seasons. But by this the
Jewess was by no means relegated from the religious life
in which, on the contrary, she had **at least** as high a
standing as women in any of the Occidental Churches ever
had. If we do not consider the nuns as religious functionaries, we have to admit that no Occidental Church
ever entrusted women with priestly functions. If the
women in the synagogue were separated in galleries not
accessible to men, while the church did not care for
separation, we cannot designate this as Orientalism,
since--on the contrary--the Church, **returning back to
the Oriental Istar-motif** in religion, did not care, as
she was not entitled, to go in demands of purity as far
as Judaism went. We may think differently today as to
the advisability of separation of sexes, but separation
is by no means a lessening of the woman's standing in
the synagogue. And in the home woman had exclusive
religious functions, such as **challah,** Sabbath candles,
etc., unknown to the Occidental Church. The only real
case in point is the debarment of women from religious
functions, but as to this, Conservative Judaism is on a
par not only with all Occidental Churches but also with
Reform Judaism. As yet we have no woman rabbi, no woman
cantor, even no woman **shamash** in the synagogue, nor do
we find her in the councils of the **kehila** (see, however,
the new attempt with the sisterhoods).

True, Judaism in the Talmudic period and in past ages in general did not care as much for the religious training of the girl as it did for that of the boy. But the fact of the matter is that the average girl in past ages in some respects knew more of Judaism than does the modern girl of today after finishing all courses in Sunday school. Women lomedot in old-fashioned Judaism are not rare; I personally know quite a number of them. As to the practical question involved, I am perfectly in accord with the suggestion to abolish Bar Mitzvah ceremony in favor of the Confirmation on Shavuot for boys and girls alike. But in synagogues where the Bar Mitzvah ceremony for boys is still in practice, I would be in favor of letting the boy come to the Torah, whether to read himself from the Torah--as is the custom in some synagogues--or only to say the Benediction and to read from the Prophets. In the synagogues where this is practiced, it is considered as a **religious function** (which it really is, historically considered), and as such the boy is called upon to perform it, while the girl is deprived of that privilege, even within Reform Judaism. And this appears strongly justified by the fact that a boy of thirteen may be called upon soon to decide to enter the Hebrew Union College, where he is admitted after completing his fourteenth year; this possibility is practically out of the question in the case of a girl.

D. Neumark

32. BAT MITZVAH
(Vol. LXIV, 1954, pp. 81-83)

QUESTION: For the past few years I have been with a congregation where some of the parents believe in Bar Mitzvah. I get the boys ready for the ceremony and attend the extravagant parties staged. Some of my colleagues, who are more impressed than I am, are even planning to introduce Bat Mitzvah. Frankly, I am puzzled. What actuated the early Reformers in their decisive stand against the Bar Mitzvah idea? Are those reasons no longer tenable? And what about Bat Mitzvah, concerning which the rabbis of yesterday had no occasion to formulate an opinion?

I may not understand the whole historical process. But the question I should like to have you answer is whether Reform Judaism has changed

its course, or is it just drifting into another
port?

ANSWER: A religion that seeks to mold a certain type
of character will necessarily impose definite duties
upon each individual life. It will also deem it within
its province to determine when the age of individual
responsibility shall begin, since the human personality
develops but slowly and gradually.

In Biblical times a man was thought to have attained his majority at the age of twenty, when he became
fully liable for any act of misconduct (Num. 14:29).   In
the Rabbinic period, a downward revision in the age of
accountability took place.   "For the first thirteen
years of his son's life," a Rabbinic authority declared,
"a father is obligated to attend to his son's conduct;
thereafter, he should say, 'Praised be He who has exempted me from the liability now resting upon **him**'"
(**Genesis Rabba**, 63.14).

When the Mishnaic teacher affirmed that at thirteen
the age is reached for the fulfillment of the commandments (Avot 5.24), he did not mean to indicate the time
when one's training in the performance of duty began,
but rather the time when one began to bear full responsibility for any dereliction in the performance of his
duties.

Accordingly, a boy who had attained his thirteenth
year joined the "congregation," as it were.   He formed
part of the "quorum" required for public worship; he
wore the phylacteries during the morning prayers; and,
he fasted on the Day of Atonement.   In short, he became
a full-fledged "Son of the Covenant"--a Bar Mitzvah.

To mark the importance of the occasion, the father
would take his Bar Mitzvah to a man of learning, who
would bless him and pray for him, beseeching God to make
him worthy of a life devoted to the study of Torah and
good deeds (Soferim 18).   The more elaborate Bar Mitzvah
celebration, of which our latter day extravaganza is a
curious offspring, seems to have originated in the 14th
century, when a family party would be held in honor of
the Bar Mitzvah (Abrahams, **J.L.M.A.**, pp. 23, 144).

The exclusion of girls from this form of initiation
might, of course, be interpreted as an act of discrimination, mirroring the time when women stood none too high
in the intellectual and social scale.   Yet, when we
consider the fact that women were legally exempt from
religious duties the performance of which was linked to
a specified time, we may discern in the Rabbinic attitude not a disparagement of woman, but a more just ap-
praisal of the value of her time.   What she had to do at
a given time--the Rabbis may well have held--was of

infinitely greater importance than the punctilious observance of some ritual practice.

At any rate, when Reform Judaism arose, the leaders
felt quite acutely that the time had come for an upward
revision of the age at which maturity and moral responsibility began. The Rabbinic estimate of the degree of
maturity which a boy of thirteen was capable of achiev-
ing might have been true in days long past; it surely
did not hold true in the opening days of the 19th century. Nor were these leaders satisfied that in an age of
shifting emphases--when not conformity to ritual, but
adjustment to life, became the chief concern of men--the
religious instruction represented by the requirements
for the Bar Mitzvah ceremony was adequate or even pertinent. Then, too, eager as they were to raise the status
of women in the synagogue, they could not but view the
conspicuous Bar Mitzvah ceremony as a striking reminder
of the dominant role the male chose to play in the house
of God.

Confirmation, as instituted by the early Reformers,
put boys and girls on a plane of equality. It also
opened the way for a modification of the age of maturity
as fixed by the Rabbis. Above all, it initiated, and
has since helped to develop, a new system of religious
education, which has vitally affected the course of
American Judaism.

Yet, despite its feeble basis in the realities of
religious living, Bar Mitzvah has retained its old appeal for many parents in some of our Reform congregations. In fact, in many recently organized congregations, it has assumed a position of importance which it
had never before attained. It would seem that when the
substance eludes our grasp, we tighten our hold on the
shell.

But the Reform synagogue, committed to the principle that it is the function of religion to serve human
needs, stands ready to respond to any call for service
that may come from its members. Our rabbis do well when
they comply with the wishes of parents and prepare their
sons for the Bar Mitzvah ceremony. However devoid of
substance the rite may be, if the boy's training in the
religious school is not discontinued, the nostalgic
indulgence of the parents may be productive of some
good. Surely, the special type of instruction offered
for the occasion should serve to stimulate interest in
the language of the Bible.

Quite different, however, must be our attitude to
the proposed Bat Mitzvah ceremony, which goes counter to
tradition and for which there is no popular demand.
When a new religious practice is urged upon us, of whose
value our fathers had no estimate and we have had no
convincing demonstration, it is not enough to point to

some by-product of possible utility, as we attempt to do in the case of the Bar Mitzvah ceremony. Unless the new project recommends itself to us by its inherent worth and direct positive purpose, none of its strained qualities shall ever win and hold our active interest.

It is surely vain to hope that we shall keep Bar Mitzvah alive by reinforcing it with Bat Mitzvah--two figments do not make one fact. Reform Judaism has not changed its course. In striving to meet the needs of men, in countenancing even dubious experiments, the Reform synagogue is true to itself and to the principle that gave it birth.

Israel Bettan

33.   REFORM ATTITUDE TOWARD BAR MITZVAH AND BAT MITZVAH
(1979)

QUESTION: What is the Reform attitude toward Bar and Bat Mitzvah? Has it changed over the years? What is their relationship to Confirmation?

ANSWER: Bar and Bat Mitzvah are, virtually, universally observed by Reform Jews. They celebrate the coming to maturity for boys and girls (**Yad.**, Hil. Ishut, 2.9, 10) and the accompanying obligations (Yoma 82a, etc.).

The ceremony possesses considerable meaning both to the young people and to their parents. It strengthens their bonds to Judaism and the synagogue, helps cement family ties, and marks a step in the religious education of each child. The nature of the ceremony and the participation of the child and his/her parents varies from congregation to congregation, but always includes reading from the Torah and the **Haftara** (on Shabbat morning), as well as a blessing by the rabbi. Bar and Bat Mitzvahs are normally conducted on Shabbat morning or at any other service at which the Torah is regularly read.

The ceremony celebrates the entrance into the initial stages of adult life. It marks a change toward physical maturity and a new degree of intellectual maturity, as demonstrated by the curricula of the Middle School and a wide variety of ancillary programs. Most important of all, it demands responsibility for **mitzvot** within the framework of the modern family and society. The actual responsibility assumed may be modest, but the process of decision-making must now be undertaken in a more serious manner.

The ceremony of Bar Mitzvah as a separate institution was first mentioned in the 14th century by Mordecai ben Hillel (cited by Isserles to **Tur**, O.Ch. 225.1), and was not welcomed by all (**Yam Shel Shelomo**, Bava Kama 7.37). The Talmud did not know it, and called coming of age "**Bar Oneshin.**"

In any case, it has become widely established and followed by all segments of the Jewish community. It has now become thoroughly a part of congregational and family Jewish life and is a major portion of the youngster's life as he or she grows up. Every effort should be made to have the youngster participate in the Torah service in keeping with his/her age, but not to the exclusion of the rest of the congregation. The child may also participate in the regular service in keeping with the general pattern of worship, so that all congregants will continue to feel that the service has meaning for them.

Many Reform congregations have always conducted the Bar and Bat Mitzvah ceremony, while others omitted it for some decades in preference to Confirmation. The ceremony of Confirmation was introduced by Ehrenberg in Wolfenbuettel in 1807 (J.R. Marcus, **Israel Jacobson**, p. 146). This communal ceremony soon involved both boys and girls (Denmark, 1817, or Hamburg, 1822; D. Philipson, "Confirmation," **Central Conference of American Rabbis Yearbook**, vol. 1, p. 44), and therefore clearly emphasized the equality of men and women in modern Jewish practice. Furthermore, it generally occurred later than Bar Mitzvah, and thus extended the religious education of the child. This ceremony continues to be of major importance in most congregations and is usually conducted when the class has reached the age of sixteen. Most children who are Bar and Bat Mitzvah are also confirmed and see the former ceremony as a step to the latter. Some attempts have been made from time to time by the Conservative Movement to change the age of the Bar and Bat Mitzvah, but these have not received popular support, and no such efforts have been made in the Reform Movement. The classic position for Confirmation in place of Bar Mitzvah was made by Kaufmann Kohler, who felt that we must recognize that true maturity had not been reached in our society by the age of thirteen, and therefore this tradition from the past should be discarded (Kaufmann Kohler, **CCAR Yearbook**, vol. 23, pp. 170ff). We disagree with these assumptions and see the ceremony as valuable for the child, the family, and the synagogue ("Symposium," **CCAR Yearbook**, vol. 72, p. 157ff).

In contrast to the early Reform Movement, we now see no conflict between Bar/Bat Mitzvah and Confirmation. One emphasizes the individual child, the other the role which he/she plays in the congregation and community. Bar/Bat Mitzvah particularly reinforces the study of Hebrew. Each marks a different level of maturity and intellectual attainment.

Bat Mitzvah is a new ceremony introduced by Mordecai Kaplan in the 1920s (although it was mentioned in the 19th century by Joseph Hayim b. Elijah in **Ben Ish Chai**). It has been widely accepted by the Reform and Conservative movements in Judaism, and among some modern Orthodox congregations, although the ceremony has been much modified among those Orthodox Jews where accepted (**Seridei Esh** III.93; Feinstein, **Igerot Mosheh** I.97,104; **Noam**, vol. 7, p. 8). Tradition has set the age of majority at twelve and one day for girls and thirteen and one day for boys (**Aruch Hashulchan** 225.4, etc.), and these are the ages for Bar and Bat Mitzvah among Conservative and Orthodox Jews. We recommend that the ceremony for both be held at age thirteen. Little was made of this ceremony until the Middle Ages, although it is clear that from age thirteen onward, a boy was considered to have reached his majority in every way and he was responsible for his own sins (Avot 5.21; Nid. 5.6).

Majority originally depended upon the appearance of two pubic hairs, and if they did not appear, then the attainment of majority was delayed (Maimonides, **Yad**, Hil. Ishut 2.9,10); but by the 14th century the physical characteristics were simply assumed and there was no examination for them unless there was some question raised. In earlier times, minors were called to the Torah (Meg. 23a; **Tur**, Orach Chayim 282), and put on **Tefilin**, but this was protested beginning in the 12th century (**Itur** II, 26c; Isserles to **Shulchan Aruch**, Orach Chayim 37.1, contrary to the Talmud, Sukka 42a). A boy may now begin to use **Tefilin** a few months before the Bar Mitzvah in traditional circles (**Ba-er Heitev** to Shulchan Aruch, Orach Chayim 37.1; **Aruch Hashulchan**, O.Ch. 37.9). On the occasion of the boy being called to the Torah at age thirteen, the father read the special blessing, "**Baruch shepetarani me-onsho shel zeh**," (for a discussion of the blessing see **Noam**, vol. 7, pp. 1ff), which freed him from responsibilities in the future (Isserles, **Darchei Mosheh** to **Tur**, O. Ch. 225.1, citing Maharil and Mordecai; **Genesis Rabba**, 63.10; Epstein, **Aruch Hashulchan**, O.Ch. 225.4).

The social festivities connected with Bar/Bat Mitzvah also began in the Middle Ages (**Yam Shel Shelomo**, Bava Kama 7.37). Every effort should be exerted to maintain the family festivities in the religious mood of the Bar/Bat Mitzvah. Some of the efforts of early Reform in favor of Confirmation against Bar Mitzvah were prompted by the extravagant celebration of Bar Mitzvah, which had removed its primary religious significance.

We vigorously oppose such excesses, as they destroy the
meaning of Bar/Bat Mitzvah. Our emphasis will continue
to be placed upon the growing physical and intellectual
maturity of the children and upon their assumption of
responsibility for **mitzvot**.
　　　We encourage the celebration of the Bar/Bat Mitzvah
at the age of thirteen as an initial step toward maturity. The ceremony must lead to continued Jewish education, Confirmation, and high school graduation. The
mood of that day should be religious and festive, so
that the child and the parents feel a sense of **mitzvah**.

> Walter Jacob, Chairman
> Leonard S. Kravitz
> Eugene Lipman
> W. Gunther Plaut
> Harry A. Roth
> Rav A. Soloff
> Bernard Zlotowitz

34. BAR MITZVAH FOR AN UNCIRCUMCISED BOY
(Vol. LXXVI, 1966, pp. 79ff)

QUESTION: If a boy is uncircumcised, may he be
permitted to be Bar Mitzvah, and what is the practice in Reform synagogues in America in this matter?

ANSWER: It happens occasionally that an Orthodox rabbi
will refuse Bar Mitzvah to the son of a woman who had
been converted to Judaism by a Reform rabbi. The reason
for his refusal has some relationship to our question.
Since this woman was not taken to the **Mikveh**, the Orthodox rabbi considers her conversion invalid. Therefore
she is not a Jewess and her child is not a Jew. It is
obvious that if a boy is not authentically a Jew, he
cannot be Bar Mitzvah, because non-Jews are obligated
only to the seven commandments of Noah.
　　　The question therefore is: Is this uncircumcised
boy about whom you ask a Jew, or is he not? There is no
basis for saying that he is not a Jew. The **Shulchan
Aruch** (in Yoreh De-a 261) says that it is the duty of a
father to have his son circumcised. If the father fails
to do so, it is the duty of the community (the **Beit Din**)
to do it. If the **Beit Din** fails to do so, the duty
reposes on the boy himself when he grows up; and if he
does not have himself circumcised, then he has committed

a sin and will be punished at the hands of heaven
(**chayav karet**).   Obviously, if he were not a Jew and
uncircumcised, this commandment of circumcision would
not be incumbent upon him.   No one doubts that the boy
is a Jew.   Since he is a Jew, you have no right to keep
him from Bar Mitzvah.

However, a **Beit Din** (i.e., a rabbi or a community)
has the right to make special prohibitory laws in times
of emergency (**Lemigdar Milta**).   If, for example, there
were in Paris at this time a growing habit of parents to
refuse to have their children circumcised, you would
have the right to protect the community in this emergency by refusing to allow this boy to be Bar Mitzvah.   But
if there is no such emergency, you have no such right.
If I am not mistaken, a Hungarian community refused
burial in the cemetery to uncircumcised men.   It was at
the time of a radical anti-Orthodox movement in Hungary.

This boy's not being circumcised may be nobody's
fault.   It may be that his brothers were hemophiliacs
and therefore, according to law, he may be free from
having to be circumcised altogether under certain drastic condition of sickness; or there may be some other
reason.   By the way, if the father is dead, the duty of
circumcision is not incumbent upon the mother at all.
So if he is the son of a widow, his mother has committed
no sin.

It is your duty to persuade the family to have the
boy circumcised; but whether they do or not, he is a Jew
if his mother is Jewish, and he has the right to Bar
Mitzvah.

You ask about Reform practice in America.   I do not
know of any Reform congregation that would refuse such a
boy Bar Mitzvah.

Solomon B. Freehof

NOTE:

Bar Mitzvah refers to any adult male Jew who is
thirteen years of age and therefore obligated to
fulfill the **mitzvot**.   That this obligation begins
at the age of thirteen is based on Rabbi Judah ben
Tema's maxim (Avot 5.24), "A son of thirteen years
of age is obligated to fulfill the commandments."
The official act marking this event is for the boy
to be called to the Torah.   In traditional Judaism
it also calls for the wearing of **Tefilin** during
morning prayers on weekdays.
The celebrations which are a part of the Bar Mitzvah ceremony today are of comparatively recent

medieval origin and have no basis in religious law. Nothing indicates specifically that an uncircumcised boy or adult may not be called to the Torah.

Responsa Committee (1980)

See also:

W. Jacob, Responsum #64 below, "Status of an Uncircumcised Retarded Adult."

35. TIME OF A BAR MITZVAH
(Vol. LXIII, 1953, pp. 156-157)

QUESTION: What would be your attitude to holding a Bar Mitzvah service on Sunday afternoon? Is there a definite **din** about the time?

ANSWER: As far as **din** is concerned, the "feast" should take place on the day the Bar Mitzvah boy has attained his thirteenth year, plus one day. The honor of reading from the Torah, ordinarily extended to the Bar Mitzvah boy on the preceding Sabbath, may be given to him on any day of the week when the Torah is read in public, that is, either on Monday or on Thursday.

Reform Judaism, in its effort to make the practice of religion less of a routine, as well as to give it a more modern and more realistic tone, virtually abolished the Bar Mitzvah ceremony, not to supplant but to supplement the Confirmation service, coming somewhat later. The innovation has met with little opposition, since we are all eager to strengthen and enrich our Sabbath worship by all the means we can muster. And indeed, however disturbing some of its aspects, the restored ceremony has, in some measure, the spirit of worship on the Sabbath Day.

The suggestion that, for the greater convenience of relatives and friends, the Bar Mitzvah ceremony be shifted from the Sabbath Day to Sunday afternoon would, we fear, nullify all the good it can do, leaving us with no compensation for some of the unattractive features it so frequently reveals.

Israel Bettan

See also:

S.B. Freehof, "Bar Mitzvah on Saturday Afternoon,"
    Recent Reform Responsa, pp. 19ff; "Bar Mitzvah
    on Sunday," **Reform Responsa,** pp. 19ff;"Bar
    Mitzvah on Yom Kippur," **Reform Responsa,** pp.
    38ff; "Havdala Bar Mitzvah," **Reform Responsa
    for Our Time,** pp. 33ff.

36.   HAVDALA BAR/BAT MITZVAH
(Vol. XCII, 1982, pp. 216-218)

QUESTION: It has been the practice of my congregation and other small congregations to hold Bar/Bat
Mitzvot at the normal congregational service, either on Shabbat morning or, where Shabbat morning
service was not possible, on Friday evenings.   In
smaller communities there is only a limited number
of Bar/Bat Mitzvot a year, and they have become a
focal point of communal activity.   Some families
have heard of the custom in larger cities to hold
Havdala Bar Mitzvot on late Shabbat afternoons for
the convenience of the family (as this would make
travel easier for out-of-town guests and permit the
social functions to be connected to the Bar/Bat
Mitzvah). Is such a late Shabbat afternoon Bar/Bat
Mitzvah ceremony permissible?   (Rabbi Robert J.
Orkand, Rockford, Illinois)

ANSWER: A number of different questions must be answered in connection with this matter. We must inquire
about the general setting in which a Bar/Bat Mitzvah can
take place. We must ask about the purpose of a Bar/Bat
Mitzvah, and whether it requires a "public" service.
What is the standing of the festivities conducted with a
Bar/Bat Mitzvah in Jewish law and tradition?   What is
the relationship of private desires and the communal
welfare?
     It is quite clear that a Bar/Bat Mitzvah can be
conducted at any service during which the Torah is normally read.   For traditional Jews, this means Shabbat
morning and afternoon, as well as Monday and Thursday
morning, in addition to **Rosh Chodesh** and festivals. For
many smaller congregations in our liberal movement, this
would also include Friday evening services at which time
the Torah is normally read.   The Torah reading during
the **Mincha** service is certainly a part of Jewish tradition, although very few of our congregations have regu-

lar **Mincha** services. According to the Mishna, a **Mincha**
service should be held during the afternoon rather than
the early evening, but it can be held as late as the
last hour before sunset (Rabbi Judah in Mishna, Ber.
4.1). In times of absolute necessity, it is possible to
move the **Mincha** service even a little later and make
Havdala before it is absolutely dark (Ber. 27b and **Tosafot; Shulchan Aruch**, Orach Chayim 293.2). It would,
therefore, be technically possible to have a service
late on Shabbat afternoon, read the Torah, conclude
Shabbat, and begin with the festivities.

There was very little discussion until recent times
of the festivities connected with a Bar/Bat Mitzvah.
Among the first to deal with them at all was Solomon
Luria **(Yam Shel Shelomo** to B.K., ch. 7, #37). There he
stated that the festivities provided by the Ashkenazim
for a Bar/Bat Mitzvah were to be considered religious
occasions **(Se-udat Mitzvah)**. There are, of course,
numerous modern authorities who have discussed these
festivities and have tried to keep them within some
reasonable bounds, although this has proven to be very
difficult in contemporary America. We, too, would object to undue emphasis on the social aspect of the
Bar/Bat Mitzvah at the expense of its religious significance.

The purpose of the Bar/Bat Mitzvah was a public
proclamation that the young individual could now be
counted as part of the **Minyan** (Meg. 23a); it was an
announcement to the community. Today it accomplishes
this, and also provides recognition for accomplishments
in religious studies before the congregation. It should
furthermore encourage attendance at regular services.
The public element of this service is, therefore, essential. The private family festivities are also important, but less so. It would, therefore, be wrong to
change the occasion into a completely private service
and hold it at a time during which the normal services
are not held, unless there are unusual circumstances.

In a small congregation, a Bar/Bat Mitzvah also
serves to strengthen the existing religious services.
There is good precedent for this. Despite private **Min-
yanim**, the community was always given the power to
strengthen the communal synagogue **(Yad**, Hil. Tefila
11.1; **Tur**, Orach Chayim 10.5). A small congregation
could make attendance at services mandatory to insure a
Minyan (Adret, **Responsa**, V.222; Isaac bar Sheshet, **Responsa** I, #518; Sh.A., Orach Chayim 150.1; 55.20). It
is clear (**Sho-el Umeshiv**, vol. 3, part A, #8) that the
strength of the community and its regular religious
services was always uppermost in the minds of the religious authorities and the congregation. In a small community, obviously, a communal Bar/Bat Mitzvah is of

great significance. It attracts additional people from
the outside and serves as a focal point for the year's
religious life. Therefore, it is important that it be
held during the normal hours of religious services.

Havdala, or late Shabbat afternoon, Bar/Bat Mitzvah, may serve a different function in a very large
congregation. There, one may find three or more Bar/Bat
Mitzvah ceremonies scheduled for every Shabbat. Therefore the ceremony may become unmanageable, and the **Benei
Mitzvah** may overwhelm the service rather than fit into
the general service. Under these circumstances, it
might be beneficial for the congregation to provide the
opportunity to schedule Bar/Bat Mitzvah on occasions
other than the Shabbat morning service (S.B. Freehof,
Recent Reform Responsa, pp. 19ff).

We therefore recommend that Bar/Bat Mitzvah be
scheduled during the regular services at which time the
Torah is read, unless circumstances which would benefit
the congregation dictate a change. The ceremony must
emphasize the religious nature of this day for the
Bar/Bat Mitzvah and the family, not the social aspect of
the occasion. Bar and Bat Mitzvah ceremonies should
strengthen the congregation and encourage all members of
the congregation, both young and old, to attend regular
services.

Walter Jacob, Chairman
Simeon Maslin
W. Gunther Plaut
Harry A. Roth
Rav A. Soloff
Sheldon Zimmerman
Bernard Zlotowitz

37.   READING THE TORAH PORTION IN THE VERNACULAR
(Vol. XXIII, 1913, pp. 167-170)

To begin with a question of liturgy submitted to
this Conference by the congregation Temple Emanuel of
San Francisco through its rabbi, Dr. Martin Meyer: the
query is whether it is advisable and proper to read the
portion from the Torah in the vernacular.

Let us state that from the point of view of the
ancient tradition there can be no doubt that the proper
way is to read the Scriptural portion of the Torah first
in the original from the Scroll, and then translate it
to the assembly of worshipers in the language which they
understand or speak (whether verse by verse or the whole

portion together). This is evidenced by the first mention of the public reading from the Law in Nehemiah 8:8, instituted by Ezra the Scribe. When, in the course of time, the reading of the portions of the Torah assigned to each successive Sabbath and the Holy Days was made an integral part of the divine service, it became the regular custom of the ancient synagogue to have the same read from the Scroll and then translated into the vernacular. This was at first done in Aramaic by one especially appointed for this function, called the **Meturgeman**. The translation was known as the **Targum**, and this name was thereafter given to the Aramaic translation of the Scripture. As the Jewish people moved into the various lands, there arose translations of the Bible in various languages, all owing to the custom of having the Torah reading **(Mikra)** translated for the congregation into the vernacular. The oldest translation which has come down to us preserved in its totality, but at variance with our traditional (Masoretic) text, is the one made for the Jews of Alexandria in their Greek vernacular, the so-called **Septuagint**, named thus after the seventy (-two) elders to whom legend or tradition ascribed the work. It appears, however, that when this Greek translation was introduced in the synagogues of Alexandria, the reading of the text from the Scroll fell into abeyance, and the Hebrew was soon forgotten altogether, as is amply shown by the writing of the philosopher Philo and other Jewish authors of Alexandria. In consequence of this neglect of the Hebrew original, the Alexandrian Jews, while working during several centuries for a great Jewish propaganda in the spirit of prophetic universalism, were sooner or later led away from many views and practices of Palestinian Judaism and were ultimately absorbed by Greek-speaking Christendom. This deplorable fact ought to serve today as a warning against omitting the reading from the Scroll--**Mikra**--while the Scriptural lesson of the day is--as it should be--brought home to the congregation in the vernacular, the language which the great majority of the worshipers understand.

On the other hand, a no less deplorable change took place in the main synagogue. In the same measure as the surrounding world of humanity, to which the synagogue was to bring its prophetic message, had been lost sight of by the framers of our liturgy, the ancient practice of reading from the Torah and the Prophets was allowed to become petrified, "a work of men done by rote." No cognizance was taken any longer of the multitude of people who failed to understand the Hebrew, and the translation into the vernacular was dropped altogether. The whole institution intended to make the whole people of Israel conversant with the law, with the ideas, and

with the ideals of Judaism, became for an ever-growing
number of Jewish worshipers a soulless custom, void of
meaning and impressiveness.

Only as the modern era of reason and enlightenment
aroused the spirit of reform in Judaism, ushering in all
those innovations in the liturgy which tend to revive
the ancient spirit of genuine devotion, changes were
introduced also in regard to the Scriptural readings.
The beginning was made with the so-called **Haftara**, the
prophetic lesson of the day, which in most Reform synagogues is read exclusively in the vernacular. In regard
to the Torah lesson, however, no common practice has
been established as yet. As a rule, the rabbi selects a
small portion of the Sabbath or Holy Day **Parasha** for
translation before reading the **Haftara** or prophetic
lesson, leaving the rest untranslated. The reason for
this practice is obvious. First of all, the **Parasha**
assigned by the synagogue for the day is too lengthy to
hold the interest of the congregation all the while,
and, secondly, there are too many statutes and sentences
that would, when translated, offend the taste and the
sensibility of the hearers, passages concerning which
the Mishna has already set down the rule: "**Nikra-in ve-
ein mitargemin**," "They are to be read [in the original],
but not translated to the people."

Now, the logical conclusion of this very Mishnaic
rule and all that has been stated here seems to be that
our aim and endeavor in our divine service should be to
transform the Torah Reading from the mechanical and
meaningless function into which it has lapsed during the
past ages, into a real and genuine source of instruction
and inspiration, as it was intended to be at the outset.

Accordingly, it should be recommended that the
Torah lesson of the day--however small a portion of the
same may be selected--be read from the Scroll in the
original and then translated into the vernacular, the
same to be followed by a Scriptural lesson from the
Prophets or the Psalms or any other of the sacred writings read solely in the vernacular. By reading the
Torah lesson in the Hebrew original previous to the
translation of the same into the vernacular, the impressiveness of the ancient custom is greatly enhanced and
at the same time the continuity of the synagogue tradition is maintained.

Another question well to be considered is, whether
such chapters as **Tazria-Metsora** and similar portions
offensive to our taste and void of all religious meaning
for us, ought not be omitted altogether and replaced by
those beautiful and inspiring portions of Deuteronomy
which, according to our calendar, are assigned to the
hot season of the year when the synagogues are empty,
and which ought by all means to be read before larger

assemblies, being of such highly educational, ethical, and prophetic character. Of course, at present this must be left to individual discretion.

K. Kohler and D. Neumark

38. WHO SHALL READ FROM THE TORAH?
(Vol. XXXIV, 1924, pp. 71-74)

QUESTION: Shall the person called to the Torah recite only the Benediction? Will you please explain to me when and how the custom originated that the person who is called up to the Torah merely recites the Benediction before and after the section from the Torah is read, while the reading itself is done by the **Chazan**? Was it due to a decrease in the knowledge of Hebrew among the people? I recall that in one of the classes in Talmud I took with you we read a Talmudic saying to the effect that consideration for the ignorant caused the Rabbis to institute the practice that when a person who was inexperienced in reading had to recite some passages from the Torah, an expert reader would do it in his stead. But I regret to say I no longer remember where the passage is found.

ANSWER: In the Mishna Bikurim 3.6 there is reported the institution that an expert should recite with the farmer, who brings the first fruit offering, the section from Deut. 26:5-10, which is the duty of the farmer to recite on this occasion. It is also stated there in the Mishna that formerly the farmer, who was himself able to read, would recite this section from the Torah by himself, and only those farmers who were unable to read refrained from bringing the offering, not wishing to display their ignorance in public. The authorities therefore instituted the custom that an expert reader should recite the passage with every farmer, even with those who could read it by themselves. The ignorant could therefore bring his offering without running the risk of having to show his ignorance. But there is, to my knowledge, no express statement found in the Talmud that a similar practice has been instituted in connection with the regular readings from the Torah in the synagogue on Sabbaths, holidays, fast days, or Monday and Thursday.

The Mishna (Megila 4.1-2), prescribing the number of people who would participate in the reading on week-days, holidays, and Sabbaths, presupposes that these people would divide among themselves the section to be read on that day and each one would read his part without any assistance from the official reader. Nowhere is it stated that an expert reader would assist the individual who took part in the reading or read his portion for him. As a matter of fact, there was no need for instituting such a practice. In the case of the farmer bringing his first fruit offering, it was his duty to recite the passage from Deuteronomy, and when he was unable to do so, one had to help him in the performing of his duty. But in the case of the public reading in the synagogue, the main duty was that the section from the Torah be read to the public. This duty could be-- and actually was--performed by those who were able to read, and there was no need to call up only such as were able to read (comp. **Or Zarua** II, Hilchot Shabbat 42, p. 19, and **Shibolei Haleket**, chapter 36).

There are, however, indications--though no express report--which would justify one in assuming that already in Talmudic times (in some localities at least) the custom was introduced that an expert reader would read the entire section for the Sabbath or holiday, or assist the ignorant in reading their portion. For, as can well be imagined, it must have happened in some small communities that there were not in the entire congregation seven persons expert in reading who could divide among themselves the section to be read on the Sabbath. In such a case, one man who knew how to read would have to read the entire weekly section or a large part of it. This would especially be the case in communities outside of Palestine, where the people were not so familiar with the Hebrew language. It is instead reported in Yer. Megila IV.75a, that the people speaking a language other than Hebrew did not follow the rule prescribed in the Mishna that seven people should read the section for the Sabbath, but one person would read the entire section: "Veha-aliyot lo nahagu ken ela echad kore et kol haparasha." Evidently this was done for the simple reason that there were among them few persons who could read Hebrew (comp. also Tosefta, Megila IV.13). But even in Palestine it must have happened in some very small communities that there was but one man in the congregation who could read, and he had to read the entire section (comp. Tosefta, **ibid.**, 4.12). It seems, however, that the people even in smaller communities-- and possibly even outside of Palestine--were anxious to retain the Mishnaic custom of seven people getting up to read from the Torah on a Saturday. And the only way this custom could be retained in those congregations in

which there were not seven persons able to read, was to
have the **Chazan** or an expert reader assist those who
were not expert in reading the portion assigned to them.
Such a practice probably caused the Talmudic discussion
of the question whether two persons may read together
from the Torah. One baraita (quoted in B. Megila 21b
and Yer. Megila IV.1, 77d) declares that it is forbidden
for two persons to read together, and the reason given
in the Yerushalmi (l.c.) is that two voices together
cannot be distinctly heard: "**Mipenei she-ein shenei
kolot nichnasin be-ozen achat.**" But another **baraita**
(quoted in Yerushalmi, l.c.) makes a distinction between
the reading from the Torah and the reading from the
Prophets, declaring that from the latter, two may not
read together, but from the former it is permissible for
two to read together: "**Shenayim korin baTorah, ve-ein
shenayim korin benavi.**"

Evidently, the reason for this distinction was because the section from the Prophets was assigned to one
person only, and they would rather call up one who is an
expert in reading to read the same. But in the case of
the Torah, the section to be read was divided among
seven persons, so they had to permit two reading together; that is, in case one or more of the seven persons
could not read well, an expert could assist him in reading. They must have met the objection that two voices
cannot well be heard together by the arrangement that
the **Chazan** or the expert who assisted in the reading
would lower his voice while the person who was honored
to be called up to read would raise his voice so that he
could well be heard distinctly.

According to Rashi (B. Shabbat 12b, **s.v.** "**rashei
parashiyot**"), the custom of the **Chazan** assisting the
reader was prevalent, at least in Babylon, already in
Talmudic times. Possibly this was one of the differences between the Babylonians and Palestinians (see
Chiluf Minhagim, no. 47, and Mueller's comments), though
from the fact that the Yerushalmi quotes the **baraita**
that two may read together and from Tractate Soferim
XI.4 it would seem that even in Palestine this custom
was not unknown. But in Gaonic times this custom was
already established in Babylon. Amram, p. 29a, expressly declares it permissible for the **Chazan** to assist the
one who is to read a portion from the Torah ("**Aval
hechazan mutar lesayea et hakore**"). Likewise Chai Gaon
in a responsum (collection **Sha-arei Teshuva**, no. 59)
permits the **Chazan** to render assistance to the one who
is called up to read, but expressly forbids the practice
of the **Chazan** reading for the one who is called up:
"**Umidivrei rabavuta kuleho mashma disevira leho shelo
yikra hechazan avur hakore.**"

From another Gaonic responsum (Ginzberg, **Geonica** II, p. 102, lines 28-29) it is also evident that the practice of the **Chazan** reading for those who are called up to the Torah was not favored. But from the very fact that Chai Gaon declares that the authorities forbid the **Chazan** to do the reading for those who are called up to read, one might conclude that some people in his time would occasionally follow the practice of letting the **Chazan** do the reading for the one who was called up, if the latter was ignorant. In fact, Tractate Soferim 11.9 could be interpreted to allude to such a practice. At any rate, one can easily see how, out of the custom to let the **Chazan** assist the one who was to read, developed the practice of letting the **Chazan** do the entire reading and having those who were called merely recite the benediction. For assistance might be understood differently by different people: some people, when asking another person to assist them in any work which they have to do, really mean that the other person should do their work for them. After the custom was established of honoring people inexperienced in reading by calling them up to the Torah and relying upon the **Chazan** to assist them in reading their portion, it became necessary to extend this honor also to those people whose inexperience in reading amounted to total ignorance, relying upon the **Chazan** to do the reading for them. This custom is mentioned by R. Jacob Tam in **Tosafot** to B.B. 15a, **s.v.** "**shemona pesukim**," and in **Eshkol** II, p. 67. The latter explains that the reason for the custom is not to put to shame those who are unable to read. It should be added, though, that the custom was not universally accepted. In some countries the older practice continued that the person called up to the Torah recite the Benedictions and read the portion assigned to him (see **Sh. A.**, Orach Chayim 139.1).

Jacob Z. Lauterbach

NOTE:

1. We consider it improper for the Torah to be read by a pre-Bar/Bat Mitzvah child during a Shabbat or festival or weekday service conducted by and for adults, with the traditional exceptions (i.e., Simchat Torah or the Tochacha in Parashat "**Ki Tavo**"). This would also apply to the Torah **berachot**.

2.   We make no distinction between men and women
either in the reading of the Torah or in the recitation of the **berachot**.

Responsa Committee (1980)

See also:

S.B. Freehof, "Blind Person with Dog at Services,"
Current Reform Responsa, pp. 74ff; "Women
Called to Torah," **Reform Responsa**, pp. 40ff.

39.   UNWORTHY MAN CALLED TO TORAH
(Vol. LXII, 1962, pp. 119-124)

QUESTION: At the regular Sabbath service, it is
the custom of the congregation to call two men up
to recite the blessings over the Torah reading.
One Sabbath morning, after the service, an officer
of the congregation protested the fact that a certain man had been called up to the Torah that day.
He said that the man (who was a lawyer) did not
have a good reputation in his professional career.
Is it justified to debar a man from being called up
to the Torah because his character is open to question? Or is his reputation or character irrelevant
to his being called to perform this religious function?

ANSWER: The question asked is of considerable importance because the answer given to it might well be applied to various other religious functions for which
people are called up to the pulpit.   The subject has
been discussed sporadically in the literature.   Simon
ben Zemach Duran (14th-15th century, **Tashbets** II.261)
was asked whether unmarried youths may be prohibited
from reading the Torah, either because the honor of the
Torah requires only mature married adults to be called
or because an unmarried youth could not remain clean-
minded. He answered that, according to the law, a young
man is permitted to be called up to the Torah, and added
that even sinners are not forbidden to be called to the
Torah; but, nevertheless, if the congregation, in order
to make "a fence against evil," desires to forbid certain groups to come up, the congregation is always permitted to do so.

Duran is cited in a recent volume of responsa, **Mispar Hasofer**, by Isaac Zvi Sofer (Jerusalem, 1961, Responsum #5), not with regard to the calling up of young unmarried men, but with regard to the more characteristically modern question as to whether a public violator of the Sabbath may be called up to the Torah. Sofer follows the decision of Duran, namely, that whatever be the actual rights of the individual in this matter, the congregation always has the right, as a congregation, to make decisions excluding sinners from being called up. He adds that many Hungarian congregations have long made such a decision as a "fence against evil doers."

The difficulties involved in this question are reflected in the very wording of the dispute as it was presented to Simon ben Zemach Duran. Some of the disputants considered that what was involved was **kevod haTorah** (the honor due to the Torah), and therefore the dignity of the service. Other disputants insisted that to come up to the Torah reading was an obligation, a **mitzvah**, and therefore we have no right to keep a man from his religious duty.

The fact is that the legal literature never clearly defines the true status of this function. For example, is being called up to the Torah to be deemed as a religious **duty** incumbent upon every Jew, just as praying three times a day is a duty? If it **is** a duty, then it would not be possible to debar a man from it, and thus prevent him from performing **mitzvah**. Maimonides says (Hilchot Tefila XIV.6) in a somewhat analogous situation, speaking of a priest who had sinned: "We do not tell a man to add to his sin by neglecting a **mitzvah**."

But being called up to the Torah may not be a **mitzvah** at all. It may be a **right** that any Jew can claim, and therefore one could protest if he were not called up to the Torah for a long time. There is no doubt that many pious Jews consider this a right which they can demand. A Yemenite, some time ago in Israel, sued the officers of his congregation on the ground that they were prejudiced against him and had not called him up to the Torah for a long time. He was suing for what he called his rights as a Jew. Certainly many Jews have that feeling, whether or not it is so in the law. Then again, it may be neither a duty on a man's part, which he may fulfill, nor a right, which he may demand, but a privilege which the congregation confers. In that case, the congregation can bestow that privilege upon whomever it deems worthy and withhold it from whomever it judges unworthy.

Since this basic definition of what the status of the ceremony is (duty, right, or privilege), has not been clarified in the law, the probabilities are that

the status is vague, and that it has the nature of all
three of these possible classifications. It is necessary, therefore, to see to what extent it partakes of
each.

Is it a duty, a **mitzvah**, incumbent upon every Jew,
to be called up to the Torah? When a boy who is to be
Bar Mitzvah is called up to the Torah, his father is
required to recite the blessing "**Baruch shepetarani**."
Now, clearly in this case, this is a religious duty
incumbent upon the father. How could we possibly prevent him from performing this **mitzvah**, even if he were a
notorious sinner? Yet, even in this case, it is to be
observed that it is doubtful whether the blessing is
really **required**. The requirement is found in a note by
Isserles in Orach Chayim 225.1, and even he is uncertain
about it, and, therefore, suggests that in reciting the
blessing, the father should leave out God's name--a
practice which is followed in the case of all blessings
of dubious validity, so that God's name not be recited
in vain).

If, then, it is not--broadly speaking--a duty to go
up to the Torah, is it a **right** which a Jew can claim?
To some extent this may be so. Certainly a **Kohen** can
count it as his right to be called up to the Torah
first. The law frequently discusses who should be called up to the Torah (after the **Kohen** and the Levite have
been called up for the first two portions): a bridegroom
in the week of his marriage has precedence over a Bar
Mitzvah; next, a father whose child is circumcised that
week; then a mourner, on his **Yahrzeit**. Are all these
rights which a man can demand? The most that can be
said is that they have become customary rights. The law
does not make them firm rights, but a man can well be
aggrieved if he is denied them. If, for example, someone gives a large sum of money for the privilege of
being called up, the old congregations would certainly
call him up, and no one of the categories above would
feel that they had a right to dispute.

Certainly, the calling up partakes also of the
nature of a privilege, because the congregation often
calls up a man in order to honor him. It will call up
the rabbi for the third portion, which is the first to
which a non-**Kohen** or non-Levite can be called up. That
honor is certainly involved in the Torah reading is
clear from the statement in B. Megila 23a, where it is
said that while women may be called up as one of the
seven on the Sabbath, we do not call up women because of
"the dignity of the congregation" (**mipenei kevod hatsi-
bur**). Thus, the dignity and propriety of the situation
involved is a significant consideration.

Is it possible to decide the matter more closely
than merely upon the vague fact that being called up to

the Torah partakes **somewhat** of the nature of all three
(a duty, a right, or a privilege)?   Ephraim Margolies,
the famous scholar of Brody (1762-1828), wrote a book
dealing specifically with the questions involved in the
reading of the Torah (**Sha-arei Efrayim**, many editions).
In section I, paragraph 32, he discusses who should not
be called up to the Torah.   Most of this discussion is
based chiefly upon two passages in the **Shulchan Aruch**
which provide some material analogous to our problem.
One, in Orach Chayim 128, deals with sinful priests and
their rights to go up to bless the people; and the other, in Yoreh De-a 334 (also Orach Chayim 55.11), speaks
of a man who has been put under ban, as to whether he
may be included in the **Minyan**, etc.   The implications of
these two laws and their bearing on our question about
calling an unworthy man up to the Torah have been rather
fully explored in an interesting responsa sequence.   It
is found in **Shetei Halechem** (331) by Moses Hagiz, a
Palestinian rabbi who lived in Amsterdam (1671-1750).

The incident which evoked this series of responsa
throws some light on the social conditions of the time.
In one of the Sephardic congregations (Amsterdam or
London), a man embezzled the money of the **Chazan** and ran
away with the **Chazan**'s wife.   The guilty couple fled to
Spain, but, terrified by the Inquisition, they came to
London.   Meantime, the **Chazan**, in poverty and anguish,
died.   The culprit in London was told by the **Chacham** to
make a public confession of guilt.   This he did in the
synagogue, in the presence of the congregation.   Thereafter he was frequently called up to the Torah.   One Yom
Kippur, the brother of the dead **Chazan** was in London and
saw this man holding the Torah at "Kol Nidrei."   He bitterly protested.   He said that this man had not returned
the embezzled money or made any attempt to do so; his
repentance is, therefore, insincere, and such a scoun-
drel should not be called up to the Torah.

Although this was a quarrel within the Sephardic
community, many Ashkenazic scholars were consulted, as
well as the rabbis of Mantua, etc., and among the Ashkenazim were the famous scholars Jacob Reischer of Metz
(**Shevut Ya-akov**) and Jacob Emden of Altona.   Between
them, they dealt with the implications of the references
to the sinful priest in Orach Chayim and the excommunicated man in Yoreh De-a.   Most of the opinions were to
the effect that since the man had made no attempt to
restore what he had stolen, his repentance was incomplete, and therefore he should not be called up to the
Torah.   This would indicate the feeling, at least on the
part of most of the scholars, that a non-repentant sinner should not be called up to the Torah.   This opinion
is generally based on the Orach Chayim statement that if
a **Kohen** has committed certain crucial sins, such as

marrying a divorced woman or willfully defiling himself
by contact with the dead, then if he is not repentant,
he is not permitted to bless the people.

Two of the scholars--one anonymous and the other
Jacob Emden--say that this is a bad analogy. A **Kohen**,
if he repents, may bless the people because blessing the
people is a **mitzvah**, a commandment imposed upon him
("Thus shall ye bless," Numbers 6:23). Thus, it is
clear in the mind of these scholars that being called up
to the Torah is **not** a commandment before which he may
not put obstacles. As for the analogy with the law in
Yoreh De-a, that a man who is under ban may not be
counted in the **Minyan**, Jacob Emden says that the law
clearly states that only the man who has been officially
put under ban is debarred. As long as a sinner has not
been put officially under ban, he may still be counted
in the **Minyan**. This sinner in London has not been put
under ban officially; therefore, he may still be counted
in the **Minyan**. Jacob Emden then adds that being called
up to the Torah is less important than being counted in
the **Minyan**. Women and children, although they may not
be counted in the **Minyan**, may nevertheless (according to
the Talmud, Megila 23a) be called up to the Torah. So
it is conceivable that this wicked man in London could
be excluded from the **Minyan** and yet be called up to the
Torah. But Jacob Emden says that since he was not put
under ban, and since, anyhow, being called up to the
Torah is not as strict a matter as being counted to a
Minyan, then it might be a kindness to let him be called
to the Torah. This might help him towards righteousness. Besides, he adds, we "must not close the door in
the face of the would-be repentant." In fact, Ephraim
Margolies in his handbook says that if it is not definitely proved that a man is a sinner, we ought to allow
him to be called up.

Ephraim Margolies, in his handbook, is specific
about who should not be called up. A man who is known
to have taken bribes should not be called up to read the
passage dealing with justice and laws; and a man whose
wife neglects the **Mikveh**, etc., should not be called up
to read the passage which deals with these matters. On
fast days, a man who is not fasting is not called up to
the Torah (**Sha-arei Efrayim** 1.17). The commentator
Sabbatai Lifschitz (**Sha-arei Rachamim**) bases an explanation of these selective restrictions upon the **Peri Megadim** (Joseph Teomim) to Orach Chayim 141, end of paragraph 8, in which he indicates that such a man would be
bearing false witness to the passage being read. But in
spite of these selective restrictions, where there would
be a shocking contrast between the reading from Scripture and the character of the man called up, Margolies
concludes that, in the spirit of Jacob Emden: "If we

call him up and some indignant worshiper scolds him, the
embarrassment may lead the sinner to full repentance."
The commentary in **Sha-arei Rachamim** to this passage in
Margolies adds another leniency as follows: Although it
is not permissible to call a blind man to the Torah,
nevertheless, we do call up blind people and illiterates
because (they do not read the Torah and) we rely upon
the reading by the official reader. Thus, he continues,
we can call up sinners who should not be permitted to
read the Torah (themselves) because nowadays we count on
the reading by the official reader.

We may, therefore, conclude as follows: While it is
not clear in the law whether being called up is a duty,
a right, or a privilege, the ceremony clearly partakes
of each of these. A man of dubious reputation should
not be called up for certain specific passages, where
his character contradicts the reading. Nor, of course,
should a notoriously evil man, as the one mentioned by
Moses Hagiz, be allowed to shame the congregation by
being called up to the Torah. But in general, in less
heinous offenses, as long as the man has not been excluded or ostracized by the community, we should not
"shut the door in his face." We should always consider
the honor of the congregation, yet be lenient and avoid
complete exclusion.

Solomon B. Freehof

40.   OWNERSHIP OF A **SEFER TORAH**
(Vol. LXXXIV, 1974, pp. 50-53)

QUESTION: In the city in question there were two
congregations, one of which was unable to maintain
itself. Most of its members joined the other congregation as individual families, although it was
not a formal merger. These individuals turned over
to the larger congregation the various religious
articles belonging to the defunct congregation,
including some **Sifrei Torah**. Now a woman who had
once belonged to the defunct congregation, but who
now belongs to another in another city, demands
that one of the **Sifrei Torah** given to the larger
congregation be restored to her. Her reason is
that her father had donated this Torah in memory of
her mother, and that the members who now joined the
larger congregation had no right to turn this Torah
over to it. The rabbi of the larger congregation
suggested that she speak to those members of the

now-defunct smaller congregation and ask them for
that **Sefer Torah**. She did so, but they did not
wish to give it to her. The question is: What
rights of ownership does this woman have in the
Sefer Torah in question? (Rabbi Sidney Ballon,
Nassau Community Temple, West Hempstead, New York)

ANSWER: The question involved here has, tragically,
become highly relevant these days, due to the fading of
our inner cities.   The defunct congregation spoken of
here may have faded for causes other than the decay of
the environment, but the problem involved is the same as
the one now widely relevant--namely, who has the right
to dispose of the sacred objects of a defunct congregation?
     Since there is a claimant, in this case the daugh-
ter of the donor of the **Sefer Torah** in question, her
rights should be considered first of all.   In general,
the question of the ownership of a **Sefer Torah** under the
circumstances mentioned has come up in various forms
rather frequently in the legal literature.   By and
large, the various opinions expressed over the centuries
have come to a fairly clear consensus.
     On the face of it, the situation is completely
covered by the rules in the laws of **Tsedaka** in the **Shulchan Aruch**, Yoreh De-a 259.   There it is stated as a
general principle (section I) that a donor may change
the purpose of the gift or the recipient of the gift.
But this right to change the recipient or the purpose
exists only before the gift has come into the hands of
the proper officials (**Gaba-im**).   If, for example, a
donor sets aside money for one charity, and still has
possession of the money which he has set aside, he may
change his gift to any other charitable purpose; but if
he has already turned the money over to the officials
(in this case, the officers of the synagogue), he can no
longer change the purpose or the recipients (see Yoreh
De-a 259.1).
     By this general rule, it would seem obvious that
since the Torah was in the possession of the synagogue
to which her father had given it, she, her father's
daughter, no longer has the right to give it to any
other recipient.   Yet, it must be stated that this
general negation of her rights to change purpose or
recipient is in itself weakened by two considerations:
One, there is at least one opinion (Israel Rappaport,
Mahari Hakohen, Yoreh De-a #47) that all synagogues are
to be of equal status, and that, therefore, giving it to
one synagogue after intending to give it to another is
not deemed to be, by this one authority, an invalid or
non-permitted change.   The only question in this case

would be whether she still has any rights of ownership
at all on this Torah, once it had been given to the
synagogue.

The other mitigation of the rule (prohibiting any
change after it had been officially received) is the
custom mentioned by a number of scholars, that in certain communities it had become an established custom for
people to have **Sifrei Torah** written and to deposit them
in the synagogue, remembering always that it is **their
Sefer Torah**, without at all intending to transfer the
ownership to the synagogue. According to this custom,
then, the Torah, although used in the synagogue, is
deemed to be still the property of its original owners,
and they can take it, sell it, or give it to somebody
else. (See this custom of retaining ownership as described in the responsa **She-erit Yosef** by Joseph B.
Mordecai, Aldorf, 1767, Responsum #41. He describes
this custom of retaining ownership of the Torah and
agrees that the owner has the right to sell it for a
debt.) The other description of such a custom is much
older. In the responsa of Joseph Colon (**Maharik**, first
edition, #161, near the end; in the later edition, p.
173, col. 2), the questioner likewise describes such a
custom in which people gave or lent the Torah to the
synagogue and carefully insisted that they still owned
it.

To this situation Joseph Colon (Italy, 15th century), who is one of the prime authorities, gives the
following answer, which has become, one might say, classic: He says that once the Torah has been used in the
synagogue and had the mantle on it, it is sacred and
belongs to the sanctuary and cannot be sold or transferred, except by the decision of the officers and the
community. In this case, the members of the congregation are, therefore, the only ones who have the right to
transfer the Torah. As for the statement of the questioner to Maharik that they had the custom of retaining
ownership of the Torah, he dismisses this argument. He
says that no custom is valid enough to overturn a law
unless it is a widespread custom and one established by
scholars (**Vatikin**). This opinion of Joseph Colon is
repeated almost exactly by the 16th-century Polish authority, Solomon Luria (Maharshal) in his **Responsa**, #15.

The case of the questioner is almost precisely the
case in this question asked today, namely: the sons of
the man gave or loaned the Torah and now are moving to
another city and want to give or loan the Torah to the
synagogue in this other city. Solomon Luria is even
more specific in his answer than Joseph Colon. He says
that once the mantle was on the Torah it can no longer
be returned or be sold, even if the man who gave it
claims he never intended to give it outright. Such a

claim would be valid only if, before he gave it, he had declared formally--in the presence of two witnesses--that he is not giving the Torah as an outright gift, but is merely loaning it to the congregation. If he had not made such a formal declaration previously, then now that the Torah had been used (once the mantle is put upon it), he may never take it back, whatever may have been the unspoken intention. The opinion of these great authorities is respected by Joseph Caro in his **Beit Yosef** to the **Tur**, Yoreh De-a 259, and also by Joel Sirkes (**ibid.**). Isserles to Yoreh De-a (**ibid.**) comes substantially to the same conclusion.

If, then, it is clear that the donor or his descendants do not have the right of the disposal of this **Sefer Torah**, who does have the right? The law speaks of "shiv-a tovei ha-ir," "The seven good men of the city"--as we say today, "Twelve good men and true"--i.e., the officers. Sometimes it speaks of the membership (**benei ha-ir**). In either case, we have the right to assume that those who decided to carry over their congregational life to the congregation which now has the Torah include what was left of the officers and many of the members. They are the ones (and the only ones) who have the right of disposal of the sacred objects. In fact, they were consulted by the claimant, and they decided to give the Torah to your congregation. Their decision is valid. Moreover, their decision is strengthened by the fact that they did not sell the Torah but gave it to another congregation, thus maintaining its sanctity.

If they had decided to give the Torah to the claimant, this decision would also have been valid, since she intended to place the Torah in another congregation, and thus its sanctity would not be diminished. But they decided otherwise. Perhaps they wanted to avoid the danger that all the other original donors of sacred objects might now claim their gifts and thus the objects would be scattered. They wanted the **Sifrei Torah** of their former congregation to be in the congregation where they now worship. Whatever was their motivation, the decision was theirs to make.

To sum up, the situation is as follows: If there was a well-established custom in the community that people would loan their **Sifrei Torah** to the synagogue with the express intention to keep their ownership of them, such a custom--if established in consultation with learned authorities--might have some validity. But even that is doubtful. Further, if the woman's father had made a specific declaration that the Torah in question was not given outright to the synagogue, but was only a loan in order to be read in the services--only then could it now be reclaimed. But since this Torah has now been transferred to the larger congregation by the majority, and perhaps also the officers remaining in the now defunct congregation, this transfer is a valid act. The weight of tradition is on the side of the opinion that this Torah may not be removed from the synagogue in which it is now placed.

Solomon B. Freehof

41. FABRIC USED IN A TORAH MANTLE
(1977)

QUESTION: May a Torah mantle be made of a fabric which contains a blend of two different fibers? May the **Talit** of the deceased boy in whose memory the Torah mantle will be given be used as part of the mantle? (Rabbi Stephen H. Pinsky, Tenafly, New Jersey)

ANSWER: The concern expressed here deals with **Sha-atnez** and the Biblical prohibition against the **wearing** of fabrics which contain a mixture of wool and linen (Lev. 19:19; Deut. 21:11). This matter has been of little concern to Reform Jews and also puzzled our traditional ancestors. The commandment was given without any reason. Maimonides felt that it was intended to avoid imitation of heathen practices (**Moreh Nevuchim** 3.37). Nahmanides considered this as a prohibition against man's attempt to improve upon God's creation (**Commentary** to Lev. 19:19), but none of these interpretations proves satisfying. The Biblical ordinance which dealt only with wool which had been carded, woven, and twisted (Kil. 9.8, where the term **Sha-atnez** is explained) was extended by the Rabbis to include wool for which any of these operations had been done (Nidda 61b). We should, however, note that the Rabbinic prohibition was limited to the wool of sheep, rams, and lambs; it did not include camel or goat wool, or any other wool. If these were mixed with sheep wool, but remained dominant, then it was not considered as "wool" (Kil. 9.1). The prohibition against such mixtures was temporarily extended to silk and hemp because of their appearance (Kil. 9.3; **Yad**, Hil. Kil-ayim 10.2), but this restriction was later removed (Sh.A., Yoreh De-a 298.1). From this it is clear that the restrictions of **Sha-atnez** are very limited and certainly would not apply to any of the modern artificial fibers or to any other mixtures.

Even in the matter of wearing such fabrics the
prohibition was concerned with their being woven or sewn
together, but it was perfectly permissible to wear a
woolen cloak over a linen garment, though an item of
Sha-atnez could not be worn or slept upon, "even on top
of ten other garments." Such an item might be carried
(Beitsa 15a) and may be used in curtains or cushions
which do not touch the bare body (Kil. 9.2) and warm it.
Therefore, chair-seats and bedspreads should not contain
Sha-atnez as they will form a warm contact with the body
(Yoma 69a). Yet, felt soles on shoes with heels were
permitted, as they were stiff and would not warm the
feet (Beitsa 15a), as were various kinds of **Sha-atnez**
rags (**Misheh Torah**, Hil. Kil-ayim 10.19). The general
rule being that items which warmed the body were prohibited while those which did not, or provided only random
contact, were permitted. **Sha-atnez** was excluded from
tablecloths as well as from the cover on the reading
desk in the synagogue, as it might warm the hands
(Sh.A., Yoreh De-a 300.9, Isserles note). It was also
excluded specifically from the binder around a Torah
(Kil-ayim 9.3; **Mishneh Torah**, Hil. Kil-ayim 10.22);
there is some controversy with the majority permitting
the use, but R. Eliezer prohibited it, and the law followed R. Eliezer (Bartenura, **ad loc.**). We should note
that the ancient priestly garments were exempt from
these restrictions (Ex. 39:290). Similarly, the **Tsitsit**
on a **Talit** may interweave wool and linen, or woolen
Tsitsit may be attached to a linen garment (Yev. 4b,
5b). In other words, in these sacred appurtenances the
restrictions did not apply.

Tradition would then permit any mixture for a Torah
mantle except wool and linen. We, as Reform Jews, would
permit this mixture (**Sha-atnez**) as well, for the following reasons: (a) it was permitted by the Mishna and
prohibited only by R. Eliezer; (b) it fits into our
general pattern of life, which has rejected these prohibitions.

There might be some question about the use of a
Talit for a Torah mantle as it is sometimes buried with
the dead, but is this obligatory? The **Shulchan Aruch**
states that we bury the dead in a **Talit**, and there is
some controversy whether the **Tsitsiyot** should remain on
it or not (Yoreh De-a 351.2). The **Tur** provided the
varying opinions on this matter. Nahmanides felt that
the **Tsitsiyot** should remain; another authority felt that
they should be snipped off; and a third said that the
Talit was placed on the dead during the funeral procession, but then removed at graveside. In other words,
burial with a **Talit** is optional. In fact, in Israel the
custom is the reverse, and no one is buried with his
Talit (**Gesher Hachayim** II, pp. 122ff; S.B. Freehof,

Modern Reform Responsa, pp. 269ff). A Talit might, therefore, well be available after an individual's death, and there should be no hesitation about using it.

The disposal of a worn-out Talit or Tsitsit presented few problems as they were considered "utensils of mitzvot" (Tashmishei Mitzvot), not "holy utensils" (Tashmishei Kodesh) (Shulchan Aruch, Orach Chayim 21.3). Like the items connected with the Sukka, they could be cast off, but it was to be done with care, i.e., Tsitsiyot were removed from the Talit, rendering it unsuitable. It was recommended that the Tsitsiyot be used in some good fashion as bookmarks (Turei Zahav, ad loc.). The pieces of a Talit rendered unfit could be used even to fashion clothing for a Gentile (Ba-er Heitev, ad loc.). All of this clearly indicates that a parallel use, as for a Torah mantle, would certainly be appropriate.

We must still inquire about the suitability of various items for inclusion in a Torah mantle. Very little has been written about this in the usual sources, and most concern with Torah and Ark decorations dealt with gold and silver objects (Yad, Hilchot Tefila 10.4; Tur, Yoreh De-a 282; Shulchan Aruch, Orach Chayim 154.6, Isserles). We can more properly rely on the mantles which have come down to us, especially on the large collection now in the Jewish Museum of Prague, which has been well described by H. Volavkova in The Synagogue Treasures of Bohemia and Moravia. This collection clearly indicates that all kinds of brocades, textiles, and precious fabrics were used in Ark curtains and Torah mantles. The variety was endless and represented the economic circumstances of the donor; and so we find decorative embroidered kitchen towels, sections of old wedding dresses, rococo waistcoats, as well as Japanese embroidery (Synagogue Treasures, p. ix). A great number of fabrics were also freely used. We should also recall the custom of preparing "Wimples," Torah wrappers, from linen diapers. This was done in the Rhineland and Bavaria. It would, therefore, be appropriate to use a Talit or a segment of it in this fashion.

There is nothing in our Reform practice which would keep a Talit or any mixture of fabrics from being used to make a Torah mantle. The Talit of the deceased boy may be used. Such special gifts to the synagogue have been encouraged for centuries.

Walter Jacob

See also:

S.B. Freehof, "Sha'atnez with Regard to Tzitzis,"
Reform Responsa for Our Time, pp. 296ff.

42. SALTING BREAD BEFORE THE BLESSING
(1978)

QUESTION: Should salt be used during the blessing
over bread before a meal? What is the history of
this usage? (Mrs. B. Finegold, Pittsburgh, Pennsylvania)

ANSWER: The connection of salt with Jewish religious
rituals is ancient and can be traced to the Bible. It
was considered as absolutely necessary at sacrifices
(Lev. 21:22). This applied not only to meal offerings,
but also to burnt offerings of animals (Ezekiel 43:24).
Salt was also used in the preparation of the show breads
(Lev. 24:7). It seems that each of these uses rein-
forced the covenant between God and Israel, so the expression "salt of the covenant" is used in Leviticus
2:13, Numbers 18:19, and Chronicles 13:5. This means
that aside from normal useful connotations, salt possessed a religious meaning. It is, of course, used in
other ways in the Bible as well, for example: as wholesome and useful for animals (Isaiah 30:24), as a way of
protecting new-born infants from illness, by rubbing
them with it (Ezekiel 16:4), and as a means of purifying
bad water (II Kings 2:19). On the other hand, too much
salt was recognized as bad, so when Abimelech conquered
and destroyed Shechem, he sowed it with salt (Jud.
9:45).
     The Rabbis wished to continue the thought of the
sacrifice, i.e., sharing a meal with God and having God
present at each meal after the destruction of the Temple. They did so by stating that every table set for a
meal was akin to the altar, and, therefore, as salt was
used for each sacrifice, it was also to be used for each
meal. A meal without salt was not considered a meal at
all (Ber. 44a). The law finally stated that when bread
of poor quality was used (probably without salt), then
salt was to be placed upon it, and a man could even
request salt before consuming a portion of bread, but
after the recitation of the beracha (a time when there
was to be no conversation). If, however, the bread is
of good quality, then one need not use salt or interrupt

to ask for it (Ber. 40a; **Shulchan Aruch**, Orach Chayim 167.5).

This custom of utilizing salt fell into disuse during the time of the Tosafists. The bread was considered of good quality, and the addition of the salt was thought to be unnecessary. One Tosafist (Menahem) was, however, recorded as feeling that it was still necessary to do so (**Tosafot** to Ber. 40a). Sometime during the Middle Ages the custom was revived, and is frequently part of present-day practice (Isserles in his note to **Shulchan Aruch**, Orach Chayim 167.5).

Although you have asked about eating salt at the beginning of the meal, there are a considerable number of statements as well about eating it at the end of a meal. All of these are utilitarian and without religious overtones. Some rabbis felt that it would cleanse the mouth and prevent unpleasant odors, and so suggested that it be used at the conclusion of every meal (Ber. 40a; **Sh.A.**, Orach Chayim 179.6). They also felt that certain kinds of salt were so strong that it was wise to wash one's hands after using them (Ker. 6a). Many other uses of salt, as for **koshering** meat, etc., are recorded, but they are not related to the use about which you have inquired.

As far as using it for the blessing before the meal, tradition would state that it is optional, although it has become customary among some Jews.

Walter Jacob

See also:

S.B. Freehof, "Salt for the Bread Blessing," **New Reform Responsa**, pp. 247ff.

43.   SABBATH OBSERVANCE
(Vol. LXII, 1952, pp. 129-132)

For some time now many of the questions directed to the Committee on Responsa have had to do with situations in which traditional observance of the Sabbath is involved. In some instances, the correspondents are irritated by the widely accepted restrictions, in the face of which no innovations designed to improve temple attendance or expand its recreational program, could be introduced. Thus, one rabbi, disturbed by the fact that the local high school attracts too many of the young

people of his congregation to its Friday evening dances,
wonders "if there is a real objection to holding dances
in the Temple vestry on Friday evening after services."
Another rabbi, eager to promote athletics among his
young people, wishes to know "the attitude of Reform
Judaism to synagogue-sponsored recreation on the Sabbath." Specifically, he should like to have his teenage
baseball team practice on Saturday afternoons. But "one
of the leaders of a local Orthodox synagogue has demanded that this not be held on the Sabbath."

In other instances, our members seem more concerned
with the impact of strict Sabbath observance on their
social and communal relations than on their purely synagogal activities and plans. Thus, one of our members,
who has had considerable experience in the field of
public relations, feels put out by the refusal of some
rabbis "to participate in public ceremonies such as
flag-raising, a welcome-to-the-city to a distinguished
visitor, or the like, if they occur on a Friday evening
or a Saturday." He asks in rhetorical vein: "Should a
rabbi refuse to accept an invitation to represent the
Jews of his community at... public occasions held Saturday afternoon at which there will be representatives of
the three faiths and a rabbi's presence is desired?"
Another rabbi, who is earnestly pursuing "an inquiry
concerning Sabbath observance and its violation by various Jewish organizations in the community which are
accustomed to having meetings on that day," raises the
question "as to which kind of meetings might properly be
proscribed and which type of meetings might, within the
spirit of the Sabbath, be given sanction?"

Of course, most of the above questions, and others
of like nature, find their clear answer within the body
of traditional law. We are, for example, left in no
doubt as to what activities one may freely engage in on
the Sabbath. One may attend any kind of meeting the
purpose of which is to deal with some pressing communal
problem. The law permits both the pledging of funds for
the care of the poor and the holding of special convoca-
tions in the synagogue for that purpose. One may even
complete arrangements on the Sabbath to have his son
placed in some desirable trade. The Rabbinic princi-
ple--resting on the passage in Isaiah wherein, in connection with the proper observance of the Sabbath, the
prophet accentuates "nor doing **thy** business, nor seeking
thereof" (Isaiah 58:13)--excludes from among the prohibited categories any business, or the speaking thereof, which is dedicated to some important social and
religious purpose (Shab. 150a).

Likewise, in the light of this Rabbinic principle,
it is quite obvious that one may join on the Sabbath any
assembly of men who have been brought together in re-

sponse to some public good--provided, of course, that there is nothing that conflicts with such participation, as, for instance, the call to public worship, or (in the case of those who abstain from any kind of travel on that day) the forced use of public or private conveyance.

Nor is the prohibition against dancing on the Sabbath anything more than a precautionary measure, aimed to forestall a possible breach of grave character, such as might occur were one led to construct on the selfsame day a musical instrument to accompany the dance (Beitsa 36b). It is interesting to note, though, that later Rabbinic authorities, in admonishing congregations not to sanction the holding of public dances on the Sabbath, to which some communities had grown accustomed, based their reason on the moral laxness which the free mingling of the sexes might induce, rather than on the older Talmudic ground (**She-elot Uteshuvot Zichron Yosef**, no. 17).

Yet, however wide an area of freedom we may still discover within the narrow limits of traditional law, no one who is acquainted with the vast bulk of restrictive measures designed to keep the Sabbath inviolate will question the accuracy of the Mishnaic observation, that the Sabbath laws represent "mountains suspended from a hair" (Chagiga 10a). But, unfortunately, we have chosen to avert our gaze from these mountains. We prefer to ignore their presence. In doing so, however, we have willfully turned away from the opportunity that was ours to bring the institution of the Sabbath under the searching light of liberal thought.

To be sure, no effort to liberalize our Sabbath laws will get us nearer to a solution of the Sabbath question, as long as the masses of our people must engage in bread-winning employment on that day. The heart of the Sabbath is today what it has always been--rest from week-day labors. Our goal must ever be to help create those conditions which will make it possible for the Jew to observe the Sabbath day and keep it holy. And with the rise of the five-day week in modern industry, the partial fulfillment of our aim may not long be delayed. Yet many of us might even today be true Sabbath observers in the essential meaning of the term, if we could but rescue the Sabbath from the host of unreasonable restrictions which mar its character and weaken its appeal to the modern mind.

There can be little doubt as to the real intent of the primary laws governing the Sabbath. We are to let go of the toil which occupied our energies during the week: "Six days thou shalt work, but on the seventh day thou shalt rest" (Ex. 34:21). The Biblical idea of labor thus embraced the agricultural occupations in

which men were engaged to obtain their livelihood. When
Jeremiah denounced the men of his time for bearing burdens on the Sabbath day, he clearly had reference to
their persistent practice of carrying the produce of the
field and the articles manufactured in the home to the
marketplace, just as they were wont to do on week-days
(Jer. 7:21-22). Even the injunction against the kin-
dling of fire on the Sabbath (Ex. 35:3) was closely
associated with the daily occupational tasks of the
people, in which fire was an essential element, as the
context of the passage clearly reveals, and as Bahya ben
Asher properly points out (Vayakhel, **Be-ur**). And so,
too, the thirty-nine principal classes of acts forbidden
on the Sabbath, as they are enumerated in the Mishna,
have to do mostly with the agricultural and industrial
occupations of the people.

The principle that fences must be built around the
law, which has led to the enactment of countless precautionary regulations, is a principle that we today must
boldly reject in the interest of a saner observance of
the Sabbath. Instead, we should reaffirm and employ as
our constant guide the more important and fruitful Rabbinic principle: That the Sabbath has been placed in our
control, and that we are not under the control of the
Sabbath (Yoma 85b).

Taking our stand on this principle, we shall, of
course, continue to stress the twofold nature of our
Sabbath, namely, that it is our Jewish day of rest, and
that, moreover, it is a day dedicated to the delights of
the soul. But we shall not seek, in the name of Judaism, to deny men the freedom to perform such necessary
acts and to engage in such additional delights as they
have learned to associate with their periods of rest.
In an age like ours, when we have come to view sports
and games of all sorts as proper forms of relaxation on
rest days; to hark back to the puritanic rigors of the
Rabbinic Sabbath is to call in question the relevancy of
religion to modern life.

Israel Bettan

See also:

"Resolution," **National Federation of Temple
    Sisterhoods**, 1948, 1949.
S.B. Freehof, "Congregational Meeting on the Sab-
    bath," **Reform Responsa**, pp. 46ff; "Gift Corner
    Open on the Sabbath," **Reform Responsa**, pp.
    51ff; "School Dance on the Sabbath," **Recent
    Reform Responsa**, pp. 32ff; "Caterer Working on

the Sabbath," **Current Reform Responsa,** pp. 225ff; "Muggers and Money on the Sabbath," **Reform Responsa for Our Time,** pp. 28ff; "Gentile Funerals on the Sabbath," **Reform Responsa for Our Time,** pp. 142ff; "Sports on the Sabbath in Community Center," **Reform Responsa for Our Time,** pp. 11ff; "Wedding on Saturday Before Dark," **Recent Reform Responsa,** pp. 167ff; "Shofar on New Year Sabbath," **Recent Reform Responsa,** pp. 36ff; "Memorial Services on the Sabbath," **New Reform Responsa,** pp. 130ff; "Preparing the Body on the Sabbath," **Reform Responsa,** pp. 126ff.

44.   ORTHODOX JEW AS PARTNER IN FIRM KEEPING OPEN ON SABBATH
(Vol. XLII, 1932, pp. 82-83)

QUESTION: An Orthodox Jew desires to become a member of a law firm, the present members of which are all Reform Jews. He consulted a rabbinic authority and was advised that he could not allow his name to appear as a member of the firm if the offices of the firm were open on the Sabbath. They are closed only on Rosh Hashana and Yom Kippur. He was informed that if a Christian became a member of the firm, even nominally, this objection would be waived. He has declined to appeal to any other rabbinic authority. I have no objection to the decision as such. If, however, you find any contrary precedent which would be binding on an Orthodox Jew, I shall be happy to know it.

ANSWER: In regard to the question, I could not find any possible argument--not to mention a precedent--which would invalidate the decision given by the rabbinic authority consulted on this matter. In fact, the rabbinic authority in question went to the limit of liberal interpretation of the law in waiving any objection in case a non-Jew would nominally become a partner of the firm. According to the stricter interpretation of the law, there would be objection in this case even if there were a non-Jewish partner.

The principle of the law is that the Jew is not to receive any profit from work done on his behalf on a Sabbath even when done by a non-Jew. In case of an ordinary partnership with a non-Jew, the Jew may stipulate in the arrangement or partnership agreement that the non-Jew should do the work--and take the entire proceeds therefrom--on the Sabbath day, while the Jew would instead do the work on any other day of the week and take the entire proceeds therefrom (Talmud, Avoda Zara 22a). In a partnership of the nature of your case, where the profit accruing from the work on one day cannot be specified, and the work cannot be so divided between the partners that one should work on one day and the other on another, some authorities permit the Jew to take his share of the total profit, even though a certain percentage of that profit accrued from the work done by the non-Jewish partner on the Sabbath day (Isserles in **Shulchan Aruch**, Orach Chayim 241.1, quoting R. Nissim). The assumption upon which this decision is based is that the non-Jewish partner is his own boss and not the agent of the Jew. He, as a partner, has the right to attend to business even at times when his Jewish partner neglects to do so. He may, if he so wishes, stay in the office and work, e.g., in the evening after his Jewish partner closes his week of work. And even though the profits of the business increase by this extra work of the non-Jew, since that part of the profit accruing from the non-Jew's work on the Sabbath is not clearly specified as profit from Sabbath work but is figured in the total of the profits from the whole week, month, or year, the Jew need have no compunction in accepting it. In your case, however, the observant Jew would receive not only the unspecified part of the profit resulting from the work on the Sabbath by the nominal non-Jew partner, but also the profit resulting from the work done by the Jewish partners and all the clerks in the office partly employed by him, and, therefore, his agents. But, of course, I am not going to be stricter than the rabbinical authority consulted on this point.

Jacob Z. Lauterbach

45. BLOWING OF THE **SHOFAR** ON SABBATH
(Vol. XXIII, 1913, pp. 182-183)

QUESTION: I wish to broach a question to which my attention has been called during the last few years. I have been asked whether it is right that in some Reform congregations the blowing of the **Shofar** is omitted on Rosh Hashana, if the same happens to fall on a Sabbath Day. This is most certainly an **error**. The Mishna (R.H. IV.1) tells us that as long as the Temple existed in Jerusalem the **Shofar** was blown only there on a Sabbath Day, but not in other places. After the destruction of the Temple, R. Yochanan ben Zakkai declared that in Yavneh, it being the seat of the Sanhedrin, the **Shofar** should be blown on Sabbath as well, the seat of the Torah being tantamount to the Holy of Holies. This decision of R. Yochanan ben Zakkai was afterward applied to every place where a court of justice sat or the spiritual head of the Jewish people resided (see Asheri, R.H. IV).

ANSWER: The reason for not having the **Shofar** blown on Sabbath outside of the Temple, stated by the older Amoraim in the Jerusalem and Babylonian Talmud is rather strange. The term "**Yom Teru-a**," "Day of Blowing," is said to refer to **Jerusalem** only as the place where the day of the new month was fixed; whereas for **other** places "**Zichron Teru-a**," "Remembrance of the Blowing" (by the recital of the Scriptural verses) is sufficient. Afterward, another--and more whimsical--reason was given: A man who does not know how to use the **Shofar** might be induced to carry it through public places on a Sabbath to an expert in order to learn how to blow it, and so violate the Sabbath, and for this reason the Rabbis forbade the blowing of the **Shofar** on Sabbath altogether. Of course, since Rosh Hashana has two days all through the Diaspora, the second day was considered as good as the first for the blowing of the **Shofar**. Now we ask, can this Rabbinical prohibition apply to us, who no longer have a second day of Rosh Hashana? Furthermore, we ask, have we not our organ playing in our temples on Sabbath in spite of the Rabbinical prohibition of using a musical instrument, based upon fear lest one might **repair** it, should it suffer any damage? (The making of music itself was not regarded as labor by Rabbinic law--"**Chochma ve-einah melacha**," "It is art, not labor".) Nay, more: the very spirit of Reform that empowers R. Yochanan ben Zakkai to declare the sanctuary of learning of Yavneh to be as holy as the Temple at Jerusalem ought by all means to empower us to assign our temples the same divine character of holiness as the ancient Temple, with its sacrificial cult, possessed. The very name "Temple" given to the Reform synagogue was no doubt meant to accentuate this very principle voiced by R. Yochanan ben Zakkai.

To sum up all we have said: We must in all matters of reform and progress agree upon the leading **principles** and not allow them to become arbitrary and individualistic. Let each member of the Conference who has practical questions to submit, bring his cases to the knowl-

edge of this or any other similar committee, so that we
may reach at least a mutual understanding.

K. Kohler and D. Neumark

46. BLOWING OF THE SHOFAR
(Vol. XXXIII, 1923, pp. 60-61)

QUESTION: In answer to a question by a younger
colleague whether the Shofar should be blown on
Rosh Hashana happening, as it did, on Saturday,
Rabbi Martin A. Meyer of San Francisco gave his
opinion "that in view of the attitude of Reform,
there was no reason why we should omit this characteristic custom."
        This opinion of Rabbi Meyer was sent to the
chairman of this committee for endorsement and
possible elaboration, both of which are given below.

ANSWER: There is no reason why the Shofar should not
be blown on a Rosh Hashana which falls on a Saturday in
congregations where only one day of Rosh Hashana is
observed.   During Temple times the distinction was made
between the Temple in Jerusalem and the synagogues in
the provinces, in that only in the former was the Shofar
blown on a Saturday. After the Temple was destroyed, R.
Yochanan ben Zakkai instituted the practice that wherever there is a Beit Din, that is, a rabbinical tribunal, the Shofar should be blown on Saturday (Mishna, Rosh
Hashana IV.1).   Commenting upon this Mishna, the Babylonian Gemara (Rosh Hashana 29b) declares that blowing
of the Shofar is an art but not work, and hence, by
Biblical law, is permitted on Saturday, but that Rabbinical law prohibits it on Saturday lest it might happen
that the one who is to perform the ceremony would wish
to go to an expert in order to practice, and thus carry
with him the Shofar on the Sabbath day, which act (that
is, the carrying of it) is prohibited on the Sabbath
("Shema yitelenu beyado veyelech etsel baki veya-avirenu
arba amot birshut harabim").   The same consideration
also prompted the Rabbis to discard the ceremony of
"taking the Lulav" on the first day of Sukkot when it
happens on a Saturday. Thus, the only reason for not
blowing the Shofar on a Sabbath is the fear that it
might lead to a violation of the law prohibiting the
carrying of burdens on Saturday. It is interesting to

notice that this consideration was not shared by all the Rabbis, for we are told that R. Abahu once came to Alexandria, and he made the congregation there perform the ceremony of "taking the **Lulav**" on the first day of Sukkot, which happened to be on a Saturday (Yer. Eruvin III, 21c), not letting the consideration that it might lead to the sin of carrying a burden on Sabbath interfere with the duty of performing the ceremony. We may safely assume that had Abahu visited Alexandria on a Rosh Hashana which happened to fall on Saturday, he would have made them perform the ceremony of blowing the **Shofar**.

Furthermore, this consideration that it might lead to a violation of a law, might be carried to the extreme. For, as some of the Rabbinical authorities rightly say, on the same ground one could argue that the ceremony should be altogether prohibited, even on Rosh Hashana falling on a week day, for fear that it might happen that the **Shofar** might need repairing, and this will lead to doing work which is prohibited on a holiday (comp. **Turei Zahav** and **Magen Avraham** to Shulchan Aruch, Orach Chayim, 588.5). Of course, they answer that, in this case, the fear that it might lead to the sin of doing repair work on **Yom Tov** is not to be entertained, for it would have the result of entirely abolishing the ceremony. This latter argument is quite correct, and it applies with equal force to the question of blowing the **Shofar** on Rosh Hashana which falls on a Sabbath Day in those congregations where only one day of Rosh Hashana is observed. For if we allow the fear that the **Shofar** might be carried on the street to interfere with the performance of the ceremony, the result will be that--for that year at least--the ceremony will be entirely omitted; and we should not abolish this characteristic ceremony, even for one year.

Jacob Z. Lauterbach and Committee

See also:

S.B. Freehof, "Shofar on New Year Sabbath," **Recent Reform Responsa**, pp. 36ff.

47. FERMENTED WINE NOT REQUIRED FOR SACRAMENTAL PURPOSES
(Vol. XXX, 1920, pp. 108-112)

QUESTION: With the adoption of the Eighteenth Amendment to the Constitution of the United States, the law prohibiting the use, manufacture, or sale of wine, beer, or alcoholic beverage in any form went into effect. And while the Law expressly permits the use of sacramental wine, there is so much inconvenience connected with the obtaining of some wine that I have been asked for an opinion to the following questions:

    I.   Is it absolutely necessary to use fermented wine for:
        a. **Kiddush** (Blessing on eve of Sabbath or Holiday)?
        b. **Havdala** (Blessing at the close of Sabbath or Holiday)?
        c. Grace after meals?
        d. **Berit Mila** (Circumcision)
        e. Four Cups (on the Passover Eve)
        f. Marriage Ceremony?
    II. Assuming that fermented wine is not essential, is it necessary to use any beverage at all?

I rendered the opinion given below.

ANSWER: A. The custom among Jews to use wine in connection with certain religious ceremonies is a very old one. Its origin reaches back to hoary antiquity. In a land like that of the ancient Hebrews, preeminently known as "a land of wine and vineyards" (Deut. 7:8; II Kings 18:32), it was but natural that the use of wine should be universal. Also it is but reasonable that the primitive Hebrew would offer his Deity the same fare he himself enjoyed so much. In the earliest stages of the Temple ritual we find, therefore, that a libation of wine was the regular concomitant of the daily burnt-offering and the numerous other offerings: a half of a hin of wine with a ram, a third of a hin with a bullock, and a fourth of a hin with a lamb (Num. 28:14; 15:5; Ben Sira 50:4; Josephus, Ant. 3, 9.4). The pouring out of the wine upon the base of the altar was the signal for the choir of the Levites to begin their chanting of the Psalm for the day (Rosh Hashana 31). The practice of reciting hymns with the offering of wine is, according to Samuel b. Nachman (third century), already indicated in the Biblical words "Wine which cheereth God and man" (Judges 19:13). How could God be cheered with wine? Only when hymns are recited at its offering. Hence, the rule: "**Ein omerim shira ela al hayayin,**" "No anthem should be sung without wine" (T. Ber. 35, Arachin 11). Hence also the rule: "**Ein mekadeshin ve-ein mevarechin ela al hayayin,**" "No Kiddush and no Grace are proper without wine" (T. Pes. 107; B. Batra 97; Men. 87). Some of the teachers, indeed, imagined they could find a reference to the use of wine for **Kiddush** implied in the words of the Bible: "**Zachor et yom hashabbat lekadesho,**" "Remember the Sabbath day to sanctify it" (Ex. 20:8). "It is evident," they argue, "that **lekadesho** refers to **Kiddush,** while "**Zachor** can only have reference to wine, as it is said: **zichro,** his remembering, is like wine of Lebanon" (Hosea 14:8). Or as it also is said: "**Naz-kira,**" "We remember thy love in wine" (Song of Songs, 1:4; see T. Pes. 106).

Thus, it may be seen that the practice of using wine for sacramental purposes is a very old custom. For **Kiddush** and **Havdala,** we are told, the custom of using wine was established by the Men of the Great Assembly (Ber. 33), while wine for "Grace" and the "Four Cups" is mentioned in the Mishna (Ber. 8.1; Pes. 10.1) and spoken of as something firmly established long ago. The effort at a later age, however, to trace the **Kiddush** back to Biblical rule was never meant seriously. Already Rashi (1040-1105) and the Tosafists declare it to be mere **Atmachta,** homiletical (**Pardes,** Hil. Shab. 112; Tos., Pes. 106, voce "Zochrehu"; Nazir 4, voce "**Mai**"; **Sefer Ha-itim** 181). Using wine in connection with **Berit Mila** is first mentioned by Mordecai B. Hillel (d. 1295; see **Be-er Hagola** to Yoreh De-a 265).

As for the practice of using wine at wedding ceremonies, it was known already to the compiler of the Tractate of Soferim (cf. 19.11)--about the eighth century--where such custom is first mentioned.

In the Talmud, however, where all the benedictions of the marriage ritual are enumerated in proper order (Ket. 8), no mention whatsoever is made of wine as yet. Only six benedictions are enumerated there. In fact, we are told that when Levi b. Sissi (second century) attended the wedding of Simon, son of Judah I, only **five** benedictions were recited, while when R. Assi attended the wedding of Tabyomi, son of R. Ashi (end of fifth century) he used **six** benedictions (**ibid.**). Of the seven wedding benedictions in our ritual, the first--which is supposed to be said over a cup of wine--seems as yet unknown. Maimonides in his Code, as well as Joseph Caro in **Shulchan Aruch,** still speak of and enumerate only the six mentioned in the Talmud, as stated above (see **Yad,** Hil. Ishut X, 3:iii, 4; Even Ha-ezer, 62.1). However, both Maimonides and Caro know already of the custom, and they observe: "It is customary to arrange these benedictions so as to say first a blessing over a cup of wine

[adding the significant remark:] if wine is at hand."
(**Yad, ibid.**, Even Ha-ezer 34.2; 62.1). The popular
number seven in the Jewish ritual seemed to have gained
in favor from the time of the Geonim onward (see Asheri,
Ket. I.12; Rashi, Ket. 8, voce "**Sos tasis**"; Tos., Pes.
102, voce "**She-ein**", 104, voce "**Chuts**"). The mystic
number seven was also seized upon by the Kabbalists, who
declared that seven benedictions are to be recited, as
the number is symbolical of the seven canopies which God
made for Adam and Eve in Paradise (**Zohar**, Ex. 169). We
might make mention here also that in the procession,
when the bride is led to the home of her future husband,
"a cup of good cheer"--**Kos shel besora**--was carried
before the procession (Ket. 16b). This, however, had no
connection with the wedding ceremony.

      B. And now, having established the origin of the
practice for using wine for sacramental purposes as
being, on the one hand, reminiscent of the libations of
the ancient sacrificial cult in the Temple of old, and,
on the other hand, grounded in the daily habits of the
wine-growing Hebrews in Palestine, we may approach the
solution of the question: "Is it absolutely necessary to
use fermented wine in the Jewish ceremonial for **Kiddush,
Havdala**, Grace, and **Berit Mila**?"
      Our answer to this must be in the negative. Fer-
mented wine is not essential, especially if wine is not
easily obtainable. In fact, the following principle was
established by the teachers: "One may press out the
juice of grapes and use it immediately for **Kiddush**" (B.
Batra 97b). This ruling was adopted by the Geonim Mar
Amram (d. 875), Chai (939-1038), and Samuel Ibn Nagdelo
(993-1055) (see **Sefer Ha-itim**, pp. 203, 206), as well as
by Maimonides (**Yad,** Hil. Shab. 29.17) and Asheri (B.
Batra 6.10), and so decided by Joseph Caro (Orach Chayim
272.2). And thus, the rule may be safely followed that
one may use the following for **Kiddush, Havdala**, Grace,
and **Berit Mila** instead of fermented wine: (1) grape
juice (or Must), or (2) raisin wine (**yein tsimukin**).
      Moreover, as to the question, "Is it necessary to
use some kind of beverage at all?"--to this we must also
reply in the negative. It is not necessary to use any
beverage at all. Many of the teachers expressly state
about Grace that "**Einah te-una kos**," no cup of wine is
necessary for it (Ber. 52; Orach Chayim 182). And as to
Kiddush, we may surely rely upon Abba Arecha (d. 247),
who "at times used wine and at other times used bread
for **Kiddush**" ("**Zimnin mekadesh arifta**") (Pes. 106b).
Hence, such authorities as the Geonim Mar Amram, Mar
Zemach, and Natronai (all of the ninth century; see
Sefer Ha-itim, pp. 180, 203, 204) and Rashi (1040-1105)
(T. Ber. 51b, voce "**Shehayayin**"; Pes. 114, voce "**Meva-**

rech"; **Pardes**, Hil. Shabbat 112) and Joseph Caro (Orach
Chayim 271.4; 272.9)--all agree that instead of wine one
may use bread for **Kiddush** and **Havdala**. Also, if **Yom Tov**
happens to fall on a Sunday, he may include the ritual
for **Havdala** in the **Kiddush** while making **Kiddush** over
bread on Saturday night.

Again, originally the Men of the Great Assembly
instituted that the ritual for **Kiddush** and **Havdala**
should be included in the evening prayer--"**Tefila ikar
takanata**" (Ber. 33). Moreover, some of the old teachers
maintain that "he who includes **Havdala** in the evening
prayer does better than he who recites it over a cup of
wine" (**ibid.**). R. Bun reports that "in our place it is
customary that, if wine is not at hand, the reader includes the **Kiddush** in the evening prayer--"**Omer beracha
achat me-ein sheva**" (T. Ber. 10.17). We may, therefore,
safely rule that where wine is not easily obtainable,
the recital of the words of the ritual without any beverage is sufficient, to be embodied either in the evening prayer or as a separate formula (see also Rashi,
Pes. 105, voce "**Shema**," 106, voce "**dechaviba**"; **Sefer
Ha-itim**, 203, 204; **Yad**, Hil. Shab. 29.1; Orach Chayim,
296.7).

C. As to the wine for the "Four Cups" of Passover
Eve, the Mishna enjoins it upon the poorest of the poor
to make every effort to obtain it "even if he receives
his support from the **Tamchui** (charity bowl)" (Pes. 10.1;
Yad, Hil. Matzah 6.7, Orach Chayim 472.13). Yet it is
but reasonable to state that if, as we have seen, one
may use unfermented wine for **Kiddush**, which some teachers regard as a Biblical ordinance, he may certainly use
unfermented wine for the "Four Cups" of Passover. Such,
indeed, is the ruling of good authorities like Amram
Gaon, who stated that "if wine is not obtainable, one
may press out the juice of grapes or soak raisins and
use the juice for the four cups" (**Sefer Ha-itim**, 203).
This decision was adopted by R. David b. Samuel in his
Turei Zahav (see Orach Chayim 472.12) and Judah Ashkenazi in his **Ba-er Heitev** (**ibid.**). Again, if grape
juice or raisin wine is not obtainable, one may use
bread (that is, **Matzot**) for the first cup, which is for
Kiddush, while the mere words of the ritual are sufficient instead of the other three cups. Such is the
opinion of Zemach Gaon (**Sefer Ha-itim**, 204), of Rashi
(Pes. 114, voce "**Mevarech**"), of Asheri (Pes. 10.36), and
of Joseph Caro (Orach Chayim 483.1). According to Judah
Ashkenazi, we may use apple cider (**Ba-er Heitev** to O.
Ch. 483.4), while Moses Isserles rules, "Mead is as good
as wine" (Rema to O. Ch. 483). Accordingly, we have the
choice of using the following for the "Four Cups," instead of fermented wine: (1) grape juice; (2) raisin

wine; (3) mead; (4) apple cider; (5) **Matzot** (for the first cup); and (6) words of the ritual (for the other three cups).

D. As to wine for the marriage ceremony: There are two formulas of benedictions used in the marriage ceremony--the "Benediction of Betrothal," **Birkat Erusin**, which in olden times was said perhaps months before the second, and the "Benedictions of Nuptial," **Birchot Nisu-in**, recited at the consummation of the actual marriage, on the wedding day. The former was recited in the house of the bride, the latter in the house of the groom. In modern times both are recited at the same time, on the wedding day. In reference to the Benediction of Betrothal--Erusin--Joseph Caro, in his code (**Even Ha-ezer** 34.2), quoting verbatim the words of Maimonides, (**Yad**, Hil. Ishut 3.24), lays down the following rule: The custom prevails now to recite the Benediction [of Betrothal] after having said a blessing over a cup of wine first, "if there is wine at hand; but if there is no wine there, he recites the Benediction alone, that is, without the wine."

Regarding the second formula, Benediction of Nuptial--Nisu-in--Joseph Caro (Even Ha-ezer 62.1), quoting again verbatim the words of Maimonides (**Yad**, Hil. Ishut 10.3), rules as follows: The Benedictions of Nuptial (Maimonides here enumerates them in consecutive order) should be recited immediately before the nuptials. In all, there are **Six Benedictions**, and "if there is wine at hand, one says first the blessing over a cup of wine, so that there may be altogether seven benedictions. But if there is no wine [or beer] the six benedictions are recited without wine (see **Ba-er Heitev** of Judah Ashkenazi to Even Ha-ezer 62.1), **as wine is not essential.**" However, Asheri (Ket. 1:16) and his son, R. Jacob (**Tur**, Even Ha-ezer 62), decide that if fermented wine is not at hand, one should use raisin wine. We may, therefore, safely state that for the marriage ceremony, if no wine can be had, one may use: (1) raisin wine, (2) grape juice, (3) apple cider, or (4) the words of the ritual without any beverage whatsoever.

Julius Rappaport

See also:

S.B. Freehof, "A Seder Without Wine," **Current Reform Responsa**, pp. 43ff.

48. THE JEWISH JUBILEE
(Vol. XLII, 1932, pp. 85-86)

QUESTION: Will you please let us know whether
there is any record of the year in which the Jewish
Jubilee was celebrated, and if there is any way of
figuring in what year the next Jubilee would be
celebrated if it had continued to be celebrated
each fifty years since Biblical days?

ANSWER: According to the Talmud (Arachin 32b), the
laws about the Jubilee year prescribed in Leviticus were
to be observed only as long as all Israel (i.e., all the
twelve tribes) lived in Palestine, but not after some of
the tribes had been exiled. Accordingly, the Jubilee
year could not have been observed during the Second
Jewish Commonwealth.

But, while not observing the Jubilee year in practice, the Jewish people may have preserved the memory of
it in their reckoning of the years. According to a
Talmudic tradition (ibid., 12a), "the fourteenth year
after the city was smitten," referred to in Ezek. 40:1,
was a Jubilee year. Since the city (i.e., Jerusalem)
was destroyed by Nebuchadnezzar in the year 586 B.C.E.,
then the year 573 B.C.E. (i.e., the fourteenth year
after the destruction) was a Jubilee year. On the basis
of this tradition, we could figure that, had the Jubilee
continued to be celebrated each fifty years, adding 1932
to 573, which total 2505, and dividing by fifty, the
present year would be the fifth in the Jubilee period,
and the next Jubilee year would then have to be in 1977.
Of course, this figure would not hold true according to
the reckoning of R. Judah, who maintains that the fifti-
eth year, while being the Jubilee year, is at the same
time counted as the first year of the following Jubilee
period: "Shenat chamishim ola lechan ulechan" (ibid.,
212b).

Jacob Z. Lauterbach

49. KASHRUT IN REFORM JUDAISM
(1979)

QUESTION: What is the Reform attitude toward Kashrut? What should be done for those who observe
Kashrut in wartime or during other emergencies?

ANSWER: The dietary laws have been discussed by reformers virtually since the beginning of Reform Judaism.
This was prompted by the widespread neglect of all the
dietary laws among a large segment of the Jewish population even during the middle of the last century. Holdheim and Einhorn suggested that they be completely eliminated, as they were part of the ceremonial laws which
dealt with Levitical and priestly purity and therefore
did not apply after the Temple ceased to be in existence
(**Sinai**, 1859-1860).   Slightly later, Kohler expressed
similar sentiments (**Jewish Times of New York**, 1872).
Others suggested that they be modified so that the basic
Biblical ideas continue, while the vast Talmudic legis-
lation--often based on the slimmest Biblical premise--be
eliminated.   This was the point of view of Wiener (**Die
Juedischen Speisegesetz**, 1895), Creiznach (cited in
Plaut, **The Rise of Reform Judaism**, p. 212), and Monte-
fiore (**The Jewish Quarterly Review**, vol. 8, pp. 392ff),
while Geiger suggested that they either be kept in toto
or be entirely eliminated (**Zeitschrift**, vol. 8, p. 24).
The Hungarian reformer, Chorin, also felt that they
should be eliminated (Philipson, **The Reform Movement in
Judaism**, p. 276).   The Leipzig Synod rejected them,
along with the various other ceremonial and ritual laws,
following a paper presented by Fuerst (**Verhandlungen der
ersten israelitischen Synod zu Leipzig**, p. 254).   A
resolution was introduced at the Philadelphia Conference
of 1869 which recommended that the dietary laws be eliminated.   Dr. Adler suggested that a commission be appointed and a report be made to the next conference
(Appendix XI, S.D. Temkin, **The New World of Reform**, p.
111).   The Pittsburgh Platform clearly rejected dietary
laws along with other laws which dealt with priestly
purity: "We hold that all such Mosaic and rabbinical
laws as regulate diet, priestly purity, and dress, originated in ages and under the influence of ideas altogether foreign to our present mental and spiritual
state.   They fail to impress the modern Jew with a spirit of priestly holiness; their observance in our days is
apt rather to obstruct than to further modern spiritual
elevation." Although this blanket rejection of the dietary laws as outmoded represented the 'official' position of the Reform Movement through most of a century,
it did not prevent individual Reform Jews and Reform
congregations from adopting certain of the dietary laws
for a variety of reasons, including the desire not to
offend traditional relatives or guests" (Philipson, **The
Reform Movement in Judaism**, p. 356).   On the other hand,
neither the Columbus Platform in 1937, nor the Centenary
Statement of 1975 made any specific mention of dietary
laws, but rather called for "the development of such
customs, symbols, and ceremonies as possess inspiration-

al value" (**The Central Conference of American Rabbis
Yearbook**, 1937, p. 100), while the Centenary Statement
recognized divergent trends within the Reform Movement
while encouraging observances and customs ("A Centenary
Perspective" in Borowitz, **Reform Judaism Today**, vol. I,
p. xxiii).

Although dietary laws were discussed at length
during the last century and early in this century, they
ceased to be a matter of primary concern for Reform
Jews.   This is also clearly indicated by the lack of
questions regarding dietary laws addressed to the Responsa Committee through the decades.   Yet, "Judaism has
always recognized a religious dimension to the consumption of food.   Being a gift of God, food was never to be
taken for granted.   And if this was true of food generally, it was especially true of meat, fish, and fowl,
which involve the taking of life."   Those Reform Jews
who observe the dietary laws, totally or in part, seem
to do so because (a) it adds to their personal expression of Judaism; the daily meals serve as reminders of
Jewish ideals; (b) it provides an additional link with
other Jews and a link to history; it enables Jews of all
groups to eat in their home or their synagogue; (c) it
encourages ethical discipline; a large number of Reform
Jews observe a modified form of the dietary laws by
abstaining from pork products, animals specifically
prohibited, seafood, and the mixing of meat and milk.
Some form of dietary observance may be carried out as a
daily reminder of Judaism; the form may be left to the
individual or congregation.   "One might opt to eat only
kosher meat or even to adopt some form of vegetarianism
so as to avoid the necessity of taking a life.   (This
would be in consonance with the principle of **tsa-ar ba-
alei chayim**--prevention of cruelty to animals.)   The
range of options available to the Reform Jew is from
full observance of the Biblical and Rabbinic regulations
to total non-observance.   Reform Judaism does not take
an 'all or nothing' approach" (**Gates of Mitzvah**, p.
132).

In times of emergency and danger of life, the dietary laws lapse and may clearly be transgressed.   The
only laws which remain in force are those which prohibit
idolatry, sex crimes, and murder (Shab. 132a; **Shulchan
Aruch**, Orach Chayim 328.10-17).   If there is danger of
life or even danger of someone becoming unnecessarily
weakened, then the dietary laws may be given up (Yoma
83a; Rosh to the above; **Tur**, Orach Chayim 618; **Yad**, Hil.
Yesodei Ha-Torah 5, 6).   The only occasions when the
dietary laws may not be breached are instances when an
oppressor attempts to use them to force the rejection of
Judaism.   However, this was discussed at length during
the period of the Holocaust and the difficult times

immediately preceding it (Oshry, **Mima-amakim**, vol. 1, 13). It was considered wrong for an individual to refuse proper food even if it meant that the dietary laws had to be trespassed (see also **Shibolei Haleket**, 117; **Pachad Yitschak**, Pikuach Nefesh). It is quite clear, therefore, that even in the strictest Orthodox tradition, the dietary laws may be transgressed during times of war or periods of danger.

We should note that the National Jewish Welfare Board has made every effort during the First and Second World Wars and subsequently to provide for Jews in military service who observe the dietary laws. In 1942, there was a suggestion by the Department of the Army to provide vegetarian tables in mess halls. This suggestion was, however, rejected. Consequently, the Department of Defense has found no feasible plan for providing food for this special group. Two pamphlets in our possession deal with the Jewish soldier in the German army in the First World War, and do not mention the question of **Kashrut**. It was left to the individual to carry out as best he could. We would, therefore, suggest that in wartime a soldier contact the chaplain and see what can be done about proper observance. Certainly, that individual would be provided with some special foods and could refrain from eating certain items. Under conditions of actual emergency, he or she would be free to eat anything which might be available.

Walter Jacob, Chairman
Leonard S. Kravitz
Eugene Lipman
W. Gunther Plaut
Harry A. Roth
Rav A. Soloff
Bernard Zlotowitz

50. **KOSHER** KITCHEN IN MILITARY CAMPS
(Vol. XXVIII, 1918, pp. 124-127)

QUESTION: An Orthodox organization started an agitation to demand of the government that a **kosher** kitchen be provided in military camps. Is it necessary for Jewish soldiers to observe the dietary laws while in active service?

ANSWER: The principle on the ground of which this question is to be treated, is the Talmudic rule "**Dina**

demalchuta dina" (Gittin 10b, and in many other places).
This principle has often been misinterpreted, as if any
state law would supersede the religious law. The fallacy of such an interpretation is evident, or else the
whole history of Israel from the time of Antiochus Epiphanes down to Nicholas II would be a rebellion against
the Rabbinic interpretation of Judaism. The rule that
obedience to the law of the state is to the Jew a religious duty, refers first of all to such laws which do
not conflict with the religious duties, as tax and custom laws. Even then, the best authorities limit such
duty to laws which do not discriminate against the Jews
(Tosafot, Bava Kama 58a; Meir of Rothenburg, Responsa,
ed. Prague, no. 134, ed. Berlin, no. 122; and Asher ben
Yechiel, Nedarim 3.11, Kitsur Piskei Rosh). The clearest definition of the limitation is given by Mordecai
Yafeh (1530-1612), who says: The principle of "Dina
demalchuta dina" is restricted to cases in which the
king derives a benefit from the law and which is needed
for the welfare of the country (Lebush, Ir Shushan, sec.
369, Cracow, 1569).

Application to War

The application of this principle to war is given
in the Rabbinic interpretation of Deut. 20:19-20, which
says that the Sabbath law shall not stand in the way of
any war operation (Sifrei, l.c., ed. Friedman, p. 111b).
Historic facts prove that this principle was actually
observed in the Jewish state. The Book of Maccabees
reports that the heroes who fought for the preservation
of their religion resolved that they would fight on
Sabbath, if it was necessary (I Macc. 3:41).
Until the end of the 18th century the Jews were not
compelled to perform military duty. We have, however,
individual instances during the whole period of the
Middle Ages from all countries, and during the great
wars of the 17th century we hear of instances in Germany
as well as in Poland.[1]

---

[1] A few instances will be given briefly: From Spain in
the 12th century--Guedemann, Erziehungswesen I, 111;
from Worms in the 13th century--ibid., 137; from
Salzburg, 1382--Altmann, Geschichte der Jueden in S.,
pp. 103-105; from Thiengen, 1499: Guedemann, ibid., III,
p. 165; from Hamburg, 1665--Jahrbuch der Jued. Lit. Ges.
X, 279; from Poland, 1650-1660--Oest. Wochenschrift,
1910, no. 31-32; also from Poland in the 17th century--
Resp. no. 2, Chemnitz, Der...Schwedische Krieg II, pp.
356 and 647. Settin (1648) speaks of a Jewish colonel
who served in the Imperial Army.

It is reasonably certain, and in the case of Worms expressly reported, that these Jewish soldiers fought on the Sabbath.   Also, it is not likely that they could have observed the dietary laws under the exigencies of camp life. There is, however, the great difference that these Jewish soldiers were volunteers and therefore had the choice of violating their religion or keeping out of the army.

Compulsory Service

The first case in which the conflict between religious laws and military exigency was submitted to a rabbinic authority occurred, as far as I am aware, in Prague.   During the siege of the city, which was the last act of the bloody drama of the Thirty Years War, the Jews had to do duty in repairing fortifications and in putting out fires caused by the bombardment (1648).[2] Similar exigencies occurred in 1744, when the city was besieged by the Prussian army. The Jews again had to work on the Sabbath, and in spite of their urgent pleas they had even to work on Yom Kippur, Sept. 16, 1744, just the day before the city surrendered.[3] Inasmuch as the Sabbath stands higher than the dietary laws (because the penalty for violating the dietary laws is stripes, while the penalty for breaking the Sabbath is death), and inasmuch as the Talmud places Sabbath observance so high as to say that it will wipe out the sin of idolatry (Shabbat 118b, an evidently hyperbolical, but significant expression), it is clear that the exigencies of the military service justify the breaking of the dietary laws.

Direct Application to Dietary Laws

Whatever higher critics may think of the chronological relations between I Samuel and Leviticus, it is clear that the report that Ahimelech gave to David the holy showbread means to convey that exigencies of military service supersede the dietary law (I Sam. 21:2-7). That this interpretation is old is clearly proven by the New Testament,[4] where this incident is quoted as proof that necessity--and in this particular case, military

---

[2] **Milchama Beshalom**, Prague, 1649, reprinted in **Bikurei Ha-itim** IV, pp. 103-130.

[3] Report of the eyewitness, Bezalel Brandeis, in Freimann, **Beitrage zur Geschichte der Juden in Prag** etc., p. 24 (Berlin, 1898).

[4] Matthew 12:5; Mark 2:26; Luke 6:4.

necessity (I Sam. 21:3)--supersedes the dietary law. This is also the opinion of Rashi (Comm., l.c.) and of the Midrash (**Yalkut**, I. Sam, sec. 130), although Kimchi tries to explain the difficulty away by saying that the bread was not showbread, but the bread of thanksgiving offering, which lay people may eat.

The question could not come before Orthodox authorities until recent times, because the first case of Jews being drafted into the army dates from 1788, when Joseph II of Austria introduced this duty by a law dated February 13. Complaints were heard by many observant Jews, but the humane emperor decided in an order of August 17, 1786, that nothing more shall be required of the Jews "als was die Not fordert."[5]

In the same sense Ezekiel Landau (1713-1793), then Chief Rabbi of Prague, and one of the most celebrated rabbinical authors of the time, addressed the first contingent of Jewish soldiers and admonished them to observe the Jewish practices as far as possible.[6] Moses Sofer (1762-1839), the greatest casuist of his age, condemns the practice, then extant, that the rich evade military service by bribery, so that the contingent is filled by drafting the poor. He says that no one has the right to make his fellow-Jew violate the laws, among which he mentions the dietary laws specifically as permissible under the exigencies of the military service.[7]

Conclusion

Military service is **Dina Demalchuta**. It is intended for the welfare of the country, and it applies to Jews and non-Jews alike. Therefore, it supersedes ceremonial law, including the dietary laws. It would be absolutely unfair to demand of the military administration to provide a **kosher** kitchen, which in some instances would be an impossibility, and in every case a hardship. Very observant young men, while in a camp

---

[5] Allg. **Zeitg. des Judentums,** 1872, pp. 981-982.

[6] Klein, **Sollen die Juden Soldaten Werden?** (Vienna, 1783); Wolf, "Die Juden im oest. Heere." in **Oester. Militaerzeitung,** of which an abstract is given in **Allg. Zeitg. des Judentums,** 1869, p. 565; Grunwald, **Die Feldzuege Napoleons,** p. 7 (Vienna, 1913).

[7] **Resp. Chatam Sofer** VI, no. 29. See also: Geiger, **Rabbinisches Gutachten ueber die Militaerpflichtigkeit der Juden,** Breslau, 1842. Eli Rust (Pseudonym for L. Landshuth), "Die Verbindlichkeit des Zeremonialgesetzes fuer Juedische Krieger," in Heinemann, **Allg. Archiv** etc. 1842, vol. II, pp. 236-238.

which is in the vicinity of a large city, can easily provide themselves with **kosher** food, or Orthodox organizations may provide it for them, if they wish to do so, but from the strictest Orthodox viewpoint this is absolutely unnecessary.

G. Deutsch

51. USE OF PYREX DISHES FOR MEAT AND MILK
(Vol. XXIX, 1919, pp. 78-79)

Not knowing what Pyrex is, I must be guided by the information that it is glass, and on this presumption give the following information in reply to a question submitted to me.

The Mosaic law (Exodus 23:19, 34:26 and Deuteronomy 14:21) says: "Thou shalt not seethe a kid in its mother's milk." This the Rabbinical law explains to prohibit the mixture of any milk or milk product with the meat of animals and fowls (**Shulchan Aruch**, Yoreh De-a 87.1-3). I am always quoting the latest standard authorities on Rabbinical law.

This prohibition is extended to the use of vessels, so that a vessel used for milk must not be used for meat and vice versa (Yoreh De-a 93.1).

"Glass vessels, even when used for permanent preservation of food, including hot food, require no purification (if, e.g., they were used for boiling milk and subsequently are to be used for boiling meat), for they do not absorb anything of their contents, and mere rinsing before using them again is sufficient" (Joseph Caro, Orach Chayim, 451.27). The glossarist Moses Isserles adds: "Some authorities take a rigorous view and declare that even washing the vessels in hot water does not help. This is the practice in Germany and Poland." The glossarist David Halevi, author of **Turei Zahav**, adds: "This rigorous view is based on the assumption that glassware is equal to earthen ware. If, however, the glass dishes [usually used for milk or meat] had been accidentally used [for the other kind], there is certainly no prohibition" (**ibid.**, 30).

"Earthen vessels used for the permanent preservation of prohibited wine are, according to some authorities, not to be used [for **kosher** food], but all authorities are unanimous in the opinion that this prohibition does not include glass vessels" (Yoreh De-a 135.8). The glossarists Shabbetai Kohen (**Shak, ibid.**, 23) and David Halevi (**Turei Zahav, ibid.**, 11) give as a reason for this exception the fact that glass vessels have a smooth surface and do not absorb anything of their contents.

These quotations should suffice to prove that Pyrex, presuming that it is glassware, may be used for both milk and meat dishes and would therefore mean both a convenience and a saving in **kosher** households. Inspection of the article would seem necessary to convince the man who gives the decision that Pyrex is what it is represented to be.

Ritualistic questions are to be submitted to an authorized rabbi. There is, however, no guarantee that a decision given by one rabbi would be recognized by others, for Judaism has no ecclesiastic authority in an hierarchical sense. New York had last year a heated controversy between two sections of Orthodox rabbis, led by R. Wolf Margolis, on the one hand, and Moses Zebulun Margolis on the other. It may be presumed, however, that if a few recognized authorities would subscribe to this opinion, it would be respected by the vast majority of observant Jews. It ought to be translated into Hebrew and Yiddish, for a Hebrew endorsement (**Hechsher**) put on the goods would, to most people, be a sufficient guarantee.

G. Deutsch

52.   SUBSTITUTING FOR CHRISTIANS ON CHRISTMAS
(Vol. LXXXII, 1972, pp. 53-55)

QUESTION: The Men's Club of Temple Beth El, Detroit, substituted for Christian volunteer hospital aides on Christmas last year (1971). That year Christmas fell on the Sabbath, and questions arose in the Detroit community as to whether it was proper for a Jewish congregation thus openly (and also with newspaper publicity) to violate the Sabbath. Since then, other Men's Clubs are planning to volunteer for such duties on Christmas. This has raised the wider question: first, as mentioned about the Sabbath, and secondly, about the value or propriety of this sort of substitute volunteering. (Rabbi Richard Hertz, Detroit, Michigan)

ANSWER: There are one or two general statements which must be made before going into the detailed laws involved in this matter. The first concerns the propriety of violating the Sabbath. It is, of course, obvious that most modern individuals--not only in Reform congregations but in others, too--do not, in their personal lives, follow with any degree of strictness the laws dealing with working, traveling, opening letters, and the like on the Sabbath. Nevertheless, there is a difference between what is done privately and what is done publicly. This difference has long been recognized in Jewish law. The building of a house by contract (**Kablanut**) may go on any day of the week, including the Sabbath, for the Gentile contractor works not by day-by-day orders from the Jewish owner, but by his own orders. But while such Sabbath work would be permitted, let us say, outside of the city, in the city--where everybody sees the work going on--it is prohibited (see Orach Chayim 244).

The Responsa Committee of the Conference receives many inquiries about the propriety of the Sabbath observance in our synagogues. May we, for instance, permit a caterer, preparing for a Bar Mitzvah meal, to prepare the meal on the Sabbath? May the congregation have its business meeting on Friday night? May the Gift Corner (Judaica Shop) be open for business on Friday night? Whatever the personal observance of individuals may be, there is considerable sensitivity as to public violation of the Sabbath by the congregation itself. The question, therefore, is whether such activities as substituting on Christmas for hospital work would justify the various public violations of the Sabbath that might be involved in transportation, copying of records, and other concomitant duties.

First of all, it must be recorded that the motivation which led this Men's Club and leads other Men's Clubs to such help to Christians is a well-established and honored motivation since ancient times. There are both the negative motive to avoid ill will (**Mishum Eiva**) and the positive one to increase comradely relationship (**Mipenei Darchei Shalom**). See the full discussion of these two motives in Dr. Lauterbach's magnificent paper, "The Attitude of the Jew towards the Non-Jew," **CCAR Yearbook**, XXXI, p. 186. The motivation for these volunteer substitutes, therefore, is not only worthy, it is also traditional.

But there is a more specific concern because this substitution takes place on Christmas. The Talmud (the beginning of tractate on idolatry, **Avoda Zara**) prohibits any association with the heathens on or within days of their holidays, lest we become involved in their worship, or lest the money that they earn in business dealings with us be contributed to the idol worship. This law of non-association at the non-Jewish holidays is carried over in the **Shulchan Aruch**, Yoreh De-a 147, but it is a well-established principle in Jewish law that

such laws refer to actual idol worshipers. Christians
and Mohammedans are not deemed to be idolaters in Jewish
law, and therefore there is no objection to associating
with them on Christian and Moslem holidays (see Yoreh
De-a 147.12, especially the long note by Isserles).
Furthermore, it has long become an unobjectionable custom to give gifts to Christians on their holidays. The
great 15th-century authority, Israel Isserlein (**Terumat
Hadeshen**, #195), discusses the propriety of giving gifts
on New Year's Day, which of course was a religious holiday (as he himself mentions), namely, the Christian
Feast of Circumcision, eight days after Christmas.

Since the motivation of comradeship is traditionally praiseworthy, and since there is no objection to
associating with Gentiles on the days of their religious
festivals, the question now arises: What sort of activity is most suitable for this expression of good will?
The Talmud lists certain types of what we would call
"social service" today, which it is our duty to do for
non-Jews. This is discussed in the Talmud, Gittin 61a,
where it says that we sustain the poor of the Gentiles,
comfort their mourners, and bury their dead as we do
with fellow Israelites. In the Palestinian Talmud (Yer.
Gittin 47c) it is added that in cities where Jews and
Gentiles live together there is even joint collection
and expenditures of funds, that is, a sort of Community
Chest. And all this social service referred even to
idolaters, from whom Israelites were expected to keep
away in those ancient days. Then how much more is it
our duty to perform these social services for Christians, who are not idolaters at all and with whom we
associate freely.

Now, the final question should be: Which of these
praiseworthy acts of social service and comradeship may
be done on the Sabbath whenever, as occurred in 1971,
Christmas falls on that day? First of all, any seriously sick person may be helped on the Sabbath, and, in
fact, it is considered a sin to hesitate and inquire
whether to violate the Sabbath or not (see especially
Orach Chayim 328). It may be properly considered that
sick people in the hospital are under the class of "seriously sick," and it is a duty to help them on the Sabbath. It is not only for the seriously sick that the
Sabbath may be violated. The violation of the Sabbath
is likewise permitted in order to rescue anybody from
danger (see Orach Chayim 329 and 330). Since saving
people from danger permits the violation of the Sabbath,
we can properly include our substituting not only for
hospital workers, but also for firemen and policemen on
these days, even if the days occur on the Sabbath.

However, it would not be proper (even though still
comradely) to substitute in violation of the Sabbath for

salesmen, postal clerks, and similar workers. There is no objection (and, indeed, it is comradely and in accordance with the spirit of Jewish tradition) to substitute for **any** workers on their holidays, provided Sabbath violation by a congregation is not involved. But in those years in which Christmas falls on the Sabbath, it would be in consonance with Jewish tradition and the sentiment of the general Jewish community if these voluntary, comradely acts were confined to hospitals and to the institutions of public safety.

Solomon B. Freehof

53. RESPONSIBILITY OF CHILDREN TO THEIR PARENTS
(Vol. XCII, 1982, pp. 207-209)

QUESTION: A newly married couple wishes to know the extent of their responsibility towards their parents according to the Reform view of Halacha. What are the limits of the command, "Honor your father and your mother," beyond the obvious duty of care and support in infirmity, sickness, and old age? Where is the boundary between independence and filial responsibility? (L.F.-W.R., Pittsburgh, Pennsylvania)

ANSWER: The commandment to honor your father is the fifth of the Decalogue. This along with the statement, "You shall each revere his father and his mother and keep My Sabbath: I am the Lord your God" (Lev. 19:3), is the Biblical source of **kibud av va-em**. This **mitzvah**, however, may come into direct conflict with other **mitzvot** such as, "Therefore a man leaves his father and mother and clings to his wife so that they may become one flesh" (Gen. 2:24). The possibility of tension between these **mitzvot** has always existed. The **mitzvah** of a new home take precedence without voiding the other (Kimchi).

The same kind of difficulty could arise with other **mitzvot**, too; for example, that of settling in the Land of Israel. The **mitzva** of **Aliya** took precedence (Meir Rothenburg, **Responsa**, vol. 2, pp. 120ff, 129). There are other areas of potential conflict, such as choice of residence, occupation, etc., but we are principally concerned with the tension which may arise between marriage and filial devotion.

Possible conflict in these matters is somewhat
clouded by the fact that the father had complete rights
over his daughter until she reached puberty and became a
bogeret (M. Kid. 2.1; Kid. 41a), although he was cau-
tioned to try to fulfill her wishes. On the other hand,
the father had no such power over his son, though at
various times the father, nevertheless, controlled the
marriage completely (as, for example, in medieval Germany; see Moses Mintz, **Responsa**, #98). As children were
likely to take matters into their own hands, various
medieval synods tried to control them through ordinances
(Friedmann, **Toledot Erusin Venisu-in**, pp. 138ff).

This question arises a number of times in the responsa literature. In most instances the authorities
decided in favor of the children, as they alone could
really decide what was proper for them. One of them put
it beautifully and said that the couple was best able to
judge the heavenly verdict in this matter. Others felt
that marriage would be good only with those who truly
loved one another; therefore, no element of compulsion
could be introduced (Solomon ben Adret, **Responsa**, vol.
1, #272; Joseph Colon, **Responsa**, 174.3).

The authority of parents expressed only for its own
sake, without need or frailty as a factor, was rejected
in favor of those areas in which direct help should be
provided for parents (**Tos.** to Kid. 32a; Yev. 5b). This
point of view was reflected frequently in the resonpsa
of the Middle Ages (Simon ben Zemah Duran, **Responsa**,
vol. 3, #130), sec. 5; Samuel de Modena, **Responsa**, Yoreh
De-a 90, 95; Isaac ben Sheshet, **Responsa**, #127). This
point of view was later expressed in the **Shulchan Aruch**
by Moses Isserles (Yoreh De-a 240.25).

Matters were seen somewhat differently in the case
of a daughter, since a father might suffer financial
loss through her actions. But many felt that daughters
should be treated like sons and ruled for equality
(Simon ben Zemach of Duran, **ibid.**, sec. 5; David Pardo,
Michtam LeDavid, #32; Ezekiel Landau, **Noda BiYehuda** 2,
Even Ha-ezer, #45). Although this represented the majority view, another body of opinion ruled that the
daughter must obey her father under all circumstances,
even in the choice of a mate (**Sefer Chasidim**, sec. 564).
Joseph of Trani followed the same line of reasoning
(**Responsa** 2, Yoreh De-a, #27, as did Yehiel Weinberg,
Seridei Esh III, p. 300). At the very least, a daughter
should listen to the advice of her parents and be urged
to make her decision accordingly.

Subsequent to marriage, the new wife owed her first
allegiance to her husband, so honoring of parents became
more the husband's duty than hers (Tosefta, Kid. 1.11;
Kid. 30b). The tension can be seen in some sad discussions. Should a deceased daughter be buried with her

father or in her husband's future burial place (Semachot 14)? Either way was considered proper (**Shulchan Aruch,** Yoreh De-a 361.3). Of course, if the wife had children, then she is definitely to be buried in her husband's plot rather than her father's. This shows that a family with children represented a much more independent unit.

In cases of conflict between mother-in-law and daughter-in-law who could no longer get along in the same household, the husband was obliged to move his family out of the house (**Gaonic Responsa,** cited by Meir of Rothenburg, **Responsa II,** 81). This rule was followed especially if the financial issues at stake were considerable (**Teshuvot Hage-onim,** Ket. 134, p. 292; **Yad,** Hil. Ishut 13.14). In another instance, both Maimonides and the earlier Alfasi recommended that a neutral person try to adjust the matter (Alfasi, **Responsa,** #235, p. 65a; **Yad,** Hil. Ishut 21.10). **Sefer Chasidim** took a different course and counseled that the young couple submit to the wishes of the parents (sec. 562ff), but the codes did not follow that path.

The medieval text encouraged children to settle near their parents, but they were not expected to make unusual sacrifices in order to accomplish that. They should be close enough to look after their needs (**Sefer Chasidim,** sec. 564). On the other hand, if father and son could not get along, it was better if they separated (**ibid.,** sec. 343).

All of the preceding material makes it quite clear that everything was done to balance the interest of the older and younger generations. Normative Judaism encouraged freedom for the younger generation. The children remained responsible for the maintenance of their parents and were to look after their physical and psychological needs, but the children were not to be subjected to every whim and desire of the older generation. Through this, the full personal development of the younger generation was constantly encouraged.

Walter Jacob

54. CIRCUMCISION OF INFANTS
(Vol. XCII, 1982, pp. 218-219)

QUESTION: During the last thirty or forty years most American children have been routinely circumcised in the hospital after birth. This was considered good preventive medicine and was recommended by most doctors. The medical profession has now changed its attitude on this matter. Some doctors no longer feel the operation is necessary and therefore do not routinely suggest it. It is clear that traditional Judaism demands circumcision for all males. What is the stand of Reform Judaism on this matter today?   (L.O., Pittsburgh, Pennsylvania)

ANSWER: The rite of circumcision is one of the most ancient practices of Judaism. This commandment was given to Abraham with the injunction that male children be circumcised on the eighth day (Gen. 17:11). The commandment is repeated later in the Torah (Lev. 12:3), and has remained throughout our history as one of the most important commandments. It already led to martyrdom in Maccabean times (I Macc. 1:48,60). The exact details of the circumcision itself have been provided in every Jewish code (**Yad,** Hil. Mila; **Tur** and **Shulchan Aruch,** Yoreh De-a 260ff; **Gates of Mitzvah,** pp. 13ff). The ritual itself is incumbent upon the father, who may delegate a **Mohel,** a Jewish physician, or any qualified Jew. It must be performed on the eighth day after birth (**Shulchan Aruch,** Yoreh De-a 262.1; **Gates of Mitzvah,** p. 14; see Responsa #55-58 below). This remains the accepted practice for Reform Jews.

There was considerable discussion in the middle of the last century among radical reformers about the need for circumcision. The question was raised in 1843 by the Frankfurt Reform Association, which encouraged its members to abandon the rite. The Orthodox Chief Rabbi of the city, Solomon Abraham Trier, did his best to dissuade the association and its members. He and others indicated that those who had not been circumcised would not and should not be considered as Jews (W.G. Plaut, **The Rise of Reform Judaism,** pp. 206ff). The entire matter was debated at the Leipzig Synod in 1869 without any resolution and was referred to the Augsburg Synod, which in 1871 declared "the supreme importance of circumcision in Judaism," though those who had not been circumcised would continue to be considered as Jews. A similar resolution was passed by the Philadelphia Conference in 1869 (**CCAR Yearbook,** 1890, pp. 118-120). Subsequently there was considerable debate about the need for circumcision on the part of converts (**CCAR Yearbook,** 1892, pp. 66ff, and 1893, pp. 69ff). However, no one further questioned the necessity for infant circumcision. This is reflected in every subsequent manual or guide (**Rabbi's Manual,** p. 110; S.B. Freehof, **Reform Jewish Practice,** vol. 1, p. 113; see Responsa #55-58 below; **Gates of Mitzvah,** pp. 118ff).

Current medical fashions are irrelevant in this matter as we consider circumcision to be a religious rite, not a health measure. Unless ill health or serious medical problems prevent the circumcision of a male infant on the eighth day, he should be circumcised on that day. If such a child is not circumcised, he would nevertheless be considered a Jew (San. 44a; Hoffmann, **Melamed Leho-il**, Yoreh De-a, #79). It would be incumbent upon such an individual to be circumcised later in life (Kid. 29a; **Shulchan Aruch**, Yoreh De-a 261.1). We would encourage uncircumcised children to be circumcised later. Certainly parents would not want to inflict this much more serious and painful operation on their adult son when it can be done easily on the eighth day.

Circumcision remains for us an essential sign of the covenant. We have affirmed it since the days of Abraham, our Father, and continue to affirm it.

Walter Jacob, Chairman
Simeon Maslin
W. Gunther Plaut
Harry A. Roth
Rav A. Soloff
Sheldon Zimmerman

55. CIRCUMCISION ON A DAY OTHER THAN THE EIGHTH DAY OF BIRTH
(Vol. LXIV, 1954, pp. 78-79)

QUESTION: It is common practice now for hospitals to discharge mother and baby within a week after birth. Since doctors and parents prefer to have the circumcision performed in the hospital, I am getting an increasing number of requests to conduct the service before the eighth day.

I discussed this matter with one of our leading obstetricians who performs many circumcisions shortly after birth. He has written a paper on the subject in which he seeks to prove by facts and figures that the immediate circumcision of the newborn male is followed by no ill effects. He further states that the procedure is now endorsed by seven-eighths of the community's pediatricians and all but one of the obstetricians and gynecologists.

Is it permissible to have the **Berit** before the eighth day?

ANSWER: It would appear from the approach to the question that, in the mind of the correspondent, there is a close relationship between the testimony of the men of science and the specific question posed. Yet, in reality, the two are in no way related. To the physician, circumcision is a surgical operation indicated by hygienic factors; in Jewish tradition circumcision is a religious rite prescribed in the Mosaic law and designated as a sign of the everlasting covenant between God and Abraham's descendants (Gen. 17:11-14). The day on which the rite is to be performed, the eighth from birth, is also specified in the law, although the reason for it is not given and is still unknown (**ibid.**, 17:12; Lev. 12:3). Hence, it is that on the eighth day the **Berit Mila** is solemnized with a special religious ceremony which--though neither of Biblical nor Talmudic origin--has been scrupulously practiced by our people for many centuries and has served to enhance the significance of this ancient symbolic rite.

The question, therefore, is not whether it is physically safe to perform the act of circumcision before the eighth day. The answer to such a question, even if it proves inconclusive, must be left to the men in the medical profession. The real question for us to answer is whether it is wise in this instance to depart from the Biblical law which is universally observed by the Sons of the Covenant. Will circumcision shortly after birth, to which our neighbors presumably submit for hygienic reasons, retain its symbolic significance for us? Shall we not be running the risk of converting a religious rite into just another surgical operation? Have we more to gain from turning hygienists than from remaining religionists?

Viewed in this light, the question raised by the correspondent must be answered in the negative. The proposed change is bound to alter, in time, the character of the rite, and it would be sheer folly to persist in an ancient practice and yet have it divested of its religious meaning and purpose.

The slight inconvenience involved in returning the baby to the hospital on the eighth day, where the traditional **Berit Mila** could be properly solemnized, need hardly enter into our consideration of the question. No religious discipline could long endure were we to consult at every step our personal convenience, whether it be of parents, physicians, or hospital superintendents.

Israel Bettan

56. CIRCUMCISION PRIOR TO THE EIGHTH DAY
(1977)

QUESTION: May the circumcision of a new-born child be conducted prior to the eighth day? Would such a circumcision be considered as fulfilling the religious obligation of circumcising a child?

ANSWER: Circumcision is the oldest ritual connected with Judaism. It ties us to Abraham and our beginnings: "God further said to Abraham: 'As for you, you shall keep My covenant, you and your offerings to come throughout the ages. Such shall be the covenant, which you shall keep, between Me and you and your offspring to follow. Every male among you shall be circumcised. You shall circumcise the flesh of your foreskin, and that shall be a sign of the covenant between Me and you. At the age of eight days, every male among you throughout the generations shall be circumcised" (Gen. 17:9-13). The commandment is repeated in Leviticus 12:3. This has remained throughout our history as one of the most important commandments, and led to martyrdom already in Maccabean times (I Macc. 1:48, 60). The precise details of the nature of circumcision have been discussed in every Jewish code (**Yad**, Hil. Mila; **Tur**, Yoreh De-a 360ff; **Shulchan Aruch**, Yoreh De-a 260ff; see also **Gates of Mitzvah**, pp. 13ff). The ritual itself is done by the father, a **Mohel**, or a Jewish physician, though any Jew is qualified, on the eighth day after birth (**Shulchan Aruch**, Yoreh De-a 262.1). The exact day is most important, and the circumcision should take place on that day, even if it falls on Sabbath or the Day of Atonement, unless illness or weakness of the baby demands postponement.

If the circumcision was done prior to the eighth day, it is still considered valid **bedi-avad** (Asher ben Yehiel to Shab. 135a; Nathaniel Weil, **Korban Netan-el**, **ibid.**; Isserles to **Shulchan Aruch**, Yoreh De-a 262.1). Others have felt that if the circumcision took place before the eighth day, at least a drop of blood should be taken on the eighth day (Shabatai Cohen to **Shulchan Aruch**, Yoreh De-a 262.1; Aryeh Lev, **Sha-agat Aryeh**, #52). We would consider it valid without that.

Circumcision and the accompanying prayers are an act of affirmation of Judaism by the parents. As such, it should be done on the traditional day. The mere surgical act of **Mila** will not suffice for a **Berit Mila.**

We strongly urge parents to have the circumcision on the eighth day, even if it might take place at home. Hundreds of generations have observed this rite on the

eighth day.   Through the observance of this ritual on
the eighth day, we teach each new generation the importance of the keeping of the covenant of Abraham.   This
presents only a slight inconvenience to the family and
to the **Mohel** or Jewish physician.   If that is impossible, then it should be done as soon after the eighth day
as possible.   The ritual of circumcision must retain its
religious significance and not simply be a hygienic
device.   For this reason, we continue to stress circumcision on the eighth day.

Walter Jacob, Chairman
Leonard S. Kravitz
Eugene Lipman
W. Gunther Plaut
Harry A. Roth
Rav A. Soloff
Bernard Zlotowitz

See also:

S.B. Freehof, "Circumcision Before Eighth Day,"
Reform Responsa, pp. 90ff.

57.   ANESTHETIC FOR CIRCUMCISION
(Vol. LXXV, 1965, pp. 99-101)

QUESTION: A physician performing a circumcision
insisted upon using an anesthetic.   Should this be
permitted or even encouraged from the point of view
of Jewish legal tradition?

ANSWER: This question has been asked a number of times
in recent years when the use of anesthetics (even for
minor surgery) has come into general use.   The question
is asked usually with regard to adult converts.   Sometimes a convert will not consent to circumcision unless
an anesthetic be used.   In one case the circumstances
were reversed, and the convert insisted that no anesthetic be used because he wanted to feel pain, since he
considered the pain to be sacrificial.   Sometimes it is
asked with regard to children.   A Jewish child had not
been circumcised in infancy (for reasons of ill health).
Now, at the age of five, he is to be circumcised and the
mother insists that a local anesthetic be used.   Out of
these various cases a general attitude has emerged as to

the use of anesthetics in circumcision for adults and
for children.

Perhaps the first discussion of the question was by
Meir Arik, the great Galician authority in the past
generation. In his responsa (**Imrei Yosher II, 140**) he
decides definitely in the negative. His arguments are
worth notice because they reveal the general mood of the
authorities of the time to all new suggestions which may
affect the ceremonial laws. He calls attention to the
Talmudic debate (in Kiddushin 21b) which deals with the
piercing of the ear of a Hebrew slave who refuses to be
set free. The Talmud there speaks of **sam** (an anesthetic
medicine). This provides, he said, that the Talmud was
well acquainted with such medicines. Yet, since the
Talmud does not mention the use of anesthetic medicines
in circumcision, it clearly was opposed to their use.
Furthermore, he says that the Midrash (**Genesis Rabba**
47.9) tells that Abraham was in pain because of his
circumcision, and it was for that pain that God gave him
additional reward. Then he concludes with a general
statement in the nature of a warning, namely, that we
have never used anesthetics in the past and, God forbid,
that we should introduce any novelties.

This firm and indignant negative is not shared by
the majority of the scholars who have dealt with the
question. For example, Bezalel Shafran (**Responsa Rabaz,**
#125) refutes the prohibitory opinion found in the book
Sefer Haberit, which insisted that the circumcised must
be awake for the reason that the fulfillments of
commandments require conscious intention (**Kavana**).
Shafran proves that a child may be asleep during the
operation and this fact would not impair the legal
validity of the circumcision.

The strongest opinion in favor of the use of anesthetics comes from the famous Rabbi of Kishinev, Judah
Lev Zirelsohn (who was murdered by the Nazis). It was
he who dealt with the question of the five-year-old boy
mentioned above. In his **Ma-archei Lev**, #53, after reviewing various arguments, he comes to the general conclusion that the Torah nowhere requires pain in the
circumcision, and therefore, he agrees in the case mentioned to the use of anesthetics.

Gedalia Felder of Toronto, who has done yeoman
service in collecting and organizing the Law and Customs
in his four-volume work **Yesodei Yeshurun**, has now written a special work on adoption, conversion, etc. In
this work (**Nachalat Tsevi**, p. 57) he summarizes the
various opinions on this question and also doubts the
negative opinion of Meir Arik.

In the light of the above, we may conclude that
there is no objection to anesthetics. The law does not
insist upon pain in the fulfillment of this commandment.

However, to this extent Meir Arik is correct: that we should not introduce novelties unless there is a good reason for them. If the child is likely to be naturally asleep during the operation (as often happens), the law does not require that he be wakened (cf. the opinion of Bezalel Shafran). However, if the operation is done by a doctor, and he insists that an anesthetic be used, then we may assume that he has a good reason for it, and we should not raise any objections. In general, we should not institute the use of anesthetics as a regular procedure, but we should permit them when the surgeon or the parent asks that they be used.

Addendum

You now ask about the popular idea that the wine which is (sometimes) given the infant during circumcision is for the purpose of allaying the pain of circumcision.

It is customary for the **Mohel** to give a drop or a touch of wine with his fingertip after the two blessings, when the phrase from Ezekiel is used: "Live in thy blood." This custom is mentioned by Joseph Caro in **Shulchan Aruch** (Yoreh De-a 265.2). Of all the classic commentators, only the Spaniard Abudarham gives an explanation; but his explanation has to do with the sinful Israelites being given to drink the water into which their Golden Calf had been ground. A later commentator tries to connect it with the word "live" in the Ezekiel quotation, and attempts to have the drop of wine symbolize eternal life.

These explanations are obviously forced. One may say that no explanation is given for the drop of wine. Nowadays they sometimes give the child a bit of cloth or cake soaked in wine. This would lend itself to the notion that it was for the purpose of allaying pain. But the texts only speak of a "drop" or a finger touch. This could hardly have any pain-allaying effect, and therefore, this could not be the reason.

For the sake of completeness, it might be added that another taste of wine is sometimes given the child on fast-days at the blessing. The **Mohel** recites the blessing, but since it is a fast-day, he may not taste the wine. Therefore (in order that the blessing not be a "vain blessing"), a taste of the wine is given to the child (cf. Isserles to Yoreh Dea 265.4, Orach Chayim 621:3). But Abudarham quotes Ibn Gayyat and Maimonides, who object to the practice and who prefer that on fast-days the wine blessing be omitted entirely. There is a wide variance in the **minhagim** about this practice. Some say: Give it to the **Sandak** to taste; some say: Give it to the young boys present to taste; some say: Give it to the mother; and some say: Give it to the child. **Mishna Berura** (The **Chafets Chayim**) to #621, says: It all depends on custom, and each custom has its basis. For a fuller discussion, see **Edut LeYisra-el** by Jacob Werdiger (Benei Berak, 1963), p. 127, #3.

The present custom of giving the child a wine-soaked object to suck, which leads to the notion of allaying pain, is not authentic. Only a drop was used, and pain alleviation is neither mentioned in the sources nor possible.

Solomon B. Freehof

58. NOLAD MAHUL (BORN CIRCUMCISED)
(Vol. XXVIII, 1918, p. 117-118)

QUESTION: The following message was received by the Chairman of the Responsa Committee, and his wired reply is appended:

> Have case of a **Nolad Mahul**, six weeks old; **Mohel** examined eighth day and said nothing to be done; then physician examined yesterday. Organ absolutely clean from **Orla** and prohibited operation. Am asked to name child. Please wire opinion at my expense upon receipt of this.

Rabbi Kohler's Opinion

Physician's opinion is paramount. Name child without the **Mila**.

K. Kohler

Rabbi Deutch dissents from this opinion:

Rabbi Deutsch's Opinion

Dr. Kohler's responsum on **Nolad Mahul** is wrongly conceived. No rabbinic authority can decide to circumcise, where there is nothing to circumcise. The point would be, whether the old practice of letting blood, "**Matif dam berit**," should be followed.

G. Deutsch

(Vol. XXIX, 1919, pp. 74-75)

I beg leave as Chairman of the Committee on Responsa to recur to my incomplete report in last year's proceedings of the Central Conference of American Rabbis, pp. 117ff. When sending it in I was at the hospital and had then and there no opportunity of elaborating on it and of explaining my telegram concerning the **Nolad Mahul**. I intentionally avoided referring to the halachic rule of "letting blood" in the telegram in order not to offend the laymen for whom the **Mila** should always have a spiritual and not a mere physiological character. Dr. Deutsch in his remarks leaves unanswered the question whether, from our Reform point of view, "the old practice of letting blood" ("**Tsarich lehatif dam berit**") should be followed or not.

Here, then, I would first of all call attention to the fact that the Mosaic law, despite the term "blood circumcision" in Ex. 4:26, does by no means imply that the bloodletting is essential, as if the sacrificial blood would constitute the covenant as in Ex. 24:8. In fact, the School of Hillel, according to the older version, does not regard it as a Biblical command, and therefore, would not have it done on a Sabbath day (Shab. 135a), though Rav insists on it (Yer., Yev. 8.8d). It was considered more essential in the case of proselytes, wherefore a special benediction is to be recited at the circumcision of proselytes emphasizing the letting of blood of the covenant with reference to Jeremiah 33:25 (Shab. 137b; Yoreh De-a 268.8). Be that as it may, we can neither admit that the case of the **Nolad Mahul** is simply an **orla kevusha** ("a suppressed foreskin"), as is the view of those who require the letting of blood, nor do we believe in the idea of sacrifice (as at a former Conference we have decided in the case of adult proselytes to do away with the circumcision altogether, laying all the stress on the spiritual idea of the Covenant). I hope that this opinion of mine will be ratified by the members of the committee and endorsed by the Conference.

K. Kohler

NOTE:

In the case of **Nolad Mahul** it is not necessary, if not impossible, to perform **Mila**, so the only question remaining concerns **Hatafat Dam**, the letting of blood (Ex. 4:26). And there is a very marked distinction between **Mila** and **Hatafat Dam**. **Berit Mila**

must take place on the eighth day, even if it is
Sabbath or Yom Kippur, but where **Hatafat Dam** is
required, the School of Hillel did not regard it as
a Biblical command, and therefore would not have it
done on the Sabbath (Shab. 135a).

Since we do not consider **Hatafat Dam** for a child
born circumcised **(Nolad Mahul)** as being a Biblical
commandment, we should continue to abide by the
responsum of K. Kohler, as it appears in the **CCAR
Yearbook** (vol. 28, 1918, p. 117), which clearly
states: **Nolad Mahul** should be named without **Mila.**

There are also references to the early Reformers
who named and consecrated uncircumcised baby boys
(though we do not subscribe to this practice) in
the synagogue (based on Jer. 31:30ff; see also
Gunther Plaut, **The Growth of Reform Judaism**, p.
228). If the uncircumcised was treated so, then
surely the **Nolad Mahul** should pose no question.

Responsa Committee (1980)

59. NAMING OF CHILDREN
(Vol. XLII, 1932, pp. 316-360)

Names of persons, among the Jews as among other
peoples of antiquity, were considered of great importance and regarded as possessing special significance.
They were not merely designations whereby a person might
be distinguished from other persons in the group. They
were believed to serve other purposes besides those of
identification and recognition. To the question, "What
is in a name?" the ancient Jews--and, to a certain extent, their later descendants--would answer: "There is a
whole lot in it." Hence, great importance has been
attached among the Jews of all times to the selection of
a proper and fitting name for the newly born child.

The Bible does not expressly tell us by what considerations one should be guided in the selection of a
name, nor does it clearly formulate any definite theories about the significance of names. But from various
casual remarks about individual names, scattered through
the Bible, we may gather what ideas and beliefs prevailed among the people of Biblical times, in connection
with personal names and their significance.

Without entering into a lengthy discussion of the
Biblical names, their meaning and significance,[1] we may

----

[1] Comp. on these questions Cheyne-Black, **Encyclopedia**

safely state that the following ideas concerning the purpose, function, and significance of personal names were current among the people of Biblical times.[2]

(1) The purpose of a name is to describe adequately the personality of its bearer, to identify him, and to make him recognizable as a distinct individual not only by his fellow human beings, but also in the world of the spirits by angels or demons, who might have something to do with him as a distinct individual. This purpose of adequately describing the person and marking him as a distinct individual is accomplished by choosing a name which would point to some characteristic or indicate some peculiarity in the person himself, or allude to his origin, to the station or social position into which he was born, or to the circumstances surrounding his birth in the world in general or in his family or group.

(2) The name has still another purpose in that it may be prophetic of the fortunes and the experiences of the person to whom it is given. It has, accordingly, the function of suggesting what the person is to be. It predicts his future and determines his fate.[3] It presages his history and experiences in life, pointing to the great things he will accomplish--as in the case of Noah (Gen. 5:29)--or to the conditions that will prevail or the events that will happen during his lifetime--as in the case of Peleg (Gen. 10:25) and of Solomon (I Chron. 22:9). In other words, **nomina sunt omina**.

(3) Even more: the belief in the power of the uttered word, namely, that by merely saying something we might actually bring it about--a belief current among Jews in Biblical times as among other ancient peoples--caused another notion to be cherished in connection with proper names. This was that by giving the child a certain name, we produce in him the qualities indicated by that name. The name given to a person, so it was believed, may influence his character and actually make him what the name would suggest him to be. Thus Jacob's conduct towards his brother Esau was suggested and, as it were, predetermined by his very name (Gen. 27:36). A man's character, so it was believed, is what his name

---

Biblica III, pp. 3264-3307.

[2] Comp. Walter Schulze, "Der Namensglaube bei den Babylonern," in **Anthropos** XXVI (1931), pp. 895-928, where the ideas as to the significance of names in Biblical times among the Hebrews and other Semitic peoples are discussed and the literature on the subject given.

[3] Comp. Schulze, **op. cit.**, p. 909.

pronounces it to be: "For, as his name is, so is he" (I Sam. 25:25).

(4) As a corollary of the belief in the absolute identity of the name with the personality, there was another belief current in Biblical times, namely, that when the two no longer coincide, they must be made to coincide. When a change takes place in the person, there must go with it a corresponding change in the name.[4] In other words, when a person's name, for one reason or another, no longer adequately describes his personality or expresses his character and fortunes, or when a change in the character and fortunes or position is wished for, the name must accordingly be changed. The practice of changing the name of a person is recorded in many instances in the Bible. The names of Abram and Sarai are changed to Abraham and Sarah (Gen. 17:5 and 15) to suggest and, in a manner, make possible the change in their position and fortunes. Jacob's name is changed to Israel to indicate a change in his character and to point to his achievements which gave him a new position (Gen. 32:29; 35:10). Jacob changes the name of his second child from Rachel, whom the mother had called Ben Oni ("the son of my sorrow") to Benjamin ("the son of my right hand"), probably to suggest better luck for the child. Likewise, Moses changes the name of Hosea the Son of Nun to Joshua (Num. 13:16), probably also to suggest success and good luck on his trip with the spies.[5] And Naomi expressly says, "Call me not Naomi, that is, Pleasant; call me Marah, that is Bitter, for the Almighty hath dealt very bitterly with me" (Ruth 1:20).

(5) Still another belief intimately connected with, or resulting from, the belief in the mystical identity of the personality with the name, was that one cannot exist without the other. Just as a man's name lives with him as long as he is kept alive, so also he lives with his name as long as the latter is kept alive. It was believed, then, that if, and as long as, a person's

---

[4] Comp. **ibid.**, p. 906. The changes in the names of Joseph (Gen. 41:45), of Elyakim (II Kings 23:34), of Mattaniah (**ibid.**, 24:17), and of Daniel, Hananiah, Mishael, and Azariah (Dan. 1:17) were made because of the change that had taken place in their position. Likewise, when--as the prophet predicts--God will in the future "call His servants by another name" (Isa. 65:15), it will be in order to indicate the change in their fortunes or position. See also **ibid.**, 62:2.

[5] So it was understood by the rabbis of the Talmud (Sota 34b). Comp. also **Mechilta**, Amalek III (Friedmann, 57ab).

name is kept alive and remembered, the person himself
continues to live. Complete obliteration of a man's
name meant his utter destruction. He is "cut off from
the land of the living and his name is no more remembered" (Jer. 11:19). "To make their memory (i.e., of
people) cease from among men" meant to "make an end of
them" (Deut. 32:26).

Hence, great importance was attached to the preservation of the name of a person, which meant the securing
of a sort of immortality for that person. Preservation
of the name merely meant remembering that name. This
remembering of the name, however, was--in Biblical times
at least--not to be achieved by calling other persons,
children or descendants, by the same name. It was to be
insured by leaving someone or something, children or
property, which--having belonged to that person--would
always be identified with his name, so that subsequent
generations, in referring to his descendants or his
property, would mention the name of the person who was
the ancestor of those descendants or the original owner
or builder of that property. In this manner would his
name be recalled and remembered. That this--and not the
naming of descendants by the same name--was the manner
in which the memory of a name was to be insured, is
evident from a few instances in the Bible. Thus, the
daughters of Zelophehad could see no way of preventing
their dead father's name from being "done away from
among his family" other than by obtaining a possession
among the brethren of their father (Num. 2:4), for this
possession which was due their father would be known as
their inheritance from their father Zelophehad, and thus
his name would be remembered. If the name of the father
could have been kept alive and remembered merely by
naming their children after their father, they would
have had no valid reason for their claim to a possession
among the brethren of their father.

Again: Absalom, who had no son to keep his name in
remembrance, erected for himself a pillar which was
called "Absalom's Monument," and thus caused his name to
be remembered (II Sam. 18:18). Likewise: to prevent the
name of the brother who died childless from being blotted out of Israel, the firstborn that his widow bears to
his brother, her second husband, must "succeed in the
name of the brother that is dead" (Deut. 25:5-6). This
means not that he should be named like the dead brother,
but that he should be known as and called the dead
brother's son, thus keeping the dead brother's name in
remembrance. It did not mean that he should be called
by the same name as the dead brother.[6] This is evident

---

[6] The possibility of such an interpretation of the
phrase "**Yakum al shem achiv hamet**" is rejected by the

from the fact that the son that Ruth bore to Boaz was called Oved and not Mahlon, like Ruth's first husband (Ruth 4:17). But he must have been called Oved the son Mahlon, so that the women, in calling him by this name, could well say: "There is a son born to Naomi." For Naomi's husband Mahlon was in a manner reborn because his name would from then on be kept alive and remembered.

Likewise, when Jacob, in blessing Joseph and his children, said, "And let my home and the names of my fathers Abraham and Isaac be called on them" (Gen. 48:16), he only meant that when people will call or refer to Ephraim and Manasseh as the descendants of Abraham, Isaac, and Jacob, the latter names thus would be recalled and remembered. He certainly did not mean that Ephraim and Manasseh, or any of their children, should be named after their grandfathers and be given the name of Abraham, Isaac, or Jacob.[7] For, as far as the Bible records show, no child was ever named after Abraham, Isaac, or Jacob. In fact, with but one possible exception, we do not find in the Bible any instances of, or references to, the custom in pre-exilic times[8] of naming children after parents or grandparents, deceased or alive. This absolute and persistent silence about such a custom strongly suggests that not only was such a custom not in vogue, but that there were definite objections to, and a determined avoidance of such a practice. These objections to, or avoidance of this practice would seem to have been based upon the very belief in the mystical identity of the name with the personality.

This belief in the absolute identity of the person with the name precluded, at least in the popular mind, the possibility of two persons in the same family, or

---

rabbis of the Talmud. See **Sifrei**, Deut. 289 (Friedmann, 125b) and Yevamot 24a.

[7] Comp., however, **Mechilta**, Pischa 5 (Friedmann, 5a), where the passage "**Ve-omer hamal-ach hago-el**" is probably a later interpolation.

[8] It is true that in I Chron. 3:6-8, in the list of David's children, Eliphelet is mentioned twice, and according to Rashi, **ad loc.**, David had two children by the name of Eliphelet, and the second child was named after the one that had died. But aside from the fact that these lists are not reliable (comp. the list of David's children in II Sam. 5:14-16, where it is stated that only one child by the name of Eliphelet was born to David), the Book of Chronicles was written at a later period, and it reflects the ideas of its time, not those of the time of David.

the same group, having the same name. For it would mean
having one and the same individuality (designated by and
identical with that name) exist as two, which, of
course, is impossible. There could be two persons having the same first name given to them in order to predict success or describe similar circumstances which
prevailed at the time of the birth of both (or of each
one) of them, or to express the same ambitions cherished
for each by its parents. In such a case, each one--
being further described as "the son of so-and-so"--would
thus be marked off as a separate and distinct individuality, different from the one with the similar name
belonging to a different group or family. But in one
and the same family no two persons could conceivably
have one and the same name.

The individuality and character which are expressed
by, and are absolutely identical with a certain name,
could belong to only one person in the same group or
family. To give the name of one person to another of
the same group or family would, according to popular
conception, mean to transfer the very being, the individuality, of the one person who is identified with the
name to another person in the family, with the result
that the one from whom the name (with the personality
identical with it) is taken must cease to exist. The
same consideration would keep people from naming children after deceased relatives or ancestors. To give the
child the name of a departed ancestor would, according
to the popular conception in Biblical times, not have
the effect of keeping the memory of the name of the
deceased alive. It would have just the opposite effect.
It would destroy and wipe out the remembrance of the
departed. For all that goes with his name--his very
being, his memory, and the mystical associations connected with it--would have been transferred to another
person to whom the name had been given and who would now
be identical with that other individual. At the mention
or recall of that name, subsequent generations would
have in mind and keep alive the memory of the second
bearer and not the original bearer of the name from whom
it had been taken.

It may, therefore, be stated with absolute certainty that in pre-exilic times the selection of a name for
a child was determined solely by consideration for the
child itself. The name was to serve the purpose of
adequately describing and identifying the person by
pointing to his origin and history, suggesting his
character, or predicting his future. Consideration of
the memory of another person, parent or grandparent,
never entered into the selection of a name for a child.
For the name **per se** given to any person was not to serve
as a reminder of any person who may have previously had

the same name. We do not find in the Bible any indication of the pre-exilic custom of naming children after
their ancestors. We have no record in the Bible of a
person in pre-exilic times being named after his grandfather, with but one exception. Nachor, the brother of
Abraham, had the same name as his grandfather. For
Terach's father's name was likewise Nachor (Gen. 11:25-
26).[9] But even in this one exceptional case, we have no
indication that the reason Terach named his son Nachor
was to keep alive the memory of his father. Most likely
the same circumstances or conditions that determined the
selection of the name for the grandfather prevailed also
in the case--or at the time of the birth--of the grandson, and these (not the consideration for the memory of
the grandfather) determined the selection of the name.
In the genealogical list of the kings of the House of
David, no two persons appear with the same name.[10]
Likewise, in the list of the High Priests of the First
Temple, as given in Ezra 7:1-5 and I Chron. 6:35-38, no
name is repeated.[11]

In post-exilic times, however, and especially with
the Hellenistic period, we notice a remarkable change in
the practice of selecting names for children. In the
list of the names of the High Priests of the Second
Temple, of the Maccabean rulers, and later on in the
family of Hillel (as well as of later Talmudic teachers)
we find many instances of a grandson having the same
name as the father. This clearly points to the prevalent practice of naming children after their grandpar-

---

[9] Perhaps it was thought that since the father of the
grandfather was named Serug (so that the grandfather's
full name was "Nachor, the son of Serug"), he was by his
full name sufficiently distinguished from the grandson
(whose full name was "Nachor, son of Terach"), and was
thus marked as a separate individual. Hence, since the
circumstances at birth, or other considerations, made it
desirable to call the child Nachor, it was deemed proper
and safe to call him so. A custom, however, to name
after grandparents would involve the repetition of the
full name; e.g., if Nachor, the son of Terach, would
name his son Terach, there would be two persons by the
full name of "Terach, son of Nachor," indistinguishable
from one another. This was inconceivable.

[10] Comp. L. Loew, **Die Lebensalter in der juedischen
Literatur** (Szegedin, 1875), p. 94, and note 49 on p.
385.

[11] The list in I Chron. 5:30-41, which disagrees with
the two lists in Ezra, is not to be considered as
authentic. Comp. Loew, **op. cit.**, p. 385, note 50.

ents. Now, among the Greeks it was the general custom to give the children the names of their grandparents. It would, however, be a mistake to assume with L. Loew[12] that the Palestinian Jews of the period of the Second Temple borrowed this custom from the Greeks. For we find instances of a grandson having the same name as his grandfather among the Palestinian Jews of post-exilic times even before they came in contact with the Greeks.[13] Then again, we find that among the Elephantine Jews, children were named after their grandparents.[14] As the custom of naming children after ancestors was prevalent among the Egyptians, the Elephantine Jews no doubt borrowed this custom from their Egyptian neighbors. And it is reasonable to assume that from the Elephantine Jews the custom came to the Palestinian Jews (if they did not get it from the Egyptians directly). But, no doubt, changed conditions or beliefs among the Palestinian Jews must have helped to make this foreign custom generally accepted. Certainly the innovation of a practice unknown in pre-exilic times could not have been introduced without corresponding changes of ideas--or at least certain modifications of those ideas--prevailing in the pre-exilic times, which precluded or prevented the practice represented by the innovation. The fact that this new custom of naming children after ancestors represented a departure from the custom which prevailed in pre-exilic times and was recognized by the people as such, is expressly stated by two rabbis of the second century, who also advanced theories of their own as to the reasons for this innovation. The statements of these two teachers, R. Jose b. Chalafta and R. Simon b. Gamliel, are found in the Midrash Gen. R. 37.10, and read as follows: "**Rabbi Yosei omer: 'Harishonim, al yedei shehayu makirim yachaseihem, hayu motsi-in leshem hame-ora, aval anachnu, she-ein anu yode-in et yechaseinu, anu motsi-in leshem avoteinu.'**

---

[12] Op. cit., pp. 94-95.

[13] Against Zunz, "Namen der Juden," in **Gesammelte Schriften** II (Berlin, 1876), p. 19. The name Jadua mentioned in Neh. 12:11 and 22 is probably the same as Yojada. So Jadua had the same name as his grandfather (or great grandfather?), and he was given this name long before Alexander came to Palestine, that is, before the Jews had any contact with the Greeks.

[14] See G. Buchanan Gray, "Children Named after Ancestors in the Aramaic Papyri; from Elephantine and Assuan," in **Studien zur Semitischen Philologie und Religionsgeschichte, Julius Wellhausen zum Siebzigsten Geburtstag** (Glessen, 1914), pp. 163ff.

Rabban Shim-on ben Gamli-el omer: 'Harishonim, al yedei shehayu mishtameshin beruach hakodesh, hayu motsi-in leshem hame-ora, aval anu, she-einenu mishtameshin beruach hakodesh, anu motsi-in leshem avoteinu.'"   "R. Jose says: 'The ancients [or former generations], who well knew their genealogical descent, would name their children according to special occasions or with refer- ence to some event. We, who do not so well know our genealogical descent, give our children the names of our ancestors.' R. Simon b. Gamliel says: 'The ancients, because they could make use of the Holy Spirit, would name their children according to special occasions or with reference of some event. We, who cannot make use of the Holy Spirit, give our children the names of our ancestors.'"[15]

It should be stated first that both these teachers agree as to the time of the period in which the new practice came into vogue; they differ only as to the reason for, or the cause of the innovation. For the term "the ancients" or "former generations" ("harisho- nim") is understood by both to mean the people of pre- exilic times or the generations up to Ezra (as contrast- ed with the generations after Ezra, or the people during the time of the Second Temple and after its destruc- tion).

According to Talmudic tradition, there were espe- cially two features which distinguished the period of the Second Temple from that of the First Temple, marking off the former as inferior in comparison with the lat- ter. The one characteristic of the period of the Second Temple was the absence of the revelation of the Holy Spirit (or the cessation of prophecy). For "with the death of the last of the prophets, Haggai, Zachariah, and Malachi [i.e., at the beginning of the period of the Second Temple], prophecy ceased in Israel and the Holy Spirit no longer revealed itself" (Tosefta, Sota 13.2, and B. Yoma 9b). The other feature was the presence, to a considerable proportion, of foreign elements in the population. Among the people who returned with Ezra and formed the new community--not to mention those who had remained in the land and later formed a part of the new community--there were many people of non-Jewish descent or at least people who were unable to trace their gene-

---

[15] I quote according to the reading in the edition of Theodor Albeck (comp. Commentaries). The reading given in **Yalkut** to Chronicles, 1073 ("**Harishonim, al yedei shelo hayu makirin et yichusan, hayu motsi-in leshem hame-ora, aval anu, she-anu makirin et yichusenu, anu motsi-in leshem avoteinu**") is a gross mistake, based upon a misunderstanding of the purport and meaning of R. Jose's saying.

alogies and could not prove their Jewish descent (M. Kiddushin 4.1).[16]

It was one or the other of these conditions which prevailed during the time of the Second Temple and distinguished it from the period preceding it, that--according to the respective opinions of R. Jose and R. Simon b. Gamliel--was responsible for the innovation of naming children after ancestors. According to R. Jose, it was the composite character of the population--the fact that not all the people could accurately trace their genealogy and prove with certainty their purely Jewish descent--that prompted many people to call their children by the names of their fathers, thus pointing to their Jewish origin and indicating by their very names that they were descended from Jewish ancestors. This theory of R. Jose, however, is insufficient to explain the change in the practice. For, on the one hand, we find, as far as our records show, that the practice of naming children after their grandparents was first introduced among the families of the High Priests, about whose pure Jewish descent there was not the least doubt, and who, therefore, did not need to indicate by the names which they gave their children that the latter were descended from good Jewish families. On the other hand, we find that proselytes were called by such names as Judah and Benjamin.[17] Hence, even names of great Jewish forefathers would not necessarily prove the pure Jewish descent of their bearers. These two facts are sufficient to disprove the theory of R. Jose.

----

[16] The term "Shetuki" ("a silent one") designates one who could not prove his pure Jewish descent, as the records were silent about him. Hence Abba Saul would designate him as "Beduki" ("one who is to be investigated"). The meaning of those terms was misunderstood, hence the fanciful interpretations in the Gamara (Kiddushin 70a and 74a; Yevamot 100b). As to these records on family registers which were kept in the archives of the Temple, see Lauterbach, **The Three Books Found in the Temple at Jerusalem** (New York, 1918), and comp. also S. Klein in **Tsiyon** (Jerusalem, 1930), vol. IV, who, without having seen my essay, independently arrived at almost the same conclusion (i.e., that the three books kept in the Temple were genealogical records and not Torah copies).

[17] An Ammonite proselyte by the name of Judah (**Yehuda ger Amoni**) is mentioned in the Mishna (Yadayim 4.4), and an Egyptian proselyte, a disciple of R. Akiba, by the name of Benjamin is mentioned in the Tosefta (Kiddushin 5.4), though some texts have the reading **Minyamin** instead of **Binyamin**, but it is the same name.

According to R. Simon b. Gamliel, it was the absence of the Holy Spirit--the fact that they could no
longer make use of divine inspiration in order to suggest or determine by the very name which they gave their
children what the latter's fate and destiny should be--
that caused the people to name their children after
their ancestors. This theory is not satisfactory, either. In the first place, even in pre-exilic times, in
the age of prophecy, the Holy Spirit was not poured out
over all flesh, and not all the people were favored with
divine inspiration; and yet all the people gave their
children's names **leshem hame-ora**, according to the occasion, or alluding to certain conditions or events. And
in post-exilic times, notwithstanding the fact that
prophecy had ceased, the Holy Spirit was not altogether
absent and there were, according to Talmudic reports,
instances of manifestations of the Holy Spirit even
during the times of the Second Temple.[18]
     Accordingly, the difference between the pre-exilic
and post-exilic times as regards the manifestation of
the Holy Spirit was merely one of degree. Furthermore:
in general the people during the period of the Second
Temple and even after its destruction, without claiming
any prophetic powers, nevertheless believed--as we shall
see--in the suggestive, if not the absolutely determinative, influence of the names upon the fortunes and char-
acters of their bearers. Hence, the cessation of prophecy or the infrequency of the manifestation of the Holy
Spirit could have been no reason why the people should
not continue as in former times to give their children
such names as would express their hopes and aspirations
for their fortunes. At any rate, such names as are not
of a prophetic nature and do not seek to express any
hopes for the future, but which merely point to a characteristic of the child or refer to the circumstances at
the time of its birth (e.g., Isaac, Perez, and Zerah),
could certainly have continued to be given by people who
not only disclaimed any prophetic powers but even dis-
believed in the suggestive powers of any uttered name.
     Accordingly, neither R. Jose nor R. Simon b. Gam-
liel with their respective theories satisfactorily explain why the older practice of pre-exilic times should
not have continued in post-exilic times. In fact, upon
a closer scrutiny of their statements, we find that
these two rabbis do not even say that the older practice
was discarded. For they do not say: "**Ein anu motsi-in
leshem hame-ora**," "We no longer give our children names

---

[18] Comp. A. Marmorstein, "Der heilige Geist in der
rabbinischen Legende," in **Archiv fuer Religions-
wissenschaft** XXVIII (1930), pp. 286-303, especially pp.
291ff.

referring to an occasion or event." All they say is: "We give our children names like the names of our ancestors." This by no means implies an abolition of the older practice. Indeed, the older custom was never abolished or discarded. It has continued, though not so universally as before, throughout the Talmudic period and up to the present day.[19] Hence, what is historically accurate in the statements of these two teachers is that the innovation of naming children after ancestors came into use not to the exclusion, but alongside, of the older practice. Their theories as to the cause of, or reason for, the innovation we have found to be insufficient. But if the older practice was never abolished and the innovation merely represented an additional practice which gradually became more and more universally accepted, it is perhaps a mistake to ascribe it to one cause or to seek to account for it by one reason only. Undoubtedly, the custom of naming children after their ancestors, so prevalent in Talmudic times and ever since, was the result of a long and gradual process whereby a foreign custom, finding its way into the life of the people, was helped and furthered by, and in turn effected, changes and modifications in some popular beliefs which were opposed to such a practice.

We must, therefore, seek to ascertain what ideas were current among the people in Talmudic times in regard to the function, purpose, and possible effects of proper names, and examine to what degree they represent developments in and modifications of ideas of Biblical times. This will explain how a custom unknown in pre-exilic times came to be so prevalent in post-exilic times, and will also help us to understand all the practices that obtained in Talmudic times in connection with naming children.

There is especially one popular belief current in Talmudic times which will help us understand the ideas which the people entertained in regard to the selection of names. This is the belief in the power of the uttered word--or at any rate intimately connected with it--i.e., the notion that the agents of the heavenly

---

[19] Thus, Jesus is reported to have been given his name **Yeshua** to suggest or predict that "he will save his people from their sins" (Matt. 1:21). Whether this actually was the intention of those who gave him his name, or they merely named him after a relative, is for our purpose irrelevant. At any rate, it shows that the writers of the Gospel assumed the prevalence of the custom of naming children **leshem hame-ora**. The names **Chisda** and **Tavyomi** in Talmudic times were names **leshem hame-ora**. So also, no doubt, were the names **Kidor** and **Lichluchit**.

administration, both good and bad angels, or angels and demons, were, like human agents, liable to misunderstanding and mistakes.

When three heavenly agents or floating spirits hear the word uttered by any human being, they are not always quick to recognize that it is a human voice speaking. They sometimes mistake it for the voice of a spirit or of a heavenly authority giving them an order which they must carry out.[20] If the uttered word pronounces something good, the good angels--eager to do good--hasten to fulfill it in the belief that they are carrying out a command from on high. On the other hand, if the word uttered is of an evil nature, the floating bad angels or demons--always eager to do harm--seize upon it quickly and hasten to bring about the evil,[21] believing that in doing so they act under the authority of a higher command. These two beliefs, the one in the power of the uttered word and the other in the fallibility of the spirits, largely determined the attitude of the people in the selection of names for their children.

Because of the power attached to the uttered word, it was believed that the name given to a person actually influenced his character and determined his destiny and his future. This belief is clearly expressed in the following statement of the Talmud (B. Berachot 7b): "Mina lan dishma garem? Amar Rabbi El-azar: 'De-amar kera, Lechu chazu mif-alot YHWH asher sam shamot ba-arets. Al tikrei shamot ela shemot.'" ("How do we know that the name is a determining factor in the character and destiny of a person? Said R. Eleazar: 'Scripture says: Come, behold the workings of the Lord who hath accomplished **shamot** in the earth (Ps. 46:9). Do not read **Ahamot** which is rendered **desolations** but read shemot, meaning **names**'"). In this verse, then, R. Eleazar finds expressed the idea that in dealing with human

---

[20] This, in my opinion, is the meaning of the phrase "Havei kishgaga sheyotse-a milifnei hashalit," which occurs in the Talmud (Ketubot 62b, and **passim**) in explanation of how the evil spoken, even without the intention to wish it, came to happen. I hope to deal with this subject more exhaustively elsewhere.

[21] Hence, one should never open his mouth to say something which Satan might hasten to bring about: "Al yiftach adam piv lasatan" (Berachot 19a, and parallel). There is another aspect to this belief which is not connected with the belief in the fallibility of the angel; and this is that Satan may simply cite the statement uttered by the person as an argument against him, claiming that the person himself admitted his guilt or invited the misfortune.

beings the Lord, through His agents, carries out what their names suggest, or, as Rabbi Samuel Eidels in his comment on this passage explains it: "**Shepe-ulot Hashem nimshachim acharei hashem shel adam shehu gorem**" ("The divine workings are controlled by or follow the suggestions contained in the name of the person"). This simply means that the heavenly agents take a person at his name's value. Believing that the name of a person had been decreed or pronounced upon him by a higher authority, they proceed to carry out all that the name implies and endow that person with goodness or wickedness, or bestow upon him happiness or misery, according to the meaning of the name. R. Meir, a famous teacher of the second century, seems to have been very much addicted to this belief, and he always paid special attention to names. From the very name of a man he would draw conclusions about his character. Thus, in the well-known story told in Yoma 83b, he concluded from the very name of an innkeeper that he was a wicked man, and he proved to be right. Here the Biblical idea that a man is what his name pronounces him to be again comes to the fore. The name given to a person cannot remain ineffective. It is bound to make his character coincide with it. Hence, in a later Midrash it is strongly recommended that one should be careful in examining the meaning of names, so as to call his son by a name which would destine him to become a righteous man, for indeed often[22] the very name causes goodness or badness of character: "**Le-olam yivdok adam bashemot likro livno hara-uy lihyot tsadik, ki lif-amim hashem gorem tov o gorem ra**" (Midrash Tanchuma, Ha-azinu 7).

The idea which we find current in Biblical times (i.e., that the identity of the name with the person demands that they coincide and that a change in the one of necessity requires or automatically produces a corresponding change in the other) was also current in Talmudic times. In Talmudic times, however, one aspect of it--namely, that a change in the name effects a change in the status or destiny of the person--is more developed and more emphasized. The other aspect of this idea--namely, that a change in status or position requires a corresponding change of the name--is not so much emphasized, though from many indications we may conclude that it also obtained in Talmudic times. Thus, e.g., R. Meir, whose original name was Me'asha, is said to have been given the name Meir, which means "enlightener," after he had become a great scholar, one who

---

22 The expression "**lif-amim**" ("sometimes" or "often") is merely put in in order not to deny the principle of free will.

enlightened the eyes of the wise in the study of the Law
(Eruvin 13b; see **Dikdukei Soferim, ad loc.**).

The belief that a change in the name effects a
change in the status was strongly developed and almost
generally accepted in Talmudic times, because of its
connection with, or the support it derived from, the
other notion so generally accepted in Talmudic times,
namely, the fallibility of the spirits. It was believed
that if a person is called by another name, the spirits,
angels, or demons, who look for him under his old name,
cannot find him. For under the new name they imagine
him to be another person, a person about whom they have
no order or against whom they have no charge or grudge.
Thus, to escape danger from demons, it was considered an
effective protection for husband and wife to exchange
their names: he called himself by her name and she by
his. The demons who might seek to harm the gentleman
would find a person who, judging by his name, was a
lady, whom they would refrain from harming. Likewise,
the demons who might pursue the lady would give up their
evil designs if they should find instead of the lady a
person who, as the new name indicated, was a gentleman.
The Talmud (Shabbat 67b) describes this practice of
exchanging names as heathen superstition (**Darchei Ha-
Emori**),[23] and is inclined to object to it. Yet the
Talmud considers it perfectly good Jewish belief, that
by a change of name one might escape the punishment
decreed against him by the heavenly court. There are
four procedures by which a person may cause the evil
decree issued against him to be torn and destroyed, says
the baraita R.H. 16b, and one of them is changing the
person's name. Some people say that a change of place
or residence may have the same effect.[24]

It is possible--though rather doubtful--that the
old idea that a man's character is what his name declares it to be, and that by changing the name an actual
change in the character is effected, also underlies the
belief that a change of name can nullify the verdict
against the person (as indeed some medieval authorities

---

[23] "Hu ve-ishto machlifin shemoteihen balaila mishum
nichush." And Rashi comments on this: "Hu bishmah vehi
bishmo yesh bo mishum darchei ha-Emori."

[24] "Arba-a devarim mekare-in gezar dino shel adam. Elu
hen: tsedaka, tse-aka, shinui hashem veshinui ma-
aseh....veyesh omerim, af shinui makom." Yet there is
no instance of an actual practice of changing the name
in case of sickness recorded in the Talmud. Comp. Loew,
op. cit., p. 108.

would explain it).[25]   The person whose name has been
changed--so these authorities rationalize--has by repentance actually become another, better person no longer capable of persisting in the sins committed by the
person with the other name and the wicked character.
Hence, he is not to suffer punishments for them.   But
the real reason for the favorable effects of the change
of name--at least to the popular mind--was that the
change of name, like the change of residence, furnishes
the person an escape from the danger of the evil decreed
against him.   The decree against him simply cannot be
executed; the agent charged with carrying out the decree
simply cannot locate or is unable to identify him.[26]
The angels go only by name and address.   If they come to
the given address and, looking there for a person with a
certain name, do not find such a person (either because
he has moved away or because the occupant goes by a name
different from the one they are looking for), they report that they could not find him or that no such man
can be found in the designated residence.   The verdict
is then destroyed as useless.   That the angels can and
do make such mistakes in persons--mistakes which might
even result in a miscarriage of justice by the heavenly
administration--is evident from the following story told
in the Talmud (Chagiga 3b-4a): The Angel of Death was
ordered to put to death Mary the hairdresser,[27] but by

----

[25] See R. Nissim (Gerondi) in his commentary to Alfasi,
ad loc., who explains: "...Deshinui hashem gorem lo la-
asot teshuva, sheyomar belibo, Eini oto ha-ish shehayiti
kodem lachen, vetsarich ani letaken ma-asai."

[26] Thus M. Coucy in his Semag Commandments, 17 (Venice,
1547), p. 90a, plainly explains: "...Kelomar, she-ani
acher, ve-eini oto ha-ish she-oseh otan hama-asim."
(The one who changes his name as much as declares--to
the angel looking for him or to whomsoever it may
concern--"I am not the person you are looking for.   I am
not the one who committed the sins you charge me with.")
Mohammed also believed that by changing the name of a
person, the person himself also becomes changed.   See J.
Wellhausen, Reste Arabischen Heidentums (2nd ed.,
Berlin, 1897), p. 199.

[27] Some authorities would identify this Mary the
hairdresser with Mary the mother of Jesus.   See Tosafot,
ad loc., s.v. "have shechiach," and comp. S. Krauss, Das
Leben Jesu nach juedischen Quellen (Berlin, 1902), p.
276ff, note 9.   Perhaps, however, "megadela se-ar nasi"
does not mean "hairdresser," but one who herself had
long hair, and there may be here an allusion to the Mary
who "anointed the feet of Jesus and wiped his feet with

mistake he put to death an innocent little schoolteacher by the name of Mary, whom, because of the similarity of names, he mistook for the woman sentenced to death.[28] And while the heavenly superiors pointed out to the Angel of Death the mistake he had made, and perhaps reprimanded him, the life of young Mary the schoolteacher was not restored; she remained in the other world whither she had been transferred by the mistake of the angel.[29] When giving their children names like those of their ancestors, people were influenced to a great extent by those beliefs in the suggestiveness of the name and in the fallibility of the angels and demons. They would select the name of an ancestor whom they believed to have been a good man and a successful man. The benefits of such a name for the child were twofold: in the first place, since **shema garem**, i.e., the name is a determining factor in the destiny of the person, this name which manifestly had been so successful in the case of its former bearer (i.e., the ancestor) would presumably have the same good effects upon the destiny and

---

her hair" (John 12:3).

[28] As to the heavenly agents carrying out their orders, sometimes without exact knowledge as to what they are doing, see Rashbam, quoted by **Tosafot Yom Tov** to M. Avot III.16, who prefers the reading of the Mishna ("**midaatan veshelo mida-atan**"), and interprets it as referring to the agents or collectors who exact payment from man. Comp. also saying in **Mechilta**, Pischa XI (Friedmann 11b), which, according to the correct text established in my forthcoming edition of the **Mechilta** reads: "**Mishenitena reshut lamal-ach lechabel, eino mavchin bein tsadik lerasha.**"

[29] The idea that the ministering angels are liable to make mistakes in the identity of a person if that person is referred to merely by name is, in my opinion, presupposed in the following statement in the Talmud (Berachot 34a): "**Kol hamevakesh rachamim al chavero, ein tsarich lehazkir shemo, shene-emar, 'El na refa na lah,' vela kemidbar shemah deMiriam,**" "When one prays for mercy for his fellowman, it is not correct [**ein tsarich** here does not mean 'it is not necessary,' but rather **lo nachon**, 'it is not correct'; see Jacob Raischer in **Iyun Ya-akov**, commentary to **Ein Ya-akov**, ad loc.] to refer to him by merely mentioning his name. For when Moses prayed for Miriam it is said 'Heal her now, O God, I beseech Thee' (Num. 12:13). He pointed to Miriam and did not merely refer to her by name." By pointing to the person for whom one prays mistakes on the part of the angels are less likely to happen.

character of its new bearer (i.e., the child).[30] Secondly, in case the angel should make a mistake in the person by the similarity of names, it would be in favor of the child. The child might be mistaken by the spirits for the ancestor whose name he bears and be treated with the consideration due to the ancestor, or credited with the achievements recorded in heaven to the account of the ancestor.

They would avoid naming a child after an ancestor or relative who was wicked (Yoma 38b)[31] for fear of the twofold danger involved in such a procedure. In the first place, the name may actually make the child's character and destiny be like the wicked relative's. Secondly, the child might be mistaken by the spirits for the older wicked person by that name. All the evil decreed against that former bearer of the name and all the accusations recorded against him might be charged to the child, who might thus be made to suffer all the punishments for them.[32]

The primary consideration in choosing a name for the child was still the welfare, future, and destiny of the child itself--how it might be affected by the name. It seems, however, that during Talmudic times there was combined with this chief consideration a secondary consideration, namely, the effect upon the person after whom the child was to be named, whether the memory of that person should be kept alive or let rot and fall

----

[30] Thus Abba b. Abba, the father of Samuel, the famous Babylonian Amora of the first generation, called his son by the name of the prophet Samuel, no doubt, to suggest that his son may become like the prophet. He thereby wished to help bring into fulfillment the promise which R. Judah b. Bathyra had given him, that he would have a son who would be like the prophet Samuel. See Midrash to Sam. 10:3 (ed. Buber, Krakau, 1893), p. 39a.

[31] The expression "**dela maskinan bishmeihu**," which literally means "we do not bring [them] up by their name," may have an allusion to the belief that if you call the name of the ghost, it appears. Hence, we do not wish to name a child like them, for fear that whenever we will call the child by its name we might--by the mere mentioning of that name--cause the ghost, the original bearer of that name, to come up from the grave and appear before us. Comp. the remark by Schulze (op. cit., p. 92): "Der Namesruf bewirkt die Gegenwart seines Traegers. Man vermeidet deshalb Namen, deren Traeger unheilvoll sind."

[32] Comp. **Pitchei Teshuva** to Yoreh De-a 116.6, **s.v.** "**liydei sakana**."

into oblivion. Due to the gradual spread of the custom of naming children after ancestors, there developed a modification of the belief in the absolute identity of the name with the person, which had made it impossible in Biblical times for two persons belonging to the same family or group to have the same name. It is true, the persistent avoidance of giving children such names as Abraham,[33] Moses,[34] Aaron,[35] or David,[36] which is so pronounced throughout the Talmudic period, would suggest that, at least in regard to certain great names, the ancient Biblical belief was still strong.[37] In general,

----

[33] The name Abraham, it seems, was never given to a child in Talmudic times. In the passage of Gen. 49:1 the words **"Avraham, Yitschak, Ya-akov"** are omitted in some editions (see Theodor, **ad loc.**, and comp. S. Krauss, **Talmudische Archaeologie** II (Leipzig, 1911), p. 113, and note 136 on p. 440). There occurs, however, the name Abram--the original name of Abraham--as the name of an Amora (Gittin 50a). See, however, Krauss, **op. cit.**, note 138 on p. 440, and comp. H.J.D. Azulai in **Shem Hagedolim** I, **s.v.** "Avraham," no. 34 (Wien, 1865), p. 3b. It is likely to assume that since Father Abraham was not to be called by his former name Abram, there was no hesitancy felt in calling children by that name. But they would avoid calling a child Abraham.

[34] The name Moses occurs but once in the Talmud (B.B. 174b) as the name of a man, Mosheh bar Itsra, who, it seems, was not a teacher. No teacher of Talmudic times, Tanna or Amora, was ever called by the name of Moses (see Azulai, **op. cit.**, **s.v.** "Mosheh," no. 110, p. 59a, who assumes that there was a mystic reason for avoiding to give the name Moses to any teacher--**"Velo haya shum tana o amora shenikra Mosheh, vehu pele vesod."** The name "Miasheh" is not identical with "Mosheh," as assumed by Graetz (**Gesch.**, vol. 4, note 19 [Leipzig, 1908], p. 433). Comp. also Krauss, **op. cit.**, note 144 on p. 441.

[35] Aaron occurs only once (B.K. 109b) as the name of a teacher of the last generation of the Baylonian Amoraim. The saying in **Avot deRabbi Natan**, Version A., ch. XII, is merely of a homiletical nature. Comp. Krauss, **op. cit.**, p. 441, note 140.

[36] David occurs but once according to some variant reading in Yevamot 115b. See marginal note in Talmud, edition Wilna 1908. This reading, however, is doubtful. It is missing in the text of the other editions.

[37] Krauss, **op. cit.**, p. 13, assumes that it was merely

however, it seems that the fear that, by naming a child
after an ancestor, the memory of the latter would be
forgotten, because all that had been associated with his
name was transferred to the new bearer of the name, was
apparently no longer entertained. It seems that somehow
the people came to believe that it was possible for two
individuals to be referred to or designated by the same
name, and that by giving a child the name of an ancestor
the memory of the latter is thereby preserved and kept
alive. Whenever the child would be called or referred
to by that name, as it was believed, people would also
be reminded of the former or original bearer of the
name. Hence, as already stated, to the consideration of
the welfare of the child in choosing the name of an
ancestor there was added, in the popular mind, the secondary consideration of preserving the memory of the
name of the ancestor who was believed to have been a
righteous man. And to the reason for avoiding the giving of the name of a wicked person to a child because of
the danger to the child there was now added another
motive, namely, the desire to cause the name of the
wicked to rot, and to avoid preserving his memory by
having someone else bear his name.

Likewise, the fear that by giving the name of one
person to another, the very being, the personality identical with the name, is transferred to the other person,
and the one from whom the name is taken must therefore
cease to exist (a fear which, as we have seen, was also
a result of the belief in the absolute identity of the
name with the person) was also generally abandoned. Not
only were people not afraid for their lives when children were named like them, but they were even pleased
with it and welcomed it, since it meant that the preservation of their memory was thus assured them even in
their lifetime. Thus R. Nathan, a teacher of the second
half of the second century, reports that in his travels
he occasionally was able, by his advice, to save the
lives of newborn children. The parents of those children, out of gratitude to him--and probably to suggest
that their children will grow up and become men as good
as R. Nathan--named their children Nathan, after him

----

reverence for those great ancestors which prevented
people from calling a child by their name, just as
Christians would not call a child by the name of Jesus.
But mere reverence would not constitute a mystery, which
Azulai assumes as the reason. To me, it seems that the
avoidance of calling children by the names of these
ancestors was due to a hesitancy to transfer the very
being or soul of any of those ancestors to another
person. These great souls should not be disturbed and
made to come to earth again.

(Chulin 47b).   And R. Nathan was rather pleased with
this expression of gratitude.   Hence, we find throughout
the entire Talmudic period that not only would people
name their children after departed ancestors, but that
there was no hesitancy even to name children after living parents or grandparents.[38] It is true that in many
instances reported in the Talmud of a son's having the
same name as his father or grandfather, we cannot definitely ascertain whether the father or grandfather was
still living when the child was named after him.   Thus,
in the case of R. Chananiah, the son of Chananiah mentioned in the Tosefta Nida V.15, there is no doubt that
the father was living when the son was named after him.
For we are told that when the son was still a minor the
father made the vow for him which caused him to become a
Nazarite.   Likewise, in Luke 1:60 it is reported that
the child John was originally called Zachariah after the
name of his grandfather who was then still living.   One
may wonder why--in spite of the belief that the Angel of
Death was liable to get confused and mistake the one
person for another of the same name--the people were
nevertheless not afraid that when the Angel of Death
comes to call for the old grandfather he might by mistake take the child having the same name.   But one need
not expect superstition to be consistent.   The older man
may even have hoped that the stupidity of the Angel of
Death might work in his favor.   And when the Angel of
Death comes to take his life, the old man might be able
to put him off and fool him by declaring that his time
has not come yet, for a certain number of years had been
allotted to him (as the heavenly record would show on
the account of the name of his junior) which he had not
yet completed.[39]
     Which of the grandfathers--paternal or maternal--
was favored in naming the grandchild, we cannot state
definitely.   There are no regulations about this in the
Talmud.   In many instances known to us from the Talmud
of a grandson's having the same name as his grandfather,
it is the name of the paternal grandfather that the
grandson bears.   The custom among the Greeks was to name

---

[38] See for reference to some instances, Krauss (op.
cit., II, p. 440, note 131, and A.S. Herschberg, in
Hatekufa XXV, p. 396, note 4, to which many other
instances could be added.   Comp. also Jacob Mann,
"Rabbinic Studies in the Gospels," in **Hebrew Union
College Annual** 1 (Cincinnati, 1924), p. 328.

[39] This, as we shall see, was actually the belief among
the oriental Jews in later times, who would seek to
secure for the older man a prolonged life by naming his
child or grandchild after him.

after the paternal grandfather. Among the Jews in post-Talmudic times this was also the rule. It may, therefore, be assumed that in Talmudic times, likewise, the general practice was to choose the name of the paternal grandfather for the child. But it was not a fixed rule. There must have been instances where the son was given the name of his maternal grandfather. Thus, we read in the Book of Jubilees (11:14-15) that Terach's wife's name was Edna and her father's name was Bram. Terach called the son whom Edna bore him "Abram, by the name of the father of his mother, for the latter had died before his daughter had conceived a son." Although this legend is contradicted by the Talmudic tradition, according to which Abraham's mother's name was Amatlai, the daughter of Karnebo (B.B. 91a), yet the report in the Book of Jubilees at least reflects the custom in certain Jewish circles of naming the son after the maternal grandfather.

As to Hebrew or non-Hebrew names, there was in Talmudic times no real distinction made in practice. It is true that we find some Agadic utterances against the practice of changing a Hebrew name into a foreign one. And one of the virtues because of which Israel was redeemed from Egypt is said to have been that they retained their Hebrew names and did not change them to non-Hebrew ones--"**shelo shinu et shemam**" (**Mechilta**, Pischa V, and **Lev. R.** 32.5). But these utterances seem to have been directed against those who, by changing their names or calling their children by foreign names would seek to deny their Jewish identity, and not against the foreign names as such. A good Jew could well have borne a foreign name. And we find even among the rabbis themselves many whose names were non-Hebrew-like Antigonos, Alexander, Romanus, and others. In some instances, these non-Jewish names, especially among the Palestinian Jews, may have been accompanied by another, Hebrew name, as in the case of Judah Aristobolus and others. For the practice of being called by or having more than one name is already found in Talmudic times.[40] In some cases, any of those non-Hebrew names would be substitutes for or merely translations of original Hebrew names. But there are also many instances where the non-Hebrew name was the original and only name, unaccompanied by any other.[41]

Throughout the entire Talmudic period, then, the people would not hesitate to give their children non-Hebrew names. And of the Jews outside of Palestine, it

---

[40] Comp. Herschberg, **Hatekufa** XXV, pp. 392ff.

[41] Comp. Zunz, **op. cit.**, p. 15, and Herschberg, **op. cit.**, pp. 395ff.

is expressly reported that the majority of them had names like the Gentiles (Gittin 11b).

In post-Talmudic times no radical change in the attitude towards names took place, and no marked development of the ideas governing the selection of names can be noticed. In the main, the beliefs and popular notions as to the purpose, significance, and function of proper names which were current in Talmudic times have been retained almost universally throughout the post-Talmudic and later Rabbinic times. Some slight modification of one idea or the other may have been made, or more or less emphasis may have been laid upon certain notions by one group or another. In some instances, even a reversal to older, more primitive ideas, which had been suppressed or rather ignored in Talmudic times, took place. These slight modifications in the popular beliefs and mild changes in the attitude towards proper names, however, brought about some changes in practice and very often put certain restrictions upon the selection of proper names, restrictions unknown in Talmudic times. But these changes and new practices are not universal. They differ among different groups of Jewry, and sometimes even vary in different communities of the same group.

One change we notice in post-Talmudic times that is almost universally accepted is the attitude of the people towards the names Abraham, Moses, Aaron, and David. The hesitancy of calling children by these names, which we have noticed in Talmudic times, has been entirely overcome. And ever since Gaonic times these names have become very frequent among all groups of Jewry. The belief or fear upon which this hesitancy in Talmudic times rested seems to have been entirely abandoned. Only in a modified form, as we shall see, we may find it still effective in later times.[42]

As regards the other changes that took place in post-Talmudic times, we must distinguish between the Sefardic and the Ashkenazic groups of Jewry. Most of the changes developed among the latter group. Among them the superstitious elements of the ideas of Talmudic times became more pronounced and were more emphasized, while the former group in general followed a more rational course in their attitude towards names and adhered more closely to the general practices of Talmudic times. Thus, we find that among the Sefardic Jews there was no fear or hesitancy in naming a child after a living person. There are many instances of a grandson being given the name of his grandfather even when the latter is still alive. To mention but a few outstanding examples: Judah Halevi had a grandson who was likewise

---

[42] As in the case of Judah Hechasid and his father.

named Judah to whom he seems to have been much attached, for in one of his poems he refers to this grandson with the words: "How can Judah [the grandfather] ever forget Judah [the grandson]?"[43]   Likewise, R. Isaiah b. Elijah de Trani, an Italian rabbinical authority of the 13th century, was named like his maternal grandfather, R. Isaiah b. Mali de Trani.   The grandfather lived to see the grandson grow up to be a prominent scholar, and he pointed to him with pride and satisfaction as his heir and successor, who would take his place in the scholarly world.[44]   Likewise, Nahmanides said, as the paternal grandfather of a new-born child: "Although, as custom requires, the child should be called by my name [Moses], I forego the privilege and am willing that he be called Jonah, like his maternal grandfather."[45]

We also find among the Sefardic Jews the practice of calling the son by the name of the father, even when the father is still living. This practice, however, is less frequent, and some of the Sefardim consider it rather strange. Thus, H.J.D. Azulai, in his commentary to **Sefer Chasidim**, no. 460 (ed. Lemberg, 1862), p. 44b says: "A man does not call a son by his own name."[46] At the same time he mentions an instance of a man by the name of Mordecai whose son was also named Mordecai. Azulai finds this rather strange. But we know from other sources that the practice was not infrequent among the Sefardim. Thus, Jacob Saphir in his **Even Sapir I** (Lyck, 1866), p. 51, reports that it is the custom among Jews in Yemen to name the child like his father, especially in a family that has previously lost children.[47]

---

[43] "Ve-eich yishkach Yehuda et Yehuda?" **Divan**, ed. S.Z. Luzzatto (Lyck, 1864), p. 3b; comp. Luzzatto's note 9, ibid., p. 4a.

[44] See Weiss, **Dor V** (Wilna, 1904), p. 94.

[45] "Af al pi shetsarich likroto al shemi, ani rotseh sheyikare Yona, al shem zekeno avi imo, mishum yizrach hashemesh uva hashemesh.   Ad shelo zarecha (lashon nekiya tachat shake-a?) shimsho shel zeh, zarecha shimsho shel zeh."   Quoted by R. Solomon b. Simeon b. Zemah in his responsa **Sefer Harashbash**, no. 291 (Leghorn, 1742), 56d.

[46] "Ulechol haminhagim ein adam kore beno beshem atsmo." Comp. also **Sefer Sharvit Hazahav Hechadash, Hanikra Beit Avot** by R. Schabsza Lipschitz (Muncacz, 1914), ch. CIII, no. 11, p. 59b.

[47] "Zot minhagam lisgula: mi asher lo yekayemu banav, rachmana litslan, yikra livno bechayav bishmo."

It was considered a protection to give the child the name of the father. By this means, it was believed, the life of the child so named would be safeguarded and it would not share in the fate of its brothers and sisters who died young. To a certain extent this practice may have been motivated by the belief in the suggestive power of the name, **shema garem**, which would make the child grow up to be like his father or grandfather. But this was not the only determining factor in this practice. There seems to have been underlying it another superstitious idea which we found current in Talmudic times, viz., the belief in the fallibility of the angels. For in some circles of the Sefardic Jews, it was also believed that a father might be assured of a long life by naming his son like him.[48] It seems, therefore, that whatever belief in the fallibility of the Angel of Death was entertained among the Sefardic Jews, it not only did not deter them from naming children like living fathers or grandfathers, but it even encouraged the practice. For it was hoped that the mistake the Angel of Death might make by confusing the names would be in favor of the person sentenced to death (by mistaking him for another person by the same name against whom no decree of death was issued).

Among the Ashkenazic Jews, however, such risks were generally avoided. They would not rely on the hope that the Angel of Death would make a mistake in favor of the living. Hence, with a few exceptions, the general practice among the Ashkenazic Jews has been not to name a child after a living parent or relative. That this practice is based upon superstition is frankly admitted by the people who, governed by certain superstitious beliefs, avoid certain practices. Thus in **Sefer Chasidim** (ed. Wistinetzki, Berlin, 1891), no. 377, p. 114, we find the following statement: "**Kol hanichushim keneged hamakpidim. Goyim shekorin livneihem beshem avihem, ve-ein bechach kelum, viyhudim makpidim al kach. Veyesh mekomot she-ein korin oto achar shemot hachayim, ela achar shekevar metu**" ("Superstitions work harm only on those who heed them. Non-Jews call their sons by the names of their fathers and no harm results. But the Jews are careful not to do so. And in some places they do not name after living persons at all, but only after such as have already died.") What these superstitious fears were that caused the Jews to avoid naming children after living persons, is not stated here. We can learn

---

[48] See Lipschitz, op. cit., ch. VIII, no. 16 (p. 60b), quoting S.A. Wertheimer of Jerusalem: "**Etsel acheinu Benei Yisra-el anshei Erets Sefarad biYerushalayim mekubal lisgula la-arichat yemei ha-av sheyikare beno bechayav bishmo.**"

them, however, from other passages in the **Sefer Chasidim**
as well as from utterances in other sources originating
among German mystics.

One of these superstitions was that, due to the
carelessness of the Angel of Death, harm may come to a
child named like an older living person. For when the
time comes for that older person to die, the Angel of
Death, receiving instructions to take the life of the
older person by that name, might instead take the life
of the younger person of the same name. This belief in
a possible mistake on the part of the Angel of Death,
which we have found expressed in the story of the Talmud
(Chagiga 3b-4a) cited above, was especially current and
strongly believed in among the Ashkenazic Jews. This is
evident from the following story told in **Sefer Chasidim**
(ibid., no. 375, p. 114): An older teacher and a young
student happened to get married in the same week. The
young student died during the very week of the wedding.
In a dream he appeared to his mother and told her that
he actually had many years yet to live but his untimely
death was brought about by a mistake on the part of the
Angel of Death. The latter received the order to take
the life of the bridegroom who got married during that
week. Of course, the order referred to the older teacher who also had been married during the same week. But
the Angel of Death did not understand the order correctly. And when he met the young student bridegroom alone
on the street,[49] he thought the order for the bridegroom
of the week referred to him, and so he killed him. The
story goes on to tell that all the years which had been
allotted to the young student and which he had not lived
out were then--by another mistake of the heavenly
clerks--assigned to the old teacher, thus prolonging his
life. Finding on their records that the bridegroom who
got married that week--referring to the young student--
had yet so many years to live, and finding only one
living bridegroom who got married that week (the old
teacher), they accordingly credited his account with
that number of years.

There is no doubt that out of consideration for the
safety of the child, and as a precaution against possible danger resulting from mistakes on the part of the
Angel of Death, they avoided naming the child after a
living father or grandfather, or--as the custom was in
some places--after any living person. And it was not
only fear of the death of the child, but also fear of
sickness or any other punishment that might be decreed
against the older person and which the angel charged

---

[49] Which, according to popular superstition, he should
not have done (see **Pirkei deR. Eliezer**, ch. 16: "**Chatan
eino yotse lashuk levado**"; and comp. Berachot 54b).

with the execution of that decree might by mistake inflict upon the child having the same name.[50] For the
Angel of Death is not the only one among the angels that
is stupid and careless. The other heavenly officers are
not much smarter and no more careful than he.

There was still another consideration which prevented people from naming children after living parents
or grandparents, and this was fear for the life of the
parent or grandparent. This fear was based upon the old
idea of the absolute identity of the soul or the very
being of the person with his name, according to which it
would be impossible for two persons to have one and the
same name. This old idea was revived and found strong
expression among German mystics. Thus, in the **Sefer
Tsiyoni** by R. Menachem b. Meir of Speyer (Cremona,
1560), p. 26, we find the statement **"Shemo shel adam hu
gufo,"** "A man's name is the very essence of his being."
Tsiyoni then goes on to quote from a **Sefer Hachayim**,
probably by R. Eleazer of Worms[51] that "a man's name is

---

[50] In this connection, it should be noticed that the
warning against a marriage in case the bride has the
same name as the mother of the groom or the bride's
father has the same name as the groom, expressed in the
Testament of R. Judah Hechasid (published in **Sefer
Chasidim**, Lemberg, 1862, p. 1b), is also based upon the
fear of an error by the heavenly agent, who might not
know to distinguish between two persons by the same name
in one family or one household, and by mistake might
inflict upon the one person ills decreed against the
other with the same name. This danger is especially
great in case the names of the respective parents of the
two persons with the same name are also alike, as when,
e.g., the father of the girl is Isaac the son of Abraham
and the groom's name is also Isaac the son of Abraham,
or when the name of both is Jacob the son of Isaac the
son of Abraham **(meshulamim)**, **Sefer Chasidim**, 477,
Lemberg, 1862, p. 45d; and comp. R. Abraham Danziger in
his **Sefer Chochmat Adam**, (Warsaw, 1914), p. 140. For in
such cases the angel will be absolutely at a loss to
distinguish the one from the other. Comp. the
interesting remark in **Sefer Chasidim (ibid.)**: "Although
one should not believe in superstitions, yet it is
better to be heedful of them" ("**Af al pi shelo lenachesh
yesh lachush**"). This is a sort of an apology.

[51] See Benjacob, **Otsar Hasefarim**, no. 560. Benjacob's
suggestion (**ibid.**, no. 559) that **Tsiyoni** may have had
reference to another **Sefer Chayim**, ascribed to Ibn Ezra,
does not seem plausible.

his soul."[52]   This, in a manner, suggested the notion
that by giving the name of a living person we cause, as
it were, the soul of that person to enter the child.
The necessary consequence resulting from this notion was
the fear of naming a child after a living parent or
grandparent. For, since the one soul identical with the
name cannot at the same time be in two places or occupy
two bodies, its entrance into the body of the child
which is effected by giving the child the name identical
with that soul, would necessitate its withdrawal from
the other body, and the latter would have to die.   In
other words, only one person in possession of a certain
soul identified with a special name can be living on
earth.   Giving to children the name of a living parent
or grandparent would cause the death of the latter.[53]

   We need not be surprised to find another result of
this emphasized belief in the absolute identity of the
soul of a person with his name. If the identity of the
soul with the name made it (in the popular belief) impossible for two persons of one group or family living
on earth to have the same name (because it would mean
that one and the same soul occupies two bodies or is in
two places on earth at the same time), then it should
also preclude the possibility of two persons of one
family or group having the same name even if one of them
has already departed this earthly life. For it likewise
involves the absurdity of assuming that one soul identical with a certain name occupies two places at the same
time: that is, one in heaven in the assembly of the
souls of the righteous, and one on earth in the body of
the person to whom the name identical with the soul was
given. And just as to give a child the name of a living
parent means to remove the soul of that parent from its
abode in the body of that parent and transfer it to the
body of the child, so also to give the child the name of
a departed parent must cause the soul of the latter to
leave its heavenly abode, to come back to earth, and to
enter the body of the child. This notion, as we have
suggested above, was probably the reason why in Biblical
times no child was named after a departed parent or
grandparent. The same notion, while not common in the
Middle Ages, must have been in the mind of some mystics,

---

[52] "Umatsati beSefer Hachayim ki shemo shel adam hu
nishmato."

[53] Of course, if the older person whose life is thus
endangered by his name being given to the child does not
mind the risk, his name is given to his grandchildren.
There have been such exceptions even among Ashkenazic
Jews.   See **Noheg Ketson Yosef** by Joseph ben Moses
Kossman (Hanau, 1718), p. 22a.

who, as a consequence, would object to their descendants being named after them. This seems to me to have been the case with R. Judah b. Samuel Hechasid. One of the mandates (no. 61) in his Testament (published in the **Sefer Chasidim**, ed. Lemberg, 1862, p. 2) was that none of his descendants should be called by his name, Judah, nor by his father's name, Samuel: "**Lo yikra ish mizar-o et beno Yehuda velo Shemu-el.**" The reason for this strange request has not been satisfactorily explained, though various theories about it have been advanced.[54] One of these theories is that Judah was conscious of having committed the sin of making use of the Holy Names. And he had a tradition that the punishment for this sin is inflicted upon any of the descendants of the offender throughout all generations who are called by his name. Hence, to spare his descendants the suffering of the punishment for this sin, he commanded them not to call any of their sons by his name. Not being called by his name, they will not be held responsible for his sin.[55] The only interesting point in this theory, which is said to have been advanced by the descendants of Judah Hechasid, is the notion which it implies, i.e., that a descendant having the same name as the ancestor might be held responsible for the sins of that ancestor, but is not responsible for these sins if he does not bear the same name as the offending ancestor. This is but another way of saying that the heavenly authorities may get mixed up in the case of persons of one family having the same name, confusing the one with the other and by mistake inflicting upon one the punishment intended for the other. But as an explanation of the motive of Judah Hechasid's strange mandate, it is unsatisfactory. For at most it would only explain why he did not want any of his descendants to bear his own name, Judah. But it cannot explain why he forbade his de-

---

[54] Comp. Jacob Emden in his **Berit Migdol Oz** (Jitomir, 1874, p. 12).

[55] Comp. Responsa **Mishbetsot Zahav** by R. Nathan Amram, no. 42 (Leghorn, 1851), p. 39, and in the **Maftechot** there, p. 73d, where he cites this theory in the following words: "[Judah Hechasid] **lehora-at sha-a hishtamesh kama pe-amim bishmot hakodesh, ulefi shehaya mityare lenafsho hatehora leshema, chas vechalila, yaanishuhu al kacha tamid kol hayamim, lachen tsiva vayaamod leval yikre-u bishmo olamim, sheken haya masoret beyado, zichrono livracha, shekol mi shehishtamesh beyamav bishmot hakodesk, kol zeman shehaya nimtsa bezar-o hashem hahu atsmo, behechreach sheyegalgelu alav et hakol, velachen lo matsa terufa lazeh im lo behashbit zichro miyotse-ei chalatsav, zechuto yagen aleinu.**"

scendants to call any of their children by the name of
his father, Samuel. He could not have been so disrespectful to his father as to imply that he likewise
committed any such grave sin for which all his descendants might have to suffer. The real reason for this
strange request seems to me to have been the desire that
he and his sainted father should not be disturbed in
their heavenly bliss and should not be forced to leave
the heavenly abode, to come down to earth again, and to
enter the body of one of their descendants who would be
named after them.

This instance of R. Judah Hechasid, however, is an
exception to the rule that prevailed almost universally
of preferring to have descendants named after their
ancestors. People in general were very eager to leave,
as it were, a name behind them. Even those people who
believed in the absolute identity of the soul with the
name, and that with the name given to the child the soul
formerly identical with that name is made to come down
from heaven and enter the body of the child--even they
would not hesitate to name their children after departed
ancestors. Superstition is usually overcome by another
superstition. And, in this case, the belief that by
preserving the name of the departed ancestor we preserve
his soul (and in a manner secure for him a sort of
immortality), counteracted the superstitious fear that
he might be disturbed in his eternal rest and be forced
to come down to earth again. People, in general, it
seems, did not consider it such an unpleasant thing to
be reborn again and, as it were, renew their life here
on earth.

Of course, some people would consider it a misfortune to be reborn as a woman. For what man would like
to live the life of a woman! Certainly, not one who all
his life had daily recited the benediction thanking God
for not having made him a woman. Hence, as we shall see
below, some people objected to giving a girl the name of
a male ancestor, for this would mean making the soul of
that ancestor enter the body of the girl and thus live
the life of a woman. But otherwise it was not considered so bad for the departed to be invited again to a
visit on earth. With the gradual spread of the belief
in the transmigration of the soul, **Gilgul**, it was believed that the souls of the departed--even of the great
and righteous man--re-enter this world and are reborn.[56]
Assuming that the soul of the departed in coming down to
earth by the process of **Gilgul** would naturally prefer to
enter the body of a new-born child of his own family, it
was even considered necessary and proper to give the

---

[56] See Hayyim Vital in **Sefer Hagilgulim**, ch. IV
(Frankfurt, 1684), pp. 3bff and 35b-36b.

child into whose body it was hoped the soul of the ancestor would enter the name of that ancestor. Thus,
according to Isaac Lurya, when the father of an unborn
child dies before the birth of the child, his soul enters the body of the child when it is born, and therefore the child should also be given the name of the
father.[57]

A contemporary of Lurya, the famous Joseph Caro,
even went so far as to say that with the name which a
person receives he also receives something of the character of the very first or original bearer of that name.
Thus, if one is named Abraham he will be inclined towards kindness.[58] This is but another way of saying
that with the name there is associated and intimately
connected the soul, or at least a spark of the soul, of
the original bearer of that name. For even though the
person is named Abraham only after his grandfather by
that name, and not directly after the Biblical Abraham,
indirectly he is named after, and has at least part of
the soul or character of, the Biblical Abraham. For the
grandfather after whom the child is named was in turn
named after his grandfather, and the latter again after
another, and so forth up to the one first named after
the Biblical Abraham. All the intermediary bearers of
the name Abraham were merely temporary possessors of the
name,[59] and each one of them in turn transmitted it--
together with the spark of the soul of Abraham associated with it--to all those who in the course of time
were called Abraham. Caro, as is evident from his reference to the saying of the Talmud (Berachot 7b), has
also in mind the idea of **shema garem**, i.e., that the
name determines the fate and character of the person.
This belief in the suggestive power of the name has been
retained all through the post-Talmudic times and was
combined with the practice of naming children after
departed parents or ancestors. With Caro, however, it
seems to have undergone a slight modification. It meant
that when we give the child the name of a certain ancestor, we thereby give the angel in charge of providing
the body of the child with a soul, directions, so to
speak, as to which or what kind of soul he should put

---

[57] See Emanuel Rik in **Mishnat Chasidim** (Amsterdam,
1727), p. 33b: "**Umi shemet vehiniach ishto me-uberet
veyoledet ben, hu mitgalgel bo.**"

[58] See **Magid Meisharim** to section **Shemot** (Amsterdam,
1708), p. 21a: "**Razin dishmeihen....deman de-ikri
Avraham noteh letsad asiyat chesed.**"

[59] See **Amud Ha-avoda** by R. Baruch b. Abraham
(Czernowitz, 1854), pp. 41c,d.

into the child (namely, the soul once associated and identical with the name of that ancestor), and thus we bring it about that the character and the fate of the child be like that of the former bearer of that name. The angels, who, as we have seen, according to popular belief in the power of the uttered word, heed sometimes orders by human voices (mistaking them to come from a higher authority), in this case also heed the directions contained in the name, believing that the name was given by a higher authority. Indeed, according to Lurya, when the father gives a name to his child, it is really not the father, but God speaking through the mouth of the father, who gives the name. God puts the name into the mouth of the father, and causes him to call his son by that name.[60] Thus, even in the age when prophecy had long ceased in Israel, and when people could no longer make use of the Holy Spirit, names, even when given by any ordinary father, were believed to have been determined upon by an act of inspiration, and actually divinely ordained. No wonder, then, that the people believed in the power of the names to determine the fate and reveal the character of the persons to whom they were given. This belief in the suggestive, if not determinative, power of the name which with more or less emphasis has been current among the people throughout all time, accounts for the continuation of the practice of naming children with reference to some event, hope, or expectation (**leshem hame-ora**). This practice has been retained all through the ages up to modern times.[61] Especially frequent is the practice of determining the choice of a name for a child by the date or season of its birth. A child born on a Saturday may be called Shabetai; one born on a holiday is named Yomtov; one born on the Day of Atonement is called Rachamim; one born on the ninth of Av is called Menachem; and one born on Purim or one whose circumcision takes place on Purim is called Mordecai, or if a girl is born on Purim she is called Esther. Sometimes the name is taken from the Scriptural portion read during the week in which the

---

[60] See Jacob ibn Habib in **Hakotev** to **Ein Ya-akov** on Berachot 7b, who interprets the saying of R. Eleazar to mean that God put into the mouth of Leah the name which she gave to her son ("**Ki Hashem yitbarach sam befiha keri-at shem zeh**"). See also Emanuel Rik (**op. cit.**, p. 85): "**Vehashem shekore laben, Hakadosh Baruch Hu mazmino befiv.**" Comp. R. Bezalel b. Solomon Slutzk in his **Amudeiha Shiv-a** (Prague, 1674), no. 33, p. 4.

[61] Comp. such names as Tavyomi (Yom Tov) and Chisda in Talmudic times, and Mevaser, Chefets, or Matsliach in Gaonic times.

child was born. When the child is born during the week
when the **Sidra** "Noach" is read, he is called Noah; when
born during the week of the **Sidra** "Vayera," which contains the account of the birth of Isaac (Gen. 21), he is
named Isaac; when born during the week in which the
Sidra "Shemot," containing the story of Moses is read,
he is called Moses.[62]   But there are also names referring to special conditions prevailing at the time for
the birth.   Thus, S.D. Luzzato called one of his sons,
born at the time he was lecturing on Isaiah, by the name
of Isaiah; another son, born at the time when he was
engaged in his work on Targum Onkelos, he called Philox-
enos, or Ohev Ger.   Of course, Luzzato meant these names
merely to be commemorative, and was not influenced in
his choice of them by a belief in the suggestiveness of
names (see Hillel Della Torre in **Kerem Chemed** IV, no.
19).

   But the majority of the people, whether giving
their children names after departed relatives, or with
reference to some occasion or event, have been--and
consciously or unconsciously still are--influenced in
the selection of a name by the above-discussed beliefs
as to the possible influence of the name upon the child,
or its effect upon the one after whom it is named.   As
these beliefs or superstitions are not shared by all
people in a like degree, there developed among different
people certain restrictions upon the selection of names,
which may have been accepted and heeded by some people
(or even the majority of the people), but ignored and
disregarded by others.   These restrictions, originating
in the popular beliefs, are endorsed or rejected by the
respective authorities according to the degree in which
they, the authorities themselves, accept, share in, or
tolerate the underlying beliefs or superstitions.   In
the following I mention a number of such restrictions
without attempting to be exhaustive.

   (1) Some authorities object to the practice of
giving to a boy the name of a girl and vice versa (see
Moses Konitz in his **Sefer Hamatsref** I, no. 86. Wien,
1820, p. 56).   But this practice has been widespread.
In Talmudic times there were certain names common to men
and women.   Thus, one of the daughters of R. Hiyya was
named Pazzi (Yevamot 65b), and Pazzi is also found as
the name of a man.[63]   In medieval and modern times we

---

[62] See A.J. Glassberg, **Zichron Berit Larishonim** (Berlin,
1892), p. 256; Lipschitz, **op. cit.**, ch. VIII, no. 31, p.
62b; and comp. R. Joseph Hahn in **Yosef Omets** (Frankfurt,
1928), p. 240.

[63] See Hyman, **Toledot Tana-im Va-amora-im, s.v.**, p.
1010.   Likewise, in the Bible we find that the names

find the name Simcha used as a name for a boy as well as for a girl, though in the latter case it is sometimes translated into German, and becomes Freude (see R. Samuel b. David Halevi in his **Nachalat Shiv-a**, Koenigsberg, 1858, p. 122). And it is a common practice to name a grandson after his grandmother, and a granddaughter after her grandfather. In cases where the name of the grandmother is not thought quite suitable for a boy, they change it slightly, giving a masculine form to the feminine name (e.g., when the grandmother's name is Dinah they call the grandson Dan). Some people, however, object to calling a granddaughter after her grandfather. The reason for this objection is that it might be unpleasant to the departed grandfather, if his soul--identical with his name--would have to enter the body of a girl, and thus be made to live the life of a woman.[64]

(2) Some people would refrain from naming a child after a person who was killed or murdered by non-Jews for fear of bad luck, lest the sad fate of the former bearer of the name also befall the one named like him.[65] The same superstitious fear underlies the hesitancy to name a child after a person who died young, for it is feared that it may have been the name that caused the untimely death of that person, and the child having the same name might suffer the same fate and be as short-lived as the former bearer of that name.[66] In both of these cases, the fear is based upon the belief that the heavenly agent or Angel of Death might possibly make a mistake and confuse the one person with another of the same name. If, however, the people wish to preserve the name of the one who was killed or died young by naming someone after him, they usually combine with his name the name of another person, who lived to a ripe old age and died a natural death. The child, then--since it has two names--is clearly marked as another person, and mistakes on the part of the Angel of Death will thus be avoided.

Atalyah, Abiyah, and Noadyah were used as names for men as well as for women. See Ch. D. Ginsburg, **The Massorah**, vol. III (London, 1885), p. 194.

[64] See Lipschitz, op. cit., ch. VIII, no. 37, p. 64.

[65] Id., op. cit., ch. VIII, no. 10, p. 59a, where, however, the remark is added that if one does not mind this fear of bad luck, God will protect him from harm ("Uman dela kafed bazeh, shomer peta-im Adonai").

[66] Comp. **Sefer Chasidim**, no. 363-364.

(3) The same fear prevents some parents from naming their child after another child of theirs who died. Most authorities declare it permissible.[67] Some authorities, however, advise--for safety's sake--to combine another name with the name of the child who died, and call the new child by two names. It is reported of R. Elijah of Wilna that he recommended to a family whose children would die young to call their new child by two names--one after the dead brother or sister, and one after another person. This he is said to have declared to be a potent means by which to safeguard the life of the new child.[68] Some authorities would even permit two living children in the same family to be called by one and the same name.[69] They cite the case of R. Hisda, who had two sons who were called by the same name (see Rashi to Ketubot 89b, **s.v.** **"Mar Yenuka"**). It is, however, thought advisable to avoid such practice for fear of the "evil eye."

(4) Some authorities would declare it prohibited to give a child the name of any Biblical personage prior to Abraham. This, however, is ignored by most authorities, as indeed names like Adam, Mahalalel, Noah, Enoch, and even Jephet have been frequent among Jewish people (see H.J.D. Azulai in his **Shem Hagedolim** I, Wien, 1864, p. 3a-4a).

(5) There are a few authorities who would object to non-Hebrew or non-Jewish names (Commentary to **Sefer Chasidim**, no. 1139, edition Lemberg, 1862, p. 84a; and R. Moses Shick in his responsa **Teshuvot Moharam Shick**, Yoreh De-a, no. 169, Muncacz, 1881, p. 52d). But, as we have seen, even in Talmudic times non-Jewish names were in vogue among the Jews. And it has continued to be the practice in post-Talmudic times all through the Middle Ages and up to the present times to call children by non-Jewish names. Many great rabbinical authorities had non-Jewish names. Rabbinic law recognizes this practice and seeks to regulate the correct spelling of these non-Jewish names for use in legal documents, especially in Bills of Divorce (see **Shulchan Aruch**, Even Ha-ezer 129, and commentaries; and comp. **Nachalat Shiv-a**, pp. 110-122).

---

[67] See responsa **Adoni Paz** by Ephraim B. Samuel Hekshir, no. 25 (Altona, 1743), p. 38 (and comp. **Pitchei Teshuva** to Yoreh De-a 116.6); responsa **Beit Yitschak** by R. Isaac Schmelkes to Yoreh De-a, part II, no. 163 (Przemysl, 1895), p. 129.

[68] See **Sefer Aliyot Eliyahu** by Heshil Lewin (Wilna, 1856), p. 67, note 51.

[69] Responsa **Adoni Paz**, no. 34, p. 40a.

In most cases, however, these non-Jewish names are accompanied by a Hebrew name, designated as the **Shem Hakodesh**,[70] the latter being used especially when the person is being called up to the Torah and in certain prayers recited by or on behalf of the person. The need for calling a person by a Hebrew name in connection with any religious performance, and especially in the recitation of prayers, is based upon the belief that the heavenly administration is conducted, and all its records kept, in Hebrew. The ministering angels are not believed to be great linguists. At any rate, whether they have any knowledge of foreign languages or not, they would ignore any communication addressed in any language other than Hebrew. They would not even pay attention to petitions expressed in Aramaic, which is cognate to Hebrew (Shabbat 12b).[71] Hence, it is deemed advisable--according to popular belief--that when dealing with the heavenly administration, a person should be called and referred to by his or her Hebrew name.[72]

---

[70] This **Shem Hakodesh** is sometimes a translation of the foreign name, but in some cases it is an altogether different name. See Zunz, **op. cit.**, pp. 26ff. In this connection we should mention the ceremony of **Hollenkreisch**, which--according to some authorities-- took place when boys were given their secular name, after **Shem Hakodesh** had been given during the circumcision ceremony. As this ceremony was performed while they placed the child in the cradle, the name given to him at that occasion is designated as **Shem Haarisa**. For a description of this ceremony of **Holikreish** or **Cholekreish**, the etymology of the word, and the superstitions suggested by the ceremony, see Loew, **op. cit.**, pp. 104-105; J. Perles, "Die Berner Handschrift des kleinen Aruch," in **Jubelschrift zum Siebzigsten Geburtstage des Prof. Dr. H. Graetz** (Breslau, 1887), p. 26, and M. Guedeman, **Geschichte des Erziehungswesens** etc. III (Wien, 1888), p. 104ff.

[71] The saying in the Talmud reads "**She-ein mal-achei hasharet makirin bilshon Arami**," and Asheri (quoted in **Beit Yosef** to Orach Chayim 101) explains it to mean that the angels would not recognize the Aramaic language, and that it is disdainful to them, hence, they would not pay attention to petitions spoken in it ("**Zeh meguneh be-eineihem lehizakek lo**"). That does not mean that they do not understand Aramaic. Comp. also responsum by Sherira Gaon in Harkavy's **Teshuvot Hage-onim** (Berlin, 1885), no. 373, p. 188.

[72] In this connection, another popular belief with regard to Hebrew names and the angels should be

In this connection, another peculiar practice in regard to mentioning a person's name for purposes of accurate identification in dealings with the heavenly authorities should be mentioned.   In certain special prayers recited by or on behalf of a person,[73] it is customary to add to the name of the person, for further identification, the name of the person's mother, and not that of the person's father.   The person reciting the prayer for himself introduces himself with the phrase: "I, Thy servant So-and-so, the son of Thy handmaid So-and-so."   When others pray for him, he is described in the prayer as: "So-and-so, the son of Mrs. So-and-so." Certain popular notions, hinted at in the Talmud and expanded on and more clearly expressed in the **Zohar**, are the basis for this practice.   In certain incantations occasionally used or recommended by the Rabbis of the Talmud, the person is referred to as the son of his mother, i.e., **"Pelanya bar Pelanita,"** (Shabbat 66b, Pesachim 112a).   And Abayei quotes his nurse, who so often gave him information about popular beliefs and superstitious practices, to the effect that in all magical formulas the person must be identified by giving his mother's name (Shabbat, l.c.).   The Talmud seemingly tolerates this practice in dealings with the demons. The assumption is either that the demons do not recognize marriage and still follow the customs of the age of matriarchy, or that they have their doubts as to who a person's father is (comp. **Zohar**, Shemot, Lublin, 1872, p. 17b).   The **Zohar**, however, goes farther and assumes that even when dealing with the angels or when wishing

---

mentioned.   As soon as a man has died and been buried--so it was believed--the Angel of Death comes to his grave and beats him and asks him for his name, for the purpose of identifying him and examining his record (see **Masechet Chibut Hakever** in **Yalkut Haro-im**, Warsaw, 1885, p. 80, and comp. the commentary **Chesed Le-Avraham, ad loc.**).   Of course, the person must give his name in Hebrew, otherwise the angel would not pay any attention to his answer and keep on beating him.   It is, therefore, necessary for every person to make sure that he will remember his Hebrew name after death.   This he can do by reciting every day after his daily prayers a verse from the Bible in Hebrew which contains his name or at least some allusion to or reminder of his name (see **Tikun Chibut Hakever** in **Kitsur Shalah**, by R. Yehiel Michael Epstein, Warsaw, 1864, pp. 101b-102b).

[73] Especially in the prayer **"Mi sheberach"** for the sick; also in the prayer beginning **"Ribbono shel olam,"** recited on the Three Festivals at the opening of the Ark before taking out the Torah scrolls.

to get something from the powers above, one should identify himself in no uncertain manner, and hence mention
the name of his mother and not that of his father
(**Zohar**, Lech Lecha, Lublin, 1872, p. 84). This, of
course, is contrary to the Jewish rule that children
follow the father and should be recorded and identified
as belonging to the family of the father (comp. B.B.
109b). Furthermore, it is not quite nice--to say the
least--and rather disrespectful to the mother, if a
prayer recited by or on behalf of her son contains the
implication that there are some doubts as to who the
actual father of her son is. So one could raise serious
objections to this practice. But it has persisted and
become widespread. (Comp. R. Eliyahu Gutmacher [1796-
1874] in his work, **Sukkat Shalom**, ch. 5, Jerusalem,
1883, pp. 295-334, who discusses the question thoroughly. He would compromise and consider the practice proper in such cases where the prayer, even though addressed
to God, indirectly aims to have some restraining effect
on the demons, seeking to forestall or counteract any
harm they might seek to do.)

As a result of this belief that the heavenly authorities know and can identify a person only on the
basis of the description furnished by his full name,
"So-and-so, the son of So-and-so," there developed in
the course of time a whole system of tricks by which to
hide a person from the heavenly agents and protect him
from them. We have found that already in Talmudic times
there was current the belief that a change in the name
of a person can have the effect of nullifying the evil
decree issued against him, for heavenly agents are unable to identify and apprehend him, since he now goes by
another name.

In post-Talmudic times this belief became more
pronounced and more generally accepted. Hence, the
practice of changing a person's name when he is sick
became widespread, and a special ritual for performing
such a change of name was developed in Gaonic times.[74]

---

[74] R. Jeroham b. Meshullam (first half of the 14th
century) in his **Sefer Toledot Adam VeChava**, part I
(Kopys, 1808), p. 182a, refers to, and in part quotes, a
ritual for effecting the change of name, instituted by
the Geonim ("shetikenu hage-onim"). It is to be recited
in an assembly of ten persons by an expert reader who
also holds a scroll of the Torah in his hands. The
ritual in full is found in **Machzor Bologna** (1540), sig.
23, leaf 4, and in **Siddur Hatefila Im Hayotserot, Ritus
Rome** (Mantua, 1557), pp. 227bff. Comp. also "**Siddur
Shinui Hashem**" in **Kitsur Hashalah** by Epstein (Warsaw,
1864), p. 101b. In this ritual, the sick person is
given a new name and the heavenly authorities are

The Angel of Death, so it was--and still is--believed,
who comes to that person with a warrant to take his
life, fails to identify him. He does not recognize in
the person now going by another name the one upon whom
the death sentence was decreed. To make this change of
name more effective, and to make doubly sure that the
Angel of Death would not be able to harm the person with
the changed name, it is deemed wise to select as the new
name one which in itself suggests long life. They usually select names such as Chayim ("Life), Alter ("Old
Man"), or Zeide ("Grandfather").[75] The Angel of Death
will thus find before him not only a person against whom
he has no warrant, but one whose very name declares that
he must continue to live, grow old, and become a grandfather; certainly the Angel of Death will not dare to
touch him. But there is still another danger threaten-
ing the person, even after his name has been changed,
and this is that the Angel of Death might be looking for
him merely as the child of his parents. This he is
likely to do (especially when death has been decreed
upon the child because of the sins of his parents,[76] and
the death warrant therefore calls for a child of So-
and-so), or he may simply ignore part of the name (which
in full reads "So-and-so, the son of So-and-so"), and
seek to identify the person merely as the child of So-
and-so with no regard for its first or proper name. To
meet this danger, a very ingenious practice was developed which frustrated all possible efforts of the Angel
of Death to get at the sick child. This practice con-

notified and requested to take cognizance of this change
in name and to consider the person with the new name as
not identical with the person with the old name, so that
whatever decrees may have been issued against the person
with the old name should not be executed upon this
person with his new name: "Ve-im niknesa mita, al peloni
zeh lo niknesa; ve-im nigzera gezera ra-a, al peloni zeh
lo nigzera. De-ish acher hu, vechivriya chadasha hi,
uchekatan shenolad lechayim tovim." Comp. also H.J.D.
Azulai in his Avodat Hakodesh (Warsaw, 1879), p. 109,
where it is assumed that the change has also the effect
of bringing into the person a new and purer and holier
soul: "Lehamshich lo nefesh chadasha ukedosha."

[75] There are some who follow another method for
selecting the new name: the scroll of the Torah is
opened and the first name of any of the Biblical heroes
they happen to strike upon is selected as the new name
for the sick person. See S. Baer, Sefer Totse-ot Chayim
(Roedelheim, 1862), p. 19.

[76] See Shabbat 32b.

sists of changing the second part of its name, that part
which contains the names of the parents, so that the
child is no longer called "the son of Mr. and Mrs. A,"
but "the son of Mr. and Mrs. B." This is done not by
giving the parents another name, but by giving the child
other parents, as it were. The real parents sell their
sick child to another couple,[77] to people against whom
(judging from the fact that all their own children are
alive and healthy) there seems to be no charge in the
heavenly records. The sick child is now considered the
child of Mr. and Mrs. B, the new parents who acquired
him. This transaction absolutely confounds the Angel of
Death. If he looks for the child not under his first
personal name, but under the name of his former parents
(as the child of Mr. and Mrs. A), he cannot find it, for
the child is no longer called so; and if his order was
to punish the parents by taking their child away from
them, he finds that these parents no longer have a child
that could be taken away from them. In either case, the
Angel of Death has to report back to heaven that he
could not execute his order.

Still another method of safeguarding the life of a
child is by not giving it any name at all, or--when a
name is given--to keep it secret for a time, so that it
is not registered in the heavenly records. Of course,
when a child has no name, or when its name is not recorded, the heavenly authorities do not know it. They
cannot issue any decree against it, and there is no way
of finding it. This method is resorted to by families
whose children die in infancy. They leave the child
unnamed for a certain time until--as they believe--there
is no more danger for the child, or until it passes the
critical period of infancy. Then they give it its
name.[78] As to who should give the child the name, there
has never been any inflexible rule or fixed regulation.
In Biblical times, it was usually the father who would
give the name of his child. In many instances, however,
it was the mother. We also gave an instance of the
foster mother's naming the child, as was the case with
Moses (Ex. 2:10). Sometimes it was done by neighbors,
as was the case with Obed, the son of Ruth and Boaz

---

[77] See **Sefer Chasidim** (ed. Wistinetzki), p. 365, and
comp. Azulai's commentary to **Sefer Chasidim** (edition
Lemberg), no. 245.

[78] See Lipschitz, op. cit., VIII, no. 28, p. 62, and
comp. commentary on the Torah by **Ba-alei Hatosafot** to
Gen. 5:28 (Warsaw, 1904), p. 5: "**Metushelach hatsadik
natan lo [leLemech] etsa shelo yemaher likro lo [livno
Noach] shem, lefi she-anshei hador mechashefim hayu,
veyihyu mechashefim oto im yede-u shemo.**"

(Ruth 4:17). In one instance, the prophet, in the name of God, gave the child a name in addition to the name given by the parents, as was the case with Solomon, whom the prophet named Yedidya (II Sam. 12:25).

In Talmudic times, it seems, no change was made in the custom which obtained in Biblical times, although we have no definite report in the Talmud on this point. In **Midrash Kohelet R.** (to Kohelet 7:1) there is a reference to the name given to a person by his father and mother, and in **Pirkei deR. Eliezer** (ch. 48) it is said that both parents of Moses gave him a name. But this may only mean that both parents agreed upon the name by which he should be called, and not that they both actually pronounced the name upon him. It may be assumed that the practice in Talmudic times was the same as in Biblical times. When the father was there, he would actually name the child. When he was not there, the mother would do it. In one instance reported in the Talmud (M.K. 25b) of a child born after the death of his father, it is said that "they," the people present--neighbors or members of the family--gave the child the name of his father. This practice would correspond to the practice of neighbors naming the child as recorded in Ruth 4:7. In post-Talmudic times, and up to modern times, the same rule has obtained. It has, however, become customary that another person--the **Mohel**, the rabbi, the cantor, or whomever the father delegates to do so--actually performs the rite of naming the child. But it is still the right of the father to decide upon the name. Popular custom in some countries gives the mother the right to decide upon the name of her firstborn child and to name it after her parents or relatives.[79] But most authorities object to this custom, insisting that it is the indisputable right of the father to decide upon the name of the child.[80] In practice, however, these questions are first settled between the parents, and after they both agree upon the name, the father tells it to the officiant, who pronounces it over the child.

With respect to the time when the name should be given to the child, there have been some developments in the course of time. In Biblical times, the child was given its name immediately at its birth (see Loew, **op. cit.**, p. 94, and comp. A.S. Herschberg, **Hatekufa** CCVI, p. 257, for references). In Talmudic times, though no express regulation about it can be found, it seems that it was the usual custom to name the male child at the circumcision ceremony on the eighth day after its birth

---

[79] See Lipschitz, **op. cit.**, VIII, no. 35, pp. 63ab.

[80] **Ibid.** Comp. also Abraham Meyuhas, **Sefer Bisde Ha-arets**, part III, Responsum 22 (Leghorn, 1788), p. 41a.

(see Luke 1:59 and 2:21; and **Pirkei deR. Eliezer**, ch. 48).[81] This has become the established practice from post-Talmudic times up to this day.[82] In case the circumcision is postponed because of the sickness of the child, the naming of the child is also postponed till the time of the circumcision. In case a child is to remain uncircumcised, as when it comes from a family whose children die as a result of circumcision (**Arel shemetu echav mechamat mila**), the name is given to the child at the time when his father is called up to the Torah. And there is difference of opinion as to whether it is preferable to do so before the child is eight days old or after.[83] In the case of girls there has been no uniformity of practice. Among the Sefardim in the Orient, the naming of a baby girl is a home ceremony. The parents invite guests to a meal at which the name of the newly born daughter is announced. Among the Italian and Ashkenazic Jews it was customary to name the girl in the synagogue on the Sabbath when the mother, for the first time after birth of the child, could visit the synagogue (Loew, **op. cit.**, p. 104). There is, however, no fixed rule about this. Present day custom among Polish Ashkenazic Jews varies in different localities. In some places it is still customary to name the girl right after she is born.[84] In others, the name is given in the synagogue on the Sabbath or on a Monday or Thursday, when the father comes to the synagogue and is called up to the Torah.

The prayer recited at the naming of a boy has become part of the service at the circumcision ceremony. The prayer at the naming of a girl now usually has a very short form. In the prayer "He who blessed" ("**Mi sheberach**"), recited for the mother, there is inserted the phrase, "May also bless the girl that was born to her and whose name should be called So-and-so."[85]

---

[81] Comp. Krauss, **Archaeologie** II, ch. V, and note 123, p. 439; also J. Mann, **op. cit.**, p. 326.

[82] See **Hagahot** to **Sefer Minhagim** by Tyrnan (Warsaw, 1709), p. 67, and compare Kaufman Cohen in **Sefer Chukei Da-at** (Sadilkow, 1835), p. 66b.

[83] See Glassberg, **op. cit.**, p. 248, and Lipschitz, **op. cit.**, VIII, no. 2, p. 58b.

[84] Lipschitz, **ibid.**, no. 3, p. 58b.

[85] As to the original, longer forms of this formula, see Glassberg, **op. cit.**, pp. 256-257.

Summary

As a result of the above survey of the different attitudes towards names and the various rituals and practices resulting from them, we may state that there have never been any definite laws or uniform fixed regulations on these questions. It was all a matter of custom and usage, which were not uniform. Custom is subject to changes from time to time and from place to place, and the customs relating to the naming of children are no exception to this rule. Since these customs are governed by certain ideas and beliefs, which not all people share in the same degree, it is not strange to find that the customs themselves differ so. Some people are more superstitious, others are more rational. It is well to recall the saying, quoted above, of one who himself was inclined to superstition, the author of the **Sefer Chasidim**: "Superstitions can affect only those who believe in them." Hence, while it is but proper to follow the custom established by the community or the group, it actually makes no difference what names we give to children. For no matter what name a person is given by others, what ultimately counts is only the name which he makes for himself by his actions and his conduct.

.Jacob Z. Lauterbach

See also:

S.B. Freehof, "Naming a Child after a Gentile Grandparent," **Modern Reform Responsa**, pp. 134ff.

60. CHILDREN OF MIXED MARRIAGES
(Vol. XXIX, 1919, pp. 76-77)

On January 1, 1919, I received the following **sheela**: "A member of my congregation approached me with the following difficulty. His wife was a Christian (Methodist), and a New York rabbi had married them. The woman is now pregnant, and the man wanted me to advise him in what faith the expected child is to be raised. His wife never accepted Judaism, though she attends services more regularly than many of my Jewish women, but she goes to her Methodist Church frequently also. Her mother is a strict Methodist; his mother is a Jewess, and each wants

the child in her respective faith. I have made inquiry
of the New York rabbi who married them, and he assures
me that he never married a couple under such circumstances without getting the promise of the alien party to
raise the children in the Jewish faith and to study (by
himself or herself) some guide of Jewish instruction.
He also tells me that they abjure their old faith in his
presence and promise to cast their lot in with our people. He remembers marrying this couple and is certain
that he exacted such a promise from this woman. I have
not spoken to this couple since I saw the rabbi in question. I will, when I am ready to give my answer, even
if she denies or forgot the promise under those circumstances. (This rabbi does not go through the formality
of issuing a paper of conversion in the presence of
witnesses.)

I feel that I would not be justified in saying that
the child should be raised a Jew, if the mother is and
intends to remain a Christian. It would be dividing the
home and the child would hardly be Jewish. It would be
a mockery and hypocrisy. On the other hand, how could
I, a Jewish teacher, tell the parents to raise the child
a Christian? If the child is to be raised in the Christian faith, the father cannot remain a Jew without--in
later years--taking the consequence of having children
who would mock and scoff and deride him. If this is not
a certainty, it is--to say the least--a possibility and
a probability. Again, then, how can I, or how dare I,
advise this man who wants to remain a Jew (or he would
not belong to a congregation and be a frequent attendant
at services) to become something else? I will, of
course, urge the mother to become a Jewess. But if she
refuses, what shall my advice be? This is my **she-ela.**
I remember the passage in Kiddushin: '**Bincha haba miYis-
re-elit karuy bincha, ve-ein bincha haba min hanochrit
karuy bincha, ela benah.**' Likewise, the passages in
Shulchan Aruch, Even Ha-ezer: '**Yisra-el sheba el achat
me-elu, havalad kemotah,**' and '**Velad shifcha ve-akum
kemotan.**' Do the passages have their force with us?''

To this I reply:

The Talmud (Kid. 68b; Yev. 23) and the **Shulchan
Aruch** (ch. 44) you refer to are certainly in force, and
consequently the child of a non-Jew has its character
determined by the mother. The Christian wife of your
member should, therefore, be persuaded as far as possi-
ble--especially for the sake of the husband who wants to
have a Jewish home--to become a Jewess in order to have
her expected child born as a Jew--**leidato bikdusha.** The
mode of her conversion and adoption into Judaism might
in this case be facilitated. Of course, when raised as

a Jew, the child could afterwards, through Confirmation, be adopted into the Jewish fold like any proselyte. On the other hand, it must be stated that the rabbi who solemnized the marriage of a Jew to a non-Jewess did not act in conformity with the Jewish law, no matter whether she promised to raise her children as Jews or not. Mixed marriages belong before the civil magistrate, who is to give them legal sanction. The Jewish religion cannot consecrate a home divided by two different creeds, as you well state.

K. Kohler

61. STATUS OF CHILDREN OF DOUBTFUL RELIGIOUS BACKGROUND (Vol. LXX, 1960, pp. 95-99)

The committee has received during the past year a number of questions which involve Jewish converts to Christianity, and some questions with regard to the reversion to a non-Jewish faith on the part of converts to Judaism. A question arose about the status in Judaism of Christian children adopted and converted to Judaism, and then--because of physical or mental defects-- the adoption is canceled and the child is returned to the agency. What is the status of such a child? The questions involving apostasy may have come up generally in the following circumstances. A child is of an immigrant family in which there is a Gentile father and a Jewish mother, the family having converted to Christianity in Germany. Now a young girl from this mixed family wants to marry a Jew. May she be married to a Jew without conversion? Analogous to it is the question of a child of a Jewish mother adopted and raised by a Christian family as a Christian; can this child be married to a Jew without conversion? Does the fact that this child was not raised by her Jewish mother make a difference? As for a Christian adopted and converted to Judaism, and then--because of physical or mental defects--returned to the agency, is this child to be deemed to have remained a Jew? May he or she, for example, when grown up, be married to a Jew without question, without further reconversion?

These are all practical questions, and therefore it is important not only that we analyze the attitude of Jewish law in the past to these individuals, but also that we come to a practical conclusion for ourselves as to how we should deal with the problems mentioned above.

It is to be noted at the outset that these problems are not new. To some degree they are dealt with in the Talmud, but they come to more complete discussion in the many responsa dealing with the **Marranos**, who for centuries kept on escaping from Spain and Portugal and appearing in Jewish communities. A decision had to be made as to the status of these fugitives. Should they be reconverted to Judaism, or was the conversion unnecessary on the ground that they were still Jews? The question came up likewise in Ashkenazic Jewry due to the waves of compulsory conversion in the wake of the Crusades and later persecutions. It would be well, therefore, to take the law in its general principles from the beginning.

The Talmud (Yevamot 45b) says that a child born of a Gentile and a Jewess is **kosher**. To which Rashi comments: "Since his mother is Jewish, he is counted as one of our brothers." The Talmud (Kiddushin 68b), in discussing the verse in Deuteronomy 7:4 ("He will wean your son away from following Me"), indicates that "he" means the Gentile father of the son, who will mislead your son away, etc. Therefore, the Talmud says, this indicates that your son born of an Israelite woman is truly your son, but a son born of a Gentile woman is her son. So is the principle embodied in the codes: in the **Tur**, Even Ha-ezer 4, it says that the son of any Gentile man and a Jewish woman is **kosher** to marry a Jew; so it is also in the **Shulchan Aruch**, Even Ha-ezer 4.5 and 19. There is some question whether a child in such a mixed marriage may marry a **Kohen**, but most authorities agree that she may do so.

Therefore, there is no question that the child of a Jewish mother is fully a Jew and may be married to a Jew. Now--theoretically speaking--if this daughter of a mixed marriage also married a Gentile, her child is a child of a Jewish mother and is also Jewish. For how many generations would this Jew's status reach? While, of course, this is a theoretical question, it is interesting to note that Solomon, the son of Simon Duran of Algiers (**Rashbash**, #89) says that it applies **ad sof ha-olam**, forever. The statement of Duran is as follows: "One whose mother is Jewish, even for many generations, even if the father is Gentile, the child is Jewish, even to the end of the world, **ad sof ha-olam**."

But such a person has been raised as a Christian: either (as in the case concerning which the committee was specifically asked) the child was herself converted, or (as in the case of the **Marranos**) the child was raised in a Christian environment from the very beginning. Granted that the child is Jewish by birth, must it not be in some formal way restored to its Jewish status by some ceremony akin to conversion? This is discussed in

the law, and most of the discussion goes back to the
Talmud in Bechorot 31a and Avoda Zara 7a. There the
discussion deals specifically with the relationship
between the **Am Ha-arets** (meaning, in the Talmudic sense,
one who is not to be trusted to observe the laws of
purity and to give tithes and heave-offering properly)
and the **Chaverim** (those who are careful to keep all the
laws mentioned). The Talmud says that the **Am Ha-arets**,
before he can be accepted as trustworthy, must make a
formal promise of **Chaverut**, that is, to be one of the
Chaverim who are careful to observe the law.

The same term is used in the discussion of apostates who want to return; it is asked of the repentant
apostates to take upon themselves the promise of **Chaverut**, that is, to obey Jewish law. As to whether any
formal ceremony other than such a promise is to be required of them, there is a general agreement that the
ritual bath is not really required by strict law (**mide-
oraita**), but some would require the ritual bath as a
rabbinical caution (**miderabanan**). Thus, it is decided
by Moses Isserles in Yoreh De-a 268.12. However, it is
noteworthy that in the discussion in the Talmud (in
Bechorot), Rabbi Simon and Rabbi Joshua--speaking of the
non-observant and whether we would accept their repent-
ance--say that under all circumstances we should accept
them because of the verse in Jeremiah 3:22: "Return, ye
recreant children." And the Talmud says that the law is
according to this pair of lenient authorities. The
status of the non-observant Jew and that of the proselyte are brought together in the Tosefta (Demai II). In
the discussion on the **Shulchan Aruch** passage mentioned
above, Elijah of Wilna quotes this lenient discussion in
the Talmud as applying also to apostates who revert to
Judaism. In general, the Talmud is lenient also with
regard to children of Jewish birth who--unaware of their
Jewish origin--are raised among non-Jews ("**tinok she-
nishba bein hanochrim**"). See the discussion in Shabbat
68b, especially with regard to their being excused since
in their ignorance they violated the Sabbath.

The general mood of the law with regard to all
those who seek to return was to make as little fuss as
possible and to interpose no hindrances. The rest of
the statement of Solomon Duran as to these reverts is as
follows: "The requirements of conversion do not apply to
them at all. When they wish to return to Judaism, we do
not have to tell them about the various commandments [as
we do to Gentile converts], for they already stand sworn
as part of Israel from Mount Sinai and they do not need
the ritual bath for conversion." That this is not merely a chance liberal statement is evidenced by the fact
that it is quoted by Joseph Caro in his **Beit Yosef**
(Bedek Habayit) at the end of Yoreh De-a 268, where the

question is discussed.   It is noteworthy, too, that
Rabbenu Gershom, the Light of the Exile, speaking in the
Rhineland, also says in a similar case (in fact, with
regard to a **Kohen**) that we should be as lenient as possible and refrain carefully from reminding the apostates
of their former state lest we discourage them, thereby
to return in repentance (**Vitry**, pp. 96-97).

It is clear from this point that no ritual of observance should be required of the children of a Jewish
mother.   To do so would indeed violate the law and imply
that they were not Jews, which would be erroneous.   However, the decision of Isserles that they avow **Divrei
Chaverut** could well be accepted by us as a cautionary
action.   We should ask the person involved to promise to
maintain a Jewish home.   This, at the most, is all that
is necessary.

Now to the other, and somewhat related, question,
i.e.: What about a child born of a Gentile mother who,
in infancy, is converted to Judaism, and then--after
conversion--is returned to the general agency because of
some physical or mental defect?   Is this child, because
of the original conversion in infancy, to be deemed
permanently a Jew?   This may be a practical question if,
when the child grows up, he or she wants to marry a Jew.

In general, the law concerning an infant who is
converted is different from that governing an adult who
is converted to Judaism.   An adult accepts Judaism of
his free will after a careful explanation is made to him
of all the circumstances involved in becoming a Jew.
But an infant is converted without knowing what is involved.   The Talmud says (Ketubot 11a) that an infant
may be converted by the authority of the **Beit Din**, not,
of course, on the ground of the child's intelligent
acceptance of the conditions involved (which is impossible), but because becoming a Jew was deemed to be an
advantage, and we may do a favor for a person even without his consent.   Therefore, with regard to an adult
convert, he cannot completely discard the allegiance
which he had accepted.   He simply becomes a sinful Jew,
and he may still enter into Jewish marriage, just as an
apostate may (see Tosefta, Demai 11.5; Yoreh De-a
268.12).

This convert to Judaism who reverts to his former
faith is, of course, not deemed a Jew in the full sense
of the word.   Just as in the case of a born Jew who
apostasizes, he is, for example, not to be relied upon
with regard to the various **mitzvot**.   The wine in his
possession is Gentile wine, and his bread is Gentile
bread.   But with regard to marriage, he has the same
right as an apostate Jew.   The only exception with regard to apostates in the marriage relationship concerns
the Levirate marriage and **Chalitsa**.   If, for example, a

man dies and has no children, and his brother is an apostate, some few authorities ease the requirement that the widow obtain **Chalitsa** from this apostate. But otherwise, the apostate, whether born Jewish or having been converted as an adult, retains his Jewish status in marriage relationships (cf. Ezekiel Landau, **Noda Bi-Yehuda** II, Even Ha-ezer 150).

Thus, the adult convert, like a Jew, possesses what international lawyers call an "indelible allegiance," at least with regard to marriage and divorce. However, a child who has been converted without his own intelligent consent but merely on the theory that a favor has been done him, is given the permission to renounce the conversion when he grows up. So says Rabbi Joseph in the discussion in the Talmud (Ketubot 11a). This is embodied as law by Asher ben Yehiel in his **Compendium on the Talmud**; he adds, however, that if, when he has grown, he is known to observe Jewish law, this observance is deemed to mean consent, and then he can no longer renounce his allegiance. So it is in the **Shulchan Aruch**, Yoreh De-a 268.7,8. The child in question, therefore, has the right to determine whether his conversion in infancy remains valid or not. If he chooses to live a Jewish life as he grows up, he is a Jew, and if not, his conversion is void.

To sum up: Those who are born of Jewish mothers and those who are converted to Judaism as adults have an indelible allegiance to Judaism with regard to marriage laws. The only real exception to this is to free a woman from the need of **Chalitsa** if her husband's brother is an apostate.

Solomon B. Freehof

62.   THE STATUS OF A GENTILE-BORN CHILD ADOPTED
INTO A JEWISH FAMILY
(Vol. LXVI, 1956, pp. 107-110)

QUESTION: Certain religious groups endeavor to have legislation passed requiring that children should not be given for adoption except to parents of the same religion as the natural parent or parents of the child. Should we Jews favor such legislation? In general, what is our attitude toward a child who is to be adopted? What ritual must it go through? What is its status?

ANSWER: What is the status of a non-Jewish child offered for adoption in the eyes of Jewish law?   It should
be clear at the outset that the racial descent of the
child has absolutely no significance in Jewish law.   It
is true that the Bible (Deut. 23:4) mentions Ammonites,
Moabites, Egyptians, etc., who may not enter into the
Jewish community.   However, this law only applied to
male members and not to female members, as the Talmud
makes clear   (B. Yevamot 76b-77a).   Furthermore, all
these racial distinctions no longer have any bearing at
all.   Rabbi Akiva stated in Tosefta Kiddushin V.4 that
the Assyrian king Sennacherib, through his conquests,
"mixed up all the races," so that no race is now recognizable for specific prohibition.   This statement of
Akiva is embodied into Jewish law.   Maimonides in **Yad**,
Hil. Isurei Bi-a XII.25 says (basing his opinion on
Akiva) that now no races are distinguishable, and therefore, all may enter the Jewish community.   Thus, it is
clear that race is not involved in the question of adoption, according to Jewish law.
      But another question is involved that must be care-
fully discussed.   The same passage in Scripture which
discusses   the   inadmissibility   into   the   community   of
Moabites, Ammonites, etc. (Deut. 23:3), also says that a
Mamzer may not enter into the community.   Since many of
these children are born out of wedlock, what we must be
concerned with here is the child's personal status at
birth.   There is a considerable number of laws about the
legal status of parentless children of doubtful parentage.   These laws are basically concerned with the question of bastardy (**Mamzerut**), since a **Mamzer** is forbidden
to marry into the Jewish family.   Of course, it must be
understood at the outset that the term **Mamzer** is much
more liberally understood in Jewish law than the term
"bastard" in modern languages and law.   A child born out
of wedlock is not necessarily a **Mamzer** in Jewish law.
Only a child born out of a connection which cannot be
legitimized is a **Mamzer**, e.g., the child of a married
woman and a man not her husband, or the child of the
forbidden degrees of relationship.   The question of
Mamzerut in Jewish law applies only to a Jewish mother,
because a Gentile child, if converted, becomes a **kosher**
Jew.   But with a Jewish mother--only if it is absolutely
sure that the child is from a Jew whom she could not
possibly marry (or if there is an overwhelming presumption that this is so), that child is a **Mamzer**--and is
forbidden.   When we do not know the parents--as is generally the case nowadays--we presume that the child is
Gentile and, therefore, admissible; and even if we know
that the mother is Jewish, the general presumption is
that the child is **kosher**.

The law of the status of such children of doubtful
parentage is given first in the Mishna briefly (Kiddu-
shin IV.2), then in greater detail in the Talmud (B.
Kiddushin 73a), then in the various codes (**Yad**, Hilchot
Bi-a XV.30, 31; **Shulchan Aruch**, Even Ha-ezer, 4.31; 32).
There are two elaborate responsa on the question, one by
Ezekiel Landau (**Noda BiYehuda** I, Even Ha-ezer 7), and
Benjamin Weiss, Rabbi of Chernowitz (**Even Yekara** II,
#5). All these sources classify the dubious children
under two headings, "**Shetuki**" (those about whom the
mother is silent, i.e., "undescribed children"), and
second, "**Asufi**" ("picked-up children" or foundlings).
As for the **Shetuki** (undescribed children), if the moth-
er--on being questioned--says that the child is the
result of a relationship with someone **kosher** (i.e., not
a forbidden degree), then she is believed and the child
is **kosher**.

In his responsum (mentioned above), Ezekiel Landau
says that although the Jewish mother died and can no
longer be questioned, the overwhelming presumption is
that the intercourse was not with anyone of the forbidden degrees (i.e., with no forbidden Jew), and therefore
the child is **kosher**. Even if it were a Gentile man, the
child still follows the status of the Jewish mother and
is also Jewish, and, therefore, the child needs no conversion. He says further that if it is known that the
child is of an unmarried woman, there is absolutely no
doubt as to the child's complete acceptability. In the
responsum of Weiss, the mother first claimed that the
child was the result of sexual relationship with her
husband, who died before the child was born, but later
she admitted that it was the child of a Gentile father.
In either case, since the child follows the status of
the mother, and there is no weight of presumption that
she had relationship with a Jew who is forbidden to her,
the child is **kosher**.

Most of the children adopted nowadays are from
unknown parents. They are, therefore, children who, if
described at all under the two categories, would be
described not as **Shetuki**, "undeclared," but as **Asufi**,
foundlings. Since there is no parent to question in the
case of an **Asufi**, the Talmud considers the **Asufi** to be a
"**Safek Mamzer**" (a doubtful **Mamzer**), but even a **Safek
Mamzer** may, according to the law of the Torah (B. Kiddushin 73a), be married into the community. But the Talmud makes so many restrictions as to the term **Asufi** that
almost no child nowadays could be put in that derogatory
category. The Talmud (in Kiddushin, **loc. cit.**) says
that an **Asufi** is only such a child as has been clearly
thrown away to die (the presumption being that the child
is a **Mamzer** and that the mother is afraid to have anything to do with it). But any foundling who shows evi-

dence of care (by his dress, washing, or anointing, or
if it is put so that someone can pick it up) is not an
Asufi at all, and is presumably **kosher**.   Since, nowadays, however, the majority of the people in the cities
are Gentile, such a child is presumably Gentile, and,
therefore, must be converted.   This is, of course, not
the case with the child of a mother who is known to be a
Jewess.   Such a child does not need to be converted.

Of course, an infant should be received into the
Jewish community.   Does it need conversion?   The Talmud
(M. Ketubot IV.3 and B. Ketubot 11a) speaks of the conversion of children.   What process is to be followed?
The Orthodox would require the ritual of the bath for
all children in addition to circumcision for boys.   On
the question of the conversion of children (not specifically for adopted children, but in general), the CCAR
came to a definite decision in my Report on Marriage and
Intermarriage.   There it was decided that such children
need only attend our religious schools and that the
Confirmation Service which ends the school course be
deemed sufficient as a ceremony of conversion.   Naturally, an adopted boy would be circumcised.   Generally,
most boys are circumcised now.   In that case, a more
observant family might want to take the drop of Blood of
Covenant.

The final question is this: What is the status of
an adopted child in a Jewish family?   On this question
there are, first of all, a number of Agadic sayings
which, while not strictly legal, embody the spirit of
Jewish life with regard to adopted children.   The Talmud
says (B. Sanhedrin 19b) as follows: "Whoever raises an
orphan in his house, Scripture considers him as if he
were his physical parent."   On the same page there is an
analogous statement: "He who teaches a child the Torah
is as if he were his parent."   **Exodus Rabba** XLVI.5 is an
elaboration of the verse in Isaiah, "Thou, O God, art
our Father."   The Midrash says, "Whoever **raises** the
child is called father, not the one who begets it."

But in addition, there is clear halachic evidence
concerning the full legal status of an adopted child.
Meir of Rothenburg, in his responsum (edition Lemberg,
#242; and also found in **Teshuvot Maimoniyot,** at the end
of Mishpatim, #48) discusses the following question: If
a man writes on a **Shetar** (a note) the name of his wife's
son, whom he has raised and to whom he refers as "my
son," is the note legal?   Meir of Rothenburg says that
it is absolutely legal, and adds, as a general principle: "Since he raises an orphan in his house, the orphan
is considered his son, and he may refer to the boy as
'my son' and the son may refer to the parents as 'father' and 'mother,' and there is no legal objection to
that nomenclature."   This statement is further embodied

in the law (**Shulchan Aruch,** Choshen Mishpat 42.15).
Isserles agrees that such notes are legal.   There is
some questioning of the right of such people to call
each other "father" and "son" in the special case of
vows.   That is to say, if a man makes a vow that he will
accept no benefits from his sons, and he has natural
sons as well as an adopted son--does that vow prevent
him also from accepting benefits from his adopted son?
This question is discussed by Jacob Emden in his Responsum #165.   He adds some doubts as to the adopted son
being **always** referred to as "son," in such specific
cases, but in general, he accepts it.   See fuller discussion of this question by Eleazar Wildenberg in **Hapardes** 23:3, p. 13.

So it is clear that race or religion of parents has
no bearing with us.   A child who is adopted is accepted
in Judaism according to the practices of the branch of
Judaism to which the adopting family belongs.   Such a
child is absolutely and completely a member of the family and a full child of the parents.

Solomon B. Freehof

63.   ADOPTION AND ADOPTED CHILDREN
(1978)

QUESTION: What is the status of adoption and
adopted children in Judaism?   What steps are necessary for a conversion if such children are Gentile?
If the children are converted, should they bear the
name **ben Avraham** or **bat Sarah**?   Should there be a
special ritual for adoptions either for the naming
of such children or for bringing these children
into the covenant of Judaism?   (Rabbi Michael M.
Remson, Family Life Committee)

ANSWER: There is nothing in the legal section of the
Talmud about adoption, although the Talmud does present
agadot which discuss the status of Moses's relationship
to Pharaoh's daughter and Naomi's to her grandchild
(Talmud, Meg. 13a and San. 19b).   These discussions led
to the statement, "Whoever rears an orphan in his house
is considered as if he had begotten that child."   In
addition, on the same page we find the statement, "He
who teaches his neighbor's son Torah, is as if he had
begotten him."   **Exodus Rabba** 45 interpreted the verse of
Isaiah 64:8, "You, O God, are our Father," as meaning

that "Anyone who raised a child is called father, not the one who has begotten it." These are not halachic statements, but they indicate a climate of opinion which definitely favored adoption.

The problem with adoption is knowing the biological background of the adoptive child. If there is conclusive evidence that the child was the offspring of parents who could, under Jewish marriage law, have contracted a lawful marriage, then the child is deemed Jewish and there is no bar to adoption or any later participation in Jewish life, except that the child could not share in the traditional privileges of the Aaronite priesthood. Further, if the child is the child of a Jewish mother and a non-Jewish father, no bar to the adoption in terms of Jewish status of the child obtains. Even if the child were a foundling (an extremely rare situation today as far as Jewish infants are concerned) and the circumstances of the discovery point to a desire on the part of the natural parent(s) to insure that the baby would be found and taken in by a family to be raised, the Jewish presumption is that such a child may rightfully be considered Jewish.

Situations of doubt have always been rare, as Jewish law did everything possible to avoid them. For example, in the case of an unmarried Jewish mother, her statement about paternity was accepted; if she could not establish paternity, then the child was presumed **kosher** (Mishna, Kid. 4.2; Talmud, Kid. 73a; **Yad**, Hil. Isurei Bi-a 15.30, 31; **Shulchan Aruch**, Even Ha-ezer 4.30, 32). The sources make a distinction between two categories of children of whom nothing was known: **Shetuki**--children about whose paternity the mother was unwilling to say anything, and **Asufi**--foundlings with nothing known about mother or father. Some doubt was expressed about the acceptability of foundlings as suspicion of **Mamzerut** (a child born of an adulterous or incestuous relationship) existed, but the Talmud (Kid. 73a) surrounded this category with so many hedges that it virtually ceased to exist. In other words, most children would fall into the former category.

A considerable amount of modern discussion of these matters has been undertaken by Ezekiel Landau (**Noda BiYehuda**, vol. I, Even Ha-ezer #7), and Benjamin Weiss (**Even Yekara** 2.5). Both of these individuals discussed whether children with an unmarried Jewish mother and with doubtful paternity could be accepted. They concluded that the children were welcome even if the father was not Jewish. We can see from both ancient and more recent authorities that the main obstacle standing in the way of possible objection of Jewish children was successfully removed. Once they had entered the household, they were to be considered completely like child-

ren of the house and in no way different from natural
children. This is in accordance with the Agadic statement previously mentioned, and which was re-emphasized
by Meir of Rothenburg in Responsum #242, in which he
dealt with a question about a note (**Shetar**) and an
adopted orphan raised in the household. The orphan was
considered legally part of the household. This thought
was then embodied in the Jewish legal tradition (Isserles to **Shulchan Aruch**, Choshen Mishpat 42.15). It is
reasonable today to rely on reputable adoption agents or
agencies that should be in a position to provide information on the adoptive child's origin, not necessarily
with specific names, etc., but with an accurate statement on the background of the anonymous (to the adoptive
parents) natural parents.

If a child beyond the age of infancy is adopted--
as, for instance, in the case of a stepfather adopting
the child of his wife, where the child was born to the
wife's first marriage--there is no problem whatsoever in
clarifying the child's origins. If a couple adopts an
older child who may remember a mother or a father, there
is an obligation on the part of the adoptive parents to
find out the child's origins in order to be forewarned
of any possible problem in the child's future full participation in Jewish life, particularly in the area of
marriage. All adopted children should be told at an
appropriate time that they have been adopted.

Lastly, a child who is definitely non-Jewish may,
indeed, be adopted and converted. There is no question
at all about the acceptability of non-Jewish children as
candidates for adoption. Their background does not
matter; even people once prohibited entry into the family of Israel, such as the Ammonites, Moabites, etc.
(Deut. 23:4), were no longer forbidden by Mishnaic times
(Tosefta, Kid. 5.9; **Yad**, Isurei Bi-a 12.25). In all
such cases, we must deal with the process of conversion
to Judaism (Mishna, Ket. 4.3; Ket. 11a). It should be
pointed out that such conversion, while full and complete ritually and legally, obligates the adoptive parents to provide Jewish training, etc., for the child.
When the child reaches the age of Bar (Bat) Mitzvah,
there is a traditional mechanism by which the converted
child could reject Judaism without prejudice (**Sh.A.**,
Yoreh De-a 268.7). In earlier days, a formal process of
rejection was required because of the rigidity of Jew-
ish-Gentile relationships. Nowadays, no such rejection
mechanism is necessary, because belonging to the Jewish
people and faith are essentially voluntary. It is important, however, that the adopted child be informed at
an opportune time that he/she was adopted. In other
words, the Jewishness of the child matures along with
the child himself. Theoretically, the child could re-

ject Judaism upon becoming an adult, but that matter is
moot for us, and the conversion matures along with the
child and becomes irrevocable.   This places a special
duty upon adoptive parents to see to it that an adopted
child receives an adequate Jewish education so that the
child's sense of being Jewish would not ever come into
question.

It is clear that nothing formal should be done in
this regard until permanent jurisdiction over the child
has been obtained.   This is proper from two points of
view; first of all, it would be morally wrong, and probably illegal, to convert a child to Judaism as long as
the possibility of having to return it to its non-Jewish
parents remains; if that should occur, the child would
be raised as a non-Jew.   Secondly, it avoids the problem
of public embarrassment if a child so placed has to be
returned to its natural parent(s).   Although this situation rarely arises, it does occur and that painful experience should not be aggravated.

When such a child has been legally adopted, then he
or she should be named in the synagogue.   The name to be
provided would be **ben-** or **bat-**, and then the name of the
adopting parents.   Thenceforth, those parents are fully
his/her parents and that should be indicated through the
name.   This should be stressed rather than the fact of
conversion.   The designations **ben Avraham** or **bat Sarah**
were created for the purpose of providing a full name to
individuals whose parents remained non-Jews.   They also
helped the convert, as this was a constant reminder of
conversion to Judaism from another religion.   In our
case, both adoptive parents are Jewish and the child has
never known any other religion, so it needs no reminder
nor a special parental name (Moshe Feinstein, **Igerot
Mosheh**, Yoreh De-a 161).   Linking the Hebrew name of the
child with his/her parents will provide an additional
firm bond between them, which may be of special significance during the teenage years when this child will
become Bar or Bat Mitzvah and question his or her real
origin.

The naming of such a child should occur in the same
manner as with any other child.   This procedure should
also be followed if the adopted child is older and may
be capable of understanding the process.   In most Reform
congregations this would be considered sufficient ritual
conversion for girls and also for a large number of
boys.   This act, along with Jewish education, would
bring the child into the covenant of Judaism in the same
manner as any natural child.

In the case of boys who are not circumcised, there
should be a circumcision done precisely in the same
manner and with the same ritual as a circumcision for
natural children.   It would, of course, usually occur at

a more advanced age. If a child was already circumcised, some parents may want to undertake **tipat dam**, but that remains optional. In addition, some more traditional parents may also want to have the adopted boy or girl undergo **Tevila**. It is quite clear from tradition that if such a child at any later time undergoes **Tevila**, even though not specifically for the purpose of conversion, it would be considered the same as if he had undergone it for that purpose (**Shulchan Aruch**, Yoreh De-a, 268.3). The Talmud debated the need for both circumcision and ritual bath. R. Eliezer (Talmud, Yev. 46a) indicated that a proselyte who was circumcised and did not take the ritual bath, was considered fully Jewish. The decision went against him. Both Orthodox and Conservative rabbis in our day require it. A good case for having **Tevila** optional can be made. **Tevila** should, therefore, be considered optional, as it is with adult converts nowadays. In some cities **Tevila** has become frequent; in many other cities it is not practiced at all.

Finally, let us turn to the possibility of a new ritual for adoption. When an adopted child enters the family, the parents will probably feel quite at ease with that child and will, from the beginning, be able to treat it as if it were a natural child. Such an attitude will develop only slowly among grandparents and other relatives, who must be shown that this child is to be considered the **complete equal** of a natural child. For this reason, all procedures should follow the pattern taken with natural children. This will help the acceptance of such adopted children. For this reason, we would **not** favor adding any new ritual for adopted children. They should be treated like any other child in every way, be brought up into the covenant, and raised as Jewish children.

Walter Jacob, Chairman
Stephen M. Passamaneck
W. Gunther Plaut
Harry A. Roth
Rav A. Soloff
Bernard Zlotowitz

See also:

S.B. Freehof, "Baptism of Child Before Adoption by Jewish Couple," **Recent Reform Responsa**, pp. 97ff; "Adoption of Children of Mixed Race," **Current Reform Responsa**, pp. 196ff; "Adoption by Cohanim," **Contemporary Reform Responsa**, pp. 145ff.

64.   STATUS OF AN UNCIRCUMCISED RETARDED ADULT
(1976)

QUESTION: What is the status of an uncircumcised Jewish adult? In this case the individual is retarded and living in an institution. Would rights of burial, etc., be denied? (M.L., Pittsburgh, Pennsylvania)

ANSWER: Jewish law is very clear in its statements about circumcision. It is the father's responsibility to assure the circumcision of a male child. We would say, father or mother. If, for some reason, this has not been done, then it becomes the court's responsibility--and later, that of the child--to see to it that he is circumcised (Kiddushin 29a; Yoreh De-a 261.1). For anyone converting to Orthodox Judaism, circumcision is also required. In early Reform Judaism there was considerable controversy about circumcision. Some of the more radical reformers wished to abolish this custom. Their stand was, however, not widely adopted, and the only element of this which remains is that we would not absolutely require circumcision of a convert (CCAR, 1892). This kind of objection had previously been raised in Hellenistic times, and led to bitter controversy. Of course, in modern America this issue has become moot, as virtually all children are circumcised at birth.

A retarded individual remains a minor and therefore he would continue to be the father's or court's responsibility all his life. If the father is no longer alive, the responsibility does not fall upon the mother, as she cannot be held directly responsible for this positive commandment, according to tradition (Yoreh De-a 261.1). But as we have stressed equality between men and women, the mother would be responsible. In any case, it would be cruel to circumcise an adult male who would suffer pain while being unaware of the reasons for this ritual. In this case, it should **not** be done.

An uncircumcised adult male Jew is, however, to be considered a Jew for every ritual in his life. With a normal individual this would mean Bar Mitzvah, marriage, and burial. He might, at various stages, be encouraged to become circumcised, but if--for reason of health or other reasons--he refuses, the normal privileges given

to other Jews would not be withheld from him. If he is
a **Kohen**, he may even bless the people (Hoffman, **Melamed
Leho-il**, Yoreh De-a 79). He has sinned, but remains a
Jew (Sanhedrin 44a). The individual must consciously
refuse circumcision to be considered a **Mumar La-aralot**;
this would not be true of a retarded adult (**Tur**, Yoreh
De-a 2; **Beit Yosef**, quoting Rabbenu Yerucham).

All of this is certainly true of burial. In fact,
Jewish law goes considerably further than this. It
clearly states in Yoreh De-a 345.5 that Israelites who
are absolute sinners and cast off the "yoke of the Commandments" entirely, or even become idolaters, are still
to be buried as Israelites. We are not obligated to
mourn for them, but we are obligated to bury them (see
also **Chatam Sofer** to Yoreh De-a 341). He only stipulated that we should bury that individual at some distance
from those who are law-abiding Jews. A **Chevra Kadisha**
may make more stringent rules as a "fence around the
law" (as was done from time to time at various times in
the past). So Simon Raphael Hirsch in the last century
excluded such Jews from membership in his congregation;
Joseph Saul Nathanson refused them burial (**Sho-el
Umeshiv** III, 2.4). Others in this time of pressure
stated that, although they should not be buried directly
next to a normative Jew, it would be proper to bury them
eight feet away (see **Vayelaket Yosef** IV, 4-118).

We can see that there would be no restriction whatsoever about the burial of an uncircumcised retarded
adult in present-day America, where the few strictures
of the last century are not applicable. Furthermore,
nowadays almost all cemeteries are divided into family
plots, so families are separated from each other, and
varying degrees of observance can be marked in this
fashion without harming anyone in the community.

Walter Jacob

65. GERUT AND THE QUESTION OF BELIEF
(Vol. XCII, 1982, pp. 211-213)

QUESTION: A young woman wishes to convert to Judaism. She has given her reasons for doing so as
follows. She will marry a Jewish man and wants to
establish a home which shall be unified religiously. She has been impressed by the strength of
Jewish family life and by its close-knit unity.
Her ethical and moral values coincide with those of
Judaism; she is strongly committed to Jewish ethi-

cal values, and has considerable interest in Israel
and Zionism. She does, however, consider herself
agnostic and doubts whether her attitude will
change. In all of these matters she is in complete
agreement with her Jewish fiance. She feels no
attachment to her former Christian background. Can
we accept such an individual as a convert to Judaism? (D.O., Pittsburgh, Pennsylvania)

ANSWER: The traditional approach to converts was to
warn them that they were joining a persecuted community
and that many obligations were incumbent upon them.
This was followed by a discussion of the ritual necessary for conversion (Yev. 46, 47; **Shulchan Aruch**, Yoreh
De-a 268; **Yad**, Hil. Isurei Bi-a 15). It is clear that
the "obligations" were the **mitzvot** and, of course, it
was understood that all of these were of divine origin.
Therefore, the source of the **mitzvot** had to be accepted.
Modern Orthodox authorities have generally rejected
converts who join us for the sake of marriage. Some
would accept them in order to avoid the conversion by
Reform rabbis (Mendel Kirshbaum, **Menachem Meshiv**, #9),
because civil marriage has preceded, or because the
couple is living together (David Hoffman, **Melamed Leho-
il**, Even Ha-ezer 8, 10; Yoreh De-a 85). Similar arguments have been advanced by Meshulam Kutner in **Uketora
Ya-asu,** and by Moses Feinstein in **Igerot Mosheh**, Even
Ha-ezer 27. However, the greatest number of Orthodox
authorities have rejected these arguments (e.g., Joseph
Saul Nathanson, Jacob Ettlinger, and Yehiel Weinberg).
Their rejection, even for consideration as converts, was
based upon the ulterior motivation and the likelihood
that they would not accept all of the commandments which
are not generally observed in the Jewish community today
and probably not kept by the Jewish partner (Isaac Herzog, **Heichal Yitschak**, Even Ha-ezer I, #20; Meir Arak,
Imrei Yosher I, #176; Abraham Kook, **Da-at Kohen**, #154;
Moses Feinstein, **Igerot Mosheh**, Yoreh De-a I, #157, 160;
Even Ha-ezer III, #4; CCAR **Yearbook**, vol. 2, pp. 66ff;
Rabbi's Manual, pp. 17ff). It is, therefore, quite
clear that in Judaism, belief in God has been considered
and was implied as a basis for conversion. The nature
of that belief may have varied considerably, as there
has always been wide latitude in Judaism and many divergent concepts have been acceptable.
    The Biblical figure Ruth has generally been taken
as the prototype for all later converts. Her classical
statement (in Ruth 1:16) mentioned God only at its conclusion, leading some commentators to the conclusion
that while rejection of pagan beliefs was considered
essential, belief in God might be achieved gradually.

The Biblical Book of Job and many of the psalms display
questions verging on agnosticism. Some Spanish Jewish
philosophers and those of Renaissance Italy expressed
similar doubts. Such thoughts were, however, rejected
in the more restrictive ghettos of Central and Eastern
Europe. In modern times the writings of Mordecai Kaplan, Martin Buber, Walter Kaufman, and a host of others
have presented a variety of radical positions, sometimes
close to agnosticism. Sections of the English prayers
in the service of **Gates of Prayer** are written from this
questioning stance. Many prospective converts have been
and will be motivated by the openness of Judaism which
encourages exploration of all ideas even while demanding
that the Jewish path of life (Halacha) be followed. The
woman in question does not deny the existence of God and
is not an atheist. We would not have accepted her if
she denied the existence of God, but we should accept
this convert with the feeling that her attachment to
Judaism and the knowledge of it are sufficient to bring
her into Judaism and to help her develop a commitment to
this religion. As her Jewish life continues, she may
also change her views on the nature of God.

Walter Jacob, Chairman
Isaac Neuman
Leonard S. Kravitz
Harry A. Roth
Rav A. Soloff

66. CONVERSION WITHOUT FORMAL INSTRUCTION
(Vol. XCII, 1982, pp. 209-211)

QUESTION: A couple in a mixed marriage have maintained a Jewish life-style for more than a decade.
He is Jewish, and she came from a Protestant background. They were married civilly, and she had not
practiced her religion or believed its tenets for
many years prior to her marriage. She has received
no formal instruction in Judaism, but for the last
decade she has lived a Jewish life. She has attended services during the **Yamim Nora-im**, and
intermittently during the year, has participated in
many programs of the Temple and its sisterhood,
enrolled in some adult education classes, and
raised her children as Jews. The family observes
Jewish holidays at home by lighting candles and
making **Kiddush** each Friday evening and on the eve
of holidays; they erect a **Sukka** and light Chanuka

lights.   She considers herself Jewish, as do her
friends.   She would now like to have this "Jewishness" recognized officially.   She does not wish to
attend the Introduction to Judaism class for young
new converts.   She would also feel out of place at
the standard conversion ceremonies which her congregation conducts publicly.   How can she officially be considered as Jewish?   (F.L., Miami, Florida)

ANSWER: Let us begin by reviewing the Reform discussion and the development of the tradition.   The American
Reform discussions of conversion from 1890 onward make
it quite clear that the principal requirements were
intellectual; we have been more concerned with understanding than ritual ("Milat Gerim," CCAR Yearbook,
1947, pp. 15ff; see also responsa #69-71 below).   In
keeping with this emphasis, Introduction to Judaism
classes have been organized by virtually all congregations.   In larger communities, some of the congregations
have joined together and offered centralized classes on
a year-round basis along with individualized instruction
by the congregational rabbi.   Traditional Judaism, of
course, also requires instruction, but usually places
the emphasis upon the specific duties incumbent upon
either the man or the woman, rather than on a more general background.   For traditional Jews, the ritual of
conversion is of primary importance, irrespective of the
instruction which had taken place.
      The traditional requirements for conversion are
clear (Yev. 46, 47; Shulchan Aruch, Yoreh De-a 268; Yad,
Isurei Bi-a 15)--a court of three is necessary.   Prospective converts must be warned that they are joining a
persecuted community, and that many new obligations will
be incumbent upon them.   They were to bring a sacrifice
in the days when the Temple stood, and males had to be
circumcised and take a ritual bath.   To this day, the
requirements of a Beit Din, Tevila, and Berit still
remain for traditional Jews.   The sources are clear on
the requirements, but considerable discussion about them
exists in the Talmud.   For example, R. Eliezer stated
that if a prospective male convert was either circumcised or took a ritual bath, he was considered a proselyte.   R. Joshua insisted on both, and his point of view
was adopted (Yev. 46b).   Hillel and Shammai disagreed
about a prospective male convert who was already circumcised: Beit Shammai insisted that blood must be drawn
from him, while Beit Hillel stated that one may simply
accept that circumcision without drawing blood (Shab.
135a).   The Rabbinic authorities decided in favor of
Beit Shammai (Sh.A., Yoreh De-a 268.1; Yad, Isurei Bi-a
14.5).   There were differences of opinion about steps

necessary for the ritual of conversion in ancient times. The Talmud also contains a variety of opinions about the desirability of accepting converts. These reflect historic competition with Christianity, persecution, etc., in the early centuries of our era.

The Talmudic discussions insist that the convert must join Judaism without any ulterior motives, and if such are present, the conversion is void (Yev. 24b). Of course, the opinion applies only prospectively, not retrospectively, and **bedi-avad** they were accepted. Some authorities were more lenient in regard to ulterior motives, so Hillel (Shab. 31a) readily accepted a convert who stated that he wished eventually to become a High Priest. R. Hiya accepted a woman who wanted to marry one of his students (Men. 44a). In modern times, although most Orthodox authorities would reject converts who seek to join us for the sake of marriage, some would accept them in order to avoid the conversion by Reform rabbis (Mendel Kirshbaum, **Menachem Meshiv**, #9), because civil marriage has preceded, or because the couple is living together (David Hoffmann, **Melamed Leho-il**, Even Ha-ezer 8, 10; Yoreh De-a 85). Similar arguments have been advanced by Meshulam Kutner in **Uketora Ya-asu** and by Moses Feinstein in **Igerot Mosheh**, Even Ha-ezer I, 27. However, the greatest number of Orthodox authorities have rejected these arguments (e.g., Joseph Saul Nathanson, Jacob Ettlinger, and Yehiel Weinberg). Their rejection, even for consideration as converts, was based upon the ulterior motivation and the likelihood that they would not accept all the commandments which are not generally observed in the Jewish community today and probably not kept by the Jewish partner (Isaac Herzog, **Heichal Yitschak**, Even Ha-ezer I, #20; Meir Arak, **Imrei Yosher** I, #176; Abraham Kook, **Da-at Kohen**, #154; Moses Feinstein, **Igerot Mosheh**, Yoreh De-a I, #157, 160; Even Ha-ezer III, #4).

Some Orthodox authorities have ruled that the conduct of a Jewish way of life, even without documentation of conversion, creates a valid assumption of Jewishness (A. Karelitz, **Chazon Ish**, Yev., par. 83, #6; Beit Hadin Harabani Hagadol, Jerusalem, Appeal 1968/26, case of Chanoch and Miriam Langer). Each of these decisions was based upon Talmudic statements which indicated that this line of thought applied in cases where either father or mother was Jewish (Yev. 45b).

Now let us turn to the specifics of your question. Although the Reform Movement has insisted on instruction and intellectual understanding of Judaism, it has never specified precisely how this instruction is to be obtained. Usually, a young convert receives such instruction through Introduction to Judaism classes and reading connected with them. Such classes extend over a period

of three months to a year and meet once or several times
a week. The reading assignments are usually geared to
the intellectual level of the prospective convert. In
some instances they include only a familiarity with
basic books on holidays, liturgy, and history, while
others require a thorough knowledge of Jewish history,
philosophy, literature, and liturgy. There is nothing
which would preclude acquisition of such knowledge over
a period of years and in a more informal manner, as the
woman described in this question. She has undoubtedly
accumulated a considerable body of knowledge through her
attendance at services and programs in her synagogue,
through random reading, and through constant association
with Jewish friends. Certainly, her present knowledge
of Judaism would exceed that of anyone who completed the
customary introductory courses. Even more important is
the fact that her commitment has shown itself to be
sincere and has stood the test of time. She not only
possesses an intellectual understanding of Judaism, but
feels herself Jewish and has involved herself in many
aspects of Jewish life both inside and outside the synagogue. From the point of view of knowledge and commitment, we may therefore consider her an appropriate candidate for the final steps of conversion. We should
encourage her to move in that direction, especially as
she and her husband wish to take this step.

There is nothing in our Reform tradition which
demands a public conversion ceremony. Her formal reception into Judaism could take place privately, in the
presence of a rabbi and two witnesses.

The prospective convert would be told about **Tevila**
and, in case of a male, about circumcision or **tipat dam**.
They should be encouraged to proceed in these directions
if that is the custom of the community; however, neither
ceremony is mandatory. It is quite clear from tradition
that if such an individual at any time undergoes **Tevila**,
even though not specifically for the purpose of conversion, it would be considered the same as if he had undergone it for that purpose (**Shulchan Aruch**, Yoreh De-a
268.3). This should be considered seriously if the
family has any intention of settling in Israel. A Hebrew name of the convert's choice can be appropriately
provided at this time as well.

In summary, it would be perfectly possible to accept such a woman as a convert to Judaism with very
little further action on her part. This step should be
made as easy as possible, and we should do everything in

our power to bring **Gerei Toshav** completely into the sphere of Judaism.

Walter Jacob, Chairman
Simeon Maslin
W. Gunther Plaut
Harry A. Roth
Rav A. Soloff
Sheldon Zimmerman

67.   MENTAL COMPETENCY OF A CONVERT
(1979)

QUESTION: A prospective convert appears to be mentally unbalanced (paranoid), therefore, his understanding of Judaism is limited.   Shall we accept or reject such a convert?   (Elizabeth Levine, Congregation Beth-El, Fort Worth, Texas)

ANSWER: Conversion to Judaism is a major religious step which cannot be taken lightly; this act has legal (halachic) implications.   It is clear that Jewish law mandates that anyone acting in a legal capacity must be mentally competent (Git. 23a; **Yad**, Hil. Edut 9.9; **Shulchan Aruch**, Choshen Mishpat 188.2).   The tradition also demands that any individual engaged in a religious act, especially initially **(lechatechila)** must be completely mentally competent (Mishna 18, Rosh Hashana 8; Meg. 2.4; Chag. 1.1; Men. 9.8; Git. 2.5, etc.).   The mentally incompetent and those with other deficiencies could not engage in a valid religious act.   If certain kinds of ritual acts had been done by someone mentally incompetent and performed properly, then they were considered acceptable **bedi-avad**.
   The Talmudic authorities and the Rabbinic authorities subsequently struggled to achieve a proper definition of mental incompetence and found it as difficult as we in modern times.   They, of course, pointed to a variety of strange behavior (Chag. 3b; Nid. 17a; **Shulchan Aruch**, Yoreh De-a 1.5).   Ultimately, this was left to the insight of the presiding judge (**Yad**, Hil. Edut 9.9; Hil. San. 2.1).   These basic decisions were followed by the responsa as well (Isaac b. Sheshet, **Responsa**, #468; Rashbam, **Responsa**, vol. 2, no. 1, etc.), and were not modified in any substantial manner.
   The Rabbinic injunction that conversion be carried out before a **Beit Din** which shall consist of three mem-

bers (Yev. 46b) makes it clear that this act, although basically religious in nature, is a legal transaction. Therefore, all of the above statements would be applicable. A person who proved to be mentally incompetent, but had been converted to Judaism, is accepted **bediavad**, but certainly not **lechatechila**.

As a complete understanding of all aspects of Judaism is necessary for a sincere and complete conversion, such prospective converts must be of sound mind and mentally competent. We cannot accept individuals who do not meet these prerequisites.

Walter Jacob

68.   CIRCUMCISION FOR ADULT PROSELYTES
(Vol. III, 1893, pp. 69ff)

Mr. President and Gentlemen of the Central Conference:

Your Committee, appointed in last year's conference, to whom were referred the papers on the subject of circumcision of adult proselytes (**Milat Gerim**), beg leave to present the following report to the consideration of your honorable body.

The papers before us in your **Yearbook** of 1891-92 are as follows:

(1)   A paper by Dr. Aaron Hahn of Cleveland (**Yearbook**, pp. 56-69).
(2)   A paper by Dr. Isaac Schwab of St. Joseph (**ibid.**, pp. 69-84).
(3)   Responses to Dr. Henry Berkowitz of Kansas City (one to the Rev. Mr. Bien of Vicksburg) on the same subject by the Rev. Dr. Felsenthal of Chicago; Prof. Mielziner of Cincinnati; Sonnenschein, then of St. Louis; Gottheil of New York; Moses of Louisville; Schreiber, then of Little Rock; Landsberg of Rochester; Hecht of Milwaukee; besides a number of reprints from different denominational journals, which were not referred to your committee.

(Vol. III, 1893, pp. 73-95)

A careful perusal of all these papers resulted in the undoubted information that all but two of the authorities mentioned are in favor of discontinuing the

practice ("**Shev ve-al ta-aseh**") of circumcision of adult
proselytes, while several are in favor of retaining the
practice of the ritual bath (**Tevila**). Dr. Schreiber, in
his epistle to Dr. Berkowitz, adds to the former a respectable number of European authorities, and the reprints from denominational journals swell the number of
the former considerably.

The two authorities opposed to the discontinuance
of the rites are Professor Dr. Mielziner, from the Rabbinical standpoint, and the Rev. Dr. Schwab, also from
the Biblical standpoint. The latter, however, admits
(**Yearbook**, p. 83): "If any changes in the mode of admitting them [proselytes] have to be made, **it must**, we
propose, be done on the independent account that modern
American Reform Judaism [is] desirous of it....But it
must not be attempted under cover of a relative authority from the so-called rabbinical age."

The difference of opinion in regard to the ritual
bath (**Tevila**) and the strong negative feeling in regard
to circumcision (**Milat Gerim**), necessitated your committee to reinvestigate the entire subject with the following results.

The Union of Israel

The foundation of Judaism is the Pentateuch. This
is historical Judaism. Its provisions and teachings may
be differently expounded, reduced to practice, and applied to meet emergencies, according to different
places, ages, and circumstances (honest, free thought is
a privilege of man older than all literary works) without disturbing the unity of Judaism. The various phases
of Judaism in the prophetic time and in the time of the
Hebrews' Second Commonwealth, Tannaim, Amoraim, Savo-
raim, and Geonim, in Palestine, Persia and Alexandria;
in the philosophic, rationalistic, rabbinistic, and Kabbalistic times of all succeeding ages--all are no more
than the garments of the same body, more or less justi-
fiable in their respective times and places, or perhaps
every one legitimate at its time as far as it was based
upon the Pentateuch provisions and teachings. It follows, therefore, that American Judaism, being one of
these historical phases, is no less in union with Israel
and in unity with Judaism than any of its other phases
ever was, as long as it is based upon the Pentateuchal
provisions and teachings. This is to say that American
Judaism remains in unity with Judaism in general, as
long as it adheres to the provisions and teachings of
the Pentateuch, even according to our own construction.

The Pentateuch Permits the Reception of Proselytes

The first preliminary question, then, must be whether the Pentateuch ordains or even permits the reception of proselytes from the midst of the non-Israelites. We know that the Torah permits to receive proselytes from among the Gentiles.

1. In Deuteronomy 23:4, it is ordained: "An Ammonite or Moabite shall not enter into the congregation of the Lord; even to their tenth generation shall they not enter into the congregation of the Lord forever." The Ammonites and Moabites--the descendants of Lot and his daughters, according to Genesis 19--were two petty nations southeast of Palestine. Only these, and no other nationality, are "forever" debarred from entering the congregation of the Lord. This naturally involves the permission of the Torah to receive proselytes from the midst of other nationalities. The Rabbinical expounders understand this prohibition to refer only to the males of Ammon and Moab and not to the females, on account of the fact given in the Book of Ruth that the royal family of David descended from a Moabite woman; and they interpret the prohibition of intermarriage to mean only that the Ammonite and Moabite shall not be permitted to marry a daughter of Israel (see Rashi, Ramban, and Targum Yerushalmi in **loc. cit.**). The law, however, was understood in the Talmud (Berachot 28a, **"Yehuda ger Amoni"**) to the effect that no male proselytes from Ammon and Moab shall be received in Israel. Therefore, it proves that the Torah permits to receive proselytes from every nationality, race, and tribe (except those specified), and is neither racial nor tribal in its provisions.

2. Numbers 15:15: "The congregation [as a religious body] hath one [and the same] statute for you and the **Ger** that dwelleth permanently with you; it is an ordinance forever in your generations; as ye are, so shall be the **Ger** before the Lord." The word **Ger** occurs fifty-odd times in the law of Moses, and always signifies the non-Israelite who associated himself permanently with the Israelites. The Law guarantees to him all rights and privileges of the native Israelite (ha-ezrach). He is included in the general law of humanity, "Love thy neighbor as thyself" (Leviticus 19:19), as is specifically stated in verses 33 and 34: "And if a **Ger** sojourneth with thee in your land, ye shall not vex him. The **Ger** that dwelleth with you shall be with you as one born among you, and thou shalt love him as thyself," etc. This is repeated emphatically in Deuteronomy 10:19, preceded by the statement that God loves the **Ger**, it is enjoined, "And ye shall love the **Ger**."

Although this covers the whole ground of man's natural rights, claims, and privileges, yet the law

specifies in numerous instances what should be done for
the **Ger**, or also what he should do to exercise these
rights and privileges. Thus, in all ordinances concerning alms to the poor, benefaction and assistance to the
needy, recognition and protection by the administrators
of the law, taking part in the ritual sacrifices of
thanksgiving, rejoicing or atonement, and all services
of the priesthood to the people--the **Ger** is mentioned
specifically to have equal rights and claims with the
native Israelite. This entire negation of all racial,
tribal, or other limitations of human rights is extended
to--or rather outdone--in the case of the fugitive
slave: "Thou shalt not deliver unto his master the servant that is escaped from his master unto thee. He shall
dwell with thee, even among you, in that place which he
shall choose in one of thy gates, where it liketh him
best; thou shalt not oppress him" (Deut. 23:16-17).

To the best of our knowledge, there never existed,
and there does not now exist, any code of laws in any
other country with such provisions to protect, natural-
ize, and assimilate the alien, the foreigner, the
stranger, or the **Ger** with the dominant nation, which so
carefully enjoins respect for the dicta of humanity and
justice. It seems, therefore, that the Torah invites
non-Israelites to come and associate themselves with
Israel. It holds out inducements to the alien, not of
the seed of Abraham, which at that time no other people
offered to one not of their kin, and even now the most
enlightened nations offer with considerable limitations.
There can be no doubt that the Pentateuch permits the
reception of proselytes from all races and classes of
men. That the prophets after Moses cherished this idea
and predicted its universal success and realization, is
evident from passages of the prophetic and psalmic
scriptures. We only need to read, in order to be convinced thereof, Isaiah 2:1-4; 56:6-7; Micah 4:1-5; and
Zachariah 14:9, 17:21. Still, with all that, there is
no commandment in the Law and no suggestion in the
Prophets to enjoin upon any man the duty to go forth and
to make proselytes among the Gentiles. The fundamental
literature of Judaism only permits and favors the reception of proselytes, but ordains nowhere that this should
be done by any person.

The Torah Prescribes No Initiatory
Observance at All for the Proselyte

The Pentateuch bestows particular care upon all
particulars of man's private and public life and his
manifold relations to God and man, providing general and
special laws, ordinances, and statutes for almost every
doing of man. Furthermore, the same Torah legislates as

carefully and humanely for the protection, benefit, and well-being of the foreigner, stranger, and alien of any kind, and evidently holds out most liberal inducements to the **Ger** to come and affiliate himself with the congregation of Israel, hence the coming in of such **Gerim** was certainly sanctioned and expected by the lawgivers. If we take all this into consideration, it must appear strange that the same Torah prescribes no initiatory observance for the incoming proselyte--no law, no ordinance, no provision whatever as to what the proselyte must do or what must be done with or for him to make of the pagan a member of the congregation of Israel. The argument **e silentio**, basing on the absolute silence of the Torah on this point, would induce the common-sense reasoner to the conclusion that the author of the Torah wanted no initiatory observances imposed on the **Ger**, and that the declaration of an honest man that he is a monotheist in good faith and in perfect harmony with Israel's doctrine and canon should be all-sufficient. So, indeed, Yom Tov Lipmann Muehlhausen, in his **Sefer Hanitsachon** to Genesis 17:10 (Hackspan edition), expresses himself: "**Ein emuna teluya bamila, ela balev**," "Faith in Judaism depends not on circumcision; it depends on the heart." In the same sense, the great rabbi Elijah Mizrachi in his **Sefer Mayim Amukim** (Responsum no. 27) expresses himself thus in regard to the acceptance of a proselyte: "**Umide-oraita sagi bekabalat Torah bifnei beit din bilvad**," "According to the Torah, the acceptance of the Torah before a college of three is all-sufficient." Still clearer--and to the same effect--Rabbi Yehudah Aryeh de Modena, in his book **Bechinat Hakabala**, expressed his opinion like Elijah Mizrachi.

But we do not propose to depend on any argument **e silentio**. We only wish to establish the fact the Torah prescribes no law, ordinance, statute, or any provision in any other form, for the modus of accepting a proselyte into the congregation of Israel, from which it follows that none of those rites is law of Moses (**mideoraita**), hence they could be only Rabbinical law (**miderabanan**). And on this point we have in our favor the whole Rabbinical literature, as we shall see instantly.

We open the Rabbinical Code by Moses Maimonides and read in Hil. Melachim 10.7 "**Hamila nitstava bah Avraham vezar-o bilvad, shene-emar, 'Ata vezar-acha achareicha'.... vehem hamechuyavin bamila.**" ("Circumcision was commanded to Abraham and his seed only, as said (Genesis 17), 'Thou and thy seed after thee'.... and they are obligated to circumcision"). This decision of Maimonides (see **Kesef Mishneh**) is based upon the Talmud, Sanhedrin 59, to which we will refer below. The

same is the case with a former paragraph of Maimonides
(ibid., 8.10): "Mosheh Rabbenu lo hinchil et haTorah
vehamitzvot ela leYisra-el, shene-emar, 'Morasha kehilat
Ya-akov,' ulechol harotseh lehitgayer mishe-ar ha-umot,
shene-emar, 'Kachem kager,' aval mi shelo ratsa, ein
kofin oto lekabel Torah umitzvot." ("Moses bequeathed
the Torah and the Commandments to Israel only, as said
(Deut. 30:4), 'an inheritance of the congregation of
Jacob,' and anyone of the Gentiles who of his free will
wishes to embrace it, as said (Num. 15:15), 'Like you is
the Ger'; but none shall be coerced against his will to
embrace the Torah and the Commandments.")

Herewith the principle in regard to the Abrahamitic
rite is laid down once and for all: Circumcision is
ordained in the Torah for the children of Abraham only.
Every father in Israel (not the mother) has the duty to
circumcise, or have circumcised, his son on the eighth
day after his birth. If the father failed to perform
this duty, the Rabbis add, it devolves on the uncircumcised son every day of his life to fulfill the commandment; if he also fails, the Beit Din may enforce it.
Whoever is not of the seed of Abraham certainly is not
charged with this duty. The Ger is one not of the seed
of Abraham, one who attaches himself to the congregation
of Israel as a monotheist, in perfect harmony with Israel's doctrine and canon. Hence (mide-oraita) he is a
Ger (see also Exodus 12:48), without submitting to the
Abrahamitic rite, or even to Korban and Tevila.

It is legitimate to infer from the various statements of the Torah concerning the equality of the Ger
and the native Israelite that he--whenever he has become
a Ger--is identified with the seed of Abraham. Therefore it is an established custom to call the Ger in all
sacerdotal matters "Ben Avraham Avinu," "Son of our
Father Abraham." This is stated expressly and explicitly by Moses Maimonides, in his epistle to the learned
and very distinguished proselyte, Obadiah of Palestine,
who had asked him whether he, the Ger, should say his
prayers, "Eloheinu velohei avoteinu" (Igeret Teshuvot
HaRambam, Prague, Gersoni edition, 1726, p. 58b).
Maimonides responded that "all persons, to the very end
of all generations, who profess monotheism as it is
written in the Torah, are of the disciples of our Father
Abraham, they and all their descendants.... This shows
that Abraham, our Father, is the father of his faithful
descendants that walk in his ways, and the father of his
disciples and these are all the proselytes."

All this, however, does not say that the Ger should
be circumcised. It merely says that he, after he has
become a Ger, has also become an Abrahamite; consequently he has the same duty to have his sons circumcised as
the Abrahamite must do: "Chayav adam lamol et beno."

Evidence from the Established Mosaic Commandments

The same is evident also from all Rabbinical authorities specifying the six hundred thirteen (or
eleven) commandments of the Mosaic law. None of them--
neither the followers of **Halachot Gedolot**, such as **Sefer
Mitzvot Gadol** and **Sefer Mitzvot Katan**, who count some
Rabbinical laws among the six hundred thirteen; nor the
followers of Moses Maimonides, such as Nahmanides (with
some amendments, **hasagot**), Aaron Halevy in his **Sefer
Hachinuch**, and down to Moses Galanti's **Eleh Hamitzvot**
(Amsterdam, 1713) and Israel Landau's **Chok LeYisra-el**
(Prague, 1798), who count among the six hundred and
thirteen only those expressly stated in the Pentateuch,
and call all laws contained in the Mishna and Talmud
"Rabbinical," as stated in Maimonides' **Sefer Hamitzvot**
(2nd **kelal**) and twice in his responses[1]--none of them
count among the Mosaic commandments any of the initiatory observances for the proselyte as being ordained in
the Torah.   The former class of authors, indeed, include
among the commandatory laws **"Mitzvah al Beit Din lamol
hagerim shenitgayeru,"** to which is added in **Sefer
Charedim**: "Not of the six hundred and thirteen" (p. 29b
in the Venice, 1601, edition).   In Hirsch Jost's **Kitsur
S. Ch.** it is added, **"Be-Erets Yisra-el"** (edition Fuerth,
1849, p. 42).
This tells plainly enough that these initiatory
observances are Rabbinical ordinances, and according to
this it becomes the duty of the **Beit Din** "in Palestine"
(and not outside thereof, having no jurisdiction) to
have the **Ger** circumcised.   But the **Ger** himself, even
according to those rigid Rabbinists, has not the duty to
be circumcised.   All this, we feel convinced, proves
beyond doubt that the Torah ordains no initiatory observances for the **Ger**, and so from this standpoint of
canon law the course before us would be decided.   But
one of the papers before us (Dr. Schwab's), discussing
the matter in an extra-judicial method, is intended to
controvert our argument, and must therefore be taken
into consideration.
Our position, opposite that of Dr. Schwab, is simply this: These initiatory observances for the **Ger**, in
order to be obligatory, must be canon law, and this is
with us statutory, i.e., the existence or non-existence
of any particular statute must be proved by documentary
evidence, and by no other logical or historical argument.   Our canon law, according to all Rabbinical authorities, consists of the six hundred thirteen Mosaic

---

[1] **Igeret Teshuvot HaRambam**, Gersoni edition, Prague,
1726, p. 24b; also **Pe-er Hador**, Responsum 144, Amsterdam
edition.

commandments. All kinds of proofs attempting to show
that such law or custom existed at some time and place
amount to a mere probability (and not certainty) of the
existence or non-existence of such a statute; hence, it
is not canon law. Therefore, the authorities mentioned
above accept neither Rabbinical enactment nor deduction
or induction from the Torah as canon law. It is the
method of Dr. Schwab's argument in this connection which
makes his conclusions illegitimate. We must analyze
some of his positions to establish our own.

Circumcision

Dr. Isaac Schwab (**Yearbook**, 1891-92, pp. 69-70)
states at the outset: "It cannot be questioned that
since immemorial antiquity, the initiatory rite [of
circumcision] was insisted on in Israel as an indispensable requisite for the complete admission to their community of Gentile aspirants.... And it may be safely
asserted, too, that from the early period of Jacob's
sons to the latter of Israel's Second Commonwealth, no
Israelitish authority has ever relaxed that stern demand. The insistence of the Abrahamitic rite for the
formal entrance into the   congregation of Israel--
Kahal--was the rule laid down immovably and observed
conscientiously throughout all ages by our ancestors of
the East, who adhered faithfully to the belief and worship of God."
The position of our learned colleague is definite,
clear, and apodictic. No commentary is necessary. However, he maintains in advance that he forms his conclusions "with the aid of historical data" (p. 69), and
this is exactly the point which makes his position un-
tenable. For if he did succeed in producing such data,
demonstrating the assumption advanced--which he actually
did not, as we shall instantly see--it could only prove
that at a certain time, in a certain place, and under
such and such circumstances, there was insistence upon
submission to the Abrahamitic rite by the Gentile aspir-
ing to enter the congregation of Israel. No amount of
such data could establish the fact that the Torah,
Moses, or the prophets (at any time or anywhere) ordained, commanded, enacted, or in any other manner imposed on Israel such and such initiatory observances for
the Gentile convert. As long as this fact is not established, those observances cannot be accepted as Biblical
ordinances, as commanded in the Law (**mide-oraita**);
hence, they are not necessarily integral portions of
Judaism. The question is not: What have certain persons
at certain times done--they may have acted on their own
responsibility and been guided by their own convictions

or opinions--the question is: What are we as Israelites commanded to do? What is canon law and what is not so?

Let us see how the Rabbis of the Talmud reason on this proposition.

1. In the Gemara and Kelalei Hagemara it is laid down as an established rule: "Divrei Torah vedivrei kabala la yalfinan," i.e., "The words of the Law [in Pentateuch] must not be construed by the words of tradition." The term "Kabala" in this connection includes all post-Mosaic scriptures, as well as all narrative portions in the Mosaic books. No law can be based on or derived from any narrative and dignified as a law of the Torah (mide-oraita), which specifically ordains, "Ye shall not add" (to the Mosaic laws). This rule is certainly a wise one. If it would be considered legitimate to derive from narratives ("historical data") canon law, commandment, ordinance, or statute--these would become as boundless as all products of fantasy. One would derive from the story of Adam and Eve's sin and punishment that every sinner must be expelled from house and home, even if it was a paradise. Another would deduce from the story of Noah and his son Ham's misdeed that in similar cases not only the son but also the grandson must be punished and cursed. Again, another might derive quite a number of ugly laws and ordinances from the narratives in Numbers 31, Joshua 7, Judges 11 or 19, I Samuel 5 and 6, II Samuel 21, I Kings 2, and many more "historical data." The fact is, no historical data can be turned into Mosaic law. But the question before us is whether the initiatory observances for the proselyte are or are not ordained in the Torah.

2. If Dr. Schwab holds (as one might understand by inference) that whatever follows with logical necessity from historical data or the words of prophets recorded in Holy Writ must have the same canonic force as the commandment of the Torah; if he holds that it is anyhow "Me-ein De-oraita," i.e., similar to Mosaic law, concerning which it is maintained in the Talmud that "chavivin divrei soferim yeter midivrei Torah" ("The words of the scribes are more precious than the words of the Torah")--then we can disabuse his mind by first-class authority,[2] especially by the rule laid down by Moses Maimonides. He advances in his Sefer Hamitzvot fourteen rules, by which to ascertain what is intended in the Pentateuch as canonical law. The second of these rules states literally not to count among the 613 Mosaic laws any derived from the Torah by means of the thirteen hermeneutic rules on which the Rabbinical law is based. He explains this rule at more length in an epistle ad-

---

[2] For instance, "Ein oneshin min hadin"; or in Sifrei, Shofetim 154, "Ein chayavin mita al divrei soferim."

dressed to Rabbi Pinchas ben Meshulam. He says there
that no law or ordinance in Mishna, Baraita, or
Talmud--not even the so-called **"Halacha leMosheh
miSinai**--none at all not explicitly stated in the
Pentateuch, can be called **Din Torah**, "canonical law."
These are all **divrei soferim**, "Rabbinical law," unless
(as is the case in three or four instances only) it is
expressly stated in the Talmud that this law is
canonical and not Rabbinical (see **Igeret Teshuvot** by
Maimonides, Prague, 1726, Gersoni edition, p. 24b). It
is evident, therefore, that the most convincing
speculation on historical data or on an expressed law
cannot produce for us a canonical law. Hence, the
initiatory observances for the proselyte cannot possibly
be canonical.

But our learned essayist fails to produce historical data to support his position. He begins with pointing to Genesis 34, the story of Shechem and his people,
who were massacred by Simeon and Levi after they had
submitted to circumcision as the condition for entire
parity. This piece of vile strategy--which Jacob upon
his death-bed yet denounced (Genesis 49:5-7)--could
hardly be accepted as a testimony for anything of a
religious or moral character. If Simeon and Levi
treacherously said so to the Shechemites, it does not
prove that it was so.

However, we need not argue from this standpoint to
invalidate the demonstrative force of the historical
data cited, including Exodus 4:24. In the Gemara and
Kelalei Hagemara, the following established rule is laid
down: **"Ein mevi-in re-aya mimikra shenichtav kodem matan
Torah**," "No proof [for a law] can be brought from Scripture written prior to the Sinaic revelation."[3]

This story of Shechem is reported to have trans-
pired prior to the Sinaic revelation. It is evident
that if it had any demonstrative power (which, **prima
vista**, it does not), it could not prove that we should
abide by this rule as a part of the canonic law; or else
we could prove from Abraham and Sarah that it is lawful
to take in marriage one's half-sister (Genesis 20:12),
or from the case of Jacob that one may take in marriage
two sisters simultaneously, or--as from the story of
Yehuda and Tamar (Genesis 38)--many other things which
the law of Moses prohibits.

Dr. Schwab then states: "As far as we can judge
from extant history, there never was before the apostle
of the Gentiles, Paul, a Jewish authority that doubted

---

[3] See also **Tosafot** in Mo-ed Katan 20a, and Yerushalmi,
ibid., 111.5: **"Ulemedim davar kodem lematan Torah
bitmiha"**; ibid., in Pe-a 2: **"Hakol modin she-ein lomedin
min hama-aseh"**; see also **Sefer Keritot** 4.14.

the indispensable obligation of the initiatory rite upon
any convert from paganism, who wished to become totally
assimilated to the Israelites as to all communal and
spiritual claims." This e silentio argument might have
some value if it did not stand opposite the stubborn
fact that besides Exodus 12:48 and Joshua 5, down to
Hyrcan (end of second century B.C.E.), not a word of
law, history, or otherwise, exists in all Jewish literature regarding the initiatory rites of a pagan or any
other man wishing to embrace Judaism. It is, therefore,
just as proper and legitimate to conclude from their
complete silence on this point, down to two centuries
before the fall of Jerusalem, that no such or other
initiatory rites were established or existed at all (we
will attempt further on to prove that nothing was fixed
in this matter even after the fall of Jerusalem). Anyhow, this argument e silentio is as forcible as Dr.
Schwab's.

The next passage to which Dr. Schwab and all others
Paul's work done among the Gentiles does not concern us here, especially not in regard to the Abrahamitic rite, as he, in the earlier days of his ministry,
denounced the entire law and circumcision fiercely, and
later on he praised both, and not only ordained the
enforcement of the law in a case of adultery, but always
argued from it, especially in the case of his son and
his assistant's wages. We only take exception to the
conclusion that circumcision of proselytes must have
been the common practice among Israelites, because the
apostles insisted upon it and Paul opposed it. This
rather appears to prove that there was nothing fixed or
established in Paul's time about the initiatory rites of
proselytes, and the general difference of opinion in the
matter existed also in the apostolic church. Paul was a
stern Pharisee and remained steadfastly upon this platform, to which he added but one plank, viz., the Messiah
has come, the Last Judgment is at hand, consequently,
the laws and commandments are no longer obligatory--just
as the Pharisees maintained to be the case le-atid lavo.

The next passage to which Dr. Schwab and all others
point is Exodus 12:48, where all of them suppose to find
an express prohibition for the Ger to eat of the Paschal
lamb until circumcised. In the papers before us different arguments, pro and con, are based on this Pentateuchal ordinance which--strange to say--according to
Rabbinical interpretation, might be understood to the
contrary, viz., that one is a Ger without being circumcised. We point to Mechilta to Exodus 12, Talmud Pesachim 28, Targumim Onkelos and Yerushalmi, and Rashi and
Ramban in the same place. According to these expounders
of the Law, "bal ben nechar" (in verse 43) signifies
that no Hebrew renegade should be permitted to eat the
Paschal lamb, and "vechol arel" (in verse 49) that no

uncircumcised Hebrew should be permitted to eat of it.
So the two **mitzvot** are invariably stated in "Taryag."
The exclusion in both cases refers to the sons of Abraham only, to those who are commanded in Genesis 17:9-14
to be circumcised.   The Rabbis were evidently led to
this interpretation of **ben nechar** and **vechol arel** by the
fact that **Milat Gerim** is ordained nowhere in the Torah,
and by the fact that in Deuteronomy 16:1-8, the whole
ordinance of the Passover is repeated with several additions, without any reference to circumcision, so that
the passage in Exodus may be understood to refer only to
Pesach Mitsrayim.   The passage in Exodus, referring
literally to the original commandment in Genesis, tells
us in verse 44 that this is not a racial or tribal commandment, for the slave bought for money, if circumcised
(and thus belonging to the household of the Hebrew as a
member thereof), may eat of the Paschal sacrifice.   In
verse 45 we are informed that the **Toshav** and the
Sachir--the transient aliens (or, according to Ibn Ezra,
also the transient Israelites), persons belonging to no
Hebrew family (see 12:3)--shall not be permitted to eat
of this sacrifice.   Verse 47 expresses the commandment
that all the congregation "shall make it," viz., have
the duty to make the Paschal sacrifice, while the **Eved**,
Toshav, and **Sachir** are not commanded to do so.   And now
in verse 48 we come to the "Ger, who dwells with thee
permanently."   He is no **Eved**, **Toshav**, or **Sachir**; he is
evidently a real **Ger**, who has the duty to make the same
sacrifice (compare "**ya-asu**" and "**ve-asu**"), but he is not
circumcised; hence, a man is a **Ger** even if he is not
circumcised.   He is not forbidden to eat of this sacrifice as are **Eved**, **Sachir**, and **Toshav**.   It is not said of
him "**Lo yochal bo**," "He should not eat of it."[4]   As a
Ger, he has the duty not only to make this Paschal sacrifice, but also to have his children, servants, etc.,
circumcised, as commanded in Genesis 17.   If he wants to
perform this Paschal duty like the native Israelite, he
must do it in his family and household (Exodus 12:3-4).
By being himself a **Ger**, he has not established a family
and household in Israel as long as he has not performed
his first paternal duty as an Israelite, viz., to circumcise his sons.   Therefore, verse 48 says: "And if a
Ger dwelleth with thee, and he wisheth to make the Passover [like other Israelites], let all his males be circumcised, and then let him come near to make it, and he
will be like the native of the land, although the uncircumcised Israelite dare not eat of it ('**Vechol arla-ei**
devar Yisra-el,' Targum Yerushalmi)".   Because that

---

[4] "Rabbi Yochanan amar [in Yalkut, it is Rabbi Akiva]:
'Ein milat zecharim me-akavto mile-echol befesach'"
(Mechilta, loc. cit.).

Israelite is commanded and the **Ger** is not commanded in the Torah to be circumcised, but, being a **Ger**, he is subject to the same Torah and enjoys the same rights and privileges as the native Israelite (verse 49).   Anyhow, no unprejudiced reader of the Pentateuchal passage can get over the plain statement, that one is a genuine **Ger** before he is circumcised.

Dr. Schwab furthermore argues (**Yearbook**, p. 71), "The statement repeated several times in the Mosaic code, that one law should govern the native and the stranger [**Ger**], can literally mean nothing else than that a foreigner, settled in a Jewish land, should be bound to live up in all respects to the same laws as the Israelites have to observe." The two other points which Dr. Schwab makes on the same page have been controverted above.

The repetition of the same provision with certain special laws, we think, rather proves on the hermeneutic rule of "**shenei ketuvim haba-im be-echad**" that this provision applies to these particular laws only, and could not be extended to any other law.   If the Torah had intended to ordain that the **Ger** must observe all laws like the native Israelite, it would have ordained so once and for all, and repeated the same only where some new point in this connection was to be suggested. As the matter stands now, we can only apply it to the particular cases mentioned in the respective law or laws.   Besides, it is evident from the Torah that the **Ger** was not expected to perform all ceremonial laws like the native Israelite.   He was not forbidden to eat **nevela** (Deut. 14:21) or **gid hanasheh** (Gen. 32:33); therefore, it is stated especially in regard to eating blood, that the **Ger**, too, shall abstain from blood.   If all dietary laws had been intended for the **Ger**, this particular provision concerning the eating of blood would be entirely superfluous.   The **Ger** is exempted from dwelling in booths during the Feast of Tabernacles.   The Torah ordains: "**Kol ezrach beYisra-el yeshev basukkot**" (Leviticus 23:43).   This, however, might lead one to premise that the **Ger** is exempted also from rejoicing on the festivals; therefore, it is mentioned explicitly (Deut. 15) that this is not the case.   It is evident from those very provisions that the **Ger** was expected to observe all the moral laws like the native Israelite, including all the laws concerning the altar and the sanctuary, Sabbath and Day of Atonement, and all the national holy days.   In all other respects, the Torah only commands the Israelite what he should do for the **Ger**, what privileges are especially granted, and what protection the nation or congregation owes to him--all of which is plainly contained in the main law, "Ye shall love the **Ger**," and "Thou shalt love him like thyself."

It is correct, therefore, what is stated in **Mechilta** and **Sifrei**: "**Ba hakatuv vehishva et hager la-ezrach bechol hamitzvot shebaTorah**," "Scripture declares the equality of the **Ger** with the native Israelite in all commandments of the Torah." We must only understand that the actual signification of "**hishva**" is **lizchut** and not **lechova**, viz., the **Ger** enjoys all rights, privileges, and promises of the Torah without being expected to submit to all ceremonial laws and ordinances as the native Israelite should.[5]

Aside from all this argument, and independent thereof, Dr. Schwab's premises bear no relation to the case before us. He discusses the duties of the **Ger** after he has entered upon that state of obligation, i.e., after he is a **Ger** he must do so and so. Nobody doubts that with the new faith he embraces, he accepts also new duties. The question before us, however, is of an entirely different nature. We ask: What must a person do, or what must be done for him, to make him a **Ger**? Must he pass through certain observances or initiatory rites, and is circumcision one of them? It is only after this question is solved that the other comes up, i.e., What must the **Ger** do as a member of the congregation whose faith he embraced? The answer to our main question is that--according to the Torah, and also as the rabbis of the Talmud and the compilers of the 613 Pentateuchal commandments understand it--no initiatory rites at all are prescribed; hence the decision of Rabbi Elijah Mizrachi: "**Umide-oraita sagi bekabalat Torah bifnei beit din**, etc." ("According to the Torah, the main declaration before a college of three to accept the Torah as the canon, suffices for the proselyte [to receive him into the congregation of Israel] also, without circumcision and without the ritual bath."

It must be admitted (**leika man defalig**) that the initiatory rites in question are not canon law, are ordained nowhere in Holy Writ, and are not **mide-oraita**. This, as far as the legality of setting aside these rites "**Shev ve-al ta-aseh**," is herewith decided for this body, whose declared standpoint is the historical and not the one-sided Rabbinical legalism, especially in the case of "**Shev ve-al ta-aseh**," where even the Rabbinical casuists admit that "**Beyad beit din la-akor davar min haTorah be'Shev ve-al ta-aseh**.'"

It Cannot Properly Be Called Rabbinical Law

Still there are among the papers referred to us two--one by Professor Dr. Mielziner, and the other by Rabbi Dr. Schwab--from which it appears, although it is

---

[5] See also Ibn Ezra to Leviticus 19:1.

not stated expressly, that these initiatory rites are Rabbinical law (**miderabanan**). On the strength of this, the Amoraim adopted in the Talmud (Shabbat 137b) a passage from the Tosefta demanding of the **Ger** the blessing "**Baruch ata, Adonai Eloheinu, melech ha-olam, asher kideshanu bemitzvotav vetsivanu al milat gerim.**" They did so not because it was presumed that God commanded it, but on the basis of "**La dela tasur.**" The Amoraim did the same with other Rabbinic laws (**Mitzvot Derabanan**), such as **likro Megila, likro et haHalel, lishmoa kol shofar, netilat lulav, kiddush hayom beyom tov sheni, lehadlik ner Chanuka**--none of which is commanded in the Torah. This **beracha** was not accepted in the code before Isaac Alfasi (12th century), because it is evidently a fallacy, as God nowhere commanded the **Ger** to be circumcised, and those Amoraim would not permit the Israelite who performs the rite to say this **beracha**. He is only wanted to say "**Asher Kideshanu bemitzvotav vetsivanu al hamila.**" It is evident, therefore, that those Amoraim, like the Tosefta, held that **Milat Gerim** is a Rabbinical law just like **Milat Avadim.**

The question concerning "**La dela tasur**" has not been referred to this committee, consequently we cannot discuss it. In this particular case, however, the Talmud Yerushalmi has already decided (Pe-a 2): "**Ein lomedin lo min hahalachot velo mehagadot velo mehatosefta.**" Therefore, these **berachot**, being taken from the Tosefta, are not Rabbinical law.

What Is Rabbinical Law?

What is Rabbinical law, according to Rabbinical jurisprudence? The usual reply to this query is that it is law not stated expressly in Holy Writ, but ordained in the so-called Oral Law, **Torah Shebe-al Peh.** Here the question arises: Where is the origin and authority of this law, or these laws? The answer is this:

1. In **takanot** and **gezerot**, i.e., ordinances (commendatory or prohibitory) ordained by any lawful Sanhedrin or any other authoritative body, or by any teacher high in authority, such as Ezra and his successors. In this latter case, it is most always added "**uveit dino,**" "and his court," telling indirectly that no one person was vested with the authority to enact or ordain such law. The case before us is entirely excluded from this kind of Oral Law. For, in all collections before us--down to the works of Zachary Frankel, Jacob Bruell, Isaac Hirsch Weiss, and all the others who wrote on the subject--there is no record that at any time a **takana** or **gezera** was ordained concerning the initiatory rites of proselytes.

2.   In "Halacha leMosheh miSinai"--i.e., a law or
rule which is supposed to have been given orally to
Moses from Sinai, or rather a custom, the origin of
which is unknown and is not premised in the Torah. From
Maimonides down to the author of **Shenei Luchot Haberit**,
down to the **Yalkut Shim-oni** and to Dr. Herzfeld and to
all authorities that have written on this point--there
is no mention of such a Halacha concerning these initiatory rites.
3.   In the **Kabbala** ("the tradition"). Here it is
said in general and without any qualification: "**Im
kabala hi, nekabel.**"
4.   In laws based on the Torah by means of the
hermeneutic rules ("**Shelosh esreh midot**"), thirteen of
which were fixed by Rabbi Ishmael, to which was added
Mi-ut Veribui.

If there is anywhere in the Talmud such a **kabbala**
or such a **derasha** as named in 3 and 4 above, it has not
been pointed out in the papers before us, and we--with
all our industrious research--found none referring to
the origin of these initiatory rites. It is, therefore,
no matter of surprise to us. (Supposed exceptions will
be noticed below.)

Rabbi Yehuda Hanasi in his entire Mishna laid down
no rule, ordinance, or direction concerning the initiatory rites of the proselyte. This must be a matter of
surprise to those who consider those rites Rabbinical
law. Once in the Mishna (Keritot 2.1) there is inserted
contrary to Rabbi Yehuda's **setam mishna** (evidently an
interpolation) a dictum of Rabbi Eliezer ben Jacob: "**Ger
mechusar kapara ad sheyizarek alav hadam**," "The **Ger** is
not fully atoned [to eat of the sacrifices] till the
blood [of his sacrifice] is sprinkled upon the altar for
him or in his name." It is from this passage of doubtful authenticity that the Talmud learns that the **Ger**
must make a sacrifice as an initiatory rite. But this
was certainly not the opinion of the author of the Mishna. If it had been, he must at least have given a name
to the **Ger's** sacrifice (to be **Ola**, **Chatat**, or **Asham**),
which he does nowhere, not even in "**Eizehu mekomo**"
(Zevachim 5).

The passage in Keritot 9a proves that Rabbi Yehuda
Hanasi did not consider the initiatory rites as Rabbinical law. It says there as a baraita: "**Rabbi omer,
'Kachem ka-avoteichem; ma avoteihem lo nichnesu laberit
ela bemila utevila vehartsa-at damim, af hem lo yikanesu
laberit ela bemila utevila vehartsa-at damim.**'" This
was certainly not intended to be Halacha, Rabbinical
law, or else the Rabbi must have stated it in the Mishna. Besides this, the **derasha** is not one of Halacha.
It is evidently a reminiscence from the school chats on
"**Kachem hager.**" It is based on no commandment of the

Torah and no tradition; it is a personal and unsupported opinion of Rabbi, which never was intended to be a law, and was therefore not placed in the Mishna. This is provided that Rabbi Yehuda is indeed the author of this passage, which is at least doubtful, as the **hartsa-at damim** is contrary to Rabbi's **Setam Mishna**, and reads as if it was said by Rabbi Eliezer ben Jacob instead of plain Rabbi (the Talmud, further on, refers to him with "**Amar Mar**," which is not the usual way of referring to Rabbi Yehuda Hanasi).

This silence of the Mishna is to us a proof **e silentio** that the author of the Mishna did not consider those initiatory rites Rabbinical law. When Professor Dr. Mielziner points to **Beit Hillel**'s (or, according to another version, Rabbi Akiva's) "**Haporesh min ha-orla keforesh min hakever**," which occurs twice in the Mishna in Pesachim and in Eduyot, without having become a law anywhere in regard to the purification of the **Ger**, he does not state that it was Halacha or a moral opinion, or that the Mishna takes any further notice of it. And we--with our limited knowledge of Rabbincal law--cannot see how any rite could be called Rabbinical law if it is not based upon any of the above four points, and has not the sanction of the author of the Mishna. That the Baraita and the older Tannaim had knowledge of said rites, and yet the Mishna had nothing to say about them, can only prove that two different opinions on these rites then prevailed, **pro** and **con**, as is evident also from the disagreement of Rabbis Joshua and Eliezer on **Mila** and **Tevila**, to which we will refer again after we have cast a glance on history. Here we will but call attention to Yerushalmi, Pe-a II, as quoted in **Sefer Keritot** 4.14.

John Hyrcan and His Successor's Conversions

From the days of Joshua (Joshua 5) to the time of John Hyrcan, High Priest and Prince in Judea (134-107 B.C.E.), no record whatever exists of the practice in accepting proselytes. Like Holy Writ and the Aprocrypha, so all other records extant from that long period of history furnish not the least information as to the existence or nature of such initiatory rites. Moses himself, we are told in Deuteronomy 29 (we refer to this as an offset to the Rabbi's **derasha** on "Kachem kaavoteichem") made the covenant at the plain of Moab with an uncircumcised generation (comp. Joshua 5), among whom was also the **Ger** (Deuteronomy 29:10), who was certainly not circumcised. This covenant was made so "that He may establish thee today for a people unto Himself, and He may be unto thee a God, as He has said unto thee [including the **Ger**] and He has sworn unto thy fathers" (verse 12), after He had said, 'This day art thou become the people of the Lord, thy God.'" It is evident that, according to this part of history, circumcision is not required of the Ger in order to enter the covenant of God. After this, all history, down to John Hyrcan, is entirely silent on this topic.

In his reign, we are told in Josephus, John Hyrcan vanquished the Idumeans, and forced upon them the faith of Judea and circumcision. The same was done by his successors to other conquered tribes. These facts, however, prove nothing in regard to proselytes, for all these conquered nationalities or tribes were of the seed of Abraham (on the one side of the country, by Ishmael and Esau, and on the other side, by the sons of Keturah, Abraham's second wife [Genesis 28:1-6]). Being of the seed of Abraham, they were commanded to be circumcised. This is acknowledged in the Talmud (Sanhedrin 59b) in regard to the sons of Keturah, but not in regard to the sons of Ishmael and Esau, who--it is maintained there-- were not included in the commandment given to Abraham and his seed after him. The passage in Sanhedrin reads thus: "Mila me-ikara le-Avraham hu, deka mazher leih Rachamana, 'Ve-ata et beriti tishmor, ata vezar-acha achareicha ledorotam.' Ata vezar-acha--in; enash acha-rina--la. Ela me-ata benei Yishma-el lichayevu. 'Ki beYitschak yikare lecha zara.' Benei Esav lichayevu. 'BeYitschak'--vela kol Yitschak. Matkif leh Rav Oshaya: 'Ela me-ata benei Ketura dela lichayevu?' Ha-amar Rabbi Yosei bar Avin ve-iteima Rabbi Yosei bar Chanina: 'Et beriti hefar--lerabot benei Ketura.'"

This very piece of exegetic nicety in the Talmud, which was without any practical use in that time, is a fragment from the time of John Hyrcan, and tells one of the objections of the Pharisees to the arbitrary doings of John Hyrcan (who became in his advanced years a Sad-ducee). He decreed a circumcision of Edomites and Ish-maelites, contrary to the will and traditions of the Pharisees. John Hyrcan had no right to expound the law or to enact one. He possessed the executive power, but the judiciary and legislative powers were in the hands of the Sanhedrin, and this body was Pharisaean in his time (under Joshua ben Perachia and Nittai of Arbella). Therefore, there is no proof for the lawful existence of those initiatory rites to be derived from the doings of John Hyrcan and his successors. They forced circumci-sion upon the seed of Abraham, and applied it to Ishma-elites and Edomites, contrary to the then existing high-est authority of the law. But the latter was done by the mandate of the sovereign or the supreme executive, which the Pharisees never acknowledged as a law.

No decree of any king ever was considered law in Israel. Herod and his family, however, were obliged to

uphold that mandate of John Hyrcan as established law
(to the best of our knowledge nobody else did) because
firstly, it had become tradition of the court, and secondly, the Jewish citizenship of Herod and his family
depended on the legality of John Hyrcan's decree concerning the Edomites. Therefore, some of the Herodian
princesses would not marry uncircumcised men. With them
this was perhaps a condition **sine qua non**, but this does
not say by any means that it was law or common custom in
Israel. We are entitled to the opinion that it was not,
because of the numerous cases of Roman **Gerim** mentioned
in the Talmud; the **Yir-ei Adonai** mentioned in the later
psalms (who were neither Israelites, nor Levites, nor
Aaronites), who feared the Lord and were identical with
the "devout Gentiles" of the New Testament; and the
Roman soldiers that embraced Judaism in Palestine. In
all the proselyte stories abounding in Talmud and Midrash, no initiatory rites are even hinted at. Why? We
say, because none were established.

The story of King Izates plainly shows that there
prevailed different opinions in his time on this question, as one advised him to submit to the Abrahamitic
rite and the other advised him not to do so (and both
were Israelites, believers in the Law). Besides, with
Izates it was a personal question of conscience (and not
of formality or law) to be acknowledged as a believer in
Judaism by the congregation. The same is the case with
Antonius and Rabbi Yehuda Hanasi. "Some say Antonius
was and some say he was not proselytized," viz., without
circumcision.

The same uncertainty is most strikingly illustrated
in the **pelugta** between Rabbi Eliezer and Rabbi Joshua:
One maintains that **Mila** alone, and the other maintains
that **Tevila** alone suffices to make one a **Ger**; and according to another version both agree on **Tevila** as the
condition **sine qua non** (see **Yearbook**, Mielziner quotation, p. 97). How could those two pillars of traditional law dispute on what was then law and custom in Israel, at a time when the proselytes were so numerous in
Israel that a prayer for them was included in the daily
eighteen benedictions ("**Ve-al gerei hatsedek**")? There
was nothing certain about the matter--as said--even when
the Mishna was written. The whole question, it appears,
originated with John Hyrcan's conversion in Idumea.

The Origin of the Initiatory Rites

It appears, therefore, that it was an ancient cus-
tom--by no means a law--that the proselyte offer up a
sacrifice (**Asham**) in the Temple of Jerusalem to atone
for his past sins of idolatry, as a token of his repentance and a solemn declaration of his loyalty to Israel's

monotheism and canon. This sacrifice might have been a pair of young pigeons or a little flour (Leviticus 5:14), which--it seems--could be made by proxy or by another gift to the Temple. Foreign proselytes, also from Rome--we know--sent gifts to the Temple. This was by no means insisted upon in all cases, as Rabbi Elijah Mizrachi and others maintain that according to the Law of Moses a confession before a college of three suffices.

With the sacrifice (**Korban**) there came naturally **Tevila**, the ritual bath. As the unclean could not approach the altar, he had to cleanse his body first before he offered up his sacrifice.

Another kind of ritual bath or baptism is unknown in the laws of Moses and the Rabbis, except "**Tevilat Ba-alei Teshuva**" ("The bath of the penitent sinner"), and this--it appears--has its origin in the cleansing ordinances for him who was to make a sin offering or a trespass offering. When the sacrifice itself was abolished, the preparatory bath remained for the penitent, as was the practice among the Essenes, who made no sacrifices, but observed scrupulously the Levitical cleansing prescriptions connected with it.

After the destruction of the altar, the question arose, what should replace the sacrifices to make atonement for man's sins. The enlightened Rabbis of that age of distress and despair--among whom Rabbi Joshua ben Chananiah may be counted--taught the people that substitutes for the sacrifices may be repentance of sin, prayer, alms-giving, acts of charity, the study of the law, conscientious righteousness, and similar practices of piety and humanity, which, they maintained, were more acceptable to God than all sacrifices. With them, the bath of repentance and the confession sufficed to accept the **Ger** into the fold of Judaism. The more rigorous Rabbis of those days, however, were not satisfied with those mild substitutes for the sacrifices, and resorted to the harsher means of asceticism and self-sacrifice. To them--and Rabbi Eliezer was one of them--the mere bath of repentance did not suffice for the proselyte. They demanded a bodily sacrifice, and found this already in the opinion of the followers of the John Hyrcan decree; and so they demanded also **Mila** as a substitute for the proselyte's sacrifice. The custom, however, of demanding both **Mila** and **Tevila** was certainly not generally established till late in the Amoraim period, and never was a Rabbinical law, as no one could make one when the Sanhedrin and Tannaim were no more. It was all a matter of custom--established by the schools and scholastic wisdom--without any foundation in Scripture or by enactments of the Scribes, Tannaim, or any other authoritative body.

If anybody holds that we, in this 19th century, are
bound to uphold, as a matter of religion, customs so and
then originated, without any basis in the Torah or even
in Rabbinical law, he must be opposed to the abolition
of those initiatory rites. Those, however, who think
that customs of that kind are not obligatory for us now,
and consider it proper and advisable to dispense with
them, have undoubtedly the right to say so and do so,
when an authoritative body declares so, without endan-
gering the union of Israel and the unity of Judaism.

(Vol. III, 1893, pp. 94-95)

Your committee maintains to have established:

1.   That there are known in history three initiatory rites for the proselyte to Judaism, viz., the Sacrificial Rite, the Ritual Bath, and Circumcision.

2.   None of these three initiatory rites for the
proselyte is ordained or otherwise suggested in the
Torah, Prophets, and Hagiography.

3.   They appear not in history and literature
prior to the conquest of Idumea by John Hyrcan, who
decreed circumcision on the Edomites, contrary to law
and custom.

4.   From and after that time, initiatory rites for
the proselyte became customary, but never became canon
law, not even Rabbinical law proper, and have therefore
found no place in the Mishna; nor were, generally, all
three rites considered necessary to every one proselyte;
there existed a difference of opinion, as to which rite
was necessary, down to the last of the Tannaim.

5.   After all legislative authority had been defunct, in the time of the Amoraim, without any lawful
enactment, the two rites--the sacrifice having been
abolished--were considered necessary to make a proselyte, but this never did and never could become canon
law. It always remained custom (**minhag**) without foundation in the Torah, brought about as "**Davar Shebeminyan**,"
and the Rabbinical rule concerning such custom is:
"**Davar shebeminyan, tsarich minyan acher lehatiro**,"
"What was prohibited [or ordained] by a vote [not by
legislative authority] must be revoked by a vote," viz.,
when the cause of its existence has ceased.

Therefore be it resolved: That the Central Conference of American Rabbis, assembled this day in this city
of New York, considers it lawful and proper for any
officiating rabbi, assisted by no less than two associates, to accept into the sacred covenant of Israel and
declare fully affiliated to the congregation (**davar
shebikdusha**) any honorable and intelligent person, who

desires such affiliation, without any initiatory rite, ceremony, or observance whatever; provided, such person be sufficiently acquainted with the faith, doctrine, and canon of Israel; that nothing derogatory to such person's moral and mental character is suspected; that it is his or her free will and choice to embrace the cause of Judaism; and that he or she declare verbally and in a document signed and sealed before such officiating rabbi and his associates his or her intention and firm resolve:

(1) to worship the One, Sole, and Eternal God, and none besides Him;

(2) to be conscientiously governed in his or her doings and omissions in life by God's laws ordained for the child and image of the Maker and Father of all, the sanctified son or daughter of the divine covenant;

(3) to adhere in life and death, actively and faithfully, to the sacred cause and mission of Israel, as marked out in Holy Writ.

Be it furthermore resolved: That a committee of three be appointed to report to this conference formulas of the two documents, viz., one to be signed by the proselyte and witnesses, to remain in the hands of the officiating rabbi, and another to be signed by the officiating rabbi and his associates, to be delivered to the proselyte.

Isaac M. Wise, Chairman

NOTE:

The two other members of the committee, viz., the Rev. Dr. Landsberg, of Rochester, New York, and the Rev. Dr. Adolph Moses, of Louisville, Kentucky, being temporarily absent from the country, in full agreement on this subject with the chairman, authorized him to write and report this document to the Central Conference.

I.M.W.

See also:

S.B. Freehof, "Circumcision of Proselytes," **Reform Responsa for Our Time**, pp. 71ff.

69. PROSPECTIVE CONVERT WHO FEARS CIRCUMCISION
(1978)

QUESTION: Is there any precedent in Halacha for a prospective convert who fears circumcision to avoid it? Similarly, is there a precedent for a prospective convert who has a deeply-rooted fear of water? Must he/she proceed with the requirement of **Mikveh**? (Rabbi Lawrence A. Englander, Mississauga, Ontario)

ANSWER: The traditional requirements for conversion are clear (B. Yev. 46, 47; **Shulchan Aruch**, Yoreh De-a 268; **Yad**, Isurei Bi-a 15). A court of three is necessary, and prospective converts must be warned that they are joining a persecuted community and that many new obligations will be incumbent upon them. In the days when the Temple stood, they were to bring a sacrifice, take a ritual bath, and--in the case of males--be circumcised. To this day, the requirements of a **Beit Din**, **Tevila**, and **Berit** remain for traditional Jews. Sources are clear on the requirements, but considerable discussion about them exists in the Talmud. For example, R. Eliezer stated that if a prospective male convert was circumcised or took a ritual bath, he was considered a proselyte. R. Joshua insisted on bath, and his point of view was adopted (B. Yev. 46b). Hillel and Shammai disagreed about a prospective male convert who was already circumcised. **Beit Shammai** insisted that blood must be drawn from him, while **Beit Hillel** stated that one may simply accept the circumcision without drawing blood (B. Shab. 135a). The Rabbinic authorities decided in favor of **Beit Shammai** (**Shulchan Aruch**, Yoreh De-a 268.1; **Yad**, Isurei Bi-a 14.5). Clearly, there were differences of opinion about the steps necessary for the ritual conversion in ancient times. As is well known, the Talmud also contains a variety of opinions about the desirability of accepting converts. These reflect the historic competition with Christianity, persecution, etc. in the early centuries of our era.

As we view the rite of conversion from a Reform point of view, we should note that the Reform Movement has placed its stress on careful instruction, with more attention to intellectual rather than ritual requirements. The Central Conference of American Rabbis in 1892 abolished the requirement of any ritual, including circumcision. Most Liberal rabbis, however, require circumcision or accept the existing circumcision (in accordance with the opinion of Hillel in B. Shab. 135b). Converts were to be accepted after due instruction before "any officiating rabbi assisted by no less than two

associates." There has been very little discussion of
Tevila by Liberal Jewish authorities. The custom has
fallen into disuse, but was never actually rejected by
Liberal Judaism. There are a number of cities in the
United States and Canada in which **Tevila** has been encouraged or required for Reform conversion, as there has
been cases of **Tevila** undertaken at the express wish of
the prospective convert.

Immersion in a **Mikveh** should not prove particularly
difficult, however. The **Mikveh** itself need contain only
forty **se-a** of water, which is approximately a hundred
and twenty gallons, and must be about four feet in
depth, so that a person can easily submerge himself
completely (**Sifra** 6.3; B. Yoma 31a, Er. 4b). During
most of the conversion procedure the convert would be in
water up to his/her neck, and then for an instant be
completely submerged. In other words, as we are not
discussing a deep body of water or an extensive one, it
should not be much more difficult than entering a bath;
therefore, someone with a phobia about water should be
able to undergo the ritual. However, as it is only
rarely used for Reform conversion, we can dispense with
it for such a convert even in a community where it is
usually utilized.

Theoretically, circumcision may be viewed similarly
according to the statement of the Central Conference of
American Rabbis of 1892. In practice, circumcision has,
however, been a virtually universal requirement. It may
be made easier, especially for an adult or an older
child, by providing an anesthetic. The early authorities of the last generation were against using an anesthetic (Meir Arik, **Imrei Yosher** II, 140). This was part
of the rejection of all innovations, but more recent
authorities have not hesitated to approve the use of an
anesthetic (J.L. Zierelsohn, **Ma-archei Lev**, 53; Gedalia
Felder, **Nachalat Tsevi**, p. 57). When the operation is
done on a new-born child, it is presumed that the nervous system does not yet fully convey a sense of pain,
but as that is not true of an adult or an older child,
anesthetic may alleviate the pain and remove the fear of
the impending operation. Circumcision may, of course,
be postponed indefinitely due to health reasons, and we
might consider the phobia as such a health reason. In
this way, one could also assure the convert that he
would be acceptable even without circumcision.

The prospective convert should be encouraged to
undergo circumcision although, strictly speaking, this
requirement may also be waived according to the earlier
Reform decision.

Walter Jacob

70.   A CONVERT WITH A CHRISTIAN FAMILY
(Vol. XCII, 1982, pp. 219-220)

QUESTION: A man has studied Judaism for several
years, involved himself thoroughly in the life of
the Jewish community, participated in Jewish charitable ventures, and is currently studying Hebrew.
He wishes to convert to Judaism. His wife, however, intends to remain a Christian. Their children
are adults, and they plan no further children.
Both individuals have reached middle age. Shall we
accept this individual and thereby create a mixed
marriage?   (Rabbi Peter S. Knobel, Evanston,
Illinois)

ANSWER: It is quite clear that the motivation of the
individual's involvement is sincere and that his commitment has already been tested through study and participation in Jewish life which has extended over several
years.   Also, there is no indication of any outside
motivation which prompted him in the direction of Judaism.   He has, therefore, fulfilled the traditional requirements (Yev. 46, 47; **Yad**, Isurei Bi-a 15; **Shulchan
Aruch**, Yoreh De-a 268).   Family problems which might
arise through a conversion should be investigated and
dealt with.
The questioner has suggested that we are, however,
creating a mixed marriage, and since we consider such
marriages wrong, we may have placed a stumbling block
before this man who would join us (A. Z. 6a).   It is for
this reason that Solomon B. Freehof has answered the
question negatively (**Current Reform Responsa**, pp.
215ff).   He suggests that we advise this man to remain a
Ger Toshav and a friend of our people, thereby demonstrating his closeness to Judaism.   Such individuals
have always had a very honored status among our people,
as for example Aim Paillere.
Clearly, however, another road would also be open
to us. As this individual has shown such a long, continuous interest in Judaism, it would be wrong to exclude him.   He has lived a Jewish life, attended the
synagogue, accepted the tenets of Judaism, given to
Jewish charity, and so we should accept him as part of
our people. We have not in modern times excluded a Jew
who has married a non-Jew from any portion of Jewish
life, so we should welcome this sincere man into the

synagogue. We recommend that he be welcomed and accepted.

                                                Walter Jacob

                71. AN APOSTATE PROSELYTE
                        (1980)

    QUESTION: What is the status of a proselyte who
    has decided to return to his/her original religion?
    What is the status of the children?

ANSWER: Any convert to Judaism has acquired an entirely new status. Indeed, the Talmud has compared a proselyte to a new-born child (Yev. 22a). He or she has not
only adopted the faith of Israel, but has also become a
part of the people of Israel. For this reason, it has
been customary to name proselytes "The son or daughter
of our Father Abraham (**Beit Yosef** on **Tur**, Even Ha-ezer
129; **Shulchan Aruch**, Even Ha-ezer 129.20; Felder, **Nachalat Tsevi** 1.31, 124) or Sarah, our Mother" (**Gates of
Mitzvah**, p. 24). It is, therefore, the almost unanimous
opinion that converts who revert to their original religions remain Jewish and are to be considered Jewish for
all purposes (Bechorot 30b). Their status was the same
as that of Jewish apostates. This problem has been
dealt with again and again with the same conclusion
(Yev. 47b; Asher Ben Yehiel, **ibid.**, **Tur**, Yoreh De-a 268;
Shulchan Aruch, Yoreh De-a 268.12, as well as the commentaries on these passages; Freehof, **Reform Responsa**,
pp. 192ff). The **Shulchan Aruch** and most of its commentaries agree that the child of an apostate female proselyte, or of a male married to a Jewish woman, would be
considered Jewish and would need no formal conversion to
Judaism. An adult proselyte who has become a Jew voluntarily cannot annul this process in any way (**Shulchan
Aruch**, Yoreh De-a 268.2, 12). Isserles indicated that
the Rabbinic ordinances, however, demanded of an apostate returning to Judaism or the child of an apostate
woman (who had been born or converted to Judaism), repentance before a court of three, as well as immersion
in a **Mikveh** (Radbaz, **Responsa** III, 415; Isserles to
Yoreh De-a 268.12; Hoffman, **Melamed Leho-il** II, 84) for
full acceptance into the Jewish community. Abraham
Gumbiner (**Magen Avraham** to **Shulchan Aruch**, Orach Chayim
326.8) reminded us that ritual immersion was not legally
necessary, but was a fence around the law.

All this clearly indicates that Judaism does not recognize a permanent change in status away from the Jewish people. A convert reverting to another religion would be considered an apostate.

We cannot, of course, deny individuals the right to adopt a religion of their choice. They have the freedom to adopt Judaism and the freedom to leave it. For all practical purposes, they will then be outside the Jewish community (in contrast to Bech. 30b), but we would always be willing to accept their return to us. Their children, too, will have full rights as Jews, should they wish to exercise them.

Walter Jacob, Chairman
Leonard S. Kravitz
Eugene Lipman
W. Gunther Plaut
Harry A. Roth
Rav A. Soloff
Bernard Zlotowitz

See also:

S.B. Freehof, "Marrying Apostate Daughter of Jewish Mother," **Reform Responsa**, pp. 192ff; "Status of Apostates (Children and Adults)," **Recent Reform Responsa**, pp. 120ff.

72.   REPAIRING DAMAGED **SEFER TORAH**
(Vol. XLVI, 1936, pp. 126-127)

QUESTION: During a fire, which recently destroyed part of our Temple, our two **Sifrei Torah** were injured. One was partially smoked up, and the second was partially scorched. Is it consistent with Jewish tradition to use these **Sifrei Torah** by replacing **Yeri-ot** in those sections that suffered injury?

ANSWER: According to Yoreh De-a, ch. 280, para. 2, when a **Yeri-a** is worn out, it should be replaced in conjunction with two **Yeri-ot** adjoining it, so that the handwriting of at least three **Yeri-ot** should look alike. However, certain authorities do not insist on this, and advocate the renewal of the affected **Yeri-a** only. But it is advisable to instruct the **Sofer** to see to it that the new **Yeri-a** should approximate the rest of the **Sefer Torah** as much as possible.

J. Mann and Committee

73. RITUAL FOR DISPOSAL OF DAMAGED **SEFER TORAH** (Vol. XXXIV, 1924, pp. 74-75)

QUESTION: I am very anxious to know the ritual in connection with the remains of a **Sefer Torah** which has been injured by fire. My impression is that they are to be buried, but I do not know the form. Since we have three such relics, I am quite anxious to dispose of them in the proper manner. Will you kindly let me know both the form and the ritual which are customary?

ANSWER: In regard to the mode of disposal of the burnt **Sefer Torah** fragments, tradition prescribes no set ritual. However, it offers a helpful guidance. The Talmud lays down the law that a worn-out Scroll may be placed in a jar and buried beside a scholar. This was to express the idea that the **Sefer Torah**, though torn, is still identified with the student: "**Sefer Torah shebala, gonezin oto etsel talmid chacham, uvichli cheres, shene-emar, 'Unetatem bichlei cheres lema-an ya-amdu yamim rabim'**" (B. Megila 26b). The Shulchan Aruch (Yoreh De-a 282.10, and Orach Chayim 154.5) accepts this view (see also **Sha-arei Teshuva** to Orach Chayim, ad loc.). The reason for burying Scrolls is to avoid their further destruction by burning or otherwise being misused. Where there is fear that vandals may take them out of the graves and burn them, it is permitted to put them in earthen vessels and hide them in a secret place (Responsa of R. Solomon b. Simon Duran, 1400-1457, no. 62).

The rule of burying the old Scrolls which became spoiled or torn was in course of time extended to all Hebrew books which became torn or spoiled. This, indirectly, probably led to the well-known practice of having special places called **Geniza**, where such books were temporarily kept before being buried (see Eisenstein's **Otsar Dinim Uminhagim**, p. 77). In almost all Jewish centers, there are **Genizot** in the synagogues--under the **Bima**, within the walls, or in the garrets. As the place grew overcrowded, the content was carried to the cemetery for burial. Among the Sefardim of Palestine it is

customary to bury the accumulated **Genizot** with considerable ceremony.   They use the occasion for prayers for
relief from drought and other forms of distress (see
Lunz, **Jerusalem** I, Wien, 1882, pp. 15-16).   In Algiers,
the burial of the **Geniza** usually takes place on **Rosh
Chodesh Iyar** (**Minhagei Algier**, p. 132).   In many Russian
and Polish communities, too, torn Scrolls and worn out
books are buried in the ground.   A tent is then placed
over the grave to show that it is a holy place.   Of
course, Psalms and prayers are recited at such occasions.

Guided by these practices, we think that in your
case--when the Scrolls were injured at the occasion when
the Temple burned down--it is fitting to place your
burnt **Sefer Torah** in an earthen jar or a box, and to
deposit it in the cornerstone of your new Temple.   Psalm
74, referring to the burning of the sacred meeting
places, will be fitting for the occasion; also selections from R. Meir of Rothenburg's dirge on the "Burning
of the Law" may be recited.   A translation of this dirge
is found in Nina Davis's **Songs of Exile**, pp. 83-91.
Your sermon might be built on the statement of R. Hanina
b. Teradyon, one of the Ten Martyrs, who, when wrapped
in a **Sefer Torah** and placed on the pyre, exclaimed:
"Scrolls are burning, but the letters fly upward"
("**Gevilim nisrafim ve-otiyot porechot**"; B. Avoda Zara
18a).   Should this ceremony be observed apart from that
of laying the cornerstone, or at a special occasion at
the cemetery, you might conclude it with reading well-
known passages (see Berachot 64a) and the reciting of
Kaddish Derabanan.

Jacob Z. Lauterbach

See also:

S.B. Freehof, "Posul Torah in the Ark,"
Contemporary Reform Responsa, pp. 114ff; "Preserving a Torah Fragment," **Reform Responsa for
Our Time**, pp. 80ff; "Torah in Museum Case or
in Ark," **Contemporary Reform Responsa**, pp.
110ff.

74.   PHYSICIAN KEEPING TRUTH FROM PATIENT
(Vol. LXIV, 1954, pp. 80-81)

QUESTION: As a physician I know that in being truthful with my patients I retain their confidence as well as my own self-respect. But it is not always possible for me to disclose all I know or have reason to suspect. I feel at times that the interest of my patient is better served if I withhold from him information of a shocking nature.

Having lived all my life in religious surroundings, I have often wondered what Jewish religion has to say on the subject. Am I ever justified, on religious grounds, in keeping the truth from my patients?

ANSWER: Our ancient teachers, from whose utterances we draw deep draughts of wisdom even today, often voiced the conviction that religion was the handmaid rather than the lord of life. They held, for example, that with the exception of a number of vital negative commandments, the injunction to live in accord with the law precluded any situation in which complete obedience might prove perilous to life and health (**Sifra**, Lev. 18:5).

It is not strange, therefore, to hear these pious men express the view that in order to preserve peaceful relations among men, the bare truth may be given an appropriate disguise. In fact, they discover that on one occasion God Himself, to forestall any possible discord between Abraham and Sarah, deviated from the line of strict verocity (Yevamot 65b).

This general attitude finds embodiment in some legal enactments of the Rabbis. We are enjoined, for example, from apprising a sick person of the death of a close member of his family, lest the mental disturbance aggravate his condition (Yoreh De-a 337). Again, when one is about to die, and confession of his sins is in order, he shall be summoned to this last rite in a hopeful tone and in an atmosphere free from any display of grief. The prescribed formula reads: "Many men, after having made their final confession, continued to live; many others, having failed to confess, also failed to recover. You who are about to confess your sins will surely be rewarded with renewed life. Also, confession assures one of his due portion of the world to come" (**ibid.**, 338).

The physician, who respects the truth and maintains truthful relations with all men, need have no qualms of conscience when, in certain special cases, in the pursuit of the good of a patient, he complies with the requirements of the situation and suppresses what appears to him to be the truth.

Israel Bettan

See also:

S.B. Freehof, "Dying Patient Informed of his Condition," in **Reform Responsa**, pp. 122ff.

75.   CHOOSING WHICH PATIENT TO SAVE
(Vol. LXXVIII, 1968, pp. 111-118)

QUESTION: The head of a clinic in Boston asked, following a forum session at the last Biennial Convention of the Union of American Hebrew Congregations in Montreal (November, 1967): "What guidance can Jewish tradition give us in the excruciating, ethical dilemma of selecting one patient over many others to keep him alive by means of a mechanical kidney machine? Since such facilities are extremely limited, many patients must be rejected and are certain to die. The same question may also be raised with reference to the very limited supply of organs for transplantation. On what basis can a conscientious doctor make the decision as to which patient is to live or die?"

ANSWER: Solomon Landau, in a responsum embodied in the collection of his father Ezekiel Landau's responsa (**Noda biYehuda**, vol. II, #74), was asked whether a man sought by the government as a criminal should be turned over or not. He says at the outset: "It is difficult to make a decision in matters which involve the life of a human being." Such a decision is always a difficult one in any decent tradition, religious or social. The question asked here by the physician of the clinic is especially difficult to decide on the basis of Jewish traditional literature. Obviously, there were in those days no such remarkable inventions, or the means for the preservation of vital organs, as there are today. In those days, when a person was dying, they would discourage any artificial attempt to keep him alive for another hour or so, because a man has a right to die when the time comes (cf. "Ran" to Nedarim 40a). But nowadays it is possible, in the case of moribund patients, to effect what often amounts to a cure. So there is no real precedent for the problem in the traditional literature.

Nevertheless, there are quite a number of somewhat different discussions which involve the question of choosing one person to live or another person to die. In the discussion of these various dilemmas there may perhaps be found an ethical principle, or at least an ethical mood, which might help indicate what Jewish tradition **would have said** in a situation such as this one which now occurs frequently in modern hospitals.

The Mishna (in Oholot VII.6) deals with a question which involves the choosing between one life and another. A mother is apparently dying because of the childbirth. Either she or her child can be saved. Which one should it be? The law is that the child is looked upon as an assailant and therefore may be destroyed before he kills the mother. Therefore, the unborn child should be destroyed, and the mother saved. If, however, the child puts forth its head, then it may no longer be destroyed. It is now considered a separate person, and now the law is thus stated: "We do not dispose of [or push aside] one person in favor of another" (cf. also Sanhedrin 72b). This is stated as the fixed law in the **Shulchan Aruch**, Choshen Mishpat 425.2).

This clear-cut principle that we may not save one life at the expense of another seemed at first glance to be somewhat contradicted by the discussion in the Mishna and the Talmud as to the relative respect to be paid to a father and to a teacher. This Mishna (Bava Metsi-a II.11) says that if a person finds an object lost by his father and another object lost by his teacher, he must first return the one lost by his teacher. The Mishna explains the reasons as follows: "For his father has brought him into the light of this world, while his teacher, who teaches him wisdom, has brought him into the light of the world to come." Upon that basis the Mishna continues to say that if both his father and his teacher are held in captivity, he must first redeem his teacher and after that redeem his father. This is discussed in the Talmud in Bava Metsi-a 33a, and is codified as law by Maimonides in Hil. Aveda 12.2 and in the **Shulchan Aruch** in Yoreh De-a 242.34. All this seems to contradict the principle that you may not choose one life to save in preference to another, but actually this is not so. The Rabbis do not speak here of such an irreversible fact as death, but only at most of captivity in which both are to be saved (except, of course, that they give the order as to who should be saved first). When it comes to an actual matter of life or death, in which a choice is final, the principle remains that one life is as precious as another.

This principle that we do not destroy one life in order to save another is further exemplified in a discussion in Pesachim 25b. A man comes before Rava and says: "The governor of my city has given me the alternative that either I should kill so-and-so or the governor will kill me. What shall I do? Rava answered him: "Be killed rather than kill. What makes you think that your blood is redder than his?"

This Talmudic phrase, "Your blood is redder than his," was used in rather a reverse sense in the latest volume of **Tsits Eli-ezer**, vol. 9, 45, Eliezer Wildenberg, Jerusalem, 1967. In this volume, devoted to a large extent to modern medical questions, the author concludes that a person is certainly not **required** by law to donate an organ of his body in order that it may be planted into the body of another. If he is endangered by the removal of the organ, then he is actually forbidden to risk his life. Of course, if the danger to him were minimal and the benefit to the recipient were maximal, it would be a good deed; but, otherwise, one should not endanger his life in this way because one life--in this case his own--is as valuable as the life he wishes to save. Wildenberg then uses the Talmudic dictum cited above: "What makes you think (that **his** blood is redder than yours)?" But whichever way the phrase is taken, its meaning is clear enough: Every life is as equally valuable as any other life.

The two instances--that of the infant and that of the man ordered to become a murderer--both differ from the case inquired about here because these two cases involve actually taking steps to put people to death, while the case of the clinic involves merely allowing dying people to die. Nevertheless, in spite of this difference, this much at least is relevant: we have no right to say that one person's life is more important than that of the other--the mother's or the child's, or the man's or his intended victim's. From the standpoint of religion, all people are alike in status as to the right to life.

There is still another set of circumstances developed in a series of discussions in the literature, all of which spring from the same Biblical account. These discussions, different from those above, do not deal with the worth of one person rather than another, but with the safety of a social group as against the life of one person. The question now is whether a city or a group may save itself by handing over one of its number to death. In the Second Book of Samuel, chapter 20, Sheva ben Bichri, who rebelled against King David, takes refuge in the city of Abel. There he is pursued by Joab and his army, which surrounds the city and threatens to destroy it. The wise woman of the city gives up Sheva to Joab, and thus the city is spared. This incident is discussed in the Tosefta (Terumot, end of chapter 7) and in the Palestinian Talmud (Terumot, end of chapter 8), where it is cited as a guide in the following situation. A group of travelers is stopped by brigands who say to the travelers: "Give us one of your number. We will kill him and let the rest of you go." May they do so? This, now, is a case of saving a large number of people by having one person die. The decision is that they must say: "No, we would rather all be killed than give up one of our number to death" (since the shedding of blood is one of the three sins for which a person must be willing to die rather than commit it, the other two being idolatry and immorality). The conclusion is, so far, that rather than commit what amounts to one murder, we would rather be killed ourselves, even though there are twenty of us and the victim would be only one.

However, the discussion in the Tosefta and in the Talmud continues as follows: This wholesale self-sacrifice applies only when the brigands are not specific and merely say "one of you," thus compelling us to choose the man to be killed. But if they are specific and they are searching for a certain man who they mention by name, then we do not all have to be killed for his sake, since it is not we who selected him for death. This, however, is only one opinion. The opposite opinion is that this one man, even though specifically named, may not be turned over to the brigands unless he is criminal, as Sheva was in the Biblical account, since he rebelled against King David. This distinction is embodied in the law (see Maimonides, Hilchot Yesodei Torah V.5). There is some disagreement about whether the man needs to be a known criminal before he is surrendered to save the lives of all the others, or whether it is sufficient if the brigands named him and it is not we who have selected him. See the discussion by Joseph Caro in **Kesef Mishneh** to the law in Maimonides.

The bearing of this discussion on the case in point is that actually the other patients, who will not be given the rare remedy, have not been directly selected for death. They have already been marked for death by forces beyond the physician's control (as by the brigands in this case), and if they die, it is not directly the physician's fault. They would die anyhow. It is not he who has really named them for death.

It is also clear from this aversion against turning someone over to death in order to save someone else, or even a group, that it would be absolutely forbidden by the spirit of Jewish law to hasten the death of some terminal patient already marked for death in order to take something from his body in order to save another patient or for the increase of medical knowledge.

But so far all of the incidents cited involve a direct choice between living and healthy people as to who should live and who should die. The case involved in the question asked is of people who are dying. Is there any guidance in the law for choosing between people who are already marked for death? It is possible to say that, since they are already dying, we should just let them all die and not attempt the bitter choice of picking one of them to live. Is such a "hands-off" attitude permissible?

This very question, by close analogy, is discussed in the Talmud (Bava Metsi-a, 62a). The case is stated as follows: Two men are walking (presumably in the desert). They have one pitcher of water which contains enough to keep only one of them alive long enough to cross the desert safely. If both of them drink, they will both die. If one drinks, he will be saved and the other will die. What shall be done? Ben Petura said: "Let them both die and let not one be a witness to the death of his fellow man." But Rabbi Akiva's greater authority is cited to refute this opinion of Ben Petura. He says: "Your life comes first." In other words, a man must strive to save his own life. Although this narrative is cited in a discussion about the taking of interest and whether it should be returned, nevertheless it constitutes an independent homily (see the statement of Asher ben Yehiel to the passage). While, of course, Akiva's decision is not directly helpful to the question of deciding which shall live (since it does not indicate in which manner the matter will be settled with each one trying to save his own life); nevertheless, this much is clear: We may not permit both men to die when at least one of them can be saved. The passage is unfortunately too terse, and therefore we cannot tell the method of selection, but it is clear enough that a selection will and should be made, and that it is not right to allow both of them to die merely because it would be painful to make a decision. Thus, the final problem still remains. He should choose, but which one?

As to whom he chooses, there is, in a sense, a negative guideline. The passage which speaks of the brigands or captors demanding one of the group of men to be given up for death, speaks first of a group of captive women. The captors ask for one woman to be given to them for sexual abuse. The sexual fate of a captive woman receives considerable discussion in the law. The married status of the captive wife may be affected by what had happened to her during her captivity. If one of the women in the group has already been abused, the other women may not say that since this unfortunate one has already been abused, she is the one who should be given up. (See **Kesef Mishneh** to **Yad**, Hil. Yesodei

Torah, V. 5, where Caro cites the responsa of Solomon b. Aderet to this effect.) They have no right to decide on the basis of her unhappy past and so select her in order to save themselves.

In other words, in matters which are equivalent to life or death (as this was considered to be), the past status or character of the prospective victim may not be considered. We may not say: "This one's life may be set aside in favor of the other's." All are of equal status in relation to life or death.

There is, however, some other standard of choice before the physician, one which is precisely relevant. There is a discussion in the Talmud (in Avoda Zara 27b) which is developed in the legal literature into a principle. It can be stated as follows: [When there is a chance for a cure] we do not put too much value upon the last hours of a dying man ("Ein mashgichim lechayei sha-a"). In other words, these last few hours are not so valuable that we may not risk them if we want to try out some new and hitherto untried remedy. These last hours are fading anyhow. So Jacob Reischer, Rabbi of Metz (died 1733), in his responsa (Shevut Ya-akov III, #75) concludes that we may risk the few hours of a dying man and try an untried remedy, if there is a fair prospect that he can be cured enough to have, say, a year of life. He says at first that even the chayei sha-a (the remaining hours of life) are important and we must guard them (i.e., we never hasten death); nevertheless, if there is a remedy by use of which it is possible to cure him, then in that case we may risk it. The same decision was arrived at in a responsum published this past year by Mordecai Jacob Breisch (Chelkat Ya-akov III, #141). From this we conclude that the physician must endeavor to decide not on the basis of personality reasons, but on medical grounds. He must select the patient--rich or poor, good or bad--who has the better prospect of survival and of getting more of relatively healthy life. As for the others, no direct action should be taken by him against them. Their sickness will run its course.

This same conclusion, i.e., that the one who will benefit most should receive the remedy, was arrived at over a hundred and fifty years ago by Joseph Teomim (1727-1793). Of course, he could not have had any knowledge of modern transplants, nor of the special problems involved in them. He came to his conclusion purely on the basis of the spirit of the law. His statement is in his commentary Peri Megadim to Orach Chayim 328 (commenting on the Magen David). The Shulchan Aruch at that point deals with the question of which patients may have the Sabbath violated for them and to what extent. The discussion involves the ques-

tion of which patient is in real danger and which is not in immediate danger.   Joseph Teomim then widens his conclusion from the Sabbath law to a more general appli- cation and says: If there is doubt about whether one patient is in danger, and there is no doubt that the other patient is in danger--if there is not enough medi- cine for both of them, we give it to the one who is in greater danger.
     From all this discussion in the Talmudic and later literature, a certain mood emerges.   First, that one life is as important as another; and this must certainly be so in the eyes of the physician.   Second, that ac- tively to take steps to destroy another life for our own benefit is not permitted.   Third, that when it comes to a choice between people who are dying anyway, the choice cannot be evaded, but **must** be made (nothing is gained by allowing both men to die in the desert!).   But as to whom to choose for survival, it must be on purely medi- cal grounds, selecting the one who has a better chance of benefiting from the remedy.   Of course, this is not an absolute test, because out of ten patients there may be two or three who could greatly benefit from the reme- dy.   But at least this principle narrows the choice and in many cases can decide the case.   So, while there is no case in Jewish legal tradition precisely like this modern question, there is enough in it to give at least this much guidance.

Addendum

     Dr. Julius Kravetz, a member of our committee, calls my attention to a sequence of passages in Mishna and Talmud which points in the opposite direction from the conclusion arrived at above.   These passages should be mentioned, not only for the sake of completeness, but also as a possible balance to the opinion expressed in the responsum.
     The Mishna (in Horayot III.7,8) says that a man precedes a woman (i.e., has prior right) "to be kept alive" (lehachayot) and to have his lost articles re- turned.   But a woman precedes a man in being provided with clothing and being redeemed from captivity.   A Cohen has precedence over a Levi, a Levi over an Israel- ite, and an Israelite over an illegitimate, etc.
     The Talmud discusses this Mishna in two places: Horayot 13bff and Nazir 47b.   In both passages the Tal- mud gives the reasons for the various priorities.   There is, however, a further development in the passage in Nazir.   Mar Ukba says that the priority (of the Battle- priest over the **Segan**) means that he has precedence in our duty to keep him alive.   The **Tosafot** are still more specific, saying that if a heap has fallen on both, it

is he who must be rescued first. Rabbi Untermann (in **HaTorah Veha-medina** IV, 22-29) takes this as the meaning of the discussion in the Mishna and applies it in the case of a pharmacist having a limited supply of penicillin, etc.

This, then, is a halachic discussion which points to an order of precedence in the saving of lives (a man before a woman, a Priest before a Levite, etc.). However, it seems to me that the discussion, in spite of the **Tosafot**, does not necessarily refer to the rescue of endangered lives. The Mishna uses the word **lehachayot**. If the Mishna meant "to rescue from danger," we would have expected it to use the word **lehatsil**. In fact, the **Shach** (to Yoreh De-a 351.14) says that the word does mean **lehatsil** and interprets accordingly. But the Mishna uses this word in precisely the same way in which it is used in Psalm 33:19. The Psalm makes use of both words, **lehatsil** and **lehachayot**, each for a specific thought. It says "to rescue (**lehatsil**) thee from death, and to sustain thee (**lehachayot**) in famine." So our Mishna here uses the word **lehachayot** precisely in connection with providing clothing and ransoming from captivity. If our Mishna had actually meant "to rescue from death," then we would expect that the Codifiers, when giving the laws of rescue, would refer to this priority. But neither Maimonides, nor the **Tur**, nor the **Shulchan Aruch** mention any of these priorities in the laws of rescue (cf. **Yad**, Hilchot Rotseach I 14; **Tur** and **Shulchan Aruch**, Choshen Mishpat 42b).

Judging by the context of this Mishna and by the Biblical use of the word in the Psalm, **lehachayot** is not used here loosely as meaning the same as **lehatsil**, but precisely as meaning "to keep alive," in the sense of "to sustain or to support."

This is clearly the way in which the Codifiers understood the discussion. They do mention the list of personal priorities, but only in connection with charity. So Maimonides in **Yad** (Matnat Aniyim VIII.15-17), the **Tur**, and **Shulchan Aruch** (Yoreh De-a 251).

Solomon B. Freehof

76. RELIEVING PAIN OF A DYING PATIENT
(Vol. LXXXV, 1975, pp. 83-85)

QUESTION: A dying patient is suffering great pain. There are medicines available which will relieve his agony. However, the physician says that the

pain-relieving medicine might react on the weakened
respiratory system of the patient and bring death
sooner. May, then, such medicine be used for the
alleviation of the patient's agony? Would it make
a difference to our conclusion if the patient himself gave permission for the use of this pain-
killing medicine? (Rabbi Sidney H. Brooks, Omaha,
Nebraska)

ANSWER: Let us discuss the second question first,
namely, what difference would it make if the patient
himself gives permission for the use of this medicine,
though he knows it may hasten his death? There have
been some discussions in the law in recent years of the
difference it would make if a dying patient gave certain
permissions with regard to the handling of his body
after death. For example, he might ask for certain
parts of the usual funeral ritual to be omitted; and
some authorities say that he may permit autopsy. If I
remember rightly, this permission was given by the late
Rabbi Hillel Posek of Tel Aviv. But all these statements, giving the dying man the right to make such requests, deal with what should be done with his body
after death, but not with any permission that he may
give for hastening his death. After all, for a man to
ask that his life be ended sooner is the equivalent of
his committing suicide (or asking someone else to short-
en his life for him). Suicide is definitely forbidden
by Jewish law.
    However, we are dealing with a person who is in
great physical agony. That fact makes an important
difference. A person under great stress is no longer
considered in Jewish law to be a free agent. He is, as
the phrase has it, **Anus**, "under stress or compulsion."
Such a person is forgiven the act of suicide, and the
usual funeral rites--which generally are forbidden in
the case of suicide--are permitted to the man whose
suicide is under great stress. The classic example for
this permissibility is King Saul on Mount Gilboa. His
death (falling on his sword) and the forgiveness granted
him gave rise to the classic phrase, in this case, "**Anus
keSha-ul.**" Thus, in many cases in the legal literature
the person committing suicide was forgiven and given
full religious rites after death, if in his last days he
was under great stress. (See the various references
given in **Recent Reform Responsa**, pages 114ff, especially
the example of the boys and girls being taken captive to
Rome who committed suicide [B. Gittin 57b]; the responsum of Jacob Weil, 114; and that of Mordecai Benet, **Parashat Mordechai**, Yoreh De-a 25; and the other responsa
given in **Recent Reform Responsa.**)

However, a caution must be observed here. The law
does not mean that a person may ask for death if he is
in agony, but it means that if in his agony he does so,
it is pardonable. In other words, here we must apply
the well-known principle in Jewish law, the distinction
between **Lechatechila**, "doing an action to begin with,"
and **Bedi-avad**, "after the action is done." Thus, we do
not say that **Lechatechila** it is permissible for a man to
ask for death, but **Bedi-avad**, if under great stress he
has done so, it is forgivable.

So far we have discussed the situation from the
point of view of the action of the patient. Now we must
consider the question from the point of view of the
physician. Is a physician justified in administering a
pain reliever to a dying patient in agony when the physician knows beforehand that the medicine will tend to
weaken his heart and perhaps hasten his death?

Jewish traditional law absolutely forbids hastening
the death of a dying patient. It requires meticulous
care in the environs of the dying patient, not to do
anything that might hasten his death. All these laws
are codified in the **Shulchan Aruch**, Yoreh De-a 339. See
the full discussion in **Modern Reform Responsa**, pp.
197ff. If, therefore, this were definitely a lethal
medicine, the direct effect of which would be to put an
end to the patient's life, the use of such medicine
would be absolutely forbidden. But this medicine is
neither immediately, nor intentionally, directly lethal;
its prime purpose and main effect is the alleviation of
pain. The harmful effect on the heart of the patient is
only incidental to its purpose and is only a possible
secondary reaction. The question, therefore, amounts to
this: May we take that amount of **risk** to the patient's
life in order to relieve the great agony which he is now
suffering?

Interestingly enough, there is very little discussion in the classic legal literature, beginning with the
Talmud, about the relief of pain. Most of the discussion deals with the theological question of why pain is
sent to us and how we are to endure it and with our
attitude to God because of it. As for the paucity of
reference on the **relief** of pain--that can be understood
because, after all, in those days they had very little
knowledge of opiates or narcotics. However, the Talmud
does mention one pain-killing medicine which could be
used in the ceremony of piercing the ear of a slave
(Kiddushin 21b). This is the basis of all modern legal
discussion as to whether anesthetic may be used in circumcision (see **Current Reform Responsa**, pp. 102ff). It
should be noted in that responsum that most of the
scholars agree on the permissibility of the relief of
pain, at least in that ceremony.

But in the case which we are discussing, it is more
than a question of relieving pain of a wound or an operation. It is a question of relieving pain at the risk
of shortening life. Now, granted that it is forbidden
to take any steps that will definitely shorten the life
of the patient (as mentioned heretofore)--may it not be
permitted in the case of a dying patient to take some
risk with his remaining hours or days, if the risk is
taken for his benefit?

This question may be answered in the affirmative.
The law in this regard is based upon the Talmud (Avoda
Zara 27a-b). There the question is whether we may make
use of a Gentile physician (in that case, an idolater).
What is involved is the enmity on the part of an idolater toward the Israelite, and the fact that the physician may--out of enmity--do harm to the patient. It
makes a difference in the law whether the man is an
amateur or a professional. The latter may generally
always be employed. Also it makes a difference as to
the present state of the patient's health, as follows:
If the patient is dying anyhow, more risks may be taken
for the chance of his possible benefit. The phrase used
for these last dying hours is **chayei sha-a**, and the
general statement of the law is that we may risk these
fragile closing hours and take a chance on a medicine
that may benefit the patient (cf. **Shulchan Aruch**, Yoreh
De-a 154). See **Modern Reform Responsa**, p. 199, and
especially the classic responsum on this subject by
Jacob Reischer of Metz, **Shevut Ya-akov** III, 75. In
other words, this is the case of a **dying** patient, and
the law permits us in such a case to risk the **chayei
sha-a** for his potential benefit.

However, this does not quite solve the problem.
The law permits risking these last hours on the chance
of **curing** the patient. But may we conclude from that
permission also the right to risk those last hours, not
with the hope of curing the patient, but for the purpose
of relieving him of pain? Interestingly enough, there
is a precedent in Talmudic literature precisely on this
question (see the references in **Modern Reform Responsa**,
197ff). The incident referred to is in Ketubot 104a.
Rabbi Judah the Prince was dying in great agony. The
Rabbis surrounded his house in concerted prayer for his
healing. But Rabbi Judah's servant (who is honored and
praised in the Talmud) knew better than the Rabbis how
much agony the rabbi was suffering. She therefore dis-
rupted their prayers in order that he might die and his
agony end.

In other words, we may take definite action to
relieve pain, even if it is of some risk to the **chayei
sha-a**, the last hours. In fact, it is possible to reason as follows: It is true that the medicine to relieve

his pain may weaken his heart, but does not the great
pain itself weaken his heart? And: May it not be that
relieving the pain may strengthen him more than the
medicine might weaken him? At all events, it is a matter of judgment, and in general we may say that in order
to relieve his pain, we may incur some risk as to his
final hours.

Solomon B. Freehof

77. ALLOWING A TERMINAL PATIENT TO DIE
(Vol. LXXIX, 1969, pp. 118-121)

QUESTION: A terminal patient was dying as a result
of a series of strokes. Two physicians, one of
whom was the patient's son, decided--with the consent of the family--to hasten the end by with-
drawing all medication and fluids given intraven-
ously. Is such procedure permitted by Jewish law?

ANSWER: This is a complex question and, therefore, is
not quite clear in the law. However, there is enough in
the legal literature to permit us to arrive at a conclusion.
    First, let us dispose of a secondary question. It
is not altogether irrelevant that one of the physicians,
a noted surgeon, was the son of the patient. There is a
great deal of discussion in Jewish law as to the relationship between a physician and a patient who is his
father. There are many responsa which--even nowadays--
discuss the question whether a son who is a surgeon may
operate on his father.
    The basis of this legal debate is Exodus 21:15,
which states that he who smites his father must be put
to death; and the law is that "smiting" is not considered so grave a sin unless it creates a wound. Therefore it is the creating of a wound on the body of one's
father which is considered a grave sin. Hence the Mishna (Sanhedrin XI.1) and the Talmud (Sanhedrin 84b) discuss whether a son may perform the operation of bloodletting on his father as part of his work as a physician, or make a wound on his body. This is discussed by
Maimonides in **Yad**, Hilchot Mamrim, V.7, and in the **Shulchan Aruch**, Yoreh De-a 241.3. In the **Shulchan Aruch**,
Caro states the law that a son may not operate on a
father, but Isserles says that if there is no one else
available for the operation, he may do so. Isserles

bases his opinion on the opinion of Maimonides (loc. cit.). This would be the general conclusion of the law. All this, of course, is incidental to our question.

The real question is: What is the limit on the freedom of action of a physician with regard to a dying patient? By "dying patient" we do not mean a patient who is in danger of death but only who can yet be healed. If, for example, a person has a heart attack and can be healed (as many are from one attack or even two), or if a patient has been rescued from drowning and can be saved with resuscitation (but if no resuscitation is given he will die)--such dying patients, all of whom have a prospect for recovery, must be given the full resources of medicine in the attempt to save them. One may even risk a remedy that might possibly kill them, provided there is a fair chance that the remedy might save them. Thus, the Talmud, in Avoda Zara 27b, says clearly that one may risk otherwise forbidden remedies (e.g., from a heathen healer) if the dying patient has a chance to be cured by the remedy. See the full discussion of this permission to risk death if there is a fair chance to cure in **Shevut Ya-akov** III.75 (Jacob Reischer of Metz, d. 1733).

But in the case under consideration we are not dealing with a dying patient who has a chance for recovery if given the proper medication. We are dealing with a patient with regard to whom all the physicians present, including his own son, agree that he has no chance for recovery. In other words, he is a **terminal** patient. What, then, are the limits of freedom of action of a physician with a terminal patient?

Is it the physician's duty to keep this hopeless patient (who is also in all likelihood suffering great pain) alive a little longer, maybe a day or two? Jewish law is quite clear on this question. He is not in duty bound to force him to live a few more days or hours. This law is based on the famous incident in B. Ketubot 104a. Rabbi Judah the Prince was dying in great suffering. The Rabbis insisted on ceaselessly praying so that he might thus be kept alive a little longer. But his servant-woman (who is often referred to with honor in the Talmud) threw down an earthen jar from the roof of the house into the midst of the praying Rabbis, in order to stop their prayers so that Rabbi Judah might peacefully die. The Spanish scholar Nissim Gerondi (to Nedarim 40a, top) says that while it is our duty to pray for a sick person that he may recover, there comes a time when we should pray for God's mercy that he should die. So, too, **Sefer Chasidim** (#315-318, edition Frankfurt)-- basing its opinion on the statement of Ecclesiastes, "There is a time to live and a time to die"--says as follows: "If a man is dying, we do not pray too hard

that his soul return and that he revive from the coma;
he can at best live only a few days and in those days
will endure great suffering; so 'there is a time to
die.'"   (See other such references in **Reform Responsa**,
pp. 117ff).   In other words, according to the spirit of
Jewish tradition, just as a man has a right to live, so
there comes a time when he has a right to die.   Thus,
there is no duty incumbent upon the physician to force a
terminal patient to live a little longer.

But what, under these circumstances, is a physician
permitted actually to do?   Here again the law is clear.
He may do nothing positive to hasten death.   The Mishna
(in Shabbat XXIII.5) says that we may not close the eyes
of a dying patient.   The Talmud (Shabbat 151b) compares
the dying patient to a guttering candle that is about to
go out.   If a man touches his fingertip to the candle
flame, it will go out at once.   This he must not do.   In
other words, he must not hasten the death of a dying
patient by closing his eyes.   The Talmudic discussion is
elaborated on in the post-Talmudic treatise, **Semachot**,
chapter 1, and finally is codified in the **Shulchan
Aruch**, Yoreh De-a 339, where it is clear that no action
must be taken to hasten death, i.e., you may not remove
a pillow from under his head.   However (see Isserles,
ibid.), if someone outside is chopping wood and that
rhythmic sound focuses the mind of the dying patient and
prevents his soul from departing, you may stop the
wood-chopping so that the patient may relax and die in
peace.   Or, if there is salt on the patient's tongue and
the tartness of the salt focuses his mind and keeps him
from relaxing into death, you may wipe the salt from his
tongue and thus allow him to die.   The **Taz** expresses
some doubt about the permission to wipe the patient's
tongue, for that would shake and disturb the patient and
would be an overt act.

The fullest discussion as to what is a permitted
act and what is a non-permitted act is found in **Shiltei
Hagiborim** (Joshua Boaz) to Mo-ed Katan, third chapter
(in Wilna edition, Alfasi, 16b).   He concludes that
while you must not do anything to hasten death, you may
remove the causes of the delay of death.   He bases his
discussion upon the **Sefer Chasidim** (edition Frankfurt,
#315), which says: "We may not put salt on his tongue in
order to prevent his dying."   And so Isserles in the
Shulchan Aruch (loc. cit.) sums up what is permitted and
what is not permitted by saying that such things are
permitted "which do not involve action at all, but merely remove that which hinders the death."

All this brings us to a clearer understanding as to
the limits of freedom of action of the physician in
relation to the hopelessly dying patient.   He may not
take any overt action to hasten death, such as giving

him, perhaps, an overdose of an opiate, but he may refrain from doing that which will prevent his dying. Of course, in this case, if he ordered the removal of the intravenous apparatus, there may be some ground for objection if the removal of the apparatus was a rather forcible procedure and shook up the patient. But if, for example, the removal of the apparatus was so gentle as not to disturb him, it would be like the wiping off of the salt on his tongue, which Isserles permits. If he does not even do this, but merely gives the order that the bottle containing the nutriment not be refilled when it is emptied out, then, too, he committed no sin at all. He is merely, as the law says, preventing that which delays the death.

We have mentioned that Isserles states (in Yoreh De-a 339.1) that one may remove that which prevents the person from dying, and thus, one may stop someone who is chopping wood outside because the regular sound concentrates the patient's mind, and one may also remove some salt from his lips. The **Taz** objects only to wiping away the salt from the lips, because this action might move or shake the patient, and this would be an overt action hastening his death.

On the basis of this objection of the **Taz**, there might be some question, as we have mentioned, about removing the tubes from his arm through which the intravenous feeding enters his body. Of course, if this is done gently, the objection of the **Taz** would be obviated. Perhaps it would be better still if the tubes were not removed at all until the patient were dead. There might also be some question if the intravenous feeding would be continued automatically until the physician gives a direct order that it be stopped. It would be less objectionable if it is the practice in the hospital to have each day's intravenous feeding kept up by the direct daily order of the physician, and if, on that particular day, he simply refrains from ordering it to be continued. Thus, in no way would he be taking any direct action. Here, then, the principle (Eruvin 100a) "**Shev ve-al ta-aseh adif**" would certainly apply.

To sum up: If the patient is a hopelessly dying patient, the physician has no duty to keep him alive a little longer. He is entitled to die. If the physician attempts actively to hasten the death, that is against the ethics of Jewish law. In the case as described, the term used in the question, "to hasten death," is perhaps not correct, or at least should be modified. The physician is not really hastening the death; he has simply ceased his efforts to delay it.

Solomon B. Freehof

78. EUTHANASIA
(Vol. LX, 1950, pp. 107-120)

QUESTION: At the convention of the Central Conference of American Rabbis, held in Kansas City, Mis-
souri, 1948, the following resolution emanating
from the Commission on Justice and Peace, was
adopted:

> This Conference notes that a committee of two
> thousand physicians in the State of New York
> has drafted a bill for presentation to the New
> York Legislature seeking to legalize the prac-
> tice of orderly scientific euthanasia.   We
> recommend that a special committee of the
> Conference be appointed to study this impor-
> tant question in the light of Jewish teaching
> and to bring in a report at the next meeting.
> (**Yearbook**, vol. 58, p. 129)

ANSWER: To carry out the mandate of this resolution,
the President of the Conference appointed a committee
consisting of the Committee on Responsa and Rabbis Abram
V. Goodman and Leon Fram.   This committee submits the
following report.

Neither in its theoretical nor in its practical
aspects does euthanasia present anything new.   Among
certain primitive peoples, as Westermarck has pointed
out, some form of euthanasia has always been prevalent.
In ancient Greece, euthanasia was countenanced in some
city states, and in Sparta it was rigidly practiced by
the state itself.   Plato and Aristotle, we know, endorsed it in principle.   In the Renaissance period, no
less important a person than Sir Thomas More advocated
the practice of euthanasia in its voluntary form.   He
made special provision for it in his **Utopia**.   In modern
times, during the brief rule of the Nazis, systematic
euthanasia, involving the lives of the "useless" and the
incurably ill, was authorized by the head of the State
and prosecuted with customary ruthlessness (**New Repub-
lic**, May 5, 1941; **Berlin Diary**, William L. Shirer, pp.
454-459).
It is a curious but incontrovertible fact that the
theory of euthanasia, even in its most restricted construction, has never invaded Jewish thought, though
"sufferance is the badge of our tribe."   In the history
of our people, from remotest antiquity to days most
recent, we come upon pages that tell of men in agony and
despair turning to self-destruction for relief.   We also

read of men in high places counseling their followers,
when faced with sure defeat by a cruel enemy, to welcome
self-inflicted death rather than to submit to capture
and disgrace. But nowhere do we encounter the suggestion that such examples merit praise and emulation.

The Bible, which affirms religious doctrine more
often by implication than by direct command, leaves no
doubt as to what the religious man's attitude toward a
life of affliction should be. He will accept the lot
apportioned to him. He surely will not tamper with the
life given him. When Job's wife, herself prostrate at
the sight of her husband's overwhelming affliction,
cried out, "Dost thou still hold fast thine integrity?
Blaspheme God, and die," Job indignantly replied, "Thou
speakest as one of the impious women speaketh. What?
Shall we receive good at the hand of God, and shall we
not receive evil?" (Job 2:9-10).

Later, in the early Rabbinic period, the same religious temper was evidenced by a famous rabbi who suffered martyrdom for his religious convictions. When
Chananiah ben Teradion, a Tannaitic teacher of the second century, was condemned by the Romans to be burned at
the stake, his disciples counseled him, as the fires
began to flare, to let the consuming flames surge into
his frame and thus put a speedy end to his suffering.
In reply, the celebrated martyr is reported to have
said: "It is best that He Who hath given the soul should
also take it away; let no man hasten his own death"
(Avoda Zara 18a).

Both of these statements, while seemingly made in
casual manner, were by no means the stray utterances of
individual teachers; they sprang from a common ethical
tradition. They are closely related to a principle of
faith that lies at the foundation of Jewish ethics.
Human life is more than a biological phenomenon; it is
the gracious gift of God; it is the inbreathing of His
spirit. Man is more than a minute particle of the great
mass known as society; he is the child of God, created
in His image. "The spirit of God hath made me," avers
Job in the midst of his suffering, "and the breath of
the Almighty gives me life" (Job 33:4). Thus, human
life, coming from God, is sacred, and must be nurtured
with great care. And man, bearing the divine image, is
endowed with unique and hidden worth and must be treated
with reverence.

This principle--which is basic to Judaism, and to
which we probably owe whatever spiritual progress there
has been made through the centuries--finds clear embodiment in the Halacha, in Rabbinic law. The Rabbis were
no inflexible legalists; they recognized that not under
all circumstances could we condemn unfeelingly the man
who chose the way of self-destruction to escape from his

hard lot. Yet in formulating the law, they proved un-
compromising. The formal rites of mourning, they declared, shall be suspended in the case of one of sound
and mature mind who deliberately and of his own volition
has laid violent hands on himself; only those rites may
be performed the omission of which would give undue
offense to the bereaved family (Semachot 2.1-5). Likewise, in the case of one who is in dying condition, the
law prohibits anyone else from employing any positive
and direct means to hasten his death, no matter from
what protracted an ailment he may suffer (Yoreh De-a
339). To abridge in some positive and direct manner the
duration of life by a single second is tantamount to the
shedding of blood (Shab. 151b).

Yet Rabbinic law sanctions the use of indirect and
negative means to facilitate a peaceful death, such as
the elimination of noise and the withholding of stimu-
lants (Yoreh De-a 339; Avoda Zara 18a). In the eyes of
the law, the causes which may retard the natural process
and thus delay the moment of death are artificial, and
may therefore be removed. Not so, however, when that
which is withheld is a natural physical requirement and
essential to sustain life. No nourishment, however
little the amount required, may be denied a dying patient whose condition seems hopeless and his pain great,
in order to hasten his death (**Tel Talpiyot**, Letter 42,
vol. 30, 1923, Budapest).

Of course, we liberal rabbis have always claimed
the right, in the interest of a progressive faith, to
modify Rabbinic law and to remove what we regard as an
obstacle in the advance of the spirit. And, indeed, we
have eliminated many an old restriction which, though
meant to safeguard Judaism, proved to obscure its essential nature. But we have never sought to nullify an
effective Rabbinic implementation of a vital spiritual
principle.

The Jewish ideal of the sanctity of human life and
the supreme value of the individual soul would suffer
incalculable harm if, contrary to the moral law, men
were at liberty to determine the conditions under which
they might put an end to their own lives and the lives
of other men.

                                        Israel Bettan

**This report was received and referred to the Execu-
tive Board, by a vote of 109 to 56.**

Discussion

Rabbi Solomon B. Freehof: Dr. Bettan's report is in consonance with the main line of Jewish Halacha. The Halacha is never so absolutely consistent that exceptions or partial exceptions cannot be adduced. There is no question, however, that the distinction which Rabbi Bettan made is essentially correct, namely, that nothing positive must be done to shorten life. It is permitted to **refrain** from doing something positive to continue life when it seems insupportable. This is based upon the story in the Talmud telling that when Judah the Prince had such a difficult time dying and the Rabbis were gathered to pray for the continuation of his life, his beloved servant threw down some object from the roof to disturb their prayers so that they should not continue to pray to extend his unhappy life. I might quote a very interesting responsum by Rabbi Chaim Pallagi, Rabbi of Smyrna, who lived at the end of the 1700s, which expresses the same principle. A woman was dying of some lingering disease, and her husband and son were trying by every means--including prayers in the synagogue--to keep her alive. She called them to her bedside and said that she was grateful for their efforts, but asked that they please refrain from such prayers because her life was no longer bearable. The rabbi was asked whether this would be permitted, and he answered that to refrain from praying is permitted, but that nothing positive could be done to shorten her life. The law in **Shulchan Aruch** states that you may not even move a pillow from underneath the head of a dying person in order to hasten his death. Hence the Conference committee is perfectly justified in saying, "You may refrain from doing anything that will prolong a miserable life," but to do something to terminate life is forbidden by Jewish law.

Rabbi Dudley Weinberg: I merely wish to ask some questions, the answers to which should be included with the responsum. I wonder about the latter part of the passage regarding the death of Rabbi Chananiah ben Teradion.

In that case, the executioner offered to make his death easier and speedier by building up the flames and removing some protective tufts of wool from vital areas of his body. Rabbi Chananiah agreed that if the executioner did these things, he would be admitted to the **Olam Haba.** After taking these steps, which hastened the death of Rabbi Chananiah, the executioner leaped into the flames and perished. The text then states that a **bat kol** declared that the executioner had been admitted to the **Olam Haba,** thereby giving approval to his action.

Is it not also necessary to deal with the passage which states, if memory serves me correctly, that "Hakol **modim shehahoreg et haterefa patur**"? It seems to me that the passage is relevant to the discussion.

Rabbi Israel Bettan: The passage you refer to is correct. Chananiah would not inhale the fire to hasten his own death, but he allowed the executioner to remove the sponge from his heart. The sponge, keeping him alive, was an artificial means which could be removed, but nothing of a positive nature would he permit. The other reference is not quite relevant. We are not discussing the question as to whether, if a man kills one who is about to die, he should be legally punished. The Talmud decides that the death sentence cannot be imposed upon him, but Maimonides is of the opinion that while no earthly court can impose such a penalty, the man stands condemned in the eyes of God.

Rabbi Jonah B. Wise: The question of euthanasia today is not one that can be discussed on the basis of the opinion of one who lived in Smyrna in the 17th century or of our distinguished Rabbinical predecessors in Talmudic times. The moral question involved has, of course, been discussed by Dr. Bettan, but the world has progressed since that time; conditions have changed. The advances in human knowledge, which I am sure our distinguished Halachists would have recognized, are a very important factor in making a decision. It is entirely possible that had these Rabbis been aware of the circumstances which confront us, they would have changed their attitude. They passed no real legislation; the references are not to cases in which the practice of euthanasia was discussed. We have any number of records in Jewish history of Jews who took their own lives and were not thereby put into the class of those who committed immoral acts. During the Roman Wars, many committed suicide rather than fall into the hands of the Romans. They were not criticized either in the Talmud or in any other subsequent literature. During the Middle Ages, many Jews killed their wives and children rather than have them fall into the hands of the Crusaders. I believe we should very carefully weigh our decision before we act on the paper which has been presented. The paper is of great interest, but the conclusions to which it comes, and the decisions which it asks us to make, are not the kind which the Central Conference of American Rabbis should present to the American public. The time may come when we may decide that euthanasia is undesirable or immoral, but that time is not yet here. Euthanasia is not practiced in the United States; it is not legal in any of our states. The Central Conference of

American Rabbis is probably the most liberal body of
religious leaders in the world today, and for it to base
a decision on the argument brought by Rabbi Bettan would
be extremely unfortunate. I therefore hope that the
report will be received with thanks, but that it will
not in any way be approved as the decision and policy of
this progressive body of men.

   Rabbi James G. Heller: I sincerely hope that the
Central Conference of American Rabbis will not take
action today on this subject. Though I think there is
no controverting the historical side of the report, I do
not believe that the treatment that was accorded to the
question as a moral issue in our day measured up to the
factual side of the statement in regard to Jewish
sources. It is quite obvious to me that a matter upon
which there is a deep division of opinion among people
who cannot be ranked with Adolph Hitler in regard to
euthanasia, must be a question on which there is no set
certainty as to where the truth lies. You cannot dispose of the problem of euthanasia by calling attention
to the abuses which occurred in Germany. If we were to
judge moral questions by the possibility of abuse, there
is hardly any type of injunction which would stand. It
is not true that society stands upon the principle that
human life is completely sacred. As long as there is
capital punishment in a state, that is an obvious exception to such a rule. I happen to be opposed to capital
punishment; the trouble is that many of the religious
bodies which put down as an absolute principle that
human life can never be taken also sanction capital
punishment. Even in our own tradition, capital punishment is sanctioned in many cases, which obviously constitutes an exception to the general moral rule which
Rabbi Bettan enunciated. It is not a question of whether there is a place for suffering. The question is what
shall be done with people where medicine is as certain
today as it can possibly be that there is no chance for
their survival. It is the custom today in the case of
people who are dying of some incurable disease to induce
unconsciousness with some of the drugs that are available. In effect, those people die long before the actual cessation of life. It seems to me that it would have
been wise to submit simultaneously with this report a
statement as to the moral status of this problem today,
and I hope that we will take no action at the present
moment.

Opinion of Dr. Samuel Atlas

   The two previous speakers have placed the problem
of euthanasia on a purely moral and religious basis, so

I would like to point out that apart from the legal aspect there is a philosophical question involved. When we speak of euthanasia, the question actually depends upon our attitude towards life: What is life? Can life be measured from the point of view of suffering and balancing the suffering with pleasure--the suffering of the patient and the suffering of those nearest to the patient against the amount of pleasure they had seeing their dearest one still living? Now, on the basis of a certain philosophy of life, as well as from a Jewish point of view, life cannot be measured in such terms. A Jewish thinker has said that "Life is more than mere living," the implication being that while the life of species other than man is a merely biological function, human life implies something more. It is the element of creativity which is the distinguishing mark of human life. If a person is ill and about to die, and the idea of repentance arises in that man's mind, that is worth more than an eternity of static existence. It is sufficient to recall the statement in **Pikrei Avot** that one hour of repentance is worth more than the whole future life. Why is one hour of repentance worth more than the whole future life? Is it because of the consideration that repentance is an act of creativity, and one hour of creative life is worth more than an eternity of static bliss? Consequently, it is wrong to deprive a hopelessly sick person of the opportunity for repentance which may arise in his mind. No man or doctor can decide that issue. And euthanasia cannot be justified on the basis of such a concept of human life.

As to the Halacha, if I may say a word on that, it has been pointed out that there is a distinction between **terefa** and **goses**. According to Jewish law, if one murders a **terefa**, there is no consequence such as capital punishment which is due to all murderers, but a **goses** is considered a normal human being with all due consequences. **Goses** means a person who is dying a natural death; **terefa** means a person in whose organs there is a deficiency. Here is a place, to my mind, for a change in the Halacha, which would be in the spirit of the Talmudic Halacha, for I am convinced that the Talmudic Halacha is so flexible that it can be made a living force and compatible with modern scientific concepts of medicine. The Halacha in itself demands an adjustment of certain elements in it which are the result of scientific conceptions of an older time no longer compatible with modern scientific developments. Only in this way could the Halacha be made existential, and a guide for life. The very meaning of the word Halacha implies a way of life, as it is derived from the Hebrew verb meaning "walking." Now, according to modern scientific conceptions of medicine, the distinction between **terefa** and **goses** has no validity whatsoever. A **goses** means one who dies a natural death; but what is natural death in medicine today? While the ancients thought that no organic change occurs in the body of a person dying a natural death, modern medicine maintains that the cause of death is always, even in the case of a very old man, the result of some deficiency in some of his organs. Consequently, there is no distinction between **goses** and **terefa**.

Maimonides, in the beginning of his Code, in Sefer Hamada, has a section dealing with medicine. You will ask, how does medicine come into a code? The reason is simply this: medicine is closely connected with law. Since there is a commandment in the Torah to preserve life, medicine is a part of that commandment; for in order to preserve life we must know medicine. Maimonides believed that he had reached the pinnacle of the science of medicine; therefore, his medicine is part of Halacha. Our medicine would accordingly be part and parcel of our Halacha. In this respect, we will have to modify the law, but it will be a change in the letter of the Halacha for the sake of preserving its spirit. And Maimonides would subscribe to our medicine which is the result of a higher development of scientific thought. Consequently, the distinction between **goses** and **terefa** does not apply to us, and the former will have to be treated in the same manner as the latter. In this respect, there is room for development, and the application of Talmudic-Rabbinic law to our times should be brought up to date in agreement with the latest development of scientific thought, for even Maimonides would agree that our present-day medicine should serve as the basis of the law, and not his medicine, which is out of date. But while we will have to identify **terefa** and **goses**, it means only that there is no consequent punishment for an act of murder in both cases; but the law "**Lo tirtsach**" ("Do not murder") which prohibits the act of cutting short a life which has in it the potentiality of creativity, obtains with regard to **terefa** as well as in respect to **goses**.

With reference to Dr. Freehof's statement on the law that a person who takes life away from the **terefa** does not suffer the consequences of capital punishment, but still has to render an account before God, I would suggest the following definition of the legal basis of the law. Taking life away from a **terefa** is an offense against the commandment, "Thou shalt not kill," for which, however, there is no consequence of capital punishment, since the murdered person is deficient and not whole. The law of "**nefesh tachat nefesh**" ("a soul for a soul") cannot be applied. For there are two aspects governing the case of murder. There is first the principle of "a soul for a soul," which does not apply in the case of the murdered person being a **terefa** (and, in our view, also in regard to a **goses**), and there is no capital punishment involved. Then there is the ethical-religious principle expressed in the commandment "Thou shalt not kill." This law is valid even in relation to a **terefa** and **goses** because of the potential activity of human life, the value of which is absolute, independent of the time element involved, and cannot be measured by the criterion of time.

I should now like to refer briefly to the Biblical story of King Saul and David's order that the Amalekite be killed for his slaying of Saul, which has a bearing on our problem. Saul had thrown himself upon his sword and he was a dying man when the Amalekite slew him, and yet David ordered capital punishment for this act of an Amalekite. This is contrary to Jewish law as explained above. The solution to this difficulty seems to be this: David's reaction to the Amalekite's report of his slaying of King Saul was motivated by political consideration, and he acted in the interest of the State. David had to show indignation at the slaying of Saul, thus dissipating any suspicion of his disloyalty to Saul which might arise in the mind of the people. In order to preserve the unity of the State and his kingship, David had to show loyalty to Saul, as is evident from his remark: "Wast thou not afraid to stretch forth thy hand against the Lord's anointed?" (II Sam. 1:14). It was thus an act of statesmanship on the part of David; it cannot therefore serve as a basis for the legal consideration of our problem.

As a proof to the correctness of this interpretation of David's act, I would like to point out another difficulty in the legal aspect of David's reaction. David meted out capital punishment on the basis of the Amalekite's confession, saying: "Thy blood is upon thy own head, for thy mouth has testified against thee," which is contrary to Jewish law, that capital punishment can be meted out only on the basis of testimony of witnesses and not on that of confession (Sanhedrin 9b). Maimonides solves this difficulty by establishing the principle that a king is entitled to accept self-confession as sufficient evidence (Hilchot Sanhedrin 18.6). And just as David was entitled to deviate from the law with regard to confession, so we may conclude that he was entitled to ignore the fact that Saul was a dying man and, according to law, no capital punishment is involved in such a case.

That a king is permitted to deviate from the law does not mean, however, that a king stands above the law and is not subject to it. Only in cases of national emergency is the king entitled to deviate from the law

(Maimonides quotes the law of the Mishna [Sanhedrin 2.4]
that a king is entitled to break a way through anybody's
property without interference and comments that it refers only to time of war). It may seem at first thought
that there is a contradiction involved in Maimonides.
As it clearly follows from his exposition of the law in
Mishna Sanhedrin, a king is subject to law and bound by
it, and yet with reference to David's acceptance of
confession as sufficient testimony, Maimonides declares
that a king is entitled to deviate from the law. This
apparent difficulty dissolves itself on the basis of our
explanation that David acted in the interest of the
State. It was a case of national emergency where the
king can make his own law and deviate from the established system of positive law. Our exposition of the
case of David is thus borne out by Maimonides' conception of the law.

I should like now to add the following: We do not
intend here to present an historically correct interpretation of the case of David. I am well aware that at
the time of David the law may have been different, and
David did not have to follow the law as it evolved at a
much later period. Our intention is merely to present
an existentially correct picture of the legal case of
David as it has been understood by the existing legal
tradition. Jewish law was an existing and living force
in Israel and underwent a long process of development,
but it always attempted to present new ideas and conceptions as if they had existed previously. Our exposition
of the legal aspect of David's reaction in the light of
the legal tradition as developed later is meant merely
as an existential interpretation of the living legal
tradition and its relation to the case of David.

Thus, in the light of our understanding of Jewish
law, an act of euthanasia is to be considered a violation of the commandment "Thou shalt not kill." Therefore, the Amalekite's slaying of the dying Saul was an
offense against this commandment. For an act of euthanasia, however, there can be no capital punishment.
Since the murdered person is deficient and not whole,
the principle of "nefesh tachat nefesh" cannot be applied. In the light of modern medicine, so it seems to
me, there should be no difference in this respect between terefa and goses, for both have organic deficiencies. David, however, meted out capital punishment for
an act of euthanasia on the basis of political considerations and in the interest of the State, just as he
deviated from the legal procedure for the sake of preserving the unity of the State.

Rabbi Israel Bettan: The discussion has taken a
peculiar turn. The committee was instructed to study

the question from the Jewish point of view. The committee has fulfilled its task. I am rather startled to find teachers of religion bemoan the fact that religious idealism comes too high. Idealism has always called for sacrifice and painful struggle. Martyrdom is a most frightful price to pay for a religious ideal, but the martyr was a man who placed a very high valuation on his religious ideals. You and I are not called upon to be martyrs, but as religious teachers, we are committed to the principle that no cost is too high to preserve a religious ideal. All your committee asks you to do is to reaffirm the traditional attitude. We as religious teachers ought to have the courage to say: This is where we have stood for two thousand years and this is where we intend to stand.

79. EUTHANASIA
(1980)

QUESTION: A patient has terminal cancer and has sunk into a deep coma. Only the artificial life support systems are keeping him alive. Would Jewish tradition permit these systems to be shut off? What is the Jewish attitude toward euthanasia? (Dr. N.H., Philadelphia, Pennsylvania)

ANSWER: Jewish tradition makes a clear distinction between, on the one hand, positive steps which may hasten death, and on the other hand, avoiding matters which may hinder a peaceful end to life. It is clear from the Decalogue (Ex. 21:14; Deut. 5:17) that any kind of murder is prohibited. The only Biblical case of euthanasia was King Saul (I Sam. 31:1ff; II Sam. 1:5ff), who asked his servant to slay him after his own attempt at suicide failed (II Sam. 1:5ff).

In the Tannaitic period, the Mishnaic tractate Semachot (1.1) considered a dying person (goses) as a living individual in every respect. That point of view has been followed by later codes such as Maimonides' Yad and Caro's Shulchan Aruch. It is clear from the Mishnaic statement that none of the acts usually performed upon the dead should be done to the dying, nor should a coffin be prepared or matters of inheritance be discussed. The additional later discussion made it clear that no positive acts which may hasten death were to be undertaken, so the Sefer Chasidim (723) stated that an individual should not be moved to a different place even if that might make dying easier.

It is further quite clear that we must use any
medicine or drug which may help an individual. All
Shabbat laws may be trespassed to save a life (Yoma 85a;
Sh.A., Orach Chayim 196.2, 319.17; Ex. 31:14; Lev.
18:5), and even the death of an individual who is seriously ill should not be hastened (Sh.A., Yoreh De-a
339.1). In all these instances, some vague hope remained. However, these injunctions were modified with a
dying individual (goses) in the throes of death. In
that case, it was considered appropriate for an individual to stop praying for the lives of those dear to him
or pray for their release (Ket. 104a; Ned. 40a; Rema to
Sh.A., Even Ha-ezer 121.7 and Choshen Mishpat 221.2).
Furthermore, it was thought appropriate to stop acts
which would hinder the soul from a departure, so Sefer
Chasidim (723) stated that if a dying person was disturbed by wood chopping, it should be halted so that the
soul might depart peacefully. Isserles (to Sh.A., Yoreh
De-a 339.1) stated that anything which stood in the way
of peaceful death should be removed. Solomon Eiger, in
his commentary to the same passage of the Shulchan
Aruch, stated that one should also not use medicine to
hinder the soul's departure; he based himself on Beit
Ya-akov (50). Clearly, as long as some form of independent life persists, nothing should be done to hasten
death and all medicines which may be helpful must be
used. Once this point has been passed, it is no longer
necessary to utilize further medical devices in the form
of drugs or mechanical apparatus.

We must now attempt to define the turning point,
when "independent life" has ceased, and we can best do
so by looking carefully at the Jewish and modern medical
criteria of death. The traditional criteria were based
on a lack of respiratory activity and heart beat (M.
Yoma 8.5; Yad, Hil. Shab. 2.19; Sh.A., Orach Chayim
329.4). Lack of respiration alone was considered conclusive if the individual lay as quietly as a stone
(Responsa Chatam Sofer, Yoreh De-a, #38). All of this
was discussed at some length in connection with the
provision of the Shulchan Aruch that an attempt be made
to save the child of a woman dying in childbirth; even
on Shabbat a knife might be brought to make an incision
in the uterus in order to remove the fetus (Sh.A., Orach
Chayim 330.5). This statement, however, conflicted with
the prohibition against moving a limb of someone who was
dying, lest that hasten the death (Sh.A., Yoreh De-a
339.1). If one waited until death was absolutely certain, then the fetus would also be dead.

Absolute certainty of death, according to the halachic authorities of the last century, had occurred when
there had been no movement for at least fifteen minutes
(Gesher Chayim I, 3, p. 48) or an hour (Responsa Yismach

Lev, Yoreh De-a, #9) after the halt of respiration and heart beat. On the other hand, a recent Israeli physician, Jacob Levy, has stated that modern medical methods change this criterion, and the lack of blood pressure as well as respiratory activity should suffice (Hama-a-yan, Tamuz, 5731).

This discussion was, of course, important in connection with the preparation for burial, as well as other matters. When death was certain, then the preparation for burial had to begin immediately (Chatam Sofer, Yoreh De-a 338; Azulai's Responsa Chayim Shaul II, #25). In ancient times it was considered necessary to examine the grave after a cave burial to be certain that the individual interred had actually died. This was recommended for a period of three days (Semachot 8.1). This procedure was not followed after Mishnaic times.

In the last years, it has been suggested that Jews accept the criteria of death set by the ad hoc committee of the Harvard Medical School, which examined the definition of brain death in 1968 (Journal of the American Medical Association, vol. 205, pp. 337ff). They recommended three criteria: (1) lack of response to external stimuli or to interral reed; (2) absence of movement and breathing as observed by physicians over a period of at least one hour; (3) absence of elicitable reflexes; and a fourth criterion to confirm the other three, (4) a flat or isoelectric electroencephalogram. They also suggested that this examination be repeated after an interval of twenty-four hours. Several Orthodox authorities have accepted these criteria, while others have rejected them. Moses Feinstein felt that they could be accepted along with shutting off the respirator briefly in order to see whether independent breathing was continuing (Igerot Mosheh, Yoreh De-a II, #174). Moses Tendler has gone somewhat further and has accepted the Harvard criteria (Journal of the American Medical Association, vol. 238, #15, pp. 165.1ff). Although David Bleich (Hapardes, Tevet 5737) and Jacob Levy (Hadarom, Nisan 5731, Tishri 5730; Noam, 5.30) have vigorously rejected this criterion, we can see that although the question has not been resolved by our Orthodox colleagues, some of them have certainly accepted the recommendations of the Harvard Medical School committee. We are satisfied that these criteria include those of the older tradition and comply with our concern that life has ended. Therefore, when circulation and respiration only continue through mechanical means, as established by the above-mentioned tests, then the suffering of the patient and his/her family may be permitted to cease, as no "natural independent life" functions have been sustained.

We would **not** endorse any positive steps leading toward death. We would recommend pain-killing drugs which would ease the remaining days of a patient's life.

We would **reject** any general endorsement of euthanasia, but where all "independent life" has ceased and where the above-mentioned criteria of death have been met, further medical support systems need not be continued.

Walter Jacob, Chairman
Leonard S. Kravitz
W. Gunther Plaut
Harry A. Roth
Rav A. Soloff
Bernard Zlotowitz

80.   CAESAREAN ON A DEAD MOTHER
(Vol. LXXXII, 1972, pp. 51-53)

QUESTION: A mother eight months pregnant has died. Does Jewish law permit a Caesarean to be performed on her body to save the child? Or, perhaps even more: Does Jewish tradition recommend or urge such an operation? (Asked by Dr. Thomas H. Redding through Rabbi Leonard S. Zoll, Cleveland, Ohio)

ANSWER: The question of cutting open the body of a mother who has died in order to remove and thus save the child is discussed as far back as the Talmud itself in Arachin 7a (cf. also B.B. 142b and Nidda 44a). The discussion is based upon the Mishnaic law dealing with a pregnant woman who is condemned to death. Do we delay execution of the sentence until she has given birth or not? In the development of that discussion, Rabbi Samuel (in Arachin) extends the discussion from that of a convicted criminal to any woman who dies when she is near to giving birth ("a woman on the **mashber**, the birth-stool, who dies"). In such circumstances, Rabbi Samuel says that we may bring a knife even on the Sabbath (bringing a knife on the Sabbath is forbidden generally), and we may cut open her body to save the child. The discussion there in the Talmud involves the question of whether the child is alive or not, and the opinion is expressed that generally the child dies immediately (or even before) the mother, and therefore the Sabbath would be violated (by bringing the instruments) in vain, since the child is already dead. But Rashi says: Even in the

case of the "doubtful saving of life," we may violate
the Sabbath; and therefore, on the chance that the child
may be alive, we bring the knife and perform the operation.

It is exactly in this form that the law is recorded
by the great legalist and physician, Moses Maimonides,
in his Hilchot Shabbat 2.15. He says: We perform the
operation even on the Sabbath, for even when there is
doubt whether we are saving a life, we may violate the
Sabbath (cf. also **Tur, ibid.**, and Ephraim Margolis, **Yad
Efrayim** to Orach Chayim 320).

A new ground for doubt arises, however, in the
Shulchan Aruch (besides the doubt of violating the Sabbath in vain if the child is already dead).   In Orach
Chayim 330.4, Joseph Caro gives the law according to the
Talmud and Maimonides; but Moses Isserles (Poland, 16th
century) says: We do not do this operation nowadays
because we are no longer skilled in determining precisely whether the mother is dead or not; perhaps she is
alive (that is, in coma) and may give birth to the child
naturally.   However, Isserles himself in his **Responsa**
does not seem concerned with this doubt (that the mother
may still be alive), and in his Responsum #40 he answers
in the affirmative--that is, that the operation should
be performed.

As for the later authorities, they all are practically unanimous in favor of permitting the operation
(even on the Sabbath, and certainly on week days). What
concerns these later authorities is whether or not the
permission to perform this operation after the mother is
dead may not imply the larger permission for autopsy in
general, which Jewish law forbids, except under special
circumstances.   Generally speaking, it is not permitted
to mutilate (**lenavel**) the body of the dead.   Therefore,
in a discussion between Moses Schick of Ofen and Jacob
Ettlinger of Hamburg (both in the first half of the 19th
century), this matter is debated (see Responsa of Ettlinger, **Binyan Tsiyon** 1.171).   Moses Schick said in
this discussion (in his **Responsa**, Yoreh De-a 347) that
we may mutilate the body of a woman to save her child,
and Ettlinger says that this permission does not justify
general mutilation (as in autopsy) because this operation (that is, the Caesarean) is not really a disfigur-
ing of the body of the woman.

Moses Kunitz (of Budapest, d. 1837) gives almost
the exact case discussed here in answer to a question
asked of him by Abraham Oppenheimer.   The woman was
eight months pregnant when she died.   A skilled doctor
said that she is definitely dead, and that the baby is
alive.   Accepting the opinion of the skilled physician,
both doubts mentioned above are canceled.   The woman is
definitely dead, so the doubt mentioned by Isserles that

we have not the skill to be sure when a person is dead is now obviated; and the physician says that the child is definitely alive, so the doubt discussed by Rashi and the Talmud that we may be violating the Sabbath (if this occurred on the Sabbath) for an unnecessary purpose (since the child may be dead) is also obviated.   Therefore, Moses Kunitz said that the physician should operate and does not even need to ask permission of the Jewish ecclesiastical court.   Moses Kunitz here actually uses the word "Caesarean," and gives the origin of the term (namely, that Julius Caesar was born by such an operation).

Jacob Reischer, Rabbi of Metz two centuries ago, in his Responsa (**Shevut Ya-akov** 1.13, at the end), not only gives permission for such an operation but ends his responsum by saying that he who performs it must be praised for doing so and his reward will be great.   See also Abraham of Buczacz (**Eshel Avraham** to Orach Chayim 330), who cites an authority who praises the physician for prompt action to save the child.

There is, of course, a possible complication somewhat related to this question.   Since the child will die unless the operation is performed very quickly, I was asked a number of years ago by a physician whether--if the mother is not quite dead, but is definitely dying (for example, of cancer)--we may not make sure to save the child by performing the operation before the mother is dead, although it is certain that the operation itself will definitely put an end to the mother's life. See the discussion of this special question in **Reform Responsa**, pp. 214ff.

But this is a special form of the question and does not apply directly here, where the physician assures us that the mother is dead.   See further discussion of the matter in Eliezer Spiro (**der Muncaczer**) in his **Minchat Eli-ezer** IV.28, and Greenwald in **Kol Bo Al Avelut**, p. 49, section 18, and pp. 43ff.

To sum up: if it is certain that the mother is dead and that the child is alive, there is no question that the Caesarean operation not only may be performed, but must be performed, and is indeed deemed praiseworthy.

Solomon B. Freehof

See also:

S.B. Freehof, "Caesarean Operation on Dying Woman," **Reform Responsa**, pp. 212ff.

81.   FREEZING BODIES FOR LATER REVIVAL (CRYOBIOLOGY)
          (Vol. LXXVII, 1967, pp. 82-83)

QUESTION: According to a newly developed scientific technique, cryobiology, it seems possible to
freeze a human body, and, after considerable
time--perhaps months or years--thaw out the body
and revive the person. The question asked is: Is
it permissible by Jewish law and Jewish legal
tradition to take the body of a person dying of a
disease at present incurable and freeze it for a
long time--even years--and then to revive him when
a cure for his sickness will have been discovered?

ANSWER: The suggestion involves many difficulties in
the law, as the questioner correctly points out, namely,
has a person the right to consent to such a procedure
with regard to himself? What is the status of his wife
and children? Are they mourning as if the person were
dead? When shall he be revived? Who will decide? etc.
     We may assume that these specific questions involv-
ing cryobiology are for the present largely theoretical.
Most of the questions raised involve freezing the body
for years and then reviving it when some cure will have
been found for the sick person's disease. It is hard to
believe that it would be possible to freeze a body for
five or ten years and then revive it without the body
having deteriorated at all. In other words, in the case
of all strange remedies discussed in the law, the question is always asked as to how provable a remedy it is,
and whether there are not dangers involved in it.
     But the basic question here is another one entire-
ly. The proposal is to freeze such bodies in cases only
of people already dying or virtually dying of an incurable disease. So it amounts to the delaying of the
death of a dying person. This is clearly prohibited by
Jewish law. While one may not do anything at all to
hasten the death of a dying person, one may also not do
anything at all to prevent his dying. Such a person has
the right to die (see **Reform Responsa**, pp. 119-122). Of
all the material contained there, the following is quoted from p. 120.

Roughly contemporary with this Spanish scholar is
the famous German mystic-legal work, **The Book of
the Pious**, from which many customs and laws are
often cited. In this book (p. 100, #315-318) it
says, "If a man is sick and in pain and dying and
asks another man to kill him mercifully, this request must **not** be fulfilled, nor may the man take

his own life. Still, you may not put salt on his
tongue to keep him alive longer." Then it continues: "Ecclesiastes says: 'There is a time to live
and a time to die.' Why does the author need to
add this obvious fact? The answer is that he has
in mind the following situation: If a man is dying,
do not pray too hard that his soul return, that is,
that he revive from the coma. He can at best live
only a few days and in those days he will endure
great suffering. So, 'There is a time to die.'"
(See also the long note, #4, in **Sefer Chasidim**, ed.
Margolies, p. 34; also note to #723).

In other words, if there were a trustworthy remedy
already available for the disease, and this remedy involved freezing, it would all be permitted. But if
there is only speculation that some day a remedy might
be discovered, and on the basis of that speculation the
process of dying is prevented, that is contrary to the
spirit of Jewish law.

Solomon B. Freehof

See also:

S.B. Freehof, "Freezing a Body for Later Funeral,"
    New Reform Responsa, pp. 100ff.

82. AUTOPSY
(Vol. XXV, 1925, pp. 130-134)

QUESTION: What is the attitude of Jewish law towards the practice of autopsy? Are there any objections to it on the part of the Jewish religious
consciousness? If there are such objections, will
you please inform me whether they are based on
valid grounds and whether, in your opinion, these
objections hold good even in our day?

ANSWER: To my knowledge no law or regulation expressly
forbidding the practice of autopsy can be found in the
Bible, the Talmud, or the **Shulchan Aruch**. It may be
safely stated that in case the autopsy would not unduly
delay the funeral, one could not find the least support
for any objection to it in these authoritative sources
of Jewish law. In case the autopsy would unduly delay

the burial, one might object to it on the ground that
the ancient Jewish law recommended burial on the same
day on which the death occurred. For the law in Deuteronomy 21:23, "But thou shalt surely bury him on the same
day," though originally prescribed for the criminal who
has been put to death as punishment for his sin, was
understood by the rabbis of the Talmud to apply to every
dead person, even to one who died a natural and peaceful
death. Hence, they recommend that, unless delay is necessary for the sake of showing honor to the dead person
or in order to have time for making the proper arrangements for the funeral, burial should take place on the
same day in which the death occurred. One might, therefore, cite this Talmudic regulation--which, however, is
nowadays generally disregarded even by the Orthodox--as
a reason for objecting to autopsy if it would unduly and
unnecessarily delay the funeral. But to the practice of
autopsy as such one cannot find any express objection in
the Talmud. On the contrary, one could cite the Talmud
in support of the practice, since it is evident from
Talmudic reports that some of the rabbis of the Tal-
mud--no doubt prompted by their interest in the science
of medicine--actually performed an autopsy.

According to the Talmudic theory of anatomy, the
human body contains 248 parts or joints, "**Ramach Eva-
rim**," and 365 sinews or veins "**Shesah Gidin**" (B. Makot
23b). Whether this theory of the Rabbis is scientifically correct or not is not our concern now. But it is
evident that they could not have obtained the knowledge
of anatomical detail upon which they based their theory
except by dissecting a human corpse and counting its
joints and sinews. Had they acquired this knowledge
indirectly from non-Jewish physicians, they would have
quoted their authority or expressly mentioned that this
was a theory of the non-Jewish scientists, **Chachmei Umot
Ha-olam**, as they do in other cases when they mention
theories of the wise men of the Gentiles (comp. B. Sanhedrin 91b, R.H. 12a, Pesachim 94b). The fact that this
theory is stated by the Rabbis in an unqualified form as
an indisputable fact certainly justifies the assumption
that they learned this fact from their own direct obser-
vations by dissecting a human body. This assumption is
confirmed by the express report found in the Talmud (B.
Bechorot 45a). There we read that the disciples of R.
Ishmael, who had learned from their teachers that the
human body contains 248 joints, had the opportunity to
test this anatomical theory of their teachers. They
obtained the body of a woman who had been sentenced to
death and executed by the Roman authorities. They
boiled the body and dissected it and counted the number
of the joints and to their great surprise they found
that it contained 252 joints instead of only 248. This

fact seemed to refute the theory which they had learned
from their teachers. They came to their master and told
him that they had found by their own observation in
dissecting a corpse that the theory about the 248 joints
was not correct. The master answered them by saying,
"**Shema be-isha bedaktem**," "Perhaps you have examined the
body of a woman." And he informed them that the theory
about the 248 joints applied only to the body of a male,
but that the female of the species had four more joints.
It is evident from this report that the practice of
autopsy was not considered by the Rabbis as forbidden or
objectionable. The master does not express any surprise
when he hears that his disciples dissected a human body.
He does not reproach them for having done such a thing.
He does not even ask where they obtained the body or
whether it was a Jewish or a non-Jewish corpse.   It
evidently made no difference to him whose body it was.
This consideration would also answer the possible argument that it was only because a woman had been sentenced
to death and executed as a criminal that they did not
mind performing the autopsy on her body.   In the first
place, it is doubtful that the Rabbis considered the
woman a criminal even though the Roman government treated her as such.   The Rabbis may have disagreed with the
Roman law on the question whether the woman in the case
deserved death or not.   Secondly, even if the woman had
been sentenced to death and executed by a Jewish court
and according to the Jewish law, the Rabbis could not
have treated her differently from any other dead person.
After she had paid the penalty for her crime, her death
brought her atonement and her body was not to be mis-
treated.   Had there been a law against dissecting a dead
body they could not have ignored such a law in this case
on the ground that the body was executed to death and
did not die a natural death.   But, above all, it is
evident from our report that when the disciples first
reported the case to their master they did not give any
details--they did not tell him whether it was the body
of a Jew or a non-Jew, man or woman, saint or crimi-
nal--and the master did not care to ask for any details.
Only when it was necessary for him to maintain the
theory about the 248 joints did it occur to him to ask:
"Was it perhaps the body of a woman that you dissected
and examined?"   It is also significant that no discussion or remarks by later teachers follow this report in
the Talmud.   This **argumentum e silencio** has some weight
considering that, usually, when some action or practice
of older teachers is reported in the Talmud, later
teachers--if they know of some law forbidding such a
practice--take up the discussion of the whole question.
Evidently in this case, the later teachers did not know
of any law forbidding the practice.

The objection to the practice of autopsy which is prevalent among Jewish people is based merely on the assumption that such a practice is a disgrace to the human body (**nivul**) and an insult to the dead person (**bizyon hamet**). And, of course, we are not permitted to treat disrespectfully a dead person. This supposition, however, that a **post-mortem** examination constitutes a disgrace to the human body has no real basis in Jewish literature. It is true, in the Talmud (Chulin 11b) it is assumed that to dissect and examine a dead body might be considered a disgrace (**nivul**) to that body, which, of course, should be avoided. This, however, holds good only in the case when it is done unnecessarily and for no good purpose. For in the same passage in the Talmud it is taken for granted that if such a **post-mortem** examination might possibly result in saving another man's life--e.g., in the case of a suspected murderer when a **post-mortem** examination of the killed person might prove the innocence of the suspected murderer--we should by all means dissect and examine the dead body, so that we may possibly avoid the loss of another life, "**Mishum ibud neshama dehai ninveleih.**"

And on general psychological grounds we have no reason to assume that the dead person would feel insulted if subjected to a **post-mortem** examination. We may rather assume the contrary. Just as a living person, while undergoing an operation, has no objection to physicians and students seeing him cut open and watching the surgeon performing the operation, so also the dead person, since it gives him no pain, would have no objection to the physicians cutting him up in order to learn the cause of his death or the nature of his disease. To apply the Talmudic phrase, "**Denicha leih le-enash lekayomei mitzva begufeih**" (Pesachim 4b)--in a somewhat different sense than the one in which it was originally used in the Talmud--we may say that it would be pleasing to the dead person to know that he is benefiting humanity, in that from his body the physicians might learn to combat disease and to alleviate the sufferings of other people. The consideration that by a **post-mortem** examination, the physicians may learn the nature of a certain disease, and thus be enabled to help other people suffering from the same disease, has indeed led two great Rabbinical authorities of the 18th and 19th centuries to permit autopsy under certain conditions. R. Ezekiel Landau (1713-1793) in his **Noda BiYehuda** (Yoreh De-a, no. 210), and, following him, R. Moses Sofer (1763-1839) in his **Chatam Sofer** (Yoreh De-a, no. 336), permit autopsy, but only when there is in the same locality another person with the same disease from which the person to be subjected to autopsy died. Their reasons for permitting the autopsy are very cogent. Since by the autopsy the

physicians may learn to understand better the nature of
the disease, and thus be enabled to save the life of the
other person afflicted with it, it is a case of **Pikuach
Nefesh.** Then, according to the Talmudic-Rabbinic law--
even if there could be found an express law in the Torah
prohibiting the dissecting of a human body--it would
have to be ignored in favor of autopsy which might lead
to the saving of a human life. Thus far we can fully
agree with these two great Rabbinical authorities. But,
with all due respect to them, we cannot see any reason
for limiting--as they do--the permission of autopsy only
to cases when there is, right then and there, another
person suffering from the same disease who might immediately be benefited by the findings of the physicians.
The Talmudic law, that consideration for the saving of a
human life sets aside any law of the Torah except the
three mentioned above, applies also to doubtful cases;
that is, when we are not sure that by the act involving
a violation of the law we shall save a human being, but
there is merely a **chance** of saving a human life, we
should nevertheless proceed with the act and ignore the
law (B. Yoma 88a). And, certainly there is more than a
mere chance of probability that the enrichment of the
medical science, and the wider knowledge and experience
gained by physicians from their findings through autopsy, will result in the saving of human life here and
now, or somewhere else and at some other time. For in
our days any discovery made in one hospital and the
knowledge acquired by one physician in one part of the
world is easily communicated through books or medical
journals to physicians living in other parts of the
world. We can, therefore, not argue against autopsy
even in an instance when we do not know of any person
suffering from the same disease. For if there is no
such case here, it may be elsewhere, and if there is
none right now, it may turn up tomorrow or next year.

I believe that in the above I have proved that
there can be no objection to autopsy on the ground of
any Talmudic-Rabbinical law. I would go still further
and state that in our days there are good reasons why
Jewish people should modify their customary attitude
towards autopsy. This attitude on the part of the Jews
has created bad feelings among Christian students of
medicine. In some universities in Europe, Jewish medical students find it very difficult and almost impossible to get admission to the medical laboratories for the
very reason that Jews ordinarily refuse to deliver Jewish corpses for purposes of anatomical dissection (comp.
CCAR Yearbook, vol. XXXIII, 1923, p. 452). The exclusion of Jewish students from the anatomical laboratories
ultimately means that Jewish students will be deprived
of the opportunity of studying medicine. For we must

consider the possibility of such an attitude towards
Jewish medical students on the part of Christian students or university authorities spreading to all other
universities outside of Poland, Austria-Hungary, and
Rumania, if we Jews persist in our unjustified objections to autopsy. These considerations have prompted
Orthodox Jewish communities in Europe to change their
attitude towards autopsy and to agree to deliver Jewish
corpses for purposes of anatomical dissection. According to a report from Bucharest, Rumania, printed in the
Jewish Daily Bulletin (March 10, 1925, p. 3), the Jewish
community in Jassy has agreed and has actually already
begun to deliver Jewish corpses for dissection to the
university of that city. No doubt, this decision of the
Jassy community had the approval of the rabbinate of
that city. Another dispatch of the Jewish Telegraphic
Agency brings the following report from Kishinev (printed in the **Jewish Daily Bulletin**, April 7, 1925, p. 1):
"An unparalleled scene took place in the hall of the
local rabbinate when an aged Jewish physician made a
declaration of his intentions with regard to his body
after death. Dr. Rabinovitch, sixty years of age, before Rabbi Zirelson and a **Minyan** (ten men, the quorum
necessary for solemn declarations) declared that after
his death his body should be delivered to the Medical
College of Jassy University for dissection, in order to
remove the cause of the anti-Semitic riots among the
Rumanian students, who claim that the Jews refuse to
submit Jewish corpses." And, according to press reports, the Jewish Burial Society in Szegedin, Hungary,
resolved to deliver Jewish corpses for purposes of anatomical dissection to the medical laboratory of the
university of that city (see **American Jewish Yearbook**
XXVII, 1925, p. 33). If all these reports are true--and
we have no reason to doubt them--they certainly prove
that the authorities of the Jewish community in Jassy
and the members of the **Chevra Kadisha** in Szegedin, as
well as Rabbi Zirelson of Kishinev and the ten men associated with him who received the declaration of Dr.
Rabinovitch, were all of the opinion that the Jewish
religious consciousness can have no valid objection to
autopsy. To this opinion I fully subscribe, as I cannot
find any law in Bible, Talmud, or **Shulchan Aruch**, which
would justify such an objection.

Jacob Z. Lauterbach

See also:

S.B. Freehof, "Donating a Body to Science," **Reform Responsa**, pp. 130ff; "Bequeathing Parts of the Body," **Contemporary Reform Responsa**, pp. 216ff.

83.   USING THE BLOOD OF THE DEAD
(Vol. LXXVII, 1967, pp. 78-81)

QUESTION: The USSR for thirty-five years has been using the blood of the recently deceased for the benefit of patients who need transfusions. This blood is usable for transfusions for up to three months; then the plasma can be extracted and frozen and be good for five years. What is the attitude of Jewish legal tradition to this procedure?

ANSWER: From the point of view of Jewish legal tradition, which in many ways expresses Jewish ethical feelings, there are many objections to this procedure insofar as it applies to the bodies of deceased Jews and insofar as the blood is to be used for the benefit of Jewish patients. The objections are as follows:
1.   The blood is deemed an integral part of the body, and it is a duty to bury the entire body of the deceased, including the blood. Thus, if a body of a murdered man or a slain soldier is found with his blood soaked into the earth around him or into his clothes, the blood-soaked objects must be buried with the body.
2.   It is forbidden for the living to derive any benefit from the bodies of the dead. This objection is often applied to the planned use of cornea and bone from a bone bank, etc.
3.   It is especially forbidden by Jewish law to eat blood. This is a Biblical prohibition and is the reason for the thorough soaking and salting of meat before it may be eaten.
The first legal principle concerning the duty of burying the entire body--limbs, eyes, blood, etc.--applies as a general rule. However, if it is demonstrable that certain parts of the body are a remedy for a sick person who is in grave danger, then the necessities for healing would constitute an exception, as it also constitutes an exception to point 2 above, namely, not to have any benefit from a dead body. It is, therefore, necessary to go into the question of the legal

status of healing, as to what may be used for healing the sick.

The laws are based upon the verse Leviticus 18:5: "Observe My commandments which a man shall do and live by them." From this verse the conclusion was drawn that whenever life is endangered, the rule is that the ritual and Sabbath laws are suspended (in fact, all laws are suspended, except those involving idolatry, murder, and immorality). In this spirit, the long chain of legal tradition is finally codified in the **Shulchan Aruch**, Yoreh De-a 155. There the law can be generally stated as follows: If a patient is **not** dangerously sick, he may use anything which is forbidden by Rabbinic law (i.e., by secondary laws), except idolatrous spells, etc. If a patient, however, **is** dangerously sick, then he may use even things prohibited by Biblical law (which is primary). Thus, the principle is that anything at any time may be used for the benefit of a patient who is gravely sick. The Sabbath must be violated in his behalf, food must be given to him on Yom Kippur, and all forbidden foods are permitted to him. But if he is not gravely sick, these permissions are, as has been mentioned, somewhat restricted.

How this works out can be seen in a responsum of Judah Lev Zirelson, the famous rabbi of Kishinev (**Lev Yehuda**, #45). He was asked the question: What should one do when the doctor recommends for a patient with anemia to eat liver (which is full of blood) cooked in butter? (Here, then, there are two prohibitions: the blood itself and the meat with butter). He answers: "If the patient has an ordinary tendency to anemia, the doctor should be asked whether there are not other more acceptable remedies, but if it is **pernicious** anemia, then the patient not only may take the remedy, i.e., the blood and the meat with butter, but it is his duty to take it, since the saving of life is primary."

More specifically with regard to the use of blood is the responsum of Jacob Reischer, Rabbi of Metz (16th-17th centuries). He says that the people of his community use as a remedy for various sicknesses (not necessarily grave ones) dried goat's blood, and he says that this is permissible because the blood has been so dried up that it has become like another substance.

A similar responsum, and more modern, is by David Hoffman, the great German legal authority of the past generation (**Melamed Leho-il**, Yoreh De-a 34). He was asked whether a man may take medicine made from blood which has been chemically broken up and is in a new form. He answered that the blood may be used, since it has now been so changed that it can be considered as another substance.

There was a number of secondary elements involved in the question. First, there is the long discussion in the legal literature as to whether the prohibition of getting benefit from a dead body is to be deemed a special restriction applying only to the bodies of Jews (for whose burial there are other special requirements, i.e., Jewish cemeteries, shrouds, etc.), or whether the prohibition of benefiting from a dead body also applies to the bodies of non-Jews. At least half of the authorities say that this is only a special Jewish requirement, like other special religious requirements that apply only to Jewish bodies. Since, therefore, the overwhelming majority of bodies would not be those of Jews, this special religious prohibition of "benefiting from the dead body" would not generally apply.

An additional special consideration involves the method by which the material is taken into the body of the patient. The law makes a distinction between "the way things are enjoyed" ("**kederech hana-atan**") and "the way things are not enjoyed" (cf. Yoreh De-a 155.3). If, for example, forbidden food is given to a patient in a way that he enjoys it as food, it would be frowned upon. But if it is taken in a way that there is no enjoyment, it is permissible. A transfusion of blood involves no direct eating or enjoyment from eating and is therefore permissible as far as that consideration is concerned.

Of course, the special difficulties in this question are due to the procedure practiced in the USSR with bodies of the dead. If it were not for that fact, it would be a rather simple problem. A well-known Orthodox authority, the late Hillel Posek of Tel Aviv, editor of the rabbinic magazine **Haposek** (in #96-97, ninth year, responsum 1082), gives a general and unrestricted permission to blood transfusions. He says that in the first place, the prohibition against the consumption of blood is essentially a prohibition against eating the blood of cattle or birds; it does not apply to the blood of fish or any other animals, including man. Of course, because it may seem like forbidden blood, then if a person's teeth or gums are injured and some blood appears on the bread he is eating, he may not eat that bread; but that is only because of the appearance of the blood. However, the unseen blood (that may be sucked from the gums and swallowed) is not forbidden. This law is clearly stated in the **Shulchan Aruch**, Yoreh De-a 66.10. Maggid Mishnah (Don Vidal), in his commentary to Maimonides' laws of forbidden foods (2, #3), says that such blood is absolutely permitted.

Then Hillel Posek comments further that whatever prohibition there is, is only a prohibition because of appearance--that the blood looks like forbidden animal blood, hence it may not be eaten or swallowed, as the

legal phrase is, "in the way of enjoyment." But if the
blood is inserted in the veins, etc.--which is not by
way of enjoyment--there is no prohibition at all against
this procedure, even with regard to sick people who are
not in danger. But this general permission applies to
blood taken from living people. Hillel Posek had not
known--as the present writer did not know--of the practice of the USSR of taking the blood from the dead;
hence, the limitations which are mentioned above.

To sum up, the general attitude of Jewish law would
be as follows. There would be some hesitation about
using the blood from Jewish bodies because of the special requirements with regard to their burial and the
prohibition against benefiting from them. But this is
only a general hesitation, because it is overridden by
the outright permission to use any valuable remedy for a
patient who is in danger. For such a patient the blood
can be used. If the patient is not in danger, then the
blood plasma--which changes the appearance of the blood
and its original form--may be used.

Solomon B. Freehof

84.   TRANSPLANTING THE EYES OF DECEASED PERSONS
       (Vol. LXIII, 1953, pp. 152-153)

QUESTION: Is there any religious objection to the
authorized removal of the eyes of a deceased person
in order to use the cornea, by transplantation, to
restore sight to a blind person?

ANSWER: The ethics of Judaism are grounded in the
doctrine that human life and the personality of each
individual are sacred. The ancient Rabbis, resting on
this fundamental principle, insisted that the very body
of man, the temple of the soul, retain a measure of
sanctity even when all life had departed from it, and
that it must, therefore, be neither marred nor degraded
in any way.

Yet, in Judaism, to save or prolong life is a supreme obligation. The law therefore permits a **post-
mortem** examination if undertaken to ascertain the cause
of death and thus absolve another person of the crime of
murder alleged against him. And so, too, is the performance of an autopsy permitted, if another person,
presumably afflicted with the same or similar disease,

might be restored to health by the findings of such a
dissection (see CCAR Yearbook, vol. XXXV, pp. 130-134).

It would seem, therefore, that in Jewish law the
dismemberment of a human body after death is not regarded as mutilation, if other lives--now imperiled or seriously impaired--might be rescued or preserved.

There is, of course, a difference between the act
of dissection and the process of transplantation. But
the difference springs from the nature of the means
employed and not from the goal pursued. In either case,
it is the life and health of a living person that stand
to benefit by the operation.

We must, therefore, conclude that the authorized
removal of the eyes of a deceased person in order to
restore sight to the blind is not an act of mutilation,
which is forbidden, but an act of healing and restoration, which in Jewish law takes precedence over almost
all other religious injunctions.

Israel Bettan

See also:

S.B. Freehof, "Donating a Body to Science," Reform
   Responsa, pp. 130ff; "Bequeathing Parts of the
   Body," Contemporary Reform Responsa, pp.
   216ff.

85.   THE USE OF THE CORNEA OF THE DEAD
(Vol. LXVI, 1956, pp. 104-107)

QUESTION: Physicians is recent years have developed a technique of transplanting the cornea from
the eyes of people who died recently onto the eyes
of the blind, and thus--in many cases--restoring
their sight. Is this procedure permitted by traditional Jewish law?

ANSWER: This question has received considerable discussion in Jewish legal literature during the last two
or three years.   There have been a number of articles on
the question in the Orthodox rabbinical magazine,
Hapardes, and also a full discussion of it by the late
Rabbi L. Greenwald, in his Kol Bo Al Avelut, p. 45.

It is necessary first to state the general attitude
of Jewish law as to the use of normally forbidden ob-

jects (blood, **trefa** meat, etc.) in case of sickness.
The law is in the fullest sense liberal and is codified
in the **Shulchan Aruch**, Yoreh De-a 155.3. An invalid who
is not in grave danger may make use in healing of all
things which are forbidden by Rabbinic law, but not of
such as are forbidden by the stricter law of the Pentateuch itself; whereas an invalid who is in imminent
danger ("**choleh sheyesh bo sakana**") may make use for his
healing even of such objects as are forbidden by the
strictest Pentateuchal law. A man who is blind in one
eye would be considered as an invalid not in immediate
danger, but one who is blind in both eyes would be considered as one who is in imminent danger. Therefore,
there is no question that a person totally blind or in
imminent danger of becoming totally blind, may make use
of **anything** that may bring him healing, in this case,
vision.

There is no question that the **invalid** is permitted
by Jewish law to make use, therefore, of the cornea of
the dead. But the question which concerns the Orthodox
writers in this matter is not whether the blind man may
use it, but whether **we** have the right to provide it.
This is another, and a more complicated matter. There
is, first of all, the question of **Tum-a**, uncleanness.
Part of the body of the dead makes one unclean by contact, and since it is the procedure to have that part of
the body available, the touching of it makes one unclean. This part of the question need not delay us
long, since uncleanness nowadays applies only to
Kohanim, Priests, and the question of uncleanness would
come up if the doctor himself were a **Kohen**. But even in
his case it is not sure that he would become unclean by
contact with the cornea of the eyeball. The doubt as to
uncleanness involves the size of the object. Does an
amount as small as this make one unclean? All of those
who discuss the matter count this amount as "less than
an olive," their usual measurement for the amount that
can make one unclean. If, then, human flesh less than
an olive in size must be buried, it does make one unclean if not buried. The two considerations are related
to each other. Does less than an olive require burial?
This is debatable. The **Minchat Chinuch** #537 (Joseph
Babad) says that even such a small amount needs to be
buried; but the authoritative commentator to the **Yad**,
namely, the **Mishneh Lamelech** (Judah Rosanes), at the end
of Hilchot Evel (the second paragraph before the end of
his comment), says that it need not be buried. Thus,
this is a question which can be decided either way.

But something further is involved. If only the
cornea itself were removed from the body of the dead, it
would be easy to decide this question permissively, but
the practice is not to take out the cornea alone, but to

remove the entire eyeball and to keep it under refrigeration until needed for the operation. If it **were** the cornea alone which is removed, then the cornea--being, as its name implies, horny, skin-like material--does **not** make unclean by contact. The law is clear that the skin of a dead human being without flesh does not make unclean, but that (practically or "Rabbinically") we treat it as unclean lest it be used irreverently (Nidda 55a). The Talmud states this figuratively: "Lest a man make floor coverings of the skin of his parents." But essentially, the cornea **per se** (being skin or horn) does not make one unclean and does not need to be buried.

However, in practice, the whole eyeball is taken out and kept. The question, therefore, depends upon whether the eyeball of the dead needs to be buried. If it does, then not burying it involves both the sin of "**Bal talin,**" "Do not delay the burial of the dead," and also uncleanness. Even if the whole eyeball may be considered by measurement as being below the mandated amount that some authorities require to be buried (i.e., less than an olive), nevertheless Greenwald in his discussion says that it should be buried for another reason. It is an **ever**, "a limb," of the body, and the "limbs" should be buried whatever their size. However, even that is doubtful, because it is not sure that the eye is counted among the "limbs" of the body. The only clear indication in the older law that the eye **is** to be counted as a "limb" which requires burial, is based upon an Agadic statement in B. Nedarim 32b. There we find an Agadic discussion as to why God called the Patriarch first "Avram" and then later "Avraham." The name Avram totals the number two hundred forty-eight, the number of the "limbs" of the body. The Agadic explanation of the difference is that God referred (by the second name) to five more "limbs" of the body, and these five are then enumerated, the two eyes being counted among them.

But, directly contrary to this Agadic statement that the eye is to be considered a "limb" which must be buried, is the halachic implication of the Mishna in Oholot I.8, in which the limbs of the body which defile are enumerated, and the eyes are **not** enumerated among them. It is, therefore, debatable in the law whether the eye is to be considered a "limb" which requires burial or not.

How then can we decide when the following crucial facts are doubtful?--Does a small amount less than an olive defile and is it required to be buried? Is the eyeball to be counted legally a "limb" (**ever**), which--whatever its size--is required to be buried? The decision can only be made on the basis of general attitude to the law. An Orthodox rabbi such as Greenwald--who in his introduction mentions the modern use of the cornea as another evidence of the laxity of our age, and who, therefore, feels obligated to guard against further laxities by being doubly strict--will decide all these doubts on the stricter side (lechumra). Whereas a more liberal teacher, more concerned with making the law viable for our changing age, will decide these doubts leniently (lekula).

My decision, therefore, which has adequate justification as seen above, is as follows: Since, the **general spirit** of the law is to allow the dangerously sick to use anything otherwise prohibited; and since there is justification in the law for not even being required to bury that which is "less than an olive"; and since it is doubtful whether the eye is one of the "limbs" which must be buried; and since at all events we have become accustomed to permit autopsies in which even limbs of the body are not buried for a while--we are justified in deciding that even though the entire eye is taken out and kept under refrigeration, the cornea may be used to restore the sight of the blind.

Solomon B. Freehof

86. SURGICAL TRANSPLANTS
(Vol. LXXVIII, 1968, pp. 118-121)

QUESTION: What is the attitude of the Jewish legal tradition to the growing surgical practice of transplanting parts of a dead body into that of a living person?

ANSWER: It should go without saying that Jewish tradition and feeling would be absolutely opposed to hastening the death of a potential donor by even one second, in order that the organ to be transplanted into another body be in good condition. Nothing must be done to hasten the death of the dying. This scrupulousness about preserving the last few moments of life is also the concern of modern medicine. There are serious discussions today among doctors--especially with regard to obtaining organs for transplanting without delay--as to exactly when the potential donor is to be considered actually dead. At first the rule was: when the heart has stopped beating. Now they are considering a further test: when the brain stops functioning. As the discussion in medical circles continues, they will devise more, and even stricter tests.

As far as deciding when the potential donor is actually dead, modern scientific opinions are much stricter than Jewish tradition. The controversy arose a century ago as to whether the Jewish law of immediate burial was too hasty an action or not. Various governments in central Europe decreed that there must be a delay of three days before the burial. The great Hungarian authority, Moses Sofer, defended the Jewish custom of immediate burial (on the same day) and said that our traditional judgment, embodied in the knowledge of the **Chevra Kadisha**, was sufficient proof of death (see his responsum in **Chatam Sofer**, Yoreh De-a 338). Let us therefore say at the outset that--at least according to the spirit of Jewish law--the stricter the test as to the time of death which physicians will arrive at, the better it is. We therefore agree with the strict judgments of modern medicine that it must be absolutely clear that the patient is dead.

But it is from this point on that the real problem begins. Is it morally or legally permissible to take away parts of the body of the dead, and is it further permissible to insert such parts into a living body? The problem is difficult, first of all, because transplanting of organs is an entirely new surgical procedure, and, therefore, there could be no direct parallel or discussion of such a procedure in the older literature. Whatever opinion is arrived at on this matter must be derived as the underlying ethical principle behind related discussions in the literature.

There is a second and more direct difficulty in analyzing this question. When we begin to study the ethical implications of related ideas in the Talmud and in the writings of later scholars, we discover that the relevant basic principles seem to be mutually contradictory. Since this fact constitutes an initial difficulty, let us consider it first.

There is a general principle as to healing and the materials used for healing which, on the face of it, is so general as to make all further discussion of this problem unnecessary. The Talmud says (Pesachim 25a): "We may use any material for healing except that which is connected with idolatry, immorality, and bloodshed." These are the three cardinal sins which a person must avoid, even if it would lead to martyrdom. But aside from three such sources of healing methods or materials, any material or any method would be permitted. Maimonides, himself a great physician, makes this Talmudic statement even clearer. He says (Hilchot Yesodei Torah 5.6): "He who is sick and in danger of death, and the physician tells him that he can be cured by a certain object or material which is forbidden by the Torah, must obey the physician and be cured." This is codified as a law in the **Shulchan Aruch**, Yoreh De-a 155.3.

Considering this general permission to use anything we need, no further discussion would seem to be necessary, except for the fact that the body of the dead has a special sacredness in Jewish law. There is a general principle that the body of the dead may not be used for the benefit of the living ("**Met asur bahana-a**," based on Sanhedrin 47b). If the two principles are taken together, the general permissiveness would then need to be restated as follows: We may use all materials except those involved in the three cardinal sins mentioned above and except, also, the body of the dead.

But this apparent prohibition of using parts of the body of the dead depends upon a closer definition of the word **hana-a** (benefit). Later scholars understand the word **hana-a** to mean not "general benefit," but rather "satisfaction" (in the sense chiefly of the satisfaction derived from food). Therefore, they speak of materials taken into the body in ways different from the way of eating, and they call such absorption of material (other than eating) "not in the way of benefit, or satisfaction" ("**Lo kederech hana-ato**"). For example, the eating of blood is forbidden, but taking a blood infusion by means of the veins is described as not by the way of **hana-a**, or satisfaction, and therefore is permitted. Thus, the question of getting **hana-a** (satisfaction) from the body of the dead depends now on whether it is taken as medicine or by way of food. If the parts of the body of the dead are taken "not by the way of satisfaction" (**derech hana-a**) but inserted into the body in another way, the law forbidding "benefit" from the dead is usually much more permissively interpreted.

There is another aspect of the principle that the dead may not be used for the benefit or satisfaction of the living. That has to do with the distinction between Jewish dead and Gentile dead. In general, we are in duty bound to heal the sick, bury the dead, comfort the mourners of Gentiles, just as we do with the bodies of Jewish dead (B. Gittin 60a). But with regard to the Jewish dead, Jewish law adds certain special regulations. For example, a **Kohen** may not be in the same building with the Jewish dead because he may not defile himself except for his own relatives. There are detailed burial requirements as to washing, shrouds, etc., which are required for the Jewish dead. These extra requirements do not apply to the Gentile dead. We are, of course, in duty bound to bury and console, but neither Gentiles nor Jews are required to obey these additional minutiae of Jewish burial laws in the case of Gentile dead. It is sufficient if Gentile dead are respectfully buried and their mourners consoled.

So there is a debate in the law as to whether the
body of the Gentile dead may or may not be used for the
benefit of the living.   The **Shulchan Aruch**, Yoreh De-a
349, is inclined to the belief that the body of the
Gentile dead may not be so used, but the majority of
opinion inclines to the opinion that such bodies may be
used for the benefit of the living (see the authorities
marshaled by Moses Feinstein, **Igerot Mosheh**, #229 and
#230).   Since, therefore, the majority of the available
bodies as sources of organs for transplant are Gentile
bodies, this doubt as to whether "benefit for the living" may come from the body of the dead does not have
heavy weight.

There is, of course, a third consideration, and
that is the duty of burying the whole body of the dead.
This duty is the source of the basic objection of Orthodox authorities to autopsy.   Therefore, the question now
is whether a part of a body which is inserted into a
living body is still to be considered part of the dead
(which must be buried), or is it now to be considered a
part of a living body.

All, or almost all, of these rather complex contra-
dictions which needed to be harmonized are discussed in
the Talmud and by its early commentators, but of course
they have no definite statement about the actual consuming or using the body of the dead for the healing of the
living.   The discussion of such methods of healing begins to appear in the literature in later centuries.

One of the strangest discussions concerning the
medical use of the dead for healing the living is found
in the responsa of David ibn Zimri (Egypt, 1479-1589).
He is asked a question which seems bizarre to us, who
are no longer aware of medieval popular medical superstitions.   It seems that mummies from the ancient Egyptian tombs were in David ibn Zimri's time a regular
article of commerce.   They were sold for medical purposes.   People would actually eat those mummies to heal
certain diseases.   He is asked whether it is permitted
to get benefit **(hana-a)** or satisfaction from these bodies of the dead (**Responsa Radbaz** III, 548).   He states
the general principle that one may not have **hana-a** from
the flesh of the dead (based on Avoda Zara 29b).   Then
he says that these bodies, embalmed so long ago with
various chemicals, are no longer human flesh but are now
another product.   The ancient embalming preserved merely
the outlines of the features but transformed the flesh
into something else entirely.   Furthermore, he says,
these were once the bodies of the ancient Egyptians,
and, of course, the law is less strict than the laws
about "benefit" from the Jewish dead.

As far as I am aware, there is no other discussion
in the responsa literature of the use of parts of a dead

body for healing. There are references to the use of
tanned skin, but that was not for medical purposes. But
in our time there are two detailed discussions of precisely our problem. They are by Moses Feinstein of New
York, who may well be considered the prime Orthodox
author of responsa (although, indeed, some extreme **Chasidim** recently denounced him for an allegedly liberal
opinion with regard to artificial insemination). Feinstein, in his **Igerot Mosheh** (volume Yoreh De-a) has two
successive responsa on the subject (#229 and #230).
These responsa, although only four or five years old, do
not yet know of heart and liver transplants, but the
author already knows of bone transplants, and that is
sufficient for him to marshal all the relevant opinions.

He discusses--as was indicated above--the exact
definition of the term "**hana-a**" (benefit) and explains
it as literally meaning "satisfaction of food." Hence,
that which is taken into the body not by way of food
(i.e., not by mouth) is to be considered more leniently.
Furthermore, he speaks of the fact that most bodies
available for organ transplants are Gentile, and therefore the stricter prohibitions do not apply to them.
Finally, he comes to a conclusion which is vital to the
whole discussion, i.e., that when a part of a body is
taken by a surgeon and put into a living body, it becomes part of a living body; its status as part of the
dead which needs to be buried is now void (**batel**).

There is a confirmation of the permissive opinion
of Feinstein in the responsa of Nahum Kornmehl, published in 1966 in New York, **Tif-eret Tsevi**, #75. His
explanation is really charming. He says with regard to
the prohibition of **hana-a** from the dead in transplants
that when the operation occurs there is certainly no
hana-a for the patient, only misery for days. The
hana-a comes when the transplant comes to life and becomes part of his body. But now it is alive, and therefore, this has nothing to do with benefit from the dead.

To sum up the discussion: The exceptional nature
and rights of the dead body do not stand in the way of
the use of parts of the body for the healing of another
body. The part used is not taken into the living body
as food, hence it is not considered **derech hana-a**. The
part becomes integrated into a living body and therefore
the requirement of its burial has lapsed. Therefore,
the general principle stated first remains unimpugned,
i.e., that "we may heal with any of the prohibited materials mentioned in Scripture." This is especially
true, as Maimonides indicates, because the patients
about to receive these implants are actually in danger

of death, and for such patients any possible help is permitted by Jewish tradition.

Solomon B. Freehof

87. OMISSION OF COMMITTAL SERVICES
(Vol. LXXXVI, 1976, pp. 96-98)

QUESTION: A custom is originating in certain western congregations to change the form of the traditional funeral service. There is no funeral service in home or chapel before the body of the dead is removed, either for interment or cremation. At the cemetery (in cases of burial), there is no service at all. On the day of burial, or sometimes a few days later, a memorial service is held. This memorial service is the only funeral ritual that is observed. Is this custom justified by tradition? Should it be encouraged?

ANSWER: It is not too surprising that such a custom can arise nowadays. There is in many quarters a desire to simplify the entire funeral ritual and to have less and less contact with the dead. The old tradition of the family sitting **Shiv-a**, seven days of mourning, and then following thirty days of half-mourning and, for a parent, a full year of partial mourning--all this is being increasingly set aside. Many now receive the consolation of their friends in the funeral parlor. This in itself is basically unobjectionable, except that in some families it supplants the **Shiv-a** entirely and leads to the entire neglect of the whole ritual of mourning.

This avoidance of any chapel or burial ritual at the time of death will easily lead to further avoidance. If the bereaved do not participate in any cemetery ritual at the time of the funeral, they will certainly not visit the grave in later times; and if such visitation is consolatory--as it must have been, for the custom is prevalent--then these bereaved are deprived of that consolation too. And as for the departed, the bitter lament of the Psalmist is fulfilled: "I am as forgotten as are the dead from the heart" (Psalm 31:13).

The new trend of avoiding contact with death and bereavement may or may not be harmful. It is, of course, for the psychologists to decide whether or not this constitutes a running away from an inescapable reality. After all, the Jewish ritual of mourning, even the completely Orthodox ritual, is meant to avoid exaggerated or unmeasured grief: "The law is to diminish mourning" (Mo-ed Katan 26b). On the next page in the Talmud it is stated that if a man mourns immoderately, God Himself rebukes him and says, "Are you more merciful than I am?" In fact, it is stated as a law in the **Shulchan Aruch**, Yoreh De-a 389.5, that when a man's friends rebuke him for excessive mourning, he should cease his mourning ritual. Thus, it is clear that our tradition has in mind a fixed and therefore limited ritual of mourning and the avoidance of excess. This certainly seems to be psychologically sound. The bereaved persons face the fact of death; do honor to the departed, as tradition requires; and when the ritual is finished, the mourner--having thus expressed himself--can now be consoled and go on with the business of living. It is a question, therefore, for psychologists to decide whether a bereaved person who avoids all ritual of mourning does not suppress his own grief thereby and actually delays his consolation.

As far as tradition is concerned, the present laws and customs are the result of an evolution of various observances. Originally there was a special ritual at the very moment of death. The law was that whoever was present when a person died had to make a tear in his garment **(Keri-a)**. This was changed because it was feared that the people present at the bedside of a dying person (especially if they were not relatives) would want to save tearing their garments and would therefore go away and leave the dead to die in loneliness. So, for that reason the **Keri-a** was shifted either to the grave side or to the funeral service. Thus, the various prayers ("Blessed be the righteous Judge..." etc.) which were originally said at the moment of death in the presence of the man just deceased were, likewise, moved to the funeral service or the grave side.

Just as these rituals (i.e., tearing the garments and the prayers) were always to be in the presence of the dead (first at the moment of death and later at the service) so, too, the eulogy is to be in the presence of the dead (see Yoreh De-a 344.12 and 17).

So definite was the tradition of having the various rituals in the presence of the dead that even in the case of sinful people the ritual was carried out. Basically the law (stemming from Semachot) was that wicked people--those who abandoned the community and those who committed suicide--were to be given no ritual at all **(Ein mit-asekin**," "We do not engage ourselves with them"). But even in the case of these individuals the law gradually changed and we are required to bury them, of course, and provide **Kaddish** and shrouds. See the references on this particular matter in **Recent Reform Responsa**, pp. 118-119:

> The strictest of all codifiers is Maimonides ("Hilchot Evel") who says that there should be no mourning rites), and so forth, but only the blessing for the mourners. The Ramban, in **Toledot Ha-adam**, says that there should be tearing of the garments. The next step is taken by Solomon ben Adret, the great legal authority of Barcelona (13th century) in his Responsum 763. He says that certainly we are in duty bound to provide shrouds and burial. Later authorities, as, for example, Moses Sofer, in his Responsa, Yoreh De-a 326, says that we certainly do say **Kaddish**; and, further, he would permit any respectable family to go through all the mourning ritual, lest the family have to bear innocently eternal disgrace if, conspicuously, they failed to exercise mourning.

Thus, it is clear that our Jewish tradition was rather insistent that a definite amount of ritual be carried out in the presence of the departed. Of course, a memorial service in the absence of the body of the departed is proper and traditional (e.g., in the case when the body is lost at sea or for some other reason cannot be found). Nor is there any objection in tradition to a memorial service taking place after the funeral, especially in the case of honored scholars, when it was a tradition to hold memorial services in various cities (therefore obviously in the absence of the body). Also, at the end of thirty days of mourning or at the anniversary of the death, such memorial services were held. But all these memorial services were never meant to be a substitute for the actual funeral service at the time of death.

As to the question we have raised above, namely, whether the avoidance of these rituals is sound psychologically, we may now say rather positively that the observance of these rituals is psychologically sound. A recent book by Jack D. Spiro, entitled **A Time to Mourn**, states the following (page 114):

> **Expressing Grief.** Through various laws, the mourner is required to remind himself of the death of his loved object, not only for the purpose of facing reality, but also to help in giving vent to his feelings. Mourning is basically an affective process which operates to relieve the tension of frustrated love impulses. But it does so only if the mourner is capable of expressing the related emotions. As Lindemann points out, one of the most

serious obstacles to accomplishing the work of mourning is that "patients try to avoid the intense distress connected with the grief experience and to avoid the expression of emotion necessary for it." When an emotion is denied expression, it is not destroyed, but only pushed down into the unconscious. The pressure builds up and may manifest itself in some disguised, unwholesome form. By giving vent to the affective tension caused by the frustration of his love impulses, the mourner moves on his way toward severing his emotional ties to the deceased. The dynamic energy itself, which had been consumed in the love relationship, seeks satisfaction. Through the expression of grief this energy is used, thus bringing emotional relief to the mourner and gradually allaying the affective force of the love relationship. The mourner thereby becomes capable of detaching himself from the deceased.

It is evident, therefore, that this new practice of avoiding committal services entirely or avoiding the family presence if there is a committal service, is both contrary to tradition and to sound mental health and should, therefore, be discouraged.

Solomon B. Freehof

See also:

S.B. Freehof, "Body Lost at Sea," **Reform Responsa,** pp. 147ff; "Funeral Services Without the Body," **Modern Reform Responsa,** pp. 110ff.

88. BURIAL FROM THE TEMPLE, ALSO WITH REFERENCE
TO BURIAL OF SUICIDES
(Vol. XXXIII, 1923, pp. 61-63)

Rabbi Henry Berkowitz has given the following opinion on two questions which are likely to come up in every congregation and at any time.

"You ask my opinion on the proposition now held under consideration by your congregation, viz.: To permit burials from the Temple at the request of the surviving members of the family, barring suicides.

In order to make my reply as clear and concise as possible, permit me to answer the two parts of this proposition separately.

First: Shall burials from the Temple be held simply at the request of the surviving members of the family, or shall the congregation, through its rabbi and officials, decide the matter?

At present, as you state, the latter condition prevails. When the congregation desires it for any reason, funerals are held from the synagogue--always, of course, with the consent of the family. I believe it should be a reciprocal rule, namely: when the family desires it, the privilege should be accorded--always, of course, with the consent of the congregation. In such cases the President or Board shall determine the practical questions (e.g., time, expense, etc.), and the rabbi shall determine the religious questions (e.g., the nature of the service and the eligibility--as, for instance in the case of a Christian wife of an Israelite, in the case of a suicide, and the like).

As burial is a religious service as much as public worship or marriage, the use of the synagogue cannot be inappropriate. As the family may have the Temple for marriage solemnities by complying with the conditions which the rabbi and the congregation require, so in the case of funerals should they have the same right, subject to the proper conditions.

Inasmuch as funerals from the Temple have been limited everywhere hitherto to such persons of special merit or distinction as the congregation desired to honor, it would no doubt be deemed a token of arrogance and a presumption of and yearning for the vanities of ostentation, for a family to make such a request. Nevertheless--you will agree with me, I believe--in recognizing that if the old Jewish sentiment in favor of equality and the leveling of all distinctions of death were carried out by having all funerals from the Temple, great, very great, good might be accomplished. The narrow, crowded quarters of private houses are rarely adequate for the decorous conduct of the services. The crowded conditions are often a menace to health and create such a state of discord and indelicacy as to harrow up the feelings of the suffering in a dangerous way and undo all the possibilities of that reverence which is essential to a religious service. Every minister has keenly felt this and should certainly welcome such a common sense innovation. Temple Emanuel, New York, adopted such a law many years ago as was imperatively demanded by the impossibility of holding funerals respectably in the flats and narrow houses of that crowded city.

Second: As to the burial of suicides from the Temple or the prohibition thereof.

We now know about mental diseases and the inducing causes of suicide more than was ever known before. As a consequence, we have more compassion in our hearts for the victim than was held in the days of old. While sometimes--and perhaps most times--the act is execrable and cowardly, and amounts to the denial of religion, we know that it is not always so. The old Jewish law recognized the nobility of suicide in some cases, e.g., that of martyr. Shall not the new Jewish law of congregational usage be as humane?

True, deception may be practiced, and the glamor of concealment may be thrown over an ignoble suicide by the publicity of the funeral. There is, therefore, a danger of condoning such dishonesty in permitting Temple burial. On the other hand, an irremediable wrong would be done if, by the enforcement of such a sweeping prohibition, one worthy person were ever branded and the family unjustly disgraced. I should say: **Do not legislate** on the subject of suicides at all. Let each case stand on its individual merits. Do not prejudge. We had a case here in Philadelphia of a woman whose eulogy will be pronounced by future ages. She discovered that the mute could be taught to speak and to understand all speech without hearing. In her effort to establish her system she threatened the old systems. She was harassed and persecuted, ridiculed and abused. The frail woman could not endure it and ended her life. Her death was the triumph of her system. Should she, whose life was so full of honor, be desecrated at death?

Trusting that these replies may be of some service to you and hoping that you will inform me of the final action of your congregation."

(Signed) Henry Berkowitz

To this I would add that, according to Jewish law, one is considered a suicide only when there is absolute certainty that he premeditated and committed the act with a clear mind not troubled by some great fear or worry which might have beset him for the moment and caused him to lose his mind temporarily. In the absence of such certain evidence, he is given the benefit of the doubt: we assume that some intense grief, fear, or worry caused him to lose his mental equilibrium, and that he committed the act in a state of mind when he could not realize what he was doing. Furthermore, consideration for his surviving relatives should, according to the Rabbis, not be ignored. And, whenever possible, we should try to spare them the disgrace which would come to them by having their relative declared a suicide.

(See **Shulchan Aruch**, Yoreh De-a 345.1-3, and responsa **Chatam Sofer**, Yoreh De-a 326.)

Henry Berkowitz
(Opinion confirmed by
Jacob Z. Lauterbach and Committee)

See also:

S.B. Freehof, "Funerals from the Temple," **Reform Responsa for Our Time**, pp. 95ff.

89. FUNERAL SERVICE FOR A SUICIDE
(Vol. LXIX, 1959, pp. 120-123)

QUESTION: A member of our congregation committed suicide and the question arose as to the funeral service. Should there be a eulogy, and should the services be simplified and the mourning ritual diminished?

ANSWER: The question of suicides and the funeral rituals which are permitted or forbidden with regard to them has long occupied the attention of Jewish legal authorities. Our Conference itself had an elaborate discussion on it in the year 1923. This discussion ended with a brief statement by the late Dr. Jacob Z. Lauterbach, chairman of our Responsa Committee. The statement consisted of one short paragraph in which Dr. Lauterbach stated the general tendency of the law to seek for reasons to keep from declaring a man to be a suicide. This question has come up very often since 1923, and occasionally involves painful discussions with the family of the deceased. Therefore, the subject, so highly complex, should now be clarified and some conclusion arrived at. The following responsum, therefore, is an attempt at some general line of procedure with regard to this situation.

Surprisingly enough, there is no clear law against suicide in the Bible or the Talmud. Perhaps suicide was so rare that there was no need for such a law. The Bible mentions only two suicides in the entire long span of history which it covers: King Saul on Mount Gilboa (I Samuel 31:4) and David's counselor, Ahitophel (II Samuel 17:23). Nor does the Talmud find it necessary to speak of the sin of suicide. Some of the earlier scholars base the objection to this crime upon the verse used by God to Noah when he and his family left the Ark: "Surely your blood of your lives will I require" (Genesis 9:5). But neither Maimonides nor Aaron Halevi in the **Chinuch** count this as one of the negative commandments.

The first clear-cut statement about the crime of suicide is in the post-Talmudic booklet **Semachot**, at the beginning of chapter 2. There it is stated that those who commit suicide are to receive no burial rites. The phraseology used there is important, since from this source it has found its way into all important later discussions. "He who destroys himself consciously (**lada-at**), we do not engage ourselves with his funeral in any way. We do not tear the garments, and we do not bare the shoulder in mourning, and we do not say eulogies for him; but we do stand in the mourner's row and recite the blessing of the mourners because the latter is for the honor of the living." Then follows a definition of the crime of suicide as follows: If a man is found hanged or fallen from a tree or a wall he is not to be deemed a suicide unless he says, "I am going to do so," and they see him climb up, etc. Then it is stated that a child who commits suicide is not to be counted as a suicide, clearly because he is not to be judged as acting with a clear mind (**lada-at**), which must be presupposed before the crime is to be considered a crime. Then follows the law that those convicted and executed by the Jewish courts should not be mourned for in any way lest the mourning imply that the Sanhedrin had made an unjust judgment.

From this statement in **Semachot** the law spread to all the codes and frequently appears in the Responsa literature. In this original source it is evident that only a person who commits suicide with clear mind and with an announced intention beforehand, is to be treated as a suicide. A mere presumption of suicide is not sufficient.

This desire to be cautious with the accusation of suicide had many motives, of course. One was that the law itself spoke of circumstances under which one should willingly accept death, when threatened with the compulsion to violate any of the three sins of idolatry, immorality, and murder (B. Sanhedrin 74a). This type of suicide, often carried out in wholesale fashion in the Middle Ages as well as in earlier times, was honored as noble martyrdom. Therefore, it was clear that not all surrender of life could be deemed blameworthy by the law. At times it was even noble. Thus, the Talmud speaks in praise of the mass suicide by the drowning of young boys and girls being taken captive for a shameful life in Rome (B. Gittin 57b). Besides martyrdom, the law also considered personal stresses. Thus, the tradition never seems to have blamed King Saul for his suicide. In fact, his case became a frequently cited case in the following way: King Saul was afraid that the Philistines would subject him to torture, and he saw himself as dying anyhow, and therefore, while the sin is still a sin, it was a forgivable one.

With Saul as a pardonable prototype for most suicides under stress, the Rabbis, in many a specific case that came before them, sought and found reasons why a person who took his own life should not be stigmatized legally as a suicide. They generally said that whoever is under stress as Saul was ("anus keSha-ul"), is not to be considered a suicide legally, even if he takes his own life. A number of cases will indicate their considerate mood in this regard.

Jacob Weil, a German rabbi of the 13th-14th century, in his Responsa (no. 114) speaks of the case of a Jewish criminal who was executed by the German courts. Should not such a criminal be deemed equivalent to a suicide (since he willfully risked his life) and therefore not have a regular burial and be mourned for? He gives a number of reasons why this man should be mourned for with full mourning ritual. First, he was tortured, and pain is considered a purification of sin. Then, we assume, he made confession of his sins, and that, too, brought him atonement. So Mordecai Benet, Rabbi of Nicholsburg, early 19th century (**Parashat Mordechai**, Yoreh De-a 25), discusses a criminal who was found in his cell, having committed suicide. He says that such an act is to be called suicide only if it is done with full and clear awareness (**lada-at**). This man certainly was in terror of being executed, or of being imprisoned for life in the dungeons of the city of Bruenn, which is worse than death; therefore he is to be considered as having acted under unbearable stress, as King Saul was. In general, he said that a man is not wholly responsible for what he does in his grief.

Solomon Kluger of Brody (middle of the 19th century, **Ha-elef Lecha Shelomo**, Yoreh De-a 301) speaks of a man heavily in debt who attempted suicide, failed, and some days afterwards died. First, there was a question of whether he really died because of the wound he inflicted on himself; secondly, he was under great stress; and Kluger concludes that whoever is under stress, as Saul was, is not to be considered a suicide. Also based upon the original source in the baraita **Semachot**, chapter 2, all children who for some reason or other commit suicide are not to be treated as legal suicides because they certainly cannot be assumed to act **lada-at**, with full knowledge.

A summary of the thoughtful, sympathetic attitude of the law to such unfortunates is summed up in the

latest code, **Aruch Hashulchan**, Yoreh De-a 345 (Yechiel
Epstein). He says, in general summary: "We seek all
sorts of reasons possible to explain away the man's
action, either his fear, or his pain, or temporary insanity, in order not to declare the man a suicide."
Whatever the secular coroner or medical examiner would
declare, the concern of Judaism, which deals with a
man's religious rights, depends upon what Jewish traditional law says and feels. It would amount to this:
Only a man who commits suicide calmly and with clear
resolve is to be considered a suicide. In fact, some of
the scholars say that he has first to announce his intention and then to fulfill it at once. If he announces
such intention and is found dead much later, or if he is
found dead under suspicious circumstances but did not
declare such an intention, he is not to be treated as a
suicide.

Since the definition for legal suicide was so
strict, there were many cases of presumed suicides which
were not definitely so stigmatized. Therefore, the
scholars could allow themselves to permit full funeral
rights for many whom--out of kindness--they declared as
not being legal suicides. They were frequently uncertain as to how much ritual should be permitted. The
original source in **Semachot** says that there must be no
mourning at all--no tearing of garments, no eulogies, no
mourning rituals after the burial. In fact, it begins
by saying, "We do not deal with them at all" ("Ein mit-
asekin bahem"), which would imply that we do nothing
even about burial. But, inasmuch as they were loath to
declare anybody a suicide, they proceeded, as it were,
to nibble away at the wholesale prohibitions just described.

The strictest of all codifiers is Maimonides (Hilchot Evel), who says that there should be no mourning
rites, etc., but only the blessing for the mourners.
The Ramban, in **Toledot Ha-adam**, says that there should
be tearing of the garments. The next step is taken by
Solomon ben Adret, the great legal authority of Barcelona (13th century) in his Responsum no. 763. He says
that certainly we are in duty bound to provide shrouds
and burial. A later authority, Moses Sofer, in his
Responsa, Yoreh De-a 326, says that we certainly do say
Kaddish, and he would permit any respectable family to
go through all the mourning ritual, lest the family have
to bear innocently eternal disgrace if they do not exercise mourning conspicuously.

The one part of the mourning ritual about which
there is almost no permission is the custom of giving a
eulogy of the dead. Thus, Jacob Castro, in his notes to
the **Shulchan Aruch**, while saying in general that public
mourning is forbidden but private mourning is permitted,

adds emphatically that we do not give a eulogy and certainly do not have a professional eulogist. Why they
were increasingly lenient about mourning rituals but
were firm against eulogy is easily understood. Although
the man who committed suicide may be pardoned, he should
not be praised as an example. In the words of Rabbi
Akiva, in the original source in **Semachot**: We should
neither praise nor defame him. In other words, he
should be quietly forgiven. Nevertheless, there are one
or two opinions which would permit even a eulogy. One
is Ezekiel Katzenellenbogen, Rabbi of Altona, early 18th
century (**Keneset Yechezkel**, no. 37), who says that whenever there is any sort of reason, we eulogize him. And
the other is the statement in the Talmud specifically
about Saul, the prototype, that the children of Israel
were punished because they failed to eulogize Saul adequately (B. Yevamot 78b). But, in general, the mood was
as summarized by the **Pitchei Teshuva**, Abraham Zevi
Eisenstadt, who said: "We mourn but we do not eulogize."
    The long and complicated succession of discussions
in the law on the matter of suicide amounts, then, to
this: An increasing reluctance to stigmatize a man as a
suicide, and therefore, an increasing willingness to
grant more and more rights of burial and mourning. The
only hesitation is with regard to eulogy. It would
therefore seem to be in accord with the mood of tradition if we conducted full services and omitted the eulogy, provided this omission does not cause too much grief
to the family. If the family is deeply desirous of some
address to be given in the funeral service, then the
address should be as little as possible in the form of a
eulogy of the departed and more in the form of consoling
of the survivors. For the general principle is frequently repeated in discussing this law: "That which is
for the honor of the living shall be done."

Solomon B. Freehof

90. A EULOGY FOR A SUICIDE
(1980)

QUESTION: May a eulogy be delivered for an individual who has committed suicide?

ANSWER: An answer has already been provided by my
honored predecessor. We might add that tradition has
always considered depression, mental derangement, or

other illness as removing some of the taint of suicide.
Under these circumstances, it would certainly be permissible to provide a eulogy and to treat the death as any
other in regard to the funeral ritual. Our tradition
saw the death of King Saul (I Samuel 31:4; San. 74a;
Git. 57b) as suicide which occurred under mental duress
and, anyhow, realized that Saul had suffered from de-
pressions. King Saul saw himself falling into the hands
of the Philistines, which meant a cruel death, so he
sought to end his life. Solomon Kluger, in the last
century (**Ha-elef Lecha Shelomo**, Yoreh De-a 301), dealt
with an individual who committed suicide because of
great indebtedness. He insisted that the man had been
depressed and under mental stress. Similarly, others
dealt with Jewish criminals who had been sentenced to
death and committed suicide while awaiting the sentence
(Mordecai Benet, **Parashat Mordechai**, Yoreh De-a 25).
All of these unfortunate individuals were to be given a
normal funeral. This also was the point of view adopted
by Epstein in his code (**Aruch Hashulchan**, Yoreh De-a
345).

It is possible to trace the development of the law
regarding suicide from the Talmudic tractate **Semachot**
through Maimonides to modern times. We then see that a
greater understanding of mental derangement slowly
evolved. **Semachot** and Maimonides insisted that no
mourning be observed (**Yad**, Hil. Evel). A little later,
Solomon ben Adret (Responsum #763) stated that we should
provide shrouds and a normal burial, while Moses Sofer
(Responsum, Yoreh De-a 326) added the permission to
recite **Kaddish**. Many modern Orthodox authorities would
still hesitate about a eulogy, but in the eighteenth
century Ezekiel Katzenellenbogen (**Keneset Yechezkel**,
#37) felt that a eulogy was also permissible. We would
follow that more liberal statement and provide a eulogy
(of course, adapted to the specific circumstances).

Walter Jacob, Chairman
Leonard S. Kravitz
W. Gunther Plaut
Harry A. Roth
Rav A. Soloff
Bernard Zlotowitz

91. MASONIC SERVICE AT A FUNERAL
(Vol. LVI, 1946, pp. 125-127)

QUESTION: Recently I conducted a funeral for a member of my congregation. I was told that a Masonic service would precede the regular religious service. I thought it would be of an incidental nature, but it proved to be of twenty minutes' duration and, to my amazement, seemed to be constructed on a pseudo-religious line that might well have satisfied the spiritual scruples of a number of people.

There were references to the "Grand Master of the Universe," and prayers were read for the soul of the departed, at least two of which seemed to be direct readings from the Christian Book of Common Prayer (one of them The Lord's Prayer). An apron was placed on the coffin by the "chaplain" of the Lodge (an all-Jewish one, by the way), and each Mason present--clad in white gloves and apron--placed a sprig of evergreen on the coffin as they solemnly paraded past.

To me the ceremony had all the earmarks of a separate cult, and I felt that as far as the membership might be concerned my participation as a rabbi was almost superfluous....

I do not know if this question has ever been discussed before, but to me it seemed like a separate religious service with obvious Christian and pagan roots, one that is entirely out of keeping with either Liberal or Orthodox Judaism. And the question also arises in my mind: If the Masons see fit to hold a funeral service, might not also the Knights of Pythias, the Elks, Lions, Moose, and who knows how many other fraternal and other organizations do the same thing?...

ANSWER: Among the principles controlling rabbinic decisions, there is one that partakes more of the nature of policy than of legal propriety. Our teachers were very much concerned with the need for maintaining amicable relationships with the larger community. When not called to compromise their religious position or any important belief and practice, they consulted the "ways of peace" before attempting to resolve a difficult situation.

The funeral rites of fraternal organizations, however designated, are harmless pageantry. They are intended as a spectacular tribute to a departed member. The primacy of the religion of the deceased is fully

affirmed when the rabbi insists, as he should, that the
rites of the synagogue take precedence over the fraternal ceremonies. After the Jewish service has been completed at the home or in the Chapel, outside participation, when desired by the family, may well be countenanced, even if one cannot approve of all the details of
the elaborate ceremonial.

The fraternal associations with which men of our
faith are affiliated, contend that their rituals are
free from sectarian bias. The examples cited by the
correspondent would tend to disprove the denominational
overtones and clear christological implications. At any
rate, it might not be taken amiss if the rabbi suggested
the omission of a given reference or rite.

To ban by Conference resolution all participation
of fraternal bodies in the service for the dead, because
of minor objections to some of the utterances, would
evince a degree of intolerance not at all conducive to
the peaceful relations we should strive to maintain
among the citizens of a community.

Israel Bettan and Committee

92. FUNERAL RITES OF FRATERNAL ORDERS
(Vol. LXIV, 1954, pp. 75-77)

QUESTION: Many of us, I learn from personal inquiries, are annoyed by a problem that arises from
time to time. When called to officiate at a funeral, we are often informed by members of the family
that representatives of the Masons or of some other
Lodge, to which the deceased belonged, will participate in the service. I, for one, am at a loss to
know how to handle the situation. The participants
of the fraternal groups are not always members of
our own faith, and the service they use, while not
antagonistic to our tradition, introduces a strange
element into our ritual. Then, too, the funeral
service is at times conducted in the Temple audi-
torium, where the favorite symbols of the Lodges
seem quite incongruous with our Jewish modes of
worship.

I also do not know of any fixed order of procedure, which all rabbis follow. Shall these participants perform their rites before or after my
religious service? Shall I permit them to insert
their part into the service I conduct.

I should appreciate a word of guidance in this matter.

ANSWER: The question raised, while not altogether new, presents a number of aspects not dealt with in previous responsa.

It was in the report of the Committee on Responsa submitted to the Chicago conference, in 1946, that the general question of outside participation in the services for the dead was briefly discussed. The statement of the Committee read in part as follows:

> Among the principles controlling rabbinic decisions, there is one that partakes more of the nature of policy than of legal propriety. Our teachers were very much concerned with the need for maintaining amicable relationships with the larger community. When not called to compromise their religious position, or any important belief and practice, they consulted the "ways of peace" before attempting to resolve a difficult situation.
> The funeral rites of fraternal organizations, however designated, are harmless pageantry. They are intended as a spectacular tribute to a departed member.... To ban by Conference resolution all participation of fraternal bodies in the service for the dead, because of minor objections to some of the utterances, would evince a degree of intolerance not at all conducive to the peaceful relations we should strive to maintain among the citizens of a community. (CCAR **Yearbook**, vol. 56, pp. 125-127)

From this general principle, we presume, none will care to dissent. The question, therefore, is no longer whether or not we shall countenance the prevailing practice, however annoying it may prove to be at times. The problem today is to discover, on the basis of our age-old tradition, some principle or method of control that shall enable us to preserve the dignity and integrity of our own religious expression without interfering with the customary rites of the fraternal orders.

It is well to remember, in extenuation of what we are witnessing today, that the Lodge delegation, or its "Ritual Team," makes its appearance at a given funeral not at the behest of the Order but at the invitation of the bereaved family, and, commonly, in pursuance of the express wish of the deceased. The "pretty" service of his Lodge had so impressed itself upon him that among

his last instructions he did not fail to include the
specific request that his own obsequies shall be graced
with the words and symbols of his fraternal ritual.

For one reared in the Jewish tradition, such a wish
is the expression not simply of personal vanity. From
earliest times the Jew has been taught to do honor to
the dead, to mourn their loss, to lament their departure. In fact, to accompany the dead to the grave is a
solemn religious obligation, from which not even the
diligent student of Torah is exempt (Yoreh De-a 361).
In times when funeral processions were the order of the
day, it was customary to lengthen the line of march in
order to induce large numbers of people to join the
procession, thus adding greatly to the honor paid the
dead (Sefer Hamat-amim, Bar Minan, p. 16). It is even
said of Joseph that he deliberately caused Jacob's cas-
ket to be carried "to the threshing-floor of Atad, which
is beyond the Jordan" (Gen. 50:10), in order to attract
some Moabites and Ammonites to his father's funeral
procession (N.Z. Berlin, Ha-amek Davar).

The levaya, which makes it obligatory to accompany
the dead to their resting place, is an old and honored
practice. To it we owe the deep respect we have for the
dead and the dying, as well as much of the pomp and
ceremony we often encounter at funerals. It is perhaps
when we come to view the fraternal rituals as part of
the levaya, which is designed merely to pay homage to
the dead, that we can assess their true worth and assign
them their proper place.

However elaborate and pretentious the Lodge service
may be, it is in its essential nature nothing but the
open expression of respect for a deceased member. As
such, it fulfills its purpose. The Lodge, through its
"Ritual Team," thus participates in the levaya and does
honor to the departed. But the Lodge is not a religious
body in any official sense, and its representatives
cannot be said to perform religious functions. Their
"rites" have no relation to the words of comfort and
consecration spoken by the rabbi in the name of the
religion of the deceased. Hence, while recognizing the
right of any group to honor the memory of one of its
members in its own set forms, the rabbi will carefully
avoid giving the impression that he, as the spokesman of
Judaism, attaches any religious significance to those
forms. He will not permit the intrusion of any of these
forms into his own traditional service. Nor, if the
obsequies take place in the Temple, will he acquiesce in
any arrangement that would sanction the simultaneous
performance of other rites besides those sanctified by
his Jewish tradition. It is only fit and proper that in
its own House of Worship, and while engaged in practic-

ing its own rites, every congregation shall bear rule and speak its own religious language.

Once the primacy of the religion of the deceased is affirmed by the rabbi and established in the minds of the people, the question as to whether the religious service, conducted at home or in a funeral parlor, shall be preceded or followed by the fraternal rites, will lose much of its significance. Different rabbis will view the matter in different lights. Then, too, the special conditions prevailing at the time will help determine the issue. But, questions of precedence aside, it is the rabbi who is in charge of the religious service and upon whom must devolve the responsibility of deciding all such questions as pertain to the proper conduct of his office.

Israel Bettan

NOTE:

Such rites should be placed at the end of the funeral service, where they do not detract from the Jewish religious mood or message.

Responsa Committee (1980)

93. RABBI OFFICIATING AT A FUNERAL OF A JEW
IN A NON-JEWISH CEMETERY
(Vol. LVII, 1947, pp. 136-137)

QUESTION: The other day I was called to officiate at the funeral of a non-affiliated person. The day after agreeing to officiate, I discovered that the man had been married to a non-Jew, and that he was to be interred in the Protestant section of the local Oak Woods Cemetery. Following the Conference ruling as it appears in the Kohler Responsa in the **Rabbi's Manual**, I refused to officiate. The family thereupon engaged a functionary associated with one of our large Reform synagogues here. However, the funeral director expressed much surprise at my decision, informing me that so far as he knew most of my Reform colleagues had on occasion conducted funerals in non-consecreated areas of cemeteries. I have no reason to disbelieve the assertion of the funeral director. Therefore, I find myself as a new rabbi in a very embarrassing position.

ANSWER: The question whether a rabbi may officiate at
the funeral of a Jew who is to be interred in a non-
Jewish cemetery, may well be considered anew.   The conflicting practices that prevail reflect fundamental
differences in attitude and point of view, which ought
to be composed, if possible, or expressed more clearly
and acutely.
    The responsum to which the correspondent refers, an
excerpt from which is given in the **Rabbi's Manual** (pp.
187-188), is, we fear, inconsistent with its underlying
principle; nor is it conclusive in its chain of reasoning.
    In a previous responsum, relative to the burial of
a non-Jew in a Jewish cemetery, an excerpt from which is
also quoted in the **Rabbi's Manual**--on the same page, in
fact--the author enunciated a principle the validity of
which he has never sought to impugn.   "Our cemeteries,"
he declared, "are not as a whole consecrated ground, in
the sense that it excludes those not of the Jewish
faith.   Only the spot where the body is interred becomes
sacred thereby."   If this principle holds true in the
case of a Jewish cemetery, making it permissible for a
non-Jew to be buried in a Jewish cemetery, it should be
equally valid in the case of a non-Jewish cemetery,
wherein a Jew is to find interment.   To grant legal
permission in the one instance and deny it in the other,
is to rely not on principle but on personal predilec-
tion.
    Some of the Rabbinic laws pertaining to the uses to
which cemeteries may or may not be put, together with
the reasons given therefore, clearly indicate that the
principle itself is well authenticated.   One is forbidden, for example, to use the cemetery as pasture land,
or indulge in levity there, or build a sewer there, not
because the ground is sacred, but **"mipenei kevod hametim,"** because the honor of the dead is to be safeguarded
(Yoreh De-a, Hil. Avelut 368).   On the other hand, one
may enjoy the fruit of the trees growing in a cemetery,
since they do not grow out of the graves; they are just
ordinary trees (**ibid.**).   Similarly, one may wear a garment with "fringes" when in a cemetery and not be guilty
of "mocking the dead" if these "fringes" do not actually
touch the graves (**ibid.**, 367).   It would seem, then,
that not the entire area of the cemetery, but only the
individual grave, is invested with special sanctity.
    Yet, it must be noted, it is not the author's re-
luctance to apply the same principle to both cases that
accounts for his insistence that they be clearly distinguished from one another.   The Jew who is to be buried
in a non-Jewish cemetery, he contends, should be denied
the services of a rabbi because "by this very fact evidence seems to be given in favor of his non-Jewish al-

legiance." We confess our inability to group the logic of the statement. We should rather think that, far from evidencing his non-Jewish allegiance, the Jew who desires to be buried in a non-Jewish cemetery because of his non-Jewish mate, but who yet indicates his wish that the services of the grave shall be conducted by a rabbi, is thereby affirming most emphatically his Jewish loyalty.

It is a strange logic that would permit a professing Christian to be buried in a Jewish cemetery but would prohibit a rabbi to officiate at the grave of a professing Jew who is buried in a Christian cemetery.

We cannot at this late date raise ghetto walls around our own cemeteries; nor can we ban a Jew from the benefits of his religion because he has chosen to make his abode among the dead of another faith.

Israel Bettan

See also:

S.B. Freehof, "Burial in a Christian Cemetery," **Reform Responsa**, pp. 140ff; "Disinterment of a Jew from a Jewish Cemetery for Reburial in a Christian Cemetery," **Reform Responsa for Our Time**, pp. 179ff; "Transfer of Jew to Christian Cemetery," **Current Reform Responsa**, pp. 162ff; "Convert Buried in Christian Cemetery," **Contemporary Reform Responsa**, pp. 151ff.

94. RABBI OFFICIATING AT CHRISTIAN SCIENTIST'S FUNERAL
      (Vol. XXVIII, 1918, pp. 117-119)

QUESTION: The following letter was received:

Allow me to ask your opinion in the following case, in order to know whether I have acted right or not. A member of our Temple recently died. Upon her death, I learned that she had been a devout Christian Scientist. Her husband, who is still living, is a Christian Scientist, too. In asking me to officiate, the members of the family told me that they also expect to have at the funeral service in the home a Christian Scientist, to act in conjunction with me. Thereupon I told them that I cannot officiate at such a funeral. In addition, I was told that the woman is to be buried in a Christian cemetery. I refused to officiate for three main reasons: (1) Because the deceased was a Christian Scientist and thereby has ruled herself out of the synagogue; (2) because of the inroads Christian Science is making in Judaism; and (3) because of their intention to have a Christian Scientist participate.

Now, for my own future guidance, I shall be very grateful to you, Doctor, if I could learn whether, in your opinion, I have acted rightly, and, incidentally, whether a rabbi can properly officiate at the funeral of a Jew who is to be buried in a Christian cemetery?

ANSWER: In replying to your letter just received, let me state my full approval of the attitude you took in refusing to officiate at the funeral of a Christian Scientist who was the wife of a Christian Scientist; particularly so in view of the fact that a Christian Scientist was to officiate with you at the funeral service.

Your three reasons are well taken. Moreover, the husband who, being also a Christian Scientist, has his wife buried in a Christian cemetery, shows by this very fact that he wants both himself and his deceased wife classed among Christians. No rabbi ought to officiate in such a case. That almost amounts to a desecration of the Jewish faith, a **Chilul Hashem**; and the rabbi is expected to uphold the honor of the synagogue.

K. Kohler

(Vol. XXVIII, 1918, pp. 118-119)

In answer to the following question submitted to Dr. Kohler for opinion: Shall a rabbi officiate at a funeral of a Jewish woman who was a believer in Christian Science, when the husband, also a devotee of that cult, desires that the woman be buried in a Christian cemetery and that a Christian Scientist should officiate with the rabbi?

Dr. Kohler insists emphatically that for a rabbi to officiate would be a **Chilul Hashem**, and therefore he would not permit it. Now the scholarly Doctor has certainly the plain letter of the Jewish Law on his side. The oldest source in Evel Rabbati 2.10, says: "Those that separate themselves from the community (and **Yad**,

Hil. Evel 1, and Yoreh De-a 34.5 add: and the **mumarim**
and **mutarim**, apostates and traducers)--one should not
attend to them at all at their funeral; the very brothers and nearest relatives should dress in white and eat
and drink and rejoice, as it is written (Psalm 139:21):
'I hate them, O Lord, that hate Thee.'"

Now I am sure that Dr. Kohler would be the last one
to abide by the letter of the law when the spirit and
intent thereof is contrary to our conception. It is a
fact that the Talmudic teachers were lenient with the
mumar. They considered him a sinner, who, "though he
sinned is still a Jew" (Sanh. 44a). Thus, a **mumar** is
required to give a **Get** to his wife, and **Chalitsa** to the
deceased brother's wife; as a first-born, he receives
twofold share, etc. (Even Ha-ezer 129.16; **ibid.**, 159).
Even meat slaughtered by a **mumar** is permissible for the
use of a Jew (Yoreh De-a 2.2): "**Avedat achicha, lerabot
et hamumar.**"

But during the Middle Ages, when apostates such as
Nicholas Donin, Pablo Christiani, Henrique Numes, Joseph
Pfefferkorn, and others, made the lives of their former
brothers miserable by their vile slanders and malicious
calumnies, these severe laws against the **mumarim** were
instituted. Thus, we find everywhere alongside the
mumarim also the **mutarim** as a companion (see **Tosefta**,
San. 13.5; Bavli, R.H. 17a; Gittin, 45b; Yoreh De-a
158). Like unto the **malshinim** of old, they were to
receive less consideration than one born a Gentile, over
whom funeral services may be held (Yer. Gittin 5, 47;
Bavli, Gittin 6; Yoreh De-a 367.1): "**Mipenei darchei
shalom lehaspidan.**"

It is evident that a Christian Scientist of today
cannot be classed with the **mumar** of medieval ages. They
are not **mumarim lehach-is** but **mumarim lete-avon**, purely
from personal reasons, and they are considered like
Jews. Thus, Rabbenu Gershom, we find, did mourn over
his son, who became an apostate (see **Hagahot Asheri**, to
Mo-ed Katan 25, ch. 59). Certainly none of us will subscribe to the injunction in Evel Rabbati and Yoreh De-a
to rejoice at the death of a **mumar**. Nor would we follow
the advice stated in Avoda Zara 27b, i.e., "**Moridin velo
ma-alin,**" or the rule found in Yoreh De-a 158 ("**Mitzvah
lehorgam**"). Let us be careful not to antagonize the
modern **mumarim**--Christian Scientists--too much. Let us
not push them away from us with both hands. Let us not
make the same mistake that was made once before with the
Samaritans. If we must push them away with the left
hand, let us be sure to pull them back immediately with
the right hand.

J. Rappaport

(Vol. XXIX, 1919, p. 75)

Regarding the opinion I expressed that a Christian Scientist who has expressly declared and demonstratively showed that he with his wife wanted to be classed among the adherents of Christianity should not be dignified by a Jewish funeral, I would appeal to the members of the Conference to decide whether they side with me or with the adverse view of Rabbi Julius Rappaport. I also believe in the Talmudic maxim, "We should push away with the left hand and pull back with the right hand" (Sanh. 207b, and elsewhere). I would apply it to the Christian Scientist, in general, who has not left the Jewish fold altogether; but as the one in the case before us wanted to have "no share in the God of Jacob," there is no reason for us to grant him the honor of a Jewish burial.

K. Kohler

95. BURIAL ON A HOLY DAY
(Vol. XXXI, 1921, pp. 53-55)

The seventh day of Passover this year (1921) having fallen on a Friday and the first day of Shavuot on a Sunday, an inconvenience was caused in funerals which had to be postponed two days. The question, whether a funeral may be held on a holy day, was answered exhaustively on a similar occasion by the present writer in the **American Israelite**, April 28, 1910, and October 10, 1912. The arguments shall be briefly repeated and a few new references added.

The question is definitely answered by reference to Talmud, Beitsa 6a, codified in **Shulchan Aruch**, Orach Chayim 256.1-3, which clearly says: "If a body has to be buried on the first holy day, non-Jews shall perform the labor, even if the death occurred on the same day, and it would be possible without danger of decomposition to keep the body until the next day. This, however, refers only to the work of making shrouds, while the dressing of the body, heating of water for washing it, carrying out the body and placing it in the grave may be done by Jews. If one died on the first holy day, it is prohibited to keep the body overnight[1] until the second holy

---

[1] The Rabbis declare it as a duty, based on Deut. 21:23, to bury the dead on the day of the death (Sanh. 46a; Yoreh De-a 357.1). For the account of the controversy

day in order that Jews may perform the services at the funeral."

This should settle the question. Only a few references to actual practice shall be added because of their special significance. Eleazar Fleckeles, Acting Chief Rabbi of Prague (**Jewish Enc.** V, 408), known as an opponent of the synagogue reforms introduced in the Hamburg Temple and otherwise as a rigorist in ritual law, was buried on the seventh day of Passover, 1826 (**Jahrb. Jued. Lit. Gesellsch.** X, 29, 1913). Mendel Kargau of Fuerth, one of the last representatives of Orthodoxy in this historic community, was buried on the first day of Rosh Hashana, 1842 (**ibid.**, VIII, 118, 1911). One must not forget that in these Orthodox centers funerals were conducted by the **Chevra Kadisha**, which included the most Orthodox elements so much so that they often came in conflict with the sanitary authorities, who--as in the case of early burial or of burying the dead on the bare ground--vetoed practices hallowed by tradition (see **Jewish Enc.** VI, 300). If Fuerth and Prague allowed funerals of rabbis celebrated for their orthodoxy to be held on holy days, public sentiment did not take any umbrage at it. Indeed, we find Shabbetai Cohen, the noted rigorist among the glossarists of the **Shulchan Aruch** (17th century) speak of a funeral on holy days as a common practice to which he has only the one objection that Jews, while not performing the labor of digging the grave, allow themselves the right to fill it in (Yoreh De-a 339.7). Just to prove the general practice, the following cases may be quoted at random: The Scotch Missionaries, McCheyne and Bonar, visiting Tarnapol, October 1, 1839, which was the festival of Shemini Atseret, witnessed a funeral in that city which persecuted S.L. Rappaport as a radical reformer (**Mission of Inquiry**, p. 447, Philadelphia, 1843). Simon Tarlau, son-in-law of Elijah Guttmacher of Graetz, the last "Wunderrabbi" in Germany, died September 29, 1886, and was buried on the next day, which was the first day of Rosh Hashana (**Der Israelit**, 1886, p. 1413). Two cases of the same kind are reported among the Orthodox of S.R. Hirsch's "Mensch-Jisroel" school (**ibid.**, 1893, p. 643, and 1920, no. 22, p. 3), and one from the darkest Chasidic corner of what used to be northern Hungary, where R. Hirsch Spira of Muncacz died on the first day of Sukkot and was buried on the same day (**Der Isr.**,

---

between Jacob Emden and Moses Mendelsohn on the question of how far the Jews must yield to the State law which required postponement of the funeral, see Graetz, **Gesch.** XI, 32; **Sulamith** IV, 2, pp. 155-159. Moses Sofer (Responsa to Yoreh De-a, no. 338) still insists on this practice.

1913, no. 45, p. 9). For completeness, R. Menachem Azariah Meir Castelnuovo of Leghorn may be quoted (1722-1847). He was probably the last legal authority of Italy, and uncompromisingly Orthodox, and he reported a funeral on the first day of Rosh Hashana (**Misgeret Hashulchan**, p. 207a, Leghorn, 1840).

The only question to be considered would be the influence on the public, that--not knowing the clear law and the well-established practice--would consider a funeral on a holy day a violation of sacred sentiment, and the case would therefore fall under the prohibition of "**Asur lechacham lehatir davar hatamuah, shenir-eh lerabim shehitir et ha-asur**" (Yoreh De-a 242.1), giving offense to religious people.

To this we have to answer that a rigorist such as Shebbetai Cohen declares that this does not comprise a case in which reasons for the decisions are given (ibid., 17) and that we cannot be held responsible for the ignorance of the public or even of an occasional rabbi. Finally, even rigorous authorities declare that we have no right to increase the burden of the law, as is strongly expressed in the Talmudic phrase: "**Lo dayecha ma she-asera lecha haTorah, ela she-ata mevakesh la-asor aleicha devarim hamutarim**" (Yer. Nedarim IX.1). And the greatest casuist of modern times, Chayim Hezekiah Medini (born in Jerusalem, 1834, died in Hebron, 1904), also a rigorist, who would not allow a kindergarten to be opened in Hebron, states: The rabbis have no right to prohibit something which is clearly permitted in the law ("**Davar shehetero meforash baTorah, ein beyad chachamim le-esor**," Sedeh Chemed, p. 49a, Warsaw, 1896).

G. Deutsch

(Vol. XXXII, 1922, p. 80)

Resolved, that the Central Conference of American Rabbis disapprove of conducting Jewish funerals on our holy days, except where the immediate burial is demanded in the interest of public health.

Samuel S. Cohon
Henry Englander
Abraham J. Feldman

Although in the Codes of Jewish Law there is no express prohibition against conducting funerals on the festivals (**Yearbook**, vol. XXXI, p. 53), yet, in deference to Jewish custom and sentiment, your Committee is of the opinion that the members of the Central Conference of American Rabbis should abstain from conducting funerals on these days, except where public health demands.

The recommendation of the Committee was adopted.

Resolution adopted by the CCAR

96. BURIAL OF JEWS IN SECTION OF GENERAL CEMETERY
(Vol. XXVII, 1917, p. 88)

The following answers were given to a colleague who submitted a series of questions in regard to burial rites.

(a) That the Jews, whether Orthodox or liberal, may bury their dead in a section of a cemetery in which the greater part is devoted to the burial of non-Jews is evidenced by the story of the Cave of Machpelah which, according to Genesis 23, formed part of the burial place of the Hittites. It was separated, however, by a field with its trees, as verse 17 shows. And it seems that the Jews in the Middle Ages loved to plant trees in their cemeteries, so that we find them called by Christian writers "**Hortus Judaeorum**," the "Garden of the Jews" (see Abrahams, **Jewish Life in the Middle Ages**, p. 77).

(b) and (c) In Biblical times the better classes had their family sepulchres (see, among others, Gen. 49:31; I Kings 13:22); and the burial place of the fathers endeared the desolate cities to the Jews (Neh. 2:3). Only the common people seemed to have had a common burial place (II Kings 23:6; Jer. 26:23; compare the Potter's Field in Matt. 27:7).

Later on, the acquisition of a cemetery became one of the first obligations of a Jewish congregation, as may be learned from the significant words of Ruth: "Where thou diest, will I die, and there will I be buried" (Ruth 1:17), and to visit the father's grave on special occasions was one of the religious practices of the Jew, prayers being offered there. Of course, the Jewish cemetery was always to be distinguished from the

non-Jewish ones--intrinsically, as it was to be treated
with special marks of reverence due to the sacred character of the surroundings of the dead; and externally,
as none of the signs and symbols of other creeds could
have a place there.   Thus, naturally, a separate place
was required for the Jewish cemetery.   In fact, by a
Talmudic law codified in Yoreh De-a 362.5, and based on
II Kings 13:21 (see Sanh. 47a), the burial of a wicked
person alongside of a righteous one is also regarded as
wrong.   But no law exists in our Rabbinic codes requiring either walls or fences to separate the Jewish cemetery from another one.   The walls or fences were, however, found necessary for the protection of the graves
against violation by the mobs, especially frequent during the Dark Ages.   Consequently, any form of separation, whether by granite posts or by considerably larger
pathways distinguishing the Jewish section from the
Christian ones, is sufficient.

K. Kohler and Jacob Z. Lauterbach

See also:

S.B. Freehof, "Communal Mausoleums," **Reform   Responsa**, pp. 158ff.

97.   BURIAL OF A PROSPECTIVE CONVERT
(Vol. XCI, 1981, pp. 71-72)

QUESTION: May an individual who is in the process
of converting to Judaism, but has not yet been
converted, be buried in a Jewish cemetery?   Is
his/her status different from an unconverted Gentile who has no such intentions?   (Rabbi Stephen E.
Fisch, Corpus Christi, Texas)

ANSWER: The status of a Jewish cemetery in Jewish law
has been discussed by Solomon B. Freehof in a full responsum (**Current Reform Responsa**, pp. 154ff).   It is
clear from this responsum that we are willing to bury
the non-Jewish spouse of a Jewish man or wife, that we
do so in order to maintain peace within the family, and
that this is possible because of the vague status of a
cemetery in Jewish law as a separate entity.   Naturally,
no Christian rites or symbols may be used.

In this case, however, we are not dealing with the non-Jewish husband or wife of a Jew, but with a non-Jew who simply plans to convert and has not been able to fulfill this wish at the time of death. We certainly applaud such intent and praise it as we would anyone studying Judaism for its own sake; however, until the time of conversion we cannot be sure of the individual's intent. Most converts come to us with an open mind, a desire to become Jewish, but have had little opportunity to confirm their notions of Judaism. As Reform Jews, we have emphasized study and an intellectual approach to our religion. Conversion has followed a thorough course of study. This is in contrast to the Orthodox approach which has emphasized ritual and felt it sufficient if the convert underwent the proper rituals with the thought that further study would follow later. Traditional Jewish law has placed its emphasis on ritual and it was perfectly possible for someone to convert to Judaism by undergoing **Mila** (for males) and **Tevila** along with a minimum of information (Yev. 46bff; **Yad**, Isurei Bi-a 13.7, 145, Shab. 135a; **Sh.A.**, Yoreh De-a). It is in that way that we should understand the story of Hillel and the prospective convert who wished to learn about Judaism while standing on one foot.

A convert who is sincere and really wishes to convert to Judaism could be simply converted. There is nothing within traditional or Reform Judaism which would prevent us from going ahead with the conversion at a time of serious life-threatening illness and thus bring the person into Judaism. This might then provide peace of mind to the dying individual. That person would then be buried as any other Jew. If, however, the individual died suddenly and unexpectedly we could not, in good conscience, bury that person in a Jewish cemetery as this individual at that time has only a preliminary relationship to Judaism.

Walter Jacob, Chairman
Leonard S. Kravitz
W. Gunther Plaut
Harry A. Roth
Rav A. Soloff
Bernard Zlotowitz

98. BURIAL OF NON-JEWISH WIVES IN JEWISH CEMETERIES
(Vol. XXIV, 1914, p. 154)

Only two days ago a case was reported to your Committee where a non-Jewish woman, legally married to a member of the Jewish community, died, and the question was raised, whether she might be buried in a Jewish cemetery. During my ministry in New York City I had many such cases, and I always decided in the affirmative. I took the stand that, unlike the Catholics, our cemeteries are **not as a whole consecrated ground**, in the sense that those not of the Jewish faith are excluded from them. Only the spot where the body is interred becomes sacred thereby. If, then, a Jew owns a lot in a cemetery, his right to bury his wife there is--from the Jewish standpoint--indisputable, unless the congregation or association which sells the lot has made stipulations or conditions forbidding the burial of non-Jews in the cemetery. Of course, it is understood that a non-Jewish service or symbols of another faith are prohibited.

I have here stated only my individual opinion. I would repeat my urgent request of last year, that the members of the Conference consult with this Committee in all difficult cases, in order that in the future it may become the clearinghouse for all important ritual and theological questions.

K. Kohler

(Vol. XXVI, 1916, pp. 133-134)

Your communication asking for my opinion concerning the **burial in a Jewish cemetery of non-Jewish wives or husbands** married to Jews and their children was duly received yesterday, and in answer thereto I would refer you to several reports of mine as Chairman of the Responsa Committee of the Central Conference of American Rabbis. I have always in my practice taken the stand that, while mixed marriages should not be sanctioned by the rabbi, the civil law which declares them as valid must be recognized by us to the extent that the non-Jewish wife or husband should be entitled to the right of being buried alongside the Jewish husband or wife on the plot owned by the one or the other in the Jewish cemetery. Still greater claim have their children to a regular Jewish burial, whether they have been brought up as Jews or not. Accordingly, I would have your cemetery rules changed in the sense stated.

Quite different is my view concerning the Jew who is--on account of his marriage to a non-Jewish person--to be interred in a non-Jewish cemetery. By this very fact evidence seems to be given in favor of his non-Jewish allegiance, and the rabbi has no business to officiate at his funeral in a non-Jewish cemetery.

Whether the congregational bylaws--reading that members who contract a forbidden marriage forfeit their membership, and that no person married to a non-Jew may be a member of the congregation--should be changed, is, in my opinion, an altogether different question. It seems to me that the law should stand. **Forbidden marriages** have disastrous results, especially in regard to the offspring. On the other hand, the second sentence simply aims at **preventing** mixed marriages in the congregation, but does not imply that they entail forfeiture of membership when concluded **before** the affiliation to the congregation. Self-preservation dictates the retention of the bylaw.

K. Kohler and Jacob Z. Lauterbach

(Vol. XXIX, 1919, pp. 77-78)

On January 2, I was asked for my opinion, and, at the same time, for the Jewish law on the following case: About a year ago a brother of a member of the congregation died in a distant town, and was buried on the latter's lot. Afterwards his wife died, and her wish was to be buried next to her husband. She being a Christian, the Board of Trustees wants to do nothing contrary to Jewish law and custom, and, therefore, waits for a decision, as the brother-in-law is willing to have her buried on his lot.

I answered as follows: There is no law forbidding a non-Jew to be buried in a Jewish cemetery. While there are congregations whose constitution expressly prohibits non-Jews (respectively, non-Jewish wives or husbands) to be buried in their cemeteries, such restrictions were undoubtedly made with the view of preventing mixed marriages in the congregation. At the same time, it cannot be denied that in case a Jew (whether a member of the congregation or not) has married--contrary to the Jewish law--a non-Jewish woman, she, as his legally married wife, has a just claim to being buried alongside of her husband on the plot owned by him or given him for burial by his brother. As rabbi of Temple Beth El in New York, I have frequently given this decision, and this view has been fully endorsed by my congregation.

In further explanation of this opinion I wish to say that the Talmudic rule, based on ancient practice, is that the wicked should not be buried next to the righteous, and therefore executed criminals had a special place assigned to them for burial (Sanh. 46-47a). But it is not likely that a non-Jew should ever have been buried in a Jewish cemetery, unless perhaps in the case of an unrecognized body found unburied, a **Met Mitzvah**, which humanitarian law (to judge from Philo, M. II, 629) applies to non-Jews as well.[1]

Another point for consideration is that we have no consecrated ground which would exclude non-Jews. Each plot is consecrated--**asur bahana-a**--by the body there. Hence, the owner of the plot ought to have full disposal of the same. It is his family plot.

K. Kohler

(Vol. XXIX, 1919, pp. 80-85)

The following question was submitted to me by a southern congregation:

> About a year ago a brother of one of the members of our congregation died in a distant town, and his remains were brought to this city and buried on the lot of this member of our congregation. The wife of the deceased has died, and it was her wish that her remains be buried next to her husband. She being a Christian, the Board of Trustees wants to do nothing contrary to Jewish law and custom, and desires higher authority. The member of our congregation who owns the lot is willing to bury the Christian wife of his brother on the lot. I want to make it plain that the brother of the member of our congregation who is now buried on the lot was not a member of our congregation, and did not own a lot in our

---

[1] It is superfluous to say that the halachic rule (Gittin 61a; Yer. Gittin V, 47c), **"Koverim metei Akum im metei Yisra-el"** means that the heathen (non-Jewish) dead may be buried simultaneously with the Jewish dead, but not alongside of them. The deprecatory view of heathen graves (Yev. 61b) with reference to Ezek. 34:31 has, of course, no bearing on Christians, who are regarded as **Benei Noach** (see responsa of Isaac ben Sheshet, and others).

cemetery.   In addition to your opinion, we
would like to have the Jewish law on the subject also.

The following is my reply:

My opinion is of no consequence in the matter; nor
is it germane to the question proposed whether the man
whose Christian wife is to be buried in the Jewish cemetery was a member of the congregation or not.   Such a
question is to be decided on the ground of financial
considerations and congregational policy, and would
apply to Jews and non-Jews alike.   The only point under
consideration is, what Jewish law and congregational
practice--the latter as precedent--furnish as arguments.

Bible

The most ancient records prove that it was a sacred
duty for the Jew to be buried with members of his family
in a burial ground exclusively owned by him and reserved
exclusively for the members of his family.   Abraham buys
the cave of Machpelah, declining the offer of the Hittites to use "the choicest of their sepulchres" for the
burial of Sarah, because he wishes to have a burial
place of his own as unlimited holding (**Achuzat Kever**)
(Gen. 23:4,6,20).   Jacob solemnly adjures his son Joseph
to go to considerable trouble to transport his body to
Canaan so that he may sleep with his fathers (Gen.
47:30).   It is certainly told with designed emphasis
that this was Jacob's dying wish (**ibid.**, 50:25),
which--as is twice emphatically related--was carried out
(Ex. 13:19; Joshua 24:32).   On this occasion we are also
told that Joshua and the High Priest Eleazar were buried
"on their inheritance," which is synonymous with
Abraham's **Achuzat Kever** (Joshua 24:30,33).
It was evidently the custom of wealthy and prominent men to provide during their lifetime an artistical-
ly constructed burial place, a mausoleum, usually hewn
in the rocks, as we learn from the denunciation of
Isaiah of Shevna, the king's chancellor, who "has hewed
out a sepulchre on high" (Isa. 22:16).   The same is told
in the New Testament (Matthew 27:60) of Joseph of
Arimathea, in whose tomb Jesus was buried.   Existing
monuments in Palestine bear testimony to the correctness
of these reports.   In keeping with these reports of the
sacredness of family tombs is the consolation given by
Jeremiah (34:5) to the exiled and blinded king Zedekiah,
that he shall be honored by the ceremonies like those
performed in honor of "his fathers, the former kings" in
their crematories, an obscure passage, which, however,
must refer to the practice of burning valuable articles

in the possession of the deceased (Avoda Zara 11a). All these passages prove that in Biblical times the burial places were in the private possession of the families, destined for the members of the family exclusively, and it is impossible to decide whether non-Jewish members of the family were also laid there to rest. At any rate, the community as such could have had no power in the matter.

Talmud

The only passage found in the Talmud which has a bearing on the subject (Bavli, Gittin 61a) reads: "We shall bury the dead of the non-Jews with the dead of the Jews for the sake of peace" (meaning, probably, for the sake of maintaining amicable relations with our neighbors, but it may also mean, on the ground of humanitarian principles; see Yevamot 15a). The question is whether the word **im**, translated as "with," means "just as" or "by the side of." Rashi, the classic commentator of the Talmud, decides in favor of the former view, and he is supported by another passage (Sanhedrin 47a): "We shall not bury a wicked man by the side of a righteous man," in which case the word **etsel** is used. Rashi also says: "We shall bury the non-Jews not in the cemetery of the Jews, but we shall attend to their burial when bodies of non-Jews are found slain by the side of the bodies of Jews." The view of Rashi is supported by the fact that in parallel texts (Tosefta, Gittin 5.5, ed. Zuckermandel, p. 328; Yer. Gittin 47c), the law merely reads: "We shall bury the bodies of non-Jews," omitting the dubious phrase "with those of Jews." In this form the law has been recorded in the codes (Yoreh De-a 367.1). R. Nissim of Gerona (14th century) opposes Rashi in one respect, extending the duty to assist in the burial of non-Jews to all cases, and not restricting it to a case when Jews and non-Jews are found slain side by side, but even he decides against burying them in a Jewish cemetery (R. Nissim, **Novellae**, Gittin, p. 34d, ed. Prague, 1810; see also **Beit Yosef**, Yoreh De-a 367). The same view may be supposed to be that of the **Tosafot** (Chullin 7b), though it is not expressly stated. The attempt of Rabbi M. Loewy of Temesvar to read such a permission into Maimonides' slight mention of the duty to take part in the burial of non-Jews (Hilchot Evel 14.2; Hilchot Melachim 10.2) is entirely arbitrary (**Neuzeit**, 1884, p. 43). The only legal authority who clearly permits the burial of non-Jews in a Jewish cemetery, though in a separate plot, is Joel Sirkes (**Bayit Chadash**, Yoreh De-a 151). This author, who died as Rabbi of Cracow in 1640, witnessed the frequent butcheries in Poland, caused by rebellious and foreign invasions, and ruled probably from actual occurrences, when bodies of murdered Jews and non-Jews were found heaped up in the same place. The following case is only remotely connected with the question, but deserves a place here, because Moses Sofer, who rendered the decision, is a relatively modern author (1762-1839) of high standing in the Orthodox world. The case submitted to him was that of a Jewish soldier who died in a military hospital and upon whose body a crucifix was found, so that it seemed almost certain that he had at one time become a convert to Christianity. Moses Sofer decided, nevertheless, that the body should be buried in the Jewish cemetery (**Chatam Sofer**, Yoreh De-a 341).

Precedents

A Venetian Christian who died in Avlona of the plague in 1515, requested on his deathbed that he be buried in a Jewish cemetery, because he feared that, being a Roman Catholic, the Greek Catholic Christians of the place would throw his body to the beasts. His request was granted (**Vesillo Israelitico**, 1888, pp. 190-191). Stephen de Werbocz, ex-Palatine of Hungary, who died in Buda (Ofen) in 1541, was buried in the Jewish cemetery. The reason is not clear, but was probably his conversion to Islam (Busch, **Jahrbuch** V, 83). Clearer is the case of a Mohammedan who died in Czernowitz, Bukowina, in 1869. He was buried in the Jewish cemetery because neither the Greeks nor the Roman Catholics would bury him in their cemeteries (**Am. Isr.**, June 11, 1908). Similar was the case of an unattached Catholic who was buried in the Jewish cemetery of Prague, which is governed by the strictly conservative **Chevra Kadisha** of this historic community. The man had left the Catholic Church because that was the only way in which the Austrian law allowed him to marry a Jewess (**Allgemeine Zeitung des Judentums**, 1871, p. 720). The congregation of Orgjejew, Besarabia, granted to a Mohammedan a burial in its cemetery, but yielded to the rabbi who vetoed its resolution because the body was buried beyond the fence (Hasman, **Hebrew Daily**, 1909, no. 208). Neil Primrose, the son of Lord Roseberry and of Hannah de Rothschild, who was killed in action in Palestine as a member of the Jewish Legion, was buried in the Jewish cemetery of Ramleh, although he was a professing Christian (**Jewish Courier**, Chicago, Dec. 2, 1917). Similar is the case of Moses S. Wile, the son of a Jewish father and a Christian mother, and raised as a Christian, who was buried in a Jewish cemetery (**Am. Isr.**, March 4, 1904). According to Jewish law, Neil Primrose would be regarded as a Jew, and Moses Wile as a non-Jew. The congregation of Wittenburg, Mecklenburg, buried in its cemetery a Protestant whose family objected when their Christian pastor ruled that the corpse be buried in a corner of the Protestant cemetery but refused to sell an adjoining grave to the widow (Oest. Wochenschrift, 1913, p. 504). A woman in Darmstadt who had converted to Christianity, but had expressed the wish to be buried in a Jewish cemetery, was granted this desire on the ground that her wish signified a return to Judaism (Allg. Zeitg. d. Judentums, 1889, p. 361). A Jew of Ancona, who had declared himself a Unitarian, though he never formally affiliated with that church, was refused burial in the Jewish cemetery of that city (Educatore Israelita 20, 1872, pp. 145-146). The Orthodox Chief Rabbi of Amsterdam, Joseph H. Duenner, refused to bury the child of a mixed marriage in the Jewish cemetery, although the mother, a Christian by birth, had converted to Judaism, and the child was circumcised. Rabbi Duenner did not recognize the conversion performed by Rabbi Rahmer of Magdeburg, a liberal, as valid, and therefore considered the child, as born of a Christian mother, a non-Jew (Der Israelit, 1883, p. 322). The Rabbinate of London rendered the same decision in an identical case (Allg. Zeitg. des Judentums, 1884, p. 302). The congregation of Hamburg took in a similar case a lenient view, in spite of the strong protest of the Orthodox element (ibid., 1865, p. 289). Rabbi A. Da Fano of Milan adopted a compromise, allowing such a burial, but insisting that the corpse be circumcised (Vessillo Isr., 1892, p. 384).

Similar cases in America are reported from Memphis, Tennessee, where such a child, after some opposition, was granted burial in the Jewish cemetery (Am. Isr., Nov. 3, 1876); while in Grand Rapids, Michigan, the rabbi refused burial. I.M. Wise decided against this attitude, declaring that while the Talmud does not consider the child a Jew, he is so in our eyes, because we consider civil marriage as legal (ibid., Sept. 4, 1874). In neither of the last two cases is it stated whether the child was a male and whether circumcision had been performed. Rabbi B. Schick of Temesvar, Hungary, rendered a negative decision in a similar case, and wrote a pamphlet concerning it (B. Schick, Notgedrungene Bemerkungen zum Jahresbericht der Temesvar Chewra Kadischa, 1903, Temesvar, 1904; see Der Israelit, 1904, p. 832).

Jews Buried in Non-Jewish Cemeteries

The completeness of the argument demands a discussion of the opposite case, namely, the burial of Jews in non-Jewish cemeteries. Sentiment and practice are usually against it. In Rendsburg-Schleswig, the Jewish congregation protested against it (Allg. Zeitg. des

Judentums, 1872, p. 49). In Nuremberg, which had in those days no Jewish cemetery, the pastor protested (Ziemlich, Geschichte der Juden in Nuremberg, p. 8). In M. Csaete, Hungary, the Jews, though forming an Orthodox congregation, use a cemetery in common with the Christians (Der Israelit, 1912, no. 8). Marcus Levy, Mayor of Aurora, Indiana, was buried in the local cemetery, and Isaac M. Wise approved of it indirectly, lecturing in Aurora for the benefit of a monument to be erected to the deceased (Israelite, Feb. 20, 1873). The "Oberrat" of Baden, on the other hand, refused the offer of the city to have the Jewish soldiers, killed in the war, buried in a special plot of the communal cemetery together with their Christian comrades (Allg. Zeitg. des Judentums, 1914, no. 41). Rev. Isaac Leeser of Philadelphia strongly condemned the action of Rev. Jacob de Solla, who had officiated at the funeral of a Jew in a non-denominational cemetery, and obtained an opinion to this effect from Chief Rabbis Abraham B. Piperno of Leghorn and Nathan Adler of London. He admitted, however, that he had been guilty of the same offense before, giving as an excuse that it was done before a religious authority had rendered a negative decision (Occident XXVI, 1863, pp. 181-187, 266-272).

Cases Analogous to the Proposed Question

Rabbi B. Illowy gave a favorable opinion in the case of a woman born a Christian who had married a Jew, on the grounds that she had converted, when Orthodox extremists in Nashville, Tennessee, objected even to this (Occident XIV, 1856, p. 84-88). Rabbi Samfield of Memphis, Tennessee, rendered a decision favorable to the burial of non-Jewish members of a family in Jewish family lots (Am. Isr., Feb. 5, 1875). The Orthodox rabbi of Breslau, F. Rosenthal, once permitted the remains of a cremated corpse of the Christian wife to be buried with her Jewish husband, because these remains were not a corpse (Jued. Presse, 1911, p. 465). He was still more liberal when he permitted a baptized Jew to be buried in this cemetery upon the request of his wife, who had remained a Jewess (Deutsche Isr. Zeitg., 1913, no. 40). The congregations of Berlin (1883), of Leipzig (1884), and of Dresden (1897) passed resolutions permitting the non-Jewish parties in a mixed marriage to be buried in the Jewish cemetery (Allg. Z. d. J., 1884, p. 10; 1885, p. 319; 1897, no. 26). The Rabbinate of Leghorn rendered an adverse opinion, which, however, was not respected by the congregation (Vessillo Isr., 1892, pp. 321-322).

Conclusion

I.   The Bible gives no clear evidence by which the question can be decided, though--speaking of family graves--its testimony would be rather negative.

II.   The Talmudic writings do not decide the case clearly, but glossarists and codifiers derive from the Talmud a negative view, with the exception of one authority who limits the burial of non-Jews in Jewish cemeteries to emergency cases, such as battles and epidemics.

III. The practice in modern congregations is divided on this point as on others--the Orthodox congregations taking a negative view, and the liberal congregations an affirmative view.

IV.   The question of congregational policy--and its relation to the danger of encouraging intermarriage or religious indifference--has to be decided on the ground of local conditions and does not lie within the line of theological argument.

G. Deutsch

(Vol. XLVI, 1936, pp. 124-126)

The member of the Conference who submitted this inquiry dealt with the case of a non-Jewish woman who is an active member of a Christian church. He took his stand upon the responsum of the late Dr. Kohler (**Yearbook XXVI**, 1916, p. 133; cited in the **Rabbi's Manual**, 1928, p. 187), according to which such burial was permissible. He inquired, however, whether her Christian minister "was to be permitted to officiate at her grave in the Jewish cemetery," or whether it should be stipulated "that she may be buried alongside her Jewish husband only if the commitment service is conducted by a rabbi."

Further information showed that the Jewish husband--since his marriage 32 years prior to his demise-- "was never a member of the Temple and rarely attended its services; only a few times did he come to the services on the High Holy Days." During this period his wife continued (and still does so) to be an active member of her church, but on the other hand--let it be stated to her credit--she tried to persuade her husband "to preserve his attachment to the Jewish people." And now, for sentimental reasons, she would like to be permitted to be buried in due course near her husband.

ANSWER: Dr. Kohler in his above-mentioned responsum has not at all discussed the data pertaining to Jewish law and custom. He only indicated his personal stand that "while mixed marriages should not be sanctioned by the rabbi, the civil law, which declares them as valid, must be recognized by us to that extent that the non-Jewish wife or husband should be entitled to the right of being buried alongside the Jewish husband or wife, on the plot owned by the one or the other in the Jewish cemetery." This argument is indeed not very logical, because the civil marriage has nothing to do with the Jewish cemetery, which is a part of the Jewish **religious organization.** The latter can so formulate its rules and regulations as not to permit such a burial, although fully recognizing the validity of a mixed marriage with regard to all marital affairs.

In this responsum we further read that if a Jew wants to be buried in a non-Jewish cemetery (say next to his Christian wife), "by this very fact evidence seems to be given in favor of his non-Jewish allegiance and the rabbi has no business to officiate at his funeral in a non-Jewish cemetery." Here the contradiction becomes evident by the realization that a cemetery is a **religious place** after all. Why, then, should the previous case be different? Either or: either it is assumed that the cemetery is non-religious ground, then logically a Jewish husband of a Gentile wife could be buried in a Christian cemetery even with the rabbi officiating; or, if the argument is that the cemetery is the **religious property** of a given denomination, then a non-Jewish wife should not be buried in a Jewish cemetery.

To discuss here at length the Jewish traditional data, would not be feasible. (See further another decision by Dr. Kohler, **Yearbook** XXIX, 1919, pp. 77-78, and Dr. Deutsch's responsum, **ibid.**, pp. 80-85; the latter discusses more fully the available data, but the matter needs still further elucidation.) But in the above case, would it be proper to bury a woman, who is "an active member of a Christian church" in a Jewish cemetery? Even according to Dr. Kohler, is this latter fact not **evidence enough for her "non-Jewish allegiance"**? Such a person, whose religious convictions should be respected, could rightly claim that her tombstone should have the symbol of her church, viz., the Cross. There is further involved the point of her clergyman officiating at the funeral. Being an active member of her church, she has a perfect right then to have her last rites performed by the accredited representative of her religion. All this tends therefore to the positive conclusion that her last resting place should not be in the Jewish cemetery, but in the burial ground of her church.

The rabbi should therefore advise the woman concerned that in view of her attachment to her religion--
which should be fully respected--arrangements for her
burial should be made with the authorities of her
church. It is not a pleasant task for the rabbi to do
so, considering the natural marital sentiments involved;
however, in order to obviate an effacement of the religious boundaries, one should take a clear stand in such
matters. In the long run, courage and honesty prevail
over weak compromises.

Jacob Mann and Majority of Committee

(Vol. XLVI, 1936, pp. 127-129)

The question of burial of a non-Jewish wife beside
her Jewish husband in a Jewish cemetery, as submitted by
the chairman of the Committee on Responsa, has been
decided in the affirmative by the late Dr. Kohler (Yearbook, vol. 26, p. 133). But now the question is proposed, "If burial is to be permitted, shall it be stipulated that a rabbi should be required to read the commitment service?"
Prof. Mann emphatically opposes Dr. Kohler's decision to permit burial of the non-Jewish wife in the
Jewish cemetery, because Dr. Kohler adduces "no traditional authorities on Jewish law and custom" in support
of his opinion, which therefore must be considered as
purely personal sentiment. Moreover, Dr. Mann alleges
that Dr. Kohler's reason in permitting the burial of
non-Jews in the Jewish cemetery on the ground that we
should respect the civil law which legalizes mixed marriages, "is indeed not a very logical argument." Dr.
Mann emphatically avers that "courage and honesty should
prevail over weak compromises," and insists that burial
of the non-Jewish wife should be denied in a Jewish
cemetery. However, the argument that it is simply a
"personal stand without any data pertaining to Jewish
law and custom" may be made against Dr. Mann himself;
for neither does he adduce any "Jewish traditional data"
in support of his decision, which therefore makes it
merely personal.
There are ample data showing the following clearly
and plainly.
A. It is proper to support the destitute...to
utter lamentation (funeral rites) and bury non-Jewish
dead with (im) Jewish dead: "Maspidim vekoverin metei
Akum im metei Yisra-el mipenei darchei shalom" (Tosefta,
end of ch. 3 to Gittin).

B.   It is proper to...bury non-Jewish dead with
Jewish dead to promote relations of peace and amity:
"Vekoverin metei Akum im metei Yisra-el mipenei darchei
shalom" (B. Gittin 61a).

C.   Alfasi quotes verbatim the above (end of ch. 5
to Gittin).

D.   Maimonides in **Yad**, Hil. Evel XIV.12) also
quotes the above, but omits the words "**im metei Yisra-
el**," leaving open the question of place of burial. He
evidently took the word "**im**"--as did also Rashi--to mean
"in the same grave."

Rashi emphatically states "not in the same grave,"
disregarding the clear terms used in the original
sources.

E.   Asheri likewise quotes the same words and
decides in **Piskei Harosh** accordingly: "**maspidin vekoverin**."

F.   R. Jacob, author of **Turim**, emphatically
states: "It is not only proper because it tends to promote relations of peace, but it is a **Mitzvah**, for the
ways of the Torah are pleasant and all her paths are
peace." The original itself is not accessible to me
just now; however, all the quibbling attempts at mis-
interpretation of the plain unequivocal terms of the
original sources, where we are told "**im metei Yisra-el**,"
cannot change the meaning.

G.   It is proper to support the poor...to visit
the sick...to bury the dead of non-Jews, to utter lamentation over them (**maspidim**, funeral ritual), and to
comfort their mourners, in order to promote relations of
peace (Yoreh De-a 151.12; 335; 367).

I am, therefore, strengthened in my definite conviction that "the non-Jewish wife of a Jewish husband
may be buried alongside her husband in a Jewish cemetery," in full agreement with Dr. Kohler's decision.

As to the question in point--i.e., "whether a
Christian minister was to be permitted to officiate at
her grave in the Jewish cemetery?"--to this also I am
inclined to say: It is permissible. I believe we may
safely rely upon his sense of decency to realize that he
is in a Jewish cemetery. We should not be more strict
rigorists than the authors quoted above who permit a Jew
to officiate (**maspidin**) at the grave of a Christian.
Why then shall we refuse permission to the Christian
minister to officiate at the grave of a Christian woman
simply because the cemetery is Jewish?

Julius Rappaport

Owing to certain objections raised by a member of the committee, the following alternative procedure is suggested:

In view of the custom prevalent in several congregations to permit such burials in a Jewish cemetery, the lady in question should be informed that the interment ritual would have to be of a neutral character, and that the tombstone could not bear the symbol of her church.

Alternative procedure suggested by a dissenting member of the committee

99. NON-JEWISH BURIAL IN A JEWISH CEMETERY
(Vol. LXXIII, 1963, pp. 85-90)

QUESTION: The question of whether a Gentile wife or children of a mixed marriage may be buried in our cemeteries was answered for the Conference by Dr. Kaufmann Kohler in 1914, and reprinted in the **Rabbi's Manual**.
      The answer, although substantially correct, needs some elaboration and development. In recent years we have been getting many more and slightly different inquiries on the matter. For example: May the Christian father of an unconverted Gentile married to a Jew be buried in a Jewish cemetery? The status of the Jewish cemetery in the Jewish legal tradition and the permissibility of burying non-Jews in it need fuller discussion than has been hitherto available to the Conference.

ANSWER: Let us first consider the actual status of the cemetery as a sacred possession and trust of the Jewish community. It becomes clear at once that the cemetery does not have a legal status equal to that of the synagogue or the school. With regard to a synagogue or school, each community is **compelled** by Jewish law to provide them (see **Shulchan Aruch**, Orach Chayim 150.1; Yoreh De-a 245.4, note of Isserles): "The people of the community compel each other ("**kofin zeh et zeh**") to build a synagogue...to establish a school." There is no such requirement anywhere in the law that a community **must** have a cemetery. As a matter of fact, while many small communities in Europe had, of course, their own **Minyan** and provided for the instruction of children, they did not have a cemetery of their own, but transported their dead to some other larger city. A cemetery is, therefore, not one of the institutions imposed by Jewish law upon each Jewish community.

The reason for this difference in legal status between a cemetery on the one hand, and synagogue and school on the other, is perhaps due to historical reasons. In Palestine, where the foundation of the law developed, people generally were buried in privately owned caves, etc., and therefore it remains an ideal in Jewish law that it is better for a man to be buried in his own property ("betoch shelo"; B. Bava Batra 102a). When, therefore, communal cemeteries developed--mainly in Babylon where the alluvial soil made rock-cave burials impossible--there was no strong basis for requiring each community to have a cemetery. Though, of course, there is discussion about it, as to where it should be located, how far from the city, etc. (M. Bava Batra II.9; Shulchan Aruch, Choshen Mishpat 155.23), the Mishna does not actually say "cemetery," but simply "graves."

Of course, over the centuries the communal cemetery became a precious possession and sacred trust of the Jewish community, but its sanctity is based primarily on minhag. Since the basic Palestinian experience was individual burial in a man's own property, we can see why the law is so meticulous about the right of the individual grave, and has no clear statement about the sanctity of the entire cemetery. The law is extremely careful to protect the individual grave. Thus, it is asked: May the earth dug out from the grave be used by the living? May one even have the minor benefit of resting by leaning on the tombstone? May anyone benefit from the trees that draw their sustenance through their roots from the graves? There are scores of discussions on the sanctity of the individual grave, generally summed up in the principle that a grave may not be used for any living person's benefit. Even broken pieces of a tombstone are asurim bahana-a.

But there is no evidence that, for example, the unused quarter of the cemetery is in this sense sacredly and inalienably the possession of the dead. Dr. Kohler is quite right in saying that our cemeteries are not consecrated in their entirety, as are the Catholic cemeteries, but each grave is sacred by itself. Of course, it must be stated that in recent years there have developed ceremonies accompanying the opening of a new cemetery, and the rabbis, chiefly the Hungarian rabbis of the last generation (Moses Schick, Yoreh De-a 357; Eliezer Deutsch, Peri Hasadeh III, 81; Joseph Schwartz, Ginzei Yosef, #86), speak of it as a good custom. Mostly, the ceremony involves the Chevra Kadisha fasting on that day and thinking thoughts of repentance, primarily in order to avert the evil omen of suddenly providing for a large and new amount of Jewish burials. It is almost like inviting Satan to bring evil ("**Al tiftach peh lasatan**"). But this penitential fasting by the **Chevra Kadisha**, which at all events is not a widespread custom, can hardly be considered a formal consecration of a cemetery in its entirety.

Since, therefore, the communal cemetery has no firm roots in basic Jewish law, but has a strong hold in Jewish custom and affection, the authorities find great difficulty in proving legally that a Jewish cemetery must be exclusively Jewish. People feel, of course, that it **should** be such, but it is hard to prove that the law **requires** it to be such. Two rabbis of the last century tried valiantly (and rather pathetically) to prove that the cemetery should be only Jewish and sharply separated. One was Eliezer Spiro of Muncacz (**Minchat Eli-ezer** II, #41) and the other was Eliezer Deutsch of Bonyhad (**Duda-ei Hasadeh**, #66). Spiro embarrassingly tried to base the reason for keeping Christian bodies separate from Jewish bodies on the Talmudic dictum: "We do not bury the wicked next to the righteous (B. Sanhedrin 47a)." This analogy has already been used by Joel Sirkes (**Bach** to Yoreh De-a 151), who says simply that even a wicked fellow-Jew is not buried next to a righteous one; so it is certainly not proper to bury a non-Jew next to a Jew. Eliezer Deutsch tried to base the prohibition on a sort of Kabbalistic classification of souls.

In the 1880s, there was considerable halachic discussion of this whole question. A rather original article on the matter was written by Meir Friedmann (**Beit Talmud** IV, #3). He concludes that the burying of non-Jews in the same cemetery as Jews was actually a regular practice in the time of the Mishna. The line of argument is of interest. Primarily it is based upon the Mishna, Gittin V.8: "We do not hinder the poor of Gentiles from gleaning the corner of the field," etc. On this mishna the Babylonian Talmud (the baraita in Gittin 61a) says: "We sustain the poor of non-Jews, comfort their mourners, and bury their dead with the dead of Israel." The Yerushalmi, in the same chapter (Gittin 47c), adds some significant details as follows: "In a city where there are Gentiles and Jews, we establish Jewish and Gentile officials who will collect for charity from Gentiles and Jews"; and then it continues more or less as in the Talmud, i.e., "and we sustain the poor, bury the dead, etc."

From this, Friedmann concludes that there was a joint social service. As for the separateness in burial, as implied in the dictum, "We do not bury the wicked, etc.," it meant, "We do not bury them together in

the same cave," since it is the same enclosure. But for
the poor they also had separate and distinct graves in a
cemetery (much like ours); and since each grave was
separate with the proper partition, it was there that
the co-operative social service authorities buried Jews
and Christians, i.e., each in his own grave, but in the
same cemetery. Meir Friedmann's famous colleague, Isaac
Hirsch Weiss, agrees with this conclusion and says that
Rashi's restrictive comment (to the baraita in Gittin
61a) that "with" does not mean "in the same cemetery,"
is an unjustified restriction based upon the presupposi-
tion that the baraita cannot mean what it clearly does
mean.   It is of interest that Joel Sirkes (to the **Tur**,
Yoreh De-a 151) says that while Rashi means that Jews
and non-Jews should not be buried side by side as a
general practice, he admits--according to Sirkes--that
if a body of a slain Gentile is found, he may be buried
in the same courtyard with Jews.

Friedmann's article, endorsed by Weiss, evoked a
response from an Orthodox scholar, Eliezer (Louis) Hausdorff. He published a booklet on this subject (**Responsum with Regard to the Burial of a Non-Jew in the Jewish
Cemetery**, Leipzig, 1884). He attacks all of Friedmann's
conclusions,   yet   nevertheless   makes   an   interesting
statement which is of concern to our discussion.   He
says (and in this he is clearly correct) that the dictum, "We do not bury the righteous by the wicked, etc.,"
which is used as the basis of the argument against burial of Jews and Gentiles side by side, is not at all a
matter of law.   It is only a matter of feeling with
regard to the dignity of the dead.   A community has no
right to bury a wicked person next to a departed person
of good reputation, inasmuch as we are sure that if the
departed worthy person had in his lifetime known that
this wicked person would be buried next to him, he would
have objected.   Therefore, out of respect to the dead
(whose sensitiveness in lifetime we may assume), we do
not bury such people next to them, when worthy people
would have felt--as far as they personally were con-
cerned--that they should not be at their side.   But
Hausdorff continues that where the communal cemetery is
not involved, this makes no difference: If a man buries
in his own property, he has the right to say that he
does not care who is buried by his side; he may bury
whom he wishes.   There is no actual legal prohibition
involved.

So it is clear that even in a vigorous, polemical
article by an Orthodox writer, it is difficult to prove
legally that we may not bury a Christian near a Jewish
grave.   But, of course, again, Jewish feelings require
that the Jewish cemetery should remain Jewish.

This being the state of the law, what are our present-day feelings in the matter, and what should our attitude be to this question? Of course it is obvious that it is not a simple matter to speak of "our" feelings. The feelings of a mixed family that wants to have the deceased of their family buried side by side are not the same as the feelings of other members of the congregation who have not this type of family bond. But, in general, even as a Jewish religious community, we do have a certain moral duty with regard to burial of the non-Jewish dead. As the Talmud says (Gittin 61a): "We feed the poor of non-Jews, comfort their mourners, and bury their dead with the Jewish dead 'for the sake of peace.'" Although Rashi (as we have said) immediately explains the word "with" to mean not in Jewish cemeteries, but as we would bury the Jewish dead, at least it is clear that being concerned with their burial, when needed, certainly remains a religious duty with us. More than that, the consensus of opinion in Jewish law is that one may say **Kaddish** for a Gentile relative (see forthcoming **Recent Reform Responsa**). Aaron Walkin, Rabbi of Pinsk-Karlin, in a responsum written in 1933 (**Zekan Aharon** II, 87), says that a proselyte may say **Kaddish** for a Gentile father; and Abraham Zvi Klein, rabbi in Hungary in the past century, in **Be-erot Avraham**, #11, says that if a Christian woman gives a gift to the synagogue, there is no prohibition against the **Chevra Kadisha** recording her name and reciting "**El Male Rachamim**" for her.

In the light of the above, the practical decisions to which the Conference has come in the past ought to be continued, and somewhat elaborated as follows: If a man owns a lot in our cemetery and he wishes his Gentile spouse or their children buried in his lot, we should not object. Even if one of her parents is to be buried in that lot, we should permit it. The Jewish owner's lot is to be considered "**betoch shelo**," his property, and he does not object to his Gentile relative being buried near where he himself will be buried.

The overwhelming number of such requests will come from a mixed family that wants to be buried side by side. But if it is a question of a single grave not in a family plot, the situation is different. A Jew may object to a Gentile who is a stranger being buried next to his parent or other close relative. Here, then, where there is no family bond between the Jew and the Gentile, we have no right to force the burial of a Christian next to the grave of a Jew (in spite of the argument of Friedmann mentioned above). Therefore, for single graves (not in a family plot), the cemetery may set aside a small section for such infrequent requests.

This section of single graves for Gentile relatives would then be no different than a municipal cemetery (common in Europe) in which there is a Jewish section and a Gentile section, side by side.

Since the exclusive Jewishness of the Jewish cemetery is rooted deeply in Jewish sentiment, if not in formal Jewish law, any Christian service held in it awakens protest on the part of our people, as many of us have discovered. Such protests have come from "the most liberal," who objected to a christological service conducted near the graves of their parents. The best solution, therefore, is the one that is generally followed: The Christian minister conducts the service in the funeral chapel or the home; the rabbi conducts the service in the Jewish cemetery (since at all events it is our duty to participate, if needed, in the burial of a non-Jew, as stated above). If it is unavoidable that the Christian minister officiate in the Jewish cemetery, then he must either use our **Manual** or just selections from the Psalms, etc. Certainly no Christian type of tombstone must ever be permitted in a Jewish cemetery.

In essence, it may be said that the point of view consistently followed by the Conference, and now developed more fully, is based upon the following considerations: The communal (or congregational) cemetery has an honored status rooted in custom but not in law, except insofar as custom becomes law (**"Minhag Yisra-el Torah hi"**). There is a special and older status for a man's own lot (**betoch shelo**). Also, we have a moral obligation to be concerned, when needed, with funerals of non-Jews. **Kaddish** and **"El Male Rachamim"** may be said for them, especially when there is a special relationship or situation involved. Close Gentile relatives, therefore, may, at the request of the family, be buried in the family plot; but as to single graves in a row, the congregation should not, on its own initiative, bury Jews and unrelated Gentiles side by side. Whatever service is conducted by a Christian minister in the home or funeral chapel does not concern us, but the service in the cemetery should always be a Jewish service.

Solomon B. Freehof

Cemeteries generally are run according to laws and regulations enacted by more than one governing body. These laws and regulations in state codes, association charters, bylaws, or official minutes must be respected. Families who purchase burial plots in the light of certain stated cemetery policies have every right to demand continued adherence to those policies.

Responsa Committee (1980)

100. CREMATION FROM THE JEWISH STANDPOINT
(Vol. II, 1891, pp. 33-40)

The CCAR discussion of "Cremation from the Jewish Standpoint" begins in the **CCAR Yearbook**, vol. II, 1891, pp. 33-40), with a paper prepared by Dr. M. Schlessinger at the direction of the Executive Committee. This paper was referred to a special committee of five "to report at the next Conference whether or not cremation is in accord with the spirit of Judaism."

The discussion continues in the following **CCAR Yearbook** (vol. III, 1893, pp. 40-41, 53-58) with a paper written by Dr. B. Felsenthal, challenging the interpretations marshaled in favor of cremation by Dr. Schlessinger. The arguments are of limited interest, but the textual references and conclusions are summarized below.

We turn to the phrase **"Ve-anochi afar va-efer,"** "I am but dust and ashes (Gen. 18:27), of which it has been said that it too points to the fact that in a previous age burning of the dead must have been customary. In answer to this we have to say that the phrase **"Ve-anochi afar ve-efer"** is a semi-poetical one, and that the author used therein a paronomastic play of words. But is it right to press such a poetic figure of speech in order to find a meaning which the author certainly did not think of when he wrote down those words? Furthermore, **efer** does not always mean "ashes." In Mal. 3:21 it stands as a synonym for **afar**, and means "dust," dust upon the roads.

In Gen. 38:24 it is said, "Take her away and she shall be burned." Judah, who spoke thus, intended to have a capital punishment executed. Is it possible to find in these words a hint that in those times cremation of dead human bodies was a prevailing custom?

Similar it is with the laws in Lev. 20:14 and 21:9. Burning is prescribed there as a punitive measure against persons who had been sentenced for having committed certain crimes.

In Josh. 7:25 it is said, "And all Israel stoned him with stones, and burned them in the fire, after they had stoned them with stones." This verse speaks of the execution of Achan and his sons and daughters, who had become guilty of a great crime. After they had been stoned, the punishment was further aggravated by burning their corpses.

In I Samuel 31:12-13, the inhabitants of Yabesh-Gilead, after they had learned that the Philistines had hung the bodies of Saul and his sons to the wall of Beth-Shan, went forth "and walked all the night, and took the body of Saul and his sons from the wall of Beth-Shan, and they came to Yabesh and burned them there; and they took their bones and buried them under the tamarisk-tree at Yabesh, etc." Compare hereto the parallel passage in I Chron. 10:12; also II Sam. 2:4. In these latter passages, in which the burial of Saul and his sons is made mention of, nothing is said of the burning of the corpses at all, and therefore certain Bible critics have proposed to emend the text in I Sam. 31:12 so as to harmonize the differing passages and to read "vayikberu" instead of "vayisrefu." But such an emendation is not necessary. We accept as correct the reading in I Samuel as it stands in the Masoretic text, and take it as a fact that the corpses (i.e., the fleshy parts thereof) were burned, and the bones were interred. As the corpses had been exposed to the air and sun for several days, perhaps for several weeks, before the men of Yabesh came to rescue them, putrefaction had certainly set in, and burning of the decaying fleshy portions of the corpses had, in this exceptional instance, become a necessity. Rabbi David Qimhi, in his commentary **ad locum**, is evidently correct, and every unbiased Bible student must agree with him when he says: "**Yitachen lefaresh ki habasar sarefu, shehe-ela rima, velo ratsu lekovram im hatola-im ki lo haya derech kavod, vayisrefu habasar vayikberu ha-atsamot.**"

In II Chron. 16:14 the burial of King Asa is spoken of in these words: "And they buried him in his own sepulchre, which he had dug for himself in the city of David, and they laid him in the couch, which was filled with sweet odors and diverse kinds of spices mixed by the apothecary's art; and they made for him a burning uncommonly great." Mark well, the text says, "**Vayisrefu lo,**" "They burned **for him** a burning," and it does not say "**Vayisrefu oto,**" "They burned **him.**" There is a difference between **for him** and **him.** The meaning of the quoted passage is: The people paid particularly great honors to the departed king by burning perfumes and spices when they brought the corpse to the sepulchre, and by arranging a funeral of unusual cost and magnificence. That the corpse itself was burned, is an interpretation of the verse (which, indeed, the language of the same will not admit at all). In the same way we have to understand II Chron. 21:19, where the death and burial of King Jehoram is spoken of, and where the remark is made "Velo asu lo amo serefa," "His people made no burning for him [mark: for him] like the burning of his fathers"; that is, King Jehoram had no such funeral honors as kings before him had.

Similar it is with the words of encouragement and consolation by the prophet Jeremiah to King Zedekiah (Jer. 34:5), "In peace thou shalt die, and as burnings were made for thy fathers...so they shall burn for thee, etc." (for thee, not thee; lecha, not otecha). The prophet desired to say: Thou, O Zedekiah, wilt see great national calamities, the conquest and destruction of Jerusalem, etc.; yet thy life will be spared and thou shalt have such an honorable and distinguished funeral as thy fathers had. Pompous and costly funerals of this kind, arranged in honor of great men, took place in later times, too (for instance, when they buried Rabban Gamliel the Elder, Avoda Zara 11a).

One other passage of the Bible we have yet to consider and make its real meaning clear. It is in Amos 6:10. We shall translate it here in its connection with the two preceding verses, and will try to elucidate it by explanatory words in brackets. Thus said the prophet (Amos 6:8-10): "The Lord Eternal has sworn by His own existence, says the Lord, the God of Hosts, I abhor the pride of Jacob and his palaces do I hate; therefore will I surrender up [to the enemy] the city with all that filleth it. And it shall come to pass that if there remain ten men in one house [as, for instance, a father and his nine sons who happened to have not been killed by the sword of the enemy], they shall die [they too shall die--by the plague which will become prevailing in the city]. And should a man's friend or relative come to carry him away [some friend of him who thus has died and who attends now to the said duty of removing the body, because no one of the family, or in the house, or of the neighbors, has been left to perform this pious act of burying the dead], and he will bring out the bones from the house and shall say unto him that is in the innermost parts of the house [perhaps some servant or other person who has been spared from sword and from pestilence, but who is afraid of coming near]: 'Is there yet any one with thee?' He will say: 'There is no one left.' Then he will say: 'Be silent, for we will not make mention of the name of the Lord.'" Thus far the prophet.

In the entire passage, as we have it here before us, cremation is not in the least hinted at. However, we have to state here that there are translations differing from that here given. In King James' Bible the words in the original, "Unesa-o dodo umesarefo," are rendered thus: "And a man's uncle shall take him up, and he that burneth him." Those who prefer this latter

translation will now ask: Is not here the word **mesarefo**
(he that burneth him) proof enough that once cremation
was in use among the Israelites?

Let us first consider whether this translation is
correct. The word **mesaref** (with a **Samech**) in the original text is a so-called **hapax legomenon**, that is, it
occurs only once in the Hebrew Bible. Now it is true
that already the Targumist and others in ancient times
took the word **mesaref** with a **Samech** as equivalent to
mesaref with a **Sin**, and that many after them, following
their translation of the word, rendered also **mesarefo**
(with a **Samech**) as "his combustor," or "he that burneth
him." Not all translators and commentators agree herein. R. David Qimhi, for instance, who does not omit
stating that some explain **mesaref** (with a **Samech**) as
though it were spelled with a **Sin**, begins his commentary
on the phrase by saying that, according to others, **dod**
means a father's brother, and **mesaref** (with a **Samech**)--a
mother's brother. He does not say who his "**Yesh mefa-
reshim**" are. The name of one of them, however, we learn
from Ibn Ezra. In his commentary, **ad locum**, Ibn Ezra
says that Judah Ibn Qoreish explained **dod** as meaning a
father's brother, and **mesaref** (with a **Samech**) as meaning
a mother's brother. May this Ibn Qoreish not have been
correct? He was an excellent Hebrew philologist, though
he lived almost a thousand years ago, and he pursued
good comparative methods in his grammatical writings.
He was the first Hebrew grammarian who insisted upon the
necessity of comparing the Hebrew with Aramaic, Arabic,
and the other Semitic dialects, if one really desires to
understand the Hebrew thoroughly and correctly. He
himself spoke and wrote Arabic fluently, which was his
mother's tongue, and he, in all likelihood, found in a
kindred Arabic word the key for the explanation of the
strange Hebrew **mesaref** (with a **Samech**). It is he that
we followed in our translation given above. Suppose,
however, that, as others say, **mesaref** with a **Samech** is
the same as **mesaref** with a **Sin**, and that it means "he
who burneth him"--would we then be justified if we drew
the conclusion from the words of Amos that cremation was
customary, and that there was a standing class of men
called "**Mesarefim**" among the ancient Israelites whose
regular business it was to cremate the bodies of those
who had died? Is it not clear that the prophet speaks
of an exceptional case of a terrible visitation on the
nation; that he speaks of times when people will die by
the hundreds, and no on will be near who will decently
bury them?

From what has been said thus far, it is clear and
evident that the Bible does not record one single fact
of cremation except the one of Saul and his sons, whose
bodies, however, had already commenced to be in a state

of decomposition and decay when the men of Yabesh came
and arranged for them a decent and becoming burial.

The Bible proves beyond any doubt that since the
day on which Abraham bought the Cave at Machpela for a
family sepulchre, burying was the one and exclusive
manner of disposing of corpses.

The Bible proves further that the idea of being
left unburied was an abhorrent one to the Israelites.

In dealing with post-Biblical times, we can be more
brief; for it is admitted on all sides, and no one gain-
says it, that during all these long centuries, burying
the dead was **de facto** the ruling custom and **de jure** the
binding statute among the Jewish people. To bury the
dead the Jew was obliged; he was commanded to do so.

Commanded? Yes. Emphatically so. Rabbi Simon ben
Yochai (second century) said that to bury the dead was a
duty prescribed by the Torah, and he found this command
indicated in the words of Deut. 21:23, "**Kavor tikberenu,**" "Bury, yes, bury shalt thou him," shalt thou every
Israelite who has died, and not only him who has been
executed in accordance with a judicial sentence (comp.
Rashi **ad locum**: "**Meribui derish kol hametim**"). The
Rabbis in those days had still other ways for basing the
law upon Biblical grounds. Thus, immediately after the
record of the saying of R. Simon ben Yochai (Sanhedrin
46b), we find it reported that the Persian king Shabur
once asked R. Chama: "Have you any indication in your
Torah that corpses must be interred?" R. Chama was
perplexed for a moment and did not know what to answer.
When R. Acha bar Jacob heard of that, he grew quite
angry, and in his anger exclaimed: "Is then the word
given over into the hands of ignorant fools? Chama
should have reminded the king of the word 'kavor' in
Deut. 21:23."--"But then the king might have said that
from this word it may merely be deduced that a coffin
has to be provided for one who has died, but not a
grave."--"Well, the word "**tikberenu**" is added, and this
word..."--"Hold on! The heathen king might not have
admitted that such a deduction ("**meribui**") was correct."--"Then it might have been said to him: 'See, the
Patriarchs already were buried.'"--"Ah, that was a mere
custom."--"Consider, then, the Lord Himself buried
Moses."--"The Lord would not alter a previously existing
custom."--"Remember then, that it is written (I Kings
14:13): 'And all Israel shall mourn for Abuyah and bury
him.'"--"This was all because an ancient custom should
not be altered."--"Then think of the words of Jeremiah
(16:13): 'They shall not be lamented for, nor shall they
be buried, like dung upon the face of the earth they
shall be.' These words, having reference to wicked
people, have been said by a divinely inspired prophet.
In regard to them what you call 'a mere old custom' was

not to be adhered to.   Therefore it follows that God
Himself approved of **kevura** as the lawful thing" (Rashi,
ad locum).

On the same page of the Talmud (Sanh. 46b) the
Halacha is laid down that if anyone should order before
his demise that his body should not be buried, this
order must be disregarded.   And this halacha is iterated
and reiterated by all the later halachic authorities.
(Comp. Maimonides , Hil. Evel 12.1; Hil. Zechiya Umatana
11.24; **Tur** and **Sh.A.**, Yoreh De-a 348; and others.)

Let us quote another Talmudic passage, which will
also show that the teachers of the Talmudical age considered **kevura** as a law, or--if you prefer it--as a
religious custom which was hallowed by the most eminent
authority, by God Himself.   It is to be found in Sota
14a.   Rav Chama bar Chanina said, "What does that verse
in the Scriptures mean, 'After the Lord your God you
shall walk' (Deut. 13:5)?   Can mortal man walk after the
Divine Being?   It means--so the Agadist continued--that
we shall follow the ethical attributes of the Holy One,
blessed be His Name.   As He, the Holy One, clothed the
naked (cf. Gen. 3:21), as He visited the sick (Gen.
18:1), as He consoled the mourners (Gen. 25:11)--so must
you do likewise.   And as He buried the dead (Deut.
34:6), so must you also bury the dead."

Though some might have considered the burying of
the dead merely as a **minhag** (a custom), not as a **mitzvah**
(an explicit law), it is certain that this **minhag** was
very deeply rooted and was consecrated in the consciousness of the people, and such a **minhag**, such an unwritten
law, is--according to very ancient Jewish legal princi-
ples--superior to the written law, and even supersedes
it ("**Haminhag mevatel et hahalacha**").   It is further
certain that since the eighth century all authorities,
without exception, agree that **kevura** is one of the six
hundred and thirteen commandments of the Torah.   The
first one who specified the six hundred thirteen commandments (which, according to a dictum of Rabbi Simlai,
are prescribed in the Torah) was R. Simon of Kahira, and
in his enumeration of the same he included also "**likbor
et hametim**" (Halachot Gedolot, ed. Hildesheimer, p. 13).

Compare also Maimonides, **Sefer Hamitzvot** (mandatory
laws), no. 231; Moses of Councy, **Semag**, no. 104; Aharon
Halevi, **Sefer Hachinnuch**, no. 537; **Ma-amar Haskel** VI.8;
and so forth.   Compare further the various Rabbinical
codices in the proper places--all maintain that **kevura**
is a great **Mitzvah**, a divinely ordained law.

But what about cremation?   Our committee is charged
to report on the question whether or not cremation is in
accord with the spirit of Judaism.   What answer shall we
give to that question?   Shall religion have anything to
say in regard to the final disposal of the bodies of our

deceased friends?   Shall we be perfectly callous and
indifferent in regard to such disposals?
   No! Religion has the right and the duty to demand
that its voice be heard on this question. Religion in
general, and the spirit of Judaism especially, has to
step forward and claim emphatically that the dead bodies
of our dear deceased ones must be treated with decency,
with propriety, and with serious-mindedness; that in the
last rites performed at the funerals of mortal men, rich
and poor be considered alike; that all unnecessary pom-
pousness and ostentatious display of riches be avoided
on such occasion; that at cremations as well as at burials, words of faith and hope, words of consolation and
encouragement, words of religious uplifting and of recalling to the duties of life be spoken. And no rab-
bi--I should think, even no rabbi who entertains conservative views--has a right to decline, if invited, to
speak such words at the cremation of a deceased co-religionist.

   We conclude now by saying that only the following
motion, or one similar to it, may probably be in order
in a rabbinical conference:

   Be it resolved that, in case we should be
   invited to officiate as ministers of religion
   at the cremation of a departed co-religionist,
   we ought not to refuse on the plea that cremation is anti-Jewish or irreligious.

   **On motion, the resolution was adopted, and the
   views of the report in general endorsed.**

NOTE:

   It is nine decades since the first Executive Committee of the Central Conference of American Rabbis
   called for a scholarly discussion of "Cremation
   from a Jewish Standpoint." A resolution was adopted two years later (1893) and remains unchallenged
   policy within our Conference. "Resolved: That in
   case we should be invited to officiate as ministers
   of religion at the cremation of a departed co-
   religionist, we ought not to refuse on the plea
   that cremation is anti-Jewish or irreligious."
   In this generation of the Holocaust we are sensitive to terrible images associated with the burning
   of a body. Rabbis may, therefore, choose to discourage the option of cremation. The practice
   remains permissible, however, for our families.
   Ashes of a cremation should be treated with respect
   as human remains. They may be interred in our

cemeteries, subject to the rules of the cemetery
(see Freehof, **Contemporary Reform Responsa**, pp.
169ff). The ancient Jewish preference for burial
within a person's personal property (see Freehof,
Modern Reform Responsa, p. 257) may be honored more
easily in the case of ashes than in the case of a
body, according to some State laws, but we still
favor use of a Jewish communal cemetery or mausoleum. Because a building in which the ashes of a
Jew are permanently entombed might well seem to a
Cohen to be like a cemetery which he would hesitate
to enter (see Freehof, **Reform Responsa for Our
Time**, pp. 167ff), we oppose keeping ashes in a
home.

Responsa Committee (1980)

See also:

S.B. Freehof, Talit for the Dead and Cremation,"
Modern Reform Responsa, pp. 269ff; "Remains of
Bodies Donated to Science," **Modern Reform
Responsa**, pp. 278ff; "Cremation Ashes Buried
at Home," **Contemporary Reform Responsa**, pp.
169ff; "Family Disagreement over Cremation,"
Contemporary Reform Responsa, pp. 228ff;
"Ashes of Cremation in a Temple Cornerstone,"
Reform Responsa for Our Time, pp. 167ff;
"Mother's Ashes in Son's Grave," **Current Re-
form Responsa**, pp. 145ff; "Wife's Ashes in
Husband's Coffin," **Modern Reform Responsa**, pp.
237ff.

101.   CHOICE OF A CEMETERY
(Vol. XXVII, 1917, pp. 88-89)

There is no law requiring the burial of the dead in
the nearest cemetery. As a matter of fact, the only
consideration in the choice of a cemetery was either the
probable preference by the dead of the place where relatives of his were buried or the better security of the
body against bad conditions of environment such as inun-
dation.

K. Kohler and Jacob Z. Lauterbach

NOTE:

Our society has become very mobile. The nuclear
family has replaced the extended family, and we
find more and more often that families are spread
out over vast distances.
The family cemetery plot, which at one time served
the burial needs for generations of families, can,
in today's society, often create unforeseen problems at the most difficult of times. In addition,
our mobile society--beginning with the years when
our youngsters attend colleges great distances from
their home, and where they often meet future mates
from still more distant regions--has added to the
problems of dispersion. We also see families in
their search for employment opportunities moving to
different locations in the span of their working
years. Therefore, it would be advisable for families to discuss in full their choice and preference
for place of burial when the matter can be discussed rationally and without pressure.

Responsa Committee (1980)

102. PREFERRED BURIAL SITE
(1978)

QUESTION: One parent is buried in New York; the
other is about to die in Houston. One son lives in
Houston, and the second in California. Should the
burial of the mother take place in Houston, where
one son can from time to time visit the grave, or
should the burial take place by her husband's side
in New York? (Rabbi Samuel E. Karff, Houston,
Texas)

ANSWER: In this question, we have a clash of two **Mitzvot**: one is concerned with burial, the other with visitation of the grave in subsequent years. In the case
where a family plot has been established, tradition
would clearly state that the wife should be buried
alongside her husband, and it is the duty of the husband
to provide for the burial of his wife, and not vice

versa (**Shulchan Aruch**, Even Ha-ezer 89; 118.18).   Furthermore, our tradition sought to establish family burial sites similar to the Cave of Machpela, in which Abraham, Isaac, and Jacob, as well as most of their wives,
were buried.   The Talmud, in a legend, speaks of a rabbi
who died, and whose friends, upon seeking to bury him,
found a snake obstructing the way into the cave.   The
snake was told to move so that the son could be buried
with his father (Talmud, Bava Metsi-a 85a).   The only
discussions in the halachic literature which dealt with
the burial site of husband and wife in two cities treated the question of disinterment for the sake of instituting a family plot.   This has been discussed by Isaac
Glick (**Yad Yitschak**, vol. II, #249), as well as by Saul
Schwadron (**Maharsham**, vol. III, #343).   Glick decided
that the husband may not be disinterred to be buried
with his wife unless other members of the family were
already buried in the same plot as his wife.   In the
case of Schwadron, it was a question of whether the wife
might be disinterred.   He decided positively because a
number of other burials had already taken place in the
husband's plot.   Both of these decisions are based on
Sh.A., Yoreh De-a #363, which listed reasons for disinterment, and among them is "burial with his fathers."
In the case cited in our question, no family plot has
yet been established, and at first glance it would seem
preferable to bury her in New York, as the husband is
buried there.   If, however, the children intend the
Houston plot to become a family plot, and will later
inter other members of their family there, then--even
according to the tradition--this would be permissible.
     The other matter which enters the discussion is the
future visitation of graves.   It is a **mitzvah** to visit
graves on the **Yahrzeit** (Rashi to Yevamot 122a, who has
cited the responsa of the Geonim; **Ketav Sofer**, Yoreh
De-a #178).   This custom was established in the days of
the Geonim for scholars, but subsequently applied to all
Jews: if it was possible to visit the grave it was done;
if not, then the family might send someone else to visit
the grave as Chatam Sofer stated.   Visiting the grave on
Yahrzeit is clearly a well-established custom.   It does
not have the same weight as statements connected with
burial which are law, in this case **mide-oraita**, yet for
us this custom may be at least as important as the law.
It will be comforting to the family to be able to visit
the grave.   This reason, and the fact that the family
intends the Houston plot to become the family plot,
would lead me to decide in favor of burial in Houston.

Walter Jacob

103. DIRECTION OF GRAVES IN THE CEMETERY
(Vol. XXXIII, 1923, p. 58)

QUESTION: Our congregation has just purchased adjoining territory to its burial grounds. The plot runs north and south. It runs from street to street and our plans are to make an entrance by the north side and the exit on the south side. This would mean that the graves and lots, when laid out, would either be facing north or south, and not east, as is customary. The question, therefore, which I desire to ask, is this: Is there anything in traditional Judaism concerning this matter? Is there any prohibition concerning the burying in graves that run north and south or vice versa?

ANSWER: There is, to my knowledge, no prohibition of this kind in Rabbinic Judaism. Neither the Talmud nor the **Shulchan Aruch** has any definite ruling about the direction in which the graves should run. On the contrary, from the Mishna, Bava Batra VI.8, and the discussion of the Gemara (**ibid.**, 101b), it is evident that they would have graves in every direction. Lest it be argued that this was only in Palestine, we have now the evidence from the Jewish catacombs in Rome, Italy, that some of the graves were arranged so that the head was in the direction of northwest and the feet towards the southeast, and others again in the opposite direction, i.e., head southeast and feet northwest (see Nikolaus Mueller, **Die Juedische Katakombe am Monteverde zu Rom,** Leipzig, 1912, pp. 48-49). And R. Moses Sofer, in his Responsum, **Chatam Sofer**, Yoreh De-a, no. 332, expresses his surprise at certain people who would fix the direction in which graves should run. In Pressburg, where he was rabbi, the cemetery was so laid out that the graves ran west-east, that is, the head was placed towards the north, and the feet towards the south. It would seem that certain people, believing that at the time of the resurrection the dead will get up and march to Palestine, would be careful to place the body in the grave with the feet toward Palestine, so that when the time comes the dead would be able to get up and walk right ahead without having to turn around. But, argues R. Moses Sofer, there are many roads toward Palestine, since from European countries one can go first south to a Mediterranean harbor and then by ship east, or one can go east by land to Constantinople first, and thence to

Palestine; therefore, he concludes that there is absolutely no difference in what direction the graves run.

                    Jacob Z. Lauterbach and Committee

        104. DIRECTION OF GRAVES IN A CEMETERY
                        (1980)

        QUESTION: Must the graves in the cemetery all face
        in one direction?

ANSWER: My honored predecessor, Jacob Z. Lauterbach,
has provided most of the traditional material on this
matter. It is clear that neither the Mishna, nor the
Talmud, nor the later codes established any regulations
about the direction of graves. The Talmud (B.B. 101b)
was concerned with graves in a cavern and established
that all walls of the cavern could be used for graves
regardless of the direction in which they faced. Greenwald (Kol Bo Al Avelut, pp. 177ff) has provided the more
recent material on the subject. It is clear that Jewish
cemeteries generally faced all graves in one direction,
east-west or north-south. This was cited as a hallmark
of a Jewish cemetery (Oppenheimer responsum, as an ad-
dendum to Bachrach's Chavat Ya-ir). Some felt that
graves should face east-west so that at the beginning of
the Messianic age the dead could rise and march toward
the Land of Israel. Moses Sofer suggested that if this
were not possible, then the graves should face a gate
for the same purpose. A new gate might be erected just
for this reason (Responsa, Yoreh De-a, #332). All authorities, however, agreed that it was possible to arrange graves differently in various sections of the
cemetery in order to conform with the contours of the
land. So, Abraham Glick (Yad Yitschak III, 83) felt
that the continuous alignment of graves might only be
changed for a famous person. In order to produce uniformity, he suggested that an offending gravestone might
be moved to conform with the others, even if it then no
longer stood precisely at the head of the grave.
    We may then conclude that it would be equally pos-
sible to align graves east-west, north-south, or in
conformity with the contour of the land. It would,
however, be within the power of a local cemetery associ-

ation to insist on uniformity of direction of graves within that cemetery or a portion thereof.

Walter Jacob, Chairman
Leonard S. Kravitz
W. Gunther Plaut
Harry A. Roth
Rav A. Soloff
Bernard Zlotowitz

See also:

S.B. Freehof, "The Alignment of Graves," **Current Reform Responsa**, pp. 132ff; "Position of the Body in the Grave," **Contemporary Reform Responsa**, pp. 172ff.

105. EMPLOYMENT OF NON-JEWS IN A JEWISH CEMETERY
(Vol. XXVII, 1917, p. 89)

For digging the grave or doing other mechanical work preparatory to the burial, non-Jews may be, and always have been, employed. Only such services as are performed directly for the dead during the burial are obligatory to his fellow-Jews.

K. Kohler and Jacob Z. Lauterbach

NOTE:

References are: Beitsa 61a; **Yad**, Hil. Yom Tov 1.23; **Shulchan Aruch**, Orach Chayim 626.1.

Responsa Committee (1980)

106. REMOVAL OF DEAD BODY TO ANOTHER GRAVE
(Vol. XXXII, 1922, pp. 41-42)

QUESTION: A man in my congregation (in a western city) wishes to remove the body of his mother who is buried in our city, to New York, in order to

have her rest by the side of his recently deceased
father, who had to be buried in New York. Is there
any objection on the part of Jewish law or custom
to his doing so? And, if so, on what ground does
Jewish practice base its objection?

ANSWER: Ordinarily, Jewish practice objects to the
removal of a dead body from one grave to another out of
consideration and respect for the dead. It was believed
that after having been put to rest the dead should not
be disturbed by removal. If, however, there is any
valid reason for the removal (especially if there is any
consideration which would justify the assumption that
were the dead alive, he or she would consent to the
change in the resting place), Jewish law and practice
permit such a removal. Thus, e.g., the **Shulchan Aruch,**
Yoreh De-a 363.1, permits the disinterment and removal
of a dead body in order to bury the same in another
place together with his or her relatives. This is exactly like the case you state, i.e., the son being desirous of having his mother rest in the same place where
his father is buried.

Jacob Z. Lauterbach

NOTE:

Practice permitted such a removal. Thus, the **Shulchan Aruch,** Yoreh De-a 363.1, states:

> We do not move the dead body or human bones,
> not from an honorable grave to another honor-
> able grave, not from a dishonorable grave to
> another dishonorable grave, not from a dis-
> honorable grave to an honorable grave, and, it
> goes without saying, not from an honorable
> grave to a dishonorable grave. But it must be
> kept in mind that one may be moved even from
> an honorable to a dishonorable grave in order
> that one may rest with ancestors. In addi-
> tion, one may be moved and buried in the Land
> of Israel [from outside the land]. If one was
> buried [temporarily] with the conscious under-
> standing that removal would take place, it is
> permitted under all circumstances. If one
> suspects that idolaters may be planning to
> remove the body [for pagan worship or orgias-
> tic purposes], or that water may seep into the

grave, or that it is the wrong grave-site, it
is a **mitzvah** to remove it.

The **Shulchan Aruch**'s prescription fits not only the
case above, but provides a reasonable response to
many questions which arise on this subject. We see
no basis for altering it.

Responsa Committee (1980)

See also:

S.B. Freehof, "Disinterment Due to a Labor Strike,"
    Contemporary Reform Responsa, pp. 160ff; "Dis-
    interment from a Christian Cemetery," **Reform
    Responsa for Our Time**, pp. 175ff.

107. TWO COFFINS IN ONE GRAVE
(Vol. LXXXV, 1975, pp. 85-87)

QUESTION: Space in the cemetery is becoming scarc-
er every year. The question has, therefore, arisen
whether or not we may bury one coffin above another
in the same grave. (Sidney Kluger, Executive Director, Temple Sherith Israel, San Francisco, California)

ANSWER: It is obvious that to open a grave and to put
another coffin above the one already there is not desirable, and so most of the scholars who deal with the
question say that this should not be done, nevertheless
find a reason to permit it after all. For example, the
great Chasidic scholar of the last century, Chaim Hal-
berstam in his **Divrei Chayim** (Yoreh De-a 136), says
simply that it should not be done; but then he adds that
if it is an established custom in the community to do
so, then it should be permitted to continue. Similarly,
other scholars dealing with the question indicate that
whatever the strict letter of the law may be in that
matter, it is a widespread custom in many communities to
do so. Thus, for example, see the responsum of Jacob
Reischer (died in Metz, 1733) in his **Shevut Ya-akov**,
II:95. It is not surprising, therefore, that when the
Shulchan Aruch states the law, it also exhibits this
same double attitude. In Yoreh De-a 362.4, the law is
given at first bluntly as follows: "We may not bury one

coffin above another." But then the law continues: "But
if there is six handbreadths of earth between the coffins, it is permitted." Thus we might say, the general
attitude of the law is ambivalent, namely, that such
superimposed burial is not desirable, but it is not
forbidden.

It would be desirable to trace the development of
the law, especially this ambivalent attitude in it,
since the various elements involved may help each congregation to make its decision on the matter. Basically
the law involving the distance between one buried body
and another is based upon the mishna in Bava Batra VI.8.
The discussion there revolves around a cave and how many
burial inches may be dug in it, in what direction, and
how close to each other. The mishna then is discussed
in Bava Batra 101ff, and most later discussions base
themselves upon this passage.

The Gaon Hai is cited in the **Tur**, Yoreh De-a 363,
to the effect that each grave is entitled to three handbreadths of earth around it (**Tefisat Hakever**). Joel
Sirkes (**Bach** to the **Tur**) explains the fact that some
authorities say that there ought to be six handbreadths
and some authorities say only three handbreadths intervening as follows: each coffin is entitled to three
handbreadths of its own. Hence, between the lower coffin and the upper coffin, there should be six handbreadths (three for each coffin). Even this amount of
space is not insisted upon by all authorities. The
fullest discussion of the whole matter is by Abraham
Danzig in his **Chochmat Adam** in the section Matzevat
Mosheh, #10. He says (on the basis of some text varia-
tion) that it may be possible to have the width of only
six **fingers** of earth between the coffins.

The justification for such a small intervening
amount of earth came up in connection with the question
which arose in the city of Paris in the 17th century.
At that time, the Jews of Paris were not permitted to
have a cemetery of their own. They buried in some city
lots and the question, therefore, of coffin above coffin
immediately arose. They asked a question of Aryeh Lev
of Metz (18th century). (See the second volume of his
Sha-agat Aryeh, Wilna edition, 1873, p. 120, Responsum
#17.) He told them that they may bury in this way, but
to be sure to have six handbreadths between coffins.

Those who would permit superimposed burial with
less than six handbreadths (as Danzig does, requiring
only six fingers) base themselves generally upon the
statement of Simon ben Gamliel in the mishna cited
above, who ends the discussion in the mishna by saying
that it all depends on the rockiness of the soil. This
is understood to mean that if the soil is firm and would
not disperse easily, even less than six handbreadths

would be sufficient. So, for example, Zvi Ashkenazi
(**Chacham Tsevi**) in his Responsum #149, is dealing with a
situation in the cemetery of Amsterdam where the soil is
loose and thin. There he would require even more than
six handbreadths. However, Isaac Schmelkes of Lemberg,
in his **Beit Yitschak**, Yoreh De-a 153, says that in Paris
they put a slab of stone between the graves and that
even if it were only an inch wide, it is sufficient to
separate coffins.

In fact, Abraham Danzig cites **Torat Chesed**, in
which the statement is made that all these laws as to
how much intervening earth there must be, were based
upon the earlier custom of burying the bodies without
coffins; but that nowadays when we bury in coffins, we
do not need to consider the necessity for intervening
earth at all.

In fact we may say that if--as is frequently the
custom nowadays in some cemeteries--the coffin itself is
enclosed in a cement casing, then the top of the casing
of the lower coffin and the bottom of the casing of the
upper coffin could fulfill completely the requirement of
even the strictest opinion. Moses Feinstein (**Igerot
Mosheh**, Yoreh De-a 234) believes that even with cement
intervening, there should be an interval of three to six
handbreadths.

Frequently in his discussion of the question, the
authority will say that all these laws of intervening
earth were meant for the time when we had plenty of room
and therefore we could leave sufficient earth between
each coffin; but nowadays our land is crowded and so the
custom to bury closely side by side and one above the
other has become widespread and must be deemed permissible. See especially the statement of Jacob Reischer of
Metz cited heretofore.

To sum up, then: Nowadays cemetery space is becoming scarce. We bury in coffins and sometimes even with
cement casing around the coffins. This is to be considered sufficient to fulfill the requirement of the
strictest authorities. Yet it must be stated in explaining the double attitude of the law that it would be
preferable if we had the space for each coffin to have
its own grave.

Solomon B. Freehof

NOTE:

Cemeteries generally are run according to laws and
regulations enacted by more than one governing
body. These laws and regulations in State codes

and association charters, bylaws, or official minutes must be respected.

Responsa Committee (1980)

108.   LAPSE OF TIME BEFORE SETTING A TOMBSTONE
(Vol. XLII, 1932, pp. 84-85)

QUESTION: Can you inform me as to the origin of
the custom of waiting at least eleven months after
death before setting a tombstone? And will you
please let me know if I am correct in holding that
there is no good reason for waiting that long if
one does not wish to.

ANSWER: There is, to my knowledge, no basis whatever
for the custom of waiting eleven months after the death
of a person before setting up a tombstone upon a grave.
I doubt very much whether there is such a custom observed in any community. The people in the case you
refer to, probably confuse the time for setting a tombstone with the time when the recitation of the **Kaddish**
stops, that is, after eleven months. In fact, there is
no fixed time for the setting of the tombstone. In many
communities it is the custom to wait till twelve months
after death. The origin of this custom is not very old.
The first, to my knowledge, to mention this custom is R.
Elijah Spira (died 1712) in his work **Eliya Rabba** on
Orach Chayim (Sulzbach, 1756), ch. 224, p. 81a. He
says: "**Haminhag she-ein omedin matseva ad achar 12 chodesh mishum dehamatseva nir-a lachashivuta uve-12 chodesh yesh lo tsa-ar. Inamei dehata-am dehamatseva shelo
yishkechu oto milev, yehamet eino nishkach ad le-achar
sheneim asar chodesh.**"[1]
The reasons for this practice as given by R. Elijah
Spira are not satisfactory. R. Zevi Hirsch b. Azriel of
Wilna in his work **Beit Lechem Yehuda** on the **Shulchan
Aruch,** Yoreh De-a 376.7 (Polnoi, 1804, p. 120a) also
mentions this custom as obtaining in some communities,
but does not give any reason for it. He merely says:

---

[1] Resp. **Chatam Sofer** VI, no. 29. See also: Geiger,
**Rabbinisches Gutachten ueber die Militaerpflichtigkeit
der Juden,** Breslau, 1842; Eli Rust (pseudonym for L.
Landshuth), "Die Verbindlichkeit des Zeremonialgesetzes
fuer Juedische Krieger in," Heinemann, **Allg. Archiv,**
etc., 1842, vol. II, pp. 236-238.

"Haminhag pashut berov hamekomot she-ein omedin matseva
ela le-achar sheneim asar chodesh." But I know personally of many communities in which the custom is to put
up the stone as soon as possible after the seven days of
mourning are over. From Genesis 35:19 it would appear
that Jacob put up the stone upon Rachel's grave immediately after burial, if we may cite this as a precedent.
At any rate, you are correct in holding that there is no
good reason for waiting that long if one does not wish
to.

                                    Jacob Z. Lauterbach

              109.   THE SETTING OF A TOMBSTONE
                          (1979)

        QUESTION: Is there a specific time after the fu-
        neral when the tombstone should be set? Must one
        wait twelve months or may this be done sooner?

ANSWER: There is no fixed time period which must
elapse before the tombstone can be set. It has become
customary among the modern Orthodox Jews to wait twelve
months (Chidushei Akiva Eiger to Shulchan Aruch, Yoreh
De-a 376.4). However, there are many opinions which
state that the tombstone can be set as early as the
conclusion of the Shiv-a period (Tosafot to Ket. 5a).
In fact, it was even possible for a mourner to interrupt
the period of mourning to concern himself with the tombstone (Siftei Kohen to Shulchan Aruch, Yoreh De-a 375,
note 12). In Israel, it is often the practice to erect
the tombstone at the end of thirty days of mourning
(Sheloshim). Greenwald, after citing all the customs
which have been followed in both ancient and modern
times, quite properly declared that the tombstone itself
was erected to honor the dead. As we feel that we honor
our dead more (kibud hamet) by waiting a year, that
should be done; it would, however, be within the framework of tradition to erect a stone earlier. Both ways
are agreeable with custom and tradition (Greenwald, Kol
Bo Al Avelut, p. 370). For guidance on a consecration
service for the stone, see Gates of Mitzvah, p. 64. As
waiting a year has become a widespread custom among us

in America, we should generally wait till a year has
elapsed.

Walter Jacob, Chairman
Leonard S. Kravitz
Eugene Lipman
W. Gunther Plaut
Harry A. Roth
Rav A. Soloff
Bernard Zlotowitz

110.   INSIGNIA ON A TOMBSTONE
(1980)

QUESTION: Is a Jewish cemetery justified in its
rule that each headstone or family memorial must
have the insignia of either the Star of David or a
Menora? (Dr. Frederick C. Scwartz, Chicago, Illinois)

ANSWER: This question should be answered in two parts.
First, let me deal with regulations, with the tradition
and its statements about tombstones. The Bible already
records marking graves of various individuals through a
special monument, e.g., Jacob set up a pillar for Rachel
(Gen. 35:20). It seems that rather grand markers were
placed over the graves of kings (II Kings 23:17), and
this custom was continued by some of the Maccabean rulers (I Macc. 13:27ff; B. San. 96b). We now know a good
deal about grave markers and sarcophagi from the Greco-
Roman period through the efforts of modern archaeology.
Many of them used both Jewish and Greek symbols as decoration. The grave markers as discussed by the Talmud
not only honored the dead, but also warned priests of
the presence of a grave, as priests were forbidden to
come into any kind of contact with the dead (M. Mo-ed
Katan 1.2).
     Every effort has been made through the centuries to
simplify everything connected with the funeral and burial, and to make burial democratic. Thus, Rabban Gamliel
of the Mishnaic period had himself buried in a simple
linen garment as an example, although he was a man of
considerable wealth (B. Ket. 8b, Mo-ed Katan 27b). An
extreme statement in this regard concerning tombstones
is found in the Jerusalem Talmud, which, in one instance, stated that "righteous people do not need a
tombstone, as their words are their memorial" (Yer.

Shek. 2.6). Subsequently, everything has been done to
assure simplicity of tombstones; so Moses Schick (**Responsa Maharam Schick**, Yoreh De-a, #170) objected
strongly to a tombstone on which a portrait was to be
engraved, as that violated the spirit of uniformity and
democracy. Abraham Isaac Glick similarly emphasized
uniformity (**Yad Yitschak**, 3.83). Parallel objections
have been raised to placing photographs on tombstones as
occurred in some Orthodox cemeteries (Greenwald, **Kol Bo
Al Avelut**, pp. 380ff).

The emphasis, therefore, has always been on simplicity, and it is certainly within the prerogative of
any burial society or cemetery association to enforce
rules which demand simplicity and uniformity (Joseph
Schwartz, **Hadrat Kodesh**, pp. 30bff). There could be no
objection to requiring the Star of David or a **Menora** on
every tombstone.

A word should be said about the two symbols which
have been prescribed by the cemetery association. Although the Star of David is an old symbol, and has been
used by many people throughout history, its Jewish association began with mystical circles of the 12th century.
A broader use of the Star of David as a Jewish designation had its inception in the Prague Jewish community,
which had been given the privilege of its own flag by
Charles IV in 1354. The insignia chosen was the Star of
David. It eventually spread from the flag to ritual
items and books. No world-wide use of the Star of David
occurred until the 19th century, when Jews felt the need
for a universally recognized symbol, and adopted the
Star, which eventually also became the symbol on the
flag of the State of Israel.

The **Menora** is, of course, the oldest symbol of
Judaism associated with the ancient desert tabernacle,
as well as Solomon's Temple, and was used in many ways,
including frequent use as decoration on tombstones in
the Greco-Roman period and in subsequent times.

We can see that both the Star of David and the
Menorah are appropriate symbols for Jewish tombstones.
It is within the prerogative of a cemetery association
to require their use on each stone as a way of emphasizing the uniformity and the democratic spirit of Judaism.

Walter Jacob

111.   EMBLEM OF THE TRIBE OF LEVI
(Vol. XXXIII, 1923, p. 60)

QUESTION: A friend would like to know what ensign or emblem the Tribe of Levi had, if any. If not, is there anything that he could use as a seal which might have some connection with the name of the Tribe of Levi?

ANSWER: The Tribe of Levi did not have any special standard or emblem.   On the breastplate of the High Priest the name of Levi was, according to tradition, engraved upon an emerald stone (Targum Jonathan to Exodus 28:17; comp. also **Yalkut Re-uveni** to **Tetsaveh**, Warsaw, 1901, p. 149, where some mystic reasons are given for it).   In later times, the Levites used as an emblem on their seal, a pitcher, or a pitcher with a basin, which is symbolic of the function of the Levites in assisting the priests.   The Levites pour out the water upon the hands of the priests when the latter prepare to go up to recite the priestly benedictions.   These emblems are also found engraved on the tombstones of Levites. Comp. B. Wachstein, **Die Inschriften des alten Judenfriedhofes in Wien** I (Wien, 1912, p. XLVIII).

Jacob Z. Lauterbach and Committee

112.   TOMBSTONE IN THE ABSENCE OF A BODY (CENOTAPH)
(Vol. LXXIV, 1964, pp. 101-104)

QUESTION: A group of former immigrants from Central Europe feel the need of visiting the graves of their parents, as is traditional. But the parents and other close relatives were murdered during the Nazi period, and there is no possible way of finding their graves (if, indeed, there are any graves). Their question, therefore, is this: May they (in the Jewish cemetery of Milwaukee, where they live) set up a tombstone where they can visit and count it as a grave of their parents and other dear ones who have perished?

ANSWER: Jewish burial and mourning traditions have frequently needed adjustment to the uncertain circumstances of the Jewish life in the Old World.   Some of

the adjustments made in the law and the customs prove
the flexibility of the tradition in providing for the
emotional needs of mourning families when the circumstances of the death are unusual. Most of the questions
which needed adjustment concern the problem of mourning:
When should **Shiv-a** begin?   When should **Yahrzeit** be observed in the case when a deceased man's body is no
longer to be found; or, indeed, in cases when there can
no longer be any proof that the person is actually dead?
     The classical decision was made in the 12th century
in the Rhineland by Isaac Or Zarua of Vienna, who said
that the moment the family gives up hope, that moment of
despair shall be counted as the moment of death, and
mourning, etc., shall begin from that date (**Or Zarua II**,
Hilchot Avelut, #424; see also Yoreh De-a 375.6).   This
indicates at least the willingness of the tradition to
adjust itself to the emotional needs of mourners when
violence or accident creates the exceptional circumstance that the body is not available for burial.
     However, the specific question asked here concerns
the permissibility of setting up a tombstone in the
absence of the body. As far as I know, this question
has never come up in the legal literature.   It is
strange that it has not come up. If the question was
frequently asked, "May we say **Kaddish** when the body was
never found?" then the question could easily also have
been asked, "May we put up a tombstone when the body was
never found?" It would be interesting to speculate as
to why this natural question was not asked. It may be
because the historic Jewish cemeteries in the Rhineland
and in Prague, etc., were so crowded with tombstones
that it was often difficult to find a place for those
who were actually buried there, much less so for those
whose bodies were not laid to rest there.
     Nowadays the question arises often. Bodies are
frequently lost at sea or in airplane accidents and are
never recovered. The American military, in cemeteries
overseas, have a stone on which are inscribed the names
of the missing, who, therefore, are not buried in the
cemetery. In London there is a cenotaph right in the
middle of one of the main streets, in honor of soldiers
who are buried elsewhere or who are missing.
     Thus, while there is no discussion in the legal
literature about setting up a tombstone where there is
no body buried, there is nevertheless a great deal of
discussion about tombstones in general, and part of this
complex discussion has some relevance here. There is a
long debate--going back to the beginnings of Jewish law
in the Talmud--as to whether tombstones are meant to be
for the honor of the dead or (also) for the benefit of
the living. What would be involved in the discussion
was whether survivors may dispose of tombstones in case

bodies are moved. The whole discussion was summed up in both the **Tur** and the **Shulchan Aruch**, Yoreh De-a 364. Also, there is a handy summary of the debate in the responsa of Abraham Isaac Glick, **Yad Yitschak**, III.38 (published in Satmar, 1908). What is relevant to our question is that there is a growing body of opinion that the tombstones are also for the benefit of the living. As it is said in the above-mentioned responsum, the tombstone is for the purpose of directing the survivors to where they can go and pray.

This side of the discussion--i.e., that the purpose of the tombstone is also spiritually to benefit the survivors--was used in the one responsum which actually deals with almost the same question that you ask. Ephraim Oshry, now rabbi in New York, was, during the Nazi period, in the Kovno concentration ghetto to which Jews were sent from all over Europe. The Nazis destroyed and ploughed over the Jewish cemeteries in the neighborhood. A man came to Rabbi Oshry after the liberation with the following question: Since it was now impossible to locate the graves of his parents, and he was accustomed to go to the graves of his parents to pray, what should he do? Rabbi Oshry advised (Responsum **Mima-amakim** I, 28) that he set up a tombstone anywhere in the cemetery, and that would be an appropriate memorial where he could pray. Oshry uses the argument that tombstones are for the benefit of the living, and also calls attention to the fact that we put up memorials (even memorial plaques with the names of the deceased) in many synagogues and schools, far away from where the bodies are buried.

Rabbi Oshry has recently published a second volume of **Mima-amakim**, in which he returns to the problem in an interesting and rather touching way. The stones from the Jewish cemeteries had been taken during the Nazi occupation and used as paving stones in certain towns. The question was: How could Jewish people walk on such paving stones, the inscriptions on which were still legible? He urges that efforts be made to buy these stones; and since the graves to which they belong can no longer be located (because the cemeteries are ploughed up), the tombstones should be set up anywhere in a Jewish cemetery (**Mima-amakim** II, 20).

Hoffman, in **Melamed Leho-il**, vol. II, Responsum #139, deals with the question of putting up a tombstone for a body that was lost at sea. He finds no objection to doing it except, perhaps, the possible objection of using up a grave space that might be needed for someone else.

Let us, therefore, sum up the situation in Jewish tradition. From the earliest medieval days, adjustments were made (with regard to mourning) when bodies could not be found. With regard to the tombstones, one body of opinion is that they are put up for the spiritual benefit of the living. On the basis of the above, Rabbi Oshry decided that tombstones may be put up, even when the bodies can no longer be located. Therefore, on the basis of the above, a group of you who wish to do so, should set up a tombstone with the inscription of the names that you wish to remember. There can be two or three such stones, perhaps classified according to the cemeteries where they **might** have been buried had they died normally. Your members from Frankfurt could put up one stone, with the names of all their dead recorded, and so could other groups. You are free to have one or many stones, as you wish.

The inscription can easily be worked out. It is suggested that you have the usual five Hebrew letters-- **Tav, Nun, Tsadi, Beit, He**--which are appropriate because they say, "May their souls be bound up in eternal life." This can be followed, in English, with "To the unforgettable memory of our martyred dear ones," and the list of names. All this is justified on the basis of Jewish law and tradition.

Solomon B. Freehof

113. EXCHANGING A TOMBSTONE
(Vol. LXXX, 1970, pp. 53-55)

QUESTION: A surviving child desires to exchange the tombstone on her father's grave, presumably for a more elaborate one. She states that the proposed second tombstone conforms to a request that her father had made. Is it permissible to make such an exchange?

ANSWER: In general, it is deemed praiseworthy in the legal tradition to fulfill a behest of a departed parent. The Talmud, in Ta-anit 21a, states that "It is a **mitzvah** to fulfill the command of the departed." This **mitzvah** applies not only to the disposing of his estate, but also to matters relating to the funeral and to the grave. However, there is a definite restriction as to such requests. No request may be fulfilled which is contrary to the law. Thus, if a man says, "Do not have any funeral eulogies for me," this request must be fulfilled because the funeral eulogy is for the honor of the dead, and he may, if he wishes, say that he does not desire that honor. But if he says, "Do not bury me in the ground," this request may not be fulfilled, because it is contrary to the law, which requires that the body be buried in the ground.

Now, assuming that the father had requested or expressed a wish for some other type of tombstone than the one that is already on his grave, may this wish to substitute another tombstone be fulfilled? Is it permitted to exchange a tombstone once it is on the grave? The question involves the status of the tombstone: Is it an integral part of the grave (in which case it may not be removed, since it belongs, as it were, to the dead), or is it merely a convenience for the survivors so that they may easily find the grave? If it is merely the latter, then the survivors may do with the tombstone what they wish. They may take it down, put up another, or sell the old tombstone, since it is theirs and does not really belong to the grave. This basic question as to whether it is an essential part of the grave or not was discussed in relation to another tombstone question in **Current Reform Responsa**, pp. 149ff. But since the question asked here is really different from the one discussed there, it needs to be gone into once more.

Greenwald, in his compendium on funeral practices, **Kol Bo**, p. 385, leaves the matter unsettled as to whether a tombstone may be exchanged. The reason for his uncertainty is that the earlier sources are themselves divided on the larger question as to whether the living may consider the stone as theirs and may therefore benefit from it. Most of the discussion in the earlier sources is dealt with by Joel Sirkes ("The **Bach**") in the **Tur**, 364. And so Isserles to the **Shulchan Aruch** (the same reference) leaves the discussion open, saying: Some forbid the living to sit on the tombstone, but some differ; that is, it is not quite settled whether the tombstone belongs to the grave and therefore the living may not benefit in any way from it.

Interestingly enough, almost precisely the same question that is asked here was asked centuries ago and is referred to by Azulai in his **Birkei Yosef**, to Yoreh De-a 342. A widow was dissatisfied when she saw the tombstone that had been put on her husband's grave. She therefore ordered a larger tombstone, but wanted to turn in the smaller tombstone for credit on the cost of the larger tombstone. This was forbidden (namely, to turn in the smaller tombstone for credit), but there was no objection to her exchanging it for a larger tombstone, for that was for the honor of the dead.

So actually there is no real objection to substituting a larger tombstone. The real question is: What may be done with the first tombstone which has been removed? Since there is a large body of opinion among the scholars that the stone actually belongs to the grave, and that, therefore, the living may not benefit from it, there is a strong limitation as to what must be done with the original stone. This specific question has come up frequently. For example, the community of Budapest had to excavate a cemetery (on which it had only a lease), and it was left with tons of tombstones. It would have been too expensive to transport them to the new cemetery. Besides, where should they be placed there? (Cf. **Responsum Maharsham Swadron II**, 122.) A similar question arose in Italy: Owing to a lack of cemetery space, tons of earth to a considerable depth were spread to cover all the old graves so that bodies could be buried in the newly placed earth. The old tombstones therefore were not even visible. Perhaps they should have been left there buried, but they were removed from the graves before the new earth was put in. So again there was a question of what to do with the old tombstones. See Isaac of Aboab (Venice, 1610-1694) in his **Devar Shemu-el**, #342; also Menachem Azariah da Fano, Responsum #56 (rabbi in Venice, 16th century). The answer usually is given that the stones may not be used for private benefit (just as the aforementioned widow could not turn her husband's tombstone in for credit), but may be used for the benefit of the cemetery or other communal causes.

Therefore, the family--in the question asked here--may substitute a new stone, but the old stone cannot be sold. It may be given to some poor family to be rechiseled for use on its graves, or it may simply be buried somewhere else in the cemetery.

Solomon B. Freehof

114. MOTHER'S NAME ON SON'S TOMBSTONE
(Vol. LXXXVI, 1976, pp. 91-94)

QUESTION: A young chaplain-rabbi was killed in Thailand. His family belong to the Hartford Reform Congregation, Beth Israel. His mother is an active National Sisterhood Board member. She asked that the Hebrew inscription on her son's tombstone should include her name as mother of the deceased. The local funeral director said that this request is improper, that only the father's name be used with that of the deceased. Is this correct? What traditional law is involved in this matter? (Rabbi Harold S. Silver, Hartford, Connecticut)

ANSWER: There is very little firm law governing tombstones.   Even the latest works that specialize in these
matters have comparatively little to say.   Greenwald in
his **Kol Bo** has only a few pages, beginning with page
379, and Shalom Schachne Cherniak, in his **Minsheret
Shalom**, has only a few columns.   The reason for the
paucity of the law on the matter has some bearing on
this discussion.

The main purpose of having a tombstone has changed
in the passing years.   Originally the stone was meant
merely to mark a grave as a warning to **Kohanim** to know
what spot to avoid, a warning which would be especially
necessary if the grave were in some open field.   Later,
this purpose of the tombstone changed, since cemeteries
(and not scattered graves or caves) developed, and the
Kohen could simply avoid the cemetery.   Now the purpose
of the tombstone is not so much to be a warning to the
Kohanim to keep away, but as a guide to the family, to
tell them where to come to honor the dead or to pray.
In other words, the tombstone is now for the benefit of
the family.   See, for example, the responsum by Isaac
Glick (**Yad Yitschak III**, #38) who says that the tombstone is for the benefit of the living to know where to
come and pray.   This change of mood as to the purpose of
the tombstone should indicate to us in our specific
discussion that the feelings of the bereaved family
deserve sympathetic consideration in all the discussions
about the tombstone.

The discussions that **have** arisen in recent law
about the tombstone usually involve three questions:
First, whether it is permitted (as is the custom in
certain Orthodox cemeteries) to have a photograph of the
deceased on the tombstone (cf. Greenwald, p. 380, note
1).   The second discussion is whether the secular date
may be used on the tombstone.   The third question is
whether the tombstone may be used for the benefit of the
living (for example, to sit down and rest upon it).
This third question has more meaning in the Orient,
where the tombstones are not vertical as with us, but
are laid horizontally, somewhat elevated, like a bench
over the grave.

As for the answers to these questions: (1) The
photograph on the tombstone is generally frowned upon as
a practice; (2) The secular date is reluctantly permitted, if it is at least accompanied by the Hebrew date;
(3) As for sitting on the tombstone, that question has
some bearing on our question, because what is involved
is the question of whether or not the tombstone is not
also for the benefit of the living, as mentioned above.
Generally that is answered in the affirmative.   So, as
mentioned above, the desires of the living should have
consideration in the discussion of the tombstone.

Now as to the specific question: May the tombstone bearing the name of the deceased give the name as the son of his mother, rather than--as is generally the usage--giving his name as the son of his father? Of course, the funeral director (or the rabbi who advised him) would be quite correct if he had merely said that the general **custom** is to cite a man's name with his father's name, e.g., as "Moses, the son of Amram." This is the way a man is called up to the Torah and thus is his name used in the **Get** and other formal documents.

Nevertheless, the question must be raised--as it is raised here in this comparatively rare question--whether this general custom of using the father's name is more than custom but is actual **law**. Is it **wrong** to use the mother's name describing the man as "Moses, the son of Yocheved," instead of "Moses, the son of Amram"? the answer goes to the heart of our question. The Bible records the name of a well-known Biblical character as the son of his mother, and never as the son of his father. King David's chief general (and his nephew) was Jacob ben Zeruyah. Zeruyah was David's sister (I Chronicles 2:16). Also in the Talmud there is an Amora whose name was Rav Mari ben Rachel (Yevamot 92b).

In fact, the great authority of two centuries ago, Ezekiel Landau, in his commentary to the **Shulchan Aruch** (**Dagul Merevava** to Even Ha-ezer 129.9), speaking of the divorce document in which the proper rendering of each name is vital, says that, in the case of a proselyte, we should use his mother's name instead of his father's name, and he cites the precedent of the rabbi mentioned in the Talmud, Mari, the son of Rachel. As a matter of fact, the **Pischei Teshuvah**, at the end of paragraph 26 to the same divorce section, says that if a man's name is better known by his mother's name than by his father's name, that should be used in the **Get**, and he says that it is obvious that if it is written thus, the **Get** is **kasher**.

This permissibility with regard to the divorce document in which the names have to be precise is crucial in all discussion of the specific matter involved here. As a matter of fact, there were communities which actually had an established custom of using the mother's instead of the father's name on the tombstone. One such community (and it could hardly have been the only one) wrote to David Hoffman telling of their established custom and wanting to know whether it is correct. He answers (**Melamed Leho-il**, Orach Chayim 23) and says that the tombstones which he had seen of all the great Rabbis give the father's name and not the mother's. Nevertheless, if it is an established custom in the community to use the mother's name, the custom should be continued, or at least not be objected to.

Now, why should such an Orthodox authority as David Hoffman permit the custom of using the mother's name, when he himself says that the tombstones of the great Rabbis that he saw had the father's name? The answer clearly must be that although most tombstones have the father's name, that is because this is the usual way of referring to a man, but that does not mean that the mother's name may **not** be used. In fact, in his responsum, he gives some examples in which the mother's name is used **exclusively**. In the prayer before the taking out of the Torah on holidays ("**Ribbono Shel Olam**"), the suppliant refers to himself by his mother's name. Also in the regular text of the **Yizkor** on holidays, the deceased is referred to as the child of the mother. (In our **Union Prayer Book**, we merely say "father" or "mother" or "brother," and do not use the personal name at all, but in all the **Machzorim** where the personal name of the deceased is used in the **Yizkor**, it is always as the child of the mother.) Also, as he correctly points out, it is a well-established custom when we pray for the sick to refer to the sick person by the mother's name only. This custom is based upon the verse in Psalms 116:16, where the suppliant says, "I am Thy servant, the son of Thy **handmaiden**."

Because of all these reasons and established precedents, and in spite of the fact that most of the tombstones that he had seen used the father's name, David Hoffman nevertheless was unwilling, in those communities where the custom was established to use the mother's name on the tombstone, to recommend that the custom be no longer followed.

To sum up: The tombstone was not a matter of strict detailed law, but largely of custom. When legal disputes have occurred, they emphasized the benefit that the custom might bring to the living. Hence their feelings must be consulted and considered. The devotional literature has many examples in which the mother's name is used to the exclusion of the father's name, and there are communities (or there **were** in Europe) in which the mother's names were used regularly on the tombstones. In this specific case, therefore, we can say that there is no real objection to the son's being called the son of his mother. In fact, we might follow the decision of Greenwald (pp. 380-381) with regard to the use of the secular date on the tombstone, namely, if the secular date is used together with the Hebrew date, the use of both dates would be permissible. So here, too, we might say that if the mother would consent to having the name of both parents--hers and her husband's--there could be no objection at all. But if with her husband's consent (as the inquirer states), her name alone is used as the parent, there is no real ground for objection.

Solomon B. Freehof

115. THE VANDALIZED CEMETERY
(Vol. LXXXIV, 1974, pp. 48-50)

QUESTION: The congregation in Poughkeepsie has been given the title to an old Jewish cemetery which has not been used for more than seventy years. The neighborhood in which the cemetery is located has become a slum. It is impossible to keep the cemetery decent. It is constantly being desecrated. It would cost a great deal of money to shield this cemetery from abuse, and even so, it is doubtful whether any effort could succeed. Besides, there is a possibility of neighborhood urban renewal, and it will be difficult to keep the cemetery anyhow. What should be done in this case? (Rabbi Henry Bamberger, Poughkeepsie, New York)

ANSWER: This tragic situation is, alas, not new. It has arisen time and time again in the past. In Europe, frequently the ruler of the neighborhood would send his cattle to graze in the Jewish cemetery. Such a case is mentioned by Israel Isserlein (14th century) in his **Terumat Hadeshen**, #284. This was deemed to be a particularly offensive desecration, with the cattle trampling over the graves and befouling them, and especially because the Talmud specifically forbids grazing cattle in the cemetery (Megila 29a). Worse than that, sometimes the government would want to run a new roadway through the cemetery. Sometimes--still worse--the government would want to repossess the cemetery. All these situations came up again and again, and the questions always are: What can we do? How much effort should we expend in the attempt to overcome these various threats?

Isserlein himself suggested that the congregation should not tax itself too heavily in order to bribe the officer of the king to keep his cattle out of the cemetery. After all, it is not the Jews themselves who are committing this desecration. As for the second situation, this arose in the city of Cracow, where some of the rabbis, including Moses Isserles, are buried (cited by Moses Feinstein in his **Igerot Mosheh**, Yoreh De-a 247). Of course, great effort should be expended to prevent, if possible, so permanent a desecration. But what if it fails? And what to do when the ruler repossesses a cemetery entirely? In the latter case, of course, there is no recourse other than disinterment. In fact, Moses Feinstein (who is the present head of the **Agudat Harabbanim** in America) suggested disinterment in the case of the old cemetery in New Orleans, which was in the same condition as the one in Poughkeepsie, mentioned in the question. He suggests that disinterment is the only permitted solution (**Igerot Mosheh**, Yoreh De-a 246), and he prescribes that while all the bones taken out of the old cemetery need not be put in separate graves, and may be put in one large grave, nevertheless they should not be mixed up with each other, but kept separated by ridges of earth or stone.

This solution--disinterment--is, of course, the optimal solution, for once the bodies or the bones are removed, there is no sanctity left in the land from which they were removed. The land is then considered **Karka Olam**, the world's earth, which cannot be prohibited for any ritual reason.

Nevertheless, although Moses Feinstein's suggestion is basically the best, it entails many difficulties. If the cemetery has not been used for almost seventy years, the bones, while they still exist, may well be scattered and unrecoverable. In this regard, it must be remembered also that disinterment is always a cause for sorrow. In traditional law a person must sit on the ground as in **Shiv-a** for a whole day while the bones of his close kin are being disinterred (Yoreh De-a 403.1). In fact, Moses Sofer, in the case of Budapest, where the whole cemetery was taken away from the Jewish community, actually forbade the **Chevra Kadisha** to make public the date and the hour of the disinterment, so that a large portion of the community should not need to sit on the ground as in **Shiv-a (Chatam Sofer**, Yoreh De-a 353).

Perhaps the best thing to do under the circumstances would be, first of all, to remove all the tombstones and to set them up in a special place in the existing protected cemetery. Thus, the memorial of the departed will not be forgotten. Secondly, if there are traceable descendants of those buried in that old cemetery, they should be gathered in a meeting and asked to decide whether they are content with the preservation of the tombstones, or would also wish that the bones be disinterred. The chances are that they will be content with leaving the bones at rest, since they will very likely consider that it is to the honor of the dead not to disturb their bones, and much is permitted in Jewish legal tradition if it is for the honor of the dead.

Finally, the community can do what Rabbi Moses Goldberg of New Orleans suggested in his question to

Moses Feinstein--namely, that a layer of earth three handbreadths or more be spread over the entire cemetery. Moses Feinstein rejects this; yet it is, nevertheless, a possible suggestion, since when a layer of earth that thick--three handbreadths, or, according to the **Shulchan Aruch**, six handbreadths (Yoreh De-a 362.4)--is laid down, the rights of those already buried below have been fully protected, since, if need be, new bodies may then be buried over the old graves. While it is debatable that such an earth-covering would cancel the sanctity of the old cemetery, at least the rights of those buried in it would be completely provided for.

One additional thing, however, must also be provided for, if possible--namely, to see to it by all means available that if the area is taken over in an urban renewal (the possibility of which is suggested in the question), then this particular section of land should never be dug up for foundations for houses (which would disturb and scatter the bones of the dead), but should become one of the open areas converted into a park; and the very trees and grass would be an evidence of respect to those who sleep below the surface.

Solomon B. Freehof

116. PUTTING SMALL STICKS IN THE HANDS OF THE DECEASED WHEN PLACING IN THE GRAVE
(Vol. XXXIII, 1923, p. 59)

QUESTION: Will you please tell me what is the origin and the significance of the custom to put small sticks of wood into the hands of the dead body when placing it in the grave.

ANSWER: This custom is not universally observed, and is not mentioned in the codes. R. Moses Sofer, in his Responsa (**Chatam Sofer**, Yoreh De-a, no. 327), mentions the custom and states that when he was in Prossnitz, he heard from the members of the **Chevra Kadisha** there that the purpose of the custom was to indicate the belief in the resurrection of the dead. The dead are provided with these sticks on which to lean and support themselves when getting up at the time of the resurrection. To this explanation of the **Chevra Kadisha** men of Prossnitz, R. Moses Sofer remarks that it is rather weak and unsound, just as the thin wooden sticks are weak and not strong enough to lean upon them. With all due respect

to R. Moses Sofer, however, I must say that he forgot or
overlooked a passage in the Palestinian Talmud (Kilayim
IX.4, 32b), where it is related that R. Jeremiah requested, among other things, that a staff be put into
his hand when placed into the grave, so that when the
Messiah will come, he, R. Jeremiah, should be ready to
get up and march.

Jacob Z. Lauterbach and Committee

See also:

S.B. Freehof, "Funeral Folklore," **Reform Responsa**,
pp. 174ff; "Funeral Folklore," **Recent Reform
Responsa**, pp. 149ff; "Funeral Folklore," **New
Reform Responsa**, pp. 262ff.

117. MOURNING CUSTOMS
(Vol. XXIII, 1913, pp. 176-179)

It is perhaps not out of place to state in this
connection certain principles that are to guide the
Reform rabbi in matters pertaining to mourning customs
in general. We are here altogether too much influenced
by the legalistic view of tradition to have our own
attitude toward the ancient practice clearly defined.
Most people, the rabbis included, find only that we have
abandoned much that was formerly observed, and consequently our attitude is too negative to lead to a proper
appreciation of the Reform principle. The ancient
mourning customs, such as the tearing of the garments
(**Keri-a**), the sitting on the ground during the seven
days (**Shiv-a**), and similar practices modified in the
Mishna and the **Shulchan Aruch** have been simply dropped
by the people as militating against the spirit of modern
times, and the abrogation of the same was ratified by
the members of the Breslau Conference after their validity had been discussed in scholarly articles (especially
in Geiger's **Theologische Zeitschrift** III and IV) some
time before. Still, neither the falling into disuse nor
the abrogation could satisfy the Jewish conscience,
which demands a positive religious principle to go by.
Consequently, we are still asked questions such as: How
long does the time of mourning last? What form should
the mourning take for parents, children, or relatives?
That is to say, the people want to be guided by us,
expecting our religious advice in matters which are of

the deepest and holiest concern to them, when their innermost feelings cry for an outward expression.

Now, it cannot be denied, nor should the fact be ignored, that the Talmudic Halacha based the laws of mourning upon Biblical narratives which are contradictory to the very spirit, if not also to the letter, of the law. The Deuteronomic Law expressly says (Deut. 14:1): "Children, Ye are of the Lord your God, and therefore ye shall not cut yourselves in the flesh nor make your heads bald on account of the dead." In other words, all the rites and ceremonies which the heathen practiced while mourning for their dead, showing thereby their terrors of a cruel fate ruling human life, should be discarded by the people of Israel, who are--even in the midst of woe and affliction--to realize that they are children of a benign Father Who sends trials to man only to test and chasten him in order to strengthen his faith in and love for Him, as well as his whole character.

Death should not cast its disheartening gloom upon a life which is forever to serve the higher purpose of the Divine Master above. Therefore, it was especially the priest in the sanctuary who was prohibited from practicing these mourning customs, in order that he might offer the people a pattern of perfect submission to the will of God on high (Lev. 21:5, 10).

Indeed, an ethnological and historical study of the mourning customs among the various tribes brings out the fact that the entire heathen world was filled with fear not merely of death, but even more so of the dead, who, while departing into the land of the shades, could ever claim anew what he had possessed here on earth (the things he wore on his body, the weapons he owned, nay, even the human beings that were his). Accordingly, all funeral rites and mourning customs of yore have the character of fear rather than of love and pious devotion. All this the prophetic spirit of Judaism was to change. "Do not cry over the dead," says the prophet (Jer. 22:10); "Tear your hearts, not your garments," says another (Joel 11:13).

The entire pessimistic conception of life and death should give way to that optimism which made R. Meir write down on the margin of his Bible, where it says, "And God saw all that He made, and behold, it was very good"--"even death" (**Bereshit Rabba** 9.5). Accordingly, a person is far more in accord with Jewish teaching if he avoids ostentatious signs of mourning, manifesting instead the true spirit of submissiveness in hours of affliction and loss. The Rabbis of the Talmud themselves must have felt that all the signs of mourning are but a concession to the people when they set down the rule that in all these matters we should follow the less rigid rule ("Ba-avelut holechim achar hamekel," Mo-ed Katan 18a).

Nevertheless, we must not lose sight of the respect and pious regard we owe to the departed, and of the true sentiment of tender love and affection that must find its proper expression at the loss of the beloved. Here the customs of each land and age prescribe certain forms to honor him whose life work is done, and also to guard the sorrowing against any intrusion that may encroach upon their feelings. And religion, above all, must step in to offer its balm of comfort to the bruised heart and to hallow the grief by special hours of devotion and prayer, by abstention from the daily pursuit of business for a certain period, and by some expression of sympathy on the part of friends and fellow-members of the congregation. Only the particulars as to time and form are better left to the individuals or to local customs.

At no time, however, should we speak in deprecating terms of the so-called "Kaddish Jews," whom only affliction reminds of their sacred obligations and allegiance to the synagogue or to religion in general. For, after all, we are taught by our sages: "Mitoch shelo lishmah ba lishmah." Often people act from lower motives, but are led to act from higher motives, "learning to aspire more and more to the higher ideal." We know full well that piety cannot take the place of religion. And yet how many have, through filial piety, been awakened to become religious Jews! Professor Lazarus voices a great truth when he pleads for the revival of the beautiful custom of blessing the children and grandchildren on Sabbath eve at the family reunion as forming a source of religious regeneration from week to week (Treu und Frei, pp. 305ff), and I wish that Dr. Berkowitz, in a revised edition of his Sabbath Eve Service, would accord a place to this sweet old custom by which our domestic religion would be greatly enriched. For is not parental love the stepping-stone to the love of God?

K. Kohler and D. Neumark

See also:

S.B. Freehof, "Funeral Folklore," Reform Responsa, pp. 174ff; "Greeting Mourners," Current Reform Responsa, pp. 125ff.

118. KADDISH
(1980)

QUESTION: What is the origin of the Kaddish? For what length of time should the surviving family recite Kaddish? For whom is it obligatory to recite Kaddish?

ANSWER: The most frequently recited prayer of the traditional synagogue service is the Kaddish. It was originally not a prayer commemorating the dead, but a great doxology which served as a way of separating various segments of the service (Ismar Elbogen, Der juedische Gottesdienst in seiner geschichtlichen Entwicklung, 1924, pp. 92ff). It was also used at the conclusion of segments of the study of Rabbinic literature, and only later became a prayer recited at the burial service.

Originally, the Kaddish was recited as the congregational response to a sermonic discourse with the main emphasis on the words "Yehe Shemeh Rabba..." (Sota 49a), and so the Talmud knew the Kaddish by these words ("May His great name be praised"). It seems, therefore, that the origin of the Kaddish lies in Beit Midrash (house of study) rather than in the synagogue (J. Heinemann, Hatefila Bitkufat Hatana-im Veha-emora-im, p. 173, and "The Background of Jesus' Prayer in the Jewish Liturgy," The Lord's Prayer and Jewish Liturgy, ed. J. Petuchowski and M. Brocke, pp. 81ff).

The first connection between the Kaddish and the mourner came about in the following fashion: At the conclusion of the Musaf service on Shabbat, the leader of the congregation would comfort the mourners and then recite the Kaddish (Soferim 19.12). However, we do not find the Kaddish recited by mourners themselves till the 13th century (Machzor Vitry, ed. Horvitz, p. 74). Isaac Or Zarua stated that this was customary in Bohemia and the Rhineland, but not in France (Or Zarua, 754). The practice of reciting Kaddish for the dead may have been influenced by a medieval Midrash which stated that such a prayer could help the soul after death (Seder Eliyahu Zuta, ed. Friedmann, p. 23, note 52; Menorat Hama-or 1.1).

It became customary to recite the Kaddish for an entire year following death, as the Talmud stated that the piety of a son could help the deceased father or grandfather (Sanh. 104a); therefore, sons were to be instructed to say the Kaddish properly (Sefer Chasidim, ed. Margolis, 722). It was felt that the tortures of the netherworld could last twelve months (Mishna, Eduyot

II.10; R.H. 17a). Both thoughts together led to the recital of the **Kaddish** by a son for twelve months (**Kol Bo**, 114). Eventually, that custom was changed to a recital of only eleven months, as the Mishna just cited asserted that the wicked are judged for a year, and no one wished to imply that his/her parents were wicked (Isserles to **Shulchan Aruch**, Yoreh De-a 376.4; **Aruch Hashulchan**, 376.15). Most Reform congregations have rejected this line of reasoning and returned to a recital of the **Kaddish** for twelve months (**Gates of Mitzvah**, p. 62).

At first, only a son recited **Kaddish** for his dead father, but, according to Ashkenazic custom, a daughter was similarly permitted to recite **Kaddish** (**Chavat Chemed**, 60). Isserles stated that in some places it was customary to recite **Kaddish** for all of one's dead kin (to **Shulchan Aruch**, Yoreh De-a, 376.4). Certainly, this would extend to the seven relatives for whom one would observe mourning. They are: father, mother, brother, sister, son, daughter, and husband or wife (Lev. 21:2 provided a primary list which was expanded in Mo-ed Katan 20b; **Shulchan Aruch**, Yoreh De-a, 374.4). Some would extend this list even further, and, certainly, we could agree that it may be so extended as prompted by individual feelings. We would include scholars or people who had particular influence on an individual's life.

In some communities it has become customary for the entire congregation to stand and recite the **Kaddish** in commemoration of the martyrs of the Holocaust. **Kaddish** for the dead should be recited at daily services at the synagogue whenever such services are held on a regular basis, privately at home, or at the weekly synagogue services, for a period of twelve months (Isserles to **Sh.A.**, Yoreh De-a, 376.4).

Traditionally, the recitation of **Kaddish** has required a **Minyan** (**Shulchan Aruch**, Orach Chayim, 55.1), as public prayer was preferred over private prayer (**Sh.A.**, Orach Chayim 90.9). It emphasized the presence of the **Shechina** in a community of worshipers. During the period of mourning, the presence of a congregation will help overcome sorrow. By reciting **Kaddish** in a congregation, "we declare the merit of those whose parting we mourn, that they have instilled in us loyalty to God and devotion to His service and the serene acceptance of His Will, so that in the presence of the congregation when we think of the departed, we praise God's Name in serenity of heart" (S.B. Freehof, **Reform Jewish Practice**, vol. I, p. 170). It is for this reason that friends of the family will join in a service (with or without a **Minyan**) at the house of mourning during the **Shiv-a**

(Gates of Mitzvah, pp. 62ff). The year of regular Kaddish recital begins with these services.

The prayer--as a doxology--praises God, and thereby lets the mourner reaffirm his faith in God despite all that has happened. It has become a prayer which expresses acceptance, loyalty, and devotion to God, and as such has become part of every Jewish service throughout the world. The Kaddish may, therefore, be appropriately repeated by all at any and every service; and any worshiper may stand during its recital. This is especially appropriate if done in commemoration of the Holocaust. Through this prayer, we express sorrow for unknown martyrs who have died and sympathy toward friends who have suffered bereavement.

Walter Jacob, Chairman
Leonard S. Kravitz
Eugene Lipman
W. Gunther Plaut
Harry A. Roth
Rav A. Soloff
Bernard Zlotowitz

119. TITLES ON A KADDISH LIST
(1979)

QUESTION: Is it permissible to include titles for individuals listed on the weekly Kaddish list read at the Shabbat service? (Rabbi Stephen Pinsky, Temple Sinai of Bergen County, Tenafly, New Jersey)

ANSWER: The origin of reading names of deceased individuals at services seems to lie in the period immediately following the Crusades. The martyrs of that dreaded period in the Rhineland were memorialized on the anniversary date of their death by the entire community. Subsequently, similar memorial lists were created for the Black Death, as well as other tragedies in the Rhineland and neighboring communities. In addition, it became customary to remember those who had been generous to the synagogue, especially during the concluding day of the Shalosh Regalim, as the reading from Deuteronomy 16:17 stated, "Everyone shall give in accordance with the gift of his hand." Solomon B. Freehof, in his article on "Hazkarat Neshamot" (Hebrew Union College Annual, vol. 36, 1965) has theorized, along with others, that the custom of praising those individuals on the festival

soon spread to the Shabbat with the saying of a "Mi
Sheberach" when some member of the family, yet alive,
was called to the Torah.   Isserles has noted a custom
similar to this in **Shulchan Aruch** (Orach Chayim 284.6):
"It is customary, after the reading of the Torah, to
mention those who have departed and to bless those who
support the congregation."   Here we do not have lists,
but individuals arranging to have the names of dear
departed read.   After a while, the custom became oppres-
sive, especially as a "Mi Sheberach" was recited for
each individual and the list could be long.   This has
been discussed by Ephraim Margolis in **Sha-ar Efrayim**,
and also by Samuel Lipschitz, in his commentary **Sha-arei
Rachamim**.   The Reform Movement has moved the reading of
the names of deceased members from the Torah service to
the conclusion of the service when our mourner's **Kaddish**
is recited.

     None of these discussions deals with titles of
individuals, nor does Gruenwald's **Kol Bo Al Avelut**.   We
must, therefore, treat this subject by analogy with
customs connected with the tombstone.   In past centuries, tombstones were often very elaborate, and virtually
an entire eulogy was inscribed on them.   For example,
the tombstone of Meir of Rothenburg reported all the
details of his capture by bandits, who then turned him
over to King Rudolf, who imprisoned him while seeking
ransom from the Jewish community; and of his eventual
death in prison, as well as of the ransom paid for his
body by a pious follower.   Other tombstones listed all
the accomplishments or offices held by individuals.   By
contrast, nowadays our tombstones rarely do more than
provide the name of the deceased, dates of birth and
death, and perhaps a verse which suitably characterizes
his or her life.   In other words, our period has become
democratic and rather reticent about excessive use of
praise or titles.   That mood is probably appropriate for
the memorial lists of the congregation.   On the other
hand, if a strongly fixed local tradition of reading
names with titles exists, it would be proper to continue
it.

                                        Walter Jacob

           120.   STANDING DURING RECITAL OF **KADDISH**
                  (Vol. XXIV, 1914, pp. 152-153)

     The question of the propriety of standing during
the recital of the mourner's **Kaddish** must be answered

from the viewpoint of the **Kaddish** in general.   The
mourner's **Kaddish** had its origin in early Talmudic, if
not pre-Talmudic times, as can be seen in the **Testament
of Abraham**, Version A, XIV (see **Jewish Encyclopedia,
s.v.** "Kaddish"), according to which Abraham is the auth-
or of the **Kaddish Yatom** (cf. also Tobit IV:17, and my
Toledot Ha-ikarim I, 80).   But this was only in connection with the **Birkat Avelim** in the first week of mourning (Soferim XIX.12: "**Umotse sham ha-avelim...ve-omer
aleihem beracha, ve-achar kach omer Kaddish**").   The
Kaddish of the mourner during the first year is a late
institution, first introduced about the 12th century in
Germany, and from all that I can see, the mourner was
regarded as the substitute for the **Chazan**.
    Now there is a controversy whether the congregation
should rise for every **Kaddish** or only for special ones.
(Cf. Rambam, **Yad**, Hil. Tefila IX.1,5,8; **Sh.A.**, Orach
Chayim, Hil. Berachot 53.1; **Turei Zahav**, 1 and 56; 1
Haggah, and **Magen Avraham** 4).   This controversy has
never been authoritatively decided, and the **minhag** varies according to the countries and congregations (in
Poland the congregation remains seated; in Bohemia it
rises).   But there is no doubt that the **Chazan** should
always recite the **Kaddish** standing.   Consequently, the
mourner, who is considered the substitute of the **Chazan**,
should also stand.   In some congregations, only one of
the mourners (according to the established order of
precedence) is admitted to the front row to recite the
Kaddish aloud, while the rest of the mourners repeat silently or in a low voice.   In our Reform congregations,
where the rabbi recites the **Kaddish** and the mourners
repeat silently, none of them evidently can be considered a substitute for the **Chazan**.   Nevertheless, it is
evident that the old idea of the mourner reciting the
Kaddish before the congregation still exists, and this
minhag should be continued, except in rare cases where
there is definite and sufficient reason for not doing
so.

Can a Distinction Be Made Between the Dead?

    If this question refers to the preceding, I would
suggest that the mourners stand at all recitals of the
Kaddish for the dead, for whom mourning is a legal duty
(viz., relative in the first degree).   If this question
is general, I refer to Yoreh De-a, Hil. Avelut, where
certain distinctions are set forth as the established
din and **minhag**.

The Educational Value of Yahrzeit

The **Yahrzeit** as a permanent institution in connection with the recital of **Kaddish** appears first in Germany about the 14th century, but since it goes back to an ancient practice known in Talmudic literature ("**Ta-anit beyom shemet bo aviv ve-imo**," Nedarim), and since its good influence is evident in manifold ways, I would strongly favor its retention as far as possible.

In addition, as chairman of the committee, I would say that while much may be adduced in favor of the individual mourner's rising for the **Kaddish** as the outflow of the soul, longing for comfort to be found in submission to God's will, in conformity with tradition--there is also a consideration for, and a sense of sympathy with, the mourner expressed by the whole congregation rising for **Kaddish**, wherever it is introduced. The decision of the question must therefore be left to the congregation.

In general, I would here refer to the ancient Rabbinical dictum, "**Mitoch shelo lishmah ba lishmah**," "A good practice, even if not done for its own sake, but for some less spiritual motive, should still be encouraged, since it may eventually lead to a more spiritual view," because it applies to the so-called "Kaddish Jew," who attends divine service only in honor of his dead parents. While religion is not merely piety, nevertheless, filial piety shown by the mourners may in the end lead to a more permanently religious attitude.

K. Kohler

NOTE:

In some Reform congregations the traditional custom has been continued of having all mourners who desire to do so--men and women alike--rise for the **Kaddish**. We concur in Dr. Kohler's judgment, appended to the 1914 responsum above, that there is no reason to press for discontinuing that custom.
But it is clear that in a large number of congregations, the custom has grown and flourished to have the entire congregation rise and recite the **Kaddish** as a community. The original reason for the institution of this custom was to provide a sense of unity and community support for the mourners. Tragically, a second reason has evolved. The Holocaust makes mourners out of all Jews, and that ongoing sense of loss is expressed through the

congregation's rising and unison recitation of the Kaddish.

Responsa Committee (1980)

121. LENGTH OF TIME FOR RECITAL OF **KADDISH**
(Vol. XXIII, 1913, pp. 173-176)

Historically of no great significance, one ritual question looms up large in the estimate of the people and is therefore most frequently brought before the rabbi of today for decision, viz.: How long after the death or burial of the relative is the **Kaddish** to be recited, and on what day is the **Yahrzeit** to be observed, and the like. An elucidation of the whole practice seems to me, therefore, quite in place. The name **Kaddish**, which--like the prayer itself--is Aramaic, is found first, as far as I can see, in Mas. Soferim (16.12, 19.19, 21.1). The Talmudic term is "**Yehe Shemeh Rabba.**" It is the congregational response to the reader's call to praise the Lord,[1] and the idea underlying it is the messianic hope as expressed in Ezekiel 38:23: "**Vehitgadalti vehitkadashti,**" somewhat corresponding to the original form of the so-called Lord's Prayer in the New Testament.[2] In the Babylonian schoolhouse or synagogue it was recited as a doxology at the conclusion of the Agadic lesson or homily addressed to large assemblies, and hence it was recited in Aramaic.[3] The more value and importance was attached to this **Kaddish** recital, the more mystic power was ascribed to it.

Originating, no doubt, in the primitive pagan belief that the son must, by some rite (originally by offering food and drink), keep the father's soul from perdition in the grave, the view took shape in Jewish circles that by having the son or grandson study and teach the Law, the father escapes from the fire of Gehenna.[4] And the same magic power was ascribed to the recital of the "**Barechu**" (Praise the Lord) or of the

---

[1] Sifrei, Deut. 30:6.

[2] See **J.E.**, s.v. "**Kaddish**" and "**Lord's Prayer.**"

[3] Sota 49a; Shab. 119b; Ber. 3a; comp. Tosafot **eadem**; Kol Bo, VII; **Tur**, Orach Chayim LVI.

[4] **Tana d.b. Eliyahu Rabba**, XVII; **Zuta**, XII; Sanh. 104a; **Sefer Chasidim**, Vislinezki, 12.

Kaddish. Quite a number of legends illustrative of this
idea circulated in Gaonic times. According to one, it
was Akiva, according to another, R. Yochanan ben Zakkai,
who saved a poor soul from Gehenna's fire by teaching
the son either the Torah or the prayer "**Barechu.**"[5]

However, this very belief in the power of prayer
for the dead can be traced to pre-Christian times, as in
the Testament of Abraham (Version A, ch. XIV), where the
Patriarch is described as saving a soul from Purgatory
by his prayer, in which the Archangel Michael joins him.
No doubt, the whole conception was adopted by the Jew
from his Persian surroundings, and the Church took it
over from the Essene circles.

Now, inasmuch as the Purgatory fires, called "the
judgment of Gehenna," were believed to last twelve
months,[6] the **Kaddish** ought by right to be recited by the
son throughout the whole year from the day of burial on.
This is indeed given as the custom in **Kol Bo,** CXIV.
But, as Moses Isserles of Cracow tells us in the name of
Isaac of Corbeil (13th century), it was felt to be rather unbecoming to a son to regard his father as so sinful
as to be subject to the full twelve months' punishment
in Gehenna, and therefore it became customary to cease
reciting the **Kaddish** eleven months after the father's
death.[7]

Much later, the custom spread to have the son recite the **Kaddish** also for the mother, and still later
for the wife, brother, sister, or son.

Originally, then, the **Kaddish** recital for the dead
rests on a view which has no root in our system of belief; but, like all the funeral rites in a later stage,
it assumed the character of pious regard for the dead.
All the more it behooves us to do away with such customs
and practices as still bear the character of crude
superstitions. Accordingly, Dr. Solomon of Hamburg
proposed at the Rabbinical Conference of Breslau[8] to
have the eleven months' recital of the **Kaddish** changed

---

[5] Seder Eliyahu Zuta, XVII; Kala Rab., II; **Menorat
Hama-or** I, A, h; **Machzor Vitry,** 144; comp. M. Friedman,
Pseudo Seder Eliyahu Zuta, pp. 23-25, and Landshut, **Ma-
avar Yabok,** ch. XXXI.

[6] Eduyot II.10. Rosh Hashana 17a; compare Tosefta,
Sanhedrin XIII.3-5, where it is an object of controversy
between the Shammaites and Hillelites.

[7] **Shulchan Aruch,** Orach Chayim 376.4, and **Darchei Mosheh**
to **Tur, eadem.**

[8] See **Protocolle d. Rabbinerversammlung zu Breslau,** p.
286.

into a recital during the whole year of mourning. Certainly, this ought to be generally adopted by the members of our Conference.

As to the **Yahrzeit**[9]--its history is also singular. The name, which is found also among the Jews of Italy and of Persia,[10] has been taken over from the Germans, who held a **Todtenfeier** annually for their dead on the day of their death on which the souls were believed to be allowed to return to look after their relatives.[11]

The name occurs in Jewish literature first among German authors at the end of the 16th and the beginning of the 17th century,[12] whereas the Spanish Jews of the Orient opposed the **Kaddish** recital on the **Yahrzeit** as casting reflection on the parental honor in the spirit expressed above. Only Isaac Luria, who was of German descent, defended the custom, saying that it was to elevate the parent's soul into a higher realm of **Gan Eden**.

On the other hand, it seems to have been an ancient custom to fast on the anniversary of the parent's death. This is mentioned in **Sefer Chasidim** and **Kol Bo**,[13] and seems to rest on the baraita:[14] "One swears to abstain from food and drink on the anniversary of the death of his father." No doubt, this day was regarded as one of ill luck, and--like the fasting after a bad dream--it was meant to avert the same.

We have here again a custom based on some superstitious notion transformed into a mark of filial piety, and it is as such that it claims our consideration.

K. Kohler and D. Neumark

---

[9] Berliner, **Rome** II, d. 55; Loew, **Ges. Schr.** IV, 264, note 1.

[10] Peterman, **Reisen im Orient** II, 175.

[11] Schoenwarth, **Liter. u. Sagen aus der Oberpfalz.**

[12] Isaac of Tyana's **Minhagim**; Mordecai Jaffe, **Levush Hatechelet.**

[13] **Sefer Chasidim**, ed. Wistenetzki, 200; **Kol Bo**, CXIV.

[14] Nedarim 12a; Shevu-ot 20b.

122. KADDISH AND DISTINCTIONS BETWEEN THE DEAD
(Vol. XXIV, 1914, p. 153)

If this question refers to the preceding, I would suggest that the mourners stand at all recitals of the **Kaddish** for the dead, for whom mourning is a legal duty (viz., relatives in the first degree). If this question be general, I refer to Yoreh De-a, Hil. Avelut, where certain distinctions are set forth as the established **din** and **minhag**.

K. Kohler

See also:

S.B. Freehof, "Kaddish for First Wife," **Reform Responsa**, pp. 162ff; "Kaddish and Yahrzeit for a Child," **ibid.**, pp. 165ff; "Kaddish for Apostates and Gentiles," **Recent Reform Responsa**, pp. 132ff; "Some Kaddish Customs," **Current Reform Responsa**, pp. 178ff; "Kaddish and the Three Steps Backward," **Recent Reform Responsa**, pp. 217ff; "Gentile Visitors and the Kaddish," **Modern Reform Responsa**, pp. 62ff; "Kaddish When Worshiping Alone," **Recent Reform Responsa**, pp. 14ff.

123. A PROSELYTE RECITING KADDISH FOR DECEASED PARENTS
(Vol. LXV, 1955, pp. 90-91)

QUESTION: A woman of my congregation, who had been officially converted to Judaism, requested that the names of her deceased parents be read before the **Kaddish**, on the occasion of the **Yahrzeit**. A member of my Board desired to know whether traditional law would favor such a practice.

ANSWER: To the Rabbinic view of the proselyte and his parentage, there are two aspects--a theoretical and a practical one. Theoretically, the convert is a new-born babe. The old self has been replaced by a new self (Yevamot 48a). In practice, however, when confronted by a real situation, the Rabbis flung their theory aside. They permitted a proselyte to exercise the right of inheritance upon the death of his parents (Demai 6.10).

They also imposed upon the proselyte the obligation to honor his natural parents, holding him responsible for any misconduct toward them (Yoreh De-a 241).

The Rabbis, it would seem, had too keen a sense of the real and the practical to follow slavishly their own theories. There is no good reason, therefore, why we should not be as realistic and practical as the Rabbis of old and permit the converted woman to give full expression to her filial sentiment and obligation.

Israel Bettan

124. KADDISH FOR A UNITARIAN SISTER
(Vol. LXVII, 1957, pp. 82-85)

QUESTION: "Should a sister who is a devout Jewess say **Kaddish** for a sister who had become a Unitarian?" I also received a question asking me the following: "A widow had a husband who was half-Jewish, and he was not affiliated with any Jewish congregation, but bequeathed his home to the Temple. The woman wants to have her husband included in the congregational **Kaddish** list."

ANSWER: Both questions have certain complications, but there is a basic problem common to them both. Let us dispose of the complications first. With regard to the Unitarian, the complication concerns the Jewish status of the woman who died. Does the fact that she joined a Unitarian church make her an apostate, since, after all, she added no deity to her belief in the one God? And: May not the fact that she asked to be buried in a Jewish cemetery indicate repentance of whatever apostasy may have been involved?

With regard to the man who was half-Jewish--if his mother was Jewish, then he is fully a Jew, since in mixed marriages we follow the status of the mother; if his mother was Gentile, he was a Gentile. Thus, his status is not quite clear from the question.

But behind both these complications there is a clear and basic question, i.e.: May we say **Kaddish**-- first for an apostate, or, secondly, for a born Gentile who never was connected with Judaism? As to the apostate, he is involved in special laws with regard to his burial. The laws are derived from the saying in the Talmud (B. Sanhedrin 46a) that relatives should not mourn for those that had been sentenced by the court.

This was fixed and developed as a law in the tractate Semachot II that we should not concern ourselves with one who "goes aside from the path of the community" ("**Ein mit-asekim imahem**"). This is embodied as law in the **Shulchan Aruch**, Yoreh De-a 345.5. Of course, the question still is: What does it mean when we say that we should not be concerned with them? Generally, the commentators take it to mean that we do not give them the full ritual, such as standing in the line of mourners, giving eulogies, etc.; but even the strict Moses Sofer of Pressburg says that, nevertheless, we must provide a burial place for them in our cemeteries (see his responsum Yoreh De-a 341). However, should we say **Kaddish** for them? This brings us closer to our question.

This question--whether we should say **Kaddish** for them--has its precedent during the time when **Marranos** escaped from Spain and there was often a difference in religious status between the generations in one family. We might combine this question with the clearer question, namely: Should we say **Kaddish** for a non-Jew who is not an apostate, since he had never been a Jew? This, too, can be, and is, a practical question. It can come up in the case of a man converted to Judaism whose father remains a non-Jew. May the Jewish son say **Kaddish** for that Gentile father? Let us, therefore, deal with the question basically, beginning first with the question of whether to say **Kaddish** for an apostate, and then whether one may say **Kaddish** for a Gentile.

The question as to apostates, which arises first in the 16th century with regard to **Marranos**, is itself based upon an older Talmudic precedent.

Many legends were told about Rabbi Meir and the famous apostate Elisha ben Abuyah **(Acher)**. In B. Chagiga 15b it is told that Rabbi Meir made great efforts to redeem the soul of this apostate from Gehinnom and to bring him into Paradise. Since the purpose of the **Kaddish** is the redemption of the father, and since the dictum is quoted in discussions of the **Kaddish** that "The son brings merit to the father," therefore, the precedent of Rabbi Meir is used in the discussion of whether a Jewish son may do merit, i.e., redeem his apostate father by saying **Kaddish** for him. This question came as a practical enquiry before Rabbi David Cohen of the Island of Corfu in the 16th century (see his Responsa, section 30). He concludes that the son should say **Kaddish** for his father, even though some might argue that the **Kaddish** will not avail this apostate. Nevertheless, it is the duty of the son to honor his father and to benefit him as much as he can by saying **Kaddish**.

So Moses Isserles, in his commentary, **Darchei Mosheh** to the **Tur** (Yoreh De-a #376) says that a son

should say **Kaddish** for an apostate father, but not if
that father died a natural death; only if the father was
slain should the child say **Kaddish** for him, since the
slaying was a means to atonement, for the father certainly would have repented before he was slain. Isserles repeats this opinion in his commentary to the **Shulchan Aruch** (same reference). The commentators Taz and
Shach, to the **Shulchan Aruch** at this point, underline
Isserles' limitation that the **Kaddish** be said only if
the father is slain. However, Solomon Eiger, son of
Akiva Eiger (Gilion Maharsha) says that if the deceased
apostate has no other mourners, then the one mourner
should say **Kaddish** for him even if he was not slain but
died on his bed.

Abraham Toomim, a Galician rabbi (end of the 19th
century), in his Responsa **Chesed Le-Avraham**, Tinyana,
Yoreh De-a #84, says that if the father is slain, the
son is **in duty bound** to say **Kaddish**, but if the father
dies on his bed, the son is not in duty bound, but he is
not prohibited from saying it. And he adds, "There
certainly can be no **prohibition** to utter this praise to
the Almighty, i.e., the **Kaddish**."

A more recent responsum (written in 1933) by Aaron
Walkin, Rabbi of Pinsk-Karlin, bridges the gap between
the matter of apostates discussed above and the second
question which was asked about Christians (see his **Zekan
Aharon** II, #87). He is asked specifically whether one
may say **Kaddish** for a Christian. The question comes to
him in the following way: A man is converted to Judaism.
His father is not converted to Judaism. Then the father
dies. The son, being a Jew, wants to say **Kaddish** for
his Gentile father. May he do so? Aaron Walkin, upon
the basis of most of the material which I have cited
above, decides that he certainly may. He argues **a fortiori**, if a son may say **Kaddish** for an apostate who
wilfully deserted Judaism, certainly a son may say **Kaddish** for a man who is naturally following the religion
in which he was brought up. Then he adds that if it
would not seem too surprising to say so, he would even
express the opinion that not only **may** this son say **Kaddish**, but actually he **must** say **Kaddish**; he is in duty
bound to do so.

In the responsa of Abraham Zvi Klein, rabbi in
Hungary during the past century (**Be-erot Avraham**, #11)
the author is asked whether we may accept a gift for the
synagogue from a Gentile woman. He answers that we may
do so. Then he is asked whether we may pray for her,
which she requested. To this his answer is that of
course we may; and he gives the following reasons: In
the Temple in Jerusalem they sacrificed seventy oxen in
behalf of the seventy nations. Further, it is accepted
by all Israel that the righteous of all nations have a

portion in the world to come. In B. Gittin 60a we learn
that for the sake of peace we should visit the sick of
the Gentiles and bury their dead.   When Maimonides records this law in chapter 10 of his Hilchot Melachim, he
adds: "For the Lord is good to all and His tender mer-
cies are over all His works."   So there is no prohibition of the **Chevra Kadisha** to record her name and her
good deed, and we should recite for her an "**El Male
Rachamim**" on **Yizkor** Days.

Thus, while there is not much discussion on this
matter, yet whoever discussed it answers in the affirmative. There may be some opinions in the negative, but I
have not seen them.   It seems clear that according to
the law, you are completely justified (as Rabbi Toomim
said) "to utter this praise of God" in honor of a deceased Christian or "apostate."

Solomon B. Freehof

125.   MEMORIALIZING CHRISTIAN RELATIVES
(1977)

QUESTION: A Christian woman, converted to Judaism
and married to a Jew, arranged for her parents and
other (Gentile) relatives to be memorialized in the
Kaddish list of the congregation which is read
annually.   She died, and her Jewish-born husband
has since remarried. Now he wants the names of the
Gentile relatives of his late wife removed from the
Kaddish list. He and his late wife had had children, so these names are the names of the grandparents and other relatives of the man's children.
(Rabbi P. Irving Bloom, Mobile, Alabama)

ANSWER: There are a number of questions involved in
this inquiry. First, is it proper to have the names of
Christians on the regular memorial list for annual **Kaddish**? Second, has the husband--now that he has married
again--any justification for wanting to remove these
names? In other words, may his second wife have grounds
for objecting that her husband is still memorializing
the relations of his first wife? Third, since a contribution was made to the congregation for putting these
names on the annual **Kaddish** list, is it now possible to
rescind and cancel such a contribution and so remove the
names?

First, as to saying **Kaddish** for Gentiles, and also
as to the congregation keeping on the **Kaddish** list a
Gentile relative of a convert, this question was discussed fully in the Conference **Yearbook**, vol. LXVII, 1957.
One might imagine that there is no religious bond between a daughter and her Gentile father, since a convert
is a "new-born child." However, Maimonides in Hilchot
Mamrim, V.11, says (based upon the Talmud), that a convert should honor his Gentile father. Rabbi Aaron Walkin, in a responsum written in 1933, states that honoring
his father involves saying **Kaddish** for him. Since a son
may say **Kaddish** for his Jewish-born **apostate** father (who
had wilfully deserted Judaism), then certainly a proselyte may say **Kaddish** for a Gentile father who is naturally following the religion in which he was brought up.
So, too, Abraham Zvi Klein, a rabbi in Hungary (**Be-erot
Avraham** II), speaks of receiving a gift from a Gentile
woman who wants her name memorialized (i.e., not even a
relative of a convert), and he concludes: "There is no
prohibition against recording her name and her good deed
in the **Chevra Kadisha**, and we should recite an "**El male
rachamim**" for her on **Yizkor** days."
     As for the second question, there is some sort of
justification for an objection on the part of the man,
or of his second wife, to his first wife (and possibly
also her relatives) being memorialized now the man is
married to this second woman. This question has come up
quite often in the literature and has been dealt with in
Reform Responsa, p. 162. For example, Eleazar Deutsch
(1850-1916) in his **Duda-ei Hasadeh**, 14, was asked whether a remarried man may recite **Yizkor** for his first wife.
He says no; but that if it was the custom of the syna-
gogue--as it is in some communities--for the cantor to
read a list of all the names memorialized, there was no
objection to the remarried man being present. The general conclusion of all who discussed the question is
that such memorial rites as might occur at home (the
Yahrzeit light, etc.) should certainly not be observed
any more. In the synagogue, however, if there is no one
to say **Kaddish** for his first wife, the husband may do
so. Of course, if there are children, it is better that
they should say **Kaddish**. In the question asked, the
names include not only the name of the first wife, but
those of her relatives, so the second wife can have less
objection to their names being read than if it were the
first wife's name alone. Furthermore, there **are** grandchildren who want to honor their grandparents, which
certainly should be permitted.
     Now there is the third question: Since a contribu-
tion was made to the congregation (a number of years
ago) to put these names on the regular **Kaddish** list, and
since the congregation had accepted this specific con-

tribution, can it now undo this memorial and cancel it
and remove the names? A related question was asked of
me by Rabbi William Braude of Providence. It was with
regard to a memorial window. Someone wanted to pay
money to have its dedication changed. This could not be
permitted. Once the gift has been accepted by the congregation, no donor has any authority over it. The
conclusion to the question asked about the memorial
window applies here: "Once the gift has been received by
the congregation, the donor has no more rights over it."
Of course, the congregation has more rights in the matter than the original donor, but even if the congregation itself wanted to change the memorial donation from
one purpose to another, the law is full of many restrictions as to just which changes they can make. There is
no need to go into this complicated question.

From all the above, we come to the following conclusions: First, there is nothing wrong with a Gentile
being permanently memorialized in the **Kaddish** list.
Secondly, the husband--while justly sensitive to memorializing his first wife in the presence of his second
wife--has no right to deprive his children of the privilege of memorializing their mother, grandparents, and
other close relatives. Finally, once a gift has been
received by the congregation, it is virtually impossible
for an individual to have it changed, and there are
considerable restrictions as to the right of the congregation itself.

Walter Jacob

See also:

S.B. Freehof, "Kaddish for Apostates and Gentiles,"
Recent Reform Responsa, pp. 132ff.

126.   THE EDUCATIONAL VALUE OF **YAHRZEIT**
(Vol. XXIV, 1914, p. 153)

The **Yahrzeit** as a permanent institution in connection with the recital of **Kaddish** appears first in Germany about the 14th century, but since it goes back to
an ancient practice known in Talmudic literature ("**Ta-
anit beyom shemet bo aviv ve-imo**," Nedarim), and since
its good influence is evident in manifold ways, I would
strongly favor its retention as far as possible.

In addition, as Chairman of the Committee, I would
say that while much may be adduced in favor of the individual mourner's rising for the Kaddish as the outflow
of the soul, longing for comfort to be found in submission to God's will, in conformity with tradition--there
is also a consideration for, and a sense of sympathy
with, the mourner expressed by the whole congregation
rising for Kaddish, wherever it is introduced.   The
decision of this question must therefore be left to the
congregation.
        In general, I would here refer to the ancient rab-
binical dictum, **"Mitoch shelo lishmah ba lishmah,"** "A
good practice, even if not done for its own sake, but
for some less spiritual motive, should still be encouraged, since it may eventually lead to a more spiritual
view," because it applies to the so-called "Kaddish
Jew," who attends divine service only in honor of his
dead parents.   While religion is not merely piety,
nevertheless, filial piety shown by the mourners may in
the end lead to a more permanently religious attitude.

                                    K. Kohler and D. Neumark

                        127.   YAHRZEIT
                          (1980)

QUESTION: What is the status of **Yahrzeit** within
the Reform Movement?   When shall the **Yahrzeit** be
commemorated--should the Hebrew or secular calendar
be used?

ANSWER: The origin of the custom of observing **Yahrzeit**--commemorating the deaths of parents, children,
siblings, and spouses--is obscure.   The Talmud mentioned
hazkarat neshamot, but not as a widely-observed custom.
We first find **Yahrzeit** as such in the writings of the
16th century authorities, Tyrnau and Jaffe (Isaac
Tyrnau, **Minhagim**, and Mordecai Jaffe, **Levush Techelet**,
133).   Its name would indicate that the custom arose in
Germany.   Guedemann has suggested that it was derived
from a similar custom among German Catholics (**Geschichte**
III, 132).   The custom may also have evolved from the
traditional commemoration of the deaths of great indi-
viduals such as Moses (seventh Adar) and Gedaliah (third
Tishri), or of great Rabbis (Rashi to Yev. 22a, quoting
Gaonic responsa).

Yahrzeit quickly became established among Ashkenazic Jews. The Sefardim were late in adopting the custom, feeling that **Kaddish** recited after twelve months of mourning reflects poorly on the deceased. They interpreted **Kaddish** as a prayer intended to assure a better status for the deceased in the world to come. Isaac Luria, the German Kabbalist who settled in Safed, countered this by stating that the **Yahrzeit Kaddish** elevated the soul of the deceased to a higher level year by year (Sperling, **Ta-amei Haminhagim Umekorei Minhagim**, p. 488; A. Lewysohn, **Mekorei Minhagim**, 98). Of course, this is not necessarily our reason for reciting **Kaddish**. We do so to honor and to remember our dead, and to praise God for their lives and accomplishments.

The custom of lighting a **Yahrzeit** candle is medieval (Solomon Luria, **Responsa**, 46; Joseph Schwartz, **Hadrat Kodesh**, p. 18). If candles are unavailable or impractical, an electric light may be used (**Gesher Hachayim** I, p. 343). The **Yahrzeit** candle is lit on the evening before the day of **Yahrzeit**, and is burned for twenty-four hours. On Shabbat or Yom Tov, the candle is lit before the Shabbat or holiday candles. In case one forgets to light it, it is lit upon remembering, or after the Shabbat or holiday is completed.

The date of the **Yahrzeit** is the date of death, not the date of burial. If the date is unknown or is questionable, then an appropriate date may be chosen and maintained in succeeding years. The Hebrew calendar should be used for the **Yahrzeit**, as it provides a Jewish rhythm for the year. It forms an additional link to tradition. In those cases where special calendar problems arise--as with Adar II or two days of Rosh Chodesh--a rabbi should be consulted. There is precedent, however, for the use of the secular calendar when the Hebrew calendar cannot be used. Analogously, the Mishna utilized it (albeit reluctantly) for dating divorces (Gittin VIII.6); Rabbinic authorities sometimes dated their responsa by it; it is generally used on tombstones, along with the Hebrew date.

For us, the recitation of **Kaddish** is incumbent upon both men and women at congregational services held on the date of the **Yahrzeit** or on the Shabbat nearest the date, if no service is available on the date itself (Isserles to **Shulchan Aruch**, Yoreh De-a 376.4; **Gates of Mitzvah**, p. 62). In some congregations, a family member is called up to the Torah on the Shabbat preceding the **Yarhzeit**. Many observe the custom of visiting the cemetery. In addition, the donation of a charitable gift in memory of the deceased is recommended.

Tradition does not demand that **Yahrzeit** be commemorated for those who died before they were thirty days old, while some restrict that to twenty days (Joseph

Schwartz, **Vayitsbor Yosef**, 21). Yet, there are sound
psychological reasons for commemorating all deceased
through **Yahrzeit** observance. Such a death is difficult
for a young couple; they and the family need the cathar-
sis of mourning and the comfort provided by others.

Someone who has remarried after the death of a
spouse should continue to recite **Kaddish** in the synagogue on the **Yahrzeit**. Because tradition has always
been sensitive to the feelings of a second spouse, the
Yahrzeit candle at home may be omitted (Mo-ed Katan 21b;
Shulchan Aruch, Yoreh De-a 385.2). Anyone who has forgotten to commemorate a **Yahrzeit** should do so upon remembering (Greenwald, Kol Bo Al Avelut, p. 394).

Yahrzeit is well-established among us, and everything should be done to encourage it as a valid expression of religious feeling.

Walter Jacob, Chairman
Leonard S. Kravitz
Eugene Lipman
W. Gunther Plaut
Harry A. Roth
Rav A. Soloff
Bernard Zlotowitz

See also:

S.B. Freehof, "Secular Date for Yahrzeit," **Reform
Responsa**, pp. 168ff; "Kaddish When Worshipping
Alone," **Recent Reform Responsa**, pp. 14ff;
"Kaddish and Yahrzeit for a Child," **Reform
Responsa**, pp. 165ff.

128.   OBSERVANCE OF **YAHRZEIT** BY WIDOW WHO HAS REMARRIED
              (Vol. LXV, 1955, p. 90)

QUESTION: As a consequence of the Korean War, one
of our young women was left a widow. She has remarried since, and together with her husband attends services regularly. She desires to know
whether she ought to observe the **Yahrzeit** of her
first husband.

It is the custom in our congregation to honor
the memory of a loved one by rising for the **Kaddish**, no matter what one's relationship to the
deceased may have been--sister, cousin, or wife.

ANSWER: The Rabbis regarded it as improper to offer
condolences to a widower **in his home** when--because of
certain exigencies--he had to remarry before the period
of mourning was over; although one may properly whisper
words of comfort to him on a chance encounter in the
street (Yoreh De-a 385).   This provision seems intended
to legitimatize the natural desire to keep out of the
new home life the unhappy memories of a previous union.
     Since the observance of the **Yahrzeit**--dictated in
this instance by custom--is calculated to revive just
such memories, we may conclude that its omission under
the stated circumstances would be in full conformity
with the intent of the Rabbinic regulation.

Israel Bettan

129.   THE TABLE OF CONSANGUINITY
(Vol. LXXXVIII, 1978, pp. 55-56)

QUESTION: The Table of Consanguinity currently
used by the Reform Movement is male-centered, and
clearly discriminates against women.   Should we
change the Table to reflect our equal treatment of
men and women?

ANSWER: The Table of Consanguinity as produced in the
Rabbis' Manual is based largely upon Biblical law (Lev.
18:11-21; Deut. 23:3, 27:20-23; Kid. 67b; Yoma 67b;
Maimonides, **Yad**, Hil. Ishut IV, Isurei Bi-a II; **Shulchan
Aruch**, Even Ha-ezer 15:44.6).   The Biblical laws were
somewhat modified and expanded by the Talmud.   A full
discussion of those modifications may be found in Mielziner, **Jewish Marriage Laws**, 1897.   Each of these statements has approached the entire matter from a male point
of view.   It would, of course, be possible to rewrite
these statements so that they would reflect the views of
the current feminist movement.   This, however, would add
a number of prohibitions, if we simply paralleled masculine prohibitions which exist already.   It would be
unwise and unrealistic to follow this path for the following reasons: (1) The last major change in Jewish
marriage laws was made in the 11th century through the
decree of Rabbenu Gershom, which prohibited polygamy.
This decree was effective because polygamy had largely
ceased in practice by Ashkenazic Jews, as the general
population among whom they lived did not practice it
either.   The decree, however, was not followed by the

remainder of world Jewry, and polygamy continued to be practiced up to modern times by Jews in various Eastern countries. In other words, the decree was effective only because it fitted into the mood of the time and place. Such additional restrictions would, however, not evoke a similar response in our age. The decree of Rabbenu Gershom had long been completely accepted by Ashkenazic Jewry. (2) The presumption of inequality for women has led Judaism to adopt the most lenient definition of bastardy in the Western world. Only the offspring of those prohibited from marrying by the laws of consanguinity and adultery on the part of a married woman are considered **Mamzerim**. Any change would also alter this definition to the disadvantage of infant children. (3) It is extremely doubtful whether our rabbis or our laymen would follow any additional restrictions in the field of marriage. It is difficult enough to enforce some strictures which we have now, much less impose others. In other words, any restrictive decision on the part of our committee in this matter would represent a mere gesture toward the feminist movement rather than an effective effort. Anyhow, one should not legislate when it is obvious that no one will follow what has been decreed (Yev. 65b, Shabbat 148b).

In addition, our Reform Movement has made some changes: (1) We have recognized the marriage of divorcees to those of priestly descent. This permissive change was made as we no longer recognize priestly privileges. (2) We have accepted civil divorce as sufficient for remarriage. The reliance on civil divorce is, **ipso facto**, an effective and realistic measure toward equality of the sexes, since women can and do institute divorce proceedings in their own right under State laws. Both changes have gained complete acceptance by Reform Jews and also by a large percentage of the American Jewish community.

The existing Table could be rewritten in a more permissive way. That also does not seem appropriate for us for the following reasons: (1) We are continuing to try to work out distinctive, but naturally agreeable, approaches to family law along with our Conservative and Orthodox coreligionists in order to avoid conflict over family matters in the Land of Israel. A decision such as this on our part would increase the difficulties of this task. (2) Most State legal systems parallel our Table of Consanguinity or are very close to it. Any changes we might make would only raise additional problems. In this case, the abstract notion of complete equality would hinder rather than help us or the feminist movement.

For these reasons the Table of Consanguinity should remain as it now stands.

Walter Jacob, Chairman
Solomon B. Freehof, Honorary Chairman
Leonard S. Kravitz
Stephen M. Passamaneck
Harry A. Roth
Herman E. Schaalman
Bernard Zlotowitz

130.   RABBI'S PREROGATIVE TO OFFICIATE AT WEDDINGS
          (Vol. LXV, 1955, pp. 85-88)

QUESTION: May cantors perform Jewish marriage services without an ordained rabbi presiding over the ceremony?

ANSWER: Basically, a Jewish marriage ceremony may be described as informal.   A man, theoretically at least, can marry simply by cohabitation with a woman he wants to be his wife (**bi-a**).   Moreover, even in the more regular type of marriage, if a man lives in a small village in which there is no **Minyan** of Jews available, he can marry without the recitation of the seven blessings. If, then, the whole procedure is basically so informal, it would stand to reason that anybody can perform the ceremony.   In fact, the literature is full of reference to the **Mesader Kiddushin**, "The performer of the marriage," who--as is clear from the discussion in the various responsa--is not a rabbi.   This point of view (namely, that anybody can perform the ceremony, provided--of course--that he performs it correctly) is stated quite plainly in the famous responsum by Isaac bar Sheshet in Spain in the 14th century.   This is in his Responsum #271, in which he is astonished at the new furor over "ordination" in France.   The case came to him about a man who claimed to be the duly ordained Chief Rabbi of France, and who declared that the religious ceremonies performed by his rival are invalid.   Isaac bar Sheshet is puzzled by this Franco-German emphasis on a so-called ordination, and says that if the ceremony or the documents (in the case of a divorce) are correct, on what ground can anyone dare to declare them invalid? Whenever this "open door policy" is mentioned in the law, reference is always made to this responsum of bar

Sheshet (as, for example, in the note of Isserles to Yoreh De-a 242.14).

However, this unlimited permission was long abandoned in the Ashkenazic lands, and Isserles in the note referred to says, "and some say [with Isserles, "some say" usually means a weighty opinion] that he who has not been ordained as a **Morenu** but nevertheless gives divorces and **Chalitsot**, the documents are invalid. Some, however, are lenient on the matter [and he again refers to bar Sheshet]."

It is clear that in the Ashkenazic lands the tendency was strong to restrict the permission of officiating in divorces and marriages to ordained rabbis and indeed to the chosen rabbi in the locality. There are two main reasons for it. One might be described as professional privilege and the other as technical ability.

We mention the historically later reason first, namely, the emphasis on professional privilege. There are two opinions of the most important authorities of the 18th century. Ezekiel Landau in Prague (**Noda Bi-Yehuda**, vol. 2, #83) speaks of a case in which the local rabbi disappointed the family and neglected to come to the marriage and someone else presumed to officiate. He says that from the point of view of the prevailing custom no one else (but the regular rabbi) may officiate at the wedding. Moses Sofer of Pressburg in his responsa (Yoreh De-a, #230), discussing the fees from weddings, etc., finds it necessary to explain an opinion of Israel Isserlein of the 15th century, who, in discussing the dispute between two rabbis, said that he was ashamed that we take fees for such **mitzvot**. On this Moses Sofer makes a pertinent statement. He says that the situation is now different from what it was in those days. In the days of Isserlein the rabbi was not engaged by the community. He had other means of livelihood, and he settled where he wished. Since he was in this status (we would say an amateur), he could not object if another rabbi settled in the same community or if someone else officiated at weddings, etc. But nowadays, says Moses Sofer, a rabbi is engaged like a workman by the community, and the fees from weddings, etc., are part of his agreed upon income. Therefore, anyone who comes in and takes these away from him commits actual robbery, as one would in taking away the livelihood of any other workman.

However, there is a deeper ground than professional privilege for the strong objection in the Ashkenazic lands against non-rabbis officiating, and that is rooted in the field of technical and legal competence. This goes back to a statement found a number of times in the Talmud (see B. Kiddushin 6a), namely, that "He who does not understand thoroughly the nature of marriages and divorces shall have no dealings (esek) with them." Rashi there comments that this statement means that he who is not expert shall make no decisions on marital problems when and if consulted. But the later respondents say that Rashi did not mean to restrict his interpretation of the Talmudic statement merely to the making of legal decisions on marital problems. The word esek (dealings) means that the unskilled may not even officiate at marriages, etc. This is the opinion of Jacob Reischer of Metz, 16th-17th century (see his Shevut Ya-akov III, 121). So, too, Jacob Weil, a century earlier, said that no one should officiate unless he received special permission from the rabbi. If he did not get such authorization, the divorce, for example, which he gave in the case discussed, is invalid (see his Responsum #85).

The strongest reference is in Keneset Yechezkel (Ezekiel Katzenellenbogen, in Altona, early 18th century), which declares that it is a decision (takana) coming from the old rabbis of France and Rabbenu Tam himself, that no one should officiate except the one who is chosen to be the rabbi of the community. This makes clear the statement by Zvi Hirsch Eisenstaedter in his Pischei Teshuva to Shulchan Aruch, Even Ha-ezer 49.3, in which he says, "therefore not in vain have they become accustomed in these generations not to officiate at weddings without the permission of the rabbi." See also Shevut Ya-akov III, 121, cited above, in which Reischer says that the custom is spread in all the regions of Israel to appoint a rabbi and that no marriages and divorces take place without the knowledge of the rabbi, i.e., he must give consent to all marriages.

A very strong opinion on this question is given by Joseph Saul Nathanson, Rabbi of Lemberg, in his Sho-el Ueshiv III, A, 239. He says, addressing the rabbi: "No one has permission to officiate at marriages and divorces other than you, the rabbi, and thus to hurt your income, and [since the community has given you that right to officiate], it is obvious that the marriages performed by someone else are void." Shalom Mordecai Schwadron (Maharsham I, 160) agrees that such marriages should not be performed, but that if they are performed, they are not void, since the recital of the blessings themselves is essential.

It is clear that the varied experiences of the Jews in Northern Europe, in France, Germany and the Slavic lands, led them--for the reasons given above--to restrict the right to marry to the duly selected rabbi. Isserles, in the note to Yoreh De-a 242.14, speaks indeed of the possibility of giving the title Morenu to someone and enabling him to officiate, even though our

ordination is not comparable in strictness to the ancient ordination.   But generally it is clear that only
the rabbi--or someone else, by his express commission in
each specific ceremony--could officiate at marriages and
divorces.
     This general principle, it seems to me, should
apply in our Reform Jewish life likewise.   While our
Reform rabbis are not as strict as Orthodox rabbis have
been on the question of divorce and **Chalitsa**, yet with
regard to marriage, conversion, etc., we have in many
ways even stricter standards of instruction, inquiry,
etc.   We are correct, therefore, in following the tendency of traditional law, and saying that the performing
of marriages is professionally, technically, and spiritually the exclusive function of the rabbi.   In specific
cases it may be possible for the rabbi who approves a
certain marriage but cannot himself officiate to give
permission to a cantor to officiate for him.   But that
must never serve as a general commission to officiate at
all marriages, but only as a permission for a specifically approved marriage.   This is no time in the history
of marriage and morals for us to take any steps to les-
sen the solemnity, dignity, and impressiveness of marriage.

                                        Solomon B. Freehof

     See also:

     S.B. Freehof, "Marriage Without Rabbi or Hebrew,"
       Reform Responsa for Our Time, pp. 200ff.

     131. A LAYMAN OFFICIATING AT A JEWISH WEDDING
                         (1979)

     QUESTION: May the president of a congregation or
     any other designated layman perform Jewish marriage
     ceremonies?   In South Dakota there are no rabbis
     except in Sioux Falls, nor is there any rabbi
     available east or west for hundreds of miles.   Und-
     er these circumstances, can weddings be performed
     by an authorized layman?   (Mr. Stanford M. Adel-
     stein, Rapid City, South Dakota)

ANSWER: The Talmud cited three ways of effecting a marriage--through a document, through money, or by intercourse (Kid. 2a; **Shulchan Aruch**, Even Ha-ezer 26.4).

(a)   The most common form featured a deed witnessed by two competent individuals and handed by the groom to the bride (Kid. 9a; **Shulchan Aruch**, Even Ha-ezer 32.1-4).   This has remained the essential covenant of the modern wedding.   The deed is akin to the modern **Ketuba** signed by the two witnesses.

(b)   In addition, it was possible to effect a marriage through the transfer of an item of value (**kesef**) in the presence of two competent witnesses.   This remains as part of the modern wedding in the form of giving a ring with the formula "**Harei at mekudeshet...**" (Kid. 2a, b; **Shulchan Aruch**, Even Ha-ezer 27.1).

(c)   Finally,   marriage   can   be   effected   through intercourse (**bi-a**) preceded by a statement indicating the wish to take this woman as wife and with two witnesses who saw the couple leave for a private place (Kid. 9b; **Shulchan Aruch**, Even Ha-ezer 33.1).   This last method was, of course, severely frowned upon by the Rabbis, but **bedi-avad** it was certainly valid.   Consent was, of course, necessary (**Shulchan Aruch**, E.H. 42.1).   The wedding in Talmudic times was also divided into two segments, **Erusin** and **Nisu-in**; the latter often took place up to a year after **Erusin**.   In the Middle Ages, both parts of the marriage ceremony were united, as mentioned by Simhah of Vitry, 11th century (**Machzor Vitry**, pp. 587f).   In the Eastern lands, this union of the two ceremonies already occurred in Gaonic times (**Otsar Hage-onim**, Yev. 381).   It is clear from these statements that Talmudic law did not stipulate the presence of a rabbi, nor did it, in this connection, mention many other matters which have later become important (e.g., **Minyan**, **Chupa**, etc.).

The matter of who may actually conduct the ceremony was hardly discussed, though there is a reference in the apocryphal book Tobit to the father conducting the ceremony which united the couple (Tobit 7:12).   Among the Samaritans, the priest participated in the ceremony, but we do not know how ancient this practice may be (Mann, **Texts**, vol. II, p. 184).   It seems that in earliest times any knowledgeable individual could conduct the ceremony (Kid. 6a, 13a).   A little later, emphasis was placed on having a **Minyan** present, so that the ceremony was conducted in public, and, therefore, could not be taken lightly as was possible before merely two witnesses at home (Ket. 7b).   Some Geonim suggested that the groom might be considered as one of the ten in order to make the **Minyan** a little easier (**Otsar Hage-onim**, Ket. 7b).   Furthermore, the same Gaonic text stated that if no one sufficiently expert to pronounce the blessings was available, then the groom himself might pronounce them for himself. As the Jewish legal system in the entire Near East developed, the **Nagid** (head of the community) was given judicial powers, including the appointment of rabbis to various cities and towns within his jurisdiction. They supervised the religious life throughout the land, including marriages. Eleventh and twelfth century documents show this clearly (Abraham Freiman, **Seder Kiddushin Venisu-in**, p. 22ff). Maimonides, therefore, decreed that there could be no marriage or divorce except by an ordained rabbi within the Jewish community (Maimonides, **Responsa**, 156).

By the 14th century, this practice had spread to Europe and was subsequently generally accepted (Maharil, **Hil. Nisu-in**). In the succeeding centuries rabbinic involvement in weddings has become virtually automatic.

Thus, it has been customary for a rabbi (or occasionally a cantor) to officiate at weddings for the last six centuries, and it would be wrong to change that practice nowadays, especially with the ease of transportation from one place to another. A rabbi five hundred miles away is today no more distant than was a rabbi in the nearby town for our Polish or Russian ancestors a century ago. A rabbi should be asked to perform such weddings.

The reason for the insistence that rabbis officiate at weddings, of course, involved much more than the ceremony itself and was already indicated by R. Judah. He said in the name of Samuel (Kid. 6a) that those who are not well acquainted with the procedures of weddings and divorce should not deal with them; this means the ability to deal with all the ramifications of marriage, which include pre-nuptial counseling, as well as the ability to counsel afterwards. It would extend to assistance in the establishment of a Jewish home, which would be even more important in a remote area than in large Jewish centers. It would also involve, in such a location, more assistance with the ceremony itself and the nuances involved with weddings. We must, of course, also insist that the requirements of the State in which the ceremony is to be performed must always be met; and many, though not all, insist on ordained clergy.

Walter Jacob, Chairman
Stephen M. Passamaneck
W. Gunther Plaut
Harry A. Roth
Rav A. Soloff
Bernard Zlotowitz

132.   JEWISH MARRIAGE WITHOUT CHILDREN
(1979)

QUESTION: Is it possible to have a valid Jewish marriage without children? Should a rabbi perform such a marriage when a couple specifically states that they plan to have no children? (Michael A. Robinson, Croton-on-Hudson, New York)

ANSWER: First, we should address the validity of a marriage without children.   There is no doubt that procreation, companionship, joy, unity of the family, etc., are basic elements of marriage as seen by the Jewish tradition (Ket. 8a).   Procreation was considered essential as already stated by the Mishna: "A man may not desist from the duty of procreation unless he already has children" (Yev. 6.6).   The Gemara to this concluded that a man may marry a barren woman if he has fulfilled this **mitzvah** of procreation, as in any case he should not remain unmarried (Yev. 61b).   If the parties marry beyond the years when child-bearing is possible, or if one of them is sterile, the same wedding blessings are, nevertheless, recited (Abudarham, **Birchot Erusin**, 98a). There was a difference between the schools of Hillel and Shammai about what was required to fulfill the **mitzvah** of procreation.   The tradition followed Hillel, who minimally required a son and daughter, yet the codes all emphasize the need to produce children beyond that number (Tos. Yev. 8; **Yad**, Hil. Ishut, 15.6; **Shulchan Aruch**, Even Ha-ezer 1.5).

Tradition emphasized the need for a greater number of children as the fulfillment of two Biblical verses: Is. 45:18, "He created the world for habitation (**la-shevet**)," and Eccl. 11:6, the obligation to sow seed in the evening (**la-erev**) as well as in the morning.   In other words, one should constantly expand the Jewish population (Yev. 62a,b).   This was also in keeping with the thought that before the Messiah could come, all the souls waiting for bodies will have to be placed into the world (**ibid.**; Nidda 13b).   During our entire history, persecution and natural disaster have decimated our people, and so repopulation has always been emphasized. Lack of children was considered grounds for divorce after a decade of childless marriage, but Isserles indicated that nowadays we do not force the issue and permit the couple to remain together (Isserles to **Shulchan Aruch**, Even Ha-ezer 1.3 and 8; also Isserles to 154.10). This was particularly true if the man had already had children by a previous marriage.   All of this makes it clear that children were considered essential to a mar-

riage, and it was considered desirable to have a large
number of children, but a marriage without them was also
condoned (Abraham di Boton, **Lechem Mishneh** to **Yad**, Hil.
Ishut 4.10; Yair Hayyim Bacharach, **Chavat Ya-ir**, #221).

The strictest interpretation of the traditional
Halacha which makes a distinction between the obligations of men and women (a distinction not accepted by
Reform Jews) would allow a woman to marry a sterile
male, since the obligation of procreation was not incumbent upon her. When the husband or wife was sterile and
it was not possible to have children, the marriage was
always considered valid (**bedi-avad**); i.e., since it had
been entered in good faith, it need not be terminated,
as mentioned earlier. This was stressed by Maimonides,
who considered such a marriage valid under any circumstances (**Yad**, Hil. Ishut 4.10), whether the individual
was born sterile or was sterilized later. Later authorities went somewhat further, and Yair Hayyim Bacharach
stated that as long as the prospective wife realized
that her prospective husband was infertile, though sexually potent, and she had agreed to the marriage, it was
valid and acceptable (**Chavat Ya-ir**, #221). Isaac b.
Sheshet (**Responsa**, #15) permitted a couple who knew that
they would not have children to become married. As long
as both were fully aware of the situation, it was permissible, even **lechatechila**.

In sum, the traditional attitude was as follows:
our tradition encourages marriage for the purpose of
procreation and would strongly urge all couples to have
children. However, if they enter the marriage fully
aware of the refusal of one or the other to have child-
ren--either because of a physical defect or because of
an attitude--the marriage can be considered valid, either **lechatechila** or **bedi-avad**. Nothing should prevent a
rabbi from conducting such a marriage; although some
rabbis would refuse to officiate. In light of the Holocaust and the current diminution of the world Jewish
population, it is incumbent upon each of us to urge
Jewish couples to have two or more children. Although
young people may marry reluctantly and late, the marriage at least represents a step in the direction of
children.

In Jewish law, the marriage is valid, yet given the
Reform emphasis on the underlying spirit of the law as a
guide to modern practice, marriage without children is
very distant from the Jewish ideal of marriage. The

letter may permit it, but we must encourage every couple to have at least two children.

Walter Jacob, Chairman
Leonard S. Kravitz
W. Gunther Plaut
Harry A. Roth
Rav A. Soloff
Bernard Zlotowitz

See also:

S.B. Freehof, "A Wife Who Cannot Bear Children," **Recent Reform Responsa**, pp. 155ff.

133. CONCUBINAGE AS AN ALTERNATIVE TO MARRIAGE
(1979)

QUESTION: Does Reform Judaism recognize concubinage as an alternative to formal marriage? If a man cannot or does not wish to divorce his disabled wife, may his "arrangements" with another woman be formalized? Can formal Jewish status be given to two retired individuals living together without marriage? Can these "arrangements" be formalized in a manner akin to the ancient form of concubinage? (CCAR Family Life Committee)

ANSWER: Each of the arrangements suggested by the question is clearly illegal and violates the laws of all the states within the United States and of the provinces of Canada. Therefore, no rabbi can formalize such an arrangement through a Jewish ceremony. Since the Paris Sanhedrin of 1807, we have recognized the supremacy of State in matter of marriage (See M.D. Tama, **Transactions of the Parisian Sanhedrin**, pp. 133ff). This has been accepted by most modern Jews. It would be helpful, however, to discuss briefly the forms of marriage and concubinage. We should understand that concubinage in Biblical times seems to have referred solely to wives in addition to the primary wife. From the Hellenistic period on, a concubine could be any wife of lower status. As is well known, Rabbinic tradition recognizes three forms of entering a full marriage. Consent was, of course, always necessary (**Shulchan Aruch**, Even Ha-ezer 42.1), and all three forms were combined in the

Jewish concept of marriage as developed during the Middle Ages.

The three ways of effecting a marriage cited by the Talmud are: through a document, through money, or by intercourse (Kid. 2a; **Shulchan Aruch**, Even Ha-ezer 25.4).

(a) The most common form featured a deed witnessed by two competent individuals and handed by the groom to the bride (Kid. 9a; **Shulchan Aruch**, Even Ha-ezer 32.1-4). This has remained the essential covenant of the modern wedding. The deed is the modern **Ketuba** signed by two witnesses.

(b) In addition, it was possible to effect a marriage through the transfer of an item of value (**kesef**) in the presence of two competent witnesses. This remains as part of the modern wedding in the form of presenting a ring with the formula "**Harei at mekudeshet...**" (Kid. 2a,b; **Shulchan Aruch**, Even Ha-ezer 27.1).

(c) Finally, marriage can be effected through intercourse (**bi-a**) preceded by a statement indicating the wish to take this woman as wife and with two witnesses who saw the couple leave for a private place (Kid. 9b; **Shulchan Aruch**, Even Ha-ezer 33.1). This last method was severely frowned upon by the Rabbis, but **bediavad** it was valid. Marriage simply through intercourse with proper intent would be akin to "common law" marriage.

There is an additional form of marriage--the concubine (**Pilegesh**)--which needs to be discussed. Concubines were mentioned fairly frequently in the Biblical literature, especially for kings (II Sam. 3:7, 21:8ff, 5:13; I Kings 11:3; II Chron. 11:21, etc.). These references dealt with women who possessed the status of an inferior wife. We should remember that the nature of concubinage changed radically from the Biblical period to the Greco-Roman period (Louis Epstein, "The Institution of Concubinage Among Jews," **Proceedings of the American Academy for Jewish Research**, vol. 6, pp. 153ff). Epstein has pointed out that the status of the Biblical concubine was determined by the ancient Near Eastern corporate family with the head of the household (**Ba-al**) possibly consorting with wives at various levels ranging from his main wife to a slave girl. The legal relationship of the half-dozen subsidiary wives is no longer clear to us. According to some ancient codes, the **Pilegesh** was second to the main wife and had definite rights as did her children. This was also her status in ancient Israel. The custom of concubinage died out during the late Biblical period, according to Epstein, and was then reintroduced among the Hellenistic Jews of the Roman Empire into a family structure which was no longer corporate, but monogamous. Among the

Romans and Greco-Roman Jews, the **Pilegesh** became a mistress of doubtful legal status, and in Roman law, she had no legal status. Nevertheless, concubinage became an accepted institution during this period, and was carried over into the Christian era; concubines were frequently found among the ruling and upper classes, as well as among Christian priests. This was the form of concubinage known to the Talmud and the medieval Jewish literature, and it was read back into the Biblical period.

In the Talmud, according to R. Judah, quoting Rav, the difference between a wife and a concubine was that the latter had neither **Kiddushin** nor **Ketuba** (San. 21a; Maimonides, **Yad**, Melachim 4.4, and commentaries to this section). However, according to the Palestinian Talmud, a concubine had **Kiddushin**, but no **Ketuba** (Yerushalmi, Ket. 5.2; 29b). The former, not the latter, definition, was generally followed by most of the authorities (Caro to **Yad**, Melachim 4.4; de Boton to **Yad**, Melachim; Radbaz, **Responsa**, vol. IV, #225, vol. VII, #33; Adret, **Responsa**, vol. IV, #314; but Rashi, Ribash, Maggid Mishneh, and others followed the latter. The two definitions may refer to two levels of concubinage, as will be discussed later, or they may reflect errors in the original Talmudic text (G. Ellinson, **Nisu-in Shelo Kedat Mosheh VeYisra-el**, pp. 40ff). The sources clearly indicated that we are dealing with an individual of intermediate status who did not have all the rights of a married wife, but on the other hand was not to be considered as a prostitute either.

Maimonides protested vigorously against concubinage, and sought to eliminate it by claiming that it was a right limited to royalty and not permitted to ordinary Jews (**Yad**, Melachim 4.4). The woman was, therefore, to be considered a prostitute (**Zona**), and both she and the male involved could be whipped (**Yad**, Ishut 1.4). Jacob b. Asher and Caro later also prohibited concubines (**Tur** and **Shulchan Aruch**, E.H. 26.1 and 2.6). This prohibition was accepted by most Jews, but not all. Concubines were permitted by many Spanish and Provencal authorities--such as Abraham ben David, Abulafia, R. Jonah, A. Nissim, R. Adret, R. Asher Meiri, etc. (Ellinson, **op. cit.**, p. 54)--although they disagreed of their precise status. Nahmanides also accepted concubines (**Responsa**, #284; commentary to Gen. 25:6), although he warned against the moral evil involved. Concubines were discussed in the Middle Ages among both Sefardic and Ashkenazic Jews, and were often considered outside the **Cherem** of R. Gershom (**Tseida Laderech III**, #1, 2; Adret, **Responsa**, vol. I, #1205, IV, #314; Rabbenu Nissim, #68; Asheri, #37.1; Meir of Padua, #19; **Sh.A.**, Even Ha-ezer 13.7; **Otsar Haposekim**, Even Ha-ezer 26.3ff). Isserles

permitted concubines as long as they were careful about
Mikveh (Isserles to **Sh.A.**, Even Ha-ezer 26.1).   Most
authorities previously cited based their prohibition and
cautions on the Deuteronomic law prohibiting prostitu-
tion in Israel (Deut. 23:19ff; Lev. 19:29, 21:9).

The general mood of the Rabbinic authorities was to
prohibit concubines or accept them only reluctantly.
The latter position was partially the result of embarrassment about Biblical concubines.   Concubinage was
further restricted by the **Cherem** of Rabbenu Gershom
(**Sh.A.**, Even Ha-ezer 1.10; **Aruch Hashulchan** 1.23).   This
ordinance prohibited the individual from marrying an
additional wife, unless special permissions were provided by one hundred rabbis from three districts.   It also
prohibited a husband from divorcing a wife against her
will.   This ordinance has continued in force for Ashkenazic Jews, but was not made universally effective among
Sefardic Jews until 1950 (Schereschewsky, **Dinei Mishpacha**, pp. 72ff).   These decrees and their legal interpretations virtually eliminated concubinage.   An exception to the general prohibition of concubinage was the
18th century Jacob Emden, who favored the institution as
a way of increasing the population of the Jewish community (Emden, **She-elot Ya-avets** II, 16).

The status of a concubine with **Kiddushin**, but no
Ketuba, was as follows: Regarding adultery and incest,
she was considered a wife; in financial matters, her
consort's responsibility was limited, and he was obligated for neither maintenance nor ransom, but, if he
became tired of her, he had to divorce her (Adret, **Responsa** V, #242).

A concubine actually needed no formal divorce
(**Get**), but some felt that for the sake of public appearance, she should have a **Get**.   If the man with whom she
lived did not wish it, or had simply disappeared, she
could remarry without a **Get** (**Shulchan Aruch**, Even Ha-
ezer 26, 26.1).   The children of a concubine bore no
blemish and possessed all the rights of other children,
i.e., inheritance, etc. (Adret, **Responsa**, vol. IV, #14,
315).   A concubine who entered the relationship without
Kiddushin or **Ketuba** needed no divorce when the relationship ended; in fact, a man could simply give her to his
son (Asheri, #32.1; Ribash, #395).   This woman was simply a mistress; she could not be charged with adultery,
although she could be flogged for lewd conduct, and she
had no legal or financial standing.

All this would show that two forms of concubinage
have existed in Jewish tradition till the beginning of
the 19th century.   Both of them were accepted only reluctantly (**bedi-avad**).   The practice of concubinage was
rare in northern Europe and became infrequent even in
the Mediterranean basin after the 16th century.   It

continued to be discussed in the codes and in occasional responsa.

This discussion has clearly shown us that Judaism sought to remove the practice of concubinage, and various authorities prohibited it. Only the Biblical example made it difficult to eliminate it entirely as a recognized form of marriage. We cannot validate this form of marriage, as it violates our ideals of marriage and the laws of the states or provinces in which we live. It is contrary to the general development of Jewish law in the last eight hundred years.

Walter Jacob, Chairman
Leonard S. Kravitz
W. Gunther Plaut
Harry A. Roth
Rav A. Soloff
Bernard Zlotowitz

See also:

S.B. Freehof, "Wedding Without a License," **Contemporary Reform Responsa**, pp. 98ff.

134. TIMES WHEN WEDDINGS SHOULD NOT TAKE PLACE
(Vol. XXIII, 1913, pp. 179-180)

Ritual questions of another nature brought before us most frequently are those concerning weddings, and I shall first touch upon those that have the least religious significance, viz., the days when no weddings should take place.

(1) The so-called **Omer** or **Sefira** weeks, still observed by the Orthodox Jews in accordance with the **Tur** and **Shulchan Aruch**, Orach Chayim 493, have been treated by Dr. Landsberger of Darmstadt in Geiger's **Jued. Zeitschrift** VII, 81-96, who shows them to have been originally identical with the May weeks in French, Scottish, and English custom, while they have their parallel (if not their origin) in ancient Roman superstition, or rather mythology. They came up for discussion and were abrogated at the Augsburg Synod.[1] It is strange, however, that many Jews in America who have long since forgotten the Jewish custom with its supposed reason (the legendary death of the 12,000 pupils of R. Akiva

---

[1] See Philipson's **Reform Movement**, p. 439.

during these weeks), observe instead the English custom of not marrying in May, which ought to be denounced as an ancient heathenish superstition.

(2) The so-called Three Weeks between the seventeenth day of Tamuz and the Ninth of Av, commemorative of the destruction of Jerusalem, on which weddings are prohibited in the later codes[2] were also declared by the Augsburg Synod to have no longer any prohibiting character for us. And they need all the less be mentioned by me, as even the Memorial Day of the Destruction of Jerusalem (which ought to be observed in some form in our service, if only on the Sabbath preceding the same) remains unnoticed in our Reform Temples.

(3) There is, however, a simpler custom found in certain Jewish circles, the existence of which I learned only in New York some forty years ago, and I suspect it to be of Portuguese origin, viz., to have no wedding ceremony performed during the Penitential Days between Rosh Hashana and Yom Kippur. It seems to be based on a wrong conception of the Penitential Days, which are nowhere regarded as gloomy,[3] and it is altogether contrary to the Jewish law of marriage, which is a **mitzvah**--a sacred command that should not be postponed except on Sabbath and Holy Days when all juridical or legal actions are forbidden.[4]

(4) As to the half-holy days (**Chol Hamo-ed**) on which the Mishnaic code expressly prohibits marriages[5]--our Reform rabbis never felt that they bear a festive character which would have the rule applied that there should be no combination of two different festivities ("**Ein me-arevin simcha besimcha**").

K. Kohler and D. Neumark

See also:

S.B. Freehof, "Weddings and Other Ceremonies on Hoshana Rabba," **Recent Reform Responsa**, pp. 170ff; "Wedding on the Ninth of Av," **Recent Reform Responsa**, pp. 173ff.

---

[2] **Shulchan Aruch**, Orach Chayim, 551.2, Isserles' note: Only 1-8 Av, based on the baraita Bab. Yev. 43b.

[3] Philipson, **ibid**.

[4] Beitsa 36b.

[5] Mo-ed Katan 8b.

135.   MARRIAGES BETWEEN NEW YEAR AND ATONEMENT
(Vol. XXXII, 1922, p. 41)

QUESTION: Is there any Jewish law or custom which would prohibit the celebration of marriages during the days between New Year's Day and the Day of Atonement?

ANSWER: There is no Jewish law to this effect, neither can any reference to such a custom be found in the **Shulchan Aruch** or in any of the older Rabbinic authorities. The first one, to my knowledge, who mentioned such a custom is Rabbi Ephraim.   But this custom was not widespread, and it is not generally accepted.   Even Rabbi Margalioth himself declares it permissible to celebrate marriages during these penitential days, if for some reason or other no other date for the wedding could conveniently be fixed by the parties contracting the marriage.   Comp. also **Sedeh Chemed** II, Ma-arechet Chatan Vechala, no. 23.

Jacob Z. Lauterbach

136.   MARRIAGE ON SHABBAT OR YOM TOV
(Vol. LXXXVII, 1977, pp. 97-99)

QUESTION: May a marriage be performed on Shabbat or Yom Tov?   (Referred to the Responsa Committee by the Central Conference of American Rabbis, June 1976)

ANSWER: The question before us deals with the sanctity of Shabbat as understood and encouraged by the Reform Movement and the social and religious context of modern Jewish marriage.
 The **Shulchan Aruch** twice states that marriages are not to be performed on Shabbat and Yom Tov (Orach Chayim 339.4 and Even Ha-ezer 64.3).   This prohibition is based on the Talmudic statement (Beitsa 36b) and the underlying mishna.   These prohibitions mentioned in the several texts do not relate to Biblically prohibited work, but were issued by the Rabbis in an effort to protect the sanctity of the Shabbat.*   This, however, engenders a

---

* The Rabbinic arguments against a marriage on Shabbat

contradiction between the Mishnaic prohibition and the weighty and esteemed **mitzvah** of marriage. The problem was resolved by stating that the prohibition referred only to an individual who had already been married and had children by that marriage. In that case, if he wished to be married a second time, the wedding could not be held on Shabbat.

The brief Talmudic discussion led to a controversy between Rashi and Rabbenu Tam. Rashi would prohibit any marriage on Shabbat while Rabbenu Tam might be permissive; he, nevertheless, refrained from conducting such a marriage because of the injunction against writing on Shabbat, and he would permit it only in an emergency.

The entire matter is also touched upon in the case of the High Priest, ministering on Yom Kippur, who must remarry immediately, even on Yom Kippur, if his first wife died, or else be unfit to continue as High Priest (Yoma 38b). There the Jerusalem Talmud asks how such a marriage could occur, since marriage involves an act of acquisition, which is prohibited on Shabbat. The specific case of the High Priest was solved by stating that Rabbinic prohibition had no validity with the High Priest serving in the Temple. The general prohibition against marriage on Yom Tov is discussed in **Shulchan Aruch**, O. Ch. 546.1.

Our tradition has also dealt with the rare emergency in which a wedding has occurred or could occur on Shabbat, and with the pressing circumstances leading authorities to violate the Shabbat in order to conduct a marriage. Moses Isserles stated (note to Orach Chayim 339.4) that "it was permitted under certain conditions," and gave as his authority Rabbenu Tam, who followed the Talmudic line of reasoning and stated (**Sefer Hayashar** 101.10): "I have permitted the marriage of a woman on Shabbat to a man who had no children from a previous marriage," and then continued that he had also made exceptions for other unusual circumstances.

Isserles himself dealt with such an exception in his Responsum #125, where he reported that he had conducted the wedding of an orphan bride on Friday evening, two hours after Shabbat had commenced (a disciple also reported that Isserles did not say his Shabbat prayers until after the wedding). There had been a lengthy argument about the dowry to be furnished by relatives of the orphan, and rather than shame the girl, Isserles insisted that negotiations continue until the groom was satisfied; then the marriage was performed. The occasion must have led to considerable complaints, for the

---

rest on weak foundations. The arguments are paralleled by those which prohibit climbing a tree, riding an animal, or swimming on the Sabbath.

responsum reports them.   The **mitzvah** of marrying the
girl overrode any objection which might have been raised
in this case, especially since the Rabbinic prohibition
was made only to keep individuals from writing the **Ketuba** on Shabbat or acquiring property (as the man might do
in this case).   Isserles did not feel that the general
rule against marrying on Shabbat was challenged by him
as he had acted only under the pressure of an emergency.
Here the "honor of people" took precedence.   He cites,
in addition, **Hagahot Asheri** and the Semag, while acknow-
ledging that Alfasi, Rambam, and others opposed such
leniency.

It is clear from these sources that under emergency
conditions weddings were certainly permissible on Shabbat.   It is equally clear that the **bedi-avad** weddings
conducted on Shabbat were to be considered completely
valid.

We, however, are not concerned with an emergency,
but with the usual social context for a modern wedding
planned well in advance in the largest number of cases.
From the sources cited above, we can see that the traditional prohibition against marriage on Shabbat as given
in the **Shulchan Aruch** rests on foundations in the Talmudic tradition which we, as Reform Jews, no longer
observe.   One might, therefore, be led to argue that
inasmuch as marriage is a **mitzvah**, it should override
any objections to its performance on Shabbat.   We disagree with that point of view for the following reasons:

(1) Despite weak foundations, the custom of re-
fraining from conducting weddings on Shabbat has been
universally accepted for many centuries.   Although the
Talmudic foundation is slim, the statement in the **Shulchan Aruch** is clear, and has had the support of Reform
Jews.   It continues to receive such support now.   (Although technically such a marriage may reflect only a
minor infringement of Shabbat, it is a major matter,
especially when related to the general level of Shabbat
observance.)   Since it has the weight of a widely observed **minhag** which supports the spirit of Shabbat, it
should not be dismissed or disregarded.

(2) The Reform Movement has encouraged Shabbat
observance in creative ways for more than a decade.   We
have published a **Shabbat Manual,** and we encourage our
members to make Shabbat a "special day" upon which we do
not carry out duties and acts performed on other days.
Countenancing marriages on Shabbat would detract from
this objective and weaken our efforts.   We would, therefore, go further and discourage weddings being held even
on Saturday evening, for they involve preparations on
Shabbat which are not in keeping with the spirit of rest
and holiness of Shabbat.   (See Ket. 2a: "Wedding preparations should not disturb the Shabbat.")

(3) We have a great respect for **Kelal Yisra-el** and wish to do everything possible to advance the unity of the Jewish people. There are, to be sure, certain matters of principle for which we must stand alone, but this does not qualify as one of them. We are here discussing a **matter of mere convenience**, because a marriage can easily be performed on any other day except in extreme emergency caused by persecution or war.

(4) Our tradition has always emphasized that in addition to all else, marriage has as its basis companionship, procreation, and family life; but there are also various economic aspects which form an important element of the traditional **Ketuba**, and are not stressed by us. However, economic considerations do play a considerable role at a time when the family is about to be established in terms of property rights, insurance benefits, etc., in many states, and an equally large role when such a family is dissolved. These may not be readily apparent to the couple. Although they may not be "transactions" in the ordinary sense, Shabbat is not the time to initiate them. Economic considerations prompted Isserles to act boldly, but he kept some distinction between the financial negotiations and Shabbat by delaying his evening prayers. His act does not seem to be a precedent for interrupting Shabbat. We should not engage in transactions with these overtones on Shabbat.

(5) We should not elevate an emergency procedure to a normal standard of conduct. We are opposed to the performance of marriages on Shabbat, as we prefer to give allegiance to a hallowed tradition rather than to honor mere convenience.

For all these reasons, we, as a committee, after due deliberation, recommend that the generally prevailing practice be continued, that is to say, marriage ceremonies should not be conducted on Shabbat or on Yom Tov.

Walter Jacob, Chairman
Solomon B. Freehof, Honorary Chairman
Stephen M. Passamaneck
W. Gunther Plaut
Harry A. Roth
Herman E. Schaalman

See also:

S.B. Freehof, "Wedding on Saturday Before Dark," **Recent Reform Responsa**, pp. 167ff.

137.   MARRIAGE AFTER A SEX-CHANGE OPERATION
(Vol. LXXXVIII, 1978, pp. 52-54)

QUESTION: May a rabbi officiate at a marriage of
two Jews, one of whom has undergone a surgical
operation which has changed his/her sex?

ANSWER: Our responsum will deal with an individual who
has undergone an operation for sexual change for physical or psychological reasons. We will presume (a) that
the operation is done for valid, serious reasons, and
not frivolously; (b) that the best available medical
tests (chromosome analysis, etc.) will be utilized as
aids; and (c) that this in no way constitutes a homosexual marriage.
There is some discussion in traditional literature
about the propriety of this kind of operation. In addition, we must recall that tradition sought to avoid any
operation which would seriously endanger life (Yoreh
De-a 116; Chulin 10a). The Mishna dealt with the problem of individuals whose sex was undetermined. It divided them into two separate categories, **Tumtum** and
Androginos. A **Tumtum** is a person whose genitals are
hidden or undeveloped and whose sex, therefore, is unknown. R. Ammi recorded an operation on one such individual who was found to be male and who then fathered
seven children (Yev. 83b). Solomon B. Freehof has discussed such operations most recently; he **permits** such an
operation for a **Tumtum**, but not for an **Androginos** (**Modern Reform Responsa**, pp. 128ff). The **Androginos** is a
hermaphrodite and clearly carries characteristics of
both sexes (M. Bik. IV.5). The former was a condition
which could be corrected and the latter, as far as the
ancients were concerned, could not, so the Mishna and
later tradition treated the **Androginos** sometimes as a
male, sometimes as a female, and sometimes as a separate
category. However, with regard to marriage, the Mishna
(Bik. IV.2) states unequivocally: "He can take a wife,
but not be taken as a wife like men." If married, they
were free from the obligation of bearing children (**Yad**,
Hil. Yibum Vachalitsa 6.2), but some doubted the validity of their marriages (Yev. 81a; **Yad**, Hil. Ishut 4.11;
also **Sh.A.**, Even Ha-ezer 44.6). The Talmud has also
dealt with **Ailonit**, a masculine woman, who was barren
(**Yad**, Hil. Ishut 2.4; Nid. 47b; Yev. 80b). If she married and her husband was aware of her condition, then
this was a valid marriage (**Yad**, Hil. Ishut 4.11); although the ancient authorities felt that such a marriage
would only be permitted if the prospective husband had
children by a previous marriage, otherwise, he could

divorce her in order to have children (Yev. 61a; M. Yev. 24.1). Later authorities would simply permit such a marriage to stand.

We, however, are dealing either with a situation in which the lack of sexual development has been corrected and the individual has been provided with a sexual identity, or with a situation in which the psychological makeup of the individual clashed with the physical characteristics, and this was corrected through surgery. In other words, our question deals with an individual who now possesses definite physical characteristics of a man or a woman, but has obtained them through surgical procedure, and whose status is recognized by the civil government. The problem before us is that such an individual is sterile, and the question is whether under such circumstances he or she may be married. Our question, therefore, must deal with the nature of marriage for such individuals. Can a Jewish marriage be conducted under these circumstances?

There is no doubt that both procreation and sexual satisfaction are basic elements of marriage as seen by Jewish tradition. Procreation was considered essential, as is already stated in the Mishna: "A man may not desist from the duty of procreation unless he already has children." The Gemara to this concluded that he may marry a barren woman if he has fulfilled this **mitzvah**; in any case, he should not remain unmarried (Yev. 61b). There was a difference between the Schools of Hillel and Shammai about what was required to fulfill the **mitzvah** of procreation. Tradition followed Hillel, who minimally required a son and a daughter, yet the codes all emphasize the need to produce children beyond that number (**Tos.**, Yev. 8; **Yad**, Hil. Ishut 15.16, etc.). The sources also clearly indicate that this **mitzvah** is only incumbent upon the male (**Tos.**, Yev. 8), although some later authorities would include women in the obligation, perhaps in a secondary sense (**Aruch Hashulchan**, Even Ha-ezer 1.4; **Chatam Sofer**, Even Ha-ezer, #20). Abraham Hirsh (**Noam**, vol. 16, pp. 152ff) has recently discussed the matter of granting a divorce when one spouse has had a transsexual operation. Aside from opposing the operation generally, he also states that no essential biological changes have taken place and that the operation, therefore, was akin to sterilization (which is prohibited) and cosmetic surgery.

Hirsh also mentions a case related to our situation. A male in the time of R. Hananel added an orifice to his body, and R. Hananel decided that a male having intercourse with this individual has committed a homosexual act. This statement is quoted by Ibn Ezra in his commentary on Lev. 18:22. We, however, are not dealing with this kind of situation, but with a complete sexual change operation.

Despite the strong emphasis on procreation, companionship and joy also played a major role in the Jewish concept of marriage. Thus, the seven marriage blessings deal with joy, companionship, the unity of family, restoration of Zion, etc., as well as with children (Ket. 8a). These same blessings were to be recited for those beyond child-bearing age, or those who were sterile (Abudarham, **Birchot Erusin** 98a).

Most traditional authorities who discussed childless marriages were considering a marriage already in existence (**bedi-avad**) and not the entrance into such a union. Under such circumstances the marriage would be considered valid and need not result in divorce for the sake of procreation, although that possibility existed (Sh.A., Even Ha-ezer 23; see Isserles' note on 154.10). This was the only alternative solution, since bigamy was no longer even theoretically possible after the decree of Rabbenu Gershom in the 11th century in those countries where this decree was accepted (Oriental Jews did not accept the **Cherem** of Rabbenu Gershom). Maimonides considered such a marriage valid under any circumstances (**Yad**, Hil. Ishut 4.10), whether this individual was born sterile or was sterilized later. The commentator, Abraham di Boton, emphasized the validity of such a marriage if sterility has been caused by an accident or surgery (**Lechem Mishneh** to Yad, Hil. Ishut 4.10). Yair Hayyim Bacharach stated that as long as the prospective wife realized that her prospective husband was infertile though sexually potent, and had agreed to the marriage, it was valid and acceptable (**Chavat Yair**, #221). Traditional Halacha, which makes a distinction between the obligations of men and women (a distinction not accepted by Reform Judaism) would allow a woman to marry a sterile male, since the obligation of procreation did not affect her (as mentioned earlier).

There was some difference of opinion when a change of status in the male member of a wedded couple had taken place. R. Asher discussed this, but came to no conclusion, though he felt that a male whose sexual organs had been removed could not contract a valid marriage (**Besamim Rosh**, #340--attributed to R. Asher). The contemporary Orthodox R. Waldenberg assumed that a sexual change has occurred, and terminated the marriage without a divorce (**Tsits Eli-ezer** X, #25). Joseph Pellagi came to a similar conclusion earlier (**Ahav Et Yosef** 3.5).

Perhaps the clearest statement about entering into such a marriage was made by Isaac bar Sheshet, who felt that the couple was permitted to marry and then be left alone, although they entered the marriage with full awareness of the situation (**Ribash**, #15; **Sh.A.**, Even Ha-ezer 1.3; see Isserles' note). Similarly, traditional authorities who usually oppose contraception permitted it to a couple if one partner was in ill health. The permission was granted so that the couple could remain happily married, a solution favored over abstinence (Moses Feinstein, **Igerot Mosheh**, Even Ha-ezer, #63 and #67, where he permits marriage under these circumstances).

Our discussion clearly indicates that individuals whose sex has been changed by a surgical procedure and who are now sterile may be married according to Jewish tradition. We agree with this conclusion. Both partners should be aware of each other's condition. The ceremony need not be changed in any way for the sake of these individuals.

Walter Jacob, Chairman
Solomon B. Freehof, Honorary Chairman
Stephen M. Passamaneck
W. Gunther Plaut
Harry A. Roth
Herman E. Schaalman
Bernard Zlotowitz

See also:

S.B. Freehof, "Marrying a Trans-Sexual," **Reform Responsa for Our Time**, pp. 196ff.

138. MARRIAGE WITH BROTHER'S WIDOW
(Vol. XXXV, 1925, pp. 364-379)

The leaders of Reform Judaism have for some time been confronted with the following question: Why should the marriage with a deceased brother's wife be prohibited by Jewish religious practice while the marriage with a deceased wife's sister be permitted, and, on occasion, even encouraged? It led to a heated controversy between Drs. E. Cohn and I.M. Wise on the one hand, and Drs. Samuel Hirsch, David Einhorn, and B. Felsenthal on the other. It received the attention of the Central Conference of American Rabbis at two or three of its sessions, and especially at the Charlevoix Meeting (1915) in Dr. K. Kohler's comprehensive paper on "Harmonization of Marriage and Divorce Laws," and in Rabbi A. Simon's Summary. Since Rabbi David Philipson's request, at the second Cape May Conference, in 1923, that the Conference consider the Jewish attitude towards the marriage of a deceased brother's wife, the question is again before us.   The issue derives its vitality from the fact that the laws of the various states of our Union place such marriages on a par with those contracted with a deceased wife's sister.

Before taking a definite stand on the matter, it becomes necessary to survey the ground historically and to note carefully the reasons for the prohibition.

Modern Biblical scholarship has bared the gradual evolution of the marriage laws of ancient Israel. Whereas Abraham married Sarah (his sister by the same father),[1] Jacob married two sisters,[2] and Amram married his aunt[3]; and whereas Absalom appropriated his father's concubines[4] and Adonijah claimed the hand of Abishag (his father's youngest wife), while Solomon considered it as part of his regal inheritance[5]--the law, as formulated in Leviticus 18 (which appears to belong to the latest stratum of Biblical legislation), prohibits all such marriages as incestuous. Leviticus 28:16, as well as 20:21, unconditionally forbids the marriage of the brother's wife.[6]   On the other hand, the Deuteronomic Code lays down the law that "If brethren dwell together, and one of them die, and have no child, the wife of the dead shall not be married abroad unto one not of his kin; her husband's brother shall go in unto her, and take her unto him to wife, and perform the duty of a husband's brother unto her.   And it shall be, that the first born she bearest shall succeed in the name of his

---

[1] Gen. 20:12; cf. II Sam. 13:13 and Ezek. 20:11.

[2] Gen. 29.

[3] Ex. 6:20.

[4] II Sam. 16:21.

[5] I Kings 17-22.   "Such unions were still common in Jerusalem in the time of Ezekiel (XXII, 10), but they were offensive to the higher morality of the prophetic religion" (W.R. Smith, **Kinship and Marriage**, 1903, p. 110).

[6] Through marriage husband and wife are united into "one flesh" ("**levasar echad**").   Accordingly, the son's wife is considered as a daughter, and the brother's wife as a sister.   See Maimonides, **Moreh**, 3.49; "**Vecha-asher ne-esra ha-achot ne-esra achot ha-isha ve-eshet ha-ach.**" B. Felsenthal, "Beitraege zum Verstaendnis der biblischen Ehegesetze," **Jewish Times**, July 12, 1872.

brother that is dead, that his name be not blotted out
of Israel."[7] In the light of Genesis 38 and Ruth 5, it
is evident that previous to the Deuteronomic Law any
near kinsman was eligible to discharge this duty. The
omission of this important law in Leviticus could not
have been accidental. It is quite likely that the
priestly legislator, viewing all human relations from
the exalted heights of holiness, regarded even the
Levirate marriage with aversion. Be that as it may, his
point of view did not prevail. When, in consequence of
Ezra's reformation, the Pentateuch as an undivided whole
came to be viewed as the revealed will of God and as the
unquestioned basis for Jewish life, the Levirate marriage was retained. Subsequent Jewish thought interpreted it as an exception to the general prohibition of
marrying the brother's wife. Accordingly, Jonathan
renders Lev. 18:16 thus: "'Ervat eshet achicha lo
tegaleh, ervat achicha hi.' Eryat itat achuch la tivzeh
bechayei achuch uvatar moteih in it leih banin, iryata
de-achuch hi" ("The wife of thy brother shalt thou not
defile during the life of thy brother and after his
death, if he has children, she is thy brother's naked-
ness").[8]

The Levirate marriage is not a peculiarly Jewish
institution. As the evidence in Westermarck's History
of Human Marriage[9] and in Frazer's Folk Lore of the Old
Testament[10] shows, it was practiced among primitive and
semi-primitive peoples in many parts of the world. J.F.
McLennan,[11] followed by W.R. Smith,[12] Wellhausen,[13]

---

[7] Deut. 25:5-6: "Ki yeshevu achim yachdav umet echad
mehem uven ein lo, lo tihyeh eshet hamet hachutsa le-ish
zar. Yevamah yavo aleiha ulekachah lo le-isha veyibema.
Vehaya habechor asher teled yakum al shem achiv hamet,
velo yimacheh shemo miYisra-el."

[8] Similarly Jonathan renders Lev. 20:21 by "itat achoi
becheivei."

[9] Vol. III, pp. 207-220, 261-266.

[10] Vol. II, pp. 263-341.

[11] Studies in Ancient History I, pp. 109-114.

[12] Kinship, pp. 85ff.

[13] Nachtrichten der Kgl. Gesell. der Wiss. zu Goett.,
1893, pp. 460ff, 474ff, and 479ff.

Buhl,[14] Benzinger,[15] and Barton[16] regard it as a survival of fraternal polyandry of the Tibetan type, in which
a group of brothers living together share a single wife,
and the children of the brotherhood are all, by legal
fiction, reckoned as belonging to the eldest brother.
As this form of polyandry was practiced in Arabia, it
may adequately explain both the Levirate marriage in
ancient Israel and the general aversion to that state of
society as embodied in the prohibition of the marriage
of the deceased brother's wife. Other scholars, such as
Post, Starcke, Driver,[17] and Frazer, seek the origin of
the Levirate marriage in a particular form of group
marriage, namely, in the marriage of a group of brothers
to a group of sisters.[18] Westermarck, while rejecting
the hypothesis of group marriage, accounts for the Levirate on the basis of inheritance of the brother's property.[19] In keeping with the inferior status of women in
primitive society, she was treated as an important part
of her husband's estate, and, upon his death, passed
together with the children and property to the new head
of the family, who assumed toward them the position of
guardian and owner.

In line with this view is Tarbari's statement in
his commentary to the Koran: "In the Jahiliya, when a
man's father or brother or son died and left a widow,
the dead man's heir, if he came at once and threw his
garment over her, had the right to marry her under the
dowry (Mahr) of (i.e., already paid by) her (deceased)
lord (Sahib), or to give her in marriage and take her
dowry. But if she anticipated him and went off to her
own people, the disposal of her hand belonged to herself."[20] With the weakening of the family unity, the
brother, while still called upon to look after the widow, often only retained the right rather than assume the
obligation of taking her as a wife. The Jewish law

[14] Die sozialen Verhaeltnisse der Israeliten, 1899, pp.
28ff.

[15] Hebraeische Archaeologie, 1894, p. 134.

[16] Semitic Origins, pp. 66ff.

[17] International Critical Commentary, Deuteronomy, pp.
284-285.

[18] Op. cit., p. 339.

[19] Op. cit.

[20] Cited by W.R. Smith, op. cit., p. 105. Compare the
symbolical act spoken of here with Ruth 3:9.

furnished him, through the ceremony of the **Chalitsa** with the means of evading this marriage.

This institution survived in Israel--as among other peoples[21]--because of two reasons. In the first place, the practice of purchasing wives rendered the widow a valuable part of the inheritance, who could not pass out of the family, and had therefore to go to the rightful heir. The second reason was the desire to preserve the name of the dead (**"Velo yimacheh shemo miYisra-el"**). As man's eternal welfare in the beyond was supposed to depend upon his leaving children behind him who could perform the rite necessary for his soul's salvation, it was the duty of the survivors to remedy the perilous state of a kinsman who died childless. Hence, what was once held to be the heir's right of succession became a burdensome and repulsive obligation imposed on the surviving brother, who submitted to it out of a sense of duty to the deceased.[22]

This aversion to the Levirate marriage accompanied it throughout its development among the Jewish people. Thus, the Samaritans, who--as is well known--represent an old point of view, allowed the Levirate marriage only where the woman was **betrothed** but not actually married to the deceased brother.[23]

Geiger has argued that this was also the position of the Sadducees.[24] Some of the early Karaites took the same position. Benjamin Nehavendi was the first to make the following compromise: While the betrothed is to be married by the brother of the deceased, the widowed wife (**min hanisu-in**) is to be married to a kinsman of the deceased, construing--on the basis of the story of Boaz and Ruth--the word **achim** in Deut. 25:5 not as literally "brothers," but rather in its wider sense of "kinsmen." Furthermore, since the Levirate marriage is bound up with the inherited land estate (i.e., in Palestine) of the deceased, the Karaites hold it no longer valid, owing to the changed conditions in the **Galut**.[25]

---

[21] Frazer, **op. cit.**, 341n.

[22] Op. **cit.**, p. 340.

[23] Kid. 75b-76a: "Shehem **meyabemim et ha-arusot ufoterim et hanesu-ot**"; Yer. Gitt. 1.4; Yev. 1.6, and Masechet Kutim, end.

[24] Geiger, **Kevutsat Ma-amarim**, Warsaw, 1910, p. 87; "Die Levirate Ehe," **Juedische Zeitschrift** I, 28f.

[25] **Ibid.**, Aaron b. Eliyahu of Nikomodio, **Gan Eden**, ch. 30: "**Ata bagalut, keivan she-ein lanu yeshivat yichud benachala, ein lanu chiyuv hayibum**"; Solomon Troki,

Moreover, even the Pharisees were embarrassed by this institution. The Shammaites upheld the Samaritan view of the Levirate.[26] The Hillelites, too, placed various restrictions upon its application.[27] Thus, they interpreted the reference to "**ben ein lo**" to mean that the law does not apply in case female as well as male offspring were left by the deceased brother. This view appears also in the Septuagint and in Josephus.[28] Abba Saul declares: "He who marries his deceased brother's wife on account of her beauty or of her possessions commits an act of fornication, and the issue of such a marriage comes near to bastardy."[29] This view was adopted in the Mishna: "In the former days the Levirate marriage was considered preferable to the **Chalitsa**, because the marriage was entered into with the sole purpose of fulfilling the law, but nowadays when this pure motive no longer prevails the **Chalitsa** is preferable."[30] Bar Kappara shares this view.[31] Rav and R. Judah held that it is optional with the man to marry the woman or to give her **Chalitsa**.[32] After considerable

---

"Apiryon," in Neubauer's **Geschichte des Karaertums** (Hebrew part), pp. 54-55; Pinsker, **Likutei Kadmoniyot** II, pp. 66ff.

[26] Yer. Yev. 1.6.

[27] **Sifrei**, Ki Tetse, 288ff; Mishna and Gemara, Yevamot; also **Shulchan Aruch**, Even Ha-ezer, Hilchot Yibum.

[28] **Ant.** IV.8, no. 23; comp. Mark XII:19. Philo makes no reference to the Levirate in his discussion of prohibited marriages. **Special Laws** (Younge's transl.), III, pp. 303.

[29] Tos. Yev. VI:9: "**Haba al yevimto leshum noy uleshum nechasim, harei zo be-ilat zenut, vekarov havalad lihyot mamzer.**" Yev. 39b quotes this saying in a different version: "**Hakones et yevimto leshum noy uleshum ishut uleshem davar acher, ke-ilu paga be-erva, vekarov ani be-einai lihyot havalad mamzer.**"

[30] Yev. 39b: "**Mitzvat yibum kodemet lemitzvat chalitsa, barishona shehayu mitkavenim leshem mitzva. Achshav she-ein mitkavenim leshem mitzva, ameru mitzvat chalitsa kodemet lemitzvat yibum.**"

[31] See also Ket. 64 and Bechorot 13. See Tosafot, Yev. 39b (referring to Ket. 64): "**Ein kofin... i ba-ei chiluts i ba-ei yibum.**"

[32] Yev. 39b.

fluctuation of opinion as to which is preferable, the
Codes gave preference to the Levirate marriage.[33] This
is still the practice of Oriental Jewry. A new turn was
given to the question in consequence of Rabbenu Gershom's (960-1028) interdict of polygamy for Ashkenazic
Jewry. Levirate marriage was abandoned and **Chalitsa**
took its place.[34] We can only see in this development
the assertion of the moral repugnance of the Jewish
people toward the marriage of the brother's wife.

When Dr. I.M. Wise, in 1872, solemnized such a
marriage, he took the view that since the widow was
childless, the marriage was imperative according to
Mosaic legislation, for "whatever is made a personal
duty by the Law of Moses, can at no time be wrong among
Israelites." On the other hand, "Rabbi Gershom has no
binding power in this century or in this country." In
taking this position, he frankly maintained that the
object of Reform must be "to lighten the burden and not
to aggravate it."[35] He was stoutly opposed by B. Felsenthal, who pointed out that certain "personal duties,"
such as blood revenge, though forming part of the Mosaic
legislation, were eventually abolished. Their practice
today would, therefore, be "wrong among Israelites." He
further maintained that the marriage laws of Leviticus
18 have not lost their validity for Reform Judaism.

---

[33] The **Shulchan Aruch**, Even Ha-ezer, Hil. Yibum still
follows the same view.

[34] See Kohler, op. cit., p. 369, and Loew, **Eherectliche
Studien** 74-78. Caro writes: "Rabbenu Gershom hecherim
al hanose al ishto aval biyevama lo hecherim." (And in
the Hagahot: "Omnam yesh cholekim, usevira leih
decherem Rabbenu Gershom noheg afilu bimkom mitzva va-
afilu bimkom yibum, vetsarich lachalots," Even Ha-ezer
1.10). See also Holdheim **Ma-amar Ha-ishut**, p. 18.

[35] **American Israelite**, July 12, 1872. Dr. Wise argued
that if it is abolished, it is because (1) it is a
penalty, and the Mosaic penal code is no longer in
force; and (2) it is a mere mockery of an ancient law
without any effect. "The conception of **Chalitsa** as a
penalty can hardly be substantiated by a careful
consideration of the matter." In an editorial (**ibid.**,
July 12) he advanced this somewhat casuistic argument
for the non-validity of the ban of R. Gershom: The
Portuguese or Spanish Jews never submitted to it, and
since they "were in America and established
congregations prior to the German Jews" it follows that
"in customs and usages, those of the Portuguese,
according to the Orthodox sect, have the authority of
priority."

Similarly, the ban of Rabbi Gershom holds in modern times because it expresses the moral sentiments of the Jewish people.[36] Samuel Hirsch, too, stressed the universal nature of these laws, emphasizing their applicability to all times and places. As to Lev. 18:16, he maintained that it is so reasonable that no European legislation permits a man to marry his deceased brother's wife. "And shall we in America treat this law lightly?" he demanded. "Shall we perchance set the stage in our homes for tragedies of the type of the 'Hostile Brothers'?"[37] B. Felsenthal's and Samuel Hirsch's views received the zealous endorsement of David Einhorn.[38] Dr. Kohler, in his aforementioned paper,

---

[36] "Beitraege zum Verstaendnis der biblischen Ehegesetze," **Jewish Times**, July 12 and 19, and August 2, 1872. At the end of his exhaustive paper, Dr. Felsenthal exclaims: "Behuete uns ein Gott in Gnaden vor solch einer Reform, die selbst in Punkt der Sittlichkeites den Leuten 'leicht machen will!'"

[37] "Das Gesetz ueber verbotene Ehen kuendigt sich als ein allgemein menschliches, von keiner Zeit und von keiner Lokalitaet abhaengiges an! Egypten und Kanaan wird es (Lev. 18:3) zum argen Vorwurf gemacht, dass sie diese Verbote nicht beachteten. Gerade weil sie diese Verwirrung aller sittlichen Verhaeltnisse duldeten, hat das Land seine Bewohner ausgespieen (18, 24 und 25). Dieses Gesetz ist so vernuenftig, dass keine europaeische Gesetzgebung die Ehe mit der Frau der Bruders Zulaesst.
Und wir in Amerika sollen mit diesem Gesetz leichtsinning umgehen? Sollen wir vielleicht in unsern Haeusern Tragoedien nach dem Muster der 'feindlichen Brueder' zur Auffuehrung bringen? Auf die Reinheit unserer Familienbeziehungen, unserer Familienliebe setzten wir bisher unseren ganzen Stolz. Der Bruder sollte den Bruder bruederlich lieben koennen und auch die Veranlassung zur Eigersucht sollte ausgeschlossen bleiben!" (**Jewish Times**, July 19, 1872)
In his answer to Dr. Elkan Cohn (**Jewish Times**, August 2, 1872), he writes: "Aber weshalb ist es denn erlaubt, die Schwester der verstorbenen Gattin zu heiraten? Nun, das Gesetz setzt voraus, dass die unverheiratete Tochter im Hause ihres Vaters **"beveit aviha"** lebt; sie hat keine Gelegenheit, im Hause ihrer Schwester stoerend einzuwirken. Und gerade diese Stoerung ist (Lev. 18:18) ausdruecklich verboten. Fuer die mutterlosen Waisen dagegen sieht das Gesetz allerdings die Tante als die beste Mutter an."

[38] **Jewish Times**, August 9, and September 27, 1872. His

discussing Dr. Wise's attitude in the matter, has justly remarked that it can hardly be said that there is great consistency in this view. "Either the Levirate law is in force (otherwise the marriage is incestuous from the Mosaic-Talmudic point of view), or the entire law, pro-hibiting the marriage of the deceased brother's wife as incestuous, has--together with the Levirate law--lost all meaning and binding force for us, and the brother-in-law may marry his brother's widow as he may marry his deceased wife's sister." For the sake of consistency Dr. Kohler advocates the formal adoption of the latter alternative.

However, it cannot be maintained that the desire for logical consistency can overrule the feeling of the people in the establishment of the prohibited degrees of marriage. The feeling of repugnance toward the marriage of the deceased brother's wife has helped to safeguard the integrity of the family. Nothing has occurred in modern times to warrant the removal of this safeguard. The prohibition works hardship on comparatively few people, whereas through upholding a high standard of chastity, its moral benefits are considerable. The circumstance that the laws of our states do not forbid such marriages can have little moral weight with us, who realize all too well the imperfection of our State laws on marriage, and who for two thousand years have main-tained our own high moral standards of the family, in every land in which we lived. If formal logic rather than human experience is to guide us in our marriage laws, the inequality of the law that permits a man to marry his deceased wife's sister and forbids the mar-riage of the wife of his deceased brother may be more profitably removed by declaring both of these forms of marriage as incestuous. This has actually been the position of a large body of Christendom. Above all, we must guard against separating ourselves from **Kelal Yisra-el** as might be the result of such a radical and hardly called-for change in our marriage laws.

Samuel S. Cohon

Discussion

Rabbi Jacob Z. Lauterbach: Rabbi Cohon is a pupil of Dr. Kohler, and, in admiration of his teacher, he

---

articles were written in reply to Dr. Elkan Cohn's letters to the **Jewish Times** of August 2, and September 13.

endorses the statement of Dr. Kohler that there was an inconsistency in Dr. Wise's view.

I have the highest regard for Dr. Kohler personally, but I cannot subscribe to this statement of his. Dr. Wise was consistent. For it should be remembered that **Yibum** has not been formerly abolished by any authoritative rabbinical assembly. The **Shulchan Aruch** still has the law that **Yibum** is to be preferred to **Chalitsa**, though it also records the other opinion that **Chalitsa** is preferable. A change of attitude towards this law took place in the course of time, as recorded in the Talmud Yevamot, but they finally came to recognize that **Yibum** is preferable. It was Abba Saul who expressed the opinion that if one marries his sister-in-law because of her beauty, and not merely because of the religious duty to raise a child for his deceased brother, such a marriage is almost incestuous. This view of Abba Saul seemed to have influenced Franco-German rabbis, and, fearing that the brother-in-law in preferring **Yibum** may be influenced in his decision by the beauty of his sister-in-law and not by considerations for the **mitzvah**, they recommended that **Chalitsa** should be preferred to **Yibum**. And among Ashkenazic Jews **Yibum**, except in a few rare cases, has not been practiced. But remember: It has never been abolished. So Dr. Wise was perfectly consistent in permitting **Yibum**, that is, the marriage of a deceased childless brother's wife.

Now, what does Dr. Kohler say? If we permit the marriage of a sister-in-law in case the brother left no children, then we should also permit such a marriage even when the brother left children. I cannot see any logical consistency in this view. The law in Leviticus unqualifiedly prohibits the marriage of a sister-in-law. The law in Deuteronomy permits, and even recommends, the marriage of a sister-in-law in case the brother died childless. We can either assume with the Rabbis of the Talmud that the law in Leviticus had reference only to cases when the brother left children; or we can, if one is antipharisaically inclined (which, by the way, is no longer fashionable), assume with the Samaritans that the law in Deuteronomy applied only to the brother's betrothed **Arusa**, but not to the brother's wife. In either case, there is no conflict between the law in Leviticus and the law in Deuteronomy. And the law in Leviticus has not been abrogated and still has its binding force. To argue that if we disregard one part of the law of Deuteronomy according to the Rabbinic interpretation which permits the marriage of a sister-in-law in case there are no children, we should also violate the law in Leviticus which according to all interpretations prohibits the marriage of a sister-in-law, at least when there

are children, is, to say the least, not a very cogent
argument.   There is absolutely no warrant for declaring
the law of Leviticus abrogated.   I would much rather
favor the abolition of **Yibum**, that is, forbid the marriage of a sister-in-law, even when the brother died
childless, although the Mosaic-Rabbinic law permits such
a marriage.   For, after all, the Jewish ideal is "Kadesh
atsmecha bamutar lecha," to refrain from doing things
even though you may be within the law in doing them.
And this brings me to the discussion of the argument of
"Dina demalchuta dina" which has been raised by one of
the previous speakers.   The principle "Dina demalchuta
dina" does not mean that we must do everything that the
law of the country permits us to do; it only means that
we should not do what the law of the country forbids us
to do.   There are many things for which the law could
not and would not put us into prison if we practiced
them, but as Jews, as religious and moral persons, we
should not practice such things.   In every case when a
marriage is prohibited by the law of the State, even
though the Jewish religious law has no objection to such
a marriage, the rabbi cannot and should not permit such
a marriage.   If he does, he not only violates the law of
the State, but he also violates the religious law contained in the principle "Dina **demalchuta dina**," which
bids every Jew obey the law of the country in which he
lives.   But if the law of the State has no objection to
a certain marriage, but the Jewish law has serious objections, the rabbi must refuse to perform such a marriage, even though a Justice of the Peace would perform
the same.   Not to do all that the law permits you to do
does not constitute a breaking of the law.   If your
religious consciousness makes you close your business on
Yom Kippur and refrain from any work and spend that
entire day in the synagogue, do you thereby violate the
principle of "Dina **demalchuta dina**" because the law of
the State has no objection to your keeping your store
open, and working or going to the baseball game on that
day?

Rabbi Cohon: I wanted to answer one question that
was raised which may easily be dismissed.   Someone
wanted to know in regard to "Dina demalchuta dina."   I
want to give an example.   The Episcopal Church as a
Church is opposed to the deceased wife's sister marrying
the husband.   However, in the United States, where there
are no objections in the State laws, the Book of Common
Prayer, drawn up by the Episcopalian Church, states that
the minister need not solemnize such marriages if his
conscience does not permit him.   If his conscience does
permit him, he may, but they do not surrender their own
ground to that.

Rabbi Brickner: May I ask Rabbi Cohon what he would do in Canada, for example, where there is no State marriage, where the minister becomes an agent of the State, and every marriage, in order to be a marriage, must be solemnized by a minister of religion? If Jews came to you in such a case and ask you to marry them, and the Jewish law will not permit you, they would be compelled in those circumstances to go to an Episcopalian for marriage.

Rabbi Cohon: Then let them go.

Rabbi Philipson: I regret extremely that I came too late to hear Dr. Cohon's paper. I precipitated this discussion, when, two years ago at Cape May, I brought the matter before the Conference as a very practical issue.

There may be some of you who were not at Cape May, and, with the indulgence of those who were, I should like to tell what induced me to bring this matter to the Conference. In the preceding spring of that year I was asked to officiate at the marriage of a man and his sister-in-law. The brother had died; there was a son. I refused. I refused on the ground that I felt that as long as no rabbinical conference had taken any action in this matter I would not set myself up against **Kelal Yisra-el** and act individually. To my amazement, several months later this man resigned from my congregation for the following reason. He had written to a friend in another city. The friend consulted the rabbi of that city, who said that he would officiate at the marriage. So the couple went to that city, and were married by that rabbi. I then felt that I should bring the matter before the Conference.

The committee had no report last year; they have a report this year. I heard only the conclusion, and I do not know whether I heard right, but it seems to me that the writer of the paper is of the opinion that the law should not be abolished, and if I understood Dr. Lauterbach right, he feels that we should keep up the practice of not officiating at such marriages, but not base it on the legal point at all; but--whether there are children or not--that we shall not officiate at these marriages. My difficulty is this. I am living in a different age from the ancient Palestinian. I may have a sort of abhorrent feeling against officiating at a wedding of that kind. I confess that I have; it seems to me somewhat incestuous. But if that is incestuous, then for a woman to marry her deceased husband's brother is also incestuous, from my point of view. I cannot separate those two things. There may have been reasons in ancient Palestine for allowing a woman to marry her deceased husband's brother while forbidding a man to marry his deceased wife's sister. It seems to me that we must take a stand in this matter. Either we ought to declare ourselves against both marriage of a deceased wife's sister and a deceased husband's brother, or we ought to be brave enough to say: In the light of modern conditions we cannot retain either. That is the problem.

I agree with Dr. Lauterbach that if we do it at all, we shall do it whether there are children or not, but I want to make it all inclusive.

Rabbi Jacobson: I do not recognize the law. I will perform any marriage that is recognized by the State, and I would have done exactly as this man did, even if I had consulted you and found out why you refused. But I want to ask this question: If you refused to marry this man on the ground of Mosaic law, then that man--by being married and living with his brother's wife--is guilty of incest. What right then did you have to take him back into your congregation?

Rabbi Philipson: According to the laws of the land that marriage is legal.

Rabbi Schulman: I am very glad that Rabbi Cohon strongly recommends the retention of the present usage in Israel with respect to the prohibition of the marriage of a man to his deceased brother's widow.

You can discuss here a number of aspects of this question. The possibility of bringing about unanimity of obedience to any resolution of this Conference is impossible. The Conference is on record as opposed to mixed marriages. It adopted the resolution after a very thorough debate at a convention at which two papers were read on the subject, and yet there are individuals in this country who are solemnizing mixed marriages. We cannot help that. Our duty is to express the sincere convictions of the majority of this Conference on any question. That is, of course, a moral influence that is a guide, and as we have not yet spoken on this matter we will do so, but not--I hope--in the sense in which Dr. Philipson suggests. We cannot, of course, say that because the State allows something we must immediately go and do it. That young colleague who asked that question, if he will do me the honor and read my paper on mixed marriages, read in New York in 1911 (it is in print), he will find that this aspect of the question is discussed in that paper. "**Dina demalchuta dina**" does not mean that you have to do what the State allows. You can refuse, as a rabbi, to officiate, because that person can get married according to the laws of the State and his marriage is legal. But if he has enough religious conscience to ask a rabbi whether he should marry this person, teach him as a rabbi and tell him, "No." Then it is for him to decide whether he will obey you as a rabbi or not. Your duty as a rabbi is, above all, to act according to your conscience with respect to this matter. I would like to know from Rabbi Cohon the date of the opinion of Dr. Isaac M. Wise, when he solemnized such a marriage. It is exceedingly interesting to me because Dr. Isaac M. Wise did change his opinion afterward.

Rabbi Cohon: In 1872.

Rabbi Schulman: Long after that he changed his opinion. I will tell you why I say so. As a young rabbi in one of my earlier ministries, before I came to New York, I refused to officiate at such a marriage, when asked by one of the high officers of my congregation. He said to me: "I can go to another city and be married by a rabbi." I said: "That doesn't concern me. I am the guardian of my own conscience. I refuse to marry you." I said: "Do not think I do so lightheartedly. I am very, very sorry that you did not speak of this matter to me before. I cannot do it. But I will tell you what I will do. In order to show you that I do not wish as a young man to force you to abide by my opinion or to seem to you to act arbitrarily, I will write to older rabbis--not that I for a moment expect that they will differ with me, but to show you that I am not giving you a subjective opinion." I wrote to Isaac M. Wise, Felsenthal, Mielziner, and to Gottheil, with whom I had personal relations. I got four letters from these men, saying that my stand was absolutely right, and that they were glad that I had the courage to do what I did and the humility of asking an opinion of older rabbis. Therefore, I know that at that date, long after 1872, Isaac M. Wise was clear in his own mind.

Now I believe that this prohibition should be upheld. When this gentleman whom I refused to marry asked me, "Are we not Reform Jews, have we not changed and abolished many Mosaic laws? Who then shall decide which shall be kept and which shall not?" I said: "Reform Judaism does not abolish laws lightly; it does not change laws merely to make life convenient for people. When it abolishes an old law, it abolishes it because of an ethical motive, whether correctly or mistakenly. It says that this law no longer expresses our own ethical feeling. But suppose Reform Judaism still feels that the ethics which is in this law appeals to it; it does not abolish it. I feel that way as your rabbi, and I agree with those men who feel that this prohibition should still be maintained." The man married. His marriage was legal.

I will answer directly the question of Rabbi Jacobson. The man remained in the congregation. It never entered his mind to leave. As to putting him out of the congregation--that is an entirely different matter as to what should compel expulsion of a member from a congregation, as our congregations are at present constituted. We all maintain the sanctity of Yom Kippur. To my horror, there is the growing custom of people attending to their business on Yom Kippur. Shall we say that we shall expel these people from the congregation? That is a practical question, and let me tell you that it is a question many an Orthodox rabbi would have difficulty in answering. It is not for me to enforce my decisions upon this man in the form of an excommunication; that is what expulsion from membership would mean. As a rabbi, I have told him the law, have made him feel uncomfortable. I am not his judge, and I socially continued my relationship with him, but my record was complete and consistent, and in the end he had respect for me. We are not ready to excommunicate our people for every violation of the law. Does the ethics in this prohibition still appeal to us? Most decidedly it does; therefore, we should retain it. The prohibition has for us--at least speaking for myself--ethical force, and I will never perform such a marriage, even if this Conference should allow me.

Now, with respect to Dr. Philipson's suggestion, I would say: He is quite right, logically; but life is not logical. It is quite true that if there is that sense of repugnance, and if there is that feeling about the continued ethical validity of this prohibition with respect to the marriage of a widow to her deceased husband's brother, then--analogously--that feeling ought to exist with respect to the marriage of a man to his deceased wife's sister. But we are not making new laws. I would have no objection; but just imagine what that would mean--today in American Israel--if you undertook to legislate and extend your prohibitions. It might have a tremendous influence upon the strengthening and deepening and heightening of the spiritual authority of the rabbinate. But because I am not prepared to make new legislation, that does not by any means mean that I should deliberately abolish a prohibition the ethical sanction of which I still feel in my own heart. Now, as to the hardship, there is this to be said. The older I become, the more I feel that to be a loyal Jew and to maintain the religion of Israel with its sanctities in the midst of a large overwhelming non-Jewish environment is impossible without some kind of sacrifice and without some kind of hardship. And if this Conference would envisage this side of the problem once for all, perhaps it might mean a new epoch in the history of modern Judaism. If our people were impressed with the fact that we, the representatives of our great historic religion, have the courage to ask them to make some sacrifice sometimes for this religion, I think it would heighten our influence and it would impress their imagination; because for something for which you never make a sacrifice you eventually come not to care for at all. Therefore I say, by all means maintain this prohibition.

Now, if this Conference maintains this prohibition, that will not prevent some individuals from going and doing what they like. That we cannot help. And still I am hopeful and optimistic enough, and have that confidence in human nature, that if we have the courage of our conviction, eventually our moral influence will grow and grow, and then it will come about that a man will be ashamed to act deliberately against the formal expressed opinion of the overwhelming majority of his colleagues; and if he is not ashamed, we shall have created a Jewish public opinion in this country which will make him ashamed.

I therefore hope that the prohibition will be maintained, and that we do not weaken the possibility of our expressing a fairly unanimous opinion for the maintenance of this by bringing in this new point of view by new legislation.

NOTE:

This question is a very complex one. The discussion in the **CCAR Yearbook** (vol. XXXV, 1925, pp. 364-379) is very lengthy, annotated, and of opposing opinions, each stated by revered and respected teachers within Reform Judaism. This discussion, based upon traditional interpretation of Halacha, affirms the conclusion of the traditional rabbis that there is a prohibition against the marriage of a man to his deceased brother's widow. This opinion has evidently remained as accepted practice within Reform, even though Rabbi I.M. Wise did not abide by it, and solemnized such a marriage in 1872. He followed the Biblical commandment found in Deut. 25:5-6. The decision rendered in 1925, affirming the prohibition of the Levirate marriage, required re-evaluation and quite possibly reinterpretation.

Responsa Committee (1980)

139.   MARRIAGE OF A COHEN TO A DIVORCEE PROHIBITED
(Vol. LIII, 1943, pp. 85-86)

QUESTION: There is a problem which I am trying to
help a young couple solve.   The young woman is a
divorcee; the boy is a Cohen.   The man's father
objects to the marriage.   I wonder: Is there any
argument, based on Jewish law, which I can use with
the father to keep him from making his son's life
miserable because of this marriage?

ANSWER: The status of the modern Cohen has long been
questioned by leading authorities in Jewish law.   As
early as the 14th century, Isaac ben Sheshet differenti-
ated between the ancient Priest and the modern Cohen in
no uncertain terms.   He contended that the Cohen of his
time, lacking any documentary evidence of his rightful
claim to the priestly title, owed his special privileges
and obligations, not to the express mandate of the law,
but rather to the force of custom or common usage: "Kol
sheken kohanim shebedorenu she-ein lahem ketav hayachas
ela mipenei chezkatan nahagu hayom likro rishon baTorah.
Kohen afilu am ha-arets lifnei chacham gadol shebe-
Yisra-el" (Sefer Bar Sheshet, Responsum 94, Lemberg,
1805).
     Solomon Luria, the well-known 16th century authori-
ty, states it categorically that because of the frequent
persecutions and expulsions of the Jews, the original
priestly families, in most instances, failed to preserve
the purity of their descent: "Uva-avonoteinu, merov
arichut hagalut, gezerot vegerushim, nitbalbelu.
Vehalevai shelo yehe nitbalbel zera kodesh bechol, aval
zera kohanim uleviyim karov levadai shenitbalbelu, ve-im
lo kulo, harov nitbalbel" (Yam Shel Shelomo, B.K., ch.
5, sec. 35).
     Likewise, the author of the Magen Avraham assumes
the impurity of the modern Cohen's descent when he seeks
to account for the doubtful status accorded him in the
law: "She-ein machazikin oto kechohen vadai dedilema
nitchalela achat me-imotav" (Magen Avraham, Orach Chayim, Hil. Pesach, sec. 457).
     Jacob Emden was so impressed with the questionable
character of the Cohen's claims that, while hesitating
to invoke the power of the law, he urged upon the Cohen
the wisdom to refund the sum given him for the redemption of the first-born, and thus preserve his own moral
integrity.   Since he could not be sure of his priestly
origin, Emden declared, the Cohen, in keeping the
redemption fee, ran the risk of pocketing money to which
he had no legal claim: "Nir-eh she-ein kohen yafeh

lehafkia mamon bechezkato hageru-a. Vechim-at she-ani
omer demidina tserichin lehachzir, ulefachot kol kohen
yachush la-atsmo lifrosh misafek gadol shema eino kohen"
(She-elot Ya-avets, part I, Responsum 155).

When, therefore, Reform Judaism chose to ignore the
nominal distinction between the ordinary Israelite and
the Cohen--a distinction which has persisted to this
very day--it did not so much depart from tradition as it
did display the resolute will to surrender a notion the
validity of which eminent Rabbinic authorities had repeatedly called in question.

Israel Bettan

140. MARRIAGE WITH STEP-AUNT
(Vol. XXVII, 1917, p. 87)

There is a saying that one swallow does not make a
summer. For years no **she-ela** or ritual question came
before me; and if any was submitted, it was scarcely
important enough to bring for a decision before so large
a committee as this one. One question that I received
was also submitted simultaneously to two other members
of this committee who are also members of the faculty of
the Hebrew Union College, namely, Rabbis Deutsch and
Lauterbach. The question was asked by a colleague who
wished to know whether he--living in New York--might go
to Providence, Rhode Island, to solemnize the marriage
of a nephew to his aunt (called by him "step-aunt")--she
being the daughter of his grandfather by a second wife.

It is superfluous to state that such a marriage is
prohibited by the law as incestuous, and, accordingly,
the opinion given by the three of us was negative.

K. Kohler and Jacob Z. Lauterbach

141. MARRIAGE WITH A MOTHER'S SISTER OR HALF-SISTER
(AUNT OR HALF-AUNT)
(Vol. XXIV, 1914, pp. 153-154)

QUESTION: The following question was submitted to
your committee: Is it prohibited to perform the
marriage ceremony in the case of a man who has

married before a civil authority the half-sister of
his mother, both having had the same father?

ANSWER: My answer, sent by wire, as requested, was:
"Certainly; see Lev. 18:13 and 20:19." There marriage
with an aunt--whether on the father's or the mother's
side--is prohibited as incestuous. Now, the very fact
that this question could be asked by a member of this
Conference, who knows his Bible well, indicates a prevailing view that the law of the land is the determining
factor as to the legality of the marriage also for us
Jews. Moreover, the general presumption is that just as
marriage with the niece is permissible according to the
Mosaic code, so should an aunt also be permitted to
marry her nephew, the Mosaic view to the contrary notwithstanding. The fact has come to my notice that a
member of this Conference not long ago performed the
marriage ceremony of a Levirate, directly prohibited as
incestuous in the Mosaic Law (viz., where the brother's
widow had a child from her deceased husband). These
facts show plainly that a thorough treatment by the
Conference of this question is demanded, viz.: how far
the marriage laws of the State may be regarded as determining factors for the Jews, and how far they cannot
legalize the marriage from a Jewish viewpoint, the same
involving the legitimacy of the issue.

K. Kohler

142. MARRIAGE WITH A MOTHER'S SISTER OR HALF-SISTER
(AUNT OR HALF-AUNT)
(Vol. XXXIII, 1923, pp. 59-60)

QUESTION: A couple came to me saying they would
like to marry each other, but there was some degree
of consanguinity concerning which they were wor-
ried. This is the situation: the young lady is a
half-sister, on the father's side, of the young
man's mother. In other words, she is a half-aunt,
so to speak. Now, does the law in Leviticus forbidding marriage with a mother's sister extend also
to the half-sister? And is there no way of permitting such a marriage as we permit the marriage
between an uncle and a niece?

ANSWER: The law in Leviticus is understood by all authorities to extend to the half-sister also, and there is no way to permit such a marriage according to Jewish law.   The argument implied in your question--i.e., why distinguish between a marriage between uncle and niece and one between aunt and nephew--would rather tend to prohibit the former than to permit the latter.   Indeed, all the Jewish sects--Samaritans, Sadokites, Falashas, and Karaites--prohibit the marriage between an uncle and a niece.   And the permission or recommendation by the Talmud of a marriage between uncle and niece was probably intended as a protest against the interpretation of this law as given by the Sadducees and Samaritans (comp. S. Krauss, "Die Ehe zwischen Onkel und Nichte," in **Studies in Jewish Literature**, issued in honor of Dr. Kohler at his seventieth birthday, Berlin, 1913, pp. 165-175). It is noteworthy that in spite of the approval of such a marriage between uncle and niece by the Talmud and Rabbinic authorities, **Sefer Chasidim** (ed. Wistinetzki, no. 1116) declares that such a marriage will not be successful, which is but another way of discouraging or disapproving of it.

Jacob Z. Lauterbach and Committee

See also:

S.B. Freehof, "Marriage with a Half-Aunt," **Modern Reform Responsa**, pp. 100ff.

143.   MARRIAGE WITH KARAITES
(Vol. LXXV, 1965, pp. 97-98)

QUESTION: A young Karaite girl, whose family comes from Egypt and who says she has always considered herself Jewish, asks a rabbi to officiate at her marriage with a young Jewish man.   Shall he, as a Reform rabbi, officiate at the marriage?

ANSWER: The status of the Karaites in Jewish law has shifted a number of times.   Sometimes they are accepted and sometimes they are excluded.   For example, Isserles says plainly: We must not marry with them (Even Ha-ezer 4.37).   No one questions that they are of Jewish descent, but the question involved from time to time is the question of their legitimacy.   If their marriages were deemed invalid, then the children, of course, need not be illegitimate in Jewish law, since a child born out of wedlock is not necessarily deemed illegitimate. A child born out of a union that cannot be legitimatized is illegitimate, such as a union between a man and too close a relative, or between a man and a woman married to someone else. So it is really held against the Karaites that the general rule is that their marriages are deemed valid, but their divorces are deemed invalid. Therefore, if a woman is divorced by Karaite law and remarried by Karaite law, her offspring of the second union will be illegitimate. This is the basis for their rejection.

As important as the letter of the law is, so is the intensity of the emotions involved. In periods when the groups were hostile to each other, the laws were strictly interpreted. Therefore, nothing is to be gained by following the ups and downs of the various decisions. It is best to be guided by one of the greatest authorities, David ben Zimri of Egypt, who had perhaps more connection with Karaites than any other rabbi. He is very liberal about them (see A Treasury of Responsa, pp. 122ff). In David ben Zimri's Responsa (IV, #219 and VIII, #9) on marriage with a Falasha, he speaks by analogy about the Karaites, and he takes the general point of view that their marriages are deemed valid, but their divorces are deemed invalid; and because of this, if any Karaite is a descendant from a woman remarried after a Karaite divorce, such a person may be deemed a Mamzer and cannot marry a Jew. This is precisely the burden under which the B'nai Israel group labors in the State of Israel today. The Orthodox rabbis, on the analogy with the Karaites, consider their marriages valid and their divorces invalid. Therefore, the group is under the suspicion of Mamzerut.

However, David ben Zimri continues that, nevertheless, many of the Karaites have intermarried with Jews, and he says that by the law of averages, the likelihood of illegitimacy (i.e., the percentage of divorce and "remarriage" and of children from this "remarriage") is so small a percentage, that they could easily be considered legitimate and should be accepted into the community. David ben Zimri concludes that he agrees with Maimonides' son, the Nagid Abraham, to receive them into the community. Before coming to this conclusion, he says: "At all events, I admit that if they [the Karaites] all agreed to enter into the community, making a promise of obedience to it (Chaverut) and to accept the tradition of our Rabbis to be like us, I, with the agreement of the scholars, would permit them to enter our community."

Beyond all this, there is a special consideration involved in the fact that we are Reform Jews. We accept the validity of civil divorce, at least in the United States. In some countries the Reform congregations give a form of divorce which really does not change the situation in the eyes of Orthodoxy, since these Reform divorces are considered by the Orthodox authorities as invalid (just like the Karaite divorces). Therefore, we frequently marry people who are the children of women who had been only civilly divorced and have remarried. The children of such a union are certainly illegitimate in Orthodox law. Yet we marry them without hesitation.

The reason for refusing a Karaite certainly does not have validity for Reformers. If we accepted the old ground for refusal, we could not marry a considerable percentage of people we do marry. Since the authorities agree that Karaite marriages are valid and Karaites are of Jewish descent, and since the only objection is the validity of their divorce and the consequences drawn from it, we should have no hesitation in officiating at the marriage of a Karaite and a Jew.

Since this young lady declares that she has always considered herself to be Jewish, we might ask her to state further that she means to become part of the Jewish community, with full loyalty. In other words, she will not need conversion, but merely a statement of **Chaverut**. This would follow precisely the practice of David ben Zimri, who (as stated above) very likely had more direct contact with Karaites than any other rabbi.

Solomon B. Freehof

144. MARRIAGE OF A NEGRO MAN TO A JEWISH WOMAN
(Vol. LXIV, 1954, pp. 77-79)

QUESTION: My question has to do with the marriage of a Negro man to a Jewish woman. The man is a writer and a university graduate; the woman is still a student at the university. They are both over 21, and have been engaged for a year and a half. The man wishes to convert to Judaism. He attends services and writes reports on the Jewish books he reads. I have endeavored to discourage the union, but the couple remains steadfast in their emotions and convictions. The woman's family is violently opposed to the marriage, and insists that I do not officiate.

I am seeking a response from you as to whether Judaism sanctions such a union, and whether you feel that it is incumbent upon a rabbi to officiate.

ANSWER: The Jewish attitude to intermarriage, all through history, has been conditioned by religious, in some instances even by political, but never by purely racial considerations.   Even in the "racialism" of Ezra, the motivating force was religion, i.e., to safeguard the purity of the ancient faith.   In the Rabbinic Halacha, conversion to Judaism gives the convert the status of a Jew, qualifying him for marriage with members of our religious group.

Since the young man in question, though of Negro race, is desirous of adopting the religion of his Jewish fiancee, there is no valid reason, having its basis in Jewish law, why the couple shall not be united in matrimony by a rabbi.

Obviously, the laws of the given State interpose no objection to mixed racial marriages, or the requisite license would not be issued.   Empowered by the State to sanctify the union, and satisfied that the religious conditions have been met, the rabbi who solemnizes the marriage will be doing no more than duty requires of him.

If, because of personal relations with the members of the young woman's family, the rabbi concerned deems it inexpedient to act as the officiating minister, he can arrange with another rabbi in the area to perform the service.

Israel Bettan

145.   STATUS OF CHILDREN
(1980)

QUESTION: The child of a Jewish mother and Gentile father is normally considered as Jewish.   For how many generations does this Jewishness continue, if in the succeeding generations the mothers, though not practicing Jews, are the daughters of Jewish mothers?   (Rabbi Simeon J. Maslin, K.A.M. Congregation, Chicago)

ANSWER: As the questioner has stated, Jewish tradition
is quite clear on the status of children born to a Jewish mother and a Gentile father: That child is Jewish
(Yev. 45b; **Tur**, Even Ha-ezer 4; **Shulchan Aruch**, Even
Ha-ezer 4.5ff).   Nothing would have to be done by these
children in order to be accepted into the Jewish community, although--practically speaking--some authorities,
both ancient and modern, would encourage study and education on their part.   There would be no obstacles in
the way of such children marrying other Jews or participating in any way as Jews, provided that they wished to
be recognized as Jews.   If they held other religious
beliefs, they would be considered as apostates and the
rights and privileges accorded to them would depend upon
the particular circumstances (Zimmels, **Die Marranen in
der rabbinischen Literatur**, pp. 21ff; **Rufeisen v. Minister of Interior**, 1962-16-P.D. 2428; Schereschewsky,
Dinei Mishpacha, pp. 81ff).

        We must now consider two distinct sets of circum-
stances under which this question may arise.   Let us
first treat apostates or **Marranos** who may have returned
to Judaism after one or more generations.   This problem
received considerable discussion over a period of centuries.   After that, we will deal with the modern circumstance in which there has been an intermarriage, but
without the adoption of or inclination to adopt another
religion.

        Let us begin with the status of apostates and their
children.   We should remember that the attitude toward
apostates has fluctuated within the Rabbinic tradition.
The final view of the **Shulchan Aruch** is clear, and has
generally been accepted since the 16th century; but
other points of view also prevailed from time to time.
In the Gaonic period, the Geonim were divided both on
the matter of what the apostate must do when he returns,
and whether he should be considered as a Jew.   These
views also determined whether their children were to be
considered as Jewish.   Hai Gaon (as quoted by Adret,
Responsa VII, #292) felt that an apostate could not be
considered as a Jew.   Centuries later, the rabbis of the
Mediterranean basin had to face the problems of the
Marranos (Anusim).   Their attitudes differed greatly and
may be summarized under five headings: (1) Apostates
were Jews who had sinned, but nevertheless Jewish (Isaac
bar Sheshet; Simon ben Zemah of Duran, but on some occasions he did not grant this status; Solomon ben Simon
Duran; Zemah ben Solomon); (2) Those who considered the
apostate as Jewish only in matters of matrimony (and so
their offspring were Jewish), but not in any other area
(Samuel de Medina); (3) **Marranos (Anusim)** were non-Jews
in every respect, including matters of marriage; their
children were not considered to be Jews (Judah Berab,

Jacob Berab, Moses ben Elias Kapsali, etc.); (4) An apostate is worse than a Gentile (ben Veniste, Mercado ben Abraham); (5) Descendants of the **Marranos** who have been baptized are like Jewish children who have been taken captive by non-Jews, and their children are Jewish (Samuel ben Abraham Aboab). All of these references and excerpts from the relevant literature may be found in H.J. Zimmels, **Die Marranen in der rabbinischen Litera-tur**, pp. 21ff.

Some of the authorities cited above would terminate the Jewishness of the child with the first generation. Others would continue it. The most generous of all is Solomon ben Simon Duran (**Rashbash**, Responsum #89), who stated that such children would continue to be consider-ed Jewish forever into the future, as long as the ma-ternal line was Jewish. He also felt that nothing need-ed to be done by any generation of such apostates when they returned to Judaism: no ritual bath nor any other act was considered necessary or desirable. In fact, he emphasized that no attention be given to their previous state, for that might discourage their return. Rabbenu Gershom gave a similar view and urged the quiet accept-ance of all who returned to Judaism (**Machzor Vitry**, pp. 96 and 97).

The other extreme has been presented by Rashi (in his commentary to Kid. 68b and Lev. 24:10). He felt that any returning apostate or the children of a Jewish mother who had apostacized were potentially Jewish, but must undergo a process akin to conversion if they wish to become part of the Jewish community. That point of view was rejected by most later scholars (as, for exam-ple, Nahmanides, in his commentary to Leviticus 24:10; **Shulchan Aruch**, Yoreh De-a 268.10f; Ezekiel Landau, **Responsa**, #150, etc.). We, therefore, have two extremes in the Rabbinic literature; both, of course, represented reaction to particular historic conditions.

Solomon ben Simon of Duran wished to make it easy for a large number of **Marranos** to return to Judaism. Unfortunately, this did not occur; even when it was possible for Jews to leave Spain, the majority chose to remain. Rashi's harsh statement probably reflected his generation's attitude toward the small number of apos-tates who were a thorn in the side of the French commu-nity. Normative Rabbinic Judaism chose a middle path; it accepted the child of an apostate as Jewish, and encouraged the child's return along with some studies, but without a formal conversion process.

The modern State of Israel has taken a somewhat different position on apostates. For purposes of the Law of Return, it does not recognize an apostate who remains a member of another religious faith. Such indi-viduals would not qualify for automatic entry into Israel under the Law of Return (Rufeisen v. Minister of Interior, 1962-16-P.D. 2428). The latest amendment to the Law of Return retained this interpretation (Law of Return, Amendment No. 2, March, 1970).

Modern cases likely to come to our attention involve entirely different circumstances. We would generally deal with a mixed marriage in which no conversion has taken place; there would also be no attempt to conceal the Jewish identity of the mother or her children. In many such cases the children receive no formal Jewish education and are only vaguely aware of any Jewish identity, perhaps through the celebration of a holiday or some other random act. If the daughter of such a union also married a Gentile and this pattern continued in subsequent generations, what will the status of such offspring be?

We must again state that we are concerned solely with individuals who remain without non-Jewish religious identification. If they have converted to Christianity, then we would consider them and their children as Christian, in contrast to our tradition. In this we would follow our earlier decision and that of the Israel, courts ("Apostate Proselyte," CCAR Responsa, 1979; Rufeisen v. Minister of Interior, 1962-16-P.D. 2428). We could not consider such individuals akin to the Marranos, as no duress has led them to Christianity, but they have taken this step of their own volition.

If the offspring have remained without formal religious identification through the generation--which is perfectly possible in contemporary America--then we would follow Solomon ben Simon of Duran with modification. We would recognize the potential Jewishness of such offspring forever into the future, but we would insist on some form of education in order to understand Judaism and to express a commitment to it. No formal conversion nor any other rite would be necessary for the acceptance of such individuals, but a sincere interest and intent are required.

We may then summarize that we would accept children of mothers who are presumed Jewish despite apostasy or intermarriage on into the future, without any limitation to the generations which have passed. It would make no difference whether they have nominally adopted another religion for the sake of safety or whether they have remained without formal religious identification. In both cases, we would insist on some education and commitment before full acceptance into the Jewish community could occur.

                                        Walter Jacob

See also:

S.B. Freehof, "Status of Apostates (Children and Adults)," **Recent Reform Responsa**, pp. 120ff.

146. REFORM JUDAISM AND MIXED MARRIAGE
(Vol. XC, 1980, pp. 86-102)

QUESTION: May a Reform rabbi officiate at a marriage between a Jew and a non-Jew? What is the attitude of Reform Judaism generally to such a marriage?

ANSWER: Reform Judaism has been firmly opposed to mixed marriages. This was true in the last century and in this century. At its New York meeting in 1909, the Central Conference of American Rabbis passed the following resolution: "The Central Conference of American Rabbis declares that mixed marriages are contrary to the tradition of the Jewish religion and should, therefore, be discouraged by the American rabbinate" (CCAR **Yearbook**, vol. 19, p. 170). This resolution was reaffirmed as part of a lengthy report in 1947 (CCAR **Yearbook**, vol. 57, p. 161). A considerably stronger resolution was passed in Atlanta in 1973. Its text reads as follows:

The Central Conference of American Rabbis, recalling its stand adopted in 1909 "that mixed marriage is contrary to the Jewish tradition and should be discouraged," now declares its opposition to participation by its members in any ceremony which solemnizes a mixed marriage.
The Central Conference of American Rabbis recognizes that historically its members have held and continue to hold divergent interpretations of Jewish tradition. In order to keep open every channel to Judaism and K'lal Yisrael for those who have already entered into mixed marriage, the CCAR calls upon its members:
1.   to assist fully in educating children of such mixed marriage as Jews;
2.   to provide the opportunity for conversion of the non-Jewish spouse; and
3.   to encourage a creative and consistent cultivation of involvements in the Jewish community and the synagogue. (CCAR **Yearbook**, vol. 83, p. 97)

These resolutions clearly state the position of the Reform rabbinate in this matter. They reflect only the latest steps in the long struggle against mixed marriage which began in Biblical times and will now be traced as background for this resolution.

The Bible and Mixed Marriage

If we review the marriages of the Patriarchs, we can see that they went to considerable trouble to obtain wives within the family circle, presumably with individuals who would be friendly to the religious ideals which the Patriarchs held. It is clear that endogamous marriages were preferred to exogamous marriages: Abraham married his half-sister (Gen. 20:12); Isaac married Rebecca, the granddaughter of Abraham's brother and niece, his double first cousin once removed (Gen. 24:5); Jacob married Leah and Rachel, who also were his first cousins, the daughters of his mother's brother (Gen. 29:12); and Esau married Mahalat, the daughter of Ishmael, his uncle, also a first cousin (Gen. 28:9). It is quite clear that Abraham wished Isaac to marry someone not a Canaanite; later Esau understood that the daughters of Canaan would not please his father, Isaac. There were many instances which demonstrated that endogamous marriages were preferred for religious, family, and national reasons.

It would be appropriate to look at the Biblical legislation against mixed marriage more closely. A prohibition against marriage with Edomites and Egyptians appeared in Deuteronomy 23:8-9. Children of such unions were not to be admitted into the congregation until the third generation. The Bible reported no marriages with Edomites, but mentioned a number of marriages with Egyptians and two involved problems. Leviticus 24:10-11 dealt with the son of an Israelite woman and an Egyptian father who became a blasphemer. Solomon married many foreign wives for the purpose of political alliance, and among them was a daughter of Pharaoh (I Kings 3:1, 9:16, 11:1). The Book of Kings specifically warned against these foreign wives: "You shall not enter into marriage with them, neither shall they with you, for surely they will turn away your heart after their gods" (I Kings 11:2), which happened in the case of Solomon. Finally, there is a reference to Sheshan who married his daughter to Jarha, an Egyptian slave (I Chronicles 2:34). These three isolated incidents indicate that such marriages involved both male and female Egyptians.

Moabites and Ammonites were prohibited from being "admitted to the congregation of the Lord...even in the tenth generation" (Deut. 23:4). This statement contains no reference to mixed marriages. Negative references connected with mixed marriages to Ammonites were associated with Rehoboam, who was considered an evil king, and his mother was Ammonite (II Chronicles 12:13); in addition, Joash was slain by assassins whose mothers were Ammonite and Moabite (II Chronicles 24:26). While the Israelites were in the desert, they consorted with Moabite women and were led astray after their gods (Num. 25:1ff). In that same section we have a report of an Israelite who brought a Midianite woman into camp and was slain by a zealot. In both these instances the danger of other religions was decried. Ruth, a Moabite woman, demonstrated an opposing point of view, as she became the antecedent of David (Ruth 4:18).

The most thorough Biblical injunctions were directed against mixed marriage with the seven Canaanite nations; so the Hittites, Girgashites, Amorites, Canaanites, Perizzites, Hivites, and Jebusites (Deut. 7:1; also Exodus 34:11) were prohibited. "You shall not intermarry with them and not give your daughters to their sons or take their daughters for your sons" (Deut. 7:3). A clear exception was made for a woman taken as prisoner of war (Deut. 21:11ff). After a period of delay, her captor could marry her; and the legislation made no comments of a religious nature, nor did it mention conversion. The Bible contains few references to proselytes as well (Is. 14:1; Esther 10:27).

When the Israelites entered Canaan, they intermarried with the local inhabitants and served other gods (Judges 3:6). The most striking example of such a mixed marriage was that of Samson and Delilah (Judges 14:1). She was a Philistine, and became responsible for his downfall. Later Solomon married many foreign women as part of royal alliances (I Kings 11:1ff), and they, too, led him astray in his old age. If we look at the subsequent record of the kings of Judah and Israel, we may be surprised at the paucity of mixed marriages. Among the nineteen kings of Israel who ruled for two hundred forty-one years, we find only Ahab, who was married to Jezebel (I Kings 16:31). Among the twenty kings of Judea who ruled for three hundred ninety-three years, we have only Jehoram (II Chronicles 21:6), and possibly Jehosaphat (II Chronicles 18:1), whose mother's name may have been omitted because she was not an Israelite (Leopold Loew, "Eherechtliche Studien," **Gesammelte Schriften**, vol. 3, pp. 138ff.

The Book of Proverbs contains a number of references against associating with loose or foreign women (Prov. 2:16-17, 5:3-20, 7:5-27). These are hortatory statements, not prohibitions. The prophet Malachi denounced such marriages (Mal. 2:11).

The clearest statements against mixed marriage appeared at the end of the Biblical period in the days of Ezra and Nehemiah, when we find specific legislation prohibiting such marriages and demanding that Israelites separate themselves from foreign wives (Ezra 9:12, 10:10ff). Ezra scrutinized the marriages of the citizens of Jerusalem and neighboring villages. Considerable time was taken to complete this task against some opposition. A list of priests, Levites, and other Israelites who had intermarried and relinquished their foreign wives was provided (Ezra 10:18ff). Among those listed by Ezra as having engaged in intermarriage we find many among the High Priests' families, thirteen among other priests, ten Levites, and eighty-six Judeans. The problem was not entirely solved, as the same difficulty arose again in the days of Nehemiah, who railed against those who had taken wives from Ashdod, Ammon, and Moab. Nehemiah did not advocate the dissolution of these marriages, although he removed the son of a High Priest who had entered such an alliance.

Each of these statements prohibiting mixed marriage was subjected to detailed Talmudic discussion, which provided a totally different interpretation. We should remember that all of these Biblical statements which dealt with mixed marriage or prohibited it, did not declare such a marriage invalid. That thought was foreign to the Bible and did not appear until a later period.

Hasmonean and Hellenistic Period

Mixed marriages were discussed by the **Book of Jubilees**, which opposed them with the same vigor as Ezra and Nehemiah earlier. In it Abraham, and later Rebeccah, condemn marriages between Israelites and Canaanites (Jub. 20:4, 25:1). This theme also continued in later portions of the book (Jub. 22:16ff). Those who permitted their daughters to marry Gentiles were to die through stoning and the daughters through fire (Jub. 30:7ff). There could be no atonement for this sin, and the act was considered akin to presenting the child to Molech.

The **Book of Maccabees** reported mixed marriages as part of the general pattern of assimilation to the Hellenistic culture and condemned them (I Macc. 1:5, 11:18). The **Prayer of Esther**, an interpolation to the Biblical Esther, stressed her detestation "of the bed of the uncircumcised and of any alien." It was only necessity which brought her into the palace and into her position (**Prayer of Esther**, 115f). Charles considered this and other additions as dating from the first century of our era or earlier.

The same reluctance to engage in public intercourse or marriage with non-Jews was reflected in Josephus' tale of Joseph, who loved a pagan actress (Josephus, **Antiquities** XII, 4.6); he was eventually tricked into marrying the Jewish daughter of his own brother. Further evidence of mixed marriage is provided by some of the papyri (Tcherikover, **Hellenistic Civilization and the Jews**, p. 70). Those who left Judaism and probably were motivated by the desire to marry Gentiles were also vigorously denounced in Egypt by Philo (**Moses** I, 147) and by the author of III Maccabees (7:10ff).

Talmudic Period

The vast literature of the Talmud contains few discussions concerning mixed marriage. Each of the Biblical statements cited in the earlier section provided a basis for further development. Every effort was made to create a protective wall against the outer pagan world and to shield Jews from contact with non-Jews. During the most restrictive periods, non-Jewish bread, wine, and oil were prohibited, and anything cooked by non-Jews could not be consumed by a Jew (Avoda Zara 35b-38a); virtually all contact with non-Jews was prohibited (Nid. 34a; Shab. 16b; Avoda Zara 36b). Naturally, this prohibition extended to casual sexual contact, and those who violated this injunction faced punishment without trial in the same fashion as imposed by Phinehas (Num. 25:7f; Avoda Zara 36b). If the parties involved went further and actually married, they were subject to whipping (Avoda Zara 36b; Kid. 68b; **Yad**, Isurei Bi-a 12.1).

Not all the Talmudic authorities and not all periods were as restrictive as those previously cited, and the exchange of food, as well as social intercourse, with non-Jews was allowed, but the basic wall of separation remained (Avoda Zara 57a, 58b, and 59a).

The most significant change made during this period was the declaration of invalidity of mixed marriages. This remained a dictum of Rabbinic literature (Mishna, Kid. 6b, 68b). This Talmudic tractate provides a long list of marriages which are null and void for a variety of reasons, as well as marriages which are valid but interdictive. Marriages which involve Gentiles are declared void as no **Kiddushin** is possible. This new view may have reflected an internal Jewish development, or it may have been influenced by Roman law (Boaz Cohen, **Jewish and Roman Law**, vol. I, pp. 339f).

The Biblical laws against intermarriage were reinterpreted sometimes more strictly, and on other occasions leniently. The Schools of Hillel and Shammai expanded the list of nations excluded from intermarriage beyond the seven peoples of Canaan, to include all pagans. Simeon ben Yochai agreed with this interpretation (Avoda Zara 36b).

A very strict view was taken by Rava, who felt that the prohibition against the seven nations continued after their conversion. This was one of the many attempts to maintain absolute family purity. It meant that intercourse or marriage with pagans was seen as prohibited from a biological or racial point of view; it was **Zenut**, and would be punished through whipping (Yev. 76a; **Yad**, Isurei Bi-a 12.1).

Part of the strong feeling against mixed marriages was reflected in a general emphasis on family purity. It existed from the time of Ezra and Nehemiah to the destruction of the Temple. The loss of records at that time and in the later revolt of Bar Kochba made such genealogical practices difficult. The long genealogical lists in Chronicles reflected the mood, as did the Mishnaic concern with **Mamzerim** and **Netinim**. Degrees of family purity were established for various Israelites (Kid. 71b, 75aff). Such laws of purity were especially enforced for the priesthood (Kid. 66a, 76a, 77a).

The Tannaitic interpretation of the prohibition against marrying Ammonites and Moabites was limited to males, and did not extend to females--provided that they converted to Judaism. They could marry a native Israelite in the third generation (M., Yev. 8.3; Yev. 76bf). Rabbi Simeon sought to apply the same principle to Egyptians. Another mishna simply declared that Ammonites could no longer be clearly identified since the days of Sennacherib (M., Yadayim 4.4; Ber. 28a; **Yad**, Isurei Bi-a 12.25).

Deuteronomy had prohibited Egyptians and Edomites until the third generation, and in this case there was no tradition to make marriages with females possible after conversion, while excluding males. Although Rabbi Simeon sought to establish such a practice (M., Yev. 8.3; Yev. 76b, 77b), his view was not accepted. If the Egyptians and Edomites converted, they were not permitted to marry born Jews until the third generation (**Yad**, Isurei Bi-a 12.19).

Others rejected these interpretations, so Rav Asi stated that the century-long mingling of pagans and Jews in Babylonia meant that many might be descendants of the ten lost tribes. One could marry them without conversion or any other step, as they were Jews of doubtful status (Yev. 16b, 17a).

Similarly, Sennacherib so mixed the nations that it was no longer possible to tell who belonged to the seven prohibited peoples. This meant that they were eligible for conversion and acceptance as Jews (M., Yadayim 4.4). Rabbi Judah and Rabbi Johanan simply stated that Gentiles outside of the Land of Israel were not idolaters,

but blindly followed the habits of their fathers, so
matters of belief were no longer at issue, nor was there
a danger of being led astray by them (Avoda Zara 65a;
Chulin 13b). The principle of population mixture could
be applied to Egyptians and Edomites also, and there was
some Talmudic discussion about this (M., Yadayim 4.4;
Tos., Kid. 5.5; Yad, Isurei Bi-a 12.25).

In general, the Talmudic period expanded the prohibition against intermarriage so that it included all
pagan peoples. Restrictions against specific nations
were eliminated. This meant that they, as well as any
other pagan, could convert to Judaism and thus become
part of the Jewish people. If this occurred without
ulterior motive, but simply because of an attraction to
Judaism, then the convert--no matter what his national
origin--was treated as any other Jew.

The Talmudic invalidation of all mixed marriages
meant that an insurmountable wall had been erected between the Jewish and pagan communities. As marriage to
a pagan was simply not recognized ("Einam tofesin"),
that family unit did not exist as far as the Jewish
community was concerned, and was effectively excluded
from the community. The union had no Jewish legal status in the various Christian communities. It was then
unlikely that such unions would occur with any degree of
frequency.

The Middle Ages

The discussion of mixed marriage continued into the
Gaonic period. The responsa of the Geonim show some
incidence of mixed marriage. The prohibitions of the
Talmudic period were extended with further discussion
about their implications, but without substantial changes (B. Lewin, Otzar Hage-onim; Yev. 48b; Kid. 22b, 66b,
68b, etc.). In these instances both casual intercourse
and long-term relationships with servants, concubines,
or wives were contemplated. We should recall that in-
terdictions toward mixed marriage were expressed with
equal vigor by Christians; this occurred frequently
during the Middle Ages. The statements generally followed the pattern of those of the Council of Orleans,
adopted in 538 C.E., which declared:

Christianis quoque omnibus interdicimus, ne
Judaeorum conjugiis misceantur: quod si fecerint,
usque ad sequestrationem, quisquis ille est, com-
munione pellatur. Item Christianis convivia interdicimus Judaeorum; in quibus si forte fuisse pro-
bantur, annuali excommunicationi pro hujusmodi
contumacia subjacebunt. (Ephraim Feldman, "Inter-

marriage Historically Considered," **CCAR Yearbook**, vol. 19, p. 300).

Similar prohibitions can be found throughout the Middle Ages (Toledo, 589; Rome, 793; etc.). Their constant renewal may point to a continuing series of mixed marriages, or it may indicate the Church's desire to re-emphasize its hostility toward Jews and Judaism. The highest rate of mixed marriage in the Middle Ages occurred in Spain, and we find reports of Gentile wives and concubines. Such relations were already reported in Visigoth Spain in the fifth, sixth, and seventh centuries. The Arian Christian Church did its best to halt them and frequently adopted statements of church councils, most to no avail (Georg Caro, **Sozial und Wirtschaftsgeschichte der Juden**, vol. I, 85ff, II, 225ff). Various forms of illicit relationships between Jews and Christians are reported (Adret, **Responsa** I, 1187, IV, 257; Asher, **Responsa** VIII, 10; Baer, **Die Juden im Christlichen Spanien, Urkunden und Regesten** I, 171, 442). We should remember that there were stiff penalties for such illicit intercourse imposed by Christians; it could mean death by fire (Baer, **Die Juden im Christlichen Spanien, Urkunden und Regesten** II, 125, no. 72; Asher, **Responsa** VIII, 10; Baer, **ibid.**, I, 456, 1037-1038, II, 63, p. 48). As such transgressions could endanger the entire Jewish community, they were dealt with severely by Jewish authorities (**Zichron Yehuda,** #80, 91). There is a considerable number of cases of adultery and intercourse between Gentiles and Jewish women (Adret, **Responsa** I, 1187, 1250, IV, 257; Asher, **Responsa** VIII, 10, XVIII, 13). We also find intercourse between master and slave, presumably non-Jewish (Adret, **Responsa** I, 7.10, 6.28, 12.05, IV, 3.14; Asher, **Responsa** XXXII, 13, 15). The medieval authorities, like their Talmudic predecessors, made some distinction between relationships with Gentiles in private and in public. Although they prohibited such relationships in either direction, they tended to be a little more lenient if it was between a Gentile and a Jewess, as the possible offspring of such a union would be Jewish (Rashba to Kid. 21a in **Otzar Haposekim**, p. 253). An anonymous Spanish rabbi commanded, "You should proclaim a ban with the sounding of a horn against anyone who would have intercourse with a Gentile woman. He that is found to have done so should be severely punished, since many children have been born to Jews by their non-Jewish maid-servants" (**Zichron Yehuda,** #91). Zakuta reported that some Jews killed during the persecution of 1391 were actually slain by their own Christian sons born to Christian women (**Yochasin,** ed. Filipowski, 225a). These conditions were endemic to Spanish Jewry and continued

after the expulsion in the lands to which Jews fled
(David ben Zimri, **Responsa** I, 48, 409, III, 443, 520).
Moses of Coucy succeeded in getting a number of Spanish
coreligionists in about 1236 to set aside their Christian or Moslem wives (**Semag**, Lo Ta-aseh 112). Loew has
suggested that these marriages probably referred to
concubines (Loew, **op. cit.**, vol. III, p. 176). Isaac
Aramah (**Akedat Yitschak**, #20, etc.) denounced irregular
sexual unions in his sermons. He may have painted an
excessively gloomy picture, but was certainly dealing
with a real problem.

Among the Spanish authorities we should also mention Simon of Duran, who dealt with Jews who had more
casual relationships with Gentile women (Radbaz, **Responsa** III, 158), and Solomon Adret, who reported relationships and concubinage with Moslem women (**Responsa** V,
#242). In Adret's case it seems that this condition was
quite frequent.

Medieval Egypt seems to have been an exception to
the continuing problem of mixed marriage. S.D. Goitein
(A **Mediterranean Society**, vol. II, pp. 2277f) reported
no such marriages in the **Geniza** material; when they did
occur, then one partner converted. Marriages between
Karaites and Jews were mentioned, but none between Moslems and Jews.

Mixed marriages also occurred in Northern Europe
although there are fewer data available (G. Caro, **op.
cit.**, I, 57, 70, 94, II, 224). There were also numerous
instances of mixed marriage and sexual relationships
with non-Jews during the Renaissance in Italy (Cecil
Roth, **The Jews and the Renaissance**, pp. 45ff, 344ff).

The halachic literature of the Middle Ages which
prohibited mixed marriage had to concern itself with the
status of Moslems and Christians, who were not pagans.
The pattern for a new attitude toward these monotheistic
religions had already been set by R. Johanan (third
century), who stated that Gentiles outside the Land of
Israel were not to be considered as idolaters, but merely as people who followed the practices of their ancestors (Chul. 13b). Non-Jews could, therefore, be subdi-
vided into three categories: (a) idol worshipers, (b)
Gentiles outside of Israel, who simply continued the
habits of their ancestors, and (c) Gentiles who observed
the seven Noahide commandments, which included the prohibition of idol worship. Maimonides considered Christians and Moslems in the second of the above categories
(Commentary on M., Avoda Zara 1.3; Zimmels, p. 208). On
other occasions he went even further and categorized
Christians and Moslems as **Benei Noach**. In that category
they assisted the preparation for the messianic era
(**Yad**, Hil. Melachim XI.4). The Tosafists of Northern
Europe generally included Christians among the **Benei**

Noach (Tos. to Avoda Zara 2a), but occasionally also saw them as simply following the practices of their ancestors (responsum by Gershom b. Judah Meor Hagola). Rashi had come to a similar conclusion, quoting the Geonim about the same time (Tos., Avoda Zara 2a, 57b). There were some variations in the outlook adopted toward Christians or Moslems, depending on the economic and social circumstances of the Jewish communities, as well as on the distinction between Ashkenazim and Sefardim.

This new and friendlier outlook towards Christians and Moslems had definite limits. Sometimes they were set to cover commercial transactions; others dealt with items which could be connected with the religious ritual of these religions (Tos. to Avoda Zara 57b; Yad, Hil. Ma-achalot Asurot XL.7; Ribash, Responsa, 255, 256; Moses Schick, Responsa, Yoreh De-a 15). The restrictions definitely prohibited both sexual relations with non-Jews and mixed marriage. Marriages of Jews with Christians or Moslems were clearly prohibited by Maimonides and others (Yad, Hil. Ishut 4.15; Hil. Isurei Bi-a 12.1; Hil. Melachim 8.7; Tur, Even Ha-ezer 16.1; Shulchan Aruch, Even Ha-ezer 16.1, 44.9). All the medieval codes contain the Talmudic prohibition against mixed marriage. The codes differed in their interpretation as to whether the prohibition represented a Biblical or Rabbinic ordinance (based on Yev. 76a). Maimonides considered it Biblical, while Jacob ben Asher in his Tur invalidated such marriages on Rabbinic grounds. The codes, like the Talmud, indicate definite punishment for intercourse with Christians or for mixed marriages. Thirty-nine lashes were prescribed for such intercourse, and if a man lived with a Gentile concubine, then the punishment was to be tripled (Shulchan Aruch, Even Ha-ezer 16.1-2). In addition, the sinner was also to suffer divine punishment. Maimonides' code mentioned the Talmudic teaching that the slayer of a Jew engaged in intercourse with a non-Jew was not liable for punishment (Yad, Sanh. 18.6).

Rabbi Simon of Duran reported that the government permitted the Jewish community to stone Jews who had illicit sexual relations with a non-Jewess (Responsa III, 158). The responsa not only reported a variety of forms of such relationships, but also tried to discover solutions. So, when unions between Jewish masters and Gentile slaves were reported (Zichron Yehuda, 91, p. 44a; Baer, Die Juden im Christlichen Spanien, Urkunden und Regesten, I, 164, #6), this was sometimes used to compel a master to liberate such a slave and convert her to Judaism. In those instances, she may have become his Jewish concubine (Adret, Responsa I, 12.19).

In the 18th century, when social barriers between Jews and non-Jews decreased in England, intermarriage increased. Conversions to Judaism were rarely permitted, so such individuals usually married in the church. Intermarriage did not necessarily mean that the party wished to leave the Jewish community, but they had little choice, as they were inevitably expelled from the synagogue. Sometimes the children of such unions later converted to Judaism, and were brought back into the community. Although no numbers are provided, it seems to have been a noteworthy group (Albert M. Hyamson, **The Sephardim of England**, pp. 176ff). We find a similar phenomenon in France before and during the great French Revolution (Z. Szajkowski, "Marriage, Mixed Marriages and Conversions among French Jews During the Revolution of 1789," **Jews and the French Revolutions of 1789, 1830 and 1848**, pp. 826ff). We can see from this essay that a goodly number of individuals who entered mixed marriages subsequently converted to Catholicism. All of these incidents have been cited to demonstrate the reality of the problem throughout the medieval period. The codes and legal literature attempted to halt the process, and generally succeeded, but the same incidence continued throughout the period.

Conversion for the Sake of Marriage

Many non-Jews joined the Jewish community in the Biblical and early post-Biblical periods. Formal conversion was first discussed by the Talmud, which required sincere motivation as a prerequisite. Sincere converts could, of course, marry Jews (**Shulchan Aruch**, Even Ha-ezer 4, 8-10). Those who converted for the sake of marriage or for the sake of wealth or power, or those who were prompted by greed, were not considered proper proselytes (Yev. 24b, 76a; **Shulchan Aruch**, Yoreh De-a 268.12), but the matter is not quite as clear cut as it might seem, since various Biblical texts were interpreted as referring to conversion for the sake of marriage. This is how the captive woman (Deut. 21:13) was seen (Kid. 68b; Yev. 48a). Furthermore, prohibition against marriage with the Ammonite or a Moabite was limited to males, while females were permitted to be married immediately after conversion (Yev. 76b). Another statement in the same tractate held that we do not question the motivation of converts if they joined us during persecution or if they could gain no improvement of status by doing so (Yev. 24b). Others went even further; thus Hillel converted a Gentile who sought to become a High Priest (Shab. 31a), while Rabbi Hiya converted a woman who wished to marry a Jew (Men. 44a).

In the Middle Ages a major distinction concerning converts developed between the Spanish authorities and the Franco-German rabbis (B.Z. Wacholder, "Proselytizing in the Classical Halakhah," **Historia Judaica**, vol. 20, pp. 77ff). The former, represented chiefly by Alfasi and Maimonides, emphasized purity of purpose, and did not recognize any injunction to seek proselytes, a matter questioned by Simon ben Zemah of Duran (**Entsiklopedia Talmudit** VI, p. 426). Therefore, only those who came with noble and lofty purposes were to be accepted (**Yad**, Hil. Isurei Bi-a 13.14ff). The Tosafists, on the other hand, stressed the commandment of seeking converts and were willing to do so even if not all the technical requirements could be met (**Tosafot** to Kid. 62b; Git. 88b, 109b; Yev. 45bff; **Or Zarua** II, 26a, 99). There were a fair number of converts during the Tosafist period despite the Church injunctions against conversions. So, Wacholder found twenty-five converts in the responsa of the 12th and 13th centuries (B.Z. Wacholder, "Cases of Proselytizing in the Tosafist Responsa," **Jewish Quarterly Review**, vol. 51, pp. 288ff). A number of them were due to mixed marriages and were cited by R. Tam (Tos. to Ket. 3b; Yoma 82b) and Yehiel of Paris (**Mordechai**, San. 702; **Toledot Adam VeChava** 23.4). In addition, there were numerous converts among slaves of Jews, which in some cases involved sexual unions and concubinage.

Social relationships, mixed marriage, and conversion remained a factor in Jewish life even in the most difficult periods of the Middle Ages. They led to conversions in both directions, with probably a larger number leaving Judaism than joining it. Any conversion could endanger the life of the convert, his family, and in some instances the entire Jewish community (Jacob ben Moses, **Maharil**, 86b; J.R. Rosenblum, **Conversion to Judaism**, pp. 74ff).

The issue of converting for marriage is discussed at length by Caro and Joshua Falk in their commentaries to the **Tur** (Yoreh De-a 268). Caro concludes that some proselytes who convert for the sake of marriage may, nevertheless, be sincere; all depended on the judgment of the court ("**Hakol lefi re-ut beit din**"). Falk concludes that such conversion would be accepted **bedi-avad**. There are, therefore, good grounds in tradition for accepting such converts.

Modern Times

Mixed marriages occurred with increasing frequency beginning in the latter part of the 18th century. This was true in all lands of Western Europe and in the United States. Szajkowski has shown that such marriages occurred among the obscure and the prominent during the French Revolution (Z. Szajkowski, **op. cit.**, pp. 826ff). Mixed marriages increased rapidly during the succeeding

century as a number of careful studies have indicated
(E. Schnurmann, **La population juive en Alsace**, pp. 87ff;
N. Samter, **Judentaufen im Neunzehnten Jahrhundert**, pp.
86ff).

The largest incidence of mixed marriage and conversion to Christianity, in many cases, was found in the
German-speaking lands of Central Europe. This began in
the generation after Moses Mendelssohn, and occurred in
the fashionable circles of the upper class as well as
among those who sought upward mobility. Much has been
written about Rachel Varnhagen and her intellectual
circle, but we should note that the phenomenon also
existed among those further down the social ladder.
Eastern European Jews who settled in Central Europe in
large numbers throughout the 19th century were equally
involved in this phenomenon. If we look at the entire
19th century, we shall find that approximately ten percent of the Jewish population was intermarried (A.
Ruppin, **The Jews in the Modern World**, pp. 157ff). The
percentage remained fairly stable throughout the century, but increased in the 20th century.

The lands of Eastern Europe and the Balkans were
not entirely free from this problem, although the numbers involved were smaller (Ruppin, **op. cit.**, p. 159).

We should remember that opposition to mixed marriages remained equally strong on the part of Catholics
and Protestants. Slowly some Protestants granted concessions if the children were raised as Christians. The
Catholic Church insisted that such marriages were not
valid and that remarriage was necessary after conversion
of the non-Catholic partner, although some changes in
this view began to occur in 1821 (Leopold Loew,
"Eherechtliche Studien," (**Gesammelte Schriften**, vol. 3,
pp. 194ff). Slowly intermarriage was legalized in modern European states. This occurred in Germany in 1875,
in Hungary in 1895, and in Rumania a little later. In
1913 it was still prohibited in Austria, Russia, Spain,
Portugal, and Islamic lands. Even within the Jewish
community, marriages between subgroups like Ashkenazim
and Sefardim were rare in the 19th century.

Intermarriage was highest in lands where the number
of Jews was small and where there was little discrimination, as in Denmark, Italy, and Australia (Ruppin, **op.
cit.**, p. 161). It reached 34.1% in Italy in 1881, while
in New York in the same year it was one percent, as most
Jews had settled there only recently. The figures in
Germany between 1904-1908 were 22.2%. It should be
noted that pre-World War I Hungary ruled that those
about to "contract a mixed marriage can make an arrangement as to the religion they wish their children to
have. In the absence of such an agreement, the sons

follow the religion of the father, the daughters that of the mother" (Ruppin, **op. cit.**, p. 177).

The pattern of increasing mixed marriage, which was noted for England in the 18th century, grew especially with the establishment of civil marriages in 1837. Before that time Jews who married Christians were forced to do so in the Church (C. Roth, "The Anglo-Jewish Community in the Context of World Jewry," **Jewish Life in Modern Britain**, pp. 83ff; S.J. Prais and M. Schmool, "Statistics of Jewish Marriages in Great Britain," **Jewish Journal of Sociology IX**, no. 2).

Such marriages were also found with fair frequency in early America (M. Stern, "Jewish Marriage and Intermarriage in the Federal Period, 1776-1840," **American Jewish Archives**, vol. 19, pp. 142ff; J. Goldstein, **A Century of Judaism in New York**, pp. 328ff; H.B. Grinstein, **The Rise of the Jewish Community of New York, 1654-1860**, pp. 372ff). Studies for the mid-20th century indicated the increasing rate of mixed marriage, which has now reached approximately thirty-five percent of all Jewish marriages. Accurate broad statistics are not available, but many specialized studies have been undertaken (see Erich Rosenthal, "Studies of Jewish Intermarriage in the United States," **American Jewish Yearbook**, 1963, pp. 3ff; B. Kligfeld, "Intermarriage: A Review of the Social Science Literature on the Subject," **CCAR Yearbook**, vol. 70, pp. 135ff; "Report of Special Committee on Mixed Marriage," **CCAR Yearbook**, vol. 72, pp. 87ff; M. Davis, "Mixed Marriage in Western Jewry," **Jewish Journal of Sociology 10**, pp. 197ff; Rosenbloom, **Conversion to Judaism**, pp. 121ff).

The issue of mixed marriage was raised in a formal way by the Napoleonic Sanhedrin in 1806. Among the questions posed to this body was the following: "Can a Jewess marry a Christian, or a Jew a Christian woman, or has the law ordered that Jews should only marry among themselves?" As a result of the French Revolution, marriage and divorce had been made a concern of the State. Keenly aware of the implications, the Sanhedrin conducted lengthy discussions, in which reference was made to marriages between Jews and Christians which had taken place in France, Spain, and Germany, and which had sometimes been tolerated by the rulers. The final answer stated, "The Great Sanhedrin declared further that marriages between Israelites and Christians, contracted according to the laws of the **Code Civil**, are civilly binding, and that, although they cannot be invested with religious forms, they shall not result in anathema" (Tama, **Transaction of the Parisian Sanhedrin**, transl. F. Kirwan, p. 155; G. Plaut, **The Rise of Reform Judaism**, pp. 71ff). The French text here simply declared civil marriages between a Jew and a non-Jew valid, but avoided the issue of religious marriage; the Hebrew text deemed such marriage religiously invalid (E. Feldheim, "Intermarriage Historically Considered," **CCAR Yearbook**, vol. 19, p. 296). The Napoleonic Sanhedrin here applied the legal principle **"Dina demalchuta dina"** to civil marriage, without granting religious status. This Talmudic principle was constantly used for civil and criminal law, but never previously in matters of personal status. Some modern Orthodox authorities recognize such marriages, while others do not, and therefore require no religious divorce for them (Abraham Freimann, **Seder Kiddushin Venisu-in**, pp. 362ff; C. Ellinson, **Nisu-in Shelo Kedat Mosheh VeYisra-el**, pp. 170ff).

The Rabbinical Conference of Braunschweig in 1844 intended to endorse the declaration of the Napoleonic Sanhedrin, but as no one possessed a copy of the resolution, it actually went further by stating: "The intermarriage of Jews and Christians, and, in general, the intermarriage of Jews with adherents to any of the monotheistic religions, is not forbidden, provided that the parents are permitted by the law of the state to bring up the offspring of such marriage in the Jewish faith." A motion was also made to permit rabbis to officiate at such marriages, but that was rejected, and so no Jewish authority was authorized to conduct such marriages (for a summary of the debate, see W.G. Plaut, **The Rise of Reform Judaism**, pp. 220ff). The author of the general resolution, Ludwig Philipson, later changed his mind on this question (L. Philipson, **Israelitische Religionslehre**, vol. III, p. 350; Moses Mielziner, **The Jewish Law of Marriage and Divorce**, p. 48). Abraham Geiger similarly opposed mixed marriages (A. Geiger, **Referat ueber die der ersten Israelitischen Synode ueberreichten Antraege**, pp. 187ff). At the conference held in Breslau in 1846, Samuel Holdheim suggested that rabbis should officiate at mixed marriages, but this motion was rejected (**CCAR Yearbook**, vol. 1, p. 98). Resolutions calling for acceptance of civil marriage and marriages between Jews and Christians were introduced at the Leipzig Synod of 1869, but none was passed. The Synod of Augsburg (1871) stated that civil marriages are to be considered as valid (**CCAR Yearbook**, vol. 1, p. 113). None of the other rabbinical conferences held in Germany or in the United States during the last century passed resolutions on this subject; a number of individual rabbis dealt with the issue in essays and lectures. The radical David Einhorn called mixed marriage "a nail in the coffin of the small Jewish race" (**Jewish Times**, 1870). This citation was frequently quoted by others in the last century and in our own.

The Central Conference of American Rabbis has dealt with the question of mixed marriage extensively from its

earliest days. Mendel Silber read a lengthy historical
essay on the subject to the Conference in 1908 (Mendel
Silber, "Intermarriage," **CCAR Yearbook**, 1908, p. 207).
This represented part of the concern over the subject
and the desire to establish a policy on the question.
The following year a major portion of the Conference was
dedicated to this subject with the presentation of two
papers (E. Feldman, "Intermarriage Historically Considered," and S. Schulman, "Mixed Marriages in Their Relation to the Jewish Religion," **CCAR Yearbook**, 1909).
Both cited a considerable number of sources and reviewed
the positions taken by various Reform groups in the 19th
century. The discussion of the Conference indicated
that all the rabbis present opposed mixed marriages,
although some were willing to officiate at them. The
debate dealt with the freedom of the individual rabbi
versus the power of the Conference and the general force
of the rabbinic tradition. The debate on the subject
dealt with the question itself and with the issue of
rabbis officiating at such marriages. The resolution
which was passed read:

> The Central Conference of American Rabbis declares
> that mixed marriages are contrary to the tradition
> of the Jewish religion and should, therefore, be
> discouraged by the American rabbinate.

There was no substantial additional discussion in
the following years, but the matter was mentioned pe-
ripherally in a lengthy paper by Kaufmann Kohler ("The
Harmonization of the Jewish and Civil Laws of Marriage
and Divorce," **CCAR Yearbook**, 1915, pp. 335ff). This
essay made it clear that Reform Judaism accepts civil
marriages as valid and does so in the case of mixed
marriages as well.

The following decades saw some discussion of this
subject in responsa of the Conference ("Forfeiture of
Congregational Membership by Intermarriage," **CCAR Yearbook**, 1916, pp. 113ff; "Burial of Gentiles in a Jewish
Cemetery," **CCAR Yearbook**, 1963, pp. 85ff), and those of
Solomon B. Freehof in his various volumes. Fairly frequent articles in the **CCAR Journal** and elsewhere by
Reform rabbis demonstrated continued concern, and minor
discussion of this question occurred at conferences
through the years. It was not brought to the floor of
the Conference again until 1947, when a lengthy report
of a special committee under the chairmanship of Solomon
B. Freehof proposed a set of recommendations with considerable annotations, which were adopted after some
debate ("Report on Mixed Marriage and Intermarriage,"
CCAR Yearbook, pp. 158ff). The Conference reaffirmed
the 1909 resolution on mixed marriage and then proceeded

to deal with the specifics involved in mixed marriage through resolutions embodied in the report. These were as follows:

> II. The CCAR considers all sincere applicants for proselytizing as acceptable whether or not it is the intention of the candidate to marry a Jew.

> III. We consider civil marriage to be completely valid but lacking the sanctity which religion can bestow upon it. We recommend that whenever a civil marriage between Jews has taken place, it be followed as soon as possible by a Jewish religious marriage ceremony.

> IV. Since it is the point of view of the Conference that all sincere applicants for conversion be accepted whether marriage is involved or not, and since, too, we recognize the validity of civil marriages but urge that they be sanctified by a religious marriage ceremony, we surely would accept such a proselyte and officiate at the religious marriage. However, it should be clear that the fact that the couple is already married by civil law does not obviate the necessity of conversion of the Gentile party before the Jewish marriage service can take place.

> V. The Conference may well take the stand that wherever the state acknowledges the validity of common law marriage, we likewise consider them to be valid; but that just as in cases of civil marriage. we urge that they be changed to regular marriage by license and religious ceremony.

> VI. We cannot take quite the same attitude which traditional law has taken inasmuch as marriage, especially in England and the United States, is not only church marriage; it has also, to some extent, the status of civil marriage, at least to the extent that the license to marry was issued by the state. Nevertheless, in this case, the mood of the traditional attitude must determine our point of view. We cannot declare such a marriage invalid but would consider it highly improper and should endeavor, as much as possible, to persuade the couple to be married subsequently by Jewish ceremony. Likewise, on the basis of the unanimous attitude of traditional law, it would be improper for a rabbi to participate with a Christian minister at such a marriage.

Children of religious school age should likewise not be required to undergo a special ceremony
of conversion but should receive instruction as
regular students in the school.   The ceremony of
Confirmation at the end of the school course shall
be considered in lieu of a conversion ceremony.
Children older than confirmation age should not be
converted without their own consent.   The Talmudic
law likewise gives the child who is converted in
infancy by the court the right to reject the conversion when it becomes of religious age.   Therefore, the convert should receive regular instruction for that purpose and be converted in the regular conversion ceremony.

Considerable background material for each conclusion was provided.   These specific recommendations have
gone much farther than any other material in providing
an orderly and uniform approach to the questions connected with mixed marriages.
A further recommendation was made by a special
committee under the leadership of Eugene Mihaly in 1962
("Report of the Special Committee on Mixed Marriage,"
CCAR Yearbook, 1962, pp. 86ff).   It analyzed the problem
and recommended a resolution which would have changed
the position of 1909 and permitted rabbis to officiate
at mixed marriages.   There was considerable debate in
which all matters connected with mixed marriage were
thoroughly discussed.   The substantive portion of the
resolution failed, but it was decided to study the matter further and monitor it.
The issue of mixed marriage was raised again in
1971 with a demand for further study which was brought
to the floor of the Conference in 1973 through a report
under the chairmanship of Herman E. Schaalman ("Report
of the Committee on Mixed Marriage," CCAR Yearbook,
1973, pp. 59ff).   In this instance the majority report
was accompanied by several minority statements.   The
entire matter was then subjected to lengthy discussion.
The resolution accompanying the report urged that the
1909 statement be reaffirmed and then proposed a series
of detailed statements which sought to restrain rabbis
officiating at such marriages and co-officiating with
Christian clergy.   It also dealt with the question of
welcoming those who had already entered a mixed marriage
as well as their children.   The discussion which followed dealt again with every aspect of mixed marriage as
well as the issue of rabbinic freedom.   The resolution
finally adopted read:

The Central Conference of American Rabbis, recalling its stand adopted in 1909 that "mixed marriage

is contrary to the Jewish tradition and should be discouraged," now declares its opposition to participation by its members in any ceremony which solemnizes a mixed marriage.

The Central Conference of American Rabbis recognizes that historically its members have held and continue to hold divergent interpretations of Jewish tradition. In order to keep open every channel to Judaism and **K'lal Yisrael** for those who have already entered into mixed marriage the CCAR calls upon its members:

1. to assist fully in educating children of such mixed marriage as Jews;

2. to provide the opportunity for conversion of the non-Jewish spouse; and

3. to encourage a creative and consistent cultivation of involvement in the Jewish community and the synagogue.

The Conservative Movement felt it necessary to deal with the intermarried Jew and his rights within the synagogue and community at length ("Intermarriage and Membership in a Congregation," **Rabbinical Assembly Annual**, 1958, pp. 110ff). The statement which opposed mixed marriage also sought to deal with the non-Jewish partner in a conciliatory manner. "It should be clearly understood that in frowning upon intermarriage and in voicing opposition to the choice of a non-Jewish mate, neither Judaism at large, nor Conservative Judaism in particular, expresses any judgment about the morality of character of these non-Jewish men and women." A list of fourteen reasons for not accepting the non-Jewish partner into a congregation was provided. Congregational membership could be retained by those already holding it, even after a mixed marriage, but would not be accepted initially. Such an individual would be permitted to worship with the congregation, but could not join it. In either case, it was recommended that synagogue honors be withheld, and the non-Jewish members of the family were not granted burial rights. The statement concluded with a milder injunction considering it "a mistake to permit the unconverted non-Jewish wife to be a member of the women's organization of the congregation." The Law Committee of the Rabbinical Assembly has dealt with the question further, but not in published responsa.

Orthodox Judaism has not changed its approach to this question. Civil marriages are not recognized by most Orthodox authorities. When a civil marriage has united a Jew and a non-Jew and, subsequently, the non-Jew converts to Judaism, some Orthodox authorities have refused to conduct a religious marriage (Mishna, Yev. II.8), while others have followed a more lenient point of view, as did Ben Zion Uziel (**Mishpetei Uzi-el**, Yoreh De-a, #14; also see B. Schereschewsky, **Dinei Hamish-pacha**, pp. 80ff).

There are a number of responsa by David Hoffman (**Melamed Leho-il**, vol. 3, #10, 14, etc.) which dealt with the status of intermarried individuals, especially in cases of a later desire to convert, or where there was some concern about the future of the offspring of such a union. Such converts were refused. Similar responsa are also found in Moses Feinstein's **Igerot Mosheh**, Even Ha-ezer, #73, 44, etc.) and elsewhere. All of them simply reported the incidence of intermarriage and decried it.

Israeli law has followed Orthodox law in matters involving family and personal status. It has, however, recognized civil marriages conducted in other lands in accordance with international law (**Skornik v. Skornik**, 1951, 8:155-156). For Purposes of the Law of Return, a non-Jewish spouse and his/her children possess similar rights of immigration as Jews (Law of Return, Amendment, 2, 4a, March, 1970).

Summary

Reform Judaism and the Central Conference of American Rabbis has opposed mixed marriages. We recognize the problem as significant in every period of Jewish history. It has become more severe in 20th-century America, and, therefore we have made provisions for families of mixed marriages and their children. They are welcome in our congregations, and we continue to urge them to convert to Judaism. The Conference resolution of 1973 succinctly summarizes our position:

The Central Conference of American Rabbis, recalling its stand adopted in 1909 that "mixed marriage is contrary to the Jewish tradition and should be discouraged," now declares its opposition to participation by its members in any ceremony which solemnizes a mixed marriage.

The Central Conference of American Rabbis recognizes that historically its members have held and continue to hold divergent interpretations of Jewish tradition. In order to keep open every channel to Judaism and K'lal Yisrael for those who have already entered into mixed marriage, the CCAR calls upon its members:

1. to assist fully in educating children of such mixed marriage as Jews;

2. to provide the opportunity for conversion of the non-Jewish spouse; and

3.   to encourage a creative and consistent cultivation of involvement in the Jewish community and
the synagogue.

Walter Jacob, Chairman
Eugene J. Lipman
W. Gunther Plaut
Harry A. Roth
Rav A. Soloff
Bernard Zlotowitz

See also:

Resolution, **CCAR Yearbook**, vol. 19, 1909, p. 170.
Resolution, **CCAR Yearbook**, vol. 57, 1973, p. 97.

147.   PRAYER FOR COUPLE CONTEMPLATING INTERMARRIAGE
(1979)

QUESTION: May a rabbi recite a prayer at the regular synagogue service for a couple contemplating
intermarriage?   One of the parties is Christian.

ANSWER: Intermarriage is not normative within Judaism.
Some deem such marriages as a sinful act regardless of
who conducts them (Deut. 7:2; San. 82a; **Sh.A.**, Even Ha-
ezer 16.1), or as not being **Kiddushin** (**Yad.**, Hil. Ishut
15; **Sh.A.**, Even Ha-ezer 154.23).   All Reform Jews discourage them to the best of their ability.   We could not
then, in good conscience, offer public prayer for such a
couple in advance of the wedding, as it is done for the
marriage of two Jews at a public synagogue service,
because such action would lend public approval to such a
marriage **lechatechila**.   We may, however, be willing to
recognize such a marriage **bedi-avad**: accept the Jewish
partner as a member of the congregation, do everything
possible to make the non-Jewish partner feel at ease and
at home in our midst, and raise their children as Jews.
It is our duty to continue warning against the contemplated intermarriage.   This is our task in this matter
as in all other areas in which "warning" plays a major
role.   Judaism disapproves of intermarriage, and we

should do everything possible to strengthen this position.

Walter Jacob, Chairman
Leonard S. Kravitz
Eugene J. Lipman
W. Gunther Plaut
Harry A. Roth
Rav A. Soloff
Bernard Zlotowitz

148.   RABBI OFFICIATING AT MIXED MARRIAGES
       (Vol. XXIX, 1919, pp. 75-76)

On October 30, 1918, I received the following letter:

> I have been asked by a Jewish gentleman of my con-
> gregation to unite him in wedlock with a Gentile.
> Is it compatible with Judaism for a rabbi to per-
> form such a marriage when the Gentile does not
> accept the Jewish religion? And is it in keeping
> with his position and dignity as rabbi to perform
> such a marriage when the Gentile does not accept
> the Jewish faith? Secondly, can a rabbi consist-
> ently perform such a marriage in the capacity of a
> layman without lending it the religious sanction as
> a rabbi?

To this I replied: "Unless the person whom a Jew or
Jewess is to marry adopts in some form the Jewish reli-
gion--after having learned its tenets in order to know
what the steps taken by him or her mean, no rabbi who
wants to be true to the tradition of Judaism can perform
the marriage ceremony, as may be learned from Dr. Mielziner's book, **The Jewish Law of Marriage and Divorce,**
pp. 45-54, and from my **Jewish Theology**, p. 446, in which
the resolutions passed by the Conference of 1909 are
referred to. As to the question whether a rabbi can in
the capacity of a layman consecrate mixed marriage, let
me simply say that neither Judaism nor the State law
acknowledges such a marriage as legal."
In a second letter, which stated that the gentleman
in question expressed his surprise at the narrowness of
Judaism and contemplated going to a Christian minister
to be married by him, the writer asked whether there was
"no possibility of performing the marriage when the
assurance is given that the non-Jew will accept the

Jewish faith after the marriage and whether a rabbi can perform the marriage of both non-Jews." To this I answered: "No matter whether said member thinks Judaism is too narrow for him or not, the question is whether religion or he who represents it stands for a certain principle or not. Certainly the Jewish home, which is the object of marriage, must be conducted according to the Jewish principles. A Christian minister cannot consecrate a Jewish home, nor can a Jewish minister consecrate a Christian home; and if man and wife belong to two different religions, it will be a house divided against itself. Without harmony of views in a matter so vital to the future there is no real unity. For those who think that the Jewish home needs no religious consecration the State law provides that they may apply to the civil magistrate to perform the marriage and have the sanction of the State for their union."

K. Kohler

149. RABBI OFFICIATING AT A MIXED MARRIAGE
(Vol. XCII, 1982, pp. 213-215)

QUESTION: Would there be any halachic justification for a rabbi officiating at an intermarriage? What reasons halachic and non-halachic, for refusal can be cited? (Mr. R. B. I., New York, New York)

ANSWER: It is clear from the committee's earlier responsum on "Reform Judaism and Mixed Marriage" that there can be no halachic basis for a mixed marriage. That responsum (CCAR **Yearbook**, 1980) presents a long and detailed history of mixed marriage and the halachic arguments. The last resolution of the Conference, passed in Atlanta in 1973 (CCAR **Yearbook**, vol. 83, p. 97), clearly states the position of the Conference:

The Central Conference of American Rabbis, recalling its stand adopted in 1909 "that mixed marriage is contrary to the Jewish tradition and should be discouraged," now declares its opposition to participation by its members in any ceremony which solemnizes a mixed marriage.
The Central Conference of American Rabbis recognizes that historically its members have held and continue to hold divergent interpretations of Jewish tradition. In order to keep open every channel

to Judaism and **K'lal Yisrael** for those who have already entered into mixed marriage the CCAR calls upon its members:
1.   to assist fully in educating children of such mixed marriage as Jews;
2.   to provide the opportunity for conversion of the non-Jewish spouse; and
3.   to encourage a creative and consistent cultivation of involvements in the Jewish community and synagogue.

The position of the Halacha and its development through the ages is outlined in the earlier responsum. However, as this question is interested in the contemporary arguments which might be useful in a discussion of this matter, let us suggest the following:
1.   The rabbi, as **Mesader Kiddushin**, acts in a legal capacity not only for the State but also for Judaism. Judaism has always held that only two Jews can be married to each other through a religious ceremony performed by a rabbi. This would not preclude a civil ceremony nor a ceremony performed by the couples themselves (as permitted in Pennsylvania). Such ceremonies can, and frequently do, contain prayers but they are obviously not **Kiddushin**, nor could they be even if performed by a rabbi, as **Kiddushin** between a Jew and a non-Jew would be a contradiction in terms.
2.   A Jewish ceremony performed for one individual who is Jewish and another who is non-Jewish violates the conscience of the rabbi and infringes upon the rights of the non-Jewish party and his/her religious affiliation. Furthermore, even if he/she would agree to such a ceremony he/she could not in good conscience say, "Be consecrated unto me as my wife/husband according to the laws of ᴹoses and Israel," as he/she has not accepted these laws.
3.   It is the task of a rabbi to strengthen Judaism and the Jewish community. Mixed marriage tends to weaken these ties. It raises doubts about the couple's will to remain a Jewish family or to assure that future offspring will be Jewish. Even if their children are circumcised, named in the synagogue, or some effort is made to raise them as Jews, this is still not as effective as raising children in a Jewish household in which both parties actively participate in Jewish ceremonies. Judaism is a religion of the home and the family, with emphasis upon the atmosphere of the home and upon the influence of extended family; therefore, it is important that there be a minimum of confusion between the couple and their in-laws about the Jewishness of the home. After a mixed marriage, the couple certainly may agree to raise their children as Jews. A Reform congre-

gation would encourage such an agreement, permit these children to attend the religious school, and encourage the Jewish partner to join the congregation. Most Reform Jews would consider the children Jewish as long as they affiliate in some fashion and do not accept another religion. Yet we also realize that their Judaism might well be diluted through the problems of a religiously mixed home.

4. The agreement to officiate at intermarriages would be a clear signal to others in the community, especially children, that this is a matter of indifference or less than paramount concern to the rabbi.

5. Religious considerations in marriage do not seem paramount to young couples, but they are necessarily of primary importance to the rabbi. The young couple should be prepared to make a decision on their religious future at this point, or, if they are not prepared to do so, should remain on neutral ground until such a decision can be properly made.

6. The statement by a rabbi that he will not marry a young couple in which one party is Jewish and the other non-Jewish is not a rejection of that couple. The request made of the rabbi to marry them is improper and betrays insensitivity to the rabbi's feelings and integrity. To the extent that identity is expressed through choice and commitment, it is the out-marrying Jewish individual who is doing the "rejecting." This should be explained as gently as possible to the family.

7. The anger of parents and grandparents sometimes displayed when the rabbi refuses to officiate at a mixed marriage is misdirected when turned toward the rabbi in the synagogue. The problems lie with the couple, not with Judaism, its institutions, or its leaders. This needs to be made clear to them.

8. Many couples nowadays want to be fair to both religions and both sets of parents; therefore, they ask that a rabbi and priest/minister participate in the ceremony, or that there be two separate religious ceremonies reflecting the two religious traditions. Such an effort must be rejected, for it demonstrates religious indifference or syncretism.

9. A mixed marriage conducted by a rabbi may have the semblance of a Jewish wedding but it cannot be **Kiddushin** by definition and will not be accepted as **Kiddushin** by most Jews, be they Orthodox, Conservative, or Reform.

10. In times of family tension and difficulty, everything which leads to further division within the family will make the marriage more unstable. Common religious bonds will enable the couple to face adversity better than divided religious allegiances.

11. In times of prejudice and anti-Semitism, families with a mixed marriage will be subject to greater pressures and will have fewer resources through which they can withstand such pressure.

12. Rabbis officiating at mixed marriages create a further and very basic division in the Jewish community, both in the United States and in Israel.

13. At the present time, the American Jewish community gains approximately 10,000 converts a year, mainly from non-Jews who contemplate marriage to Jewish partners. Some of these conversions would probably occur under any circumstances, but a large number would not. Through officiating at mixed marriages we will lose that large number of converts. At present, the number of converts to Judaism roughly balances those who are lost to us through mixed marriage and indifference.

14. Later conversions of the non-Jewish partner is possible and should be encouraged. But experience has taught us that early family patterns generally continue. Tensions which may later develop in the family make such a religious change even more difficult and unlikely.

15. It is clear that mixed marriages will continue and that the percentage will rise and fall depending upon circumstances beyond our control. That is a risk of living in an open society. Some non-Jewish partners will convert, others will not. Some children will be raised as Jews, others will not. But we have never depended upon numbers alone. It is far more important to have a strong commitment from a smaller group than a vague commitment from a large number who are at the very periphery.

For all the foregoing reasons we reaffirm the position taken by the Central Conference of American Rabbis, "that mixed marriage is contrary to Jewish tradition and should be discouraged; it now declares its opposition to participation by its members in any ceremony which solemnizes mixed marriage."

Walter Jacob, Chairman
Leonard S. Kravitz
Isaac Neuman
Harry A. Roth
Rav A. Soloff
Bernard Zlotowitz

150.   MARRIAGE WITH A "MESSIANIC JEW"
(Vol. XCI, 1981, pp. 67-69)

QUESTION: May a Reform rabbi officiate at a marriage between a Jewish girl and a boy who was born
a Jew but now considers himself a "Messianic Jew"?
Is this in consonance with Reform Judaism?   (Rabbi
Seymour Prystowsky, Lafayette Hill, Pennsylvania)

ANSWER: Reform Judaism has been firmly opposed to
mixed marriages.   This was true in the last century and
in this century.   At its New York meeting in 1909, the
Central Conference of American Rabbis passed the resolution, "The Central Conference of American Rabbis declares that mixed marriages are contrary to the tradition of the Jewish religion and should, therefore, be
discouraged by the American rabbinate" (CCAR Yearbook,
vol. 19, p. 170).   This resolution was reaffirmed as
part of a lengthy report in 1947 (CCAR Yearbook, vol.
57, p. 161).   A considerably stronger resolution was
passed in Atlanta in 1973.   Its text reads as follows:

> The Central Conference of American Rabbis, recal-
> ling its stand adopted in 1909 that "mixed marriage
> is contrary to the Jewish tradition and should be
> discouraged," now declares its opposition to par-
> ticipation by its members in any ceremony which
> solemnizes a mixed marriage.
> The Central Conference of American Rabbis recog-
> nizes that historically its members have held and
> continue to hold divergent interpretations of Jew-
> ish tradition.   In order to keep open every channel
> to Judaism and K'lal Yisrael for those who have
> already entered into mixed marriage the CCAR calls
> upon its members:
> 1.   to assist fully in educating children of such
> mixed marriage as Jews;
> 2.   to provide the opportunity for conversion of
> the non-Jewish spouse; and
> 3.   to encourage a creative and consistent culti-
> vation of involvements in the Jewish community and
> synagogue.   (CCAR Yearbook, vol. 83, p. 97)

These resolutions clearly state the position of the
Reform rabbinate in this matter.   They reflect only the
latest steps in the long struggle against mixed marriage
which began in Biblical times and will now be traced as
background for this resolution.   The Responsa Committee
has written a long responsum on this subject.   It is
printed in the 1980 Yearbook (pp. 86-102) and presents a
good deal of additional background material.

If we consider a "Messianic Jew" as an apostate
Jew, what would his status be for us? Judaism has always considered those who left us as sinners, but still
remaining as Jews. They could always return to Judaism
through **Teshuva** and the exact response of Judaism depended very much on the conditions of the time. Hai
Gaon (as quoted by Adret, **Responsa** VII, #292) felt that
an apostate could not be considered as a Jew. Centuries
later the rabbis of the Mediterranean Basin had to face
the problems of the **Marranos (Anusim)**. Their attitude
differed greatly and may be summarized under five headings: (1) Apostates are Jews who sinned but, nevertheless, are considered Jewish (Isaac bar Sheshet; Simon
ben Zemah of Duran, but on some occasions he did not
grant this status; Solomon ben Simon Duran; Zemah ben
Solomon). (2) The apostates are considered Jewish only
in matters of matrimony (and so their offspring are
Jewish), but not in any other area (Samuel de Medina).
(3) **Marranos (Anusim)** are considered non-Jews in every
respect, including matters of marriage; their children
are not considered to be Jews (Judah Berab, Jacob Berab,
"oses ben Elias Kapsali, etc.). (4) An apostate is
worse than a Gentile (ben Veniste, Mercado ben Abraham).
(5) Descendants of the **Marranos** who have been baptized
are like Jewish children who have been taken captive by
non-Jews and their children are Jewish (Samuel ben Abraham Aboab). All of these references and excerpts from
the relevant literature may be found in H.J. Zimmels **Die
Marranen in der Rabbinischen Literatur**, pp. 21ff. One
extreme position was held by Solomon ben Simon Duran
(Rashbash **Responsa**, #89) who felt that not only the
apostate, but also the children would continue to be
considered Jewish forever into the future as long as the
maternal line was Jewish. He also felt that nothing
needed to be done by any generation of such apostates
when they returned to Judaism. No ritual bath nor any
other act was considered necessary or desirable. In
fact he emphasized that no attention be given to their
previous state, for that might discourage their return.
Rabbenu Gershom gave a similar view and urged the quiet
acceptance of all who returned to Judaism (**Machzor Vitry**, pp. 96 and 97).

The other extreme has been presented by Rashi (in
his commentary to Kid. 68b and Lev. 24:10). He felt
that any returning apostate, or the children of a Jewish
mother who had apostacized, are potentially Jewish, but
most undergo a process akin to conversion if they wish
to become part of the Jewish community. That point of
view was rejected by most later scholars, as for example
Nahmanides (in his commentary to Leviticus 24:10; **Shulchan Aruch** ᵛoreh De-a 268.10f; Ezekiel Landau, **Responsa**, #150, etc.). We, therefore, have two extremes in

the Rabbinic literature; both, of course, represented reaction to particular historic conditions. Solomon ben Simon of Duran wished to make it easy for a large number of **Marranos** to return to Judaism; unfortunately, this did not occur. Even when it was possible for Jews to leave Spain, the majority chose to remain. Rashi's harsh attitude probably reflected the small number of apostates who were a thorn in the side of the French community. Normative Rabbinic Judaism chose a middle path and encouraged the apostate's return along with some studies, but without a formal conversion process. If an apostate did not wish to return to Judaism he would, nevertheless, be considered as part of the Jewish people (San. 44a). His or her marriage, if performed according to Jewish law as **Marranos**, and therefore as unwilling apostates, were valid (Yev. 30b; **Shulchan Aruch**, Even Ha-ezer 44.9); divorce procedures for them are somewhat modified. Such an individual was not considered as reliable witness except in the case of an **Aguna**. Penalties may be imposed on his inheritance (Kid. 18a), although he does have the right to inherit (B.B. 108a ¹11a). Normal mourning rites should not be observed for such a person (M. San. 6.6; **Shulchan Aruch**, Yoreh De-a 345.5). It is clear, therefore, that an apostate stands outside the community in all but relatively few matters until he has repented. We cannot officiate at his marriage with a Jewish girl.

Could we, on the other hand, consider a "Messianic Jew" as still a Jew? He may define himself in this manner, but do we? A "Messianic Jew" is one who has designated himself as Jewish, but believes that Jesus of Nazareth is the Messiah and has come to fulfill the messianic promises. By making these assertions that individual has clearly defined himself as a Christian. He may be somewhat different from other Christians in the Jewish practices which he continues, but in belief of theology and basic life pattern he is a Christian. We should remember that there are a wide variety of Christian sects which also observe various Jewish laws and customs--so the Seventh Day Adventists who observe the Shabbat as their day of rest, some Black Christian churches which celebrate Jewish festivals, etc. It is clear, therefore, that unless the young man renounces his belief in Jesus of Nazareth and becomes a Jew rather than a "Messianic Jew," we must consider him as a Christian and cannot officiate at his marriage with a Jewish girl.

We should be much stricter in our relationship with "Messianic Jews" than with other Christians with whom we continually attempt to establish good interfaith relations. The normative Christian churches are known for their beliefs and practices and are easily distinguish-

able by our people. Although they may continue to seek
some converts from Judaism, most Churches have not pursued active missionary activities in modern times. Directly the opposite is true of "Messianic Jews." They
have established a vigorous missionary presence and
often seek to confuse Jews about the nature of their
religion. They have frequently presented themselves as
Jews rather than Christians through misleading pamphlets, advertisements, and religious services. We should
do everything in our power to correct these misconcep-
tions and to maintain a strict separation from anyone
connected with this group. We should, of course, not
officiate at such a marriage.

Walter Jacob, Chairman
Leonard S. Kravitz
W. Gunther Plaut
Harry A. Roth
Rav A. Soloff
Bernard Zlotowitz

151. NON-JEWISH CLERGY PARTICIPATING IN A
JEWISH WEDDING WITH A RABBI
(Vol. LXXXVII, 1977, pp. 100-102)

QUESTION: May non-Jewish clergymen participate in
a Jewish wedding ceremony together with a rabbi?

ANSWER: We are here concerned not with a class of
mixed marriage, but with the participation of non-Jewish
clergy in the ceremony of **two Jews**. This question involves the general status of Christians in Jewish law,
as well as their capacity in any Jewish service.
    It is clear that the Talmud, already having begun
to consider pagans of its day differently from the more
ancient heathen, did so also with Christians. The precise attitude toward Gentiles during the five centuries
of Talmudic times depended upon specific circumstances.
Thus, Simeon ben Yohai could be uncomfortably negative:
"The best of the Gentiles should be killed in time of
war" (Yer., Kid. 66c, with full reading in **Tosafot** to
A.Z. 26b; Soferim 15.10). On the other hand, it was
possible for Meir and Judah Hanasi to have warm, friendly relationships with Gentiles (B.K. 38a)   or for R.
Chiya bar Abba to say in the name of R. Johanan that
Gentiles outside of the Land of Israel are not idolat-

ers, that they merely continue to follow the customs of their fathers (Chulin 13b).

By the Middle Ages, Christians were no longer classified as idolaters (Meir of Rothenburg, Resp. #386). Rabbi Isaac of Dampierre placed Christians in the category of Noahides and not of pagans (Tosafot to San. 63b and Bech. 2b). Menachem Meiri (1249-1306) went further by stating that Christians and Moslems who lived by the discipline of their religions should be regarded as Jews in matters of social and economic relationships (Beit Habechira to Avoda Zara 20a). Maimonides stated that a Christian or a Muslim should be considered as a Ger Toshav (Yad, Hil. Melachim 8.11 and Hil. Teshuva 3.5; Hil. Edut 11.10, etc.). This point of view became normative, and Christians, as well as Muslims, were considered to be in the same category as the Gerei Toshav. This was the point of view accepted by Caro in the Shulchan Aruch (Yoreh De-a 148.12; also Tur, Yoreh De-a 148). It was expressed most forcefully by Moshe Rifkes, author of the Be-er Hagola to the Shulchan Aruch (Choshen Mishpat 425, at the end of the column). The statement is remarkable because the author himself was an exile (from Wilna to Amsterdam) who had fled from anti-Jewish riots. He says: "The sages made reference only to the idolaters of their day, who did not believe in the exodus or the creation of the world, but these people among whom we are scattered believe in the creation of the world and hold with the essentials of religion, and their whole intention is to the Creator of heaven and earth. So it is not only not prohibited to deliver them, but it is our duty to pray for their welfare," etc. The status of the Gentile in the general application of Jewish law had, therefore, changed, and thus positive opinion of Gentiles was re-emphasized at the beginning of the modern era by Emden, Bacharach, Ashkenazi, and other Orthodox authorities (see A. Shohet, "The German Jew: His Integration Within the Non-Jewish Environment in the First Half of the Eighteenth Century," Zion, vol. 21, 1956, pp. 229ff), as well as Mendelssohn ("Schreiben an Lavater," Schriften, 1843, vol. 3, pp. 39ff).

Since the Christian has been equated in the legal tradition with the Ger Toshav, we must inquire about the latter's status. In economic and social matters a Ger Toshav is considered equal to a Jew, but he has no status in connection with the ritual obligation of the Jew. A Ger Toshav would not be considered part of a Minyan, or part of the quota for Mezuman, or suitable for leading Jewish worship service (Orach Chayim 199.4).

Similar considerations would prevail in the case of a wedding. The officiating individual (Mesader Kiddushin) must be Jewish. Nothing would prevent a non-

Jewish clergyman or friend from participating in the less essential parts of the service as a social, non-religious gesture. He might add a prayer (without trinitarian references), give a homily, or be included in the wedding party. This would be considered appropriate and within the bounds of Jewish tradition. Rabbis, whose regular officiation at weddings is attested at least since the 14th century (Abrahams, **Jewish Life in the Middle Ages**, p. 216), should read the major portion of the service. The wedding liturgy could also be so arranged that the non-Jewish clergyman's participation would not interrupt the Jewish service, and, therefore, no one would have the impression that the Gentile participated in the actual ritual.

Jews who have been married by a Christian minister (with a civil license) alone would, of course, be considered civilly married, but the marriage could not be considered **Kiddushin**.

In passing, we may note that the question of the status of a marriage of two Jews or **Marranos** by Christian clergy arose following the legislation in Spain, when Jews married in this manner fled to neighboring lands where they could once again live openly as Jews. These marriages, performed by Catholic priests, were not considered valid Jewish marriages (Isaac bar Sheshet, Responsa #6 and 7). This decision may have been partly prompted by the fact that often only one partner survived the attempt to escape; if the marriage was invalid, then no proof of death was necessary, and no inheritance problems, etc arose. The only exceptions to this rule were those marriages conducted under the Inquisition which had been preceded by a Jewish ritual held privately at home before ten witnesses; in that case the marriage was considered Jewish, since the Catholic ritual was conducted only for the sake of the authorities (Duran, vol. 3, #47; for more on this see, A. Freimann, **Seder Kiddushin Venisu-in**). These decisions cast no aspersion upon marriages performed by Christians between two Christians, which were, of course, considered appropriate and valid (Isaac bar Sheshet, #6; Maimonides, **Yad**, Isurei Bi-a 14.19).

We may, therefore, summarize: At a Jewish wedding it would be improper for a Christian minister to co-officiate with a rabbi on equal terms. The essential portion of the wedding ceremony must be performed by the rabbi; the minister may, however, participate through a greeting, a homily, etc., in such a fashion as to preclude any inference that he or she is performing or validating a Jewish rite. A minister may be a member of a wedding party.

Walter Jacob, Chairman
Solomon B. Freehof, Honorary Chairman
Stephen M. Passamaneck
W. Gunther Plaut
Harry A. Roth
Herman E. Schaalman

152. AN INQUIRY ABOUT VIRGINITY
(1979)

QUESTION: What importance has tradition attached to virginity for males or females? What act specifically terminates virginity in females? Must the hymen be broken? (CCAR Family Life Committee)

ANSWER: Chastity before marriage has been considered an obvious requirement for all and was taken for granted by the tradition without specific reference, as Rabbi Eliezer already pointed out long ago (Tosefta, Kid. 1.4). There are many statements which support this point of view and demand that an unmarried person refrain from sexual intercourse. The references deal particularly with males (Pes. 113a-b; Shab. 152a). A statement of Rabbi Yochanan makes this very clear: "There is a small organ in man; he who satisfies it goes hungry and he who allows it to go hungry is satisfied" (San. 107a). Although one must also be mindful of the statement by Rabbi Illai: "If a person realizes he is overcome by lust, then he should go to a place where he is not known, dress in dark clothes, wrap his head in a black turban, and do what his heart demands, but he should not openly profane God's name" (Mo-ed Katan 17a; Tos. to Kid. 40a). For males, chastity was demanded; no stiff legal penalties were incurred, though flogging was possible (Ket. 10a).

All females were expected to be virgins at the time of their first marriage. The dowry of the non-virgin was less than that of a virgin, and anyone falsely claiming virginity was subject to severe punishment (Deut. 22:14ff). The test for virginity, which consisted of bleeding during the initial intercourse, led to considerable discussion in the Talmud. The Rabbis were aware that some women may not bleed, and wished to avoid false accusations against them, so various methods were devised to establish virginity, and the evidence was carefully assembled and examined (Ket. 10b, 46a). All this demonstrated that virginity was prized, and every effort was made to retain it until marriage.

Concern over virginity led to discussion of special problems among the handicapped. Deaf mutes, blind and retarded girls could not be accused of lacking signs of virginity (Tosefta, Ket. 1.3). Others felt that such a policy stigmatized such individuals and their families, and therefore disagreed (Tosefta, Ket. 1.5, Yerushalmi, Ket. 1.25c).

There were a number of different opinions about what constituted the loss of virginity. For example, a High Priest was not allowed to marry a girl with whom a partial intercourse had occurred, i.e., without actual penetration (Kid. 10a). Though, if this occurred during an attempted rape by an enemy soldier, she was permitted to marry the priest (Yerushalmi, Ned. 9.42d). Normally, bleeding (as mentioned above) or breaking of the hymen was considered proof of loss of virginity, though it was considered possible to have intercourse without breaking the hymen if the man involved were skillful (Ket. 6b; Nida 64b). Bleeding during the first intercourse may, in any case, come either from the breaking of the hymen or from rupturing blood vessels. Some individuals were recognized as not bleeding during first intercourse (Ket. 10b; Nida 64b). Destruction of the hymen could, of course, also occur through various kinds of injuries (Ket. 13a), climbing high steps, taking usually large steps while walking (Shab. 63b), etc. Even if this were to occur at a very young age, there was some question about the hymen healing over completely (Nida 45a).

It was presumed that all girls were virgins before their first marriage, unless there was definite knowledge to the contrary. This assumption was continued by the codes, including the **Shulchan Aruch**.

Walter Jacob, Chairman
Leonard S. Kravitz
Eugene J. Lipman
W. Gunther Plaut
Harry A. Roth
Rav A. Soloff
Bernard Zlotowitz

153. MASTURBATION
(1979)

QUESTION: What does the tradition say about masturbation? Are any distinctions made between males and females, young or old, married or unmarried? (CCAR Family Life Committee)

ANSWER: The tradition has considered masturbation as a sin and strictly prohibited it. Any seed which was brought forth in vain involved a sin punishable by God (Gen. 38:8ff; **Shulchan Aruch**, Even Ha-ezer 23.1-3; Nida 13a,b), although it was not listed among the six hundred thirteen commandments derived from Biblical texts (which raised exegetical problems). This prohibition was carried even further, and anyone who excessively touched his genitals was considered a transgressor (Nida 2.1; Shab. 108b). It might be all right for a married man to do so (Nida 13a), but certainly not for a single individual; and an especially "holy" man would try never to place his hands below his belt (Shab. 118b). These thoughts never went as far as the preoccupation with masturbation found in the prohibitions of Catholic religious thinkers. The question has been treated at length by them in every century (J. Noonan, **Contraception: A History of Its Treatment by the Catholic Theologians and Canonists**, 1965).

These prohibitions were extended even further so that no masturbation through other means occurred. For example, tight-fitting pants were prohibited (Nida 13b). Riding a camel bareback excluded such individuals from the heave offering; nor were individuals supposed to sleep lying flat on their backs, which also might have the same results (Nida 14a). Young people were not to sit and study alone (Ber. 63b). There is no mention in the Talmudic literature about the women masturbating. The only reference to it is a folk saying: "He masturbates with a pumpkin and his wife with a cucumber" (Meg. 12a). Of course, these practices are vigorously rejected. Although women often had to examine themselves to see whether they were in a state of uncleanliness, none of this was thought to lead to masturbation (Nida 13a).

There is some discussion of masturbation in Jewish medieval ethical writings, and also in the responsa, but it is limited (Trani, **Minchat Yechi-el**, vol. II, #4, 22; Jacob Ettlinger, **Binyan Tsiyon**, #137; **Penei Yehoshua**, Even Ha-ezer, vol. II, #44). The matter was taken up again in connection with the question of artificial insemination. The sperm must be obtained through masturbation or through withdrawal before completing intercourse. Orthodox authorities are divided on whether this is permitted under these special circumstances. Those who are permissive have felt that in this case the sperm is not being wasted, while the opponents reject this interpretation. A complete discussion can be found in **Noam**, vol. I, pp. 111ff, as well as in Eliezer Waldenberg's **Tsits Eli-ezer**, section 3, no. 27, and Moshe Feinstein, **Igerot Mosheh**, Even Ha-ezer.

Although the statements of tradition are very clear, we would take a different view of masturbation, in the light of current psychological thought. Masturbation should be discouraged, but we would not consider it harmful or sinful.

Walter Jacob

154.   JEWISH ATTITUDE TOWARD SEXUAL RELATIONS BETWEEN CONSENTING ADULTS (1979)

QUESTION: What is the Jewish attitude toward heterosexual relations between two consenting adult single individuals? (CCAR Committee on Family Life)

ANSWER: The tenor of halachic literature, from the Talmud to the present, is against casual sexual relationships. Some extreme statements were made. For example, Reish Lakish has stated that even one who sins with his eyes may be an adulterer (**Lev. Rabba** 23); but this did not become normative. This kind of attitude, however, led to, or was a function of, the segregation of men and women. A man was not to walk behind a woman; men and women were separated on festive occasions and in public parks (**Yad**, Hil. Yom Tov 6.21); and separate days for men and women were even set aside for visiting cemeteries. The attitude which governed such restrictions may be shown through a Talmudic passage concerning an individual who became physically ill over his desire for a certain woman. His physicians stated that he should have intercourse with her, and the rabbi said: No, let him rather die. Finally, they suggested that the woman speak to the man, and the rabbi said: No, let him rather die. This was their feeling, although the woman in the tale was not married (San. 75a).

There was, of course, some conflict over these kinds of restrictions, and so we have a statement that Rabban Gamliel offered an exclamation of thanksgiving upon seeing a beautiful non-Jewish woman (A.Z. 20a,b; Yer., A.Z. 40a). Yet, on the same page we also have statements such as the following: One should refrain from looking at the little finger of a woman to whom one was not married. This statement is of interest even though it presumably was addressed to married men.

All of this led to a good many later restrictions; for example, not touching any woman other than one's wife, not even another adult relative; not reclining to rest, even when fully dressed, or permitting personal services of any kind (e.g., washing, delousing, etc.) to be performed by a woman for a man (Adret, **Responsa** I, 1188; **Shulchan Aruch**, Even Ha-ezer 21); not conversing much with women (Ned. 20a). This, of course, led to great difficulties with the customary handshake of the western world (**Sedeh Chemed**, Chatan Vechala 26a). Certainly, no affection was to be shown to any strange woman, and no kissing was allowed (**Sh.A.**, Even Ha-ezer 21.6). We can be quite sure from this that in especially puritanical periods any relationships between the sexes was severely restricted, and every effort was made to keep men and women apart, even within the family circle.

This isolation led to tension and suspicion of illicit sexual relationships whenever men and women were alone together. A young man was supposed to be chaperoned after age nine, and a girl upon reaching the age of three (Yer., Kid. 66b). Even a divorced couple was not permitted to meet again privately or live in the same neighborhood; it was assumed that they would have sexual relations (Git. 81a; Ket. 27b, 28a; **Yad**, Hil. Isurei Bi-a 21.27; **Aruch Hashulchan**, Even Ha-ezer 119.25-28). The same assumption was made for spice peddlers who visited homes (B.K. 82a). This was permitted by a decree of Ezra, against the wishes of the townspeople, so that women could obtain perfume (B.B. 22a). It was generally assumed that all people constantly sought for sexual relations and had sinful thoughts (B.B. 164b; A.Z. 20b). In other words, the sexual drive is not only considered constant, but in many ways dominant. This was also illustrated by the statement that males who had not gotten married by the age of twenty would be plagued by immoral thoughts for the rest of their lives (Kid. 29b; **Yad**, Hil. Ishut 15.2). Unmarried women faced restrictions too numerous to be listed here.

None of these restrictive statements was entirely effective, since it is clear from the literature that sexual relations took place often outside and also before marriage, although virginity for the female was greatly prized. Generally, intercourse with an unmarried girl fell under the concept of **Zenut**, which was prohibited. If an act of intercourse was intended as a mode of lawful betrothal, the betrothal was indeed lawful (Mishna, Kid. 1.1). Children born of liaisons conducted without contemplation of marriage were completely free of any blemish, and there was no question about their legality (Kid. 4.1,2; Yev. 100b). Aside from such alliances reported in the Talmud, we also hear of them often in the Golden Age of Spain and in Renaissance Italy. Nahmanides was lenient about such illicit unions, and was willing to overlook them (Isaac b. Sheshet, quoting Nahmanides, 6, 398; also 425 and 395). They are mentioned as well in other ages, but less frequently.

We must remember that the sexual drive, when leading to marriage and procreation, has always been considered in a positive light. Its association with the **Yetser Hara** (wicked inclination) was given two interpretations: sexual relations might be sinful, but they constituted a necessary sin; sexual relations were not evil **per se**, but capable of leading to evil. Certainly, within marriage--and to some extent outside of it--sex was considered good and perfectly acceptable (A.Z. 5a; **Yad**, Hil. Isurei Bi-a 22.18f; **Tur**, Even Ha-ezer 25, etc.). There is an enormous Midrashic literature (see L. Ginzberg, **Legends of the Jews**) on the **Yetser Hara** and its sexual overtones.

Let us also deal with the question of sexual relationships between those who were engaged and might live together for some time. This has been prohibited by tradition (**Sh.A.**, Even Ha-ezer 55.1, etc.). In early times, such intercourse was reported as unobjectionable in Judea (Ket. 7b), but not in the Galilee (Ket. 12a). Some felt that the children of such a union should be declared **Mamzerim** (Yev. 69b; Kid. 75a), a view which was not adopted. In the final analysis, the stricter view prevailed. Such relations remained fairly common (Yer., Kid. 64a; **Otsar Hage-onim** 18ff, etc.; Elijah Mizrahi, **Responsa**, 4; David ben Zimri, **Responsa III**, 525). Louis Epstein felt that such looser standards, which prevailed in the Byzantine Empire, spread slowly through Rumania to Western Europe (L. Epstein, **Sex Laws and Customs in Judaism**, p. 128). This led to the combination of betrothal and marriage into a single ceremony in the medieval period and perhaps earlier. Prior to this time, the betrothed couple was faced with all the restrictions of marriage, and even needed a divorce in case of separation, but did not have the benefits of marriage. It is clear from all this that sexual intercourse between engaged couples was discouraged, but the prohibition was difficult to enforce. If the engagement had taken place through intercourse (**bi-a**), then further intercourse was not permitted until an official ceremony and **Chupa** had taken place (**Sh.A.**, Even Ha-ezer 55.1, **Yad**, Hil. Ishut 6).

Given the indubitable fact that extramarital relations have become common in our day, can Judaism give
them its approval? The answer is decidedly negative.
We consider premarital and extramarital chastity to be
our ideal.

On the question of informal heterosexual relations
outside marriage between two consenting single adult
individuals, we can then come to the following conclusions. Such relationships were prohibited and discouraged by authorities throughout the ages. Little was
done when such relationships took place between two
engaged persons, except in puritanical periods. Other
sexual relationships between single adults were prohibited, and every effort was made to enforce such prohibitions. These prohibitions were equally strong upon the
man and the woman. In times of lower moral standards,
authorities were occasionally permissive or simply looked the other way. Generally, the effort to enforce high
moral standards succeeded, and the responsa call attention to the failures. In our own period of loose standards, it would be appropriate to do everything within
our power to encourage higher standards for both men and
women. We should do whatever we can to discourage casual sexual relations.

Walter Jacob, Chairman
Leonard S. Kravitz
Eugene J. Lipman
W. Gunther Plaut
Harry A. Roth
Rav A. Soloff
Bernard Zlotowitz

155. SEXUALITY OF A MATURING CHILD
(1979)

QUESTION: How does Jewish tradition treat the
sexuality of a child maturing toward adulthood?
When is a child considered an adult in sexual matters? (CCAR Family Life Committee)

ANSWER: According to the Halacha, a boy is a minor
until he has reached the age of thirteen years and one
day. If two hairs have then appeared in the pubic re-
gion, he is considered adult (Ish). If this has not
occurred, then the change of status is delayed until the
physical evidence has become visible. In any case, both

the age of thirteen, plus the physical signs, are necessary (Nida 6.11, 46a; Maimonides, **Yad**, Hil. Ishut 2.10).
Matters are somewhat different in the case of a girl,
though there also the appearance of pubic hair was one
requirement. If this has occurred, then she ceases
being a child at the age of twelve and one day (Nida
6.11, 46a; Maimonides, **Yad**, Hil. Ishut 2.1). Here,
however, a dual change of status is involved. For the
next six months she is considered a **Na-ara**, and at the
end of that period, she goes through another change of
status and becomes a woman (**Bogeret**) (Ket. 39a; Kid.
79a; Nida 65a; Maimonides, **Yad**, Hil. Ishut 2.2). In
other words, in the case of a girl, there are two steps
involved in becoming a woman. In addition, we should
note that there is some disagreement in the Rabbinic
tradition about the varied outward signs of maturity in
a female, but all agree on the necessity for pubic hair
(Tosefta, Nida 6.4; Mishna, Nida 5.7ff; Maimonides, **Yad**,
Hil. Ishut 2.8).

Bernard Bamberger dealt with these distinctions at
some length and has come to the tentative conclusion
that the Rabbinic provision of stages for maturity in
the case of girls was an effort on the part of the Rabbis to restrict harsh punishment of all problems connected with virginity and seduction (Deut. 22:13, to end
of chapter), which were, in any case, difficult to enforce. This would have been in keeping with other efforts on the part of the Rabbis to limit the effect of
Biblical laws (Bernard Bamberger, "Quetanah, Na'rah,
Bogereth," **Hebrew Union College Annual**, vol. XXXII,
1961, pp. 281-294).

We can be quite certain, therefore that concern
with active sexuality began at age twelve and one day
for girls and thirteen and one day for boys. However
there was some concern also expressed earlier

If the physical signs of maturity were absent from
a man or a woman, they were not considered adults until
they had reached the age of twenty, according to Beit
Shammai (Nid. 5.9, 47b; Yev. 96b; **Shulchan Aruch**, Even
Ha-ezer 155.12). If a eunuch shows the normal physical
signs of maturity, then he becomes an adult at thirteen.
Nowadays, any male is presumed to have reached his majority at thirteen, a process which began in Gaonic
times (**She-iltot,** Bechukotai 116; Akiva Eiger, **Shulchan
Aruch**, Orach Chayim 615.2).

In addition to sexuality at the time of maturity,
the Talmud also concerned itself with the beginnings of
sexuality at a much earlier age, for it felt that a girl
attained an initial degree of sexuality at age three,
and a boy at nine. For these reasons various laws which
dealt with sexual relationships were in force for minors. Such a young girl could, for example, be acquired

as a wife through sexual relations; if she was sexually violated at this early age by an adult, the normal punishments were in effect. The sexual acts of males nine years old and above were also considered as those of an adult (Nida 5.5ff). A girl could also be betrothed at this early age, and there was a special simplified form of separation (**Me-un**--refusal) which would be exercised to annul such an early betrothal or be used by her to refuse such a marriage. Before the age of ten **Me-un** might be used for annulment, but was not strictly necessary (Yev. 107ab; **Yad**, Gerushin XI.3; **Shulchan Aruch**, Even Ha-ezer 155.3). The father possessed the right to give his minor daughter in marriage with or without her consent (Ket. 46b; Kid. 41a). There was some debate whether a girl in this stage of **Na-ara** could contract her own marriage, as she was completely subject to her father (Kid. 43b and 44a); but it is quite certain that once she had reached the stage of **Bogeret**, she was independent and could contract her own obligations (Nida 5.7). In the Middle Ages, strong protests against child marriages were raised (Judah Mintz, **Responsa**, #13; Isserles to **Shulchan Aruch**, Even Ha-ezer, who quotes Jacob Pollock, etc.).

This decision and the considerable detail provided by the Talmud on early sexuality before betrothal, weddings, seduction, and rape, show that these laws are far from theoretical, but representative of an actual concern on the part of the Rabbinic tradition. They are discussed to a greater or lesser extent during succeeding centuries in the responsa literature, reflecting standards of the time.

Walter Jacob, Chairman
Leonard S. Kravitz
Eugene J. Lipman
W. Gunther Plaut
Harry A. Roth
Rav A. Soloff
Bernard Zlotowitz

156. BIRTH CONTROL
(Vol. XXXVII, 1927, pp. 369-384)

In considering the question of the Talmudic-Rabbinic attitude towards birth-control we must seek to clear up the confusion that prevails in the discussion of the subject and define the principles involved in the whole question.

Some rabbis are inclined to regard all forms of birth-control, excepting self-control or continence, as "**Hotsa-at shichvat zera levatala**," and therefore put them in a class with masturbation or self-abuse. Hence, they believe that by citing Agadic sayings from the Talmud and the Midrashim against the evil practice of self-abuse, they have also proved the opposition of Rabbinic law to the various forms of birth control. Such a method, however, is unscientific and not justified in the discussion of such a serious and important question.

In the first place, the method of adjudging questions of religious practice on the basis of Agadic utterances is altogether unwarranted. The Talmudic rule is "**Ein morin min hahagadot**," i.e., that "We cannot decide the questions of practice by citing Agadic sayings" (Yer., Chagiga I.8, 76d). The Agada may set up an exalted ideal of the highest ethical living. It may teach the lofty precept "**Kadesh atsmecha bamutar lecha**," to aspire to a holy life and to avoid even such actions or practices which—though permitted by the law—do not measure up to its high standard. But it does not rest with the Agada to decide what is forbidden or permitted by the law. "The Agadist cannot declare anything forbidden or permitted, unclean or clean," says the Talmud ("**Ba-al agada she-eino lo oser velo matir, velo metame velo metaher**," Yer., Horayot III.7 48c). The answer to questions of practice—that is, as to what is permitted by Jewish law and what is not—can be given only on the basis of the teachings of the Halacha.

Secondly, it is absolutely wrong to consider cohabitation with one's wife under conditions which might result in procreation as an act of "**Hotsa-at shichvat zera levatala**," and to class it with sexual perversions such as self-abuse.

In the following, therefore, we must consider only what the Halacha teaches about the various forms of birth control and ignore what the Agada has to say in condemnation of the evil practices of self-abuse and sexual perversions.

In order to avoid confusion and for the sake of a clearer understanding and a systematic presentation of the Rabbinic teachings bearing upon our subject, it is necessary to formulate the question properly. It seems to me that the correct formulation of our question is as follows: Does the Talmudic-Rabbinic law permit cohabitation between husband and wife in such a manner or under such conditions as would make conception impossible; and if so, what are the conditions under which such cohabitation is permitted?

As to the first and main part of the question, there is no doubt that it must be answered in the affirmative. To begin with, the Rabbinic law not only permits but even commands the husband to fulfill his conjugal duties to his wife, even after she has experienced the change of life and has become incapable of having children. Likewise, the husband is permitted to have sexual intercourse with his wife even if she is congenitally incapable of conception, as, for instance, when she is **Akara**, sterile, or an **Ailonit**, that is, a wombless woman (**Tosafot** and Mordecai, quoted by Isserles in **Shulchan Aruch**, Even Ha-ezer XXIII.2). The later Rabbinic law goes even further and permits even a man who has never had children (and thus has not fulfilled the duty of propagation of the race, "**Mitzvat Periya Ureviya**") to marry a woman incapable of bearing children, that is, a sterile woman (**Akara**) or an old woman (**Zekena**) (Isaac b. Sheshet, quoted by Isserles, **op. cit.**, I.3). From all this it is evident that the act of cohabitation, even when it cannot possibly result in conception, is in itself not only not immoral or forbidden, but in some cases even mandatory. Hence, we may conclude that the discharge of sperm through sexual intercourse, even though it does not effect impregnation of the woman, is not considered an act of "wasteful discharge of semen" (**Hotsa-at shichvat zera levatala**), which is so strongly condemned by the Agadic sayings of the Talmud. For while--as regards procreation--such a discharge is without results and purposeless, yet since it results from legitimate gratification of a normal natural desire, it has fulfilled a legitimate function and is not to be considered as in vain.

Now it may be argued that only in such cases where the parties--through no fault of their own--are incapable of procreation does the law consider the mere gratification of their natural desire a legitimate act and hence does not condemn it as "**Hotsa-at shichvat zera levatala.**" We have, therefore, to inquire further whether the gratification of their legitimate desire by sexual intercourse in a manner not resulting in procreation would be permissible even to a young and normally healthy husband and wife who are capable of having children.

To my knowledge, the Halacha--aside from recommending decency and consideration for the feelings of the wife in these matters--does not put any restrictions upon the husband's gratification of his sexual desire for his wife, and certainly does not forbid him any manner of sexual intercourse with her. This is evident from the following passage in the Talmud (Nedarim 20b) where R. Johanan b. Nappaha, commenting upon a saying of R. Johanan b. Dahabai in disapproval of certain practices indulged in by some husbands, says: "These are but the words [i.e., the individual opinion] of Johanan b.

Dahabai; the sages, however, have said that the decision
of the law, i.e., the Halacha, is not according to Johanan b. Dahabai, but a husband may indulge with his
wife in whatever manner of sexual gratification he desires" ("**Amar Rabbi Yochanan, 'Zo divrei Rabbi Yochanan
ben Dahavai. Aval ameru chachamim: Ein halacha ke-
Yochanan ben Dahavai, ela kol ma she-adam rotseh la-asot
be-ishto, oseh'**").

   This Halacha of R. Johanan b. Nappaha, supported by
the decisions of Judah Hanasi and Abba Areka and reported in the Talmud (**ibid., l.c.**), has been accepted as law
by all medieval authorities, and they accordingly permit
intercourse with one's wife in any manner ("**Kedarkah
veshelo kedarkah**") (Maimonides, **Yad**, Isurei Bi-a XXI.9;
Tur, Even Ha-ezer 25; and Isserles on **Shulchan Aruch**,
Even Ha-ezer 25.2). Maimonides (**l.c.**) would limit the
permission of sexual indulgence ("**Shelo kedarkah**") only
to such forms of "**Shelo kedarkah**" which do not result in
Hotsa-at shichvat zera levatala, for he says: "**Uvilvad
shelo yotsi shichvat zera levatala.**" But other medieval
authorities permit intercourse "**Shelo kedarkah**" even
when resulting in **Hotsa-at shichvat zera levatala**. The
only restriction they would put on this permission is
that a man should not habituate himself always to do it
only in such a manner: "**Dela chashuv kema-aseh Er ve-
Onan, ela keshemitkaven lehashchit zera veragil la-asot
ken tamid. Aval be-akrai be-alma umit-aveh lavo al
ishto shelo kedarkah--shari**" (Tosafot, Yevamot 34b, s.v.
"**Velo kema-aseh Er ve-Onan**"; **Tur** and Isserles, l.c.).

   From the fact that they permit "**Shelo kedarkah**"
even when it necessarily results in "**Hotsa-at shichvat
zera levatala**" we need not, however, necessarily conclude that these authorities would also permit such
practices of "**Shelo kedarkah**" as are performed "**Mimakom
acher**" or "**Shelo bamakom zara**" (see Rashi to Yevamot
34b, **s.v.** "**Shelo kedarkah**"; and Rashi to Genesis 24:16,
compared with **Genesis R.**, XL.5), which are really sexual
perversions and not sexual intercourse. See R. Isaiah
Horowitz in his **Shenei Luchot Haberit**, Sha-ar Ha-otiyot
(Josefow, 1878, pp. 132-133). It seems rather that the
Rabbis were of the opinion that when intercourse is had
by what they euphemistically term "**Hafichat Hashulchan**,"
whether "**Hi lema-ala vehu lemata**" or "**Panim keneged
oref**," the very position of the woman is such as to
prevent conception. Compare their saying "**Isha mezana
mithapechet, kedei shelo tit-aber**" (Yevamot 35a; also
Tur, Even Ha-ezer 76 end). Hence, according to their
theory (though not sustained by modern medicine), there
are forms of sexual intercourse--"**Shelo kedarkah**"--which
cannot result in conception. These alone--not sexual
perversions--do they permit. The statement of Rava
(Sanhedrin 58b), taking for granted that an Israelite is

permitted ("DeYisra-el shari"; see Tosafot and Maharsha,
ad loc.) to have intercourse with his wife "Shelo
kedarkah" is also to be understood in this sense; though
from the phrase "Vedavak--velo shelo kedarkah" used in
the amended saying of Rava it would appear that the term
"Shelo kedarkah" means "Bi-a mimakom acher." From a
baraita in Yevamot 34b, we learn that during the period
of lactation the husband is allowed, if not commanded,
to practice coitus abruptus when having intercourse with
his wife. The baraita reads as follows: "Kol esrim ve-
arba-a chodesh dash mibifnim vezoreh mibachuts, divrei
Rabbi Eli-ezer. Ameru lo, 'Halalu eino ela kema-aseh Er
ve-Onan.'" ("During the twenty-four months in which his
wife nurses, or should nurse, the child, the husband
when having intercourse with her should, or may, practice coitus abruptus [to prevent her from becoming pregnant again; for in the latter eventuality she will not
be able to continue nursing the child and the child
might die as a result of an early weaning--Rashi, ad
loc.: 'Kedei shelo tit-aber vetigmol et benah veyamut'].
The other teachers, however, said to R. Eliezer that
such intercourse would be almost like the acts of Er and
Onan.") One may argue that this permission or recommendation of practicing coitus abruptus represents only the
opinion of R. Eliezer, and we should decide against him,
according to the principle "Yachid verabim--halacha
kerabim." But such an argument does not hold good in
our case. In the first place, when the individual opinion has a good reason in its support ("Demistaber ta-
ameih"), as--according to Rashi--R. Eliezer's opinion in
our case has, the decision may follow the individual
against the many (see Alfasi and Asheri to B.B., chapter
1, end; and comp. Maleachi Cohn, Yad Mal-achi, 296).
Secondly, we cannot here decide against R. Eliezer,
since the other teachers do not express a definite opinion contrary to his. For we notice that the other
teachers do not say, "It is forbidden to do so." They
do not even say that it is Onanism. They merely say:
"It is almost like the conduct of Er and Onan." This
certainly is not a strong and definite opposition to R.
Eliezer's opinion. It seems to me that even the other
teachers did not forbid the practice under the circumstances. They merely refused to recommend it as R.
Eliezer did, because they hesitated to recommend a practice which is so much like the acts of Er and Onan, even
under circumstances which made it imperative that conception be prevented. And we have to understand R.
Eliezer's opinion as making it obligatory for the husband to perform coitus abruptus during the period of
lactation.

That this interpretation of the respective positions of R. Eliezer and the other teachers in our ba-

raita is correct will be confirmed by our consideration
of another baraita dealing with the question of using
contraceptives. This other baraita is found in Yevamot
12b, 100b; Ketubot 35b; and Nida 45b. It reads as follows: "Tanei Rabbi Bibi kameih deRav Nachman: Shalosh
nashim meshameshot bemoch--ketana, me-uberet umeinika.
Ketana, shema tit-aber vetamut; me-uberet, shema ta-aseh
ubarah sandal; meinika, shema tigmol benah veyamut.
Ve-eizo hi ketana? Mibat 11 shanim veyom echad ad 12
shanim veyom echad; pachot mikan veyoter al ken meshameshet kedarkah veholechet. Divrei Rabbi Me-ir. Vacha-
chamim omerim: Achat zo ve-achat zo meshameshet kedarkah
veholechet, umin hashamayim yerachamu, mishum shene-emar
'Shomer peta-im Adonai.'"

    Before we proceed to interpret this baraita, we
must ascertain the correct meaning of the phrase "Meshameshot bemoch," as there are different interpretations
given to it. According to Rashi (Yevamot 12b), it means
putting cotton or other absorbent into the vagina before
the cohabitation, so the semen discharged during cohabitation will fall upon the cotton and be absorbed by it
and conception will not take place. According to R.
Jacob Tam (Tosafot ibid., s.v. "Veshalosh nashim"),
however it means using the cotton (or the absorbent)
after the act of cohabitation in order to remove the
semen and thus prevent conception. Whether the latter
is, according to modern medical science, an effective
contraceptive or not, is not our concern; the Rabbis
believed it to be such.

    It is evident that according to R. Tam, the use of
a douche or any other means of removing or destroying
the sperm would be the same as "Meshameshot bemoch."
Likewise, according to Rashi, the use of other contraceptives on the part of the woman would be the same as
"Meshameshot bemoch." Possibly R. Tam would permit the
use of chemical contraceptives, even if employed before
cohabitation. For his objection to the cotton put in
before cohabitation is that when the semen is discharged
upon the cotton, it does not touch the mucous membrane
of the vagina. This he considers "no real sexual intercourse, but like scattering the semen upon wood and
stone" ("De-ein derech tashmish bechach, vaharei hu
metil zera al ha-etsim veha-avanim keshemetil al
hamoch")--a practice which, according to the Midrash
(Genesis R. XXVI.6), was indulged in by the "generation
of the flood" (Dor Hamabul). This objection, then,
would not hold good when chemical contraceptives are
used.

    Again, according to Rashi, (Yevamot 100b) the
phrase "Meshameshot bemoch" means "Mutarot leiten moch
be-oto makom, shelo yit-aberu," that is, that in these
three conditions women are allowed to use this contra-

ceptive. This would imply that other women who do not
expose themselves or their children to danger by another
pregnancy are forbidden to do so. According to R. Tam
(**Tosafot** Ketubot 39a, **s.v.** "**Shalosh nashim**"), Asheri
and R. Nissim (on Nedarim 35b) the phrase "**Meshameshot
bemoch**" means "**tserichot.**" or as R. Nissim puts it
"**chayavot,**" that is, that these three women--because of
the danger of possible harm which might result from
pregnancy--are **obliged** to use this precaution. If we
interpret the phrase in this sense, it would imply that
other women--not threatened by any danger from pregnan-
cy--are merely not obliged to use this precaution
against conception, but are not forbidden to do so. It
would also follow from this interpretation that if the
other teachers differ from R. Meir, they differ only in
so far as they do not consider it **obligatory** upon these
three women (or, to be more correct, upon the **Ketana**) to
take this precaution; but as to **permitting** these three
women (or any other woman) to use a contraceptive, there
is no difference of opinion between R. Meir and the
other teachers. R. Solomon Lurya (1510-1573), in his
Yam Shel Shelomo to Yevamot, ch. I, no. 8 (Altona,
1739), pp. 4b,c has indeed so interpreted our baraita.
He points out that from the Talmud (Nida 3a) it is evident that Rashi's interpretation of "**Meshameshot bemoch**"
as meaning "putting in the absorbent before cohabitation
takes place," is correct. As to R. Tam's objection,
Lurya correctly states that such a practice is not to be
compared to "**Metil al etsim.**" For, after all, it is a
normal manner of having sexual intercourse, and the two
bodies derive pleasure from one another and experience
gratification of their desire. It is, therefore, not
different from any other normal sexual intercourse with
a woman who is incapable of having children: "**Ve-ein zeh
kemetil al etsim, desof sof derech tashmish bechach,
veguf neheneh min haguf.**"

Lurya further points out that since from Nida 3a it
is also evident that all women are permitted to use this
contraceptive, the meaning of the phrase "**Meshameshot
bemoch**" in our baraita must therefore be that these
three women **must** use this precaution--which implies that
all other women may use it. From this, argues Lurya, we
must conclude that even if we should decide that the law
(Halacha) follows the **Chachamim** who differ from R. Meir,
it would only mean that we would not make it obligatory
for these three women to use this precaution. But these
three women, like all other women, are permitted to use
it if they so desire. This is in essence the opinion of
Lurya.

It seems to me that a correct analysis of the baraita will show that Lurya did not go far enough in his
conclusions, and that there is no difference of opinion

between R. Meir and the other teachers on the question
of whether a pregnant or a nursing woman must take this
precaution. For this is what the baraita says: "There
are three women who, when having intercourse with their
husbands, must take the precaution of using an absorbent
to prevent conception: a minor, a pregnant woman, and a
woman nursing her baby. In the case of the minor, lest
she become pregnant and die when giving birth to the
child. [It was believed by some of the Rabbis that if a
girl became pregnant before having reached the age of
puberty, she and her child would both die at the moment
of childbirth. Comp. saying of Rabba b. Livai in Yevamot 12b and **Tosafot ad loc., s.v.** "Shema tit-aber"; also
saying in Yer., Pesachim, VIII.1, 35c: "**Iberah veyaleda,
ad shelo hevi-a shetei se-arot--hi uvenah metim.**"]   In
case of a pregnant woman, this precaution is necessary,
lest, if another conception takes place, the embryo
becomes a **foetus papyraceus** (comp. Julius Preuss, **Bib-
lisch-Talmudische Medizin**, Berlin, 1921, pp. 486-487).
In the case of a nursing mother, this precaution is
necessary, for if she should become pregnant, she will
have to wean her child before the proper time [which was
considered to extend for twenty-four months], and the
child may die as a result of such an early weaning." So
far the baraita apparently represents a unanimous statement. It then proceeds to discuss the age up to which a
woman is considered a minor in this respect. R. Meir
says that the minor in this case is a girl between the
age of eleven years and one day and twelve years and one
day, and that during that period only must she take this
precaution. Before or after this age she need not take
any precaution, but may have natural intercourse
("**Meshameshet kedarkah veholechet**"). The other teachers, however, say that even during the period when she
is a **Ketana** (i.e., between the age of eleven and
twelve), she may have natural intercourse and is not
obliged to take any precautions; for the heavenly powers
will have mercy and protect her from all danger, as it
is said, "The Lord preserveth the simple" (Ps. 116:6).
The other teachers evidently did not consider the danger
of a minor dying as a result of childbirth so probable.
They must have believed that a girl even before the age
of puberty could give birth to a living child and survive (comp. Preuss, **op. cit.**, p. 441). But as regards
the nursing or the pregnant woman, even the other teachers do not say that she may dispense with this precaution, for we notice that they do not say, "**Kulan meshameshot veholechot.**"
     The rules of law laid down in this baraita accord-
ing to our interpretation are, therefore, the following:
When there is a danger of harm resulting to the unborn
child or the child already born, all teachers agree that

it is obligatory to take the precaution of using a contraceptive. According to R. Meir, however, this obligation holds good also in the case when conception might result in danger or harm to the mother. But even if we should understand the baraita to indicate that the other teachers differed with R. Meir in all three cases, it would still only follow, as Lurya correctly points out, that in all three cases we decide the Halacha according to the Chachamim and do not make it obligatory upon these three women to take the precaution of using contraceptives; the rule indicated by the baraita would still teach us that, according to the opinion of all the teachers, it is not forbidden to use a contraceptive in cases where conception would bring harm either to the mother or to the child born or unborn. And I cannot see any difference between the protection of a minor from a conception which might prove fatal to her and the protection of a grown-up woman whose health is, according to the opinion of physicians, such that a pregnancy might be fatal to her. Neither can I see any difference between protecting a child from the danger of being deprived of the nourishment of its mother's milk, and protecting the already born children of the family from the harm which might come to them due to the competition of a larger number of sisters and brothers. For the care and the comfort which the parents can give their children already born will certainly be less if there be added to the family other children claiming attention, care, and comfort.

The Talmudic law even permits a woman to sterilize herself permanently ("Ha-isha rasha-it lishtot kos shel ikarin," Tosefta, Yevamot VIII.4). And the wife of the famous R. Hiyya is reported to have taken such a medicine ("Sama de-akarta") which made her sterile (Yevamot 65b). Whether there be such a drug according to modern medicine or not, is not our concern. The Rabbis believed that there was such a drug which, if taken internally, makes a person sterile (see Shabbat 110a,b and Preuss, op. cit., pp. 439-440 and 479-480), and they permitted the woman to take it and become sterile. According to Lurya (op. cit., Yevamot IV.44), this permission is given to a woman who experiences great pain of childbirth, which she wishes to escape, as was the case of the wife of R. Hiyya. Even more so, says Lurya, is this permitted to a woman whose children are morally corrupt and of bad character, and who fears to bring into the world other moral delinquents: "Ela lemi sheyesh lah tsa-ar leida ke-ein deveitehu deRabbi Chiya; vechol sheken im baneiha ein holechin bederech yeshara, umityare-a shelo tarbeh begidulim ka-elu, shehareshut beyadah." To these I would add the woman who, because of hereditary disease with which she or her husband is

afflicted, fears to have children who might be born with
these diseases and suffer and be a burden to their family or to society.

From the passage in the Talmud (Yevamot 65b) we
learn, however, that there is an objection which the
Jewish law might have to a man's using contraceptive
means, or having intercourse with his wife in such a
manner as to make conception impossible. This objection
is based not on the view that such an act is in itself
immoral or against the law, but merely on consideration
for another religious duty which could not be fulfilled
if such a practice would be indulged in all the time.
The wife of R. Hiyya--so the Talmud tells us--incapaci-
tated herself only after she had learned that the duty
of propagation of the race was not incumbent upon her,
since, according to the decision of the Rabbis, women
were not included in the commandment, "Be fruitful and
multiply" (Genesis 1:28), which was given to men only.
Since a man must fulfill the duty of propagation of the
race ("**Mitzvat periya ureviya**") he cannot be allowed the
practice of having intercourse with his wife only in
such a manner as to make conception impossible. For in
so doing he fails to fulfill the law commanding him to
have children. It is accordingly a sin of omission but
not of commission; for the practice as such is not immoral or against the law.

But--and this is peculiar to the Jewish point of
view on this question--the man who practices absolute
self-restraint or total abstinence is also guilty of the
same sin of omission, for he likewise fails to fulfill
the duty of propagation of the race. No distinction can
be made, according to Jewish law, between the two ways
of avoiding the duty of begetting children, whether by
total abstention from sexual intercourse or by being
careful not to have intercourse in such a manner as
would result in conception. For, as has already been
pointed out, the act of having intercourse with one's
wife in a manner not effecting conception is in itself
not forbidden by Jewish law. If, however, a man has
fulfilled the duty of propagation of the race, as when
he already has two children (i.e., two boys according to
the School of Shammai or a boy and a girl according to
the School of Hillel) and is no longer obliged by law to
beget more children (Yevamot 61b and **Shulchan Aruch**,
Even Ha-ezer 1.5), there can be no objection at all to
the practice of birth control. For while the Rabbis of
old, considering children a great blessing, would advise
a man to continue to beget children even after he has
already fulfilled the duty of propagation of the race,
yet they grant that any man has a right to avoid having
more children when, for one reason or another, he does
not consider it a blessing to have too many children and

deems it advisable in his particular case not to have more than the two that the law commands him to have.

But even in the case of one who has not yet fulfilled the duty of propagation of the race ("**Mitzvat periya ureviya**") it might, under certain conditions, be permitted to practice birth control, if it is done not for selfish purposes but for the sake of some higher ideal or worthy moral purpose. For the Rabbinic law permits a man to delay his marrying and having children or even to remain all his life unmarried (like Ben Azzai), if he is engaged in study and fears that having a family to take care of would interfere with his work and hinder in the pursuit of his studies (Kiddushin 29b; Maimonides, **Yad**, Hil. Ishut, XV.2-3; **Shulchan Aruch**, Even Ha-ezer, I.3-4).

Since, as we have seen, the act of having intercourse with one's wife in a manner not resulting in conception is in itself not against the law, there can be no difference between the failure to fulfill the commandment of propagation of the race by abstaining altogether from marriage and the failure to fulfill the commandment by practicing birth control. The considerations that permit the one permit also the other. It would even seem that the other--i.e., the practice of birth control--should be preferred to the one of total abstention. For, in granting permission to practice the latter, the Rabbis make the proviso that the man be so constituted, or so deeply engrossed in his work, as not to be troubled by his sexual desires or to be strong enough to withstand temptation ("**Vehu shelo yehe yitsro mitgaber alav**," Maimonides and **Shulchan Aruch**, l.c.). Now, if a man is so constituted that he is troubled by his desires and suffers from the lack of their gratification, and yet is engaged in some noble and moral pursuit (like the study of the Torah) which hinders him from taking on the responsibilities of a family, he may marry and avoid having children. He may say with Ben Azzai, "I am very much attached to my work and cannot afford to have a family to take care of. The propagation of the race can and will be carried on by others" ("**Efshar la-olam sheyitkayem al yedei acherim**," Yevamot 36b; Tosefta, **ibid.**, VIII, end). For the Rabbis also teach that "it is better to marry," even if not for the sake of having children, than "to burn" with passion and ungratified desires. And, as we have seen above, the Rabbinic law permits marriage even when it must result in failure to fulfill the commandment "Be fruitful and multiply," as when a young man marries an old or sterile woman. The Rabbis did not teach total abstention. They did not agree with Paul that "It is good for a man not to touch a woman" (I Corinthians VII:1). While the institution of marriage may have for its main purpose the propagation of the race, this is not its sole and exclusive purpose. And the Rabbis urge and recommend marriage as such without regard to this purpose, or even under conditions when this purpose cannot be achieved. The companionship or mutual helpfulness in leading a pure, good, and useful life, achieved by a true marriage, is also a noble purpose worthy of this divine institution. In fact, according to the Biblical account, this was the first consideration in the Divine mind when creating woman for man. He said: "It is not good that the man should be alone, I will make him a helpmeet for him" (Genesis 2:18). He did not say, "I will make him a wife that he have children by her." The commandment to have children God gave to Adam later on. When husband and wife live together and help each other to lead a good life--whether they have children or not--God is with them and their home is a place for the **Shechina**, the Divine purpose, says R. Akiva (Sota 17a). Ben Azzai did not say like Paul, "I would that all men were even as I myself" (I Corinth. VII:7). He did not set up celibacy in itself as an ideal, nor would he recommend it to others (comp. H. Graetz, **Gnosticismus und Judenthum**, Krotoshin, 1846, pp. 73ff). Ben Azzai considered marriage a divine institution and recognized the obligation of propagating the race as a religious duty. But he believed that he was exempted from this duty in consideration of the fact that it might interfere with another religious duty, e.g., the study of the Torah in which he was engaged. Of course the same right would, according to Ben Azzai, be given to others in a similar position, i.e., to those pursuing studies or being engaged in any other moral religious activities which might be interfered with by the taking on of the obligation of having children. We have seen that the medieval Rabbinic authorities have concurred in the opinion of Ben Azzai and allowed a man engaged in a religious pursuit, such as the study of the Torah, to delay--or even altogether neglect--fulfilling the commandment of "Be fruitful and multiply." And we have also found that no distinction can be made between neglecting this duty by abstaining from marriage and neglecting it by practicing birth control.

The above represents the logical conclusion which one must draw from a correct understanding and a sound interpretation of the halachic statements in the Talmud touching this question, disregarding the ideas expressed in the Agadic literature as to the advisability of having many children.

The later Jewish mystics emphasized these Agadic sayings, as well as the Agadic condemnations of the evil practices of "**Hotsa-at shichvat zera levatala**." They came to regard any discharge of semen which might have resulted in conception but did not, almost like "Hotsa-at shichvat zera levatala." Nay, even an unconscious seminal emission is regarded as a sin against which one must take all possible precautions and for which one must repent and make atonement. But even the mystics permit intercourse with one's wife even when she is incapable of having children (see Zohar, Emor 90b).

Some Rabbinic authorities of the 18th and 19th centuries--under the spell of the Agadic sayings of the Talmud and more or less influenced by the mystic litera-ture--are loath to permit birth control. But even these authorities do not altogether prohibit the practice when there is a valid reason for exercising it. The reasons given by some of them for opposing the practice are not justified in the light of the halachic statements of the Talmud which we discussed above. Their arguments are not based upon correct interpretations of the Talmudic passages bearing upon this question, and they utterly ignore or overlook the correct interpretations and the sound reasoning of R. Solomon Lurya quoted above. In the following I will present the opinions of some of the authorities of the 18th and 19th centuries on this ques-tion.

R. Solomon Zalman of Posen, rabbi in Warsaw (died 1839), in his responsa Chemdat Shelomo (quoted in Pit-chei Teshuva to Even Ha-ezer XXIII.2)--in answer to a question about a woman to whom, according to the opinion of physicians, pregnancy might be dangerous--declares that she may use a contraceptive. He permits even the putting into the vagina of an absorbent before cohabita-tion, declaring that since the intercourse takes place in the normal way, the discharge of the semen in such a case cannot be considered "Hashchatat zera."

R. Joseph Modiano, a Turkish rabbi of the second half of the 18th century, in his responsa collection Rosh Mashbir, part II (Salonica, 1840), no. 49, discus-ses the case of a woman who, during her pregnancy, be-comes extremely nervous and almost insane. He quotes the great rabbinical authority R. Michael, who declared that the woman should use a contraceptive. R. Michael argued that since the woman is exposed to the danger by pregnancy she is in a class with the three women men-tioned in the baraita of R. Bibi and should therefore, like them, use an absorbent, even putting it in before cohabitation ("Sheyeshamesh ba-alah bemoch kedei shelo tit-aber"), and her husband cannot object to it. Modiano himself does not concur with the opinion of R. Michael; he argues that the use of the absorbent could only be permitted if employed after cohabitation, and the husband who may find the use of this contraceptive inconvenient or may doubt its effectiveness should therefore be permitted to marry another woman. But even

Modiano would not forbid the use of this contraceptive if the husband had no objection to it.

R. Akiva Eiger in his Responsa (Warsaw, 1834), nos. 71 and 72, pp. 51b-53a, also permits the use of an absorbent, but only if it is employed after cohabitation. The questioner, R. Eleazar Zilz, a rabbinical authority of Posen however argued that it should be permitted even when employed before cohabitation.

R. Moses Sofer in his **Chatam Sofer** (Pressburg, 1860), Yoreh De-a, no. 172, pp. 67b-68a, likewise permits it only when used after cohabitation. R. Abraham Danzig in his **Chochmat Adam** and **Binat Adam** (Warsaw, 1914), Sha-ar Beit Hanashim, no. 36, p. 156, permits the use of an absorbent or a douche or any other method of removing or destroying the semen after cohabitation. He adds, however, that according to Rashi's interpretation, it would be permitted to the woman in question to whom pregnancy was dangerous, to use this contraceptive even before cohabitation.

R. Jacob Ettlinger (1798-1871) in his Responsa **Binyan Tsion** (Altona, 1868), no. 137, pp. 57b-58b, and R. Joseph Saul Nathanson (1808-1875) in his Responsa **Sho-el Umeshiv**, Mahadura Tenina (Lemberg, 1874), part IV, no. 13, are inclined to forbid the use of any contraceptive, even when used after cohabitation.

The authorities objecting to the use of an absorbent before cohabitation, do so, of course, on the ground that, like R. Tam, they consider such a practice "**Kemetil al ha-etsim ve-al ha-avanim.**" On the same ground they would no doubt object to the use of a condum. But, as was already pointed out above, they could have no objection to the use of chemical contraceptives on the part of the woman.

In summing up the results of our discussion, I would say that while there may be some differences of opinion about one detail or another, we can formulate the following principles in regard to the question of birth control which are based upon a correct understanding of the halachic teachings of the Talmud as accepted by the medieval Rabbinic authorities, and especially upon the sound interpretation given by R. Solomon Lurya to some of these Talmudic passages:

(1) The Talmudic-Rabbinic law does not consider the use of contraceptives as such immoral or against the law. It does not forbid birth control, but it forbids birth suppression.

(2) The Talmudic-Rabbinic law requires that every Jew have at least two children in fulfillment of the Biblical command to propagate the race, which is incumbent upon every man.

(3) There are, however, conditions under which a man may be exempt from this prime duty: (a) when a man

is engaged in religious work, such as the study of the Torah, and fears that he may be hindered in his work for taking on the responsibilities of a family; (b) when a man, because of love, or other considerations, marries a woman who is incapable of having children (i.e., an old or sterile woman); (c) when a man is married to a woman whose health is in such condition as to make it danger- ous for her to bear children; for, considerations for the saving of human life--**Pikuach Nefesh** or even **Safek Pikuach Nefesh**--set aside the obligation to fulfill a religious duty. In this last case, then, the woman is allowed to use any contraceptives or even to permanently sterilize herself in order to escape the dangers that would threaten her at childbirth.

(4) In case a man has fulfilled the duty of propa- gation of the race (as when he has already two child- ren), he is no longer obliged to beget children, and the law does not forbid him to have intercourse with his wife even in a manner which would not result in concep- tion. In such a case the woman certainly is allowed to use any kind of contraceptive or preventive.

Of course, in any case, the use of contraceptives or of any device to prevent conception is allowed only when both parties, i.e., husband and wife consent.

Some Rabbinic authorities of the 18th and 19th centuries would object to one or another of the above rules, and especially put restrictions upon the use of contraceptives. But we need not expect absolute agree- ment on questions of Rabbinic law. We must be content to have good and reliable authority for our decisions, even though other authorities may differ. We have the right to judge for ourselves which view is the sounder and which authorities are more correct. We have found that the arguments of those authorities of the 18th and 19th centuries who would oppose or restrict the use of contraceptives in cases where we would recommend it, are not convincing. With all our respect for these authori- ties, we may ignore their opinions, just as they in turn have ignored the opinions of other authorities (espe- cially those of R. Solomon Lurya) on our question.

Jacob Z. Lauterbach

See also:

S.B. Freehof, "Sterilizing Husband," **Reform Re- sponsa**, pp. 206ff.

157.   ARTIFICIAL INSEMINATION
(Vol. LXII, 1952, pp. 123-125)

QUESTION: Is artificial insemination permitted by Jewish Law?

ANSWER: The question involves many legal problems. Does the donor fulfill the duty of begetting children (Periya Ureviya) if a child is born (but the donor has no other children)? Does he commit the sin of wasting seed (zera levatala)? Is the woman henceforth forbidden to live with her husband on the ground that she has been fertilized by a man who is not her husband? Is the child a Mamzer, since he is born of a married woman (Eshet Ish) and a man not her husband? Is there not a danger that the child, when he grows up, may marry his own blood sister or the wife of his own blood brother (contrary to the Levirate laws)?

1.   Even though the technique of artificial insemination is new, nevertheless, most of the questions mentioned above are not new in the Law, since the legal literature has already discussed them with regard to certain special circumstances which are analogous to artificial insemination, namely, if, for example a woman is impregnated in a bath from seed that had been emitted there ("Ibera be-ambatei") (cf. B., Chagiga 15a, top).

2.   Joel Sirkes (1561-1640), in Bach to Tur, Yoreh De-a 195 (quoting Semak) says that the child is absolutely kasher (i.e., not a Mamzer), since there had been no actual forbidden intercourse ("Ein kan bi-at isur").

3.   On the basis of the fact that there has been no illicit intercourse, Judah Rosanes (died in Constantinople in 1727), in his Mishneh Lamelech to Maimonides, Hilchot Ishut XV.4, declares that the woman is not immoral and is therefore not forbidden to live with her husband.

4.   But whose son is it? Samuel b. Uri Phoebus (17th century), in his commentary Beit Shemu-el to Shulchan Aruch, Even Ha-ezer 1, note 10, says that it is the son of the donor; otherwise we would not be concerned lest the child later marry his own blood sister. If he were not, the donor's daughter would not be his sister.

5.   In modern times, since the development of the technique of artificial insemination, the subject has been discussed by Chayim Fischel Epstein in his Teshuva Shelema (Even Ha-ezer, #4), and by Ben Zion Uziel of Tel Aviv, the chief Sephardic rabbi of Palestine, in his Mishpetei Uziel, part II, Even Ha-ezer, section 19.

Epstein--because of the danger that the child may some day, out of ignorance, marry one of the forbidden degrees of relationship--opposes the use of seed from a stranger, but permits the use of the husband's own seed if that is the only way the wife can be impregnated by her husband. Ben Zion Uziel says--as do earlier authorities--that the woman is not immoral because of this act and that the child is **kasher**, but--disagreeing with **Beit Shemu-el**--he says that the child is **not** the child of the donor as to inheritance and **Chalitsa**. He adds that the woman thus impregnated (if not married) may not marry until the time of suckling the child is over.

Since he concludes that the child is not the donor's child, he therefore considers that the donor has sinned in wasting seed.

However, inasmuch as he concludes that the woman is not immoral and not forbidden to her husband, he seems to incline toward permitting the procedure at the recommendation of the physician although he hesitates to say so.

6. My own opinion would be that the possibility of the child marrying one of his own close blood kin is far-fetched, but that since, according to Jewish law, the wife has committed no sin and the child is **kasher**, then the process of artificial insemination should be permitted.

Solomon B. Freehof

158. ARTIFICIAL INSEMINATION
(Vol. LXII, 1952, pp. 125-128)

QUESTION: Is artificial insemination permitted by Jewish Law?

ANSWER: Talmudic and Rabbinic sources do not discuss, nor even mention, artificial insemination as understood (and practiced) in our day. Artificial insemination, with which we are concerned, is premeditated, planned. The physician performs it upon request by the parents, applying either the husband's sperm or that of a stranger. In the latter case, the identity of the donor must not be revealed to the parents (nor to the resulting child, of course).

Yet, since artificial insemination concerns family life--an area meticulously regulated and steadily supervised by Jewish religious leaders of all times--it is quite natural that rabbis of our day investigate the matter in order to find a solution that would be in character with Jewish practice and thought.

In an attempt at a solution of the problem, the first step, as a matter of course, is to search for sources that may have some bearing on the subject. Whereas many passages from Talmud and Rabbinic literature could be, somehow, linked to the problem (as has been done), only those passages shall be discussed here which possess (or are believed to possess) real significance for the issue:

1.   In Talmud Bavli (Chagiga 14b), the question is raised whether a virgin who became pregnant is allowed to be married by the High Priest (in view of Leviticus 21:13-14, "Isha bivtuleiha"). Subsequently (14b-15a) the possibilities of a virgin's becoming pregnant are discussed. One of the possibilities suggested is that she was impregnated in a bath (from seed deposited there by a man).

Let us keep in mind that this incident, considered by some rabbis as being analogous to artificial insemination. is, in fact an accident, a calamity; the pregnancy was undesired. It was not artificial in the sense in which this expression is being used today.

2.   **Chelkat Mechokek** (Moses ben Isaac Jehudah Lima) on **Shulchan Aruch**, Even Ha-ezer 1, note 8, raises the question (in connection with the **Mamzer**) whether the father fulfilled the commandment of **Periya Ureviya** (procreation) if his wife was impregnated in the bath, and whether the resulting child is his child in every respect. Instead of giving a clear answer, **Chelkat Mechokek** cites an incident from **Likutei Maharil**. According to this incident, Ben Sira was the result of a bath insemination (yet no blemish is attached to him).

3.   **Beit Shemu-el** (Samuel ben Uri Phoebus), **ibid.**, note 10, cites **Chelkat Mechokek**'s question and answers it by referring in brief to **Hagahot Semak,** a note by Perez (ben Elijah) on Semak (Isaac ben Joseph of Corbeil). This note is related fully in **Bach** (Joel Sirkes) on **Tur,** Yoreh De-a 195, and tells us the following: A menstruous woman may lie on the sheet of her husband but not on that of a stranger lest she become pregnant from the seed of a stranger (emitted on the sheet). But why should she not be afraid of becoming pregnant from the seed of her husband while she is menstruating and thus producing a **Ben Hanida** (child of a menstruous woman), which is prohibited? The answer: Since there is no prohibited intercourse, the child is entirely **kasher** (no stigma attached to him), even if she became pregnant (in such a way) by a stranger, since Ben Sira was **kasher** (see above). Yet, if it is a stranger, we have to be cautious (i.e., she must not lie on his sheet), because

of the possibility that the resulting child might marry his own sister by his father (whose identity is unknown). **Beit Shemu-el** concludes from this note that the child resulting from such an insemination is that of the emitter of the seed in every respect.

This conclusion, needless to say, is irreconcilable with the fundamental rule of artificial insemination, requiring that the child belong to the mother's husband, not to the donor of the seed.

4. **Mishneh Lamelech** (Judah Rosanes) on Maimonides' **Mishneh Torah**, Hilchot Ishut XV.4, besides citing **Likutei Maharil**, **Chelkat Mechokek**, **Hagahot Semak** (see above), remarks: "**Ein safek dela ne-esra leva-alah mishum de-ein kan bi-at isur**" ("There is no doubt that she does not become prohibited to her husband because no prohibited intercourse took place").

What **Mishneh Lamelech** clarifies is that accidental insemination in a bath or on a sheet (i.e., without direct contact with a man) cannot be considered as adultery, which would make her prohibited to her husband (rape of a Kohen's wife would have the same result). For our problem, this does not reveal any clue, since we are not trying to solve the question of accidental insemination. Planned artificial insemination involves some problems which do not exist at all with regard to accidental insemination. One of these problems is whether or not the emitting of seed for artificial insemination would be **Hotsa-at zera levatala** (wasting of seed), which is prohibited. Let us return to this point in a brief reference to recent responsa on the subject.

One of these is found in **Mishpetei Uzi-el** (Tel Aviv, 1938), part II, Even Ha-ezer Responsum 19, pp. 46-69, by Ben Zion Uziel. Uziel equates, basically, artificial insemination with accidental (bath, sheet) insemination. But, as to the emitting of seed for bath or artificial insemination, he can see no way whatever for permitting it. Uziel's concluding words are that the matter belongs to the category of the Halachot which bear the designation "**Halacha ve-ein morin kach**," i.e., Halacha which must not be translated into practice (cf. Michael Guttmann, **Zur Einleitung in die Halacha** II, p. 91).

Haim F. Epstein, in his **Teshuva Shelema** (St. Louis, 1941), vol. II, Even Ha-ezer, Responsum 4, pp. 8-10, like Uziel, basically equating artificial insemination with accidental insemination, finds no way of allowing the use of a stranger's sperm. However, as to the use of the husband's seed for artificial insemination, he states "**Efshar dezeh mutar**," i.e., "It is possible that this is allowed," if the physician finds that this is the only possible way for his begetting a child.

Epstein's argument as to the necessity of limiting of the concept **Hotsa-at zera levatala** (wasting of seed), based primarily on Yevamot 76a, is sound and provides at least some justification for his hesitant conclusion (cf. also Responsum 5, **ibid.**).

Let me sum up the problem of artificial insemination considered from the viewpoint of historical Judaism, as follows:

Artificial insemination, as understood and practiced today, is not mentioned in Rabbinic literature. What we find here is merely accidental, indirect insemination. We must also keep in mind that the bath insemination of the Talmud is not merely an **ex post facto** case, but it also involves the concept of **Ones**, meaning "accident." Jewish law mostly, though not always, clearly distinguishes between accidental and premeditated deed. I do not believe that we do justice to Jewish law or to Judaism by disregarding its concepts and principles in an effort to force certain conclusions, one way or the other.

Also the fact that the laws and discussions of the Rabbis with regard to bath insemination are of a theoretical nature, is of importance. Not one incident of actual bath insemination is attested to in Jewish literature. What we find, including the Ben Sira case, is mere Agada. Had such an incident actually occurred, the Rabbis might have found a solution entirely different from the known theoretical considerations. Noteworthy is the fact that the Sages never recommend bath insemination, even if this were the only means of saving a marriage, which ranks very high with the Rabbis. A case in point is an incident in Yevamot 65b (see **ibid.**).

I do not claim that the last word has been said on artificial insemination in its relation to Jewish life and practice. It is hardly possible to draw safe conclusions from the theoretical accidental insemination found in Jewish sources to the artificial insemination of our day. While indications strongly point to a negative answer (particularly if the seed of a stranger is to be used), other aspects of Judaism must be explored as well, in order to arrive at a conclusion reflecting Judaism at its best.

Whereas I do not see sufficient evidence for recommending the issuance of a prohibition against artificial insemination, I should like to caution against a hasty **Heter** (permit) for which I found no backing worth the name in our Jewish teachings.

Alexander Guttmann

See also:

S.B. Freehof, "Artificial Insemination," **Reform Responsa**, pp. 212ff.

159. SURROGATE MOTHER
(Vol. XCII, 1982, pp. 205-207)

QUESTION: What is the status of a child born to a surrogate mother who has been impregnated through artificial insemination with the sperm of a man married to another woman? The child will eventually be raised by the husband and his wife. (J.Z., New York City)

ANSWER: We must inquire about the Halacha and the use of surrogate mothers, as well as the status of the child. The Talmud and later Rabbinic literature seem to have dealt with a subject akin to the question of a surrogate mother when they discussed pregnancies which were not caused by intercourse. The Rabbis felt that a girl could conceive by taking a bath in water into which male semen has been discharged (Chag. 14b); in other words, without intercourse or penetration. This line of thought has been continued by some later commentators and respondists (Eibeschutz, **Commentary** to **Yad**, Hil. Ishut 15.6; Ettlinger, **Aruch Laner** to Yev. 12b). The medieval author of **Hagahot Semak**, Perez ben Elijah of Corbeil, felt that a woman should be careful and not lie upon linen on which a man had slept so that she might not become impregnated by his sperm (Joel Sirkes to **Tur**, Yoreh De-a 195).

Here we have instances of conception through an unknown outside source, and this was not considered to cause any halachic problem for the woman or the child, who was legitimate. Yet there is a striking difference between these situations and ours, as the child in question there was raised by its natural mother while ours will be raised by other parents. Furthermore, there is a commercial aspect in our situation, as the surrogate mother presumably has been paid for her efforts.

A Biblical parallel seems to exist in the tales of the Patriarchs (**birkayim**, Gen. 30:3, 50:23) as Hagar was given to Abraham by Sarah so that there would be a child. Similarly, Rachel gave Bilhah to Jacob. In both instances the primary wife reckoned the child as her own and was able to accept (as Rachel) or reject (as Sarah) it. The differences here, however, are as follows:

1.   the child and biological mother were part of the same household and family; and

2.   the biological mother continued to play a major role in the life of the child.

There are also some problems with an apparent Talmudic parallel, i.e., the situations of a concubine, whether of a temporary or permanent nature (see the responsum "Concubinage," #133 above). These women bore the children of a man who usually was already married to another woman as his primary wife, but the concubines raised the children themselves.

There is nothing then akin to our problem in the literature of the past. A vague example in **Noam** (vol. 14, pp. 28ff) actually deals with organ transplants, in this case ovaries. The midrash which dealt with the transfer of a fetus from Leah to Rachel and vise versa (**Targum Jonathan** to Gen. 30:12; Nida 31a; Ber. 60a) is also not relevant, as the parents seemed unaware of this.

We would, therefore, have to treat the use of a surrogate mother as a new medical way of relieving the childlessness of a couple and enabling them to fulfill the **mitzvah** of procreation. It should cause us no more problems than modern adoptions which occur frequently. There, too, the arrangement to adopt is often made far in advance of birth, with the complete consent of one or both biological parents. Here we have the additional psychological advantage of the couple knowing that part of the genetic background of the child which they will raise as their own. This may prove helpful to the adoptive parents and, at a later stage, to the child.

If we were to treat this child as the offspring of a concubine or the result of a temporary liaison between a man and an unmarried woman, there would be no doubt about its legitimacy. The issue of Biblical and Rabbinic **Arayot** does not arise.

We should look at the halachic view of artificial insemination with a mixture of sperm as is common practice. The majority of the traditional authorities consider such children legitimate (Nathanson, **Sho-el Umeshiv**, part 3, vol. 3, #132; Uziel, **Mishpetei Uziel**, Even Ha-ezer, #19; Walkin, **Zekan Aharon**, Even Ha-ezer 2, #97; Feinstein, **Igerot Mosheh**, Even Ha-ezer, #10). Waldenberg (**Tsits Eliezer**, vol. 9, no. 51.4) considered such children to be **Mamzerim**. Additional discussion of the different authorities may be found in vol. 1 of **Noam** (1958). S.B. Freehof also considered them legitimate ("Artificial Insemination," #157 above), but Guttmann was cautious (see #158 above).

We would agree that there is no question about the legitimacy of such children, as long as the surrogate

mother is not married. However, we realize that problems still exist in civil law in various states.

It is more difficult when we consider a married
surrogate mother. Different factors are involved. On
the positive side, we have the **mitzvah** of procreation to
fulfill. Certainly, that **mitzvah** ought to be encouraged
in every way possible. It is for this reason that both
adoption and artificial insemination have been encouraged by traditional Judaism and Reform Judaism. In a
period when the number of Jewish children has declined
rather rapidly, we should do everything possible to make
children available to families who wish to raise them.

Problems are raised by the marital status of both
couples in civil law and Halacha. Is this to be considered adulterous or not? Certainly, under normal circumstances sexual relations between a man and a married
woman would be adulterous. The fact that the woman with
whom the relationship is carried on has a husband who is
willing to permit it makes no difference. In this instance however, insemination would be conducted artifi-
cially and no sexual penetration would occur. It would,
therefore, not differ materially from circumstances
under which artificial insemination with sperm from an
unknown donor takes place. In that case, too, the donor
may very well be married and certainly the woman recipient is married. This form of artificial insemination
has been accepted by us (see #157-158 above), by Freehof, and with some reservations by Guttmann. At least
two of three Orthodox authorities (Baumol, **Emek Halacha**,
#68; Schwadron **Maharsham**, vol. 3, #268) have permitted
this, too, however with reservations. We would therefore not consider the use of a married surrogate mother
as adulterous, as the beginning of the process is akin
to artificial insemination. We would therefore hesi-
tantly permit the use of a married surrogate mother in
order to enable a couple to have children and await
further clarification of medical and civil legal issues.

Walter Jacob, Chairman
Leonard Kravitz
Isaac Newman
Harry Roth
Rav Soloff
Bernard Zlotowitz

160. PREDETERMINATION OF SEX
(Vol. LI, 1941, pp. 97-100)

QUESTION: A writer in leading magazines has submitted a question to me. She is preparing a manuscript that will include the attitudes of the various faiths toward predetermination of sex in babies. She says: "As the aim of scientific predetermination is not to limit families in any way, but to increase their happiness through having the sex they most desire, what does your group think on the subject?"

ANSWER: The question posed in the above statement, while avowedly premature, is not impertinent. In fact, the question is not as new as it sounds. The Rabbis of the Talmudic period gave some thought to it. They even sought to prescribe methods whereby nature, in such cases, might be guided to predetermined ends. Those were the days when parents showed undisguised elation over the birth of a male child, and accepted with due resignation the arrival of a female child. Rabbi Chiya Rabba, a Tannaitic teacher of the second century, in animadverting upon this parental preference, spoke rather approvingly of it. "There is need for wheat," he said, "and there is need for barley" **(Gen. R. 26.6)**. Accordingly, some teachers endeavored to advise parents what to do in order to achieve the desired result. Rabbi Eleazar is reported to have recommended generosity to the poor as the best method, while Rabbi Joshua, with a keener sense of the relevant, thought that when the husband aimed to predispose his wife for the act of cohabitation, male progeny would ensue: **"Ma ya-esh adam veyihyu lo banim zecharim? Rabbi Eli-ezer omer: Yefazer me-otav la-aniyim. Rabbi Yehoshua omer: Yesamach ishto lidvar mitzvah."**

Other teachers thought that by the mere process of retarded ejaculation on the part of the husband, thus inducing the wife to reach the climax first, the birth of a male child would be assured. Thus, a Babylonian Amora of the third century, Rabbi Kattina, boldly asserted that he had mastered the art of coition which would yield him only male children (Nida 31b, **"Vehainu de-amar Rav Katina: 'Yacholni la-asot kol banai zecharim.'"**).

Informed by the same impression or conviction, another Babylonian Amora, Rava, declared that the immediate repetition of the act of coition, tending to retard the ejaculation of the male, could not but produce male children (ibid., "Amar Rava: 'Harotse la-asot kol banav zecharim, yiv-ol veyishneh'").

Various other methods, we find, were suggested. Thus, Rabbi Isaac is reported to have said that when the bedstead extended in a northerly-southerly direction the sex of the offspring would be male (Ber. 5b, "Kol hanoten mitato bein tsafon ledarom, havyin leih banim zecharim.").

And so, too, is Rabbi Johanan reported to have held that abstention from intercourse immediately before the menstrual period, would result in male issue (Shev. 18b, "Kol haporesh me-ishto samuch levistah, havyin lo banim zecharim."). And, as if to disown the implication of the psychological basis for his statement, he proceeds to add that the scrupulous use of wine in the Havdala ceremony will produce the same wished-for effect (ibid., "Kol hamavdil al hayayin bemotsa-ei Shabbat, havyin lo banim zecharim").

There is also the citation of an anonymous authority, which would make the determination of the sex of the offspring conditioned by the moral and social fitness of the union, as well as by the spirit in which the act of cohabitation is performed (Nida 70a, "Amar lahem: 'Yisa isha hahogenet lo viykadesh atsmo bish-at tashmish'").

Of course, all these suggestions partake more of the nature of magic than of pure science. But whatever the value of the methods suggested,they are certainly "moral, simple and safe," even though not quite effective. Above all, they clearly indicate the Rabbinic attitude toward the question raised. The desire of parents to predetermine, if possible, the sex of their progeny, is not a reprehensible desire. The objective sought is a legitimate objective. The issue then resolves itself into this: Will the absolutely reliable method anticipated, though not too hopefully, by the author of the question, be as moral, as simple, and as safe as those projected by the early Rabbinic authorities? Judaism, it is well to state here emphatically, is not a religion that teaches the doctrine that the end justifies the means. In this case, therefore, if the means, yet to be discovered, will prove scientifically sound and morally unassailable, the Jewish teachers of that far-off day will find ample basis for their endorsement of the enterprise in the thought and tradition of their past.

Israel Bettan and Committee

161. DIVORCE (GET)
(Vol. LVI, 1946, pp. 123-125)

QUESTION: Some time ago, I officiated at the wedding of a young woman of Orthodox background. She
had previously been divorced and had been extremely
eager to secure a religious divorce from her former
husband. However, he put all sorts of humiliating
obstacles in the path of this woman, so that it was
necessary to be married without this religious
divorce. She felt very badly about it, and so did
her new husband. I suggested to...that in cases
where it is almost impossible to secure a divorce
because of the obstinacy of a spouse, the Conference issue a unilateral divorce. This divorce
would say that, inasmuch as a civil divorce had
been granted, we recognize the religious right of
the party to remarry. I feel that this would be of
great psychological value to many people. It would
solve the problem of large numbers who are now
encountering difficulty in remarrying because of
the lack of cooperation of their former spouses....
    I might add that my proposal does not pretend
to give any religious authority to the divorce, but
is rather a device whereby we give sanction for
remarriage to people who may, because of their
inability to secure a Get, feel that their remarriage is not quite according to correct procedure.

ANSWER: The proposal herein set forth, while somewhat
startling, contemplates no revolutionary change in our
attitude. The correspondent reaffirms his belief in the
adequacy of the civil decree, and disavows any desire to
restore to the religious bill of divorcement its former
character and status. He would merely invest the Conference with the power to issue, in special cases a
document similar to the Get only as a "device" to foil
the willful husband who refuses to comply with the Orthodox requirement, and thus embarrasses his scrupulous
former mate.
    It is worthy of note that the divorcee in question,
though eager to obtain a religious divorce, does not
seem to regard its absence as a serious obstacle to her
remarriage. Reared amidst Orthodox surroundings, she is
conscious of an unfulfilled requirement and betrays a
measure of mental disturbance. The suggested "device,"
in the judgment of the correspondent. would tend to ease
her perturbed mind.
    We are dealing here, then, not with a question of
law, but with a question of policy. Shall we as a religious body that has abandoned a given practice on prin-

ciple (see **CCAR Yearbook**, vol. 39, p. 43), deliberately
resolve to restore it, not as a discipline in our lives,
but as a possible palliative for the none-too-poignant
scruples of certain divorcees who still cherish a super-
ficial attachment for Orthodox practices?

The question, so put, can therefore have but one
answer. Nor, as a matter of policy, is the suggested
step free from unpleasant complications. It is necessary to remember that the leaders of Orthodoxy insist,
as is their right, that the civil decree, though binding, must be validated by a supplementary religious
divorce, if the remarriage of either party is to be
within the law. To be sure, we are not bound by this
insistence. We are at liberty to dispense with this
provision of the law. Yet, were we to adopt the proposal of the correspondent and proceed to issue this sort
of "indulgence" to all comers, as a salve to their tender consciences, we would justly be condemned for the
unwarranted attempt to interfere with the proper enforcement of an Orthodox discipline.

The proposal is neither sound in principle nor safe
in practice and cannot receive the endorsement of the
Committee.

Israel Bettan

162. REFORM JUDAISM AND DIVORCE
(Vol. XC, 1980, pp. 84-86)

QUESTION: What is the traditional Jewish attitude
toward divorce? What is the Reform attitude toward
divorce? Is a **Get** necessary before remarriage can
occur?

ANSWER: Judaism looks upon divorce with sadness (Git.
90b; San. 22a), but recognizes that it might occur. It
makes divorce easy and simple when the parties are no
longer compatible, in keeping with the Biblical statement (Deut. 24:1-2). According to the Talmud, divorce
could be given by a man for virtually any reason, even
the most minor one (Git. 90a). This was subsequently
restricted according to the decree of Rabbenu Gershom
(Finkelstein, **Jewish Self-Government in the Middle Ages**,
pp. 29ff; **Shulchan Aruch**, Even Ha-ezer 119.6). A divorce always originated with the husband, and the wife
accepted the document. A court could force the husband
to give a divorce, and a man might be punished and im-

prisoned for his refusal to give a divorce; this remains
true in modern Israel.   If he remains unwilling after
punishment, nothing further can be done (B.B. 48a; **Yad,**
Hil. Erusin 2:20; Amram, **Jewish Law of Divorce,** pp.
57ff; Schereschewsky, **Dinei Mishpacha,** 285ff).   There
are also certain circumstances under which a court may
demand a divorce, although neither one of the parties
involved has requested it.   The detailed reasons for a
divorce have been codified in the various early codes
and in the **Shulchan Aruch,** Even Ha-ezer (1.3; 11.1;
39.4; 70.3; 76.11; 115.4-5; 134; 154.1-7, etc.).   The
actual procedure and the document of divorce have been
surrounded by many restrictions in order to ensure their
complete validity.   The procedures have been prescribed
in greatest detail (**Shulchan Aruch,** Even Ha-ezer 119ff).
The various problem areas have been treated extensively
by Rabbinic law; for example, the mental incapacity of
the husband or wife, the disappearance of the husband,
or his presumed death.   In these instances and in ordinary divorce, Orthodox law has found itself in a difficult position for only the man can actually give a
divorce, and if he is unwilling or unavailable there is
little that can be done.

As divorce proceedings frequently involve a great
deal of bitterness, the husband may not be willing to
provide a religious divorce (**Get**) along with the civil
divorce unless a large payment or some other concessions
are made.   Sometimes a religious divorce is stipulated
as part of the arrangement in a secular divorce.   The
Conservative Movement has sought to remove itself from
this predicament by including a special statement in its
marriage document.   It provides for authority of a rabbinic court to grant a divorce in cases where the husband is unwilling to do so or if he becomes unavailable
(Isaac Klein, **A Guide to Jewish Religious Practice,** p.
498).   This kind of ante-nuptial agreement, as well as
other possible solutions, have been suggested by various
traditional scholars (Freimann, **Seder Kiddushin Venisu-
in;** Berkovits, **Tenai Benisu-in Uveget**), but they have
met only strong opposition among other Orthodox authorities.

The limitations of the Orthodox procedure for
granting a divorce are, therefore, quite clear.   In
theory, divorce should be easy to obtain; in practice,
the stipulation that only a male may initiate the proceedings, the lack of enforcing power of the Jewish
court, and the many details necessary for the procedure,
make the **Get** virtually unobtainable for many individuals.

The Reform Movement has concerned itself with the
problems of both marriage and divorce since its inception.   The matter was raised at the Paris Sanhedrin in

1806, when it was asked whether divorce was allowed and whether civil divorce would be recognized. It was clearly stated that a religious divorce would only be given if a valid civil divorce had preceded it (M.D. Tama [Kirwan tr.], **Transactions of the Parisian Sanhedrin**, 1807, pp. 152ff). This statement weakened the status of religious divorce, although that was not the intent of the respondents. The Brunswick Conference of 1844 appointed a committee to look into all of the questions connected with marriage and divorce. They reaffirmed the Paris statement that marriage and divorce were subject not only to Jewish law, but to the laws of the land in which Jews reside. Although various reports and motions were presented to the rabbinic conference which was held in Breslau in 1846, as well as to that of Leipzig in 1869, none of these resulted in any definite actions. In 1871, in Augsburg, another commission was appointed to study the matter and to bring definite recommendations to a further meeting (CCAR **Yearbook**, vols. I, II, III). Holdheim had earlier suggested that divorce be eliminated entirely from the set of Jewish proceedings and that civil divorce simply be accepted (Holdheim, **Ueber die Autonomie der Rabbinen**, pp. 159ff). This was the point of view accepted by the Philadelphia Conference of 1869, with only Sonnenschein and Mielziner expressing the sentiment that the **Get** should not be entirely abolished, but should be modified in some form (Mielziner, **The Jewish Law of Marriage and Divorce**, p. 135)--a view also held by Geiger (S.D. Temkin, **The New World of Reform**, p. 61). The resolution of the Philadelphia Conference remained somewhat unclear, as it permitted the rabbinic court to look into the decree of the civil court and reject some grounds for divorce.

The discussion of divorce continued at later rabbinic conferences, but without any formal action being taken. Generally, the civil decree was simply accepted (CCAR **Yearbook**, vol. 23, p. 154; Freehof, **Reform Jewish Practice**, vol. I, p. 106). One might say that this is in keeping with at least one Talmudic decision, as quoted by Ezekiel Landau when he states that the **Get** is really a matter of civil law (**Dinei Mamonot** in **Noda BiYehuda** II, Even Ha-ezer 114, based on Yev. 122b). Kaufmann Kohler, in his discussion of the problem of marriage and divorce and their relationship to civil laws, recommended that civil divorce be recognized as long as the grounds for such divorce were in consonance with those provided by previous rabbinic tradition (CCAR **Yearbook**, vol. 25, pp. 376ff). His recommendations were heard by the Conference, but not accepted in any formal manner.

Technically, of course, the child of a woman (and possibly a man) who has remarried without prior reli-

gious divorce would be considered illegitimate (**Mamzer**).
Such a child would, according to Orthodox law, be considered unlawful, and akin to one born of incestuous or
adulterous relationship (Mishna, Kid. III.12; **Yad**, 49a;
Shulchan Aruch, Even Ha-ezer 4.2). This was the attitude taken toward Karaites until recently. In fact,
however, there is nothing that Reform or Conservative
Jews can do to avoid this possible predicament. It does
not matter to the Orthodox authorities whether we simply
recognize civil divorce or proceed to initiate our own
form of **Get**. The latter is also not recognized by them.

The entire matter of divorce has come up a number
of times again more recently. Several Canadian congregations have decided that they would provide a **Get** in a
somewhat modified form, as have the Reform (not the
Liberal) congregations of Great Britain. Petuchowsky
has suggested that an appropriate **Get** be instituted by
the Reform Movement in keeping with the spirit of Jewish
tradition, i.e., both the consecration of marriage and
its dissolution should have religious forms. Others
have stressed the psychological value of a religious
divorce.

At the present time, the Central Conference of
American Rabbis makes no provision for a religious divorce and civil divorce is recognized as dissolving a
marriage by most Reform rabbis.

Walter Jacob

See also:

S.B. Freehof, "Divorce for a Doubtful   Marriage,"
     Contemporary Reform Responsa, pp. 82ff).

163. DIVORCE OF INSANE HUSBAND
(Vol. XXIX, 1919, pp. 88-94)

QUESTION: The following letter was received from a
rabbi in England:

I should be obliged to you if you could give
me an opinion concerning the giving of a **Get**
to a Jewish woman whose husband has been confined in a lunatic asylum for more than ten
years, and cannot recover sanity, according to
the diagnosis of the medical superintendent.
The woman would only consider herself free to

marry again if she could receive a **Get**, and
her husband is quite incapable of doing so.
The parties were married in Poland according
to the Jewish rite, and not before a secular
registrar, as the case would be in England.

ANSWER:

Incompetency of the Insane

Rabbinic law considers **Cheresh, Shoteh,** and **Katan**
--the deaf mute, the insane, and the minor--as incompetent to act in any case in which civil or religious law
requires responsibility. This principle is found in numerous places in the Talmud and in later Rabbinic literature, of which merely the following passages shall be
indicated: Mishna, Teruma 1.2 (and see remarks of **Tosafot Yom Tov**); **Shulchan Aruch,** Choshen Mishpat, 35.8,10;
and the remark of Joseph Habiba, in his commentary on
Alfasi, **Nimukei Yosef** ad Bava Kama 9b (Alfasi, ed. Vienna, 1805, fol. 5b): "**Cheresh, shoteh vekatan-la benei
de-a ninhu.**"

The Special Case of Divorce

The mishna Gittin 67b teaches: "If one was seized
by **cardiacus** and said, 'Write a **Get** for my wife,' his
statement has no legal force.... If he lost his speech
and people said to him, 'Shall we write a **Get** for your
wife?' and he nodded assent, he should be examined three
times; if he answered properly yes and no, the **Get** might
be written and handed [to the wife]." The word **cardiacus** is explained by Rashi, who follows the Gemara in
this case, as a demonic obsession, curiously ascribed to
overindulgence in grape juice. Maimonides, in his commentary on the Mishna (**l.c.**), gives the correct interpretation: **Cardiacus** is a disease which results from the
clogging of the cells of the brain and causes disturbance of the mind. It is a kind of falling sickness.
This is etymologically correct, the **cardiacus** (an abbre-
viation of **Morbus Cardiacus**) is perhaps used in medieval
medical literature for all forms of apoplexy (see
Preuss, **Biblische-Talmudische Medizin,** etc., pp. 368-
369, Berlin, 1917). Another passage in the Mishna
(Yevamot 112b) says: "If a man married while in the full
possession of his senses, and afterwards became deaf,
mute or insane, he can never divorce his wife...for a
man cannot divorce his wife except by an act of free
will." The Gemara in the discussion draws a distinction
in the case of a man who has lucid intervals ("**Itim
chalim, itim shoteh**") and declares that if he remained

lucid during the whole time of the procedure of issuing
Get, the divorce is valid.

The two Talmudic passages just cited are practically embodied in the codes of law (Shulchan Aruch, Even
Ha-ezer 121.1-6), and it is unnecessary to repeat the
text verbatim. It, therefore, may be laid down as the
Jewish law that a man who becomes insane after his marriage can never divorce his wife.

Two cases, found in the Responsa literature and
having a bearing on this subject, will be quoted.
Menachem Mendel Krochmal (c. 1600-1661) deals with the
case of a deaf mute who wishes to divorce his wife, and,
after consultation with Yom Tov Lipman Heller (1579-
1654), the famous author of Tosafot Yom Tov, he permits
the divorce with a modification of the usual procedure
(Tsemach Tsedek, no. 68). There is, however, in this
case, a considerable difference, inasmuch as the man was
a deaf mute at the time that he married, and the divorce
is in such case permissible according to the law of the
mishna quoted (Yevamot 112b). In addition, while the
law considers the deaf mute incompetent, the man in this
case is intelligent, having supported himself as a tai-
lor for years.

Another case, somewhat more closely resembling
ours, gave rise to a whole literature. Isaac Neuburg
married Leah Gunzenhausen in Mannheim, August 13, 1766,
and a few days later deserted his wife under peculiar
conditions, which were considered a clear evidence of
insanity. On August 26, 1766, he appeared before Israel
Lipschitz, Rabbi of Cleve, and asked for a divorce,
which the rabbi granted. The rabbis of Mannheim, where
a rabbinical college of ten rabbis--the Lemle Moses
Klausstiftung--existed, declared the Get invalid on the
ground that the man was mentally incompetent.[1] The rabbinate of Frankfurt am Main supported this view, and
Simon Copenhagen[2] published the arguments in a book
entitled Or Hayashar (Amsterdam, 1769). Israel Lip-

---

[1] Unna, The Lemle Moses Klausstiftung, Frankfurt a. M.,
1908-1909.

[2] Simon Copenhagen was a champion of Orthodoxy for his
time. In his Bechi Neharot (Amsterdam, 1784), which is
a description of a devastating flood in the Rhine
valley, he alludes to Herz Ullman of Mayence, who had
written a textbook of metaphysics, Chochmat Hashorashim
(The Hague, 1781), with the pun: "Haba litama, potechin
lo pitcho shel ulama." It is also interesting to learn
that the Copenhagen's patron who bore the expense of the
publication was Baruch Simon Mergentheim, the
grandfather of Ludwig Boerne (Roest, Katalog der
Rosenthalischen Bibliothek, Anhang, p. 49, no. 281).

schitz published his side in another book, **Or Yisra-el**
(Cleve, 1770), in which he presented his argument and
letters of most of the leading rabbis of his day who
sided with him. As is always the case in such contro-
versies, those who were not convinced from the start
remained unconvinced. Marcus Horovitz (1844-1909), as
Rabbi of Frankfurt am Main, in his history of the Frankfurt rabbinate, upholds the authority of his predecessors, while Judah Lubetzki (1850-1910), not bound by
such sentiments, indignantly exclaims, "What shall we
say, if a man in our generation dares to challenge the
authority of all the luminaries of Israel on whose words
our lives depend? Indeed, one who disputes their authority disputes the authority of the Almighty" (**Bidkei
Batim**, p. 44b, Paris, 1896). The case is not applicable
to our question, for in the controversy between Israel
Lipschitz and his opponents everything depended on the
question, whether Isaac Neuburg was sane, which Lipschitz affirmed, while his opponents denied it. If it
could be proven that Neuburg was insane, Lipschitz would
admit that the **Get** was not valid.

Conclusion: We, therefore, must arrive at the
conclusion that from the point of view of the strict
Rabbinic law, an insane man such as the one described in
the question cannot divorce his wife, and that the latter cannot marry during the lifetime of her husband.

It is different when we consider the higher principles of Rabbinic law, recognized even by the most rigorous authorities. One of these principles is the often-
repeated Talmudic rule, based on the Scriptural passage,
"Her ways are ways of pleasantness" (Prov. 3:17) that
legal decisions must be in harmony with the ideas of
humanity (Yer. Eruvin 20b, 24c-d; Yevamot 15a, 87b),
with propriety and common sense (Gittin 59b; see Abraham
Danziger, 1749-1780, one of the most rigorous authorities of the age in **Bidkei Batim** 3.19), and even with
aesthetics (Sukka, 32a-b; see also Isaiah Horowitz, c.
1560-1630, in **Shalah**, fol. 383a). The special application of this principle ("**Deracheiha darchei no-am**") to
matrimonial laws shall be presented later.

The Right to Change and to Interrupt the Law
in Accordance with the Needs of the Age

While it has to be admitted that the general principle of Rabbinic legislation is strictly to apply the
law as laid down by the older authorities, instances are
not missing in which the opposite principle is proclaimed, i.e., that changed conditions demand a liberal
application of the law. A Talmudic agada (Yoma 69b)
states that the prophets altered some of the institutions of Moses. Wherein the question is asked: How

could they set aside the authority of Moses? And the answer is given: They knew that in the eyes of God, truth stands higher than authority. This and other passages are quoted by Menahem di Lonzano (16th century, **Shetei Yadot**, Venice, 1618, ch. IV) and by Hirsch Katzenellenbogen (1796-1868) in his preface to his **Netivot Olam** (Wilna, 1822).

Estori Farhi of France, 14th century, the pioneer of Palestinian archeology among the Jews, says in the **Kaftor Vaferach**, ch. IV, p. 67, Jerusalem 1897: "The leaders and scholars of every generation have the right to abolish a prohibition when they become convinced that the reason for the prohibition has ceased to exist."

Mordecai ben Hillel Hakohen of Nuremberg, 13th century, one of the most rigorous authorities of his age, quotes Eliezer of Verdun, 12th century, as saying: "The Rabbis of the Talmud have empowered the conscientious and learned men of every generation to interpret the law in its application to the needs of their time" (Mordecai, Yevamot, ch. 16, sec. 91, fol. 56c, cd. Vienna, 1805). This view is of great importance to our question, as it is applied to a question of matrimonial law.

Joseph Caro, 1488-1575, the author of **Shulchan Aruch** who may be counted among the strictest upholders of authority, decides that Jews who occupy positions at the court may dress like non-Jews, contrary to the provisions of the law (**Sifra** ad Lev. 18:3; Yoreh De-a 178), because this adds to their dignity, which enables them to be benefactors of their people (**Kesef Mishneh** to Maim., Avoda Zara 11.3). Chayyim Benveniste of Constantinople (c. 1600-1673), an industrious compiler of notes on the code of Jacob ben Asher, declares without any attempt at apology that the Rabbinic law, prohibiting that a single man be a teacher (Kiddushin 82a), has become obsolete by universal disregard (**Keneset Hagedola**, Yoreh De-a 245, quoted by Elijah Hazan, Chief Rabbi of Alexandria, 1845-1908, **Ta-alumot Lev**, p. 18b, Leghorn, 1879). Isaac Elhanan Spector, Rabbi of Kovna (1817-1896), universally regarded as the greatest authority among the Russian rabbis of his age, allowed work to be done in the vineyards of the Palestinian colonists by non-Jews in the Sabbatical year in clear contradiction to the Mosaic law (Lev. 25:4), on the ground that otherwise the colonization would be a failure (**Luach Achi-asaf** IV, 293, Warsaw, 1896).

Another advocate of colonization in Palestine may properly be mentioned in this connection. Hirsch Kalischer (1795-1874) was guided by what is now being called "Kultur-Zionism" in the sense in which he, a strictly Orthodox Talmudist, understood it. Judaism, which suffered constant losses from the inroads made by political emancipation and secular education was to obtain a homeland where Orthodox practices and Jewish studies would be either custom or law of the land. For this purpose Kalischer advocated the reintroduction of sacrifices on Mount Moriah with the permission of the Sultan. He proved from the **Zohar** that this was necessary as the first of the four stages of the Messianic Kingdom (see his **Derishat Tsi-yon**, Lyck, 1862). So, his Orthodoxy is above all suspicion. Yet in a correspondence with Israel Hildesheimer, he asserts boldly, and as a matter of course which requires no further proof, that the laws regulating the social contact and business relations with non-Jews, found in the **Shulchan Aruch** (Yoreh De-a 153-156), are obsolete, because the laws are based on the presumption that the non-Jews are uncivilized and immoral. It is noteworthy that these views were expressed in a private correspondence and therefore not presented as an apology for the consumption of the non-Jewish world, as may have been the case with the remarks frequently found on the title page of a rabbinical work, that **Akum** does not include Christians. It is also noteworthy that Hildesheimer, who, in the course of the correspondence hurls sneering invectives against the Reform Rabbiner, Einsegnung, etc., and especially against any attempt to place philosophy above religious authority, has no objection to these views, and thus admits that parts of the **Shulchan Aruch** have become antiquated (see **Festschrift zum vierzigjaehrigen Amtsjubilaeum des...Dr. Solomon Carlebach**, pp. 263-307, Berlin, 1910, esp. p. 286).

The plain law of the Mishna (Ta-anit 19a), that in times of an epidemic public fasts shall be held, is set aside by Abraham Gombiner of Kalisch (17th century), on the ground that the weakening of vitality would be dangerous (**Notes on Shulchan Aruch**, Orach Chayim, 576.2). This view is upheld by Chayyim Joseph David Azulai (1723-1806), a famous Palestinian scholar of his age (**Birkei Yosef**, 576.4), and--which is highly important-- by Hillel Lichtenstein (1815-1891), the representative of the most eccentric Orthodoxy in the school of Moses Sofer (**Teshuvot Beit Hillel**, p. 51c, Szatmar, 1908). Moses Isserles (c. 1520-1572), whose notes to the **Shulchan Aruch** are a compilation of the most rigorous practices--often recommended with such phrases as "God will bless one who conforms with the rigorous practice"-- allows Jews to assist in extinguishing a fire on the Sabbath because by refusing to do so they would risk violence at the hands of the mob (Orach Chayim 334.26). This is quoted with approval by Ishmael Hakohen (Laudadio Sacerdoti), c. 1730-1811, Rabbi of Mantua, one of the last great teachers of Halacha in Italy (**Zera Emet**, 1, 44, Leghorn, 1786).

The examples cited, which could be almost indefinitely multiplied, prove beyond doubt that the most rigorous authorities admit that laws of the Bible and Talmud may become obsolete. Another series of quotations will prove that humanitarian regard frequently suggested the application of this principle to matrimonial laws, which, by stringent interpretation, would work hardship on women.

Some of the most burdensome laws imposing hardship on women are those that compel a childless widow to be married to her brother-in-law (**Yibum**; see Deut. 25:5-10), or be released by the ceremony of **Chalitsa**, which, to modern aesthetic feeling, is highly objectionable, and often delivers the woman helplessly to the extortion of an unscrupulous man. In the passages quoted above (Yevamot 15a, 87b), the Talmud limits these obligations on the ground of the principle that "the ways of the Torah must be ways of pleasantness." The Geonim, as the leaders of the Babylonian school from the seventh to the eleventh century are called, though usually guided by belief in authority, permit the release from a brother-in-law who is an apostate without **Chalitsa**, on the ground that "the widow would be chained forever" (Resp. **Sha-arei Tsedek** II, no. 19). Moses Maimonides (1135-1205) sets aside certain decisions of the Geonim in laws of marriage and Levirate (**Yibum**) on the grounds of unreasonable hardship ("**Devarim rechokim be-einai me-od midrachei hora-a**," **Mishneh Torah**, Gerushin 10.19). The opinion of Eliezer of Verdun, quoted above, refers to another law which entails considerable hardship on a widow. Rabbinic law required the identification of the body as proof of death, and consequently the widow of a man lost at sea, or even drowned in a river ("**Mayim she-ein lahem sof**") cannot marry again, if the body was not recovered (Yevamot 121a; Even Ha-ezer 17.32). It was with reference to such a case that R. Eliezer of Verdun declared that the rabbis should decide such a case according to the conditions of the time. And it is highly remarkable that Isaac Elhanan Spector (quoted above in his decision on the Sabbatical year) allowed the widow of a man who was a passenger on a ship lost at sea, to marry again on the ground of the opinion that the Talmudic law figured on the possibility that such a man might have saved himself on a lonely island from where he could not communicate with his family, although in our days of general postal, telegraph, and steamship connections such an eventuality was out of the question (**Ein Yitschak**, no. 22, p. 232, Wilna, 1888)

Most of the cases quoted are so complicated that a complete presentation would necessitate the disregard of all reasonable space limits. Therefore, in the cases to be quoted, as in those already quoted, only the essential part (namely, the principle of placing moral consideration above the letter of the law) is presented. In the case of a man who deserted his wife on the ground of disobedience (**Moredet**), Joseph Colon, 15th century, declares that the rights of women must be protected against the arbitrary action of the man (Resp. 57). More in line with the question under consideration is the opinion of Joshua Falk Cohen (c. 1550-1617), that the laws regarding the legal status of the deaf mute have to be interpreted with proper regard for the future of the woman in case of divorce (**Perisha**, commentary on **Tur**, Choshen Mishpat "**Bimkom tsorech mishum igun**," sec. 235).

Another law which, while originally conceived for the benefit of an orphan child, works considerable hardship on a woman, prescribes that a woman cannot remarry until her child born of a former husband is two years old (**Meineket chavero**; Yevamot 42a; Even Ha-ezer 13.11). The medieval legal literature is full of exceptions, all based on the principle that a rigorous application of the law might ruin the future of the widow, of a divorced woman, and, above all, of the mother of an illegitimate child, who thus might be deprived of her only chance to reform. Significant in this respect is the decision of Jacob Joshua, Rabbi of Frankfurt am Main, 1680-1756, who, while deploring the laxity in such decisions, allows a woman to marry before the lapse of this period, for otherwise the engagement might be broken ("**Kedei shelo lehafrid bein hadevekim**," see **Benei Yehoshua**, Ketubot, no. 150). The same reason is given by Moses Isserles, characterized above as an extreme rigorist for having performed a marriage ceremony on the Sabbath (Resp. 124). The authority of one of the bitterest antagonists to the Reform movement may be cited in conclusion. Mordecai Benet (1753-1829) rules in a case when a woman had married before her child of a former marriage was two years old that the couple should not be compelled to separate, as the law would require, because divorce is objectionable, especially in our times when divorce cases are subject to secular legislation: "**Kasheh gerushin bifrat bazeman hazeh mipenei dina demalchuta**" (Resp. **Har Hamor**, p. 20b, Vienna, 1862).

Conclusion

Humanity and regard for the conditions of the time suggest a liberal interpretation of the law. Whereas in the case of the marriage of the deaf mute, the practice, as stated by Menahem Mendel Krochmal (Resp. **Tsemach Tsedek**, no. 77) is that a relative of the bridegroom shall act as his interpreter; and whereas in the case of the divorce by a deaf mute, besides the regular **Get** which the husband hands to the wife, a special act recorded by the **Beit Din** states the fact (reported by Lipman Heller as the practice of the Cracow congregation dating from R. Meshulam Feibish, 16th century, **ibid.**, 68)--so in this case the **Beit Din** could appoint a guardian for the insane man, who would hand the **Get** to the woman, and state the facts in a document preserved in the archives of the **Beit Din** and published in the Jewish press.

From the point of view of liberal Judaism in America, the question was decided by the Philadelphia conference of 1869, which recognized--and rightly so--the **Get** as rabbinic civil law, and therefore recognized also the right of the courts of a civilized country to grant divorce just as the probate court deals with an estate, while in former centuries the Rabbis acted in such cases.

G. Deutsch

164. VALIDITY OF RABBINICAL OPINIONS
(Vol. XLII, 1932, pp. 82-84)

QUESTION: Is it true that a first opinion is legally and ethically binding on the one who asks a rabbinic authority? In other words, is there no appeal to one of equal or superior standing?

ANSWER: Your question would require a lengthy and elaborate discussion into which I cannot enter now, but may do so at some future time. For the present, I will only briefly state that to a certain degree the first opinion given by any rabbinical authority is ethically binding upon the one who consulted the rabbinical authority. For if he had no confidence in his rabbi, he should not have turned to him with his question. The Talmudic ethical rule is as follows: A person who received from the rabbi an opinion that a certain thing or act is forbidden should not go around to other rabbis seeking to find one who would permit it. But if he does receive two conflicting opinions--one declaring it prohibited and the other permitted--he should follow the opinion of the teacher who is older in years and greater in knowledge and wisdom. If they be equal, then if the question involves merely rabbinical decrees, he may follow the more lenient decision (Avoda Zara 7a).

Likewise, one rabbi should not lightly declare permitted what his colleague prohibited or vice versa (Berachot 63b, Nidda 20b). But when he feels confident that his own contrary opinion is correct--especially when he believes himself to be in possession of better information, a reliable tradition, or an established precedent in support of his opinion--he may render an opinion contrary to that of his colleague (Chulin 49a). All this is only from the ethical standpoint, or, if you wish, from the standpoint of professional ethics among the rabbis in questions that are matters of opinion.

Legally, however, the first opinion or decision given by any authority is not binding on anyone, if other authorities disagree on the basis of what they consider a more correct interpretation of the law. In Temple times there was a final appeal to the highest court in Jerusalem (Mishna, Sanhedrin 11.2; Tosefta, Sanhedrin 7.1). After the Temple was destroyed, there was no authoritatively established "highest court" in Jewish law. Hence, we cannot speak of "appeal." But a person who has some reason to think that a decision rendered by any rabbi is not correct, may present the case before another authority who might prove--on the basis of reliable authorities and correct interpretation of the statutes--that the former decision is wrong. In that case the previous decision is, of course, void. In some instances, depending on the nature of the mistake involved and on the official standing of the one who made it, the first authority who gave the wrong decision may even be liable to pay damages caused by his decision.

Jacob Z. Lauterbach

See also:

Introduction to this volume.
S.B. Freehof, "Introduction," **Reform Responsa**, pp. 3ff.
Rabbinic Authority, New York: CCAR Press, 1982.

165. RABBINICAL FEES AND SALARIES
(Vol. LXXVI, 1966, pp. 76-79)

QUESTION: A congregation had decided that whatever fees a rabbi receives from weddings and funerals should be turned over to the congregation. It was

assumed that the salary would be raised to make up
for the loss of fees, and that it is more dignified
for the rabbi to receive only a salary and no fees
from individual members. The question is asked by
a colleague as to whether this deprecation of fees
is in accordance with the ethics of the Jewish
legal tradition, and whether it would be wrong on
his part to ask to have the decision reconsidered.

ANSWER: The question of fees and salaries and the
relation between them has been an ongoing discussion in
Jewish law, almost from the beginning. The question
grew complex and needed constant reanalysis and redefi-
nition. To give a general picture of how widespread the
discussion was, we need only mention a number of references in the law in which a detailed analysis of the
question was deemed necessary.

There are full discussions of this question, for
example, in the following: a series of responsa by Simon
ben Zemach Duran, from 142-148, and his long commentary
to the **Ethics of the Fathers**, IV.5; Joseph Caro in his
Kesef Mishneh to the **Yad** (Hil. Talmud Torah, ch. III);
Moses Isserles in the **Shulchan Aruch**, Yoreh De-a 246.21,
also, to Even Ha-ezer 154.21; also, **Tosafot Yom Tov** (Yom
Tov Lipmann Heller) to Mishna, Bechorot IV.6. Then
there are the responsa by Joel Sirkes (**Bach,** #52); Meir
Eisenstadt (**Panim Me-irot,** I.79); Moses Sofer in his
responsa (Choshen Mishpat, 164).

Such a continued and elaborate discussion reveals
the fact that the question of fees and salaries is one
which has undergone considerable evolution as the rabbinate gradually evolved, becoming first a special skill
and then a full-time profession.

Originally no fees and no salary were deemed to be
justified or permissive for any of the functions which
we now look upon as the essential part of the rabbinate,
namely, for teaching the Torah, for making decisions on
the basis of Jewish law, for officiating at weddings or
at divorces, etc. There was, first of all, the general
ethical objection to getting any material benefit from
the study of the Torah, as is stated in the **Ethics of
the Fathers**: "Not to make worldly use of the Crown of
the Torah" (I.13), or, "Not to make it a spade to dig
with" (IV.5). The study of the Torah was a religious
duty incumbent upon every Jew (see Maimonides in Hilchot
Talmud Torah); therefore, how could a person take pay
for pursuing that divine mandate? Besides the duty to
study, there was also a duty to teach the Torah. It was
especially incumbent upon a father to teach his own
child the Torah. In general, teaching of the Torah to
anybody was a religious duty for which no pay should be

accepted. The Talmud, in Nedarim 37a (basing its comment upon the verse in Deut. 4:14, where Moses says: "And God commanded me to teach you"), elaborates on Moses' statement as follows: "God said to me, 'Just as I, the Lord, taught thee without pay (**bechinam**) so thou teach without pay.'"

As for the making of legal decisions, that too was deemed to be a religious duty ("And they shall judge the people," Deut. 16:18). Therefore, the Mishna in Bechorot IV.6 says: "If a man takes pay for making a legal decision, all his legal decisions thereby become void." On the basis of these various opinions for complete "amateur standing," one can understand the stern statement of Obadiah Bartenura in his commentary to this Mishna, in which he says that he was shocked at the rabbis in Germany who took fees for officiating at a divorce proceeding and also at the witnesses who took fees for signing the divorce document (the Mishna also prohibits witnesses from taking fees).

Nevertheless, even in the Talmud, as the need for special training grew, this general prohibition was mitigated step by step. A teacher could be engaged for pay to teach children. Yet could he be permitted to receive pay when the duty of teaching was religiously incumbent upon him? The Talmud says that teachers of children were paid not actually for the teaching of the Torah (which was their religious duty), but for teaching the **Pisuk Hate-amim**, the punctuation and accents, etc., which they were not required to teach (Nedarim 37a). Rav says that the teacher is paid for taking care of the children, i.e., not directly for teaching the Torah (cf. Rashi, **ad loc.**). The **Tosafot** to Bechorot 29a say that as for our present-day custom of receiving pay for the teaching of the Torah, it applies only to one who has no other means of support; or even if he does have other means of support, he is paid for the time that he is taking away from his other business. The comment of the **Tosafot** has in mind the fact that so many of the rabbis in Talmudic times were working men and made their living from their labor and not from teaching the Torah (and in the time of the **Tosafot**, they were business men).

As for taking pay for making legal decisions, the law as such is embodied in the **Shulchan Aruch** (Choshen Mishpat 9.5), namely, that if one takes pay for judging, all his decisions are void; but Caro himself adds that the judge may take pay for the time that he has taken away from his other business. This brief statement of his is more elaborately dealt with in his **Kesef Mishneh** to the **Yad** (Hil. Talmud Torah, III.11), in which he says that a man may take support from the community for all these functions (teaching, judging, etc.), if he has no other means of support; and then he adds that since the time of the Rambam the custom is for rabbis to take salaries, and he justifies this situation by the statement of the **Tosafot** mentioned above.

Caro's statement as to the changes which have occurred since the time of the Rambam are to be understood in the light of the series of responsa 142-148 of Simon ben Zemach Duran and his commentary to **Ethics of the Fathers**, IV.5. Duran, who formerly made his living as a physician, had to flee from the Belearic Islands, which were part of Spain, during the persecutions of 1396. He could no longer practice his profession in Algiers, where he was a refugee, and was forced to take a salary from the congregation. He reviews all the relevant literature to justify his taking the salary.

As for those who took pay for deciding legal questions, a distinction was made between those who were occasional judges and those who were appointed to devote all their time to judging, i.e., professionals (**Tosafot Yom Tov** to Bechorot IV.6). With regard to divorces, Isserles says (Even Ha-ezer 154.2) that the arrangements of divorces are not to be classified as legal decisions and therefore no fees are justified.

The fact of the matter is that it simply became necessary to professionalize the rabbinate, and so Isserles (with reference to the responsa of Simon ben Zemach Duran) simply says: "Therefore it has become the custom in all places that the rabbi of the city has income and support from the community in order that he need not engage in other work."

However, the memory of the older tenor of the law (before the rabbinate became a profession) still remained, and the statement is often made by the scholars, that if a person could afford to serve as a rabbi without pay, that would be the ideal situation. It is rather touching to read the responsum of Moses Sofer (Choshen Mishpat 160). A pupil of his had asked whether to accept a rabbinical position with salary, and his teacher answers: "Alas, I am suspect in this matter" (i.e., I take a salary). And then he refers to all the above opinions now permitting it.

As to the difference between fees or salary, there is really no choice as to which would be deemed worthier or more ethical. The older law objected to both. Yet, as can be seen from the arguments of Duran, the paying of a regular salary developed later than the receiving of separate fees for specific services. He bases his justification for accepting a salary (hitherto unprecedented) upon the fact that rabbis have "always" received "fees." But this was to be expected as a natural evolution: first, separate fees were justified, and then the custom of a salary was established. So there is really no historical preference for one form of income over the other. In fact, in later centuries, the rabbinical fees are considered to be the legal prerogative of the rabbi. Moses Sofer in his responsa (Yoreh De-a 230) refers to a responsum by Isserlein (three centuries earlier) in which Isserlein deprecates the acceptance of wedding fees. Moses Sofer says that since the days of Isserlein the situation of the rabbinate has changed; he is now engaged by the community (professionally) and the fees are an integral part of his income (cf. fuller discussion in the CCAR Yearbook, vol. LXV, pp. 86-87).

Of course, a congregation and a rabbi have the right to agree as to the sort of emolument the rabbi should receive. There can be no legal objection to a contract confining the rabbi to one class of income or the other. If the congregation and the rabbi have agreed at the beginning of the rabbi's term that he should not keep the fees, they have the right to make such an agreement. But if the rabbi would like to have the matter reopened and the agreement changed so that he be permitted to accept fees, there can be no objection in Jewish law to such efforts. Both salaries and fees have equal standing in the law, except perhaps that fees arose earlier than regular salary. Both were equally frowned upon at the beginning, and both became acceptable as rabbinical duties became specialized and professional.

Solomon B. Freehof

See also:

"Resolution," CCAR Yearbook, vol. 44, 1934, p. 98; vol. 50, 1940, p. 98; vol. 51, 1941, p. 142; vol. 56, 1946, p. 103; vol. 76, 1966, pp. 100ff.

166. GAMES OF CHANCE IN CONNECTION WITH FUNDRAISING
(Vol. XLVI, 1936, p. 126)

QUESTION: Several organizations of our Temple are planning to raise a special fund for the erection of a school house adjoining our present building. One of the principal means they hope to use is a bazaar. That will involve certain gambling devices such as wheels of chance and other similar contrivances. They would like to know whether such measures are ethically permissible.

ANSWER: Legally, there is no objection. We can look
at the matter from the following aspect: the Jewish law,
while disqualifying a gambler from giving evidence in
lawsuits, stipulates that this applies only to professionals whose sole occupation is gambling (see Choshen
Mishpat, 34.16).   Moreover, although one lending money
on interest is debarred from being a witness (**ibid.**,
34.10), if he does so with monies belonging to orphans
whose guardian he is, he is not disqualified "because he
thinks he is doing a **mitzvah** in order to increase the
funds of the orphans" (**ibid.**, 34.11).

There is further the case, bearing more directly on
the subject of the question, of a respected Jew of Modena (Italy) who was in straitened circumstances and was
about to sell a very valuable **Sefer Torah**. The rabbi of
Modena, R. Ishmael Sacerdote (died 1811), a famous Talmudist and author of Responsa **Zera Emet** (3 volumes),
even issued a letter of recommendation for this scheme,
urging its furtherance as a "**mitzvah**" (see **Zera Emet**
III, no. 144).

However, "ethically" there are grounds for scruples, especially if the attractive features of the bazaar are advertised and brought to the notice of the
non-Jewish clergy. The **New York Times** (June 14, 1935),
for example, devoted a column to the report of a special
committee of the United Lutheran Synod of New York,
which strongly condemned games of chance at bazaars for
raising money for the support of Lutheran churches.
Such Jewish affairs, especially if much publicized, may
lower the respect for Judaism in the eyes of non-Jews.
Hence, discretion is advisable even from this angle
alone.

Jacob Mann and Committee

167.   JEWISH ATTITUDE TOWARD GAMBLING
(Vol. LXXXIX, 1979, p. 115)

QUESTION: Is it permissible for a synagogue to use
a lottery as a means of fund raising? What is the
Jewish attitude toward gambling? (Mrs. A.S., New
York)

ANSWER: It is clear that the early tradition saw professional gambling as sinful (**Midrash Tehilim** 26.7; **Yer.**
San. 23d).   Those who were engaged in gambling were
ineligible to serve as witnesses or as judges (San.

24b); yet it was never made a criminal offense. Every effort was made to help the compulsive gambler away from his vice. Those who had taken an oath to refrain from gambling were not allowed to abrogate it, no matter how difficult the circumstances (**Pachad Yitschak**, vol. 5, Cherem); some, however, felt that this was too difficult and that vows to avoid gambling should not be enforced. Responsa have been written on both sides of the question (Leo Landman, "Jewish Attitudes toward Gambling," **Jewish Quarterly Review**, vol. 58, pp. 302ff). A wide variety of communal ordinances have been enacted, but few proved successful (Adret **Responsa** II, 35; VII, 244, 270). Gamblers were even barred from synagogue honors and from being counted toward a **Minyan**. None of these strictures against professional gambling proved to be successful, and they are repeated century after century in the responsa literature.

Despite the views held against the professional gambler, occasional gambling was permitted, and ordinances against gambling were often lifted for Chanuka, Purim, and the intermediary days of Passover and Sukkot, as well as Rosh Chodesh (Leo Landman, **op. cit.**, p. 42). Chanuka was, in fact, known as the New Year of the gamblers (I. Rivkind, **Der Kampf Kegen Azart Schpielen bei Yiden**, pp. 29ff). Elsewhere it was suggested that card playing even be permitted on fast days so that the individual would not feel excessively hungry (Finkelstein, **Jewish Self-Government in the Middle Ages**, pp. 284, 291). Although rabbinic authorities frowned upon the playing of cards and gambling within a **Sukka**, they realized that some people would not sit in a **Sukka** unless they were permitted such entertainment, so they allowed it as well (Leo Landman, **op. cit.**, pp. 46ff). It is clear from all of this that gambling was permitted with some reluctance by the Rabbis. Yet a few rabbis also participated in various forms of gambling. Leo Landman's monograph in the **Jewish Quarterly Review**, his article in **Tradition**, and Rivkind's Yiddish book have discussed gambling in great detail, and shown the ebb and flow of the changing attitudes throughout the century.

Lotteries have also been discussed, and Jews seem to have been heavily involved in them in the 18th and 19th centuries, so major winnings were reported with approval in the responsa. One rabbi ruled that he who wins a lottery should recite the blessing "**Shehecheyanu**," as well as the blessing "**Hatov vehameitiv**," if he had won with a partner (B.D. Levin, **Shemen Sason**, p. 27). Landman also reported an incident in Bresova, Hungary, in which the congregation each year purchased lottery slips with excess funds from their budget. They inquired then whether the winnings would go back to the

general treasury or be divided equally among the members
of the **Kahal** (Landman, "Gambling in the Synagogue,"
Tradition, vol. 10, pp. 81ff).   Sacerdote permitted
lottery tickets to be sold in order to save a valuable
Sefer Torah for a synagogue (**Zera Emet**, vol. 3, #144).
There are also reports of rabbis winning considerable
sums (I. Rivkind, **op. cit.**, pp. 285ff).   It is clear
from all of these statements that a lottery was considered as legitimate entertainment, unlikely to lead to
compulsive gambling, and, therefore, it should not be
generally prohibited.

We must also ask whether our tradition was concern-
ed with the source of funds used for religious purposes.
Gifts of prostitutes and criminals were rejected in
Deuteronomy: "You shall not bring the hire of a harlot
or the price of a dog to the House of the Lord, your
God, for any vow" (Deut. 23:19).   The discussion in the
Talmud (Bava Kama 65b; Temura 29a) makes it clear that
the prohibition was restricted to harlotry and idolatry
or to the bringing of the actual object used in payment.
If that object had been changed to money or into another
object, it became acceptable.   This was the view of
Maimonides (**Yad**, Hil. Isurei Mizbeach IV.14).   This law
was subsequently applied to the synagogue (**Shulchan
Aruch**, Orach Chayim 153.21); Rabbenu Yeruham (14th century, **Toledot Adam VeChava**--Chava, 23.1) and Isserles
expressed concern over such funds being used for a Torah
or for synagogue lights.   In other words, funds from a
tainted source may be used to support a synagogue, and
it is incumbent upon **all** Jews to do whatever they can to
maintain the synagogue.   It would be wrong to deny this
right even to criminals, gamblers, etc., though they
should receive no recognition for their help (Isserles
to **Shulchan Aruch**, Yoreh De-a 249.13).

We may conclude that Jewish tradition has found it
impossible to prohibit gambling and has many concessions
in this regard; it would, however, not favor lotteries
or any other form of gambling as a regular means of
raising funds for the synagogue.   It is one thing to
accept the human frailty, but another to approve it or
to encourage it through the synagogue.   Although funds
from dubious sources may be accepted by a synagogue, it
would be wrong to make such funds a basis for synagogue
life.   We would, therefore, urge synagogues to refrain

from using gambling as a way of raising funds on a regular basis.

Walter Jacob, Chairman
Leonard S. Kravitz
Eugene J. Lipman
W. Gunther Plaut
Harry A. Roth
Rav A. Soloff
Bernard Zlotowitz

See also:

"Resolution," **CCAR Yearbook**, vol. 89, 1979.
S.B. Freehof, "Gambling for the Benefit of the Synagogue " **Current Reform Responsa**, pp. 56ff; "Occasional Gambling and State Lotteries," **Reform Responsa For Our Time**, pp. 229ff;
"Resolutions," Union of American Hebrew Congregations, 1957 and 1959.

168. CARD-PLAYING IN THE SOCIAL HALL OF THE TEMPLE
(Vol. LXV, 1955, pp. 91-92)

QUESTION: Some members of my congregation feel that there is nothing improper in playing a sociable game of cards, such as bridge or canasta, in the social hall of the Temple. Does the traditional law uphold their view?

ANSWER: The ancient rabbis, although they frowned upon any kind of unearned gain, were rather chary in the use of violent epithets. They branded a man as a **gambler** and barred his testimony from a court of law, if he derived his livelihood from a game of chance such as dice (Sanhedrin 24b). All other forms of play, insofar as they crowded out more serious employments, the Rabbis did little to encourage, but resorted to no ill-tempered language to condemn them.

In our time, there are rabbis who are inclined to dub a man **gambler** if he plays a game of cards. Yet, should the laity prevail over the clergy in this matter, would the impact of the triumph be felt in our moral life. Not at all!

Some congregations, it should be noted, encourage their members to play games at social gatherings, and

impose no restrictions on those who choose to play
cards. We have yet to hear that the officers of any
such congregation have found it necessary to curtail the
privilege because of abuse.

Israel Bettan

169. HOW SHOULD A LOAN IN FOREIGN (RUSSIAN) CURRENCY, EXCHANGED IN ANOTHER COUNTRY (UNITED STATES), BE REPAID?
(Vol. XXX, 1920, pp. 113-119)

From the Scriptural injunction: "Hear the causes
between your brethren, and judge righteously," Talmudic
judicial procedure derives a rule forbidding the court
to hear one party to a litigation in the absence of the
other party; and from another Scriptural dictum is derived that the one party should not unfold to the judge
his side of the controversy in the absence of his adver-
sary (Sanh. 7b; cf. Shev. 31a). Accordingly, the
greatest rabbinic authorities have always refrained from
expressing opinions, even in an academic way, on questions involving money, unless both parties to the cause
had clearly set forth their respective allegations (Solomon Luria, **Responsa**, Fuerth, 5528.24).

In view of those just and wise regulations it may
be deemed presumptuous on the part of even a recognized
judicial authority (**Mumcheh lerabim**)--and much more on
the part of one who, like myself, is not vested with
such authority--to venture a ruling in a case the parties to which are separated by land and sea, and, consequently, on the one-sided statement of facts affecting
money matters. However, it should be considered that,
in the present case, the novelty of having before me a
debtor who is anxious to be adjudged indebted to a
greater amount than his creditor is likely to consider
his due, proved an irresistible temptation to examine
the matter and to clarify his status according to Rabbinic law. Moreover, it should be remembered that just
because I am not vested with judicial authority, I am
not bound by those restrictive regulations.

Shortly before the outbreak of the World War,
Ephraim determined to emigrate from his native Russia to
America. Before his departure from home, his chum,
Manasseh, presented him with 300 rubles in Russian cur-
rency, saying, "Here are three hundred rubles. Please
accept them from me, and carry them to the United
States; and may He 'Who maketh poor and maketh rich'

prosper your way. Providence permitting, in the course
of the next year or two, I too shall come thither, and
then if you are able and your heart prompts you (I shall
never appear as your creditor, neither shall I ever
press you), you may repay me the loan, but without interest." Ephraim accepted the proffered bills, pocketed
them, and departed. Arrived in America, he exchanged
the Russian bills for $145 in American money, and God
blessed him in all his undertakings. In the meantime
the terrible war broke out, and prevented Manasseh from
crossing the ocean. He is still in Russia, while
Ephraim has for some time been anxious to repay his
indebtedness, but does not know how to cancel his debt,
for if he sent his friend an exchange for 300 rubles,
which would cost now about $15, that would represent
only about one-tenth of the amount he realized for the
Russian money he had taken from Manasseh; and, on the
other hand, if he should repay him the sum of $145, this
would be equal to about 3,000 rubles--ten times as much
as the original sum.

I have intently listened to Ephraim's recital and
pleas, and carefully pondered his sincere utterances and
his earnest mien. I became convinced that he was anxious to repay the kindness of his friend who stuck to
him closer than a brother. At least he was desirous of
repaying his actual debt, at once and in cash if he
only knew what that debt was. He reasoned thus: "If I
should send Manasseh 300 rubles, which, at the present
rate of exchange, would amount to only $15, I should
consider myself as robbing my friend and benefactor of
90 percent of the sum he lent me (i.e., of the sum I
received in exchange for his 300 rubles); and if I sent
the value of $145 in Russian money, which would be about
3,000 rubles, I feel sure that Manasseh would be griev-
ously offended. He would think that his close friend,
who knows that he had never lent his money on interest,
now presumes to suspect that he would take usury from
his life-long friend. I know that he would never for-
give me such an offense, while I am anxious to perpetu-
ate and to strengthen the bond of friendship between
us." Therefore, he importuned me to advise him how to
proceed in this case, so that he might discharge his
obligation as he feels it, without offending his friend
or the Rabbinic law.

Bearing in mind the circumstances and details of
the transaction as portrayed by Ephraim, I find some
analogy in the following precedent. A ruling was asked
of Simeon ben Zemah Duran in this case (see **Tashbaz** II,
288):

Reuben had borrowed from Simeon 20 pounds of purple
yarn, with the distinct understanding that 20

pounds of purple yarn should eventually be returned. Subsequently the price of purple yarn
rose, and now Reuben argues that he owes him no
more than an amount equal to the value of the borrowed yarn at the time of the borrowing, while
Simeon claims that this is not so, but that purple
yarn was the loan and purple yarn must be returned.
However, he hesitates to press this claim lest it
savor of usury; he therefore seeks the sanction of
the learned in the law.

This was the answer:

From the phraseology of the question it appears
that no time for the return of the loan was stipulated; and since the price of purple yarn is known
among the dealers so long as their storehouses
contain yarn, the case is analogous to borrowing a
Se-a of wheat to be repaid with a Se-a of wheat,
which, when the price is once standardized, may be
done without setting a time for the return of the
loan, and may be returned at any time. For while
it is taught (B.M. 75a), "A woman must not lend to
her neighbor a loaf, unless she sets on it a price,
else, should wheat rise in value, the transaction
might eventuate in usury"--that is not confirmed
law. The Gemara cites the comment of Samuel, reported by R. Judah: "That is Hillel's doctrine; but
the [majority of] sages have decided that one may
lend without stipulations and repay without stipulations." Hence it appears that he [Simeon] is
likewise within his rights in demanding the present
price of the yarn; for, according to the universally approved ruling of R. Yannai (ibid., 65b):
"There is no difference in the law between the
goods and the value of the goods."

Agreeable to the principles underlying this decision, had our clients--Ephraim and Manasseh--appeared
before a rabbinical court in Russia, which apparently is
the place where the loan was consummated, they could be
viewed as standing in the same relation towards one
another as did Reuben and Simeon in their case, and the
Russian currency notes could be considered as the purple
yarn; and hence it would appear that Manasseh could
legally claim no more than 300 rubles in Russian currency. For, if at the time of the transaction, the notes
were considered as commodities (they themselves having
no intrinsic value, except as certificates of trusts,
which pass as money because the government promises to
redeem them at their face value with silver, but have as
yet not been redeemed and therefore have a fluctuating

market value), I should consider their status analogous to that of the wheat in the following baraita (B.M. 75a), where it is decided: "One may borrow a **Kor** of wheat [without setting a price]; if wheat becomes cheaper, the borrower may return wheat;[1] if it becomes dearer, he repays its value as it was at the time of the loan." And if, on the contrary, we consider the ruble notes as money--since in contradistinction to commodities they certainly are money--their status is like that of the coin in Asheri's responsum which concludes with the decision: "Where one borrows money without specifying how it is to be repaid, he may repay in the kind of coin borrowed, even if it is nowhere current; **a fortiori**, in this country where no coin is invalidated, but all are current, only one more so than another. Therefore he is obliged to repay in the coin which he borrowed."[2] Nor can Manasseh claim that, because the notes have fallen in value, silver has gone up, and should he now wish to exchange the notes for silver he would incur a loss in the weight of bullion. Should he so argue, Ephraim could rejoin in the words of Rabbi Yom Tov Lipmann Heller (**Pilpula Charifta**, B.K. 98a): "You did not lend me bullion, but coined money, and coined money I return; hence you lose nothing." Again, should Manasseh plead: Because the value of the notes has come down, the price of goods has correspondingly risen, hence I should not now get as many goods as I formerly could have for the same amount in currency notes, Ephraim could counter with the statement that the price of goods has really gone up only because the government of the country has fallen, and, consequently, the people have lost confidence in the treasury notes, although the notes themselves have been reduced neither in size nor in weight. Therefore, since Manasseh lent him Russian notes, he must accept Russian notes in return.

And were Manasseh to sue Ephraim before a rabbinical tribunal in this country--where no place for repayment is specified, because "a loan may be reclaimed anywhere" ("**Milva nitena litava bechol makom**," B.K. 118a)--in that case Ephraim could not discharge the debt with Russian currency. For a baraita provides: "When one produces a bond of indebtedness against another...no place for repayment being designated therein, if the bond is produced in Babylon, the creditor collects in Babylonian money; if it is produced in Eretz Yisrael, payment may be demanded in the money of Eretz Yisrael" (Ket. 110b). Elsewhere it is taught (B.K. 97a): "Where one lends his neighbor money on condition that repayment

---

[1] Cf. **Tosafot**, B.K. 97a, **s.v.** "Hamalveh."

[2] Asheri, **Responsa**, CIII.1.

be made in coin, Rav decides that payment must be made in the coin current at this time, while Samuel rules, the debtor may say to the creditor, Go to Meshan and spend it there." Thereupon Rav Nahman remarks: "Samuel's ruling is reasonable if the creditor is likely to go to Meshan; but if he is not likely to go to Meshan, the debtor may not pay him with coins not current here." And since Manasseh's intention is to establish himself permanently in this country, he must be considered as not likely to go to Russia. This being so, Ephraim must pay him with the money current at the place of payment, which is America; but even so, Manasseh is not entitled to more than the value, in American money, of 300 rubles at the time of repayment.

From what has been said it follows that, although there is some difference as to the kind of money with which payment can be made (this depending on the place where the claim is made), there is no difference as to the amount Manasseh may claim according to Rabbinic law; to wit: 300 rubles--in Russia of Russian currency notes; or in America, of American money to the value of 300 rubles in America the established rule applicable to this case being, as enunciated by R. Yannai: **"Ma li hen, ma li demeihen"** ("There is no difference between goods and their value in money").

Such, it seems to me, would be the judgment of a rabbinic tribunal, if we view Russia as **mekom hashiabud**, the place where the obligation was consummated. After careful consideration, however, that view is impossible. The Rabbis of the Mishna (B.K. X.6) prescribe: "If one robs another, or borrows anything from him, or accepts from him a deposit for safe-keeping, if the deed is done at an inhabited [i.e., safe] place, he cannot legally make restitution in the desert; but when the deed is conditioned on going out to the desert, he may make restitution in the desert." Hereunto the Gemara (**ibid.**, 18a) remarks: "'On condition of going out to the desert'--Why, this is self-evident! Well, it would really not have been necessary to state it, were it not intended to intimate that when the owner said, 'Let this thing stay with you, for I intend to go out to the desert,' whereupon the other said: 'I too intend going out to the desert; if I should desire to restore it to you there I might do so.'" This is variously explained. According to Rashi (**ibid.**, **l.c.**, **s.v.** "I ba-ina"), it means: "Although there is no real condition, since he says, 'If I should desire,' nevertheless, because he too goes out to the desert, he is obliged to accept it there even against his will." Bertenura interprets it thus: "It means not that one says, 'On condition that you come out into the desert and restore it to me'--that would be self-evident; but even if the one says to his friend, 'Let this remain in your custody for I am going out into the desert'; whereupon the friend says, 'I too intend going out into the desert'--even so, if he so desires he may restore it to him in the desert." The difference between these two expositors is that Rashi makes the borrower the first to say: "**Ana lamidbar ba-ina lemeifak**"; while, according to Bertenura, it is the lender who says it first. There is, however, no difference as to the legal effects whether the one or the other expresses his intention first, since both share that intention.

Now, in our case there was an express condition; for according to Ephraim's statement, the lender had said to the borrower: "Providence permitting, in the course of the next year or two ᵀ too shall come thither, and then...you may repay me the loan." Surely there need be no more express condition that this! If "even when a loan is made at an inhabited place, and the borrower says to the lender: 'I intend going out to the desert,' whereupon the lender expresses a like intention, it is legally considered as if the loan was made in the desert" (**Tur**, H.M. LXXIV), although neither loan nor repayment was mentioned by either party; **a fortiori** when, in our case, the lender plainly says: "I too shall come to the United States, and then you may repay me," it should be taken as if the loan was made in the United States. And if the loan was consummated in the United States, the United States must be considered **mekom hashi-abud**, the place where the obligation was incurred. Therefore, Ephraim must pay to Manasseh the value of the loan in United States money. This, I think, is perfectly clear.

But in view of this, the question comes back: What does Ephraim owe to Manasseh? What are we to understand by "the value of the loan"--300 rubles at the present rate of exchange or the value of 300 rubles as the rate stood at the time of the first transaction? The answer may be deduced from the following ruling (B.M. 72b): "A merchant carrying goods from market place to market place is approached by another who proposes to take the goods off his hands at the price which they are expected to bring at a certain place," where goods are rated higher (Rashi, **ad. loc.**). In this case it is ruled that, "if the risk of conveyance to that place is carried by the original vendor, the bargain is permissible; but not so if the buyer assumes that risk," for the surcharge might be construed as interest for deferring payment until after the sale of the goods at that other place (cf. Maimonides, **Yad**, Malveh IX.9). Now, if we carefully ponder Manasseh's words which accompanied the loan, as repeated by Ephraim, it appears that not only did Manasseh entrust the Russian currency notes to

Ephraim with the stipulation that they should be taken to the United States and exchanged for United States money, but also that Manasseh assumed the risk for the time being and for the future (i.e., the risk of transportation and until Ephraim should have accomplished the exchange and begin to profit by the use of the proceeds thereof as a business capital). For thus Manasseh said to Ephraim at the time of the loan: "Here are 300 rubles. Please accept them from me and carry them to the United States; and may He Who 'maketh poor and maketh rich' prosper your way. Providence permitting, in the course of the next year or two, I too shall come thither; and then, if you are able and your heart prompts you (I shall never appear as your creditor, neither shall I ever press you), you may repay me the loan, but without interest." By this Manasseh surely did not mean to intimate that Ephraim should take the Russian notes overseas and lock them up in a safe or "bury them (according to the Talmudic advice, B.M. 42a) in a wall within a handbreadth from the ground"; but that he should exchange them for American money and use that money in business. Hence, Ephraim was Manasseh's agent to convey Manasseh's goods to America, there to dispose of them at the market price. Only after thus disposing of the goods and beginning to employ the proceeds in his own business did Ephraim become the borrower of Manasseh's capital.

Accordingly, we must apply to our case Rashi's construction of the baraita just quoted: "There could be no loan until the goods have been sold; hence no matter how high a price the goods brought, all the proceeds belong to the original owner" (Rashi, B.M. 73a, **s.v.** "**Mutar**"). And since Ephraim received in exchange for the Russian notes entrusted to him by Manasseh one hundred and forty-five dollars, he owes Manasseh one hundred and forty-five dollars ($145.00), or the value of this sum in Russian currency notes, in accordance with the accepted principle enunciated by Rabbi Yannai: "There is no difference between the goods and their value in money."

Under the prevailing circumstances, Manasseh being in Russia (where United States money is not current), Ephraim is obliged to avail himself of the latter alternative, even though in following that course he will repay in rubles ten times the original sum entrusted to him. The increase can be considered neither as a "belated bonus" ("**Ribit Me-ucheret**") for the use of the money, nor as any other shade of interest ("**Avak Ribit**"). It was practically a number of dollars that Ephraim borrowed from Manasseh; and if today the dollar buys more rubles than it could buy six years ago, it is

the value of Manasseh's dollars that pays for the greater sum of rubles.

This, it appears to me, is the correct judgment,
according to Talmudic and later Rabbinic law and regulation; and so I advised Ephraim, this the seventh day of
Chanuka 5680, December 23, 1919.

                                        Samuel Mendelsohn

170. TESTIMONY AGAINST A FAMILY MEMBER
(1980)

QUESTION: Does a prisoner in a federal correction
institution have the right to refuse testimony in a
case which involves his father and other members of
the family? What is the attitude of Jewish law in
this matter? (Rabbi Stanley J. Garfein, Tallahas-
see, Florida)

ANSWER: The principle that governs all cases of the
laws of the land in which we live is, of course, "Dina
demalchuta dina" ("The law of the land is the law"), as
you properly pointed out. This Talmudic principle has
been applied in all matters except those connected with
Jewish family law (i.e., marriage and divorce), and even
in that area the decision of the Napoleonic Sanhedrin of
1806 gave civil law priority over Jewish law. This
principle has been attributed by the Talmud to Samuel of
the third century (Git. 10b; B.K. 113a; Ned. 28a; B.B.
54b; **Shulchan Aruch**, Choshen Mishpat 369.6). Of course,
in the Middle Ages Jewish communities were often autono-
mous and used the Jewish legal systems to govern other
communities. The question arose only when there was a
conflict between a Jew and a non-Jew, or when a Jew
chose to take his case to a non-Jewish court, something
that was decried by the Jewish authorities.

The earliest record of a Jew handing a Jewish criminal who had injured non-Jews to a Gentile court came
from the Gaonic period (700-1000 C.E.; J. Mueller, **Maf-
teach**, p. 182). The responsa literature contains numerous examples of Jews testifying in non-Jewish courts and
doing so willingly when the law of the land demanded it.

The codes summarize various other considerations.
Clearly, one may testify to save oneself if punishment
is threatened; then one is **Moser Be-ones**, and should
testify before a non-Jewish court (**Tur**, Choshen Mishpat
388; **Shulchan Aruch**, Ch.M. 388.8ff; **Yad**, Hil. Chovel

8.2). Furthermore, if the withholding of testimony will harm the community, then handing such an individual over to the government, as well as testimony, is mandatory (Isserles to **Shulchan Aruch**, Choshen Mishpat 388.11). Testimony in criminal cases is every witness' obligation (Lev. 5:1; B.K. 55b), while in civil cases a witness may wait until summoned (**Shulchan Aruch**, Ch.M. 28.1). A witness must possess personal knowledge of the events (Isserles to **Shulchan Aruch**, Ch.M. 19, 28.1).

In our instance, it seems that we are not dealing with a government demand for testimony--as that would certainly have to be met--but with a request to volunteer testimony. The decision then rests in the hands of the individual involved.

He may wish to be guided by the principles surrounding family witnesses in a purely Jewish court. Members of the immediate family are not eligible to act as witnesses and are disqualified. The tradition interpreted the statement of Deuteronomy 24:16 that parents should not be put to death for their children or children for their parents as a prohibition against parents testifying against children or children against parents (San. 27b; **Sifrei Deut.** 280). The Mishna expanded this list of disqualified relatives considerably so that it included father, brother, uncle, brother-in-law, stepfather, father-in-law, their sons, and sons-in-law (San. 3.4). Later the rule was extended still further to include nephews and first cousins (**Yad**, Hil. Edut 12.3; **Shulchan Aruch**, Choshen Mishpat 33.2).

A husband was disqualified in cases involving his wife (**Yad**, Hil. Edut 13.6; **Shulchan Aruch**, Choshen Mishpat 33.3). Testimony from the individuals listed above for or against the accused was not permitted in court, and it did not matter whether these relatives retained any ties with the accused or not (**Yad**, Hil. Edut 13.6; **Shulchan Aruch**, Choshen Mishpat 33.3).

Jewish tradition, therefore, very clearly eliminated all relatives from this kind of judicial involvement in contrast to other legal systems. The ancient Greek legal system had no qualms about the testimony of relatives (W. Smith, **A Dictionary of Greek and Roman Antiquities**, p. 626). In Rome, such testimony was not excluded, but it was given little weight. In English common law, relatives, except husband and wife, may testify against or for each other (H. Roscoe, **A Digest of the Law of Evidence**, pp. 112ff).

It is clear, therefore, that from the point of view of a Jewish court, such an individual should not testify against any member of his family, but he must testify (1) if it is a criminal act which endangers the community, (2) if the law of the land demands such testimony in accordance with the principle "**Dina demalchuta dina**";

this may restrain bitter family feelings which might arise from such circumstances (Gulak, **Hamishpat Ha-ivri** IV.1).

Walter Jacob

171. ABORTION
(Vol. LXVIII, 1958, pp. 120-122)

QUESTION: A young woman has contracted German measles in the third month of her pregnancy. Her doctor says that her sickness creates the possibility that the child, if born, may be deformed in body or mind. Some doctors, however, seem to doubt that this will happen. In other words, there are various opinions as to the probability of the child being born deformed. May she, according to Jewish law, or to Reform interpretation of Jewish law, have an abortion done to terminate the pregnancy?

ANSWER: The Mishna (Oholot VII.6) says that if a woman has great difficulty in giving birth to her child (and if it seems as if she cannot survive), it is permitted to destroy the child to save her life. This permission to destroy a child to save the life of a mother is cited in all the codes and is finally fixed as law in the **Shulchan Aruch** (Choshen Mishpat 425.2). This permission to destroy the child is only given in the case where it is necessary to save the mother. The law continues and says that if the child puts out its head or most of its body, it may no longer be killed to save the mother, since we do not "push aside one life for another." Therefore, this legal permission to destroy the child cannot be relevant in the case mentioned, in which the fetus in no way endangers the mother, and, therefore, on the ground of the law in Choshen Mishpat there is no basis as yet to terminate the pregnancy.

However, Rashi to B. Sanhedrin 72b--where the law of the destruction of the child is cited from the Mishna Oholot--feels it necessary to explain why the child must be spared if it puts forth its head and yet may be killed if it does not. His explanation (which is cited in later discussions) is of some relevance to our problem. He says that as long as it does not go forth "into the air of the world" it is not considered a **nefesh** and, therefore, may be slain to save the mother. From this we might conclude that an unborn fetus or infant is not considered a being, and may, if necessary, be destroyed. Yet even so, in this case, the permission is given only to save the mother.

Still, Rashi by his explanation raises the possibility that we need not be too strict about saving an unborn child. In fact, there is some assistance to this point of view from the law (codified in Choshen Mishpat 423), that if a man happens to strike a pregnant woman and the child is destroyed, he has to pay **money** damages for the harm to the mother and the loss of the child. But why should he not be guilty of a capital crime, having killed the child? Evidently one would conclude that the unborn child is not a **nefesh** in the sense that killing it would be a capital crime. Joshua Falk (16th-17th century), in his classic commentary **Me-irat Einayim** to the passage in Choshen Mishpat 425 (end of his section 8), develops the opinion of Rashi and says clearly, "While the fetus is within the body of the mother it may be destroyed even though it is alive, for every fetus that does not come out or has not come out into the light of the world is not described as a **nefesh**." He proves this from the case of a man who strikes a pregnant woman and destroys her unborn child. The man must pay damages, but is not deemed a murderer, which he would be if the fetus were considered a **nefesh**. Similarly, in Arachin 7a, if a pregnant woman was condemned to death, she was smitten in front of her body so that the child should die before she was executed. This, too, would indicate that it is at least no capital crime to slay unborn children. However, the cases mentioned above are mitigated by various arguments given in the literature, and the actual law is that a fetus may **not** be destroyed, as is seen in the following: The Talmud, in Sanhedrin 57b, gives the opinion of Rabbi Ishmael that a **Ben Noach** (i.e., a non-idolatrous non-Jew) is forbidden to destroy a fetus. It is a capital crime if **he** does it. The **Tosafot** to Chulin 33a say that this indicates that a Jew is not to be put to death (as a **Ben Noach** is) if he destroys a fetus; nevertheless, continue the **Tosafot**, while it is not a capital crime for a Jew, it is still not permitted for him to do so.

There is a modern, scientific analysis of the law in this matter by Aptowitzer, in the **Jewish Quarterly Review**, New Series, volume 15, pp. 83ff. However, it is rather remarkable that the whole question of abortion is not discussed very much in actual cases in the traditional law. As a matter of fact, I found at first only three responsa which discuss it fully. There are others which I found later. The first responsum is by a great authority, Yair Chaim Bachrach, of Worms, 17th century. In his responsum (**Chavat Ya-ir**, #31) he was asked the following question: A married woman confessed to adultery, and, finding herself pregnant, asked for an abortion. Bachrach was asked whether it is permissible by Jewish law to do so. He discusses most of the material that I have mentioned above, and at first says that it would seem that a fetus is not really a **nefesh** and it might be permitted to destroy it, except that this would encourage immorality. But he continues, from the discussion of the **Tosafot** in Chulin, that a Jew is not permitted (even though he would not be convicted) to destroy a fetus, that it **is** forbidden for him to do so.

Yet in the next century the opposite opinion is voiced, and also by a great authority, namely Jacob Emden (**Ya-avets** I, 43). He is asked concerning a pregnant adulteress whether she may have an abortion. He decides affirmatively, on the rather curious ground that if we were still under our Sanhedrin and could inflict capital punishment, such a woman would be condemned to death and her child would die with her anyhow. Then he adds boldly (though with some misgivings) that perhaps we may destroy a fetus even to save a mother excessive physical pain.

A much more thorough affirmative opinion is given by Ben Zion Uziel, the late Sephardic Chief Rabbi (in **Mishpetei Uzi-el** III, 46 and 47). He concludes, after a general analysis of the subject, that an unborn fetus is actually not a **nefesh** at all and has no independent life. It is part of its mother, and just as a person may sacrifice a limb to be cured of a worse sickness, so may this fetus be destroyed for the mother's benefit. Of course, he reckons with the statement of the **Tosafot** in Chulin 33a that a Jew is not permitted (**la shari**) to destroy a fetus, although such an act is not to be considered murder. Uziel says that, of course, one may not destroy it. One may not destroy anything without purpose. But if there is a worthwhile purpose, it may be done. The specific case before him concerned a woman who was threatened with permanent deafness if she went through with the pregnancy. Uziel decides that since the fetus is not an independent **nefesh** but is only part of the mother, there is no sin in destroying it for her sake.

In the case which you are discussing, I would, therefore, say that since there is strong preponderance of medical opinion that the child will be born imperfect physically and even mentally, then for the **mother's** sake (i.e., her mental anguish now and in the future) she may sacrifice this part of herself. This decision thus follows the opinion of Jacob Emden and Ben Zion Uziel against the earlier opinion of Yair Chaim Bachrach.

Solomon B. Freehof

See also:

S.B. Freehof, "Abortion," **Recent Reform Responsa,** pp. 188ff; "Abortion and Live Foetus Study," **Reform Responsa for Our Time,** pp. 256ff.
"Resolution," **CCAR Yearbook,** vol. 67, 1967, p. 103.
"Resolution," **Union of American Hebrew Congregations,** 1967, p. 77.
"Resolution," **National Federation of Temple Sisterhoods,** 1965.

172.   COSMETIC SURGERY
(Vol. LXXVI, 1976, pp. 94-96)

QUESTION: A young unmarried Orthodox girl wants a plastic surgery on her nose and her face lifted. She realizes that according to Halacha she must not inflict unnecessary injury to herself. Should she have a facial plastic surgery? (Dr. Abraham Bernstein, San Francisco, California)

ANSWER: In traditional law there is ground for debate whether **any** operation which cuts the human body can be freely consented to. Of course, if it is a question of saving an endangered person's life, then no prohibition among the commandments is allowed to stand in the way of the necessary operation. All commandments are waived in cases of **Pikuach Nefesh** (danger to life). But suppose the operation is not one for saving a person from real danger, but is for a relatively minor purpose, such as improving the shape of the nose. Are such operations permitted by Jewish law?
In order to answer that question, we must first look into the question of a person's giving consent to an operation. The law is fairly clear that just as a person may not wound another (**Chovel,** "wounds or injures"), so he may not wound himself (or arrange for someone else to wound him; in this case, the surgeon). This law is stated clearly by Maimonides in his Code in Hilchot Chovel V.1. However, where the law is stated in the **Shulchan Aruch,** Choshen Mishpat 420.31, it is not stated as positively as in Maimonides. The **Shulchan Aruch** says, "He who injures himself is free [from punishment], although it is not permitted to do so." The reason for this ambiguous statement of the law in the **Shulchan Aruch** (which seems to say you may and you may not injure yourself) is that Rabbi Akiva, who is the chief authority for this law himself, seems to have two

diverse opinions. In the Mishna Bava Kama 8.6, he states the law just as the **Shulchan Aruch** quotes it, namely, "You should not injure yourself, but if you do so, you are free from punishment." But in a **baraita** quoted in the Talmud (in Bava Kama 91a, at the bottom), Akiva says flatly that a man is free to injure himself. Clearly this vagueness in the law of self-injury leaves room for discussion of the question asked here and of many analogous questions.

An interesting recent discussion was given by Moshe Feinstein, the prime contemporary Orthodox authority (in his **Igerot Mosheh**, Choshen Mishpat #103). The specific question with which he was dealing was the following: May a man give his blood to the blood bank for pay? On the face of it this should be prohibited because the man is arranging for his self-injury. After a minute analysis of the two semi-contradictory statements of Rabbi Akiva, Moses Feinstein comes to the conclusion that it is permitted--first, because they used to do bloodletting in Talmudic times; secondly, the injury is slight and painless; and thirdly, the man may, of course, need the money.

On the basis of the law, the line of our inquiry must be as follows. First: How dangerous is the cosmetic surgery as a procedure? What risks does the patient incur? Secondly: How important a benefit is the beautification of the woman? Is it important enough to justify whatever danger there is in the surgery?

It may be assumed that cosmetic surgery deals mostly with the outer parts of the body and does not generally involve disturbing the vital organs. As for the benefit derived by whatever risk this surgery entails, this question has a remarkable place in Jewish traditional literature. The Bible and the Talmud pay a surprising amount of attention to cosmetic matters. First of all, the various spices and lotions used in women's beautification are mentioned many times in Scripture. In Song of Songs 3:6 and 4:10 and in Esther 2:12, various spices are mentioned. Also in the Talmud (Bava Kama 82a) we are told that when Ezra brought the people back from Babylonian captivity, among his special ordinances was one permitting peddlers of cosmetics to travel freely throughout the country so that these ointments, etc., would be readily available.

The law permits a woman to go through extensive beauty treatment on the half-holidays (see Orach Chayim 346.5). The husband must provide means for his wife's beauty material (see B. Ketubot 64b). One of the most touching narratives in the Mishna (Nedarim 9.10) concerns Rabbi Ishmael. A man had made a vow that he would not marry a certain woman on the ground that she was homely. Rabbi Ishmael then took the girl into his house and beautified her. Then he presented her to the young man who had made the vow and said to the young man, "Is this the girl you vowed you would not marry because you said she was homely?" The young man looked at this beautiful girl and said, "No, I would gladly marry her." Then follows the saying, "The daughters of Israel are beautiful. It is their poverty which makes them homely." Then we are told that when Rabbi Ishmael died, all the daughters of Israel sang a dirge for him.

It is clear from Jewish tradition that the right of a woman to beautify herself is one that is honored in Scripture and in Talmud. It is not at all to be considered a trivial matter. It is clearly the spirit of the tradition that a woman has the right to strive for beauty.

Since, therefore, the cosmetic purpose is an honored one and an important one, and since the operation is not likely to be a dangerous one, then the ambiguous law of **Chovel** against self-injury does not apply here, and this woman is not prohibited by Jewish law to undergo cosmetic surgery.

Solomon B. Freehof

Report of the Committee on Patrilineal Descent on the Status of Children of Mixed Marriages

Adopted by the Central Conference of American Rabbis
at its 94th Annual Convention, March 15, 1983

The purpose of this document is to establish the Jewish status of the children of mixed marriages in the Reform Jewish community of North America.

One of the most pressing human issues for the North American Jewish community is mixed marriage, with all its attendant implications. For our purpose mixed marriage is defined as a union between a Jew and a non-Jew. A non-Jew who joins the Jewish people through conversion is recognized as a Jew in every respect. We deal here only with the Jewish identity of children born of a union in which one parent is Jewish and the other parent is non-Jewish.

This issue arises from the social forces set in motion by the Enlightenment and the Emancipation. They are the roots of our current struggle with mixed marriage. "Social change so drastic and far reaching could not but affect on several levels the psychology of being Jewish.... The result of Emancipation was to make Jewish identity a private commitment rather than a legal status, leaving it a complex mix of destiny and choice" (Robert Seltzer, **Jewish People, Jewish Thought**, p. 544). Since the Napoleonic Assembly of Notables of 1806, the Jewish community has struggled with the tension between modernity and tradition. This tension is now a major challenge, and it is within this specific context that the Reform Movement chooses to respond. Wherever there is ground to do so, our response seeks to establish Jewish identity of the children of mixed marriages.

According to the Halacha as interpreted by traditional Jews over many centuries, the offspring of a Jewish mother and a non-Jewish father is recognized as a Jew, while the offspring of a non-Jewish mother and a Jewish father is considered a non-Jew. To become a Jew, the child of a non-Jewish mother and a Jewish father must undergo conversion.

As a Reform community, the process of determining an appropriate response has taken us to an examination of the tradition, our own earlier responses, and the most current considerations. In doing so, we seek to be sensitive to the human dimensions of this issue.

Both the Biblical and the Rabbinical traditions take for granted that ordinarily the paternal line is decisive in the tracing of descent within the Jewish

people. The Biblical genealogies in Genesis and elsewhere in the Bible attest to this point. In intertribal
marriage in ancient Israel, paternal descent was decisive. Numbers 1:2, etc., says: "By their families, by
their fathers' houses" (lemishpechotam leveit avotam),
which for the Rabbis means, "The line (literally: 'family') of the father is recognized; the line of the mother
is not" (Mishpachat av keruya mishpacha; mishpachat em
einah keruya mishpacha; Bava Batra 109b, Yevamot 54b;
cf. Yad, Nachalot 1.6).

In the Rabbinic tradition, this tradition remains
in force. The offspring of a male Kohen who marries a
Levite or Israelite is considered a Kohen, and the child
of an Israelite who marries a Kohenet is an Israelite.
Thus: yichus, lineage, regards the male line as absolutely dominant. This ruling is stated succinctly in
Mishna Kiddushin 3.12 that when kiddushin (marriage) is
licit and no transgression (ein avera) is involved, the
line follows the father. Furthermore, the most important parental responsibility to teach Torah rested with
the father (Kiddushin 29a; cf. Shulchan Aruch, Yoreh
De-a 245.1).

When, in the tradition, the marriage was considered
not to be licit, the child of that marriage followed the
status of the mother (Mishna Kiddushin 3.12, havalad
kemotah). The decisions of our ancestors thus to link
the child inseparably to the mother, which makes the
child of a Jewish mother Jewish and the child of a non-
Jewish mother non-Jewish, regardless of the father, was
based upon the fact that the woman with her child had no
recourse but to return to her own people. A Jewish
woman could not marry a non-Jewish man (cf. Shulchan
Aruch, Even Ha-ezer 4.19, la tafsei kiddushin). A Jewish man could not marry a non-Jewish woman. The only
recourse in Rabbinic law for the woman in either case
was to return to her own community and people.

Since Emancipation, Jews have faced the problem of
mixed marriage and the status of the offspring of mixed
marriage. The Reform Movement responded to the issue.
In 1947 the CCAR adopted a proposal made by the Committee on Mixed Marriage and Intermarriage:

> With regard to infants, the declaration of the
> parents to raise them as Jews shall be deemed suf-
> ficient for conversion. This could apply, for
> example, to adopted children. This decision is in
> line with the traditional procedure in which,
> according to the Talmud, the parents bring young
> children (the Talmud speaks of children earlier
> than the age of three) to be converted, and the
> Talmud comments that although an infant cannot give
> its consent, it is permissible to benefit somebody

without his consent (or presence). On the same page the Talmud also speaks of a father bringing his children for conversion, and says that the children will be satisfied with the action of their father. If the parents therefore will make a declaration to the rabbi that it is their intention to raise the child as a Jew, the child may, for the sake of impressive formality, be recorded in the Cradle-Roll of the religious school and thus be considered converted.
Children of religious school age should likewise not be required to undergo a special ceremony of conversion but should receive instruction as regular students in the school. The ceremony of Confirmation at the end of the school course shall be considered in lieu of a conversion ceremony.
Children older than confirmation age should not be converted without their own consent. The Talmudic law likewise gives the child who is converted in infancy by the court the right to reject the conversion when it becomes of religious age. Therefore the child above religious school age, if he or she consents sincerely to conversion, should receive regular instruction for that purpose and be converted in the regular conversion ceremony."
(**CCAR Yearbook**, Vol. 57)

This issue was again addressed in the 1961 edition of the **Rabbi's Manual**:

Jewish law recognizes a person as Jewish if his mother was Jewish, even though the father was not a Jew. One born of such mixed parentage may be admitted to membership in the synagogue and enter into a marital relationship with a Jew, provided he has not been reared in or formally admitted into some other faith. The child of a Jewish father and a non-Jewish mother, according to traditional law, is a Gentile; such a person would have to be formally converted in order to marry a Jew or become a synagogue member.
Reform Judaism, however, accepts such a child as Jewish without a formal conversion, if he attends a Jewish school and follows a course of studies leading to Confirmation. Such procedure is regarded as sufficient evidence that the parents and the child himself intend that he shall live as a Jew.
(**Rabbi's Manual**, p. 112)

We face today an unprecedented situation due to the changed conditions in which decisions concerning the status of the child of a mixed marriage are to be made.

There are tens of thousands of mixed marriages.   In a
vast majority of these cases the non-Jewish extended
family is a functioning part of the child's world, and
may be decisive in shaping the life of the child.   It
can no longer be assumed **a priori**, therefore, that the
child of a Jewish mother will be Jewish any more than
that the child of a non-Jewish mother will not be.

This leads us to the conclusion that the same requirements must be applied to establish the status of a
child of a mixed marriage, regardless of whether the
mother or the father is Jewish.

Therefore:

The Central Conference of American Rabbis declares
that the child of one Jewish parent is under the
presumption of Jewish descent.   This presumption of
the Jewish status of the offspring of any mixed
marriage is to be established through appropriate
and timely public and formal acts of identification
with the Jewish faith and people.   The performance
of these **mitzvot** serves to commit those who participate in them, both parent and child, to Jewish
life.
Depending on circumstances,[1] **mitzvot** leading toward
a positive and exclusive Jewish identity will include entry into the covenant, acquisition of a
Hebrew name, Torah study, Bar/Bar Mitzvah, and
Kabbalat Torah (Confirmation).[2]   For those beyond
childhood claiming Jewish identity, other public
acts or declarations may be added or substituted
after consultation with their rabbi.

---

[1] According to the age or setting, parents should
consult a rabbi to determine the specific **mitzvot** which
are necessary.

[2] A full description of these and other **mitzvot** can be
found in **Shaarei Mitzvah**.

INDEX